AIRCREW SECURITY

This book is dedicated to all those who lost their lives from the terrorist attacks in the United States on September 11, 2001.

We especially remember our fellow crewmembers who became victims of 'the system' that day. It is our hope that we never lose another crewmember because of complacency, lack of attention or effort, or inadequate training.

Aircrew Security

A Practical Guide

CLOIS WILLIAMS AND STEVEN WALTRIP
Aviation Safety and Security Association

ASHGATE

Published by
Ashgate Publishing Limited
Gower House
Croft Road
Aldershot
Hants GU11 3HR
England

Ashgate Publishing Company
Suite 420
101 Cherry Street
Burlington, VT 05401-4405
USA

Ashgate website: http://www.ashgate.com

British Library Cataloguing in Publication Data
Williams, Clois
Aircrew security : a practical guide
1.Aeronautics, Commercial - Security measures 2.Crimes aboard aircraft 3.Crimes aboard aircraft - Psychological aspects 4.Flight crews - Training of 5.Aeronautics, Commercial - Law and legislation
I.Title II.Waltrip, Steven
363.1'24

Library of Congress Cataloging-in-Publication Data
Williams, Clois.
Aircrew security : a practical guide / Clois Williams and Steven Waltrip.
p. cm.
Includes bibliographical references and index.
ISBN 0-7546-4076-0
1. Flight crews--Protection. 2. Aeronautics--Security measures. 3. Human behavior. I. Waltrip, Steven. II. Title.

TL553.6.W56 2003
629.13'028'9--dc22

2003063541

ISBN 0 7546 4076 0

Printed and bound in Great Britain by TJ International Ltd, Padstow, Cornwall

Contents

List of Tables

List of Photographs

List of Appendices

Preface

The terrorist attacks in the United States on 11 September 2001 changed all crewmember lives forever. With murderous intent in their hearts, terrorists took control of four commercial aircraft and crashed three of them into pre-selected targets killing approximately 3,000 people. Passengers fought with terrorists for control of the fourth aircraft that was destined for the White House and managed to crash it into a field in rural Pennsylvania instead. Never in the modern history of the world, have 19 murderers taken the lives of so many innocent people in such a short span of time. While most of the world mourned, many others in the radical terrorist world rejoiced in the deaths of innocent civilians. We must accept the cold reality there are people who find joy in killing people for their own twisted reasons. The terrorist attacks on 9/11 significantly affected people worldwide. We must continue to be vigilant for those who will continue to look for ways to kill us. We must accept this sad, but grim reality. Terrorists continue to threaten the safety of airline passengers and crews across the globe and to disregard such threats would be both foolish and naïve.

In November 2001, President Bush signed into law the Aviation and Transportation Security Act (ATSA). The ATSA legislated among other things that flight crewmembers would receive training in specific areas of self-defense (See Table P.1 below). For the first time in commercial aviation history, flight crewmembers were to expect more than just the 'standard' hijacking preparation of previous training. Over the past several decades, security training at the airlines had become boring, monotonous and uninteresting – a 'square-filler', often containing minimal or useless information. After 9/11, expectations changed, and many flight crews hoped that security training would now contain vital and useful information. After all, the provisions of ATSA regarding flight crew security training were quite clear, or so it seemed.

Table P.1 Eight elements regarding flight crew training from ATSA

1	Determination of the seriousness of any occurrence
2	Crew communication and coordination
3	Appropriate responses to defend oneself
4	Use of protective devices
5	Psychology of terrorists to cope with hijacker behavior and passenger response
6	Live situational training exercises regarding various threat conditions
7	Flight deck procedures or aircraft maneuvers to defend the aircraft
8	Any other subject matter deemed appropriate by the Administrator

Source: Section 144 of the Aviation and Transportation Security Act, United States.

Unfortunately, as each airline put together its security programs as dictated by 'further guidance' provided by the Transportation Security Administration (TSA) and Federal Aviation Administration (FAA), it became evident that training was for the most part, minimal. Flight crews from various major airlines have expressed their dismay and disdain for their new program. The responsibility of interpreting legislation and guidance was left to airlines as they determined what information would be provided to the crews, in what manner, and in what length of time.

The financial effects of 9/11 have pushed airlines into the worst economic period they have ever experienced. Because of this predicament, money was and continues to be extremely tight at most airlines. The costs of security program development and implementation have added to the financial woes they are experiencing. Doing what was most economically feasible compromised doing what was right. Variations between airline programs were amazing and yet all programs were eventually approved by the FAA/TSA.

A few of the major airlines' flight attendant unions rebelled against minimal training and convinced their airlines to reconsider the self-defensive portion of their training. At least two American airlines have enlisted the aid of outside vendors to provide additional self-defense training to crewmembers on a volunteer basis. Volunteer basis? Sounds like a way of skirting the issues of providing effective, mandatory self-defense training as required by ATSA. Something is wrong with this line of thinking! Yes, flight crews are protecting their own lives with self-defense training; however, in the big picture are they not defending the *company's* passengers, aircraft and cargo, not to mention thousands of people on the ground? Individual personal protection training IS highly recommended, but not as a substitute for training that should be provided for flight crews by any company operating any kind of aircraft.

With the passage of the Homeland Security Act (H.R. 5005) in the United States, American flight crews are to receive additional training in self-defense. Will this legislation be strong enough to cause a significant positive change in crewmember training? Some doubt that it will, but time will tell whether the legislation has any substance to it. However, the legislation is supposed to provide additional time requirements for training of flight attendants in self-defense tactics as well as for arming pilots. It is evident the emphasis on security training is a serious step toward correcting the deficiencies of the ATSA. It is imperative that all crewmembers receive the most current and effective training available today. Will this legislation correct the deficiencies?

There are always exceptions. One particular U.S. airline in particular we have first hand knowledge of, took impressive steps to train their crews. Their management felt very strongly their crews should receive the most comprehensive training available. Their highly successful two-day course incorporates academics and hands on self-defense methods that have been in place since May 2002. Crewmembers who work there have given it very high marks on their critiques of the course. This airline's security training should be the benchmark for all crew security training. We are not mentioning their name here for security reasons.

Since the terrorist attack on America, a good portion of the world's attention has been on aviation security. In the United States, placement of National Guard troops, law enforcement and federalization of security screeners at airport checkpoints, expansion of the sky marshal program, cockpit door modifications, and security directives from the TSA have all served to keep attention focused on airline and airport security. Any assumption by the traveling public that aviation travel is now safer because of all the attention and the many announced 'new security procedures' being implemented at the airports is a big mistake. *Activity and attention should not be mistaken for effective solutions to airport security.* Terrorists have proven themselves as determined individuals who by their training and actions will not let increased activity in and around the airports deter their homicidal goals. Unfortunately, airline travel is not as safe as it should be considering the enormity of the horrific events of 9/11. The threats continue to be real and crewmembers must react and train accordingly.

Examining Your Beliefs

We all possess beliefs that we have developed since birth. How you look at others, yourself, politics, jobs, likes, your dislikes, biases and anything else in and around your life is processed through the glasses of these experiences both good and bad. It is who we are. We may change and alter those beliefs as we go through life because something has caused us to change. We are sometimes at odds with change and must make change over a span of time as we come to accept the idea of change in our lives. For some people, change faster than others.

A strongly held personal belief is difficult to change. Especially, since there does not appear to be any need to change that opinion. However, if a tragic event occurred that is contrary to a strongly held opinion, then should we not change that belief?

The powerful belief we had in the world's airline security changed on 9/11. Who believed terrorists would board four American airliners, hijack them and then crash them into predetermined targets? Crewmembers lived and unfortunately died by this strong belief in airline security. That belief in the security system, plus a good deal of denial continues for many people. Unfortunately, many people in powerful positions with our society are in denial. A former major airline executive testified before the U.S. Congress in 2002 the airline security system is more than adequate. Additionally, we all have seen the 'aviation security experts' on news programs that claim a hijacking or an onboard attack of an airliner is no longer possible. Do you really believe them? Crewmembers are at the front line of aviation and know better.

We are living in the same dangerous world as we were before 9/11, but with rules that we all learned the hard way. Most crewmembers believed in the 'Common Strategy', established hijacker procedures, because the 'experts' said we should. [Author's note: The term 'Common Strategy' describes a set of principles flight crews used to deal with a hijacking. Some of the tactics included having the pilots set the radar transponder on the aircraft to the hijacking code. The transponder is a device in the flight deck of the aircraft that is set by the pilots that enables ground controllers to follow the flight path of the aircraft on their radar scopes. The hijacking code was a universal code to alert the ground controllers of a hijacking. Other previous tactics proved useless on 9/11.] It is only by hindsight these procedures were in a state of failure for many years. Crewmembers did not recognize this breakdown and felt comfortable with what they believed was, for the most part, a safe security system. Some individuals still subscribe to the previously held beliefs that crewmembers should only adhere to the established roles within the previous airline security concept. These individuals have a difficult time understanding those who want to make changes. In contrast, when the automobile started to become the common mode of transportation there were those who continued to ride a horse. They felt strongly the automobile would never become a viable mode of transportation. History proved these people wrong. Likewise, the future will prove those who discourage a new role for crewmembers in airline security are also wrong.

There is a proper place in life for denial. Denial helps us deal with very traumatic things in life that, too difficult to think about occurring. Our minds push aside horrible thoughts through denial as we go through life. For example, we deny our spouse could be killed in a traffic accident or our child could be murdered. We deny these overwhelming thoughts because if we did not, we would have difficulty functioning in our everyday lives. Because denial can be dangerous from a security standpoint, we ask you to look within yourself and examine what you believe. We hope through information provided in this book, you will learn new ways to become aware of your environment, attain control of it and act appropriately when needed. We cannot stop the evil that is in this world, but we can strive to control the evil in our aviation world. To deny it exists, defeats that goal. Remaining objective to the environment in which we work and deciphering information (often ignored), enhances our abilities to recognize and defeat evil threats.

About This Book

Our intention with this book is to give each reader insights and knowledge that will be helpful in protecting him or her, other crewmembers, passengers and the aircraft from attack from hijackers or terrorists. The book is not an exposé on self-defense. It will provide crewmembers with some tools they may employ during dangerous and/or violent confrontations aboard an aircraft. No one book will arm you with everything you may need to counter a trained terrorist, however, even a small amount of information may be helpful to you in dire circumstances.

This book is intended to provoke creative thought. We base our opinions and tactics on decades of aviation experience, backgrounds in law enforcement and personal protection, research and common sense. We heartily commend all who seek training beyond that provided by their respective airlines. As you read Chapter 4 on terrorism, compare the training you have received to that of the terrorists and you may realize why we feel the way we do about aviation security.

Much of the information, personal protection techniques/tactics, and other subject matter we will discuss in this book are new to commercial aviation, at least in the context in which they will be presented. We have entered new and un-charted territory where there never has been a need to devise methods of self-preservation for crewmembers. *It should be noted that we have not knowingly divulged any information of a secure nature or of any security program that is in use at any airline worldwide. All information provided is available in the public domain.*

We are in a new reality of air transportation and must develop strategies to counteract current and future threats. Security, survival techniques and tactics must become a way of life for pilots and flight attendants. Awareness, mental and physical preparation, willingness and the ability to act should be instilled into the thinking of every crewmember. The new reality is insistent upon our approaching these efforts methodically and meticulously. The very way crewmembers go about their jobs must change to integrate this thinking into all aspects of their jobs from greeting passengers to preparing the cabin for landing and more. No matter how we may long for 'the good old days' of aviation, the world will never be the same again. There is a clear and present danger for flight crews. Accordingly, they must accept and deal with those dangers as a new way of doing business. To be unaccepting of the new reality of air transportation could prove fatal to a crewmember as well as to all of those aboard a commercial airliner. Our world changed on 9/11 and it will never be the same again. We need to deal with it intelligently. We invite you to embark with us upon an extremely important journey through the pages of this book where we will explore the importance of the flight crew to air transportation around the world and the knowledge that is necessary for airline security. We ask you to read with a critical eye and look for ways to improve the role of crewmembers in this new era of air transportation. Working cooperatively with one another as flight attendants, pilots, airline managements, security experts or as government officials is how the many difficult security issues facing the airline industry will be solved. Together, we can do it. Let the inspiring words of Todd Beamer resonate and guide you as you read this book … 'Let's roll!'

Clois Williams and Steve Waltrip
Aviation Safety and Security Association
www.as-sa.org or www.diversifiedtrainingco.com
Phoenix, Arizona USA
11 September 2003

PART I
IDENTIFYING THE THREATS

Chapter 1

Aviation Security: Crewmember Perspectives

Aviation Security – Concerns

Aviation security warnings

Before 9/11, there were many warnings by sensible, highly experienced individuals about the lack of adequate security at airports in the United States.[1] In one of the four terminals at Sky Harbor Airport in Phoenix, Arizona, a private security screening company had security lapses 125 times between July 1997 and 2001.[2] Lapses included improperly searching passengers and not finding weapons in screened bags. Since these security lapses are for only one terminal at one major airport, one can only imagine how many lapses occur at all the airports in the United States and the rest of the world. These lapses occurred while private security companies were in control of passenger screening. In the United States, the Transportation Security Administration (TSA) now employs many of the same individuals formerly employed as private screeners. Will the security lapses stop just because the Federal government has taken over this function? Let us remember the US government was the policing agency in charge of security checkpoints both before and after 9/11, was aware of the problems, and yet permitted private security companies to operate with known shortcomings.

Security lapses at airports across America have been well publicized for many years. The General Accounting Office warned in 2000 that airport security had not improved and wrote, 'the security of the air transport system remains at risk'.[3] Between 1988 and 2001, there have been at least five GAO reports, two Presidential Commissions, and major federal legislation addressing or criticizing airport security.[4] With all the taxpayer money spent on reports, commissions, and legislation, the government still did not provide adequate airport security to stop 19 terrorists from getting aboard four commercial airliners with 'legal length' knives and box cutters and causing the devastation on 9/11. One can only conclude that continued security shortcomings highlighted by the government, prove effective solutions to airline security have not been achieved despite a significant amount of attention to the issue. Just because there has been a significant amount of attention and energy spent on aviation security since 9/11 by the government and airlines, how can anyone believe airline security is satisfactory? *Do not mistake considerable government activity and attention, and the billions of dollars spent, for effective solutions to aviation security.*

The increasingly violent trend of airline hijackings

The 9/11 hijackings are the culmination of an increasing trend of violent hijackings that began with the advent of suicide bombings in the mid 1980s. After aircraft hijackings subsided in the 1980s, most crewmembers did not pay attention to international terrorism or recognize the threats to them personally. By 2001, flight crew security training was inadequate and training was minimal. If crew security training had kept up with the existing threats, 9/11 may have never happened, or at least the outcomes may have been different. We must be learn from this horrible experience and apply techniques and strategies to prevent another 9/11 from ever occurring again.

The history of airline hijackings during the last two decades indicates that a violent and horrible trend has emerged. Hijackers are no longer in fear for their lives. Instead, they look to martyrdom as a reasonable end to their goals. The hijackings on 9/11 should forever stick in our collective minds as a wakeup call for crewmembers to employ tactics and strategies to combat terrorism and violent hijackings with effective defensive measures.

Flight deck vulnerability

What became evident to us while developing a flight crew security training course at an established airline is just how vulnerable the flight deck continues to be since 9/11. After 9/11, procedures regarding flight crews coming and going from the cockpit changed. Yet, the fact remains the crew may open the flight deck door during flight and thereby create an opportunity for hijackers. We will not go into the specifics of the vulnerability of the flight deck because of the security issues involved. However, based upon our personal observations, the flight decks on commercial passenger airliners continue to be at risk of forced entry by hijackers.

Even with future development of stronger and improved flight deck doors, they will be opened during flight by crewmembers. If during one of these openings of a super-reinforced door, hijackers were to force entry and secure the door, just how are we are going to get them out? This situation does not have an easy solution, but armed pilot tactics could be implemented to defend the flight deck during times of vulnerability. By arming and adequately training pilots with firearms, the chance for a successful forced entry into the flight deck can be greatly reduced by the application of certain tactics. We trust the TSA has incorporated effective tactics into the training of pilots as Federal Flight Deck Officers that began in April 2003. Arming pilots is not the 'silver bullet' that will solve all our security problems, as some may want you to think. All crewmembers need training, education and knowledge on combating terrorism.

Hijackings are still possible

The terrorist hijacking of a commercial airliner or other type of aircraft continues to be a distinct possibility. Numerous methods exist that provide terrorists with the ability to hijack an aircraft that would not raise suspicions. Just like us, they ponder 'what if' scenarios, study aircraft movements on the surface and in the air, and will find the weak spots in our security systems. Terrorists have proven they have the monetary backing and the intelligence to carry out their missions. If you are a crewmember, or other person who is very familiar with airline travel, couple your personal knowledge of the aviation security system and the aviation industry with your imagination and it will not be difficult for you to envision scenarios that could result in the successful hijacking of commercial aircraft for any terrorist on any given day.

We may all have extreme disdain for the actions of the terrorists on 9/11, and others like them, but let us not forget they carried out their plan masterfully and are much more capable than we ever believed they were. We are not safe from fanatics like them and probably will not be for a long time to come. Let us not once again underestimate the ability of terrorists to carry out their homicidal goals. The threats remain as indicated by US officials warning of a credible hijacking threat during the summer of 2003. Intercepted al-Qaida transmissions indicate a continued interest in hijacking commercial aircraft.[5] Do not be lulled into complacency because little has occurred since 9/11. The threat is deadly serious and you must be ready for other hijacking attempts. A hijacking attempt may occur on the flight where you are working as a crewmember! Be ready, be vigilant, and be prepared! We must never let a similar attack occur again.

Constant vigilance to the maintenance of our aviation security system by crewmembers and other aviation personnel is the best method to prevent further attacks on aviation. We must continue to search for the weak spots in the aviation security system and correct them immediately. We must be *proactive*, not just *reactive*. We must not only develop new tactics and techniques, but must continually update them. We cannot afford to maintain the status quo ever again.

A 1991 report on airport screening of baggage in the United States indicated an effective reduction in hijackings by 64 per cent.[6] We do know that 100 per cent of the airplanes on 9/11 were hijacked successfully, and this report provides little assurance to us. Another way of interpreting this report is there is a 36 per cent chance that airport screening will not deter a hijacker. So, tell us, 'do you feel lucky?'

A tremendous amount of attention by governments focused on protecting the 'front doors' and the perimeters of commercial airports, with little attention paid to passengers aboard the aircraft. The crucial nerve center of aviation security, the aircraft itself, is still very vulnerable. As flight crews, we are left to chance and our own devices if terrorists are on board our aircraft. Assurances from airlines and government agencies that armed individuals will be interdicted at security checkpoints are contrary to continued reports of security violations. The need to establish and maintain over lapping responsibilities of security – a seamless security approach – will continue to be emphasized throughout this book.

With military actions in Iraq, Afghanistan and others that may occur, we can be certain there will be other hijacking attempts and/or homicidal-suicide bombings. Sabah Khodada, an Iraqi defector who was a captain in the Iraqi Army under Saddam Hussein and worked in terrorist training camps in Iraq, stated in an interview being conducted by PBS that we could expect further hijacking attempts. Iraq's terrorist training focused on a multitude of tactics primarily targeting American interests, including how to hijack aircraft. Khodada explained to the interviewer that hijack training involved taking over an aircraft by using available weapons on the aircraft, such as food utensils, pencils and pens.[7] This is what some within the law enforcement community believe to have happened aboard the doomed hijacked airliners on 9/11; the terrorists quickly instilled horror by murdering flight crewmembers causing passengers to freeze and not react, just as they had been trained. (Refer to Chapter 4 on terrorist training.) Do not fall into the complacency trap now the war within Iraq has overthrown Saddam Hussein. Without a doubt, terrorist training camps will be moved to other more hospitable countries sympathetic to terrorists such as Iran, Somalia, North Korea, the western frontier of Pakistan, or to Southeast Asia. Terrorism is a long way from being defeated, if that is even entirely possible.

Training of thousands of recruits in terrorism has not been accomplished for 'idle threats', but rather to carry out acts of destruction over a period of years. We can only account for some of those trained in terrorism. It is definitely not over yet, and terrorists get to pick the time and place for their destructive acts.

Vulnerabilities continue

Since 9/11 guns, knives, bombs, and other weapons are still making there way onto commercial airliners. Here are a few examples:

- A Florida man arrested in Atlanta after a random search had already flown on two flight segments and was preparing to board another flight when a gun was discovered in his carry-on bag.[8]
- A flight from JFK diverted after a man gave the flight crew a gun he said he had forgotten about in his bag.[9]
- Then of course there is the infamous 'shoe bomber', Richard Reid. Reid had been detained by French police before the flight, questioned, and was permitted to board the flight. He attempted to light a plastic explosive bomb imbedded in his shoes during flight.[10]
- Over America's Thanksgiving holiday in November 2002, 15,982 pocket knives and 98 boxcutters were confiscated at security checkpoints. In addition, at the 38 busiest US airports 1,072 clubs or bats were confiscated, along with 3,242 banned tools and 2,384 flammable items. Another 20,581

sharp objects such as scissors, ice picks and meat cleavers were also confiscated.[11]

- Since February 2002, TSA screeners have confiscated 1.4 million knives, 2.4 million sharp objects, 1,101 guns, 15,666 clubs, more than 125,000 incendiary items and nearly 40,000 box cutters.[12]

In an effort to demonstrate the continued weaknesses of the security at airports nationwide, reporters from the *Daily News* in New York smuggled weapons through the security checkpoints at eleven different major airports over America's Labor Day weekend in September 2002. The airports included Newark International, Boston Logan International, Washington Dulles International, Portland International Jetport in Maine, New York's La Guardia and Kennedy, Chicago's O'Hare, Los Angeles, Las Vegas, Fort Lauderdale and Santa Barbara, California. They reportedly smuggled various weapons through the checkpoints that included utility knives, rubber-handled razor knives, pocketknife, corkscrew, razor blades and pepper spray. All of the reporters managed to get through the security checkpoints without the weapons being detected by security personnel.[13] Does anyone really think security screeners will locate all the dangerous items passengers will bring through the security checkpoints? A test during the spring of 2003 by the Transportation Security Administration showed screeners found knives only 70 per cent of the time and missed 25 per cent of the guns in carry-on baggage.[14] It is just a matter of time before organized terrorists attempt to implement their murderous plans involving aviation. It is not over.

No doubt, terrorists will continue to plan airline hijackings and other violence. Those who believe that further hijackings are not possible are ignoring the obvious determination of modern terrorists. *The defenseless position of flight crews that currently exists aboard commercial aircraft against highly trained and motivated terrorists needs to be fully recognized and properly addressed.* Flight crews ultimately bear the brunt of ALL the errors and pitfalls of our present aviation security system.

The new reality of today's world is clearly violent and contains millions of people who hate Americans, and their allies. They will kill themselves, everyone aboard an aircraft, and as many innocent people on the ground as possible to make their political point. Some terrorists have been trained to create horror and fear (terror) quickly by publicly murdering one or more victims at the onset of a hijacking as a control technique for both the flight crew and passengers. This is quite a departure from the hijacker of the past who simply wanted a free ride to Cuba, or another destination, with no intent of self-destruction. How can we differentiate between the two types of hijackings in time to prevent either from happening? A good start would be proper training, continued education, individual study, practicing both individually and as a crew (team), being properly equipped to defend the aircraft, and being constantly vigilant and aware of the environment in which we live and work.

Photo 1.1 Have you been trained in how to deal with a hostage situation?

Flight crew security procedures and training

In the early 1970s the Federal Aviation Administration (FAA) designed an aviation security program known as the 'Common Strategy' that was a plan to deal with aircraft hijackings. It was a basic set of principles for airlines, crewmembers, ATC, airports and law enforcement to use when confronted with a hijacker. However, the 'Common Strategy' became known as the 'Common Knowledge'. Some of the 'Common Strategy' procedures were printed for all to read in the Airman's Informational Manual, a book available to anyone at just about any bookstore. The procedures did not change over time, giving terrorists ample time to study our aviation security weaknesses, which they then used against America on 9/11. We must not let our security procedures lapse into 'Common Knowledge'. Revision of aviation security tactics, procedures and policies should occur on a regular basis. This will have the affect of making these procedures obsolete and any inside knowledge learned by terrorist will become time critical.

As we mentioned earlier, there has been a lot of publicity about most every aspect of aviation security except flight crew security training. Flight crews are the last line of defense and must have a comprehensive security training course that gives them basic tools needed to counteract an attack. The Aviation and Transportation Security Act passed through Congress and was signed by the President of the United States on 19 November 2001 required crew security training. The crew training required is embodied in section 106 of the Act and has some very good aspects to it. As flight crewmembers, we were initially pleased with the legislation. Unfortunately, it was interpreted in widely different ways throughout the airline industry with the apparent blessing of both the FAA and the TSA.

Some airlines have taken the subject of crew training seriously and have implemented comprehensive training, while others have done as little as possible. During the process of developing a flight crew security training course for a major airline, we discovered to some degree what most American domestic airlines have for crew security training. Unfortunately, some airlines have chosen the least amount of security training for their crews. 9/11 was one of the darkest days in American history and the most cataclysmic for commercial aviation. Surprisingly, most airlines in the US provided as little training to crewmembers as the FAA would let them get away with. We know the airlines have had a difficult financial period after 9/11, but the human cargo that is carried aboard airliners is priceless. Therefore, we are very disappointed at the FAA, TSA, and the airlines by not putting as much effort into insisting upon a comprehensive security course for crewmembers as they were at protecting security checkpoints with National Guard troops. Terrorist threats remain and are very real; and the sad fact is, crewmember training at most airlines is plainly insufficient for the existing threats. Terrorists are training today to kill Americans and their allies and to think terrorists would not attempt another hijacking is the height of naiveté. We have had some pilots and flight attendants tell us that a terrorist hijacking will not happen again, as if it were an absolute certainty. We would really like to know where they get this information because government officials continue to claim threats to commercial aviation remain real. As tight and comprehensive as the security is in Israel, homicidal/suicide bombers continue to kill whenever they want. If the terrorists want to hijack an airplane, they will attempt to hijack an airplane. With the lack of security training that some airline crews have received, hijacking an airplane could be easier than one might expect. With the intelligence demonstrated by the hijackers on 9/11, devising methods to hijack airplanes is not beyond their capabilities. It is conceivable that militant terrorists could attempt to hijack an airplane just to prove the point they can terrorize the world's airline industry anytime they want. They will certainly operate on their own time and place. With the lack of credible training for crews and as more time passes from the events of 9/11, the fears of another hijacking become erased by over-confidence. We have become more vulnerable, not stronger, to another hijacking attempt.

The Aviation and Transportation Security Act of 2001 mandated security training for flight crews. However, the guidance provided by the FAA and the TSA left the development of training to the airlines in content and duration. A crewmember (who wished to remain anonymous) gave us the following observations of the security training course at the major airline where he works:

> The security training received from my airline was completely inadequate. The pilots received a few hours of training and the flight attendants just a little more. The Instructor who taught my security course had no police, military, or security training. He was reading the material from a power point presentation and could not answer any questions about the material. Each of us could have read the slides for ourselves and gotten out of class in an hour or less. In my opinion, the lack of training undermines the intent of the Aviation and Transportation Security Act and falls way short of what real security training should be. I have talked with crewmembers from other airlines

> and we have compared our training. Based on those discussions, I believe my airline security training experience is the norm in the industry.

Unfortunately, his opinion is common among crewmembers industry wide and is a sad commentary on how the airlines and government views their role in aviation security. From discussions with crewmembers in America, their airlines have provided as few as 4 hours of training while others have provided 16 hours with programs that vary significantly in quality. The crewmember training, called 'Common Strategy 2' and treated as 'guidance' by the TSA and FAA, is not mandated. Crewmembers can only conclude their approach to crew security training is only 'filling the checked boxes'. The FAA and TSA are not serious about crewmember training.

These may be strong words, but when compared to the attention and resources poured into security screeners, police, National Guard troops and the like, you can understand why crewmembers may feel slighted. In fact, there was not one security device on 9/11, nor today, that can detect the malevolent intent of a human being. Therefore, it makes sense for crewmembers to receive the best possible security training to counter terrorist threats. So far, crewmembers across the world are waiting for this quality training. When it is coming is our question.

Capitalism at its finest

When an airliner sits on the ramp, it is not producing revenue for the airline. After the remarkable manner in which all aircraft landed within a couple of hours after the terrorist events of 9/11 unfolded, airlines immediately started losing money. Passengers, crews and aircraft were stranded all over the world and needed to reach their destinations. Airlines wanted to start moving aircraft and people as soon as possible. Their bottom line demanded it.

The problem was that flight crews were not that eager to take aircraft into the air again until some changes were made that would provide some amount of protection for themselves, the passengers and the aircraft. Unfortunately, flight crews were expected to do as they were told, even though they, like most people throughout the world, were extremely upset about the events of 9/11. It would be very difficult to find any flight crewmember anywhere that did not have the nagging question on their mind of 'what would I do if similar events occurred on my next flight?'

No one could assure any flight crew their particular flight was going to be uneventful. Even worse, during those first few days after airline flight operations resumed, there was NO guidance from the airlines, the unions, or the government on what to do if similar events occurred. Flight crews invented some rather unique methods of protecting themselves, the passengers and the aircraft. Left to their own imagination and ingenuity, some of these methods were very bizarre. One captain wanted security issues handled one way while another captain wanted security issues handled completely differently. Confusion reigned in a time when flight crews needed more than ever to be knowledgeable about airline security.

Airlines expected flight crews to go about their duties as if nothing had ever happened. Flight crews were expected to instill confidence in the traveling public, an almost impossible task when totally untrained in self-defense, doubtful of abilities to respond to terrorist attacks, highly stressed, and frightened of the unknown. Airlines were quick to point out that, nothing else of significance occurred during the week following 9/11. Flying was very safe, and we could all rest a little easier now.

Initially after 9/11, most aircraft operated with full loads as stranded passengers scrambled to get to their destinations. It was not very long, however, until load factors dropped considerably. Few people wanted to go on vacations, or to attend conferences or business meetings. Many elected to drive or go by bus or train. Passengers sensed the vulnerability of air travel and of all those people who make air travel possible. They were correct, but probably did not know the full extent of that vulnerability. The fact that one-year later on 11 September 2002, scheduled airline flights that operated were virtually empty, underscores the continued tremendous lack of confidence passengers have in aviation security. A non-scientific poll taken by CNN in August 2003 showed that 55 per cent of those responding believed an aircraft hijacking is still possible.

Two years after 9/11, look at how many airlines are in deep financial trouble and continue to be at this writing. With a few exceptions, most airlines are operating at huge losses, on borrowed time, applying for bankruptcy protection, or simply going away. At a time when revenues are down sharply, additional costs of modifying aircraft, re-developing and implementing security procedures throughout the airline and airport operations are all becoming financial burdens that have taken its toll on the airlines. As if that were not enough, a US District Judge in New York opened the door for law suits to be filed against American and United airlines, the Boeing Company and the Port Authority of New York and New Jersey by victims of 9/11 by citing negligence in areas of security as contributing factors to the attacks.[15]

Federal Air Marshals

The Federal Air Marshal program began in 1968 as the Sky Marshal Program and continued through the 1970s as a program designed to stop hijackings to and from Cuba. The current Federal Air Marshal program was established by Public Law 99–83 in August 1985 in response to the hijacking of TWA 847 in June of that year. After 9/11, the FAM program received additional funding to expand its program.[16]

Since its expansion beginning in 2001, the FAM program has been plagued with allegations. During a Congressional hearing in May 2002, the TSA was accused of lowering its standards in order to hire quickly and rapidly increase the numbers of marshals. The TSA was also accused of cutting training requirements and placing new hires on flights despite their lack of advanced marksmanship skills. In an August 2002 statement prepared by the Federation of Government Employees, air marshals confirmed their lack of training, reporting the program operates like 'security guard training at a mall'.[17] In September 2002, a letter to the

TSA published in *USA Today* cited a report that 250 marshals have left the program. The paper reported marshals working a 12- to 16-hour day, with some scheduled to fly for ten consecutive days, while others are not working at all. Marshals report they are falling asleep or getting sick aboard flights.[18]

The FAM program has seen its share of other problems, as well. In one incident in July 2002, a marshal was removed from a flight in Washington, DC, after smelling of alcohol. Two other incidents involved the accidental discharge of their firearms. One incident occurred in a hotel room in Las Vegas and the other in the lavatory of an aircraft in flight. One marshal was suspended after he left his firearm in a lavatory during a flight from Washington to Las Vegas. A passenger discovered the weapon.[19]

Another controversial problem that has produced negative press for the FAM program involves their interface with the airlines. According to federal rules, each airline must assign the specific seat requested by a FAM on official duty. With the airlines desperately trying to win back business travelers, who usually occupy first class seats, the money-conscious airlines do not like to give up those seats to non-paying FAMs. Numerous confrontations have taken place over this topic resulting, in come cases, in the compromise of the identity of the FAMs and their purpose for being on the flight.[20] The nearsightedness of the airlines to turn a profit over conducting a safe and secure flight in these instances reinforces our belief that money will not be spent in adequately training flight crews, either.

In the United States alone, there are approximately 30,000 commercial flights daily. At this rate, the sky marshal program has a long way to go to assure every flight is manned. We wholeheartedly support anything that increases the security of commercial flights, but there are some important things to consider when accelerating the hiring of individuals into the sky marshal program. First, the position requires a top-secret clearance that takes time to complete. Unless time is taken in the selection process, it will be impossible to hire the tens of thousands of FAMs needed, without compromising quality. When Waltrip worked for the San Jose Police Department, they could not keep adequate levels of staffing for officers regardless of the frequent and massive recruitment drives conducted by the department.

A prospective FAM candidate could be rejected several ways during the selection process. These include written tests, physical agility, medical exam, background investigation/interview, psychological tests, psychologist interview, polygraph test, academy academics, field training, and the probationary period. Law enforcement is a demanding job and it is a difficult position to attain for anyone.

FAMs are critical to aviation security but rushing into hiring just anybody because bodies are needed is ultimately going to be a major mistake, as evidenced by a lawsuit against the TSA settled in mid-2003. A passenger detained after a flight to Philadelphia on Delta Air Lines resulted in an unusual settlement. The TSA agreed to apologize to the passenger (to be made by TSA director, James Loy), change training policies, and to pay the man US$50,000. One of the FAMs involved was a former Border Patrol agent who had been rejected by the Philadelphia police and fire departments because of his performance on a psychological exam.[21]

The FAM program received negative publicity in July and August 2003. In July, the HSD hastily canceled a plan that would have taken FAMs off long-distance flights to save the costs of overnight expenses. The plan would have left most international and cross-country flights (like those on 9/11) without the added security of FAMs. 'Those actions were premature and a mistake by the people who were involved', said the agency's spokesperson.[22] In August, lawmakers on both parties in Congress were reported to be furious over a proposal by the TSA to cut US$104 million from the FAM program to plug a budget hole. Denounced as 'mind-boggling', 'crazy', and 'foolish', the budget cut proposal was the latest of a series of stumbles by the TSA. 'Some members of Congress view the TSA as a bloated, unresponsive agency that is shirking its most important duty: ensuring safe air travel'.[23]

As much as crewmembers would like to see sky marshals on every flight, it is not going to happen any time in the near future. It is estimated that to cover all US flights would require 120,000 marshals and US$10 billion annually.[24] Homeland Security Director Tom Ridge announced in August 2003 that many of the 5,500 US Customs and Immigration agents will be trained as FAMs to give the FAM program a 'surge capability'.[25] Security and protection of the passengers on a commercial flight will always ultimately fall onto the shoulders of the captain and the flight crew. For these reasons, we believe crew security training should be comprehensive and should empower the crews with the tools to protect themselves, passengers, and the aircraft.

The Federal Air Marshal program will take many years to get up to full strength and it is unlikely the program will produce enough marshals to put them on every domestic US flight. *What is certain is that crewmembers are aboard every scheduled commercial flight.* The obvious answer is to train flight crews in comprehensive methods used in defending themselves, passengers, and the aircraft.

Aviation Security – Reconciling the Changes

Crewmembers

The advent of security changes after 9/11 has prompted many uncomfortable feelings by crewmembers. We have overheard crewmembers say, 'When are we going to be trained on airline security?', 'What is the training going to entail?', 'Is this all the training we are going to get?', 'Are we going to get any more training?', 'What do I do if I am faced with a terrorist hijacker?', 'Will we ever be attacked again?' These questions, and others, have been repeated many times by crewmembers around the world.

The many procedural changes have affected crewmember lives. Mandatory fingerprinting, background investigations, and an obvious mistrust by airlines and the government are just a few. Many of the complaints we have heard from cabin crewmembers are in regards to the unsatisfactory training they received since 9/11. Pilots often complain about why they have to be stopped and checked at the security checkpoints when they do not really need a weapon – they already have the aircraft at their fingertips. This brings up an interesting point, in fact, how does an airport security scanning machine measure a pilot's malevolent intent anyway? How do you really discover what lies in the heart of a human being with a scan of a machine? Law enforcement officers walk through security checkpoints with all their weaponry without question. Why do law enforcement officers get to go through security unmolested and pilots are 'stripped' searched? Why do law enforcement officers get to fly on our aircraft with weapons and a pilot cannot have a screw driver to tighten a loose screw on the engine cowl? While at the same time an aircraft mechanic can bring his complete toolbox onto the aircraft without passing through airport security. Thus, we can only conclude the government suspects pilots of ill intent, but permits them to fly the airplane anyway. Does this make sense to you? Subjecting flight crews to searches at security checkpoints will always be irrelevant because of these and other reasons. Trust is an important factor in life. We have to trust some people in aviation security and it is who to trust is the question. Obviously, flight crews are not to be trusted. Crewmembers must somehow deal with this skewed reality of aviation security and function without fault. This is a difficult task for anyone.

Crewmembers from around the world have many of the same concerns and worries. Since 9/11, being a crewmember has changed dramatically. How flight attendants and pilots view their jobs since 9/11 has added complications to their working relationships. Most crewmembers see their jobs as significantly different now. For those crewmembers new to the airlines after 9/11, the cold hard reality of deadly hijackings will be a part of their job they will always know. Yet, for those crewmembers that lived and survived through the horrors of 9/11, the changes may be difficult. For those of us who long for the 'days of old', must admit they are now gone forever. It is a fact that many crewmembers that lived through the ordeal of 9/11 cannot seem to find the enthusiasm they used to have for their jobs. For many crewmembers, the job is just not fun any longer. In reality, how can it be fun when crewmembers are often the very targets of suspicion while at the same time expected to do a good job and be vigilant of terrorist threats? On the one hand, they are suspects at the security checkpoint, while on the other expected to stop a terrorist from hijacking the flight they are working. Instead, of being provided the tools (in the form of education and training) to protect themselves and passengers, they are left to imaginative methods of their own invention. We work in a distorted world where crewmembers are expected to perform their duties, to act as if there were nothing wrong, and to be happy and thankful they still have a job. If crewmembers were machines, we suppose that would be possible.

How each airline or individual crewmember deals with the potential threats varies significantly. It is obvious to us that leadership is severely lacking in crewmember security training. We highly suggest that crewmembers take responsibility for their own destinies by taking the personal initiative to learn what is important for their survival. By reading this book, you are taking significant steps over the inadequate training you have received to develop many ideas and concepts on how you will go about your job. We wholeheartedly encourage this approach and believe that by searching for knowledge, you will not only be better prepared but will feel much more confident in your job. Encourage others to take control of their own lives and seek to become empowered with knowledge. Leadership within the ranks of crewmembers is desperately needed to encourage crewmembers to search for knowledge, and this is where you can make a difference. This approach could take many forms such as attending conferences, symposiums, workshops, reading books, and participating in discussion groups on security topics. Your airline security education should be taken seriously. If adequate training is not provided you by your airline, you need to seek it out for yourself.

Photo 1.2 An airline captain being screened at a security checkpoint

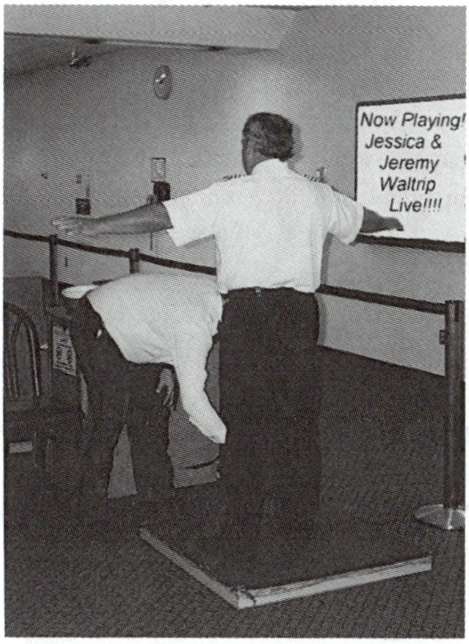

Becoming educated about our common enemy will help you to understand why terrorists want to hijack airplanes. Study and training in areas addressed by this book will be a good start to your education. Many individuals have given their lives in the advancement of aviation within the past 100 years. We too must learn from those who paid ultimate price for ignoring the threat and consequences of terrorism. With the knowledge of the brutality of our enemy, it is imperative we act before we fail to learn additional lessons from 9/11. By seeking ways to solve our security problems, we will honor those whose lives were so tragically taken from us on 9/11. If we have learned anything from the events of 9/11, it is that CREWMEMBERS NEED TO BE AN INTEGRAL PART OF AVIATION SECURITY.

Crewmember relationships

Maintaining relationships is difficult in even the best of marriages and friendships. Getting along and agreeing with others is just not possible 100 per cent of the time. Sometimes differences of opinion will persist within a relationship. The individuals may attempt to reconcile those differences and come to some common ground of agreement. Yet, differences of opinion do not usually jeopardize a relationship unless one attempts to impose their opinion on the other without their consent.

Both cabin and flight crewmembers have different priorities on what constitutes the correct approach to crewmember security issues. The 'last line of defense' is a phase that is used by both pilots and flight attendants when speaking of their roles in airline security. It is interesting to listen to how a flight attendant or pilot views the roles of the other crewmember in security. For some reason, the other crewmembers' role does not seem to be as important as their own role. We are speaking generally here, because this is not the case 100 per cent of the time. However, it appears obvious that crewmember labor unions appear to underestimate the others' importance to airline security. Instead of banding together and as a collective group seeking mutually beneficial solutions to security they are standing in their separate corners ready to do battle with the 'powers to be', as well as with one another.

The Homeland Security Act of 2002 was an example of the lack of cooperation between flight crews. The pilot unions were happy because they got what they wanted in the legislative bill in the form of the armed pilot provisions. Meanwhile, flight attendants were unhappy because what they got was a 'watered down' version of the self-defense provisions they where seeking in the bill. Unfortunately, self-serving politics played a role in the outcome of the legislation and caused bad feelings between crewmember unions. Why the unions could not have pushed collectively for what was in the overall best interest of airline security is unknown to us. We believe a cooperative approach to security would serve pilots, flight attendants, airline and the traveling public. Both flight attendants and pilots should be very concerned with each other's roles in airline security and should want the very best training for (and with) each other.

At a time in the history of airlines where crewmembers need to increase their appreciation for each other and the important job they do, they are being pulled apart by perspective. In Chapter 8, Mental Preparation: Developing a Survival Mindset, we write about camaraderie. It is imperative that crewmembers stick together and not lose sight of what is important. Our lives are so dependant upon one another in this era of terrorism and we cannot understand why crewmembers are not drawing closer together. We have observed some calloused views of what role each crewmember can play in airline security. The truth is; we need each other more than ever. Minimizing the other's job or role is not accepting the reality. We have heard flight attendants say, 'The pilots are scared to come out of the cockpit'. We have heard pilots say that 'It is impossible to train flight attendants to defend the aircraft'. Why is it so hard to believe each group serves an important role in airline security? These unrealistic opinions need to change now.

We witnessed these opposing viewpoints first hand when we were assisting in the development of a flight crew security training course for an airline that had a strained relationship between Inflight and Flight Operations personnel. Neither group was interested in designing a mutually acceptable course that addressed the concerns of both groups. One group bowed out of the development process just when their input was crucial to the unified conclusion of the course. What does this tell us about how airline flight departments view each other?

When airline flight departments, employee unions, and individual crewmembers let personal interests get into the way of such an important time in airline history, it is clearly time for change. Terrorists must really like to hear about the conflicts among aviation personnel because it shows signs of weaknesses they can use to their advantage. These conflicts must stop because the longer we argue over the importance or lack of importance over each other's jobs, we are taking a huge risk that can be avoided through respect and cooperation.

Neglecting the #1 job: Safety

'These are the times that try men's souls'. They certainly are and with all the security alerts, airline security directives and terrorism in the news, it is easy to lose sight of what is our most important job: *Safety*. Safely transporting passengers to their destinations is our main job. Becoming preoccupied with terrorist dangers that surround crewmembers can be counter-productive to their jobs. The danger of a terrorist hijacking or attack is just a reality we need to accept while we continue to focus on safety.

Aviation personnel are a strong group of people that have endured a lot of turmoil over the history of air transportation. There have been economic depressions, wars, tragic accidents involving collisions of aircraft in the air and on the ground, hijackings, bombings, and hijacked airliners used as guided missiles to kill thousands of people. All along, airline people have survived and courageously continued to provide safe, reliable transportation. Aviation personnel will prevail just as they have always prevailed, but not without problems to overcome. Life is not perfect and it is a challenge of our character to overcome terrorism while at the same time maintaining a high level of safety in air transportation.

The security knowledge we would like all crewmembers to possess is in *addition* to the high level of safety they must maintain while doing their jobs. Security is just another new aspect of crewmembers' jobs that is needed to maintain the high level of safety in airline travel. We urge all crewmembers to continue to learn and add to the professionalism of their jobs through education and knowledge. You cannot ever know too much about your job. Study before recurrent training and prepare for the simulator while seeking information to make you more knowledgeable about your job. Do not neglect your job, and remain focused on getting the job done correctly and safely. We recognize it is easy to become preoccupied with the turbulence surrounding airlines in these difficult transitionary times. Yet, you are the same caliber of crewmember that has come before you and will overcome difficulties just as they have in the years past.

Aviation Security – Making it Safer

The airline security model

Like other security models, the airline security model consists of concentric circles or rings of protection around a protected area. The center of the circle is the area to be protected with the various concentric circles or security rings, representing layers of protection/security. In this case, the center area to be protected is the aircraft where the passengers and the crew are located. This is the vital center of airline security. Although, there are other concerns such as the terminal area, we will limit our discussion to the aircraft.

Currently, the airline security systems of most of the world place an emphasis on the outer rings of the concentric circles rather than the center area. The closer you get to the vital center area, the less protected it becomes. In other words, airline security approaches security from the *outside in* while at the same time reducing protection as each ring of security is passed. For example, outer rings consist of items such as the CAPS program, which identifies potential passengers as a threat, police patrolling the terminal areas, explosive detection (EDS) machines checking luggage for explosives, security checkpoints where passengers are checked for weapons. These are just a few of the *outside in* approaches to airline security. However, the closer one gets to the passengers and crew the less protected it becomes. We are not at all suggesting the outer rings of security are not important, because they are and should continually be upgraded and improved. Using the *outside in* security approach is dangerous because it places passengers and crew at incredible risk, leaving them at their own devices to protect themselves.

With the *outside in* approach to airline security the question should be raised, what occurs if terrorists make it through the decreasing levels of the security rings and boards the flight? Not an unrealistic assumption considering the preparation the 9/11 terrorists went through to commit their serial murders.

We believe the passengers and crew, the vital center area of the airline security model, should be the most protected. It should be provided the highest level of security as opposed to the other way around. Our approach to airline security is from the *inside out,* and we believe it is the preferred method to apply to aviation security. Immediate provisions should be made to strengthen the security of the center area through more complete crew security training, continual increases in sky marshals on flights, arming pilots and on-board technological security gadgetry to compliment the other security measures taken to the outer rings of the airline security model. All the rings of security protection should compliment each other rather than relying heavily upon the outer rings as presently exists in airline security.

The US government responded to the terrorist actions of 9/11 by placing National Guard troops at the airport security checkpoints, conducting random passenger screening, using fighter jet intercepts on commercial aircraft and using other *outside in* approaches to aviation security. Yet, bombs, weapons, and dangerous individuals have gotten through the *outside in* security since 9/11. What happens then to the protection of the vital center area (aircraft and passengers)? Security of the center area is obviously left to the crew and passengers who are the least prepared to deal with a violent hijacking or other violent act. Under the current airline security model, if a plane is suspected of veering even the slightest bit off course, fighter jets will be dispatched by ATC to intercept the flight, and if certain parameters are met, to shoot it down. The possibility of being shot down by our own forces is not a calming contemplation for both passengers and crews. This is just one reason why we believe crewmembers should receive comprehensive counter-hijacking training.

Sadly, the effort the government has placed on the outside rings of its security perimeters to protect commercial aviation has not satisfactorily occurred at the core, the flight crew/passenger level. It is obvious to us that *inside out* security in the form of properly trained flight crews should be a top priority. Anything less is a major mistake of emphasis. If they had placed the emphasis at this level, we would not have to write these very critical words. We honestly wish that we could say that valiant efforts have been made at getting flight crews adequately trained. We are at the front line of commercial aviation, but the reality is that little has changed regarding crewmember security training since 9/11, when compared to other areas of security emphasis by the government and industry.

Seamless airline security

Airline security should be redundant and incorporate overlapping areas of responsibilities. All airline/airport employees, including those directly involved with security, should raise their levels of awareness and observe all areas in and around an airport. We need to develop new strategies and solutions to airport/airline security. Everyone from the janitor to the pilots need to get out of the dangerous 'WHITE' (Unaware – see Chapter 7 – Awareness for Survival) phase of awareness and pay attention to their surroundings. Unfortunately, before 9/11, the aviation community had been lulled into a corporate state of complacency. We settled upon a comfortable existence of a predictable standard of security.

The airline security system should be seamless with the concentric security rings we spoke of previously, catching what a previous security ring missed. For example, if the ticketing passenger profiling system (CAPPS) missed a terrorist, then the check-in process should identify the terrorist and stop him. If the check-in process failed to stop the terrorist then the security checkpoint should identify the terrorist and stop him. If the security checkpoint process failed to stop the terrorist then the boarding process should identify him. If every security ring failed to detect the terrorist, then it would be up to the passengers and crew to stop him. If the passengers and crew failed then it would be up to the fighter jets to shoot down the airliner to stop the terrorists.

Each ring of security should support the other and catch what the previous ring missed. No one ring of security is sufficient. The rings can also be described as layers of Swiss cheese layered upon one another (as described in James Reason's book, *Managing the Risks of Organizational Accidents*). Each piece of cheese has its own individual and unique hole positions. If a terrorist makes it through one hole of security, he will run into another piece of cheese whose holes are in another place altogether. If terrorists make it through the second security layer (piece of cheese), they should be stopped by the third layer whose holes are in another location. However, each succeeding inner layer should not be weaker then the previous layer. In other words, have fewer holes than the cheese preceding it. As each layer of cheese is passed, the holes decrease in number and not increase or begin to align making it easier to pass to the next. The holes in the cheese should become smaller and less numerous thus making passage from one layer of security to the next increasingly difficult. With this approach to a seamless security system the ultimate success of the terrorist will become significantly reduced.

We envision such a multiple-layered security system for aviation – identifying the threats, striving to learn as much as possible about the threats, designing and incorporating proactive policies to prevent the threats from coming to a conclusion and implementing self-defensive methods to defeat the threats. Unfortunately, the current airline security system does not incorporate this approach to aviation. We admit we are not the last word in security, but if we can see the weaknesses in airline security, so can the terrorists.

Airline safety versus cost considerations

Airlines are facing the largest financial challenges since airlines have been in existence. Airlines around the world have suffered incredible financial losses because of the 9/11 attacks and the downturn of the world's economies. In this unfavorable economic environment, the regulatory agencies around the world are forcing the airlines to spend millions of dollars on meeting security requirements with money that is scarce. The reality is that it is difficult to separate financial survival and meeting the post 9/11 security regulatory requirements. However, the immense financial stresses on the airlines are relevant and should not be ignored when discussing important safety issues.

Just how do the worlds' airlines reconcile doing what is needed in making crews and passengers secure as possible while at the same time making a profit? Even in the best of financial times, achieving this goal may be difficult. Let us face it; a crewmember's definition of what is secure is different from that of an airline's CEO. Therefore, an individual's opinion of the airline industry is based upon what your particular perspective happens to be. Yet, we must make an important distinction when it comes to viewing the hazards of commercial flight. An airline corporate headquarters has never been hijacked by terrorists and crashed into another building. If this were actually a serious threat, airline management personnel may feel as crewmembers do about security.

It is imperative to the future security of the airlines that airline management personnel around the world make sincere attempts to understand the threats that face their airline. Costs and profits will make little sense if procedures and policies have not stayed in touch with the threats and the airline is destroyed by another 9/11 terrorist attack. Examining the airline organization will reveal a lot about the corporate culture of an airline. With knowledgeable people doing the analysis, it may save the airline from taking steps that may ultimately lead to costly security oversights. The examination should reveal insights that may save not only money, but also through policy adjustment how to prevent the loss of equipment, employees, passengers and innocent people on the ground. Honesty and keen observational skills will produce a report that will potentially save the airline from unseen obstacles that management does not look for in the operation of their company. A brief look at important security distinctions highlights their importance in a thorough security evaluation. A complete airline security evaluation should include:

- An evaluation of security threats at operational levels and non-operational levels of the airline;
- An evaluation of security risks of employee tasks and their environment;
- A diagnosis of corporate factors that create potential security risks;
- An estimate of the levels of security risk and suggested methods to eliminate threats;
- Measures to assist those who evaluate the risks and identifying methods to reach solutions;
- Methods to detect security risks;
- Suggestions to devise overlapping security responsibilities throughout the corporate structure;
- Forecasts and predictions of future security threats based on the evaluation;
- Identifying corporate failures of procedures and policies rather than employee shortcomings; and,
- Application of informed human factors knowledge in the evaluation of employees' security mistakes.

No doubt, such an evaluation would be an unusual undertaking for any airline. Searching for errors and holes in an organization takes courage and imagination on the part of the directors. It would take time to complete such an evaluation, one that would more than likely involve a review that could be very frightening. Weaknesses and vulnerabilities are not easy for anyone to accept. Since 9/11, the governments of the world have taken steps to insure the security of the traveling public through new initiatives, equipment, and personnel. The airlines rightly acknowledge the government should handle security issues. This may be true to some degree, but this does not preclude an airline from taking reasonable steps to insure the safety of their passengers, crew and aircraft.

Once a threat is known to exist (9/11), then should not the airlines take reasonable and prudent steps to protect themselves and their employees from that threat? However, if the serious security threats are a matter for the proper authorities, then why do the airlines have to spend valuable resources during difficult economic times? Furthermore, if an evaluation is conducted and security threats are uncovered, then valuable resources would be directed into correcting the problem, which could potentially cost an untold amount of money. So why should the airlines accept this advice?

All we can offer is a reasonable argument that strikes at the ethics of an organization and their leaders. Our efforts in this book are not an attempt to place blame or preach a 'holier than thou' message, but to convince you of suggested methods to significantly reduce the risks that exist in the world around us all. We have admitted that we do not have all the answers, but if an attempt is not made to look for the weaknesses, then solutions to potential threats will not be found. We care about the airlines, their existence and want them to be profitable. We believe that searching for weaknesses will save money through proactively detecting and eliminating potential threats before they occur, and will play a significant role in airline survivability in a new violent chapter of air transportation.

With the advent of mass air transportation, violent behavior by terrorists has partly been made possible by our own desires to build 'world-class' airlines. Airlines have unknowingly contributed to their own vulnerability by encouraging the world to fly. An airliner is an inviting target to radical terrorists who would like to destroy one to make headlines for their cause, whatever that may be. The airliner represents important issues that are both good and bad for the radical terrorist. They have been able to travel around the world spreading their hateful philosophies and educating themselves on airline weaknesses. While on the other side of this equation, airliners have brought foreigners into their land whose actions, cultures, and behaviors are contrary to theirs, causing conflicts that may not ever be reconciled. The equation represents a very complex problem that ignoring will not make go away.

This is a violent world and the violence will come to us if we do not take prudent steps to look for the airline vulnerabilities and make efforts to fix them. We have the ability to address security issues at the airline level, but does airline management have the heart and desire to keep terrorism from targeting their airline? 9/11 is an example of how cruel, inhuman and violent behavior can be inflicted upon any of us anywhere in the world. Because the terrorist actions of 9/11 were so successful, it will no doubt encourage other terrorists of all stripes to plot their malevolent deeds that are just as dramatic, or more. The terrorist bar has been set, but can governments and airlines keep another 9/11 from happening? We suggest that well trained and knowledgeable crewmembers serve as effective deterrents to terrorist hijackings. Does the government or the airlines have the foresight and understanding to recognize this fact?

Aviation Security – The Human Element

Placing blame for security incidents on personnel

When a security incident occurs that involves personnel who are responsible for the secure operation of airports and airlines, it is easy to blame the person(s) whose mistake led to the situation. How many times since 9/11 have airport terminals been evacuated because of security oversights by security screeners? How often has a commercial airliners found a fighter jet along their wing because of a lack of communications (over 400 times)? How many flights have diverted and landed because crewmembers suspected a passenger was a terrorist? How many flights have been quarantined because of a suspected chemical agent was on the aircraft? Security incidents have continued to occur repeatedly. Many of the incidents involve airline or airport employees who made a mistake because of a lack of training and knowledge. Granted, it is easy to blame the operational employees for the over-reactions that resulted in the airline losing money and creating 'bad press' for the following week. Admonishing and disciplining employees is often a convenient choice of an airline management, but is this the proper approach correct the root problems?

An important issue to remember is that airline security procedures and policies have been evolving quickly since 9/11. Many individuals are new to the airline security business, but nonetheless are taking the heat for procedural shortcomings. Blaming an employee with a lack of training, knowledge, or oversight, for over-zealous performance is like blaming the automobile for the traffic accident. The car was involved, but it got to the scene of the accident by the direction of the driver. In affect, training, procedures and policies and management oversight are the drivers of the security incident. Other than outright criminal behavior, the offending employee usually just happens to be the convenient scapegoat, which often serves the purpose of the investigators/airline management looking to place the blame on someone. It is very easy to place blame on employees rather than to examine the incident further.

At one major US airline, security changes have been significant in number. By the first of January 2003, this airline has incorporated into their operations 90 security directives, 408 name lists, 48 information circulars, added six computer assisted passenger pre-screening addendums, and made nine changes to their Aircraft Operator Standard Security Program (AOSSP). All of these changes occurred after 9/11.

The security of the traveling public is so important that serious attempts should be made by governments and airlines to analyze in detail each aspect of every employee position that has something to do with airline security. How else will we discover the error-making potential of employees and their tasks? How else do we identify, assess and then eliminate serious flaws within the employee environment? How can procedural shortcomings contribute to the breakdown of security at the worst possible moment? To counter human and procedural shortcomings, can proactive methods of education be developed that consider human frailties of employees? These questions are very important and need answers to allow the continual revision of tactics designed to keep terrorists off guard to the advances within the aviation security world. Becoming satisfied with some arbitrary level of security should never occur in aviation. The system needs constant review and adaptation to the threats potentially directed at aviation and currently existing in the world at any one time. Human beings are by nature industrious and determined when searching for solutions to problems. Terrorists will no doubt continue to try to uncover aviation's weaknesses so they can exploit them to their advantage. The fact is there will always be vulnerabilities in the aviation system worldwide, but will we find the vulnerabilities and fix them or will we let the terrorists find them for us?

When incidents occur that highlight the shortcomings of individuals involved in aviation security, we need to look more closely at the situation. Human error in an airline or the TSA is not the cause, but rather a consequence of some factor. When an incident occurs it is usually because, upstream from the incident, procedures, policies and corporate culture provided an avenue of incident trajectory that lead to the outcome of the event. Only after careful examination of all of the factors involved can a conclusion actually be reached on why a certain incident occurred. The examination will usually point to procedures, policies and a working culture that contributed to the incident. To ignore this reality is to ignore behavioral science studies that have been conducted over the last 35 years regarding the causes to human error.[26]

Other scientific data points to the fact that situations are easier to control than trying to change people.[27] It is much easier for the organization to attempt to change the employee through discipline, warnings and retraining, than to admit a procedure was wrong and to change it. A consideration for those investigating a security incident involving a person, is that if a different person were faced with the same information and knowledge at the same time, would they have acted any differently than the person who made the original mistake?

Will the security changes allow a terrorist event or other serious aircraft incident to occur?

An important question we need to ask ourselves is that by developing more and more aviation security protections, are we paving the way toward allowing a terrorist event or some other serious aircraft incident or accident to occur? Many factors may upset the balance of airline safety by making numerous policy changes. Since 9/11, the governments from around the world have attempted to make airline travel safer by instituting security regulations. Even with the best intentions, will any of these regulatory efforts directly or indirectly allow a terrorist event or a serious aircraft incident to occur? This should be a major concern to the governing bodies that make the rules and those that have to enforce new security regulations.

There is nothing wrong with this noble effort by lawmakers and regulators to stop terrorism, but caution should be used, to ensure regulatory steps taken are in fact workable for those carrying out the mandates. The rules will more than likely become more and more restrictive, which will make getting the job done that much more difficult for airline employees and security workers. An unfortunate aspect of the implementation of many new rules is that potentially they may appear petty and unattainable for the employees. Furthermore, pressure from airline management may cause unnecessary stress upon employees to get the job done as efficiently as possible. The un-wanted consequence may be the employees overlook security issues that could ultimately prove very deadly. Nothing may occur the first time this oversight occurs and maybe not the 1000th time either, but this behavior may one day catch up with these actions. Emphasis on getting the job done efficiently may promote an employee culture where letting security issues slip through regulatory barriers becomes the 'norm' because 'this is the way we do it to get the job done'. Additionally, the further away the memories of 9/11 are, the less inclined aviation employees may be concerned with a terrorist event. When an environment of complacency exists, there is a higher probability that a terrorist act may become successful. Complacency and the fallacy of human behavior may prove a lethal combination unless steps are now taken to prevent them through crewmember education.

The airline's most important asset

Powered flying machines have come along way since Wilbur and Orville launched their fragile flying craft off the dunes of Kitty Hawk, North Carolina. The advancements of aerospace engineering and the drive of humans to improve aviation technology have been very impressive. Within 30 years of the Wright Flying Machine, airlines were already establishing themselves across the world. Advances in airframes, engines, navigation, aerodynamics, and abilities were advancing rapidly in an exciting human endeavor. By 1960, the airlines were flying across oceans and continents non-stop in large jet aircraft. By 1969, NASA, with the help of many companies and the incredible efforts of many people, had landed a man on the moon. A lunar landing came after a mere 66 years from the Wright brothers' flight off the dunes of Kitty Hawk with an aircraft that could barely fly. The first 100 years of aviation have been nothing short of a miraculous collective achievement. The individuals known, and unknown, who have contributed to these achievements have been many.

Unfortunately, many of the advancements of aviation have come at a very high price. From the deaths of many people whose lives were taken from them prematurely, we have collectively learned many things that have prevented the deaths of others who have followed. Sometimes, our collective stubbornness has led to the repeating of those mistakes and a rethinking of priorities. The airlines have lost many crewmembers, passengers and aircraft because of the many reasons aircraft crash. Safety initiatives by regulators, manufacturers, employee unions and airlines are an assured result of an aircraft accident. Loss of human life is devastating to crewmembers, passengers, their families, and the airlines. Even though technological advances have brought much to aviation, we should not ever forget what the true cost really was in this success – lives. Although money and time are valuable commodities, they pale in comparison to a human life. Human lives are priceless and the unnecessary loss of just one person is worth the effort at trying to find solutions to preventing a death.

In an effort to make our lives more comfortable with the material things in life we often lose sight of the most important asset – people. The 'bottom line' and 'making a profit for the stockholders' can overshadow the value of human beings and indicate by actions and words the true value of an employees' life in the eyes of the corporation. Unfortunately, the priorities of not only airlines, but also other businesses point directly to how the employees rank in relation to the operation of the enterprise. This is not about how much an airline compensates an employee, but rather how it values that employee. Do the objectives of the airline overshadow the contribution of how they are going to get there with their employees? The company is sending a mixed message to its employees when it claims it cares about every one of them, but then overlooks their individual contribution to the company and fails to provide the bare necessity of employment, training.

Deeds speak louder than words and if a company's stated objectives are more important than its employees are, then the loyalty from the workforce is limited. Loyalty from employees is derived from many factors including corporate vision, stability, employer treatment, positive environment, integrity, attitude and opportunities. People will care only enough to get a paycheck if a company's priorities do not include them. Employees will not care how much its management knows about the airline business until it knows how much management cares about them. Words will not suffice, but actual deeds that prove the worth of each person employed at the airline. It is up to the management to figure out how to prove their motives to employees and not for employees to prove theirs to management. Excellent leadership is not easy, but can pay incredible dividends in the form of employee morale, production and attitude in operation of the airline. Several excellent models of leadership from airlines around the world exist that prove the worth of valuing employees. The successes of these companies prove how well these techniques work in practice.

Leadership, teamwork and vision

Watching the news, reading the newspaper and observing what is occurring at airports across the world reveals the varied approaches to aviation security. The governments of the world state they are dedicated to protecting us by passing legislation aimed at strengthening aviation security. The airlines are concerned with enough security to keep their airplanes moving with passengers. Some aviation security companies and martial arts companies are claiming to have all the answers and want the airlines to fit into *their mold* of what security should be. Flight crews have their own agendas on what is important to them and seem unwilling to cooperate and coordinate with each other. Everyone seems to have his or her own concept as to what should be done to improve aviation security. This is not necessarily bad and shows that people are trying to find solutions to an incredibly complex problem. However, problems arise when all the entities involved fail to cooperate with each other for the common goal. Personal agendas appear to take precedence over what is right.

Among all the collective and individual movements toward improving aviation security, it is obvious there is a distinct void of leadership in this area. It is difficult to ascertain whether anyone has a distinct vision of aviation security, especially for crewmembers. No one person or company has demonstrated a vision about including others into that vision. It is going to take many people to help get airline security to get to acceptable levels, and so far, it appears there is a lot of scrambling and jockeying for self-serving positions and the almighty dollar. Understandably, aviation security is an immense and complicated problem that will not be easy to solve. Throwing as much money as a government or a company can afford at the wall of security and hoping some will stick is not the solution. Government money may put many people to work, but ultimately it is not the solution. Although, many advanced technologies should augment aviation security, we believe a direct approach with educated human involvement is paramount in its implementation. Understandably, it is impossible to build a 'perfect aviation security' system because if humans are involved, it will be imperfect. There will always be weaknesses and holes in any system to exploit by malevolent and industrious individuals. As much as we all want to stop evil things from occurring around us, it would be incorrect to think this is 100 per cent possible, 100 per cent of the time. Mentally and physically preparing those who are involved in aviation security for a 'worse case scenario' makes the most sense to effectively dealing with a security incident.

Criticizing aviation security systems has its place, but with an absence of concrete solutions it is only one side of the equation; and thus, incomplete. Many different people through the ages of humankind have had to step forward with a clear vision of how to solve a problem and have demonstrated the leadership to get through it. We need leaders with an honest desire to improve aviation security. We need leaders without hidden agendas and those not looking for a boost to their egos. We need people who are willing to serve others, demonstrating this through action and not expecting others to serve them.

We suggest the solutions to our aviation security problems can come close to being solved by the involvement of those dedicated to safety. Establishing clear objectives, gathering qualified and dedicated people from around the aviation community, and then setting out to accomplish the objectives is a good first start. Developing positive attitudes toward each other's roles and respecting what both pilots and cabin crews can bring to the table of ideas are crucial to beginning a process of equal worth. Some individuals and companies involved in aviation security are protective of their 'jurisdiction' they cannot see that sharing information can be extremely useful to crewmembers and passengers. To some degree, this is human nature, but to what lengths will we allow this to be taken while endangering others with the selfishness of knowledge and information? Are we all so proud that we cannot work with others on an equal basis to stop an attempted terrorist incident on an aircraft that is sure to happen again?

The main priority in aviation security should be to assure that a terrorist event at an airport, terminal or on an airplane is prevented from occurring. How to accomplish this goal will obviously vary, but if we do not collectively look for ways to solve these problems, we may individually discover it one day at our own peril. The government, airlines, unions, crewmembers and security companies need to recognize the worth of each other's involvement. Creating change is difficult and critics may bellow and make accusations of ineffective action, but together we must keep our eyes fixed upon what we want to accomplish – the elimination of terrorist hijackings and other serious threats on airliners.

The problems we describe in this book are challenges to all of us in aviation. The aviation world throughout its history has faced many challenges that were ultimately solved through a collective and unifying spirit. Problems are necessary for the propulsion of humankind into the future. Going to the next level of aviation security requires resistance. All of the challenges and problems of aviation security create resistance for us, but without it, progress cannot be made. The future direction of aviation security needs leadership with a vision of safety.

Safety without security is not safe

Not being concerned about airline security is like saying we should not have to be concerned about airline safety. Knowledgeable aviation personnel know that safety continually needs to be assessed and adapted to the ever-changing aviation environment. The fact will always remain that safety and security are interlinked and cannot be separated. You cannot have safety without security and you cannot have security without safety. Safety and security are one in the same. Aviation safety issues will always be a serious factor and so will the security of flight. At what level of security does a given flight become unsafe? Chances are you will get a completely different answer to that question if you ask a TSA/airline representative than if you ask a pilot or flight attendant. From a practical standpoint, who would you believe has a better perspective to observe the vulnerabilities of the airline security system? Which one of the two has the most to lose if aviation security is not at a safe level?

Conclusion

The endeavor of aviation security needs a refocusing of direction that will be difficult, but worth it. The ability to see over the fray and fodder of those involved in the day-to-day internal and external battles of aviation is a difficult skill to manage. As Nicolo Machiavelli once said, 'There is nothing more difficult to take in hand, more perilous to conduct or more uncertain in its success, than to take the lead in the introduction of a new order of things'. We, who have undertaken the journey of a difficult and challenging goal of aviation security, have embarked upon a tumultuous ride that is at the same time exciting, but also uncertain. What is certain is that we cannot do it alone. Let us illustrate with a story that you may have heard before of how we all need to work together to accomplish a common goal. This is a story of a bricklayer who tried to do it alone and what happened to him. He wrote the following on his insurance claim report:

> It would have taken too long to carry all the bricks down by hand, so I decided to put them in a barrel and lower them by a pulley, which I had fastened to the top of the building. After tying the rope securely at ground level, I then went up to the top of the building. I fastened the rope around the barrel, loaded it with bricks, and swung it over the sidewalk for the descent.
>
> Then I went down to the sidewalk and untied the rope, holding it securely to guide the barrel down slowly. But, since I weigh only 140 pounds, the 500-pound load jerked me from the ground so fast that I did not have time to think of letting go of the rope. As I passed between the second and third floors, I met the barrel coming down. This accounts for the bruises and the lacerations on my upper body.
>
> I held tightly to the rope until I reached the top where my hand became jammed in the pulley. This accounts for my broken thumb. At the same time, however, the barrel hit the sidewalk with a bang and the bottom fell out. With the weight of the bricks gone, the barrel weighed only about 40 pounds. Thus, my 140-pound body began a swift descent, and I met the empty barrel coming up. This accounts for my broken ankle.
>
> Slowed only slightly, I continued the descent and landed on the pile of bricks. This accounts for my sprained back and broken collarbone. At this point, I lost my presence of mind completely and I let go of the rope. The empty barrel came crashing down on me. This accounts for my head injuries.
>
> As for the last question on the insurance form, 'What would I do if the same situation rose again?', he answered, 'Please be advised I am finished trying to do the job alone'.[28]

If we do not work together, we risk a much worse fate then the bricklayer. Working together and striving to attain a common goal is a vision we have for the many entities of the aviation community. We want you to be part of that vision. Leadership for crewmember security has been lagging too long. In fact, no government or airline has shared with crewmembers a significant leadership vision that includes them. At the time of this writing, it has been two years since the tragic events of 9/11 unfolded, and crewmembers are still waiting for the government and airlines to make them partners in aviation security. We believe that time is now. Flight crewmember ideas and visions in aviation security must be put forth for serious discussion and debate. Whether government officials, airline personnel, union representatives or security company leaders are the ones who demonstrate leadership and share with us their vision for our roles as crewmembers, we do not care; but we cannot wait any longer for direction. Therefore, we have taken serious and significant steps to write this book for crewmembers. We will continually assert our right to prepare crewmembers for the threats they face. We hope this book will create a significant amount of discussion that brings others forward with a clear and distinct vision for crewmembers.

Notes

1 Fish, Mike, In Depth Special, Part Two: Previous Warnings, www.cnn.com, 2001.
2 Zoeller, Tom. New firm at airport has lapses, *Arizona Republic*, 22 November 2001
3 Fish, Mike, In Depth Special, Part Two: Previous Warnings, www.cnn.com, 2001.
4 Fish, Mike, In Depth Special, Part Two: Previous Warnings, www.cnn.com, 2001.
5 Schmidt, Susan, Officials warn of new hijacking plans, *Washington Post*, 29 July 2003.
6. Penn State University, Jerry Lee Center of Criminology, A Study by Easton and Wilson, *Preventingcrime.org*, 1991.
7 Interview with Sabah Khodada, PBS, *Frontline*, 14 October 2001.
8 Gun in handbag undetected on two flights, *Airwise*, 29 December 2001.
9 Man on flight from JFK hands over gun, *Airwise*, 16 November 2001.
10 Footwear focus of airport security after man tries to ignite explosives, *Associated Press*, 24 December 2001.
11 Airport's Thanksgiving seizures: 15,982 knives and a Brick, *Associated Press*, 3 December 2002.
12 TSA: More than 4.8 million items seized, *Associated Press*, 11 March 2003.
13 Reporters smuggle knives onto flights, *Arizona Republic*, 5 September 2002.
14 TSA: More than 4.8 million items seized, *Associated Press*, 11 March 2003.
15 Suits vs. airlines OK'd in Sept. 11 hijackings, *Wire Services*, 10 September 2003.
16 Fact Sheet – FAA Federal Air Marshal Program, *AA News*, Federal Aviation Administration, Washington, D.C., September 2001.
17 Airplane security: Terrorism prevention or racial profiling, www.CNN.law.com, 2 October 2002.
18 US air marshal program is plagued by problems, *USA Today*, 15 August 2002.
19 US air marshal program is plagued by problems, *USA Today*, 15 August 2002.
20 Incident may be tip of airlines-marshals conflict, *USA Today*, 6 March 2002.
21 Air marshal arrest case settled, www.philly.com/mld/inquirer/news, 1 August 2003.
22 Airline security change canceled, *USA Today*, 31 July 2003.
23 Security agency under fire for bid to cut 20% of air marshal budget, *Associated Press*, 2 August 2003.
24 Need for sky marshals soars, *Arizona Republic*, 2 March 2003.
25 Customs, immigration agents to be trained as air marshals, *Los Angeles Times*, 3 September 2003.
26 Reason, James, *Human Error*, New York: Cambridge University Press, 1990.
27 Meister, D., *Human Error in Man-made Systems*, The Open University Press, 1977.
28 Numerous web sites on the World-Wide Web.

Chapter 2

Disruptive Passengers and Sky Rage

Introduction

This chapter deals with ever-continuing problems of disruptive passengers and sky rage in aviation. Causes of disruptive passengers and sky rage vary. It is important for flight crews to be able to discern between an upset passenger and a passenger who has potential to cause a serious safety threat to the aircraft, crew and passengers. Understanding some of these issues will help crews deal with this very important safety issue without inadvertently escalating a minor incident into one that jeopardizes safety of the flight. In this chapter, we offer some solutions on how flight crews can deal with issues behind this problem in air travel. We are not going to delve into an exhaustive study of sky rage. For this, we recommend numerous articles written by the press, lawyers, dissertations by post-graduate students, and working groups such as The Skyrage Foundation. In addition, books by our colleagues, *Air Rage* by Angela Dahlberg, and *Air Rage: Crisis in the Skies* by Andrew Thomas, provide an in-depth background about the subject. What we present in this chapter is a practical guide for use by crewmembers to help understand the differences between disruptive passengers and sky rage, and deal with either of them.

In the early 1990s, the government and other organizations began to track and record incidents of disruptive passengers and air rage. Subsequently, there has been a considerable amount of attention focused on disruptive passengers by the press, FAA, and the US Congress. The press, by publishing and broadcasting incidents that have occurred, has brought attention to the problem of disruptive passengers.

Incidents will continue to occur involving disruptive and violent passengers. Unfortunately, it remains with flight crewmembers to diagnose and handle incidents that will occur on the aircraft. By being equipped with useful information that can assist you to detect, avoid, or defend against disruptive passengers or sky rage, you will be much better prepared to handle either event, should one occur on your flight.

The intent of the following information is to supplement guidance provided by the TSA, the FAA, or your company in regards to cases of disruptive behavior or sky rage. Information provided should dovetail into recommended procedures for Threat Levels as addressed in current security training programs.

Definitions

Disruptive passenger

The term is synonymous with 'unruly' passenger. One definition of 'disruptive passenger' comes from the September 2001 *Airline Pilot* magazine published by the Airline Pilots' Association. The article defines disruptive passenger as 'one who fails to respect the rules of conduct aboard an aircraft, including any passenger who refuses to comply with safety instructions'. For the purpose of this chapter, disruptive behavior is non-violent (once it becomes violent, it becomes sky rage). Verbal and/or written threats (not related to bomb threats or hijacking), unresponsiveness to instructions, abusive language, irrational or disorderly conduct or pointedly defiant acts are some behaviors included in this category. Disruptive behavior can lead to aircraft diversions and passenger arrest.

A potentially greater danger resulting from disruptive passengers is pilot error. A study by NASA analysts of 152 disruptive passenger events revealed 15 cases of pilot errors directly attributed to disturbance. Errors included flying too fast, at wrong altitudes, and incursions of taxiways or active runways – all potentially leading to disasters. Pilots elected to leave the cockpit to quell a disturbance, or were interrupted from their duties by flight attendants seeking help, in 40 of 152 events.[1] Forty-three per cent of events involved use of alcohol, a topic addressed later in the chapter.

Disruptive passengers are problems worldwide and involve people from all cultures and socio-economic backgrounds. Consider these worldwide examples of disruptive passengers:

- *US* – A US magistrate in Albuquerque released a Miami man on bail and told him to take the bus home. Authorities arrested the man after an America West flight made an emergency landing in Albuquerque to have him removed for throwing a crumpled beer can and a cup of ice at a flight attendant. After being delayed for two hours before leaving Miami bound for Phoenix, passengers 'complained about bad service' during flight. (Although it sounds like sky rage, further investigation into this case revealed the passenger was not violent, just disorderly. He was not trying to injure the flight attendant, but was simply expressing his disgust with poor service and being late. The communication with the flight deck did not accurately portray the event and directly contributed to the decision to land the aircraft short of destination.)[2]
- *UK* – A British man, jailed for nine months after an incident on a British Airways flight from London to Newcastle, was scared of flying, had been drinking beer and vodka at an airport bar prior to departure, and had taken Diazepam and Valium. During flight, the man asked a flight attendant if he could sit with her in the galley because he hated flying. After chatting with the man, the flight attendant became concerned when the man said he was a terrorist, his language deteriorated and he began swearing at her. The flight attendant served the man a vodka and coke, hoping to diffuse the situation. However, the man became more belligerent,

threatening flight attendants with clenched fists. The man remained threatening even after being arrested by police upon landing.[3]

- *France* – An Air France flight from Paris to Libreville in Africa, landed in Toulouse after a passenger on board got out of control and threatened crewmembers and passengers. Some of the 173 passengers were treated for shock before the aircraft continued its journey.[4]
- *Scotland* – A passenger who was 'not a good flier' became so drunk during a flight from Glasgow to Cyprus that he did not know what he was doing. The crew first became alarmed when they saw the man guzzling vodka from a bottle, which they took from him. Later, he removed all his clothing, exposing himself to other passengers, including families with children. The man had no recollection of what had taken place.[5]

The key in determining whether it is an incident of disruptive passenger or sky rage lies in determining whether or not a violent act has occurred, or in the view of the flight crew, has the potential to occur. A verbal threat by itself does not constitute a violent act unless the crew believes the passenger, based upon his/her behavior, capable of taking immediate violent action. A verbal threat accompanied with a violent action, such as pounding on the flight deck door, clearly constitutes a violent act, or sky rage. Defining a violent act can be somewhat tricky when violence has yet to occur. However, a passenger approaching you with clenched fists, visibly angry, threatening he/she is going to cause some sort of violence against you, is a violent act since violence could occur immediately.

Rage

'Rage' has gotten a lot of attention in the past few years as incidents of 'road rage', 'rage in the workplace', and 'ground rage' and 'air or sky rage' in aviation appeared to be on the increase. A number of experts have studied the nature of rage and there are numerous publications on the subject.

A popular notion is that rage is an undesirable but completely controllable emotion. As with drug abuse, the theory goes, one can just say 'no' to it, take an anger management class and get a grip. Many people do not realize the brain is hard-wired for anger and rage, a neural circuitry shared with all kinds of other animals.[6]

An intriguing clue as to how the brain may process rage comes from a recent brain-imaging study of convicted murderers. Using a PET scan (which measures glucose metabolism in neurons), scientists compared a group of impulsive murderers with a group of premeditative murderers. According to the study, impulsive murderers had significantly lower activity in prefrontal cortex than premeditative murderers. Those who committed planned murders had equivalent prefrontal cortex activity to normal (non-murder) subjects in a control group.[7]

Prefrontal cortex, a region of the brain located just behind the eyes, serves an executive function, integrating information and inhibiting emotional impulses that arise from deeper brain centers. The resulting decrease in activity in this region by impulsive murderers means they are less able to resist or control their violent impulses. On the other hand, cold-blooded killers are able to control their violent impulses, they just choose not to.[8]

The problem in understanding rage is that it represents a final path of many causes. Like body temperature, rage can be a normal response to certain environmental stimuli or a sign of serious underlying disease. There are people who experience anger attacks as a symptom of major depression. A report from Harvard Medical School indicates that up to 40 per cent of depressed patients experience anger attacks. Impulsive aggressive behavior is linked tightly to the neurotransmitter, serotonin. Violent and impulsive patients have significantly lower levels of brain serotonin compared with normal people. Serotonin reuptake inhibitors, such as Prozac and Aoloft, enhance the function of serotonin and have an anti-aggressive effect on patients prone to rage and to those suffering from depression or personality disorders.[9]

What does this all mean to aviation personnel? We never know who will show up for a flight and we have no means to determine a person's mental state, nor do we force passengers to submit to a PET scan before boarding (God forbid!). Therefore, we can expect to be forced to deal with people suffering from depression (whether they even know it or not) and people with personality disorders (whether they know it or not) on the ground as well as in the air. In addition, we do not know what factor(s) may kick off an incident of uncontrollable rage by a passenger. We DO know that airline employees have escalated incidents in the past by improperly handling situations involving passenger rage, signaling the need for better training in this area.

From an airline perspective, rage exhibited by passengers at the ticket counters and boarding gates can become a huge problem. Take these cases for example:

- A 37-year-old investment analyst, trying to board Delta Air Lines Express flight scheduled to go from Boston to Ft Lauderdale, was told he could not get on the plane before other passengers. The passenger, a member of Delta SkyMiles program, then assaulted a gate agent and her supervisor, pushing the agent and pouring coffee over the head of her supervisor. The man claims Delta employees started the physical altercation and if cooler heads had prevailed, the incident would not have occurred. (WB56 News Cast)
- A dispute between a passenger and a gate agent at a Continental gate in Newark resulted in serious injury to the agent. The dispute began when the passenger and ten other family members began boarding a Newark to Orlando flight after a two-hour delay. As an 18-month-old daughter of the passenger wandered down a jetway, the gate agent physically stopped his wife from pursuing the child. The enraged passenger confronted the agent for allegedly pushing his wife, and a scuffle ensued. The passenger picked the agent up and slammed him into the floor. The agent was comatose for five days after the incident and permanently lost 80 per cent of the mobility of his neck. A jury acquitted the passenger of

aggravated assault charges based on testimony by witnesses who said the gate agent escalated the incident.[10]

- Two British Airways baggage handlers started a brawl in front of travelers at Heathrow Airport. The fight started in the gate area after an argument, and spilled out into the corridor beyond passport control. One witness said, 'There was blood all over the place. This was an awful sight for passengers to witness as they went to board their flights'. Colleagues tried to separate the two without success. The fight ended when paramedics arrived.[11]

Gate agents have a tough job as they frequently are the first to experience a passenger's rage. It is important gate agents attend mandatory conflict resolution and self-defense training. From our perspective, these issues are not adequately addressed at any airline. 'They've been screamed at, called names, spit on, choked and punched. If there were a Purple Heart for working people, these folks certainly deserve it', says Frank Larkin of the IAMAW union that represents customer service employees and ticket agents.[12] Reports by gate agents from various airlines include a passenger throwing a briefcase at the agent, a passenger picking up a gate agent and slamming him into a wall, passengers using countertop holiday decorations as projectiles, etc. 'We're counselors. We're baby sitters. We're nurturers. We're mediators. The job of customer service has expanded to a whole new level,' said Sharon Caldwell of Northwest Airlines.[13]

British Airways has become the first airline to address 'ground rage' proactively. The airline's soccer-style yellow cards, previously used only for air rage incidents, are now issued to passengers engaged in disruptive or aggressive behavior on the ground. BA's safety and security director, Geoff Went said,

> Recent reports from our staff suggest the number of ground rage incidents is on the increase. Our staff has to deal with aggressive behavior on a daily basis, and at least once a month this turns to physical abuse. We hope the cards will defuse the situation on the ground to avoid the behavior escalating in the air, which may put passengers and crew at risk at 35,000 feet. We know from our experience of dealing with disruptive passengers in the air that in the vast majority of cases, issuing a yellow card is successful and causes passengers to refrain from further abusive behavior.[14]

'We are living in the age of rage, where more of the 'me' generation times the millions of travelers equals explosive situations,' said Dr Leon James, a professor of traffic psychology at the University of Hawaii. 'Air rage, like road rage, is the inability to cope with the challenges of congested traffic. Air rage is so common that most travelers are unaware that they have it. It is just part of the background feeling that goes along with stress of travel and transportation.' Dr James believes airlines should, among other things, provide a continuously updated stream of accurate information and elevate the importance of the traveler's comfort.[15]

Regardless of the origins of rage and what factors may trigger outbursts, airline personnel will continue to be targeted by the minority of passengers who exhibit this violent behavior. It is up to airlines to train and equip their employees to handle rage incidents on the ground and in the air. Airlines are well aware of these requirements.

In its *Air Rage Report Card* in July 2001, the Association of Flight Attendants (AFA) said airlines have neglected to promote cabin safety, train crewmembers to deal with incidents and support workers who are victims of air rage. The AFA also gave poor marks to the US Justice Department and the FAA, alleging that both organizations failed to require airlines to report all incidents or train crewmembers to handle air rage and failed to levy and collect fines as a deterrent. The report, issued in an effort to get airlines and the federal government to act before an air rage disaster occurs, estimates there are in excess of 4,000 incidents of air rage each year. The flight attendants' group urged airlines to establish more responsible alcohol policies, including not serving alcoholic drinks before take-off, serving only one drink at a time and never using free drinks as compensation for delays or cancellations. It also called for a public education campaign including posters and notices throughout airports, including bars and restaurants that are serving alcohol, to ensure passengers understand the penalties for violent in-flight actions. The report also contends only half of the airlines have policies addressing the problem, two-thirds offer cabin crews NO training for dealing with disruptive passengers, and most do not have equipment to restrain extremely violent and aggressive passengers.[16]

Sky rage

For the purposes of this book, we define sky rage as 'violent, anger-related behavior disruptive or detrimental to aviation safety'. Pushing, grabbing, slapping, hitting, or kicking another person, or the deliberate attempt to damage another's property (including the aircraft or aircraft furnishings) are some behaviors considered to be violent in nature and are included in the category of sky rage. Use of any item to strike or throw at another individual classifies as sky rage, also. Here are some examples of sky rage from 2002:

- *US* – In January, a Southwest flight was pulling away from the gate when a very large man approached the rear of the aircraft with his shoe in his hand. When confronted by a flight attendant, he struck her in the head with his fist and managed to get the rear aircraft door open before being subdued by passengers.[17]
- *US* – An unarmed passenger on a United Airlines flight broke the lower half of the cockpit door with 'Kung Fu' style kicks about five hours into flight. The first officer hit the man on the head with the on-board crash axe as he tried to crawl through the opening into the flight deck. The captain called for help on the PA and passengers responded. Passengers and crewmembers extricated the man from the door and restrained him for the duration of the flight. The man did not appear intoxicated, but seemed completely confused. It is unknown whether he had used drugs, or whether he had mental problems.[18]

- *US* – A 50-seat US Airways Express flight with 22 passengers aboard, bound for Birmingham, Alabama, turned back to Charlotte, North Carolina after the only flight attendant was punched in the stomach by a passenger shortly after takeoff. The man was arrested upon landing.[19]
- *US* – A woman arrested at Chicago O'Hare International Airport was accused of hitting an American Airlines flight attendant during the flight from San Francisco.[20]
- *US* – A Delta flight from Atlanta to Spain diverted after a passenger bit a flight attendant. The passenger was reported to possibly be either intoxicated or under the influence of drugs.[21]
- *Canada* – A woman assaulted several flight attendants and passengers during Air Canada Flight 881 from Paris to Toronto. The woman consumed an excessive amount of alcohol, becoming progressively more intoxicated and disruptive during flight. The woman grabbed a flight attendant and struck her on the arm; then, the woman began an unprovoked attack on one of the passengers. As flight attendants tried to calm the situation, the woman punched one of the flight attendants and bit another. One flight attendant received a cut to his left finger, which required medical attention. Two other attendants and two passengers received minor injuries.[22]
- *Singapore* – A 41-year old man traveling from Paris to Singapore became so drunk after consuming an excessive number of martinis that he smashed his television screen. He was fined $549, sentenced to three weeks in prison and ordered to pay Singapore Airlines $2,582 to repair the television screen.[23]
- *South Africa* – A German woman on a South African Airways flight from Bangkok was arrested on arrival in Johannesburg after she allegedly assaulted passengers and crew. The crew had given her a verbal warning and a written warning to no avail.[24]
- *UK* – A passenger on a British Airways flight from Seattle to London changed from a 'pleasant and polite southern gentleman' into a 'nasty and foul-mouthed drunk that even his family would not recognize' after drinking about 15 glasses of wine during the flight. The man allegedly upended a serving cart, swore at the captain, ripped up a 'yellow card' warning him to behave or face arrest, splattered the cabin crew with yogurt, and tried to leave the aircraft at 35,000 feet saying he wanted 'to go home'. A witness claimed to have seen the man slip a knife under his sleeve.[25]
- *Italy* – A flight from Mexico City to Rome diverted to Boston because of an unruly passenger who had to be physically restrained after he became violent with other passengers and crewmembers. Even after being physically restrained, he continued verbal threats to crewmembers and passengers. After the man was taken into custody and arrested by Boston police upon arrival, 185 grams of cocaine was found in his possession.[26]

Sky rage also includes sexual assault (a felony), abusive sexual contact and public indecency (misdemeanors). Here are some examples of these events aboard aircraft that indicate these problems occur across international boundaries.

- A Chinese man on an All Nippon Airways flight from Tokyo to San Francisco allegedly reached under a blanket and fondled a 14-year old passenger, a Japanese resident traveling alone. Authorities charged the man with felony sexual assault.[27]
- Authorities in San Francisco arrested an economics professor traveling from Narita, Japan and charged the man from India with abusive sexual contact aboard an aircraft, a misdemeanor. A 22-year old tourist from Japan told authorities the man put his hand under her blanket and between her thighs, and continued even after she pushed him away.[28]
- A drunken passenger sexually assaulted a 15-year old girl traveling alone on a 16-hour KLM flight from Kuala Lumpur to the United Kingdom. The unaccompanied minor, seated in the center of the aircraft between two men, woke up two hours into the flight to find one of the men touching her leg. The girl's family won an unprecedented legal ruling in their favor to claim damages from KLM for psychological damages suffered by the girl.[29]
- A famous jockey was arrested after landing at London Heathrow and charged with indecently assaulting a female flight attendant on a Virgin Air flight from Narita, Japan.[30]
- A Delta passenger on a flight from Dallas was arrested upon arrival in Boston, and charged with sexually assaulting a woman during the flight.[31]
- A man traveling on an American Airlines flight from Sacramento to Chicago, with a stopover in San Francisco, observed an 18-year old female board the aircraft and sit in a window seat across the aisle and several rows behind him. The man moved from his assigned seat to the unoccupied middle seat located next to the woman. Shortly after takeoff, the man sexually assaulted her as she slept. The man received a six-year prison sentence after a jury found him guilty of sexual abuse aboard an aircraft.[32]
- A man and woman aboard an American Airlines flight from Dallas to Manchester seated next to each other, got drunk, fondled each other, and the man removed the woman's pants and top. The couple, who were strangers prior to the flight, became angry and abusive to flight attendants who intervened. Authorities arrested the pair in Britain and both were fined. Both people also lost their jobs over the event.[33]

As evident from incidents in the above paragraphs, sky rage is a worldwide problem. Numerous nations are saying 'enough is enough', and are finally beginning to crack down on offenders.

The US Congress passed H.R.1000, in March of 2000 and President Bill Clinton signed it into law. The bill provides for monetary fines up to US$25,000 for airline passengers who interfere with the duties of flight crewmembers.

Disrupting a flight can bring 20 years in prison and a US$250,000 fine.[34] To address jurisdictional issues, the bill calls for deputizing airport law enforcement officers as Special Federal Air Marshals so they can more easily make arrests on aircraft.

In 1999, 140 passengers flying into London's Heathrow Airport and 34 passengers flying into Gatwick were arrested for disruptive behavior. British airlines reported a 400 per cent increase in such cases since 1997. The British government introduced a new offense for using threatening and abusive language or behavior to flight crews in September 1999. Offenders now face a GB£2,000 fine or a two-year jail sentence.[35]

Australia's Qantas and Ansett airlines reported in year 2000 that they had experienced 571 air rage incidents. Incidents included 233 cases of unruly behavior involving offensive language and reckless behavior such as indecent exposure. There were 310 cases of behavior interfering with comfort of other passengers, such as drunken passengers, food throwing and boisterous behavior. Twenty-eight incidents involved violence or threat of violence against passengers and/or crew. Ansett has begun to force unruly passengers to pay costs if an aircraft is diverted to put them off, which can be as much as US$90,000.[36]

Japan's three largest carriers – Japan Airlines, All Nippon Airways and Japan Air System – began telling customers in April 2000 they will restrain any passenger who threatens others or refuses to heed orders from crewmembers. JAL reported 100 incidents in 1999, while All Nippon reported 190 cases, 2.5 times more than in 1998. In 1999, Japan Air System reported 15 cases, the first double-digit figure since the company began recording events in 1955.[37]

A worldwide air rage campaign organized by airline flight attendant unions in year 2000, drew attention to disruptive passenger and sky rage issues. The Transport Workers Federation, an umbrella organization for the unions, wanted governments to sign an international convention that would close loopholes to ensure prosecution of air rage offenders. Flight attendants demonstrated and handed out leaflets in Montreal, Paris, London, Cancun, Mexico City, Taipei, Oslo, Stockholm, Lagos, Zurich, Tokyo, Frankfurt and Buenos Aires.[38]

Flight crews can learn valuable lessons from all incidents involving disruptive passenger or sky rage. Some additional incidents from the past several years are provided in APPENDIX 2A at the end of this chapter for your reading pleasure. Careful study of these incidents, and of those with which you might be privy to at your own airline, should help you recognize and react to these extremes in behavior. In addition, this chapter, as well as other chapters of the book, provides some solutions for recognizing and handling confrontations. The better you develop your skills in recognizing and handling these types of incidents, the safer you, and your fellow crewmembers and passengers, will be.

The Problem

Everyone who has frequently traveled by air has probably experienced some sort of flight delay or cancellation at one time or another. The majority of flight crews have an 'on-time' mentality, and flight delays or cancellations affect our lives, as well. Table 2.1 is a compilation of these and other factors reported as causes behind disruptive behavior and sky rage. See how many of these factors you recognize from your experiences aboard aircraft or in the departure gate area.

Table 2.1 Factors contributing to disruptive passenger/sky rage incidents

Alcohol consumption, before or during flight	No upgrade to first class
Reaction to drugs, prescription or illicit	No food
Being 'stuck' on aircraft, before or after flight	Mentally deranged, unstable
Long waits at ticket counter, security checkpoint, gate	No smoking aboard aircraft
Lost or damaged luggage	Flight delays, running late
Poor service at ticket counter, gate, or on aircraft	Just plain mean
Cramped space, violation of 'personal zone'	Seat duplications
Differences in gender, sexual preference	Other passengers
Loss of control over life	Flight cancellations
Having to check carry-on baggage	Discourteous crews
No space in overhead bins	'Dirty air', no air circulation
Dirty or inoperative aircraft lavatories	Ticket price differences
Too hot or cold on the aircraft	Gate and concourse change

The growing number of incidents

One of the problems with statistics on this subject is that until just a few years ago, no one kept good records of them. In addition, conflicting statistics on disruptive passengers and air rage is found in literature on the subject. Some airlines require reports on disruptive passengers and air rage while others do not. There is reason to believe there were a lot more incidents than was reported in available reports. According to some reports, overall trends of disruptive passengers appear to have stabilized since about 1997; however, other sources we have researched reveal conflicting opinions, including information provided by Andrew Thomas in his book, *Air Rage: Crisis in the Skies*.

A United States government rule stemming from a record number of flight delays and cancellation in 1999 and 2000 went into effect in 2003. In order to determine solutions for causes of flight delays and cancellations, the Transportation Department started building a database in June 2003. At that time, it became mandatory for all airlines to report the following information on a monthly basis:

- Circumstances that were within control of the airline, such as lack of flight crew or maintenance problems;
- Extreme weather problems;
- Problems caused by the national aviation system (NAS), such as air traffic control, airport operations, or heavy air traffic;
- Security-related problems, such as airport evacuations caused by a security breach; and,
- Delays in takeoffs from late-arriving aircraft.

Table 2.2 Comparison of key data over three years[39]

Year	1999–2000	2000–2001	2001–2002
Total incident reports	1205	1205	1055
Severity			
Serious	74 (6%)	63 (5%)	52 (5%)
Significant	519 (43%)	595 (48%)	528 (50%)
Other	612 (51%)	652 (47%)	475 (45%)
Context			
Number of flights per serious incident	15,000	17,000	22,000
Number of passengers carried per serious incident	1.3 million	1.7 million	2 million
Incident details			
Violence involved	157 (13%)	139 (11%)	101 (10%)
Violence towards crew	83	71	49
Contributing factors			
Alcohol involved	607 (50%)	533 (43%)	472 (45%)
Alcohol – pre-boarding	66	198	198
Alcohol – airline	234	165	92
Alcohol – own	283	214	
Smoking involved	449 (37%)	408 (33%)	385 (36%)
Smoking in toilet	240	350	306

The Transportation Department issues monthly reports that began in August 2003. 'This has a lot of value for consumers, airlines and the government alike', said David Stempler of the Airline Travelers Association.[40] Perhaps this effort will shed light on these issues for the traveling public and create a better understanding of some of the major factors airlines must deal with just to get a flight out on time, or at all. At the same time, it will put pressure on airlines to tighten up their procedures regarding aircraft routing, crew scheduling, spare aircraft, etc. The effort will highlight National Airspace System (NAS) problems also, whether on a local or national basis.

At the request of the Department for Transport, airlines in the United Kingdom have reported incidents of disruptive behavior on board their aircraft to the Civil Aviation Authority (CAA) on a common reporting basis since April 1999. The CAA has analyzed the data submitted from April 1999 to March 2002 (Table 2.2).

The incidents categorized as 'significant' are behaviors that include smoking in the aircraft's toilet, aggressive or abusive behavior, refusing to follow instructions regarding the use of seat belts, intoxication and passengers exhibiting signs of personality disorders. The incidents categorized by the CAA as being 'serious' are incidents in which passengers were acting extremely irrationally and strongly suspected of being under the influence of drugs, excessive consumption of alcohol, varying degrees of violent, and abusive or unacceptable behavior including damage to the interior of the aircraft.

The contributory factors in overall incidents appear to be alcohol and/or tobacco use. To nobody's surprise alcohol was identified or suspected as the leading contributory cause in the last three years. The data confirms that drinking prior to boarding often has a continued negative effect on behavior on the aircraft. Smoking, or the desire to smoke, is actually not too far behind in leading to confrontations with passengers. The survey revealed that often passengers were smoking in the lavatories, implying a degree of premeditated deception that poses a significant safety risk to the aircraft.

Where do most incidents occur and who are the offenders? A study in the UK revealed:

- 78 per cent of incidents involve male passengers;
- 66 per cent of offenders are in the age group from 20 to 30 years old;
- 95 per cent of incidents occur in economy class;
- 11 per cent of the cases involve violence;
- 43 per cent involved alcohol; and,
- 33 per cent involved the desire to smoke.[41]

Ninety per cent of cabin crew surveyed by the BBC current affairs program *4X4*, said they felt air rage was putting lives at risk.[42] Intoxication tends to play a significant part in violence aboard aircraft. Since the events of 9/11, passengers consume more and more amounts of alcohol in airport terminals. Alcohol sales either remain at the same levels prior to 9/11, or have increased from 8 to 30 per cent at some airports even though passenger loads are down as much as 20 per cent from 2000.[43] We can conclude by these trends that confrontations between crew and passengers, or between passengers, will escalate into increased numbers of disruptive passenger or sky rage incidents as a direct result of the effects of alcohol. In August 2001, a spokesperson for AFA Air Safety and Health Department, Candice Colander said, 'The airlines should train flight attendants to recognize drunken behavior and how to effectively cut off passengers who have had too much.'[44]

As a police officer, Waltrip witnessed many individuals who had lost all common sense resulting from consuming too much alcohol. He concluded what most people already know, inebriated people can be a challenge to deal with, to say the least. Dealing with passengers who are upset, nervous, stressed, and intoxicated is a time bomb waiting to go off. Unfortunately, these are mental states of some passengers when they board flights everyday in every country. Some passengers pass through security checkpoints under the influence of alcohol and continue to drink at facilities on concourses as well as on aircraft. It becomes incumbent upon gate agents to determine if a passenger is intoxicated; however, negative effects of intoxication may not appear until on the aircraft or airborne, resulting in flight crew involvement. Crewmembers should not have to resolve a violent situation with an intoxicated passenger during ANY phase of flight!

Some educated guesses (predictions) can be made regarding future sky rage events based upon past incidents and the projections of airline growth in the next ten years. The latest outlook for air travel by the FAA indicates domestic passenger traffic rising over 41 per cent in the next ten years.[45] With the rise in passenger traffic, there will no doubt be additional crowding of airport space and gate delays. Without continued advances in airspace traffic controls, ATC delays will continue to be a problem. Based upon these trends, one can logically conclude disruptive passenger and sky rage incidents will continue to increase, as well.

Lack of enforcement actions and prosecutions

A look at FAA enforcement actions taken directly from their web site against disruptive passengers (Table 2.3) can lend some insight to future prosecutions. Keep in mind, this figure shows the actual amount of disruptive passenger and sky rage incidents *reported* annually.

Table 2.3 FAA Enforcement actions, violations of 14 CFR 91.11, 121.580 and 135.120, 'Unruly Passengers', calendar years 1995–2003[46]

Year	Total	Year	Total
1995	146	2000	251
1996	183	2001	299
1997	235	2002	270
1998	198	2003	195
1999	228		(as of 4 December 2003)

The number of incidents the FAA investigates is in dispute by those within the agency. There is reason to believe statistics posted on the FAA web site on disruptive passengers only reflect about half of the cases the agency actually handles. From the period of 1997 through 1999, the FAA web site reveals the agency handled 913 cases – approximately 300 a year. However, information from the FAA's security division shows 1,514 to 1,657 cases for the same time period (more than 500 a year) were investigated by the security division.[47] Research by author Andrew Thomas, for his book *Air Rage: Crisis in the Skies*, suggests that the FAA might have handled as many as 9,431 probable instances of 'interference with a flight crew' in 2000 alone.[48]

A research article on sky rage by *USA TODAY* reviewed hundreds of pages of documents and internal FAA memos, many obtained through the Freedom of Information Act. The newspaper also collected crime statistics from airport police, analyzed actions taken in unruly-passenger cases and interviewed dozens of current and former FAA officials, safety advocates, counter-terrorism experts and others.[49] Here is a summary of what they found during an analysis of 1,519 unruly-passenger cases, opened and closed from 1990 through 2000:

- In hundreds of on-board incidents that drew airport police, the FAA never opened an investigation or even sent inspectors to interview witnesses or victims.
- When the agency chose to investigate, officials either took no action or mailed unruly passengers warning letters in most cases.
- Despite an FAA pledge to crack down on unruly passengers five years ago, the agency actually was more lenient with offenders in subsequent years.
- The FAA collected fines from unruly passengers in 508 cases, or a third of the time.
- In another third of the cases, the federal agency sent a warning letter, was unable to locate the offender, or determined that a fine was 'un-collectable'.
- *The agency did nothing in 449 cases, or 30 per cent of the cases. (Italics added.)*
- 'It's beyond amazing, it's criminal', says Pat Friend, president of the Association of Flight Attendants which represents 50,000 cabin crewmembers. She has repeatedly criticized the FAA for failing to take in-flight violence issues seriously. 'The truth is, they didn't act', Friend says, 'and they acted as though they didn't care'.[50] (See the FAA's response in APPENDIX 2B)
- Among the cases federal prosecutors did not pursue:
  - On 27 May 1997, an American Airlines passenger 'beat on the cockpit door and harassed flight attendants and passengers. He then sexually harassed a female flight attendant by grabbing her buttocks', one report says. He only received a warning letter.
  - On 27 November 1997, during a Delta Air Lines flight from New York to Los Angeles, a male passenger 'grabbed a female flight attendant's hand three times and made sexual advances towards her. The passenger ... would not let the female flight attendant continue with her duties'. As a result, the report says, the flight engineer 'left the cockpit twice in an effort

to get the passenger to stop his behavior'. The passenger received a warning letter.

- On United Airlines Flight 876 from Japan to Los Angeles on 17 December 1997, a US Navy serviceman 'choked a flight attendant' and 'was restrained by three other servicemen', the report says. He received a warning letter.
- In one case in March 1997, a man aboard KLM Royal Dutch Airlines Flight 601 began bothering passengers about 2 hours into an overseas flight, resulting in a warning by the captain. The passenger was asked to stay seated by crewmembers. Six hours later, the report says, the passenger 'became violent and was wrestled to the floor by members of the flight crew and passengers and subsequently handcuffed to a seat in the rear of the aircraft. One flight attendant was elbowed in the stomach during this altercation'. More than a year later, the man only paid a $100 fine to the FAA.[51]

Unrealistic expectations

At the request of the CAA in 1999, a questionnaire was sent by researchers at London Guildhall University to 400 air carriers selected from the World Airline Rankings and the World Airline Directory. A chart was compiled by the collection of 197 useable returns as to the causes of air rage (Table 2.4). Airlines and crewmembers have high expectations for passengers. Table 2.4 clearly demonstrates some of our unrealistic expectations of travelers who do not move in and out of our airline world as well as we do.

The number one reason listed here (alcohol use – 88 per cent) is in conflict with other studies that list alcohol as being a factor in only 25 per cent to 50 per cent of the cases. However, this information is valuable to crewmembers in understanding some causes of air rage.

For example, the flight crew's mismanagement of the passenger's problem is listed as a causal factor 51 per cent of the time. Amazingly, *this report indicates that over half the time crewmembers are a contributing factor in disruptive passenger incidents.* This information leads one to believe it is not necessarily the situation, but how the situation was managed that can be a major problem.

The data points out the need for flight crews to continue to be aware of their surroundings and to be sensitive to any possible growing irritation to passengers aboard aircraft. Awareness can serve as a double purpose: 1) to show concern to our passengers which is good for customer relations; and 2), and perhaps more importantly, self-preservation in avoiding confrontations that could become violent.

We want our passengers to be knowledgeable of airline procedures regardless of how each airline's procedures differ. We expect them to be able to communicate

Table 2.4 Passenger aggressive behaviors[52]

Reason given for behavior	%
Too much alcohol consumed by the passenger	88
Passenger's demanding/intolerant personality	81
Flight delays	78
Stress of air travel	75
Smoking ban	70
Cramped conditions in aircraft cabin	66
Passenger not allowed to carry on baggage	59
Passenger expectations too great	57
*Crew mismanagement of passenger's problem**	51
Passenger denied upgrade	48

* Author's emphasis

effectively with employees and to be completely cooperative to all safety and airline rules imposed. We want them to maintain alertness at all times to briefings, to stay completely non-confrontational, and to be unaffected by fears and any alcoholic effects or tobacco withdrawals. We expect them to remain unaffected by stress, fatigue and any physical discomfort and to be submissive with a lack of information, while remaining cordial with airline personnel. Passengers should remain seated with seat belts fastened throughout the flight, regardless of the duration of the flight, especially when ordered. After all this, we expect passengers to evacuate quickly after being cramped into their seats.[53] Are these *reasonable* expectations for passengers?

Crewmembers are usually aware of the incredible pressures passengers face and the often-unrealistic expectations we demand from them; however, these factors are easy to overlook during day-to-day operations. An understanding of passenger frustrations may well be the first step in dealing with irate passengers. To 'understand' does not mean we have to be verbally abused or physically attacked; however, flight crews should exemplify what is good and honorable in how we treat those who trust us with their lives. Take this typical passenger traveling experience scenario for example:

> Passengers often stand in line to check in at the ticket counter for an hour or more. After their encounter with the ticket agent, it is off to the security checkpoint where another hour of waiting in line is possible. The passenger arrived at the airport two-and-a-half hours early just as the airline advised and they are now sweating it because it is just about departure time.
>
> The passenger empties all pockets, places their laptop in a tray, puts their carry-on articles on the conveyor belt at the security checkpoint and passed through the metal detector. It beeps. The screener tells them to go stand in another line for an additional search. The screener will probably require the person to remove their shoes, unbuckle

their pants, pull out their pants pockets, and stretch their arms out to be frisked with a wand. An additional wait is endured as shoes re-enter the x-ray machine. When cleared, the person is free to redress, accumulate all their belongings, re-pack as necessary and continue – almost.

The screener on the x-ray machine scanned their bag twice and saw something suspicious in the bag, so the screener asks the person's permission to check the bag by opening it up and going through it. The person is taken by a screener to a special screening area near the Explosive Trace Detection Machine (ETD.) Once again, they are asked to take off their shoes to check for traces of explosives and stretch out their hands so the screener can swab their hands for traces of explosives. The swab is then tested, sending out an alert for traces of explosives. All the contents of their bag are now emptied out and each item is carefully gone through by a screener. The person may be asked by the screener if they have handled any explosives. The passenger replies that they were at the firing range the day before shooting their weapon. After being searched under the scrutiny of a stern looking airport police officer, the screeners finally clear the person and they are indeed free to leave. It took another 15 minutes to clear security.

It is now ten minutes to departure and the passenger begins a mad dash to the gate. Arriving at the gate, they are relieved to discover that the flight is running late, but now they cannot find their wallet with their identification in it. They realize that it must have been left at the security checkpoint in the plastic container with their change. Running as quickly as they can back to the checkpoint, they discover no one has seen the wallet. Although stressed, they reason that they can cancel their credit cards later and then rush back to the gate where the sweat is rolling off their face. The flight is just about ready to depart, but since they do not have identification, they are flagged for additional pre-boarding screening. Once again, they are asked to take off their shoes and be searched by a screener. Their carry-on baggage is once again dumped out and searched. By this time, they can feel anger and frustration building to unbearable levels.

Finally, they get to board, only to be told by a crewmember that they do not have room for their carry-on since they are late boarding, and are going to have to check it. Hesitating, the passenger peeks down the aisle looking for any possible space in the overhead bins. The flight attendant tells the passenger that they must either check the bag now or get off the plane because they are now holding up the flight. The passenger reluctantly hands the flight attendant their bag, it is 'gate' tagged by a flustered gate agent and left near the boarding door of the aircraft. As the plane begins to move away from the gate, the passenger sees his bag sitting on the ramp. Although, angry, frustrated and stressed-out, the passenger comforts himself by knowing that they can get an alcoholic drink or two to relax after takeoff.

Is this scenario too far fetched? Unfortunately, law abiding and decent passengers are subjected to this type of treatment (or worse) time and time again. How can we expect everything to go so smoothly when passengers may have been subjected to a multitude of indignities, inconveniences and stressors that have been imposed upon them by air travel? What do you think may happen after this passenger has a few drinks to *calm down*?

Understanding Passenger Behavior

Passenger rudeness and non-compliance is often not a deliberate attempt to undermine crewmember authority. Hostility can be a symptom of a host of emotions. Fear of flying, loss of control, fatigue, and personal and environmental stresses are common experiences associated with air travel.[54]

As noted in this chapter, alcohol and tobacco often play a significant role in how passenger disturbances materialize. Alcohol use and tobacco withdrawals lower inhibitions and can lead to rage. Cabin crews 'reading the rules to a passenger' risk escalation of hostility and aggression. Passengers can be expected to become defensive to cover their embarrassment.[55] It is important for crewmembers to understand this reaction in order to better deal with a similar situation.

A sense of helplessness relates to a person's inability to change their conditions. The resultant resentment of authority with hostility or anger may be triggered by the image of the crewmember that is perceived to possess more power.[56] Being prepared for a hostile response should lower the natural defensive counter-reaction by a crewmember, whereas a negative-aggressive reaction by the flight crewmember could escalate the situation further. Although we never condone it, the unfortunate reality is that being insulted by rude passengers is part of being a flight attendant. Understanding this beforehand, flight crews will be better mentally prepared for the inevitable insults that result from the many stressors encountered by passengers. This does NOT make it right, that is just the way it is. The attitude of the crewmember in dealing with stressed-out passengers (particularly when the crewmember is also stressed-out) is a huge part of being able to adequately deal with this problem.

Crewmembers' Attitudes

Attitude toward a crewmember's job is crucial to establishing positive on-board relationships. Maintaining awareness between the duality of safety and customer service with a good communication style is very helpful. Crewmembers are always in the public eye and need to gain the passenger's respect, trust and cooperation.[57] Crewmembers must balance their safety and service roles. Repetitive service demands, time constraints, and job routine tend to erode motivation resulting in lukewarm job performance and complacency. In the interest of safety, customer service can be a powerful tactic to control passenger aggression and anger.[58] Certainly, customer service may be a challenge on short flights with quick turnarounds and multiple flight segments. However, it has been observed that the best performing cabin crews have effectively created positive short-term relationships with their passengers through service.[59] A conflict between safety role and service role is not easily reconciled for some cabin crewmembers. For the most part, passengers do not appreciate the safety roles of the cabin crew unless a need arises during an emergency. Routine actions performed by the crew during normal operations do little to reinforce the important safety role cabin crews provide.[60]

Unfortunately, conflict produces stressors for some crewmembers that negatively reflect in their job performance. The relative low value placed upon the service role by cabin crew labor unions has undermined this aspect of dealing with passenger stresses.[61] The image of professional cabin crewmember in this era of air transportation has not been clearly defined. We believe that the service role flight attendants provide should NOT take away from their more important safety and security roles.

Nothing will exemplify the safety or security role more than when the cabin crew is called upon to perform their duties in very difficult circumstances. However, service roles can be equally important to control difficult passengers on a regular basis. Cabin crewmembers perform this role everyday of the year. The exact numbers of potential conflicts avoided by performing these important functions in an exemplary manner cannot be quantified, but it is certain they occur on a regular basis. We compare the deterrent effect to police officers who routinely patrol a neighborhood. We cannot say for sure what crime was prevented by their presence, but they most assuredly have deterred some criminal activity – some days more than others have.

Some Solutions

Crewmember relationship skills

The emotional security of the crewmember and their knowledge of passenger moods and expectations are important aspects in setting the stage for a safe cabin environment. Communication with passengers should be a key aspect of the crewmembers' approach.[62] Southwest Airlines uses this approach and teaches their crewmembers to personalize contact with passengers. This approach has proven to be an effective strategy in avoiding disruptive confrontations with passengers for Southwest Airlines, reflected in the low amount of complaints about Southwest received annually by the US government.

Skills in conflict resolution and problem solving are essential in the current crewmember-working environment. Well-developed and essential skills enable crews to cope with the demands placed upon them by passengers who need reassurance, gentle guidance and direction.[63] The skills are important, not only with passengers, but with relationships with other crewmembers where conflicts can certainly occur and manifest negatively over the duration of a trip pairing. Conflict resolution is so important for flight crewmembers that we have dedicated Chapter 9 to this subject.

Recognizing and reacting to the dangers of disruptive passengers

A number of chapters in this book address tactics and techniques in awareness and desired reactions to threats. We are confident that following safety techniques we have suggested throughout this book will greatly decrease your chances of being attacked or injured. Here are a few more suggestions:

- *If possible, do not allow passengers to touch you.* Touch could be a precursor to an assault. You are making yourself vulnerable to assault if you allow someone to touch you. Do not allow an unknown person to touch you under any circumstances.
- *Keep your distance from others.* If someone is going to attack you with a weapon other than a gun, he or she will need to approach you and get in close enough to carry out the assault. Try to stay at least an arm length away from people, not your arm length, but the other person's. Remember this equation, '*Distance = Time and Space to React*'. Do not let anyone get close enough to strike you. Keeping your distance will help to reduce that threat. Realistically, in an aircraft people move back and forth down the aisles, sometimes making it impossible to keep that desired arm length. While you are in an aisle, you are within arm reach of some passengers. As hard as it may be, keep that arm length whenever possible to give you the time to react before you are attacked.
- *Maintain a balanced stance.* There are several reasons why it is desirable to maintain a bladed stance (approximately a 45 degree angle to the other person, feet apart at shoulder width, weight evenly distributed on both feet) while talking to others. A bladed stance provides a much more stable platform, making it much easier to maintain your balance if pushed or pulled by someone.
- *Keep your hands up above your waist.* Your hands should be held above the waist in a non-threatening manner so a passenger does not feel you are being aggressive toward them. Keeping your hands up in a non-threatening manner when talking, allows you to save very precious time and distance in getting your hands into position if attacked. As you keep your hands up, clasping your hands gently or make small gestures with them, passengers may think you 'talk with your hands', a natural occurrence. Having your hands up and in front of you will allow you to be ready and prepared to defend yourself.
- *Be aware of what is behind you.* Remaining aware of your surroundings and what is behind you will be to your benefit if the need arises to quickly retreat, or if a retreat is not possible, to know what your course of action should be.
- *Watch passengers' hands while the passengers are in your presence.* You might have heard the saying, 'Looks that could kill'; however, eyes do not kill, hands do. The hands are what will assault or kill you. Watching where the other person's hands are and what is in them as they talk to you will give you a definite advantage in knowing when and how an attack is coming.

- *Do not turn your back on a passenger.* We also need to be realistic and accept that there will be times we turn our back on a passenger. However, do not make yourself an even better target for a drunk, combative passenger, or a hijacker. Especially avoid turning your back when a person is close to you is agitated. You are saying by your body language, 'go ahead hit me.' Reducing the opportunities for assault is something each of us needs to practice and make a part of our everyday life.
- *Recognize when things are deteriorating.* If you have maintained self control and attempted to mediate a situation to the best of your abilities and the passenger is getting more and more upset, you will need to discern if and when this incident is about to become violent. If you determine that the situation has the potential to become violent, try to back down, alert another crewmember and the flight deck, if possible. De-escalation should be your goal, but there are times when this will not be possible, like when a passenger is inebriated and beyond reasoning.

Why do we keep emphasizing crew safety techniques? Reports indicate 20 per cent of cabin crewmembers have been physically assaulted by passengers, while up to 80 per cent of crewmembers have reported verbal abuse.[64] Many of the passengers' attacks have become personal and very brutal to cabin crewmembers. You must do everything possible to limit attacks or injuries to yourself and other crewmembers. You are the safety team on the aircraft and if you are injured, who else is going to defend the aircraft or take care of the passengers and other crewmembers?

Response techniques to an escalating incident

When faced with difficult passengers, it is easy to respond with negative responses. It is easy to feel personally insulted by their comments and treatment and it is human nature to lash back. It is unfortunate that many passengers do not care about or appreciate what crewmembers do. However, when faced with a disrespectful passenger, it does little to change the public's perspective of what cabin crewmembers do by getting into an argument over the importance of your position. For survival purposes, we suggest it is much better to get along than to continually force your views with the grace of a bull in a china shop. Yes, there is a time and place to change views and perceptions, but facing off with passengers on a flight will not accomplish what needs to be changed. Tempers cloud the underlying issues.

The following techniques may be helpful in maintaining self-control during a conflict with another person:

- *Take a breath.* Take a deep slow breathe before responding to the person.
- *Acknowledge hostility and anger.* Empathize by understanding their position. Allow the person to vent their anger while maintaining your neutral demeanor.

- *Do not take it personally.* Do not respond with anger by personal attacks. Chances are they are mad at the airline and you just happen to be the person who represents the company.
- *Clarify their position.* Asking for clarification has a way of focusing on the issue. Going point by point through their problem tends to cool things off and shows your personal concern for their problem.
- *Settle for differences.* If differences remain after fully discussing the issues, agree to disagree. If the difference is a safety item or security issue, it may be time to bring in another crewmember to attempt to settle the conflict.
- *Mediate conflict.* State the reason(s) why the issue needs to be resolved. If the difference is between two passengers ask them both to be patient and state their viewpoint. Suggest ways to end the dispute.[65]

Recognizing and reacting to passengers exhibiting potential for disruptive behavior

Okay, so you have treated an obnoxious passenger with dignity, respect, ignored the confrontational comments and served them with a smile. Yet, the anger persists and seems to be intensifying. What should you do? Communication with other crewmembers is essential when it appears a situation seems to be deteriorating. Positively identify the person to other crewmembers, including where the passenger is seated. Make note of what he/she looks like, what they are wearing, how tall and/or big they are, how many are traveling in their group and any other information you feel may be important.

Crew observations are vital to noticing any signs of trouble before departure. Giving passengers a harsh look because you think they may cause trouble will not help defuse the situation, and may in fact, escalate it. A crewmember, which wishes to remain anonymous, told us of an incident that occurred to him while traveling with his family on the airline where he is employed. We will call him Tom.

> I was with my wife and teenage kids that are 16 and 14 years old. We looked forward to the flight to visit my mother who lives near Kansas City. As we were boarding the flight, my 14-year-old son saw a can of WD-40 lubricating oil on a table at the end of the jet bridge. As teenagers tend to do, he did not think beyond the moment. He walked over to the can and pushed the nozzle dispersing the lubricant mist. I slapped his arm and discreetly told him to knock it off because I did not want us to be kept off the flight because of his actions.
>
> A flight attendant standing in the forward galley saw me slap my son on the arm and have words with him. As I entered the aircraft, I noticed the flight attendant was not smiling and was in fact giving me what I perceived as a very stern look. I told him that we had a small disciplinary problem, but it was resolved. He replied, 'That's good because you do not want to be striking him while in flight because you may upset the passengers and we will have to divert and land at another airport and you will be arrested'. You can imagine my surprise at these words spoken by the flight attendant.

> I said, 'Whoa, its cool. I am a crewmember for this airline and I am not going to cause any trouble'. He did not reply, but simply stared at me.
>
> As I started down the aircraft aisle, followed by my wife and kids, the flight attendant stopped one of my children, reached down to the carry-on bag tag, noted my name on the crew tag and wrote my name down. The flight proceeded without incident and we had a pleasant visit with my mother.

Tom told the flight attendant that he was a crewmember for the flight attendant's airline, yet, the flight attendant felt he had to note the crew tag on Tom's carry-on bag anyway. Did it matter that Tom was a fellow crewmember or if he was just another passenger? Potentially violent behavior aboard aircraft should be noted and dealt with, regardless of whether the person is an airline employee; however, do you think the flight attendant handled this situation properly? How could it have been handled better? How would you have handled it?

Crewmembers must be able to recognize the difference between a minor disruption and a potentially serious problem on-board their aircraft. Granted, this may not always be easy, but direct confrontations rarely do little to defuse any potential problem on the aircraft, especially when alcohol consumption is a factor.

Alcohol is a key factor in the escalation of air rage and when combined with other negative personality traits it can lead to an explosive combination. Passengers who have one or more of three psychological traits – a sense of entitlement, who have an opposition to authority, and a fear of losing control – are the most susceptible to becoming disruptive on flights.[66] These traits, combined with the effects of alcohol and the one of many other stressors involved in air transportation, can produce unpredictable results. How would you have handled this next difficult flight?

> While waiting for the TWA flight from Paris to Boston in January 1996, a Saudi Arabian princess, accompanied by her daughter and two female servants, went to the TWA Ambassador Club in the airport. The princess had at least one glass of champagne while waiting in the club and she smoked while seated in a nonsmoking area, and was loud.
>
> The princess's party was the last group to board the aircraft and she tripped as she came through the door, but recovered her balance. Once on board, the princess and her daughter, who was supposed to sit next to her mother in first class, had a loud argument and the daughter moved to coach, exchanging seats with one of their servants. The princess was very upset.
>
> After the aircraft pushed back from the gate, the princess got up to go to the coach section to see her daughter. The FSM asked the princess to sit down and to wait until the aircraft was airborne before going back to see her daughter, explaining that the captain would have to be informed and would stop the aircraft if she did not comply. The princess ignored the FSM's request and yelled at her after a second request was made. The princess's traveling companion took the princess to her seat. The princess obsessed on her treatment by the FSM for the remainder of the flight.
>
> Prior to takeoff, the princess had two glasses of champagne and retained her glass during both the taxi down the runway and the takeoff. About 15 minutes after takeoff, the FSM placed two landing warning cards on the princess's tray table. The princess

picked them up and threw them at the FSM. The princess screamed, 'Don't ever tell me what to do', used profanity, and demanded that the FSM get down on her knees and apologize. The FSM apologized if the tone of her voice earlier had offended the princess, but said that she would not apologize for asking the princess to return to her seat because that was a part of doing her job. This explanation only further upset the princess. As the FSM turned to get away from the princess, the princess followed her, snapping her fingers, shouting profanities, demanding that the FSM get down on her knees, and threatening to have the FSM killed. The princess ignored the FSM's instructions to be seated. Finally, two other flight attendants and the traveling companion intervened and took the princess back to her seat.

The captain went back to talk to the princess about 40 minutes after takeoff having received a report that the princess was causing a disturbance and was being very difficult. She was standing in the first-class aisle smoking a cigarette when he met her. According to the pilot, the princess was very loud and extremely angry about the way the FSM had treated her. She was so angry spittle was coming out of her mouth. The captain had to ask the princess twice to put out the cigarette before she complied. He was able to calm her down and get her to return to her seat. The captain then instructed the flight attendant in the first-class galley not to serve the princess any more alcoholic beverages. Because the princess continued to behave in a loud and unruly fashion, the captain had to go back to see her two additional times during the flight.

Before the meal service, the princess demanded champagne from two flight attendants and they served her another glass. In addition, passengers observed the flight attendants serving her at least two glasses of red wine during her meal.

On several more occasions throughout the flight, the princess got out of her seat to find the FSM or to see her daughter. On these occasions, the princess created commotions, being loud and abusive toward the flight attendants, shouting profanities and death threats. About six hours into the flight, the princess approached the FSM, lunging at her in an attempt to grab her by the throat and screaming that she would have the FSM killed. Another flight attendant intervened, but not before the princess dug her nails into the FSM's arm.

After his last visit with the princess, the captain notified TWA flight operations that there was an unruly passenger aboard whom he wanted detained when they landed in Boston. As a result, a Massachusetts State Police Officer met the aircraft when it landed. When the officer met the princess, he described her as being very emotional and smelling strongly of alcohol. The officer stated that he would not let her drive in her condition. The princess was arrested for assault, battery and interference with the flight crew. She was later assessed a US$3,000 penalty for violating 14 CFR 91.11 by assaulting, threatening, intimidating and/or interfering with a crewmember in performance of the crewmember's duties.

In a written statement made shortly after the flight, the captain said, 'I went to the first class cabin and encountered a very agitated and upset lady. With proper training, I would probably have diagnosed her as intoxicated and filled with rage'. However, the captain's instruction not to serve the princess any additional alcohol was based on his assessment that she was intoxicated, as determined by the judge. TWA received a fine in the amount of US$40,000 for: 1) permitting the princess to board the aircraft under the influence of alcohol; 2) allowing the princess to retain her glass during taxi and takeoff; 3) continuing to serve her alcoholic beverages, even though she appeared intoxicated and after the captain had issued the instruction not to serve her additional alcoholic beverages; and, 4) not reporting the incident to the FAA. TWA appealed the decision, but lost.[67]

There were several United States Federal Aviation Regulations (FARs) cited by the judge who presided over this case:

- *Section 121.575(c)* No certificate holder may allow any person to board any of its aircraft if that person appears to be intoxicated.
- *Section 121.575(b)(1)* No certificate holder may serve any alcoholic beverage to any person aboard any of its aircraft who appears to be intoxicated.
- *Section 121.575(d)* Each certificate holder shall, within five days after the incident, report to the Administrator any disturbance caused by a person who appears to be intoxicated aboard any of its aircraft.
- *Section 121.577(a)* No certificate holder may move an airplane on the surface, take off, or land when any food, beverage, or tableware furnished by the certificate holder is located at any passenger seat.[68]

Some other examples of what a passenger disruption may look like are found in the following descriptions. It should be recognized that a passenger's disruption might not necessarily escalate progressively from mild to extreme:

- *Passive aggressive behavior:* The passenger does not comply with minor requests by flight attendants or pilots, or if they do respond, it may be slow. Often, they ignore requests of the crew and do not respond verbally.
- *Verbal/aggressive behavior*: Passenger uses abusive language that could include profanities, sarcasm and insults. Often the passenger will shout or yell at the crew. There may be defiant acts and aggressive body language and/or irrational behavior that may seem childish. They may make threats either verbally or in written form.
- *Physical aggression*: Physical contact is made between passenger and crew or between passengers. Contact may include pushing, grabbing, slapping, hitting, or kicking another person. A deliberate attempt to damage another person's property, including interior of the aircraft is also included.
- *Violent behavior*: The passenger causes or attempts to cause a serious bodily injury or death to another person. They may display a weapon or make a threat of possessing a weapon. They may cause damage to aircraft interior or other equipment.[69]

Competency in handling difficult situations is a skill that can and should be learned by crewmembers through continued practice and should be a requirement for anyone who is involved with dealing with the public.[70] Chapter 9, Conflict Management, discusses various methods that can greatly assist crewmembers in maintaining a focus on their job and controlling their environment through positive approaches to conflict resolution with others.

Meeting the needs of airline passengers

The needs of airline passengers are simple, really – comfortable, on-time passage, and efficient service from ground level to cruising altitude to destination. Whether or not those needs are met depends upon whether the industry regards the passenger as its Number One priority.

A 1998 report compiled by the W. Frank Barton School of Business at Wichita State University and the University of Nebraska at Omaha Aviation Institute demonstrates what air traveler's want, from the ground up:

- *Honest, courteous flight deck and cabin crews* – Passengers want to hear honest information broadcast from the flight deck, especially about flight delays. In the passengers' views, crewmembers ARE the airline and their performance and attitude can be the most important factors in determining the quality of the flight experience.
- *Paperless travel* – Passengers enjoy the convenience of electronic access to airlines.
- *Carrier identification* – Passengers want to know the airline they booked is the airline they will fly. As mega-alliances proliferate, the average passenger will probably become more befuddled by myriad code-sharing agreements.
- *Frequent service/direct routes* – Passengers are more eager than ever to get from here-to-there more frequently and faster.
- *Right airline, right price* – Passengers seek fares that include as many services as possible. Airfare is the most important factor in choosing an airline, according to a study by the Boeing Company. The second is flight scheduling. On short duration flights, reliability, scheduling and comfort – in that order – become the determining factors. On long-duration flights, comfort becomes four times as important followed by aircraft features.
- *Passenger-friendly airports* – Travelers want an efficient reliable transport system that will get them to the terminal without hassles and with no delays, whether it is high-speed trains, helicopters or monorails. Once there, they want to be able to check-in, find the gate and board – preferably without the aid of a global satellite navigation system.
- *More pleasant waiting areas/lounges* – Some airports are installing works of art to soothe passengers. Accessibility to retail stores and food courts is another sought-after amenity.
- *Safe, ergonomically correct cabin environment* – A clean aircraft and well-regulated temperature in the cabin are on the want list, along with adequate reading lights and reasonable levels of sound.
- *Entertainment* – The passengers want a choice of ways to fill their time. Many airlines are providing in-flight entertainment; however, the reliability of the systems in use is marginal. When the system is inoperative, passengers feel cheated.

- *Adequate personal space* – Passengers say they want as much space as possible and specify more legroom as opposed to seat width.
- *Better airline food* – People are more health-conscious today and are demanding 'light, healthy, and nutritional menus on flights'.[71]

Factors controllable by flight crews

- *Honest, courteous flight deck and cabin crews* – Keeping passengers informed and treating them with dignity should be obvious, but how often do crews fail to achieve these goals?
- *Safe, ergonomically correct cabin environment* and *entertainment* are other areas that crews can control to some extent. Paying attention to control of cabin temperatures and making timely maintenance write-ups of inoperative equipment, such as in-flight entertainment systems, reading lights and lavatories, and of aircraft furnishings, such as broken tray tables or seats, will go a long way in meeting this demand.

Conclusion

Perhaps YOU can help affect change in reducing and better handling disruptive passenger and sky rage incidents. Here are some suggestions for you to pass along to your airline and congressmen.

Demand better and more thorough security training. Conflict resolution and self-defense training should be required for all crewmembers (as well as gate agents and ticket counter personnel). Training scheduling and cost are always a determination in what and how training will be accomplished; however, time and money were found to accomplish SOME security training after 9/11. If training in these areas is not mandated and directed by regulators, it will more than likely not be accomplished. If accomplished, it will more than likely be as little as possible to satisfy the regulations.

Live situational training is a great learning tool providing flight deck and cabin crewmembers use the experience to handle other real live situations that could occur on the line. (We do not let pilots fly with passengers until they have received hands on training in a whole series of normal, abnormal and emergency scenarios.) The scenarios should include the spectrum ranging from minor passenger disturbances to those that begin or end with violence.

Passenger profiling techniques can be effective through a combination of using intuition, building rapport, conversation and behavioral observations. We cover this subject in much more detail in Chapter 11.

Self-defense techniques presented through mandated initial training with periods of recurrent training for defensive techniques are desirable for safety of the crew and passengers. The Aviation Transportation Security Act (ATSA) is weak and does not mandate that airlines actually provide defensive training for crews, but rather *separation techniques* that only provide limited escape. How long can you 'separate', how many times will you need to 'separate' in a multiple threat situation, and just where do you go to escape? At some point, you WILL have to defend yourself or others. You NEED this type of training and it must be possible to accomplish on an aircraft. Practicing martial art tactics in a large room full of mats is NOT suitable training for altercations on an aircraft. If defensive maneuvers cannot be accomplished in areas the size of a galley, in an aircraft aisle, or in the cockpit, they should not be taught for that purpose. The Homeland Security Act has mandated self-defense for flight crews, but as of the writing of this book, nothing specific pertaining to content or duration has emerged.

Use of Force training should be mandatory for all flight crewmembers. The new Federal Flight Deck Officers will receive some training on this subject; however, ANY crewmember can become involved in a situation demanding their knowledge of the use of force. Our Chapter 10 addresses this issue in detail.

Restraint training should be mandatory for all crewmembers. It is a very difficult skill to teach, but is very important for the safety and security of everyone concerned, including the aggressor. There are many restraint devices on the market and your airline may provide some type of device on your aircraft. If they are on board, do you know where they are and how to use them skillfully? A violent event is not the time to read directions or ask someone if they know how to use them. Do you know how to use alternate means of restraint?

Airline efforts at realistic customer relations will also help reduce the amount of undue expectation by the passengers. Advertising that your experience on Brand X airline will be the greatest experience you have ever had is not the truth. The truth is that airline travel can be fraught with difficulties. Delays, cancellations, diversions and cramped conditions are the reality of airline travel. Treat passengers as adults and be honest in the advertising of the airline product. This is NOT a commercial, we do not have any financial interest here, but Southwest Airlines makes no qualms about what and who they are. They do not make unrealistic claims to the consumer about what they provide. The only thing they promise is that they will try as hard as they can to get you to where you are going on time.

Zero tolerance for passenger violence aboard aircraft by airline and government alike. The arrest and prosecution of people who have been disruptive or that committed acts of sky rage aboard aircraft produce negative press for the airlines involved. Frequent events on the same airlines affect travelers' willingness to choose that airline for their personal travel, or for sending unaccompanied minors to travel on that particular airline. Nevertheless, airlines need to continually monitor these events and prosecute violators to the fullest extent of the law.

Aggressive government prosecutions of violent passengers are needed, not just slaps on the wrist with minimal fines and *warning letters.* It is an insult to the many fine men and women crewmembers to be so ignored by the law. Without a doubt, prosecutions would occur for violent acts directed against other 'more important occupations'. For instance, a verbal or physical attack on a bank manager for every time an ATM machine did not work would certainly result in the arrest of the individual committing the act. What do you think would happen if an irate passenger went to the office of the president of your airline and physically attacked him or her? Would there be a lawsuit? It is time to get TOUGH on disruptive and violent passengers.

Airlines have a Ground Security Coordinator (GSC) and an Inflight Security Coordinator (ISC) and their responsibilities and duties are spelled out in regulations. However, there are many times when the GSC and/or the ISC are not available and decisions regarding safety and security are required. Therefore, we believe there should be a *Cabin Security Coordinator (CSC)* designated, as well. The CSC would coordinate with the GSC when the ISC is not on board, such as situations that occur frequently when the ISC is tending to other duties prior to flight or when the flight is boarded and is waiting for the flight deck crew to come from a connecting flight. Once the cabin door is closed for flight and the aircraft is away from the gate, the CSC would coordinate with the ISC should any safety or security issue arise in the aircraft cabin. Additional training would be required to be designated a CSC, especially in conflict resolution, situational awareness, decision-making, and managing the use of force in the cabin.

It is up to everyone in the aviation business to continue to proactively seek solutions at all levels to problems associated with disruptive passengers and sky rage. The problems are simply not going to go away. We must be able deal effectively with them.

APPENDIX 2A

Disruptive Passenger and Sky Rage Incidents

Air rage incidents increased to 5,416 in 1997 from 1,132 in 1994
International Transport Workers Federation

As you think about crew survival tactics with regard to defending yourself against unruly, disruptive passengers, take a moment to read these cases and answer these questions. How would I have responded? What were some of the warning signs that the situation was escalating? How could the situation have been defused in any way? Would you have been able to protect yourself, other crewmembers and passengers? What kind of injuries do you think you might have sustained during your attempt to control the situation? What would have happened if the disruptive passenger had won? [Events NOT in chronological order.]

- A United flight from San Francisco to Shanghai was diverted to Alaska when intoxicated twin sisters attacked the flight crew who tried to subdue them. According to the flight attendants, the women had been acting erratic and boisterous earlier in the flight and the flight attendants decided not to allow them any more alcohol. One of the women began yelling that she had to get off the plane, and that she wanted to open the (exit) door and get out to smoke. [AviationNow.com, 10 August 2001]
- BA Flight 2069 with 398 people on board, including 19 crewmembers, plunged to 19,000 feet from its cruising altitude of 30,000 feet as a 27-year-old Kenyan man pushed the controls of the B747-400 while struggling with the First Officer. The Kenyan burst into the cockpit and attacked the pilots, biting the Captain on the ear and finger and then attacking the First Officer. The autopilot was disengaged during the fight as the Kenyan pushed against the yoke. Several passengers came to the aid of the pilots and helped remove the Kenyan from the cockpit to the aisle where three passengers sat on him. Four passengers, the Captain and a female flight attendant suffered minor injuries. [*Arizona Republic*, 21 December 2000]
- On August 11, 2000, Jonathan Burton became the first passenger to be killed by fellow passengers aboard a US commercial jet. Half-way through the one-hour Southwest Flight 1763 from Las Vegas to Salt Lake City, the 19-year-old Burton began pacing the aisles and mumbling. He reached for an apple juice that was not meant for him and then rummaged through cabinets before taking two bags of peanuts. Then he shoved a flight attendant, ran to the front of the B737 and kicked free a panel on the cockpit door. Ducking his head into the cockpit, he shouted, 'I can fly this f---ing plane!' Stories vary as to what actually happened next, but the result was that Burton was first subdued temporarily and then re-engaged in

struggles with passengers. During these last struggles, Burton died. An autopsy report later reported the cause of death from being restrained by passengers. [*USA Today*, 18 December 2000]

- A hulking, 6′ 2″ carpenter weighing 250 pounds, yelling, 'I'm going to kill you all!' and shedding his clothes, broke through the locked cockpit door of Alaska Airlines Flight 259 en route from Mexico to San Francisco. The man attacked the flight crew and grabbed the controls before he was wrestled to the floor by terrified passengers. The co-pilot used a fire ax to try to fend off the man. During the struggle, the pilot pleaded for help over the aircraft public address system and five to seven passengers sprang into action, tackling the man and sitting on him while crewmembers put him in plastic cuffs. The co-pilot needed 8 stitches to close a cut in his hand. The man received a black eye, and cuts and scratches on his face from the struggle. *[Arizona Republic*, 18 March 2000]
- The flight attendant cowered in the cockpit as the America West A320 cruised at 30,000 feet, en route from New York to Phoenix. Just outside the door, the co-pilot and a woman passenger punched and shoved each other in a racially charged struggle that left them both bloody. The woman struck the co-pilot four times in the mouth and the co-pilot pushed her into a cart in the galley. The woman stopped fighting when she noticed she was bleeding. The attack started innocently enough when a flight attendant asked the woman to use the restroom in the front of the aircraft due to a cart blocking the aisle leading to the aft restrooms. An argument ensued during which racial slurs were used by the black woman. The flight was diverted to Albuquerque where the woman was arrested. [*Arizona Republic*, no date]
- On 19 May 2000, Southwest Flight 1857 was awaiting a gate in Nashville during a gate hold due to a weather induced power outage at the airport. A passenger left his seat, approached a flight attendant at one of the aft entry doors and told her he needed some fresh air. She directed him to reseat himself three times, after which the man grabbed her hair, opened the slightly ajar door, and jumped to the tarmac. The flight attendant was able to free herself from his grip and remain aboard. The man was transported to a local clinic with a fractured wrist by airport police. [*AWA Glideslope*, November 2000]
- Former Stone Roses singer, Ian Brown, threatened to chop off a flight attendant's hands and hammered on the cockpit door on BA Flight 1611 from Paris to Manchester on 13 February 1998. [BBC News, 23 October 1998]
- A Virgin flight from Manchester to Florida diverted to New York to have a loud and abusive teenager removed. The incident started when his father asked the flight attendants to stop giving his son free alcohol. The son head-butted his father and then threatened to jump through an emergency exit. He then bit a steward on the arm and spat blood and saliva into the face of a stewardess. The son threatened to slit the throats of staff and smashed a seat before breaking free of an in-flight restraint. [BBC News, 4 September 1998]
- A 24-year-old woman who drank a lot of whiskey before boarding a flight from the US to Heathrow, was described as being in an 'emotional state'. She also

took her prescribed methadone. Five hours into the flight, the woman became 'agitated and abusive' in spite of efforts of stewardesses to calm her down. The woman head-butted two members of the staff before punching, kicking, biting, and scratching a stewardess. The First Officer had to leave the cockpit to help restrain her. [BBC News, 4 September 1998]

- In July 1998, a BA jet was forced to land in Tenerife after a passenger, who was apparently drunk, attempted to force his way into the flight deck during a flight from Rio de Janeiro to London. The passenger, a businessman, threatened to kill the pilot and head-butted a fellow passenger. [BBC News, 1 September 1998]
- In September 1998, a Britannia flight from Las Palmas to Manchester diverted to Cardiff after a 23-year-old man verbally abused the cabin crew and attempted to force his way into the cockpit. Crewmembers and a number of passengers managed to restrain the man and secured him in his seat with use of a restraint kit. [BBC News, 11 September 1998]
- A Virgin airlines flight attendant was attacked with a broken vodka bottle by a violent passenger resulting in the need for 18 stitches and for a piece of glass to be removed from her head. She said that as soon as the flight departed, she knew the man would cause trouble as he had been drinking and had immediately broken airline rules by smoking in the lavatory. When she threatened to tell Spanish police of his behavior, he attacked her. She said, 'I remember he had a vicious look in his eyes. He raised the bottle and hit me across my head. Stunned, I fell to the floor and was screaming for my colleagues to help. He continued to bash the bottle across my back. I thought he was going to kill me'. Four passengers leapt on the man and subdued him. In the interview afterwards, the man said, 'She asked me to sit down, but I did not like the way she said it. She was aggressive, so I did her. If someone starts on me, I will go for them, even if it is a woman'. [BBC News, 1 November 1998]
- Danny Walters was smashed when he kicked a passenger in the head, fondled a flight attendant, and then threatened a co-pilot with a 3½-inch knife on a flight to Charlotte, forcing an emergency landing. [ABCNEWS.com, no date.]
- Six people had to restrain a drunken plumber after he became violent at being asked to turn off pornography on his computer because it was offending fellow travelers. The man, who had been refused alcohol because he appeared intoxicated, started ranting and swearing. He then allegedly jumped up on his seat and began shouting 'You are all gay and full of Aids' before lunging at the cabin director and trying to punch him. The man tried to head-butt the steward and managed to bite him. An appeal was made by the Captain over the public address system for any passengers who had served in the army or police to help restrain the man. The man was overpowered, handcuffed, gagged, strapped down, and sedated; however, even that was not successful in controlling his anger as he head-butted the seats in front of him. He was described as behaving 'like a caged wild animal'. [BBC News, 20 May 1999]

- A man who had been drinking and flicking food and small pieces of rolled up paper at other passengers on a Continental flight from New York to Gatwick, attacked the cabin crew, head-butted passengers, and tried to kick open a door at 33,000 feet before the Second Officer left the flight deck and managed to pin him down. The Second Officer had his hat and glasses snatched off, causing a cut to his left eye. [BBC News, 6 July 1999]
- A woman aboard a Spirit Airlines flight from Ft. Lauderdale to Atlantic City gave the seat in front of her a 'mule kick' after the occupant reclined his seat towards her. The 12-year-old boy was sandwiched inside the broken seat, trapping him and causing him to hit his head. [Associated Press, 24 September 1999]
- A father and son got drunk and fought with passengers on an Air2000 flight from Birmingham to Malta. The captain diverted the plane to Milan after the father told a stewardess that he wanted to tell the pilot he loved him. Two passengers who tried to restrain the father needed hospital treatment in Milan. A prison officer who was aboard tried to subdue the father, but was head-butted in the face, knocking a tooth out. [BBC News, 16 November 1998]
- A chartered B767 made an unscheduled stop in Norfolk, Virginia while en route from London to Jamaica. Twelve people, six English and Irish couples, were removed after fighting broke out among the passengers. The trouble apparently began with shouting and a drink being thrown by one passenger at another traveler. [CNN, 1 February 1999]
- A passenger appeared to be fine during the boarding process, but trouble began after he awakened from a nap. The flight attendant said, 'About 45 minutes after takeoff, the passenger woke up screaming and pointing at no one. He locked himself in the aft lavatory, started to bang on the walls and continued to scream. I opened the door and told him his behavior was not appropriate nor would it be tolerated. He told me to go away, or he would kill me! I figured he has drunk and searched his bags where we found a big bottle of whisky. He was not served liquor on-board. We finally got him out of the lavatory. We had a minister who asked to help because the passenger was crying and upset about something. The passenger became more belligerent over the next hour, and then violent. The passenger hit me, and the #3 Flight Attendant, and threatened several times to kill us. The First Officer helped us restrain the passenger and received similar threats. The minister who helped us was punched in the face, again with threats. Because of the time of night, both the #3 Flight Attendant and I had to a spend considerable time trying to contain this passenger. We both had to suspend our normal duties including our normal jumpseats for landing. I feel other passengers were upset and fearful. We were met by police and the passenger was removed.' [ASRS Callback Report, 1997]

APPENDIX 2B

FAA Office of Pubic Affairs Press Release, July 6, 2001
Statement – Air Rage (www.faa.gov)

FOR IMMEDIATE RELEASE
July 6, 2001
Contact: Alison Duquette/Rebecca Trexler
Phone: 202-267-3462
Statement – Air Rage

Federal Aviation Administration (FAA) rules clearly prohibit passengers from assaulting, threatening, intimidating, or interfering with flight attendants. Our nation's flight attendants perform vital safety duties, especially during an aviation emergency.

Unfortunately, some passengers continue to put the flying public at risk by choosing to engage in dangerous behavior aboard an airplane. The repercussions for passengers who engage in unruly behavior can be substantial. They can be heavily fined by the FAA or prosecuted on criminal charges.

The FAA aggressively pursues each reported case and proposes substantial fines for the most egregious incidents. The FAA can propose up to $25,000 per violation for an unruly passenger case. One incident can result in multiple violations.

The FAA believes that widely publicized criminal prosecution of air rage cases serve as a strong deterrent. The FAA, FBI, local US attorneys, local law enforcement, airlines, and crewmembers are working together to help prepare cases that the Justice Department can then prosecute. At several major airports, FAA security agents respond to the more serious incidents and help interview victims, suspects, and witnesses. The FAA supports Justice Department efforts toward full criminal prosecution, when warranted.

The FAA has provided model training programs to airlines to help flight attendants manage instances of passenger misconduct.

The FAA urges passengers to do their part to make their trip as safe as possible.

An electronic version of this statement is available via the World Wide Web at: http://www.faa.gov/apa/pr/index.cfm

Notes

1 Air Rage Incidents Threaten Safety, *AirWise News*, 12 June 2000.
2 Miami Man En Route To Vegas Charged In Air Rage Incident, *AirWise News*, 1 December 2000.
3 Air Rage Man Took Beer, Vodka And Valium, *AirWise News*, 15 August 2000.
4 Passenger Problem On French Flight, *AirWise News*, 24 December 2000.
5 Drunken 'Full Monty' Demo Earns Fine And Reprimand, *AirWise News*, 1 December 2000.
6 Beyond the anger: Experts studying subconscious nature of violent rage, *New York Times*, 28 November 2002.
7 Beyond the anger: Experts studying subconscious nature of violent rage, *New York Times*, 28 November 2002.
8 Beyond the anger: Experts studying subconscious nature of violent rage, *New York Times*, 28 November 2002.
9 Beyond the anger: Experts studying subconscious nature of violent rage, *New York Times*, 28 November 2002.
10 Man is acquitted in airport attack, *Aviation Week*, 3 April 2001.
11 Drunken Brawl In Heathrow Terminal, *AirWise News*, 26 June 2000.
12 Ground Rage is a overlooked problem, airline employees say, *Aviation Week*, 5 July 2001
13 ibid.
14 Controlling cabin fever, *BBC News*, 23 July 2001.
15 Regulators, airlines grapple with how to address air rage, www.aviationnow.com, 10 August 2001.
16 FAA warns fliers of air rage penalties, *CNN News*, 1 August 2001.
17 Passenger punches flight attendant and opens plane's rear door, *Airwise.com*, 8 January 2002.
18 Copilot uses ax to keep man out of cockpit, *CNN.Worldnews*, 8 February 2002.
19 Flight returns to Charlotte after fight between passenger and attendant, *Associated Press*, 4 September 2002.
20 Flight returns to Charlotte after fight between passenger and attendant, *Associated Press*, 4 September 2002.
21 Flight returns to Charlotte after fight between passenger and attendant, *Associated Press*, 4 September 2002.
22 Woman Arrested At Toronto After Alleged Air Rage Incident, *AirWise News*, 13 September 2000.
23 Airwatch, Aviation Security International, April 2002.
24 Airwatch, Aviation Security International, April 2002.
25 REM guitarist 'lied' over attack, *CNN News*, 3 April 2002.
26 Unruly passenger tied up on plane, *Associated Press*, 6 June 2002.
27 Second Charge Of Sexual Misconduct On Board A Plane, *AirWise News*, 14 August 2000.
28 Second Charge Of Sexual Misconduct On Board A Plane, *AirWise News*, 14 August 2000.
29 Teenager Wins Damages For Psychological Harm After Sex Incident On KLM Flight, *AirWise News*, 4 December 2000.

30 Airwatch, Aviation Security International, April 2002.
31 Airwatch, Aviation Security International, June 2002.
32 Appeal from the US District Court for the Northern District of Illinois, Eastern Division. No. 91 CR 559 – Charles R. Norgle, Sr, Judge. 24 September 2002. United States Court of Appeals for the Seventh Circuit.
33 Thomas, Andrew, *Air Rage: Crisis in the Skies*. Prometheus Books, New York, 2001, pp. 50–51.
34 World Wide Air Rage Campaign, *AirWise News*, 7 July 2000.
35 UK 'Air Rage' Incidents Double, *AirWise News*, 24 January 2000.
36 Violence 'Tip Of The Iceberg' In Air Rage Incidents, *AirWise News*, 20 February 2000.
37 Japan Gets Tough On 'Air Rage' Incidents, *AirWise News*, 21 May 2000.
38 World Wide Air Rage Campaign, *AirWise News*, 7 July 2000.
39 Disruptive Behavior on Board UK Aircraft: Analysis of Incident Reports April 2001–March 2002, Department for Transport, UK
40 Airlines face explaining flight delays, *Knight Ridder Newspapers*, 29 November 2002.
41 Controlling cabin fever, www.bbc.co.uk, 23 July 2001.
42 Controlling cabin fever,www.bbc.co.uk, 23 July 2001.
43 Liquor sales jump in airports, *Airport Retail News*, 18 December 2001.
44 Regulators, airlines grapple with how to address air rage, *Aviation Week*, 10 August 2001.
45 27th Annual Commercial Aviation Forecast Conference, Mar. 2002.
46 FAA Unruly Passenger Statistics, www.faa.gov/passengers/Unruly.cfm, Dec. 2003.
47 Reporting of violence lacks standards, *USA Today*, 5 December 2001.
48 Reporting of violence lacks standards, *USA Today*, 5 December 2001.
49 FAA seldom punished violence, *USA Today*, 5 December 2001.
50 Flight attendants urge action against air rage, www.cnn.com, 6 July 2001.
51 FAA seldom punished violence, *USA Today*, 5 December 2001.
52 Flight Crew Security Training Course, Williams and Waltrip, 2002.
53 Dahlberg, Angela Dahlberg, *Air Rage*, Ashgate Publishing, Burlington, Vermont, 2001. pp. 19–20.
54 Ibid., p. 43.
55 Ibid., p. 44.
56 Ibid.
57 Ibid.
58 Ibid., p. 45.
59 Ibid.
60 Ibid., p. 44.
61 Ibid., p. 45.
62 Ibid.
63 Ibid.
64 Attacks on cabin staff have risen six-fold in the past decade, www.independent.co.uk, 6 April 2002.
65 Dahlberg, Angela, *Air Rage*, Ashgate, Aldershot, 2001, p. 46.
66 International Conference on Disruptive Passengers, *Air Line Pilot Magazine*, June/July 1997.
67 FAA Order No. 1998-11, Docket No. CP96NE0294, Served 16 June 1998. US Department of Transportation, FAA, Washington, D.C.

68 United States Department of Transportation, FAA Order No. 1998-11 served 16 June 1998.
69 Dahlberg, Angela, *Air Rage*, Ashgate, Aldershot, 2001, p. 49.
70 Ibid.
71 Passengers enraged, but does industry care?, *Aviation Week*, 14 June 1999.

Chapter 3

Aircraft Hijacking: A Continual Threat

Introduction

> A hijacking is an attack on us all, an offense to us all and a danger to us all; and we must act collectively to diminish the risk and to lessen the consequences.[1]
>
> Lord Brabazon of England
> Fifth International Aviation Security Conference, 1988

The purpose of this chapter is not to discuss specific anti-hijacking techniques since each airline addresses those topics during their flight crew security training. Although every hijacking event produces lessons learned, our focus is mainly on hijackings that have occurred in the past five years. An exploration of the background of hijacking, followed by our own analysis of more current hijackings, sets the stage for guidance on what to do if you are hijacked and what a hostage scenario may involve.

For the purposes of this chapter, the words 'hijacking' and 'hijacking attempts' are used interchangeably as flight crews may experience injury, traumatic stress, and/or captivity in either case. 'Hijacking' also includes commandeering, or the attempted commandeering, of aircraft on the ground. It does not include instances of sky rage or disruptive passengers.

The Threat

A brief history of aircraft hijackings

The first recorded *attempted* hijacking of an aircraft took place in Arequipa, Peru on 21 February 1931. The captain, approached on the ground by armed revolutionaries, refused to fly them anywhere. The first *successful* hijacking took place on 16 July 1948 and ended in disaster as the Cathay Pacific aircraft crashed into the sea off the coast of Macao after hijackers attempted to gain control of the aircraft.[2] The first US aircraft hijacking occurred on 1 May 1961 when a Puerto Rican-born man forced a National Airlines plane at gunpoint to fly to Havana, Cuba where he was granted asylum.[3]

Aircraft hijackings, although sporadic and in some years non-existent in the US, have continued to plague aviation since that first successful one in 1948. Of the 15 hijackings attempted from 1948 through 1957, none involved aircraft from the US.[4] The

82 hijackings recorded in 1969 more than doubled the total number of hijackings from 1948-1968. During the ten-year period 1967–76, the number of hijacking peaked with 385 incidents, including 27 hijackings or attempted hijacking to Cuba from the United States. In 1969, there were 82 hijacking attempts recorded, more than double the number from 1947 to 1967. From 1967 to 1976, hijackings peaked with 385 incidents recorded. From 1977–86 there were 300 incidents and from 1987–96, 212 incidents.[5] The US experienced no hijackings during the period 1992–98.[6] There were approximately 78 hijackings in the five-year period, 1997 to 2002. Since 1947, 60 per cent of hijackings have been refugee escapes.[7] In 2003, there have been hijacking attempts:

- 1 January – A British man with an aerosol can and a knife made threatening remarks about hijacking a Qantas flight at Cairns bound for Darwin.[8]
- 19 May – A man apparently intent on crashing a Qantas flight bound for the island of Tasmania from the city of Melbourne. A 40-year-old man slashed two flight attendants with sharp wooden sticks, possibly sharpened chopsticks, on his way to the cockpit. Passengers and crew wrestled the man to the floor before he could reach the cockpit.[9]

It is reasonable to believe that hijackings will continue, but will probably decline in numbers as security tightens around the world. As such, it is still important that flight crews address this subject in training and in professional education.

Fortunately, not all attempts at hijacking aircraft have been successful, and flight crews can benefit from lessons learned from these events. In the early 1980s, Williams was an Eastern Airlines first officer flying the DC-9. On an originating flight from Detroit to Atlanta, a security incident took place on his aircraft that he describes in his own words:

> Minor maintenance was required on the aircraft and a maintenance technician was in and out of the flight deck numerous times while attending to the item. All of the passengers on the full flight were on board the aircraft. A couple of minutes before scheduled departure. The gate agent working the flight entered the flight deck, closed the door and quietly said, 'We have reason to believe you have an armed hijacker on board, what do you want to do?'
>
> The captain and I briefly looked at one another and then in an attempt to delay the flight for a few minutes longer as we tried to devise a plan, he said, 'Get maintenance back up here!' The technician arrived in no time and the captain explained the situation to him, as we knew it. At the same time, I looked out to the right and saw another Eastern DC-9 sitting at the gate next to us with no lights on. I suggested to the captain that we have the maintenance technician make an announcement that our aircraft was out of service and that we would be using a spare aircraft at the gate next to us.
>
> The gate agent then made the announcement, apologizing to the passengers for the inconvenience, relating how lucky we were to have a spare aircraft, ('Look out the right and you will see it.') and that all passengers would need to gather their belongings and proceed to the next gate for processing. In the meantime, EAL operations notified airport security. During the time, it took to get the aircraft shutdown and secured, all the

> passengers exited the aircraft. We conducted a quick search of the aircraft for anything left on board and found nothing.
>
> When we arrived in the boarding area of the next gate, the gate agent was making an announcement for all passengers to take their carry-on baggage, exit the concourse and re-enter through the security-screening checkpoint. Unfortunately, all airport security agents were on the gate side of the checkpoint allowing one passenger, a woman, to depart the terminal, summon a taxi and disappear. All of the remaining passengers cleared security and we departed approximately an hour late.
>
> The entire event happened very quickly and our plan fell into place nicely with good communication and coordination between the flight deck and cabin crew, the gate agents and EAL operations, and airport security. Having had the passengers witness maintenance in and out of the flight deck and having a spare aircraft visible at the next gate helped us hastily devise a believable plan that worked in getting everyone safely off the aircraft and back into the terminal. The only weak point was that there were no security agents on the terminal side of the checkpoint, allowing the woman to escape.
>
> A further discussion with EAL operations before departure revealed that a man had called indicating his wife was on board with a pistol and had intentions of committing suicide by killing the pilots and crashing the plane. It is unknown whether the woman was apprehended, or not. I have always wondered what might have happened if we had gotten airborne.

It is very important flight crews fully realize that every security-related event is unique. Truly, no two events are ever the same – sometimes similar, but never identical. It is a rare to have a 'textbook' situation, emphasizing the importance of creativity and situational awareness in devising a plan, good communication and coordination in relaying and executing the plan, and to some degree the element of good luck in the successful outcome of an event. Listed below are some additional recent hijacking attempts that include some important points to ponder.

Hijackings: Attempted (2000–2002)

July 2000, National Airlines – One attempted hijacking event reflects some of the major weaknesses in our security system as well as the importance of CRM skills, such as crew communication and coordination. After being stopped by an airport security supervisor while trying to bypass a security checkpoint, a lone gunman ran past the airport security screening area, walked onto the aircraft entered the flight deck of a National Airlines B757 and closed the cockpit door at 10:26 p.m., four minutes before departure. After the gunman entered the flight deck, some of the passengers began screaming, rushing for the boarding door as fast as they could and escaping. About this time, one of the pilots ordered the front door closed and a flight attendant complied; however, passengers pushed the flight attendant aside, re-opened the door and fled down the jetbridge to the gate. Passengers also escaped down an emergency chute at the rear of the aircraft.[10] The hijacker released the captain at 12:10 a.m. with a list of demands and the co-pilot was released thirty minutes later. Five hours after the incident started, the gunman surrendered and authorities took the man into custody at 3:30 a.m.[11] No one was injured.

Important points to ponder:

- Security officers were unable to stop the man at the security checkpoint.
- The gate agent was unable to stop the man from boarding.
- Inattention of the flight attendant at the boarding door permitted the man to enter unimpeded.
- The flight deck door being open during the boarding process permitted easy access by the gunman to the cockpit.
- According to a first class passenger, the entire takeover took less than 10 seconds.

February 2002, United Airlines – United Airlines Flight 855 was en route from Miami to Buenos Aires when a lone male tried to kick open the flight deck door in an attempt to takeover the aircraft. The man managed to kick in the bottom half of the door (a pressure-relief panel) and attempted to crawl through the opening into the cockpit when the First Officer hit the man on the head with the crash ax. Crewmembers in the cabin, assisted by passengers, pulled the would-be hijacker back into the cabin and subdued the man.[12]

Important points to ponder:

- The 'impregnable' door may not be impregnable.
- The first officer (F/O) was hesitant to strike the hijacker due to the proximity of his body parts to the man. (The F/O had his knee on the man's neck and back.)
- Flight attendants enlisted the aid of passengers in yet another event.

June 2002, Ethiopian Airlines – Security officers on board the aircraft shot and killed two men armed with knives who attempted to hijack the aircraft shortly after takeoff. No one else was injured.[13]

Important points to ponder:

- Your flight may include Federal Air Marshals, armed law enforcement officers, and/or Federal Flight Deck Officers. How can you help them overcome hijackers armed with knives without becoming a victim of either?
- If you are one of the armed individuals named above, how good are you with your firearm? When was the last time you practiced or qualified?

August 2002, Ryanair – A Swedish man, accused of planning to hijack a flight from Vaesteraas, Sweden to Stansted Airport outside London belonged to a group headed to an Islamic conference in Birmingham, England. Airport security officers detained the man after finding a pistol hidden in the man's toiletry kit. According to police, the man, who had undergone flight training in the US in 1996–97, had planned to seize the aircraft and fly it into an American Embassy in Europe in a conspiracy with four other men. The man, with prior convictions of assault and theft, attacked a US Embassy Marine guard in Stockholm in 1999.[14]

Important points to ponder:

- Sometimes, the security checkpoint works. What would have happened if the security guards had not found the weapon? How do you subdue a man armed with a pistol?
- Where are the other four men involved in the conspiracy, or was this incident the actions of a lone, mentally deranged person?

October 2002, Saudi Arabian Airlines – An Airbus A300 en route from the Sudanese capital of Khartoum to the Saudi city of Jeddah, returned to Khartoum after a Saudi man armed with a pistol attempted to hijack the aircraft shortly after takeoff. Security guards on board the aircraft overpowered the would-be hijacker. There were no injuries.[15]

Important points to ponder:

- How did a pistol get through security?
- What were the intentions of the hijacker?
- If security guards had not been present, would the crew have known how to subdue the armed individual?

November 2002, El Al – An Arab with an Israeli passport attempted to hijack an El Al B757 en route from Tel Aviv to Istanbul just minutes before landing. The man tried unsuccessfully to kick in the cockpit door after threatening a flight attendant with a small pocketknife. Two security guards, one posing as a passenger, overpowered the man within seconds, quickly terminating the event. The flight landed in Istanbul where authorities arrested the would-be hijacker.[16]

Important points to ponder:

- How did a pocketknife get through El Al security, the 'best in the world'?
- If someone threatened you with a small pocketknife, would you know how to disarm and subdue the person?
- Usually, hijacking attempts when airborne occur within minutes after takeoff. What were the intentions of the hijacker in attempting the hijacking just before landing?

Analysis and conclusions of hijackings occurring 2000–2002

Termination of two of the six incidents cited above (33 per cent) occurred on the ground before flight. In one of these events, the would-be hijacker gained access to the flight deck during the boarding process after dashing through the security checkpoint. In the second event on the ground, a weapon detected at the security checkpoint during a search of carry-on baggage resulted in stopping the would-be hijacker. Both events involved men armed with pistols.

In three of the six events (50 per cent), security officers on board the aircraft terminated the attempted hijacking during flight. Two of the events involved the use of knives, and three events involved the use of pistols. During one of the attempts with knives, security officers shot and killed the two would-be hijackers on the aircraft.

The would-be hijackers were armed and exhibited violent behavior during five of the six events (83 per cent). In only one event was there no weapon involved.

Our conclusions from this analysis are:

- In spite of the increased number of screeners at security checkpoints, as well as increased security awareness of gate agents, armed individuals can still gain access to aircraft and the flight deck. Flight crews are continually required to face security failures in the system.
- An attempt to hijack an aircraft may occur during the boarding process when the attention of the flight deck crew is on preparation of the aircraft for flight. The many distracters of the boarding process may divert the attention of the cabin crew. Crew alertness and constant awareness is difficult to establish and maintain while performing routine tasks that demand attention. Flight crew training must address the limitations on multi-tasking functions that constitute a human frailty.
- Attempts to hijack an aircraft happen very fast. Your initial reaction to the threat is extremely important to the outcome of the situation. To help build fast reaction times, flight crews must practice as many related scenarios as possible. The short duration of a takeover attempt does not usually provide time for lengthy discussions, crew coordination or data collection. Flight crews must react decisively and without hesitation, sometimes on very limited cues, information, or help from other crewmembers.
- Violent behavior involving both armed and unarmed individuals accompanied the vast majority of attempted hijacking involving flight crews. Flight crews must know and be proficient in tactics and techniques to counter these types of attacks. From our experience in training flight crews to deal with armed and unarmed attacks, we believe these skills must be kept simple, easy to learn, and capable of being performed within the confines of an aircraft. Airlines vary greatly in their approaches to hands-on 'separation training' in both techniques taught and length of training. It is our opinion that separation techniques may be effective in 'buying time' to solicit aid from other crewmembers and/or passengers. Flight crews must learn defensive tactics for use in situations where separation is not possible, or if the confrontation continues after separation. Crews should learn the difficult skill of restraining a combatant. Continual, repetitive practice of all tactics and techniques is *essential* to creating rapid and accurate reactions to any attack.

An Analysis of Hijackings Listed in Appendix 3A

Forty randomly selected hijackings that occurred from January 1998 to November 2002 are briefly described in Appendix 3A. The analysis disregards airline, trip origin and final destination in the analysis of the 40 events. Focus is on the number of hijackers, types of weapons used, fatalities and injuries that occurred, and the duration of the event. The analysis extracts some of the conditions you might encounter during captivity, as well.

The number of hijackers involved

The 40 hijacking events listed in Appendix 3A involved 88 hijackers, making the average number of hijackers 2.2 per event. (A point-2 person is probably very intoxicated, but that is another story.) A single hijacker accomplished 28 of the 40 events (70 per cent). Two hijacking involved two hijackers, two involved three hijackers, and one involved four hijackers. Five had five hijackers, including three of the hijackings involved on 9/11. (Officials believe the Indian Airlines hijacking in 1999 by five terrorists was a rehearsal for the 9/11 attacks.[17]) One hijacking involved nine hijackers and another, twelve hijackers. It is difficult to see trends within a small sample, so to conclude there has been a drastic change from having one hijacker in the past to five hijackers now or in the future would not necessarily be a correct deduction. In three of the four hijacking events listed since 9/11, there was only one hijacker (the other involved 2). Five of the six attempted hijackings previously discussed (2000–2002) involved a single would-be hijacker.

Conclusions:

- Seventy per cent odds are that you may encounter only one hijacker.
- If the purpose is to commandeer the aircraft and use it as a weapon of mass destruction, multiple hijackers will be involved to ensure success of their terrorist mission.
- One-hijacker scenarios tend to play out with goals of bringing attention to political or religious ideologies, seeking asylum, escaping, extortion, or for unknown reasons (the mentally unstable) or suicide (mentally unstable, despondent and desperate).

Types of weapons used

In 14 of the 40 events (35 per cent), fake explosives or other associated devices were involved (or the threat of having an explosive that turned out to be a hoax). In another eight events, either actual explosive or grenades were present (20 per cent) Interpreting the data, about half the time you can expect an explosive to be involved during the event with a 3:2 chance that it is a fake. In the only actual explosive detonation event, the detonation of a grenade injured 15 passengers.

In 16 of the events (40 per cent), knives, box cutters or other edged weapons were involved. Hijackings involving the use of edged weapons (excluding the 9/11 hijackings) resulted in the deaths of one captain and one passenger, and injuries to a captain, first office and four flight attendants. Edged weapons used in all four terrorist events on 9/11, resulted in the deaths of all crewmembers and passengers (and hijackers). If these numbers were factored into the previous calculations, the use of edged weapons in 10 of the 16 events (63 per cent) caused death or injury.

In 11 of the 40 events (28 per cent), firearms of some type were involved with the hijacking event. *There were no cases of death or injuries inflicted upon passengers or crewmembers from the use of a firearm by a hijacker.* Six hijackers were shot and killed during five of the events. Two hijackings involved the use of fake pistols. In one event, the lone hijacker did not use a weapon at all.

Conclusions:

- You can expect the involvement of an edged weapon in a hijacking about half of the time.
- Injuries from the use of edged weapons can be expected approximately two-thirds of the time when edged weapons are present.
- About a fourth of the time, a firearm will be present.
- Even if a firearm is present, *probably* no one will be shot (except maybe the hijacker) – again, no guarantees, but good odds.

Fatalities and injuries that occurred

During six of the 28 events involving only one hijacker (21 per cent), there were five fatalities, four of which were the hijackers, the other a captain. Injuries were sustained by 15 passengers and four crewmembers in these six events, also. Events involving multiple hijackers resulted in deaths of 235 passengers, 22 hijackers, 26 flight attendants, eight pilots (in addition to over 3,000 people on the ground) and injuries to one soldier and one hijacker (plus hundreds on the ground).

Conclusions:

- There are never any guarantees as to the outcome of a hijacking event; however, if only one hijacker is involved, odds are greatly in your favor that no one will be killed (except maybe the hijacker).
- The chances for injuries and/or fatalities to passengers and crewmembers, as well as to the hijackers, increase dramatically as the number of hijackers increases.
- One sure conclusion: unless stopped, a multiple-hijacker scenario with terrorists bent on self-destruction will be fatal to all those aboard and possibly thousands on the ground.

The duration of the event

Some of the reports concerning the hijackings were vague as to the length of the hijacking, sometimes listing the event as 'one day'. We estimated the average length of each of those 'one day' events as four hours, based upon ground and flight time, and other variables. *The average duration for one-hijacker events is approximately 6 hours, a good figure to remember.* Although there is no guarantee things will be over that fast, this is good news for the flight crew and passengers. The stress and fatigue induced by the act on the hijacker undoubtedly becomes a factor relatively quickly in the one-man show.

During the longest hijacking event on record, passengers were held hostage for 40 days after an El Al flight from Rome was diverted to Algiers in 1968. In 1970, three aircraft (UK, US and Swiss) and 400 passengers were hijacked to Jordan and hostages were released 24 days later. During a hijacking event in Colombia in 1999, rebels took passengers into the jungle and held them for over 20 months. These are the extremely long cases, however, and by far are the exception.

When multiple hijackers were involved (excluding the 20-month ordeal), the duration of the event averaged three days. (Events on 9/11 were excluded in that computation.) The four hijackings on 9/11 are the exception to that statistic as they averaged just over an hour in duration. Multiple hijackers provide the ability for their group to be more relaxed, to take mental and physical breaks, and to gain support from each other. The ratio of hijacker-to-captives becomes less as the hijackers disperse throughout the aircraft, reducing the stress of having to watch everyone all the time. For example, during the 1999 hijacking of the Indian Airlines, one of the passengers recalled that the hijackers appeared to relax after landing in Kandahar and did not seem intimidated by the Taliban fighters surrounding the aircraft.[18]

Conclusions:

- If you are involved in the more-than-likely one-hijacker scenario, it is reasonable to expect it to be over in approximately 6 hours.
- Involvement in a multiple-hijacker event requires your mental and physical preparation, as well as that of the rest of the crew and passengers, for the long-term – maybe for up to three days in duration.
- You can expect creature comforts to deteriorate well beyond pleasant, as described in the section to follow. Personal hygiene will be difficult, if not impossible to maintain.

Conditions you may encounter

The following are some of the quotes, complications, concessions, and flight crew responses extracted from reports of some of the hijackings in Appendix 3A.

Quotes:

- 'They announced, 'This plane is hijacked' and did a lot of running up and down the aisles' – hostage.
- 'Inside the air is very bad and it smells like people have been sick' – aircraft servicing personnel.
- 'I died many times' – the captain.
- 'There were always times when we thought this was the last minute. The heat was turned up with the fumes and stench I almost passed out. Then it was turned down so it was cold and there was no circulation of air' – hostage.
- 'Sometimes it was "don't move", and sometimes it was "let's all pray together and hope for a good outcome"' – hostage.
- 'We constantly felt our lives were in danger' – hostage.
- 'To begin with they were threatening, but slowly their aggression subsided and they treated us quite well. No one was beaten or insulted. Relations were good' – hostage.
- 'There wasn't enough oxygen, there wasn't enough water, women and children were crying' – co-pilot.
- 'We lived through a dark time … they were going to kill us all' – a hostage.
- 'The crew did their best to comfort the passengers. They supported us psychologically, they managed to feed us' – hostage.

Complications:

- The passengers were without food and water for 26 hours.
- The aircraft engines shut down briefly, cutting radio communications between the hijackers and the negotiators. A mechanic was allowed to work on the engine to restore power.
- The aircraft engines shut down again due to a faulty battery.
- All hostages were forced to wear blindfolds during the entire event.
- The fifth day, people were sick, toilets had clogged and the air was foul.
- One hostage suffered from a kidney ailment.
- Some passengers developed stomach problems with diarrhea.
- Children, confused and uncomfortable, began to cry. Adults also broke down in tears when it became clear there would be no early end to the crisis.
- Some passengers fainted.

Concessions:

- The hijackers allowed some of the passengers to change clothes and briefly exercise outside the plane.
- Hijackers allowed the aircraft's doors and rear chute opened to air out the interior of the aircraft.

- Hijackers allowed a diabetic man to go to a hospital for treatment, but on the condition that he would return to the aircraft later. He complied.
- Hijackers demanded food, water and medicine for release of some hostages.
- The hijackers requested a generator to keep heat and air flowing through the aircraft.
- Hijackers allowed the captain, who won the trust of the hijackers, to walk the aisles to talk with passengers.

Flight crew responses:

- I had many passengers say, 'Let's fight', but I told them casualties would be very high and that we could not take the risk of fighting.
- The captain said he sustained himself during the eight-day ordeal with a vast reserve of patience. He only slept a few hours during the whole eight days.

As much as possible, flight crews should perform routine duties during any captivity. Doing so has two very tangible benefits. First, it takes your mind off the situation and focuses it on accomplishing your duties. It is easy to forget normal and routine items while under difficult and stressful conditions. Second, accomplishing routine tasks includes attending to the needs of passengers and other crewmembers. The passengers in particular are depending upon you for comfort, sustenance, moral support, leadership and guidance.

As you can determine from the comments listed above, conditions in the aircraft can get wretched quickly. Food and water may be scarce and its dispersal will more than likely require careful management. Crowd control techniques may be required to avoid matters from getting out of hand. Your patience and attitude will be tested to the maximum, but as a captive, they are your best assets if kept positive.

What to Expect During a Hijacking

In his book, *Everything You Need to Know Before Being Hijacked*, Dan McKinnon states that, 'The odds of being a victim in a terrorist attack or hijacking are about one in a million. But, what do you do if you're that one?' Chapter 8, dedicated to mental preparation, emphasizes the importance of mental preparation for high threat events that may occur on an aircraft. Knowledge of what to expect during a hijacking or hostage situation will further aid your being able to personally cope with the situation and help support other crewmembers and passengers during such a traumatic event.

Typically, there are four phases to a hijacking or hostage event. We label them takeover, control, delay and resolution phases, while other references use different terms for these phases. In any case, phases are divided according to what occurs during each phase.[19, 20] Understanding and being able to recognize each phase is very important to your survival both mentally and physically.

Takeover phase

The takeover phase is usually violent, aggressive and abusive. The takeover process involves victim(s) passing from a routine existence of comfortable and predictable behavior to a sudden and dramatic encounter with threats and possible death.[21] For the unprepared, this is a traumatic turn of events and the situation may seem unreal. Common feelings of control and invulnerability by the hostage are quickly overcome by opposite extremes of confusion and defenselessness. During this phase, hostages may experience mixed feelings of anger, fear, panic, fight or flight response, frozen fear, aggression and/or disbelief.

Some hostages may seek immediate relief in denial, an effective psychological mechanism put to use when the mind is so overwhelmed with trauma that it cannot handle the situation. 'I can't believe this is happening to me', or 'This can't be happening', are typical remarks indicating denial. Hostages have been known to go to sleep during denial, or to believe they are dreaming and will soon wake up. People who have not been mentally prepared for being taken hostage may panic, which is more likely to occur when the chances of a favorable outcome are perceived to diminish rapidly.

Most hijacking takeovers require no longer than 1 to 2 minutes and may be accompanied by tactics to induce terror and compliance into hostages, such as yelling, beating, threatening, or even killing passengers or crewmembers. Typical characteristics of hijackers during the intimidation phase include being violent, very verbal, vindictive, emotional and nervous. Their objectives are to establish control by instilling fear, to prevent counter-reactions, and to gain respect.

For individuals who can quickly determine what is going on and react, the best time to try to escape is during those first moments of confusion before the terrorists have established their position of control and have counted hostages. Obviously, whether or not the aircraft is airborne, the number and location of hijackers, and how they are armed are huge factors to consider in making a decision to escape.

Control phase

During the control phase, the hijacker has established control of the situation. The control phase is of utmost importance to the survival of the hostage as the behavior patterns exhibited in this phase create the foundation for hostage-hijacker interaction. Although some hostages may remain in denial, others begin to face reality and act as they do normally providing a measure of emotional relief and mental escape. Three major stressors experienced at this point – fears of isolation, claustrophobia, or the loss of a sense of time – may be very troublesome, depending upon the length of captivity. The problem is exacerbated by not knowing how long the event will actually last.

The *fear of isolation* may be particularly difficult for a person who is more outgoing. The demoralizing effect of being alone is supplemented by the realization that the only human contact is with hostile individuals.[22] Boredom and despair are fostered by the fear of isolation.

Darkness in a confined space for an extended period can lead to disorientation and *claustrophobia*. It is common for hostages to be blindfolded, or for all aircraft window shades to be closed. Hostages may be required to remain in their seats with their seatbelts fastened and the tray tables down, further restricting or limiting movement. Even the most sedentary individuals will begin to feel the stress of such conditions.[23]

The *loss of the sense of time* may actually begin during the takeover phase and continue into the control phase. Hostages may experience something similar to a 'time warp' from being focused on trying to figure out what is happening or from being focused on a particular attention-getting event and not being allowed to look at their watches. It may be difficult to remember the sequence of events or the duration of each event. Sometimes the only knowledge the hostage may have about what is going on is what the captor decides to relate – this is especially true if blindfolded.

During the control phase, terrorists and hostages are likely to be in a highly agitated emotional state. It is extremely important to your survival to remain calm and patient. If terrorists sense they are losing control during this phase, they may repeat their attention-getting tactics demonstrated in the takeover phase.

Delay phase

The delay phase is usually the longest phase of a hostage situation and hours may seem like days to hostages. Boredom may be broken up by moments of terror (as the hijackers revert to the takeover phase). Alternating between these extremes of emotions induces fatigue.

It is during the delay phase that hijackers may resort to tactics involving sexual molestation of a crewmember or passenger, a search for sky marshals or law enforcement officers, collection of cell phones/passports/ID cards, binding certain passengers, and/or switching clothing – either between hijackers or between hijackers and hostages. The hijackers may reserve certain lavatories for their own use, separate children from parents or husbands from wives, and announce captaincy of the aircraft with the goals of de-humanizing hostages and turning them into symbols of their cause.

It is also during the delay phase that negotiations may occur between the hijackers and authorities. Making hijackers aware of the lack of food or water, inadequate toilet facilities, needs for adapting to the environmental conditions, and medical conditions that need to be addressed may become bargaining chips that may serve to improve conditions on the aircraft as well as to place additional stressors on the hijackers.

As the ordeal drags on, it sets the stage for crewmembers to experience the John Wayne Syndrome, a predominately-male problem. This syndrome consists of feelings of helplessness in a crisis when the person wishes they could be the hero, but are actually helpless to respond.[24] The overwhelming feelings of helplessness can cause depression and the inability to respond in a positive manner, even if afforded the opportunity. Other feelings involved can include self-hate, despair, and giving up.

Resolution phase

Finally coming to grips with the whole ordeal through self-analysis of their feelings, hostages in the resolution phase may reveal mixed feelings toward their captors. It is during this phase that the hostage may develop the Stockholm syndrome – positive feelings for the captor accompanied by negative feelings toward authorities. This syndrome is a natural unconscious survival technique. Victims who have experienced the Stockholm syndrome reported trying unsuccessfully to resist their feeling of compassion for their captors.[25] A flight attendant who survived a hijacking offered an indication of this inner conflict.

> After it was over and we were safe I recognized that the captors had put me through hell and had caused my parents and fiancée a great deal of trauma. Yet, I am alive. I was alive because they had to let me live. You know only a few people, if any, who hold your life in their hand and then give it back to you. After it was over and we were safe, and they were in handcuffs, I walked over to them, kissed each one and said, 'Thank you for giving me my life back'. I know how foolish it sounds, but that is how I felt. [26]

The resolution phase may be achieved gradually through negotiations in the delay phase, or it may be achieved suddenly through liberation by a rescue force. The characteristics of each of these methods of resolution are quite different. If resolved by negotiation, emotional reactions may vary from hope and encouragement to disappointment and despair. If resolved by liberation, emotional reactions may include panic, frozen fear, flight or fight response, compliance and/or emotional breakdown.

Hostages: Survivors or Victims

Hostages tend to fall into one of two categories, survivors or victims, with the difference having much to do with mental preparation before the event occurring. Survivors return to a meaningful existence with strong self-esteem and live healthy, productive lives with little evidence of long-term depression, few nightmares or serious stress-induced illness. Victims may not have lived through the ordeal or upon release or rescue may require extensive psychotherapy to deal with real or imagined problems.[27]

Neither the survivors nor the victims ever completely forget the hostage experience. A positive-growth experience separates the two categories. The typical reactions of the two categories are diametrically opposed:

Survivors	**Victims**
Cling to faith	Abandon faith
Suppress hostility toward captors	Act out aggression
Value 'self'	Have self pity
Constructively fantasize	Belabor reality of the situation
Tend to rationalize	Dwell on how the situation could have been avoided
Indulge in routine behavior	Deal in antagonistic behavior
Display mature stability	Display youthful immaturity
Demonstrate flexibility and humor	Demonstrate obsessive-compulsive behavior
Blend in with peers	Are overly compliant or resistant to demands

Faith – Hostages must have faith in themselves, their God, their country and in those who are negotiating or dealing with their captors. An American hostage should know that the US government, at a variety of levels and agencies, is monitoring the situation and working towards a release or rescue. Hostages should concentrate on the positive resolution of the situation rather than sinking into depression with feelings of being abandoned and isolated. Depression is a common and can be an insurmountable enemy as time passes and there has been no apparent change in conditions, or conditions have worsened. Our discussions with Viet Nam POWs revealed that those who 'survived' never lost faith, no matter how desperate or prolonged the situation seemed.

Suppression of hostility – The psychological defense mechanism called 'suppression and isolation of affect' allows the hostage to keep aggressive feelings inside rather than challenge captors with hostile words or deeds or by insisting on better or more comfortable conditions.[28] This is the reverse of the London syndrome, a term used to describe the display of aggressive feelings toward captors that over time results in the hostage-taker resenting the captive. During the siege of the Iranian Embassy in London, one hostage continuously argued his point of view through prolonged political discussions with his captors, despite pleas of fellow hostages. His captors finally killed him, triggering an assault on the embassy during which additional hostages were killed. During the hijacking of an India Airlines flight, one hostage who repeatedly removed his blindfold and was subsequently stabbed to death, a victim of the London syndrome, also known as 'Suicide by Terrorist'.

Value of 'self' – Hostages need to remember that one of the reasons for their predicament is that they have value. No matter how demeaning the hijackers act, survivors retain their value of self-worth. This is not to be interpreted as a superior attitude with hostile actions taken against the hijackers, but an inner dignity regardless of outward appearances.

Ability to fantasize – The experiences of hostages have shown that survivors were able to occupy their minds during their captivity in a wide variety of manners. Some relate using their imagination to build or remodel homes while others planned trips or vacations. Some reduced stress by daydreaming or withdrawing into sleep. All agree that dealing with boredom is one of the major problems of the experience. By constructively fantasizing, a person can gain some self-control, fill empty hours, and mentally escape from the danger of the situation.[29]

Rationalize – It is clearly more desirable to be a live hostage than a dead martyr. Hostages must recognize and accept the reality of the situation, realize that they do not have the power to effect change, and adjust to the circumstances, making the best of the situation. Avoid the use of hindsight to see how the situation could have been avoided, but rather accentuate the positive. Give thanks for being alive, and resolutely adjust to the demeaning status of hostage.[30]

Routine behavior – As long as the behavior does not pose a threat to the captors, acting according, as close to normal routine as possible is a great stress reliever. Flight attendants have found great consolation in accomplishing routine tasks such as cleaning the galley, tending to passengers (if permitted), accounting for items served, or in writing letters. Hostages who are preoccupied with helping others have little time to reflect upon their individual plight.[31] Physical exercises, such as dynamic tension activities, provide a multitude of benefits as they occupy time and promote better physical and mental functioning. Physical exercises also enable one to sleep better and provide the very positive effects of goal setting and achievement.

Mature stability – The sense of confidence projected by the mature, stable appearance of one who is in control can have a calming effect on both the captors and other hostages. As a flight crewmember, you are the most important safety feature on the aircraft and it is important that your mature professional behavior convey this message to all concerned.[32]

Flexibility and humor – Things change during any situation, sometimes very rapidly. Being able to adapt quickly and without hesitation to those changes is a valuable trait. Although certainly not a humorous occasion, keeping a sense of humor and being able to laugh inwardly at personal idiosyncrasies is a proven way to relieve stress.

Blend in with peers – Doing exactly what one is told is recommended to ensure safety of the group. Unless passenger, aircraft or personal safety is danger, doing more than what is ordered is not a good survival tactic.[33] In fact, it may get you killed or singled out for torture if your captors identify you as 'the weakest link'. If you must assume a leadership role, try to accomplish it covertly.

Coping with captivity

The feelings you may experience during captivity are largely dependent upon the length of time involved. The chart below depicts typical characteristics of reactions as a function of time and offers some useful and productive countermeasures to overcome some of these feelings.[34]

Although these last two categories are highly unlikely for crewmembers of commercial airlines, many crewmembers are military reservists. As such, they have the potential for becoming a POW while on military assignment and could experience very long-term incarcerations; therefore, these categories are included for your consideration. The last two categories in Table 3.1 may also produce long-term symptoms requiring psychotherapy treatment.

Some major psychological problems that may be encountered during captivity, their causes and results, are depicted in Table 3.2.

Your knowledge of these problems and their results will aid you in assessing your behavior as well as the behavior exhibited by other crewmembers and/or passengers. Your correct assessment of the behavior exhibited will allow you to apply or to suggest appropriate stress reduction methods depicted in Table 3.3.

What to Expect During a Hostage Rescue

Oh God, we will all be blown to hell!

Last conscious thoughts made by a Russian journalist that survived the rescue attempt by Russian Special Forces ending the hostage situation at a theatre in Moscow in October 2002

The rescue force will probably try to use the utmost stealth in approaching the aircraft, or hostage holding area if off the aircraft. In some cases, the assault may begin with some sort of distraction that draws the attention of the terrorists in one direction while the rescue force is moving in from another. At night, lighting may be positioned so that terrorists become virtually blind to what is going on beyond a short distance from their position. The assault may involve simultaneous strikes from as many entrances as possible. Once the assault begins, the rescue force will try to create as much confusion for the terrorists as possible using smoke, flash grenades and shouting.

Table 3.1 Reactions to captivity

Major reaction	Time period	Characteristics	Countermeasures
Startle/panic	Seconds to minutes	Time distortion Frozen fear Tunnel vision Poor memory Panic Confusion	Rely on training Self discipline Deep breathing
Disbelief	Minutes to hours	Denial Hope Disappointment	Talk down the situation Try to observe
Hyper-vigilance	Hours to days	Wary Attentive to detail Vigilant	Use observational skills to their best advantage Avoid the three syndromes
Resistance/ compliance	Days to weeks	The three syndromes Listening improves	Maintain physical and mental fitness
Depression	Weeks to months	Despair Excessive sleeping Loss of appetite Feelings of guilt Suicidal tendencies Abandon of self-hygiene	Communicate Have faith/pray Communicate Engage in fantasy Plan for the future Conduct creative mental work
Gradual acceptance	Months to years	Development of ritual Acceptance of fate Development of normality within confines of captivity	Stretch out activities Communicate Engage in mental activities

Chaos is intentionally created to disorient the terrorists and put them on the defensive, not allowing them time to shoot hostages or set off explosive devices. Any lull or slowing down during the assault may give terrorists time to take cover, grab a hostage to use as a shield, or to return fire.

A successful assault should take not more than 90 seconds. The longer the assault lasts, the more likely there will be casualties among the hostages. Once under attack, most terrorists will immediately turn their attention away from the hostages and focus on the attack by the rescue force. Here are some recommendations to avoid being injured during the confusion.[35]

Table 3.2 Psychological reactions to captivity

Psychological problem	Cause(s)	Result(s)
Fear and anxiety	Unpredictability	Action paralysis Counterattack Inappropriate actions Uncontrollable laughter
Boredom and despair	Lack of stimuli Time to think	Depression 'Give-up-itis' Non-communication
Guilt	Reason needed Situation viewed as punishment John Wayne syndrome	Self-recrimination Depression Emotional breakdown
Fatalism	Loss of faith	Self-fulfilling prophesy
Pain	High stress leading to psychosomatic pain	Headache Chest/ back pain Stomachache Numbness in extremities
Psychiatric symptoms	Fear of going crazy Lack of stimulus	Auditory and/or visual hallucinations

Table 3.3 Stress reduction methods

Category	Methodology
Physical	Engage in deep breathing and physical fitness exercises, progressive muscle relaxation, and massage
Practical	Talk down the severity of the situation, actively observe
Distractive	Review life plans and memories, be creative, fantasize, study, apply humor
Mental	Stop negative thoughts, engage in meditation, apply self-hypnosis
Beliefs	Work at maintaining a positive mental attitude, engage in religious rituals such as prayer, choose activities that lead to an increase in knowledge, challenge yourself

Do:

- Lay face down immediately where you are when the shooting starts.
- Keep your head down.
- Keep your hands visible at all times, using your arms to cover your head and ears.
- Follow instructions exactly and cooperate with the rescuers.
- Make an orderly exit as directed by the rescuers.

Do not:

- Raise your head and look around.
- Move until the rescuers tell you that it is safe to do so.
- Try to be a hero – rescuers will not have time to make positive identification before shooting to kill.

Summary

No one can tell you exactly how or when a hijacking will occur; therefore, no one can tell you exactly how to react. The purpose of the material presented in this chapter was to better prepare you for an ordeal that we hope would never happen. Hijackings, and the responses and reactions to them, are not an exact science. What may occur in one may not occur in another; what works in favor for the hostages in one may not work in another. The terrorist hijackings on 9/11 were unique in their planning, in the manner in which they were carried out and in their purpose. Will they happen again that way? No one knows for sure, but with the publicity they received worldwide, it is doubtful that passengers and crewmembers will allow it to happen that way again, if it is at all possible. There is also the remote possibility that your hijacked aircraft may be shot down if it is deemed a threat to national security interests.

Various agencies, including the North American Aerospace Defense Command, FAA, TSA, FEMA, Royal Canadian Mounted Police and Transport Canada, participate in a major exercise each year called 'Amalgam Virgo'.[36] Amalgam Virgo 2002 was conducted in June 2002. The relatively free-play exercises were designed to test responses of the various agencies to aircraft that are hijacked. Responses and procedures were checked in scenarios involving aircraft in flight and on the ground with actual aircraft being flown during the exercise. The exercise was played out more as a war game where the outcome was unknown and events unfold according to the responses and tactics employed by the various agencies. Although no live fire was conducted, simulated lethal force against the aircraft was an option. If an aircraft was destroyed through simulated lethal force in the air, it was still allowed to land to test procedures and coordination of ground-based agencies at the destination. Although the results of the exercises are classified, procedures that affect flight crews may result through analysis of the data collected by the agencies.

First Officer Williams, while employed with a major US airline, participated in a similar exercise in 1988. Some of the material included in this chapter comes from his experiences aboard a B727 that was 'hijacked' from San Diego by two individuals (FBI) armed with pistols, grenades and plastic explosives. After the flight landed in Dallas, FBI negotiators secured the release of several 'hostages' being held for ransom. Refueled, the flight departed Dallas, made a low approach at Toronto, and landed at Atlantic City, New Jersey. The FBI Hostage Rescue Team terminated the flight by force after hearing shots fired aboard the aircraft. A tremendous learning experience for all involved, it is highly recommended that you volunteer to participate in any such event.

It is important for crewmembers to remain aware at all times, and to apply their basic knowledge of hijackings and survival to their circumstances as quickly and as accurately as possible. Recognition of the various phases of a hijacking and having an understanding of what to expect during each phase, better equips flight crewmembers to handle these stressful events and come out survivors instead of victims.

APPENDIX 3

Randomly selected aircraft hijackings: 1998 to 2002

Y–M	Flight/ origination/ destination	Number	Type(s) of weapons used	Fatalities/ injuries	Duration of hijacking
98–01	Atlantic Airlines Bluefield, Nicaragua to (Little Corn Island) Puerto Limon, Costa Rica[37]	1 man	Gasoline	None	4 hours ±
–02	Kibris (THY) Adana[38]	1 man	Bomb inside teddy bear (hoax)	None	1 day
–03	Kibris (THY) Cyprus to Ankara[39]	1 man	Lighter in shape of grenade	None	1 day
–05	Air Luxor (Portugal) Toronto to (Lisbon)[40]	1 man	Bomb in gym bag (hoax)	None	4 hours ±
–05	Pakistan International Airline Turbat to (Karachi) Hyderabad, Pakistan[41]	3 men	Guns, grenades	2 injured, 1 soldier, 1 hijacker	2 days
–06	Iberia Airlines Seville, Spain to (Barcelona) Valencia, Spain[42]	1 man	Television remote control	None	4 hours ±
–09	Turkish Airline THY Ankara to (Istanbul) Trabzon[43]	1 man	Plastic toy gun	None	4 hours ±
–10	Turkish Airline THY Adana, to Ankara, Turkey[44]	1 man	Grenade, handgun	1 fatality, the hijacker	9 hours
99–03	Air France Marseille, France to (Orly Airport, Paris) Roissy-Charles de Gaulle Airport, Paris[45]	1 man	Explosives (fake)	None	4 hours ±

Y–M	Flight/ origination/ destination	Number	Type(s) of weapons used	Fatalities/ injuries	Duration of hijacking
99–04	Avianca Airlines Bucaramanga, Colombia to (Bogota) San Pablo, Colombia[46]	5± rebel group	Military rifles	Whereabouts of 15 crew and passengers unknown	20 months
–7	All Nippon Airways Haneda, Tokyo to Sapporo, Japan[47]	1 man	Knife	1 fatality – the captain	1 day
–08	Royal Air Maroc Casablanca, Morocco to (Tunis, Tunisia) Barcelona, Spain[48]	1 man	Pistol	None	2 days
–10	Egyptian Air 838 Istanbul, Turkey to (Cairo, Egypt) Hamburg, Germany[49]	1 man	Knife	None	4 hours ±
–11	Zhejiang Airlines Yiwu, to Xiamen, China[50]	1 man	Explosives (fake)	None	Unknown
–12	Indian Airlines Airbus Katmandu, Nepal to (New Delhi, India) Kandahar, Afghanistan[51]	5 men	Box cutter, knives	1 fatality – passenger stabbed by hijacker	8 days
00–02	Ariana Airlines Kabul, Afghanistan to Uzbekistan to Kazakstan to Moscow to London Stansted Airport[52]	12 men	4 handguns, 5 knives, 2 grenades, 2 detonators, 1 pair of brass knuckles	None	5 days ±
–02	China Southwest Airlines[53]	1 man	Gasoline, lighter, knife	None	4 hours ±
–05	Philippine Air Lines Manila[54]	1 man	Pistol, fake grenade	1 fatality, hijacker who parachuted to his death in a homemade parachute	1 day

Y–M	Flight/ origination/ destination	Number	Type(s) of weapons used	Fatalities/ injuries	Duration of hijacking
00–05	EgyptAir Cairo to Aswan[55]	1 man	Fake bomb (hair gel)	None	4 hours ±
–07	Royal Jordanian Airlines Amman, Jordan to Damascus, Syria[56]	1 man	Pistol, stun grenade	1 fatality, hijacker: 15 wounded by grenade	1 hour ±
–07	National Airlines New York JFK[57]	1 man	Pistol	None	5 hours
–07	British Airways City Flyer Express Zurich to London[58]	1 man	Scissors, fake bomb	None	4 hours ±
–09	Royal Jordanian Airlines Sanaa to Amman[59]	1 man	Fake bomb	None	4 hours ±
–09	Xinhua Airlines Baotou to (Beijing) Jinan[60]	1 man	Knife, fake gun	1 fatality, hijacker; 2 injured, captain and F/O stabbed	4 hours ±
–09	Qatar Airways Doha, Qatar to (Aman, Jordan) Ha'il, Saudi Arabia[61]	1 man	'Big' Knife	None	1 day
–10	Sabena Airlines Brussels to (Abidjan) Malaga, Spain[62]	1 man	None	None	4 hours ±
–10	Saudi Arabian Airlines Jeddah, Saudi Arabia to (London Heathrow) Baghdad, Iraq[63]	2 men	3 bombs, handgun	None	8 hours ±
–11	Vnukovo Airlines Dagestani to Azerbaijan, Russia to Uvda, Israel (Moscow)[64]	1 man	Fake bomb (blood pressure gauge)	None	12 hours

Y–M	Flight/ origination/ destination	Number	Type(s) of weapons used	Fatalities/ injuries	Duration of hijacking
01–01	Yemenia Airways Djibouti to (Taiz, Yemen) Djibouti[65]	1 man	Suitcase full of explosives (fake)	None	1 day
–01	Gulf Air Hong Kong to Abu Dhabi	1 man flight	Knife	2 injured, flight attendants	1 day
–03	Vnukovo Airlines Istanbul, Turkey to (Moscow, Russia) Medina, Saudi Arabia[66]	3 men	Knife, fire axe (from the cockpit), explosives (threat)	3 fatalities, hijacker, flight attendant, passenger; 1 steward stabbed	24 hours ±
–04	Addis Ababa, Ethiopia Khartoum, Sudan[67]	9 men	Military explosives, grenades, pistols	None	11 hours ±
–09	American Airlines 11 Boston to (Los Angeles) World Trade Center[68]	5 men	Knives, box cutters	Fatalities: 81 passengers, 2 pilots, 9 flight attendants, 5 hijackers	0:46
–09	United Airlines 175 Boston to (Los Angeles) World Trade Center[69]	5 men	Knives, box cutters	Fatalities: 56 passengers, 2 pilots, 7 flight attendants, 5 hijackers	1:05
–09	American Airlines 77 Washington Dulles to (Los Angeles) The Pentagon[70]	5 men	Knives, box cutters	Fatalities: 58 passengers, 2 pilots, 4 flight attendants, 5 hijackers	1:28
–09	United Airlines 93 Newark to (San Francisco) Rural Pennsylvania near Pittsburgh[71]	4 men	Knives, box cutters, possible explosive device	Fatalities: 38 passengers, 2 pilots, 5 flight attendants, 4 hijackers	1:59

Y – M	Flight/ origination/ destination	Number	Type(s) of weapons used	Fatalities/ injuries	Duration of hijacking
02–04	China Northern China	1 man	Knife	None	4 hours ±
–06	Ethiopia Airlines Bahr Dar to Addis Ababa, Ethiopia[72]	2 men	Knives	2 fatalities – the 2 hijackers	Unknown
–10	Saudi Arabian Airlines Khartoum, Sudan to Khartoum (Jedda, Saudi Arabia)[73]	1 man	Pistol	None	Unknown
–11	Alitalia Airlines Bologna, Italy to Lyon Paris (Paris, France)[74]	1 man* (see 3/99)	TV remote control	None	3 hours ±

Notes

1 ICAO Seeks to Stop Airline Hijackings, *Air Line Pilot Magazine*, December 1988.
2 Aircraft hijacking, www.wikipedia.org, 25 October 2002.
3 Significant Terrorist Incidents, 1961-2001: A Brief Chronology, www.state.gov, 16 July 2003.
4 Airports, www.preventingcrime.org, 13 July 2003.
5 Aircraft hijacking, www.wikipedia.org, 25 October 2002.
6 The history of hijacking, www.suntimes.co.za, 13 July 2003.
7 Aircraft hijacking, www.wikipedia.org, 25 October 2002.
8 Qantas threat, man charged, *Herald Sun*, 2 January 2003.
9 Man Tries to Crash Qantas Plane, Stabs Crew, *Reuters*, 29 May 2003.
10 Gunman releases pilot and co-pilot from plane at New York's JFK Airport, www.cnn.com, 28 July 2000.
11 Gunman surrenders after New York airport hostage drama, www.cnn.com, 28 July 2000.
12 Drama in the Skies, www.abcnews.go.com, 7 February 2002.
13 Airline security guards hill 2 in hijack attempt, Associated Press, 10 June 2002.
14 Detained Swede planned to hijack jet, official says, Associated Press, 31 July 2002.
15 Saudi with gun seized in jet hijacking attempt, Associated Press, 16 October 2002.
16 Israel questions man seized on airliner, www.cnn.com, 18 November 2002.
17 Similarities seen between Indian Airlines, US hijackings, www.cnn.com, 27 September 2001.
18 India airline hostage recalls harrowing ordeal, www.cnn.com, 6 January 2000.
19 Barthelmess, Sharon, How to Survive In a Hijacking and Hostage Situation, *Cabin Crew Safety*, Flight Safety Foundation, July/August 1988.
20 Hijacking: From Intimidation to Resolution – Training for Reality, Violence in the Skies Seminar facilitated by Philip Baum, Green Light Limited, London, UK New Orleans, Louisiana, July 2002.
21 Barthelmess, Sharon, How to Survive In a Hijacking and Hostage Situation, *Cabin Crew Safety*, Flight Safety Foundation, July/August 1988.
22 Ibid.
23 Ibid.
24 Hijacking: From Intimidation to Resolution – Training for Reality, Violence in the Skies Seminar facilitated by Philip Baum, Green Light Limited, London, UK New Orleans, Louisiana, July 2002.
25 Barthelmess, Sharon, How to Survive In a Hijacking and Hostage Situation, *Cabin Crew Safety*, Flight Safety Foundation, July/August 1988.
26 Ibid.
27 Hijacking: From Intimidation to Resolution – Training for Reality, Violence in the Skies Seminar facilitated by Philip Baum, Green Light Limited, London, UK New Orleans, Louisiana, July 2002.
28 Barthelmess, Sharon, How to Survive In a Hijacking and Hostage Situation, *Cabin Crew Safety*, Flight Safety Foundation, July/August 1988.
29 Ibid.
30 Ibid.
31 Ibid.
32 Ibid.

33 Ibid.
34 Hijacking: From Intimidation to Resolution – Training for Reality, Violence in the Skies Seminar facilitated by Philip Baum, Green Light Limited, London, UK New Orleans, Louisiana, July 2002.
35 Kidnapping Survival Tips, www.terrorismsurvival.com/kidnap.htm, 25 October 2002.
36 NORAD Hijacking Exercise Could Lead to Simulated Shoot-down, www.aviationnow.com, 4 June 2002.
37 Significant Terrorist Incidents, 1961-2001: A Brief Chronology, www.state.gov, 16 July 2003.
38 Chronology of Hijacked Planes in Turkey, www.turkishpress.com, 29 March 2003.
39 Significant Terrorist Incidents, 1961–2001: A Brief Chronology, www.state.gov, 16 July 2003.
40 Significant Terrorist Incidents, 1961–2001: A Brief Chronology, www.state.gov, 16 July 2003.
41 PAF prevents hijacked PIA Fokker F-27 from entering India and forces the airliner to land at Hyderabad Airport, www.piads.com.pk, 24 May 1998.
42 Hijacking description, www.aviation-safety.net, 26 October 2002.
43 Significant Terrorist Incidents, 1961–2001: A Brief Chronology, www.state.gov, 16 July 2003.
44 Turkish commandos storm plane, kill hijacker, www.cnn.com, 30 October 1998.
45 France holds ex-policeman after short-haul hijacking, wwww.cnn.com, 2 March 1999.
46 Colombian hijackers release 6 captives, www.cnn.com, 13 April 1999.
47 Pilot killed in hijacking of domestic flight, www.cnn.com, 23 July 1999.
48 Hijacking ends at Barcelona airport, www.cnn.com, 25 August 1999.
49 Hijacker surrenders after seizing Egyptian airliner,www.cnn.com, 19 October 1999.
50 Chinese police detain hijacking suspect, www.cnn.com, 24 November 1999.
51 Indian airlines hijacking in third full day, www.cnn.com, 27 December 1999.
52 Hijack ordeal over, www.news.bbc.co.uk, 10 February 2000.
53 Criminal Acts Against Aviation, Federal Aviation Administration Office of Civil Aviation Security, 1997–2001.
54 Ibid.
55 Ibid.
56 Jordanian guards kill hijacker after grenade explodes on jet, www.cnn.com, 6 July 2000.
57 Criminal Acts Against Aviation, Federal Aviation Administration Office of Civil Aviation Security, 1997–2001.
58 Ibid.
59 Ibid.
60 Ibid.
61 Qatar Airways jet hijacked; man give himself up, www.cnn.com, 14 September 2000.
62 Criminal Acts Against Aviation, Federal Aviation Administration Office of Civil Aviation Security, 1997–2001.
63 Hostages arrive back in Saudi after hijack ordeal, www.cnn.com, 15 October 2000.
64 Israeli forces claim Chechen plane hijacker mentally unstable, www.cnn.com, 12 November 2000.
65 US envoy escapes Yemen hijack, www.cnn.com, 23 January 2001.
66 Three die as jet hijack ends, www.cnn.com, 16 March 2001.
67 Ethiopian plane hijacked by students, www.cnn.com, April 26, 2001.

68 History of airliner hijackings, www.news.bbc.co.uk, 3 October 2001.
69 Ibid.
70 Ibid.
71 Ibid.
72 Airline security guards kill 2 in hijack attempt, Associated Press, 10 June 2002.
73 Saudi with gun seized in jet hijacking attempt, Associated Press, 16 October 2002.
74 Hijacker of '99 flight suspected a 2nd time, Associated Press, 28 November 2002.

Chapter 4

Investigating Terrorism

Introduction

One of many things to come out of the attack on the USA in September 2001 was the fact that Americans generally did not realize, or recognize, the depth of grave danger to the nation and its citizens that existed. Terrorism experts had been predicting such an event for more than a decade. As we ignored the experts, we buried our collective heads in sands of false security, denial, complacency and ignorance. We chose to minimize or to ignore warning of danger. Were you even aware of the following warnings?

- In March 1996, 'The threat of a terrorist group using a nuclear, biological or chemical weapon of mass destruction in the United States is real', said John Sopko, who has been studying the problem for the Senate Governmental Affairs Committee. 'It is not a matter of 'if' but rather 'when' such an event will occur'.[1]
- In 1998, the World Islamic Front for Jihad Against Jews and Crusaders – a group founded by Osama bin Laden – issued a defiant warning in the London-based Arabic newspaper Al-Hayat. 'The coming days will guarantee, God willing, that America will face a black fate. Strikes will continue from everywhere, and Islamic groups will appear one after the other to fight American interests'. The group said it would 'continue shipping more American dead bodies to their unjust government until we humiliate America's arrogance and roll its dignity in the mud of defeat'.[2]
- US intelligence officials learned from several sources in June 1998 that bin Laden was considering attacks in the US, including Washington DC and New York. Officials learned in August 1998 a group of unidentified Arabs planned to fly an explosive-laden plane from a foreign country into the World Trade Center.[3]
- Officials learned in March 2000 bin Laden was eyeing ports, skyscrapers, nuclear plants, airports and the Statue of Liberty as targets.[4]
- In June 2001, CIA officials learned key bin Laden operatives were disappearing and others preparing for martyrdom.[5]
- A person returning from Afghanistan in July 2001 told the CIA, 'Everyone is talking about an impending attack'.[6]

- The National Security Agency intercepted two messages on the eve of 9/11 warning that something was going to happen the next day, but no one translated the messages until 12 September 2001.[7]
- 'A year after 9/11, America remains dangerously unprepared to prevent and respond to a catastrophic terrorist attack on US soil. In all likelihood, the next attack will result in even greater casualties and widespread disruption to our lives and economy'. From a report by a congressional panel sponsored by the Council on Foreign Relations that comes one week after the CIA Director warned Congress that, 'the terrorist threat is as grave now as it was just before the 9/11 attacks'.[8]

Realizing most of us are not privy to such information (until much later), you probably have just read most of these warnings for the first time. If you had known about any of the warnings from 1998 to 2001 – before 9/11 – what would you have done? What *could* you have done? Realistically, the answer to those two questions is probably the same, – 'nothing'. The assumption is our government can and will protect us against such events. It cannot and it did not. In fact, no government can protect its citizens ALL the time. Nor can your airline. It is an impossible task.

Without getting philosophical, in general people are *reactive*, not *proactive*. The government is reactive and airlines are reactive, not proactive. Look around. How many times in your airline career have you seen the government or an airline company do anything proactive of any significance for their flight crews? We must have accidents before training issues are addressed (windshear and upset training), aircraft design flaws corrected (rudder actuators redesigned, vertical stabilizer strengthened), enhanced ground proximity warning systems installed (many controlled flight into terrain accidents), runway and taxiway signage correctly installed (runway incursions), etc. How many flight attendants were injured, many seriously, during turbulence before it became a flight briefing item and procedures were developed for communicating levels of turbulence to the cabin crew? The list goes on indefinitely. To think that in today's airline economic climate airlines are going to voluntarily act 'proactively' on security threats alone is absurd. The vast majority of airlines will spend some money and effort to provide additional training for their personnel when absolutely mandated by the FAA – and even then, it becomes a matter of 'what is the minimum training necessary to fulfill requirements and how can we accomplish training at least cost?' Quality, content and depth of training tend not to be issues addressed at all. These statements may seem blunt, but they mirror exactly what we found in working within the industry since 9/11. The reactive posture of both the government and industry leaves the ball in your court. *Flight crewmembers must adequately prepare themselves for the shortcomings of the system.* It is our goal to help you accomplish that.

This object of this chapter is to immerse aviation personnel into the world of terrorism. That is not to imply you are ignorant on the subject, but rather like the authors, your prior knowledge may be limited to a few newspapers and TV news updates. You may have received some information on the subject as part of your 'required' airline security-training program, as well. As you will ascertain by the references to this chapter, we have conducted an in-depth study of terrorism and have attempted to bring the subject more into focus for aircrews. One dilemma we faced while writing many of the chapters of this book was keeping the chapters up-to-date on a daily basis – an almost impossible task since 'something security-related' is happening daily on a national and international basis. We will keep the chapters updated through 30 September 2003, the day of submission of our final manuscript. In spite of this effort, some of information in this chapter (and others) will be out of date before the ink is dry when published. It is our hope that you will closely follow national and world events pertaining to terrorism ... and ultimately to you as a flight crewmember.

Defining Terrorism

> Terrorism is like pornography – easy to recognize, but hard to define.[9]

When is a crime a terrorist attack? Numerous definitions of 'terrorism' are pertinent to this chapter, including:

- 'A purposeful human activity primarily directed toward the creation of a general climate of fear designed to influence, in ways desired by the protagonists, other human beings, and through them some course of action';[10]
- 'The threat of violence and the use of fear to coerce, persuade, and gain public attention';[11]
- 'The use of violence or the threat of violence, to coerce governments, authorities, or populations by inducing fear';[12]
- 'The conscious exploitation of the natural phenomenon, terror';[13]
- 'The premeditated, calculated use of force to achieve certain objectives';[14]
- 'The unlawful use of force or violence against persons or property to intimidate or coerce a government, the civilian population, or any segment thereof in furtherance of political or social objectives';[15]
- 'Premeditated, politically motivated violence perpetrated against a noncombatant target by sub-national groups or clandestine state agents, usually intended to influence an audience';[16]
- 'The systematic attempt to undermine a society with the ultimate goal of causing the collapse of law and order and the loss of confidence in the state';[17] and,
- 'The unlawful use or threatened use of force or violence by a revolutionary organization against individuals or property, with the intention of coercing or intimidating governments and societies, often for political and ideological purposes'.[18]

These different definitions are similar in concept and, either implicit or implied, share commonalities of:

- Acts of or threats of criminal, unlawful, political subversion carried out by states, individuals or private groups usually sponsored by states as part of a campaign of geographic expansion or political control, or of illicit business operations in pursuit of goals unattainable by conventional political, economic or military actions;
- Destruction of property focused on military bases and equipment, embassies, business establishments or headquarters, and national or religious monuments and icons;
- Killing of human beings, with special emphasis on high-profile individuals, heads of state, diplomats, public officials, business leaders, noncombatant soldiers, alleged spies, and 'innocents'; and,
- Tools of violence used to instill and spread fear and to jeopardize fundamental human rights and freedoms among a targeted population, such as kidnapping, hostage taking, extortion, individual or mass murder, arson, shooting and bombing.[19]

In reality, none of the traditional definitions of terrorism exactly fits its use today. Terrorism has changed. We have been slow to recognize the changes and define them, to determine what they mean to us today, and how to be successful in countering terrorism. As with other endeavors in aviation, with terrorism we are again *reactive* not *proactive*, putting all of us into a defensive mode rather than an offensive position. One only has to look at the events and aftermath of 9/11, the limited anthrax attacks in the months that followed, and all terrorist events worldwide since 9/11 to comprehend changes in use of terrorism as a weapon today. All of those events affected the lives of every American, as well as those of many other countries, either directly or indirectly. We have witnessed reactions of horror and grief by most of us, global responses by our government and other governments of other nations, reactions of the global economy, and frequent 'knee jerk' reactions of transportation and security industries.

Terrorism is the primary approach to conflict today, and if strategists are correct, terrorism is going to be the twenty-first century 'battlefield of choice' in the future among fanatics who bitterly resent the United States' status as the supreme global heavyweight. Terrorist zealots view the US as the agent of spreading 'Disney-fication', 'McDonald-ization' and vulgarization worldwide.[20] Americans tend to look into the world 'pond' and see themselves as a beautiful swan, not the ugly duckling as viewed by many people throughout the rest of the world.

Consider this statement reflecting the reason terrorism has changed:

> Terrorists traditionally had political or nationalist motives that constrained the violence, because in fact the violence was on the same population and territory that you ultimately hoped to rule. There is unfortunately in the world a new breed of terrorist with millennialist, idealistic, transcendental aims for which violence itself is in fact success. The demands for greater violence to gain attention are simply a product of our media-driven age.[21]

To better define terrorism today, we should look at terrorist organizations that are currently active and the psychology behind the use of terrorism as a weapon. In addition, we need to know more about our adversaries, the terrorists, what motivates them and the training they receive.

Terrorist Organizations

It is impossible to list all terrorist organizations today. Some are covert while others appear, disappear, and/or reappear seemingly overnight. Organizations named today may not be in existence tomorrow, or at least not under the same name. Many available books on terrorism are excellent references for those interested in learning even more about terrorism. Numerous terrorist organizations are included in this chapter; however, Osama bin Laden's al-Qaida organization, for obvious reasons, will be the primary focus.

Why do terrorist organizations hate America and its allies? There is no easy or complete answer for that question. Many highly educated and experienced people have studied the subject for years and even they cannot agree on the answer to this question. The director of the Washington Institute for Near East Policy told an independent commission studying the 9/11 attacks, 'We are resented in no small part because we are seen as using democracy as a tool or weapon against those we do not like, but never against those we do like, Saudi Arabia for instance. We are seen as mouthing the words of democracy but then supporting regimes seen as repressive'. The head of terrorism research in Singapore told the commission the US and the international community sat by for a decade, as Afghanistan became a 'terrorist Disneyland' where attackers were trained and assaults were planned.[22]

America's power is enormous as it dominates the planet at the beginning of the twenty-first century. That is far from a good thing in the eyes of many nations around the globe. America, viewed by many as a superpower out of control, 'unrestrained by any law or any convention other than its national interest', reinforced these views by spurning the Kyoto Protocol on global warming, rejecting the standing of the international court to try Americans, and shunning arms control treaties, as well as attacking Iraq without the approval of the United Nations.[23] An article in the *New Straits Times* in Malaysia expressed the rising unease and criticism about America by other nations, stating, 'The imperious and arrogant in Washington believe the rights of man come not from God, but from the generosity of Uncle Sam'.[24]

There is resentment and envy for the power of the US, the freedoms we enjoy, and the richness of our nation to be sure; however, millions of depressed and oppressed peoples around the globe who share those feelings do not retaliate by converting aircraft into weapons of mass destruction or by conducting suicide bombings against America. There is more to terrorism and the acts of terror than envy and deprivation.

For bin Laden and al-Qaida, the answer lies in *religion*. The religious element involves the idea the US is not just the enemy of the Arabs or Muslims, but is the enemy of God. In the minds of al-Qaida and other terrorist organizations, this is a holy war, a jihad, between Islam and Christianity/Judaism. This ideology, spread by Islamic extremists throughout the entire Arab world, stems from Iran's Ayatollah Khomeini who proclaimed the US 'the Great Satan'.[25] Although every Islamic country in the world has outwardly condemned the attacks of 9/11, millions of people across the Islamic world covertly agree with bin Laden and lend their support to his efforts on their behalf.[26]

It would be truly overwhelming if we actually knew the extent of both covert and overt support of al-Qaida and bin Laden. We only get to witness the tip of the proverbial iceberg on this subject. What we do know is not in our favor, either. Some of al-Qaida's covert actions include building relationships with members of Hezbollah, a radical militant organization backed by Lebanon and Iran. The fervor and international sophistication of al-Qaida members coupled with resources, organization and state backing of Hezbollah would constitute a 'volatile mix' according to terrorism experts. 'Hezbollah has a very extensive support network, not only in the Mid-East, but in Europe and the United States', a US official said.[27] Any type of union or support between these two powerful terrorist organizations could only spell additional trouble and grief for the US and its allies.

Some support of terrorism has been overt. Hamas marked its 15th anniversary in 2002 with a rally in the southern Gaza town of Khan Younis. Approximately 30,000 supporters filled the town's stadium. As the group founder, Ahmed Nimer Hamdan announced the continuation of fight against Israel, the crowd chanted; 'God is great! Hamas fighters will not lay down their weapons and will not stop firing their bullets until the end of the battle'. Hamas, an extremist militant group supported by Palestine, was founded in December 1987, just days after the first Palestinian uprising against Israeli occupation.[28] In another overt act of support, extremist Muslim clerics met in London on 11 September 2002 to celebrate the anniversary of the attacks on America and to launch an organization for Islamic militants, Al-Muhajiroun – a radical group that supports making Britain an Islamic state and is also funded by al-Qaida. The event at a north London mosque was entitled 'Sept. 11, 2001: A Towering Day in History'.[29] An obvious pun intended.

The al-Qaida terrorist organization

The notorious Taliban, virtually destroyed in the last three months of 2001, originally consisted of Afghan nationals who trained in Pakistan with former Islamic mujahedin fighters. In 1994, the Taliban protected convoys attempting to open trade routes between Pakistan and Central Asia. The Taliban developed into a full-fledged military faction by 1996, controlling approximately 90 per cent of Afghanistan by 2001. Twenty years of continuous, turmoil and fighting between warring Afghan mujahedin factions provided the perfect medium for terrorism to flourish in that country. Enter Osama bin Laden's al-Qaida organization, made up of a coalition of groups operating in up to 60 countries.[30]

In the early months after 9/11, Osama bin Laden dominated the news. A multi-millionaire, bin Laden was born in Saudi Arabia to a wealthy Yemeni family. Abdullah Azzam, an influential figure in the Muslim Brotherhood and historical leader of Hamas, heavily influenced and shaped bin Laden's view of the world. In 1979, bin Laden fought in Afghanistan against the Soviets backed by billions of dollars of US aid. He even received security training from our own CIA.[31] Between 1982 and 1984, Azzam founded the Maktab al-Khidimat – the 'Arab Afghans', in Afghanistan with bin Laden as its leader to recruit men and equipment internationally to support the fight against the Soviets. After the withdrawal of the Soviets, bin Laden and his organization turned on the US, in part because of the arrival of US troops in Saudi Arabia in 1990 during the first Gulf War against Iraq. Bin Laden considered the presence of infidels in Muhammad's birthplace a desecration. Deported from Saudi Arabia in 1992 because of anti-government activities, he spent the next five years in Sudan until expelled in 1996 under pressure from the United States, after which he returned to Afghanistan and received protection from the Taliban controlled government.[32]

In 2001, another significant event for terrorism occurred. Bin Laden married the daughter of Mohammed Atef, a member of the Egyptian Islamic Jihad – an extremist group best known for its 1981 assassination of Anwar Sadat. The wedding fused two of the world's top terror organizations and al-Qaida quickly became stronger overnight.[33]

Between 1993 and 1995, the US and some of our allies narrowly missed becoming terrorist victims in a number of huge ways. The first event was the bombing of the World Trade Center by a Pakistani engineer named Ramzi Ahmed Yousef that resulted in some damage to the building, killed six and injured over 1,000 others. The next events were the unsuccessful plots to assassinate Pope John Paul II and President Bill Clinton, followed in 1995 by an unsuccessful plot to destroy 11 US airliners on a single day traveling from Southeast Asia to the US These events signaled the beginning of a new age of terror. Bin Laden was able to build upon the Muslim rage kindled by Yousef's attempts and make the rage even more lethal.[34]

To put his ideology into practice, several hundred of bin Laden's Afghan veterans, drawn from a 50,000 strong pool of two generations of Afghan fighters, were dispatched to join Islamic groups in Asia, Africa and the Middle East to boost domestic and international terrorism efforts. In doing so, al-Qaida built strategic depth by maintaining leadership and operational links with some of the largest and deadliest Middle Eastern and Asian terrorist groups. Bin Laden's stature and personal relationships with the leaders of these groups facilitated al-Qaida links. Bin Laden's generosity with funds and words of praise enabled him to cement strong working relationships at both leadership and operational levels. Although bin Laden is an icon of terrorism to the West, in parts of the Islamic world he is seen as the only leader that can stand up to the big Satan (the US) and the little Satan (Israel). To draw maximum support, al-Qaida created the 'World Islamic Jihad against the Jews and Crusaders'. Due to superb planning and organization on their part, al-Qaida has a ready base of recruits, supporters and sympathizers. To deepen and widen al-Qaida's reach, bin

Laden departed from tradition and embraced a pan-Islamic view. As a result, al-Qaida draws the support of both Arab and non-Arab Muslims.[35]

During a May 2003 interview by the London-based magazine, *Al Majalla,* with al-Qaida spokesperson Thabet bin Qais, Qais was quoted as saying, 'Al-Qaida is way ahead of the Americans and its allies in the intelligence war, and American security agencies still are ignorant of the changes the leadership has made. The Americans only have predictions and old intelligence left and it will take them a long time to understand the new form of al-Qaida'. Qais also warned of plots 'the size of September 11 attacks being devised against the United States'. 'A strike against America is definitely coming', he said.[36]

New/re-emerging terrorist organizations

As mentioned early in this section, terrorist organizations tend to literally pop up over night. Some of the other terrorist organizations that are connected directly or indirectly to al-Qaida include:

- *The Islamic Martyr Brigade* In late September 2002, the *Washington Post* reported a new alliance known as Lashkar Fedayan-e-Islami, or the Islamic Martyrs Brigade headed by former Afghan Prime Minister Gulbuddin Hekmatyar. Hekmatyar fled to Iran in 1996 after his group was defeated by the Taliban, but has recently been seeking to incite jihad against American forces in Afghanistan. '*There will be suicide attacks, ambushes by suicide attackers and bomb blasts against soldiers as they are moving from place to place and when they go out and disperse into smaller numbers, like in searches*', he said.[37] The alliance also involves Maulvi Abdul Kabir, the Taliban's No. 3 man who is still at large. The alliance is funded by Iran and al-Qaida and its targets are US military installations.[38]
- *Laskar Jundullah* The armed wing of the Committee to Establish Islamic Shariah Law in South Sulawesi – Responsible for a fatal bombing of a McDonald's and a car dealership in Indonesia in December 2002, the group planned to blow up churches on Christmas Eve 2002. The plot was thwarted. Laskar Jundullah is linked to both Jemaah Islamiyah (JI) and al-Qaida.[39]
- *Jemaah Islamiyah* A terror group operating in Indonesia with the goal of transforming all of Indonesia into an Islamic state.[40]
- *Lashkar-e-Jhangvi* Designated a terrorist organization in January 2003 by the US, its members carry out attacks on religious minorities and Western targets in Pakistan. The group, closely linked with the remnants of the Taliban in Afghanistan and believed to have ties to al-Qaida and the Pakistani Islamic group, Jaish-e-Mohammed, is believed to be involved in the kidnapping and murder of *Wall Street Journal* correspondent, Daniel Pearl.[41]
- *Ansar al-Islam* Originally a group of several hundred Islamic militants staging in the mountains dividing Iran and Iraq that was thought to have been destroyed by Kurdish soldiers after a barrage of US cruise missiles in March 2002. The group

is re-emerging and apparently, a dozen Ansar activists sneaked into Baghdad in April 2003, before the fall of Baghdad to US troops. In June 2003, the military commander of the town of Kalar was killed when he tried to arrest a suspected Ansar militant who set off a suicide bomb. The Ansar group carried out suicide bombings, car bombings, assassinations and raids on militiamen and politicians of the Kurdish government, killing scores of people since 2001.[42]

- In a broadcast on 12 July 2003, on Al Arabiya television network in Dubai, UAE, a previously unknown terrorist group took credit for recent attacks on Allied forces in Iraq. Claiming to be an affiliate of al-Qaida and not followers of Saddam Hussein, the group warned Iraqis to expect 'a strike that will permanently break the back of America in the coming days'.[43]

The US and its allies have yet to reap the whirlwind from Operation Iraqi Freedom. Without entering the snake pit of debate as to whether the war on Iraq was justified, it occurred and repercussions are sure to take place. In late March 2003 in Cairo, Islamic leaders from Saudi Arabia, Lebanon and Iraq appealed to thousands of people massed in protest of the war on Iraq. The protests, sanctioned by Egypt, Jordan and Iran, appealed to the masses to engage in holy war and proclaimed Saddam Hussein a great Islamic warrior against the Crusaders.[44] It will be interesting to watch for new terrorist organizations spawned by the protests and the war in Iraq.

Support and Funding of al-Qaida and Terrorism

It is common knowledge bin Laden is a huge financial contributor to al-Qaida and other terrorist organizations. Bin Laden supports four types of groups, not in order of preference:

1. Groups fighting regimes led by Muslim rulers which are believed to be compromising Islamic ideals and interests, such as Egypt, Algeria and Saudi Arabia;
2. Groups fighting regimes perceived as oppressing and repressing their Muslim populace, such as Kosovo, India and Indonesia;
3. Groups fighting regimes to establish their own Islamic state, such as Palestine, Chechnya, Dagestan and Mindanao;[45] and,
4. Groups fighting America, Israel, and their allies.

The depth and breadth of bin Laden's financial support to terrorism is another unknown, in absolute terms, and the truth about his finances remains somewhat of a mystery. 'We do not know where his money is, not a single dime', said a senior US official. That is why the Treasury Department has never been able to freeze any of his 'personal' accounts. Because of the international scrutiny of bank accounts worldwide, bin Laden has shifted his use of traditional banks to an underground banking system known in South Asia as *hundi* or *hawala*. This ancient network, based largely on bonds of trust and ethnicity, is able to move millions of dollars across borders through a system of chits and credits.[46]

When the Taliban was in power in Afghanistan, they paid their taxes in gold from their treasury, also kept in gold. In 2001, the Taliban shipped large amounts of gold through Dubai to other safe havens. Swiss Attorney General Roschacher during a visit to Washington in September 2002 indicated the Taliban had converted much of its money into gold and diamonds and a UN panel report in August 2002 substantiated this statement. The UN report stated, 'Despite initial successes in locating and freezing al-Qaida assets, the network continues to have access to considerable financial and other economic resources. It is exceedingly difficult to identify these funds'.[47]

In August 2002, European and US intelligence officials highlighted three significant developments in the war on terrorism:

1 The growing number of Iranian intelligence units allied with the country's hard-line clerics in protecting and aiding al-Qaida;
2 The potential re-emergence of Sudan as a financial center for al-Qaida; and,
3 Al-Qaida has the ability to generate new sources of revenue, despite the global crackdown on its finances.

The third item on this list is extremely important. Without funding, terrorist organizations could not operate effectively. The sources of their financial support are unbelievable as indicated by the following descriptions.

International banking

Support for terrorism in the international banking arena has been huge.[48] Islamic charities claim that al-Qaida siphons off money from selected charities, mosques and relief agencies.

- In the 1980s, a Pakistani, with the backing of Sheik Zayed bin Sultan al-Nahayan, an illiterate billionaire from Abu Dhabi, created the Bank of Credit and Commerce International (BCCI). The Sheik, who funded radical Arab and Muslim groups, declared the US as 'our enemy number 2' behind Israel. The purposes of the bank were to fight the evil influence of the West, help develop an 'Islamic Bomb', launder money from a variety of illegal ventures and finance radical terrorist organizations. The primary source of money was from the drug trade.[49]
- A UN report shows that $112 million of al-Qaida resources were frozen almost immediately after 11 September 2001, but only $10 million were seized in the eight months thereafter.[50]
- A UN report from the Monitoring Group on al-Qaida indicates that financial backers in North Africa, the Middle East and Asia are managing $30–300 million

of al-Qaida investments. Suspected bank accounts of unidentified intermediaries exist in Dubai, Hong Kong, London, Malaysia and Vienna.[51]

- In May 2002, the head of the Benevolence International Foundation in Chicago was taken into custody and charged with providing logistical support, including the movements of money to fund terrorist operations. The organization is one of the most prominent Muslim charities in the US, with offices in Bosnia, Pakistan, Tajikistan, Yemen, Turkey, Georgia and China. The organization's former headquarters were raided in December 2001 and its bank accounts frozen by the US Treasury Department's Office of Foreign Assets Control.[52] On the same day, assets of another Islamic charity, Global Relief Foundation, also based in a Chicago suburb, were frozen and its offices raided.[53]
- In October 2002, an indictment said a criminal enterprise that existed for at least a decade used charitable contributions from innocent Muslims, non-Muslims and corporations to support bin Laden's al-Qaida network, Chechen rebels fighting the Russian army and armed violence in Bosnia.[54] Also in October, the New York-based Council on Foreign Relations reported that, 'Individuals and charities based in Saudi Arabia have been the most important source of funds for al-Qaida, and for years the Saudi officials have turned a "blind eye" to this problem'.[55]
- In November 2002, a congressional panel investigating financing of the attacks on 9/11 reported a money trail involving two hijackers and influential financiers in Saudi Arabia.[56] The 'charitable contributions' made by the wife of the Saudi Arabian ambassador to the US may have indirectly benefited the two hijackers that flew into the Pentagon.[57] The Saudi government acknowledged in late November the Saudi Princess thought she was making charity payments to a woman with serious medical problems, not realizing funds were endorsed over to the al-Qaida operatives.[58]
- In December, the foreign policy advisor to Crown Prince Abdullah of Saudi Arabia admitted that 'A number of our charities, especially those operating outside Saudi Arabia, did not have sufficient financial control mechanisms to ensure funds were raised and actually went where they were supposed to go. That's the area we have now fixed'.[59]
- Additional funding comes through a branch of al-Haramain Islamic Foundation (an international charity based in Saudi Arabia with offices in several Islamic countries) with money being laundered through the foundation by donors in the Middle East.[60]

Other sources of revenue for terrorist organizations include donations, criminal activities, front companies and other terrorist organizations. The following are some examples of these activities:

- Donations by wealthy Muslims, including businessmen, disaffected members of the Saudi royal family and bin Laden's own relatives, are estimated to be $16 million per year and continue unabated;[61]

- The FBI arrested an Iranian immigrant in Arizona in October 2001 after he allegedly tried to wire $16 million to Iran via banks in Kuwait and United Arab Emirates.[62]
- Al-Qaida earns cash – official estimates are $50 million a year – by protecting Afghanistan's shipments of opium and heroin bound for the West, exhorting money from wealthy merchants.[63]
- Research by the Center for the Study of Corruption and the Rule of Law has shown that since a meeting of numerous Islamic fundamentalist organizations in 1993, radical groups have cooperated in a drugs-based, global fund-raising effort. The report stated, 'America just was not paying attention. These organizations work with Latin American narcoterrorists with the goal of destabilizing legitimate states. They barter illegal arms and drugs, smuggle people and trade illegal identification documents. It's one huge criminal organization'.[64]
- From a series of raids in the Midwest US in January 2002, DEA officials determined millions of dollars from a methamphetamine drug operation conducted by Middle Eastern men were funneled to terrorist organizations through Jordan, Yemen, Lebanon and other Middle Eastern countries. Raids resulted in criminal charges against 136 people, seizure of nearly 36 tons of pseudoephedrine, 179 pounds of meth, $4.5 million in cash, eight real-estate properties and 160 cars used by drug gangs.[65]
- In November 2002, US officials announced they had foiled a plot to use drug money to buy weapons for terrorists. The reputed attempt involved two Pakistani nationals and a naturalized US citizen who lived in Minneapolis. The trio offered to trade 5 metric tons of hashish and 600 kilograms of heroin to undercover FBI agents for 4 Stinger missiles. The men said they intended to sell the missiles to members of al-Qaida.[66]
- Money laundering schemes continue to be uncovered. In December 2002, two schemes were dismantled with arrests of numerous conspirators. One involved transfer of $480,000 to sources in Yemen by a cell operating in Buffalo, NY; the other was a ring that transferred more than $12 million to Iraq. The latter group included members from Dallas, Phoenix, St Louis, Nashville, and Roanoke in the US, and others in London, Jordan, the United Arab Emirates, and Iraq. Funds were forwarded to a business in Iraq called Al-Nour Trading, after being sent from Seattle and New York to England, India, Canada, Brazil, Taiwan, Egypt, Jordan and the UAE.[67]
- Other rackets include skimming profits of drug sales, stealing and reselling baby formula, illegally redeeming quantities of grocery coupons, collecting fraudulent welfare payments, swiping credit card numbers and hawking unlicensed T-shirts, and stolen vehicle trade – all of which are thought to generate tens of millions of dollar annually.[68]
- Bin Laden's own companies have ranged from construction and currency exchange to agriculture, offering cover for operatives by providing them with jobs and legitimate identities.[69]

- Some supporters of terrorists in the US are citizens who operate legitimate businesses that are fronts for indirectly raising funds to support terrorism, or directly contribute to terrorism in other manners. For instance, Mohammed el-Atriss, a native of Egypt, was arrested in August 2002 and charged with supplying false identification papers and driver's licenses in Patterson and Elizabeth, NJ to terrorists aboard aircraft that struck the WTC and the Pentagon.[70]
- US authorities are investigating more than 500 Muslim and Arab small businesses throughout this country to determine if they are dispatching money raised through criminal activity to terrorist overseas. Funds are suspected to have gone to terrorist organizations such as Hamas and Hezbollah. 'It was not until after September 11th that we understood the magnitude of terrorist fund-raising from our own shores', said John Forbes, a former US Customs Service official who directed a financial crime task force in New York.[71]
- Many of the terrorists and their supporters are living and working in our country, among us. We invited them here and opened our arms to them. A study released in early 2002 by the Center for Immigration Studies entitled, 'The Open Door: How Militant Islamic Terrorist Entered and Remained in the United States', underscores our vulnerability. The study examined the immigration status of 48 foreign-born terrorists who had been charged, convicted, pled guilty, or admitted to involvement in terrorism within the US since 1993, and included the 19 suicide hijackers of the 9/11 attacks. The study found that 16 terrorists entered our country under legal temporary visas, posing as students, tourists, and business travelers. Seventeen resided in the US as lawful permanent residents or naturalized citizens. Three had requests for amnesty and asylum pending. Nine were here illegally (staying after their temporary visas expired). Only three came across a border illegally. Terrorists have penetrated every aspect of the US immigration system, and the INS is still ill equipped to handle the situation. According to reports, there are between seven and eight million undocumented immigrants nationwide. The INS has about 2,000 agents, or one agent for every 4,000 immigrants.[72]
- German security officials uncovered a scheme in December 2002 where militant Islamists use donations from 'charitable organizations' to buy luxury cars in Germany. After being imported to Saudi Arabia, the cars are resold. The income generated from the sales is transferred to Islamic organizations and al-Qaida elements in Pakistan. Unfortunately, the process is legal under German law and no one has been arrested.[73]
- Allegedly, al-Qaida obtained millions of dollars in financing from diamonds mined by rebels in Sierra Leone, either by trading the gems or using them to launder money.[74]
- Information revealed by al-Faruq (captured al-Qaida leader) indicates financial and operational assistance for al-Qaida from Jemaah Islamiah (IH), a militant group seeking to establish a pure Islamic state in Southeast Asia.[75]
- Other militant organizations in the region also support al-Qaida initiatives: Abu Sayyaf (notorious for kidnappings and beheadings); Indonesian Mujahedin

Council (MMI); Laskar Jundullah, involved in attacks on Christian villages in the region; and Jihad Islamic (JI), who boasts of having 20 suicide bombers waiting and ready to carry out attacks as instructed.[76]

- The fugitive Taliban, operating brazenly along the Afghanistan border in Pakistan, raised $50,000 during a three-day Muslim festival and even issued receipts that indicate the 'donations' are for the Islamic Emirate of Afghanistan – their new name for their part of the country.[77]

There has been some progress in disrupting some financial support of al-Qaida and other terrorist organizations; however, Deputy Treasury Secretary Kenneth Dam said in August 2002, 'the group still has enough cash to launch terrorist attacks, in part because its costs dropped after the fall of the Taliban. They no longer bear the expenses of supporting the Taliban government or running training camps'.[78]

There have also been seizures and freezing of some accounts. Secretary Dam said by August 2002 the Treasury Department, in conjunction with the Department of Justice, had seized $6.8 million domestically and more than $16 million in outbound currency (including more than $7 million in cash) being smuggled to Middle Eastern countries. In addition, the US and other countries have frozen more than $112 million in terrorist-related assets. More than 160 countries now have orders to block cash to charities and other groups suspected of funding terrorist activities.[79]

Additional efforts to curb terrorist funding can be found in Chapter 15, War on Terrorism. Money, although vital to terrorist organizations, is not everything. Terrorist organizations need a place to train, to plan, to receive supplies and to hide. They find these necessities in the arms of state sponsors.

State Sponsors

Given the amounts and diversities of the contributions to terrorism just discussed, it is not difficult to believe that terrorism can exist without sponsor states; however, sponsor states contribute more than just financial support. They also supply or provide:

- Physical space for training and headquarters;
- A relatively safe and secure, or in some form protected, environment in which to train and operate; and
- Recruits from poorly educated, politically and economically oppressed people.

Some countries identified as state sponsors include Iran, Iraq (before their overthrow), Sudan, Yemen, Libya, Palestine, Pakistan, Lebanon, Somalia, Syria, and of course, Afghanistan. A few of these sponsors of terrorism have attempted to portray themselves as being against terrorism to avoid repercussions from the US Some of the sponsors on the list deserve a second look.

Pakistan

- Are they not supposed to be on our side? It is a country divided. Some members of the Pakistani army protect and support Taliban fugitives from Afghanistan, even giving them jeeps to use for safe transportation. As one official said, 'Why do you think none of the top Taliban who came to Pakistan has been arrested?'[80]
- Pakistan-based guerrillas continue to fight for the independence of the Indian-ruled province of Kashmir. India accuses Pakistan of arming, training and financing the Lashkar-e-Tayyaba and Jaish-e-Mohammed terrorist groups. Pakistan claims only ideological support.[81]
- A young Afghan captured in January 2003, told of terror training camps in Afghanistan and Pakistan where he learned to carry out bomb attacks and suicide ambushes. Others trained in the same camp included Afghans, Pakistanis, Southeast Asians, and Arabs who belonged to the Taliban or al-Qaida. Many small mobile camps operate along the Afghan-Pakistani border.[82]

Iran

- An annual US State Department report to Congress reported that Iran remained the most active state sponsor of terrorism in 2001, even though they publicly condemned the 9/11 attacks and offered to assist US aircrews operating in Afghanistan if they went down.
- Iran increased its support of anti-Israel terrorist groups such as the Hezbollah and Hamas.[83]
- Iran furnishes financial support for a new alliance known as Lashkar Fedayan-e-Islami, or the Islamic Martyrs Brigade.[84]
- Al-Qaida operatives use Iran as a transit route to enter and exit Afghanistan and Turkey.

Iraq

- Before Saddam Hussein was removed from power by US led military forces, Iraq provided money, training and political support to several terrorist groups including The Palestine Liberation Front and the Popular Front for the Liberation of Palestine.
- In addition, at least a handful of ranking members of al-Qaida have taken refuge in Iraq, which may account some of the continued attack on US and UK military forces that are still stationed there. 'The fact that only Iraq would give safe haven to Abu Nidal demonstrates Iraqi regime's complicity with global terror', said White House spokesman Ari Fleischer.[85] As a side note, in August 2002 Abu Nidal allegedly committed suicide, according to Iraqi officials.[86]

Sudan

- Sudan remains a designated state sponsor because it continues to serve as a safe haven for al-Qaida, Hamas, Egyptian Islamic Jihad and Palestine Islamic Jihad terrorist organizations.[87]
- In August 2002, other large quantities of gold were shipped out of Pakistan by al-Qaida operatives to Sudan through United Arab Emirates and Iran by boat and airplane.[88]

Yemen

- Yemen has one of the most significant al-Qaida organizational links in the world, composed mainly of Yemenis who received military training in Afghanistan, according to a US official. Thousands of veterans of the Soviet-Afghan war live in Yemen and are capable of launching 'uncoordinated or coordinated attacks'. The government of Yemen said it deported about 5,000 non-Yemeni Arabs since 1998, and keeps a close eye on thousands that lead lawful lives in Yemen.[89]

Terrorism is indeed a complex problem. To understand the significance of terrorism in shaping and influencing international relations, religion, politics, related fields, we must first understand terrorism as a weapon. That will be the first of our two-part exploration of the psychology of terrorism.

Psychology of Terrorism: Part 1 – Understanding Terrorism as a Weapon

> Terrorism ... sees the whole society as an enemy, and all members of a society as appropriate objects for violent action. [90]

Matthew Levitt, a former FBI agent who now monitors terrorism for the Washington Institute for Near East Policy think tank said, 'These [terrorist] groups are no longer interested in traditional political goals such as national liberation, they are interested in undermining society. They are interested in annihilation'.[91]

This concept was clearly defined on 22 February 1998 when a new fatwa was issued in the name of the 'World Front for Jihad against Jews and Crusaders'. The fatwa, signed by bin Laden and the heads of major Islamic movements in other countries, stated,

> To kill the Americans and their allies – civilians and military – is an individual duty for every Muslim who can do it in any country in which it is possible to do it, in order to liberate the al-Aqsa Mosque [in Jerusalem] and the Holy Mosque [in Mecca] ... and to force their armies to withdraw from all the lands of Islam, defeated and unable to threaten any Muslim. [92]

'Civilians and military'? Wow! What is this all about? Many references to terrorism refer to its victims as innocents, noncombatants who were just going about their daily lives oblivious to a specific political conflict. Yet, to many terrorists, all victims are guilty. Noncombatants pay taxes to the government that may be targeted by terrorists. Noncombatants can be children who may grow up to pay taxes or be anti-terrorist and counter-terrorist personnel; or, they can be women who have the potential to be impregnated, to carry these children to term and to nurture them. Noncombatant men, women and children may give comfort, solace, and material support to anti-terrorist and counter-terrorist forces through forming logistical, social, and stress management systems improving the performance of terrorists' adversaries.[93]

This line of 'reasoning' by terrorist was underscored in November 2002 in a statement attributed to al-Qaida issued through an Arab TV reporter. The statement demanded US troops leave the Arabian Peninsula and justified killings of American civilians because they pay taxes that finance military operations.[94] During the Jerusalem Day celebration of 2001, Hezbollah leader Sheik Hassan Nasrallah echoed this statement when he said, 'There are no civilians in the Israeli society. They are all invaders, occupiers and usurpers of the land. They are all partners in crime and massacre'.[95]

It is important to realize acts of terrorism are directed at a target audience, not just the immediate victims.[96] Terrorist flying the aircraft into the World Trade Center and the Pentagon were not directing their actions against the people in those buildings, but against ALL Americans. If it had been within their power at the time, those terrorists would gladly have killed every person in the United States. Their mission was not only to destroy American financial and military nerve centers and to take American lives, but also to destroy America's sense of security and confidence in the ability of our government to protect its citizens. Unfortunately, the threat of similar or of even greater events continues today, not only in the US, but also in countries of our allies. A prime example of the continued threat comes from Osama bin Laden's al-Qaida recruitment videotape released in 2001 when he spoke of the bombing of the USS Cole: 'The heads of the unbelievers flew in all directions, and their limbs were scattered. The victory of Islam had come, and the victory we scored in Yemen will continue'.[97]

The aim of a terrorist organization today is to communicate something on a national scale about its objectives, assertions of its existence, or evidence of its power to control the course of events and to enforce subsequent demands.[98] Bin Laden and his organization wanted us to know emphatically they have declared jihad, war against Christianity and Judaism. In a videotaped statement aired on 7 October 2001, Osama bin Laden said, 'As to America, I say to it and its people a few words: I swear to God that America will not live in peace before peace reigns in Palestine, and before all the army of the infidels depart the land of Muhammad, peace be upon him'.[99] In a tape revealed during the last week in December 2001 by CNN News, bin Laden takes great pride in the damage to both the US and the world economy inflicted, as he put it, 'Not by 19 Arab nations, but by 19 high school graduates'. The attacks on 9/11 sent these messages loud and clear:

- We are vulnerable as a nation to terrorist attacks at any time and place;
- It established Osama bin Laden's Taliban-backed al-Qaida organization as a force to be dealt with; and
- Americans must remove their presence from Islamic countries and cease their support of Israel.

Although we suffered severe damage as a nation, it is very doubtful we will leave the Mid-East region any time soon or abandon Israel; therefore, not all of Osama bin Laden's goals have been achieved. This by no means is to be interpreted as meaning that the war against his organization or on terrorism is over, nor does it mean that we will not continue to fall prey to additional terrorist attacks like the attempted bombing of American Airlines Flight 63 on 22 December 2001.

Even though the fight against terrorism has realistically just begun, it is evident that Osama bin Laden underestimated a number of things. First, was physical damage inflicted upon the WTC and Pentagon buildings as evidenced by his videotaped comments released in December of 2001 in which he stated he expected the destruction of only the floors above impact of the aircraft. Second, overwhelming feelings of nationalism and unity created by events of 9/11 – the out-pouring of manpower, money, blood, and prayers as a nation was incredible. Third, development of an effective international alliance against terrorism and the intensity of the retaliation brought against Afghanistan, the Taliban and al-Qaida fighters. Last, not only the depth of economic impact of events on 9/11, but also resiliency – to some limited extent – of the American economy in recovering from such a blow.

The objectives of terrorism

The unmistakable objectives of terrorism today are to:

1. Create a climate of fear as a *psychological weapon*;
2. Deliver an unmistakable message and receive widespread publicity as a *communication weapon*;
3. Undermine a society causing chaos, collapse of law and order, and a loss of confidence in the nation's leadership and the government's ability to protect its citizens as a *political weapon*;
4. Severely damage the economy of a nation as an *economic weapon*; and,
5. Affect change in modern military strategies to cope with a new form of warfare as a *military weapon.*[100]

The intention of carefully designed attack on America in 2001 was to accomplish all of these objectives. For the most part, terrorists succeeded. In addition to massive destructions of buildings and human life, the 9/11 event resulted in a tremendous rippling effect throughout both US and world economies causing billions upon billion of dollars to be lost as stocks plummeted, businesses failed, and jobs were lost. People temporarily stopped traveling, shopping, and attending large gatherings or events. Conferences and symposiums cancelled, rescheduled for a 'later date'. Two years after 9/11, the effects of the terrorist attacks are still felt in the economy. In September 2003, half of the 100 largest US companies reported terrorism as a possible business risk. A second quarter 2003 survey of 319 small and mid-size businesses found 31 per cent of chief executives and business managers cited 'another terrorist attack' as the greatest concern to the US economic future.[101] Airlines, as well as other businesses, are teetering on the verge of bankruptcy as the death spiral of the decline in travel on top of increasing costs of airline security continues to tighten.

Every new 'event' is immediately interpreted to be another terrorist activity linked to al-Qaida, and we hold our breath until results are measured. President Bush recognized our fears as he continually urges Americans to go about business as usual, only with a greater sense of awareness, and to travel and shop; however, we as Americans have been slow to respond. We are still fearful because we do NOT know what will happen next, nor are we trained or equipped to handle the unknown. Because mass-casualty terrorism is a cheap and simple way for an enemy to take America to war without frontally engaging its superpower might, we can continue to expect terrorist attacks in America and on American interests abroad.[102]

Terrorist organizations have the advantage in choosing their methodologies and timings of terrorist acts. They also continually study worldwide reactions to their acts and make adjustments as necessary for the next round of events. This process constantly keeps potential victims off guard and unprepared, even fearful, of the next event. For instance, the Revolutionary Armed Forces of Colombia (FARC) has been responsible for over 3,000 kidnappings a year for many of the 39 years they have been fighting the Colombian government. FARC has been able to fund its organization from ransoms paid for the victims, some of which have been kidnapped more than once. What has changed in the kidnapping scheme is that FARC is now focusing on the elderly, many of which spend days or weeks trying to cope with the rigors of being held in the jungles and freezing mountains of the country.[103]

Interpol has reported, 'Terror groups may switch to attacking smaller targets in a long-lasting campaign of attrition to avoid being wiped out in the international anti-terror campaign focused on al-Qaida. Terrorists might, in the short to medium term, go "back to the basics", choosing symbolic targets with limited casualties in a long-lasting campaign, hoping over time the collective will of states to fight terrorism will wane'.[104]

Postwar Iraq in 2003 has proven to be a 'magnet for jihadists' from all over the world for Islamic militants bent on waging 'holy war' against the US and its allies. The terrorists consider Iraq a target-rich environment where tens of thousands of Crusaders exist. Unknown but large numbers of foreign fighters, some linked to the al-Qaida network, are crossing into Iraq from Syria and Iran with hopes of bloodying US soldiers and destabilizing the postwar, pro-Western government. In a recent attack on a training camp in Iraq, for instance, most of the dead were from Saudi Arabia, Syria, Yemen, and Africa. Revolutionary Guard Corps backs the Arab fighters entering Iraq from Iran, according to an official. The official said, 'The Iranians appear to believe they can drive us out of Iraq the same way they drove us out of Lebanon – with terrorist attacks against both military and civilian targets'. (Referring to the withdrawal of US troops from Lebanon after Iranian-backed terrorist attacks against the US Embassy and Marines that left more than 300 dead in 1984.)[105] Only a couple of months later in August 2003, the top civilian administrator in Iraq said fighters from Ansar al-Isam, a militant organization the US had sought to destroy during the war, had escaped to Iran and then slipped back across the border into Iraq. Bremer said, 'The intelligence suggests Ansar al-Islam is planning large-scale terrorist attacks'.[106]

Unfortunately, the objectives listed in the first paragraph of this section constitute a very real threat to the US and its allies now, and in the future. If we are to win the war on terrorism, we must counter each objective of terrorism with a viable plan. We must become proactive rather than remaining reactive.

Terrorist threats and alerts

In March 2002, the United States government established a color-coded warning system designed to warn law enforcement agencies, first responders and US citizens of known or suspected terrorist attacks. The five alert levels and the recommended government and private sector responses are:

- *RED – Severe risk of terrorist attacks*
  - Assign emergency response personnel and preposition specially trained teams
  - Monitor, redirect or constrain transportation systems
  - Close public and government facilities
  - Increase or redirect personnel to address critical emergency needs
- *ORANGE – High risk of terrorist attacks*
  - Coordinate necessary security efforts with federal, state and local law enforcement agencies or any National Guard or other appropriate armed services
  - Take additional precaution at public events and possibly consider alternative venues or cancellations
  - Prepare to work at an alternative site or with a dispersed work force
  - Restrict access to threatened facilities to essential personnel only
- *YELLOW – Elevated condition, significant risk of terrorist attacks*
  - Increase surveillance of critical locations
  - Coordinate emergency plans with nearby jurisdictions
  - Assess further refinement of protective measures within the context of the current threat information
  - Implement, as appropriate, contingency and emergency response plans
- *BLUE – Guarded condition, general risk of terrorist attacks*
  - Check communications with designated emergency response or command locations

  - Review and update emergency response procedures
  - Provide the public with necessary information
- *GREEN – Low risk of terrorist attacks*
  - Refine and exercise planned protective measures
  - Ensure emergency personnel receive training
  - Assess facilities for vulnerabilities and take measures to reduce them.

Sporadic 'non-specific' alerts and warnings issued by governmental agencies, although necessary, do not help to alleviate the general-publics' fear of unknown attacks. By mid-2002, the FBI sent out alerts that terrorists might attack stadiums, nuclear power plants, shopping centers, synagogues, apartment houses, subways, the Brooklyn Bridge, the Golden Gate Bridge, and other New York City and national landmarks. According to Kevin Giblin from the FBI, none of the alerts was meant for the public, or to provoke their alarm. Of all alarms issued, only one was meant for the public – the possibility of terrorists hitting banks in the Northeast. All other alarms were meant for law enforcement agencies and were leaked to news media, which made them big news.[107] Here are just a few alerts/warnings issued by the US government and a brief summary of their contents (in chronological order):

- *October 2001: Terrorism warning given for this week* – The Justice Department said it had credible but not specific information a new wave of attacks could strike Americans at home or overseas. The Nuclear Regulatory Commission and the FAA were adopting 'special, but undisclosed security measures'. Eighteen thousand law enforcement agencies across the nation were informed of the new alert.[108]
- *March 2002: Ashcroft: No end near for alerts* – Ashcroft said Americans should not expect any relief, possibly for their lifetimes, from a series of high alerts against ongoing threats of terrorism.[109]
- *May 2002: New attacks on US feared – Intercepted messages not specific* American intelligence agencies have intercepted vague yet troubling series of communications among al-Qaida operatives in the past few months indicating the terrorist organization is trying to carry out an operation as big as or bigger than the 11 September attacks.[110]
- *May 2002: America is warned* – The FBI announced that it had asked 56 field offices to alert managers of large apartment complexes their facilities might become terrorist targets. It was 'uncorroborated and non-specific information that al-Qaida leaders had discussed renting apartment units in the US and then planting explosives'. The warning was made to 'encourage citizens to remain vigilant in their everyday lives'.[111]
- *June 2002: Terror warning over model planes* – Al-Qaida may be planning to use model airplanes to attack passenger aircraft worldwide, a German security source has warned. The German agency said the information came from the US.[112]

- *June 2002: Color of summer: Terror alert yellow* – Ships, malls, bridges, trains, waterworks, landmarks, monuments and more – the possibilities for terrorists, as identified by the government in recent months, cover just about anywhere Americans live, work, travel and play. The State Department published a list of 27 countries Americans should avoid.[113]
- *June 2002: FBI – Terrorist may try to arrive by sea* – The FBI has received reports that al-Qaida may be making their way toward Southern California aboard a merchant ship, but has no evidence to back up the report. The report indicated that as many as 40 al-Qaida members may have boarded the ship bound for the US – possibly Catalina Island off the coast of Los Angeles.[114]
- *September 2002: US raises alert status to 'high risk'* – The nationwide threat index was raised to 'high risk' for the first time in response to information obtained from an unidentified al-Qaida operative who is in custody. The terrorist indicated al-Qaida cells in South Asia and suicide bombers in the Mid-East would launch attacks on the anniversary of the 9/11. The heightened alert precipitated the Pentagon to move live anti-aircraft missiles to launchers deployed around Washington for the first time in 40 years. The State Department closed more than a dozen embassies and consulates in Asia and elsewhere.[115]
- *September 2002: US lowers terror alert level to yellow; arrests get credit* – Administration officials credited the arrests of suspected terrorists from Buffalo to Pakistan to Bahrain, while warning the danger of another attack remains. US intelligence officials continue to believe operatives of al-Qaida are at work on American soil and they ask citizens to remain alert.[116]
- *October 2002: Expect more al-Qaida attacks, CIA director warns* – During a joint House and Senate Intelligence committee hearing, CIA Director George Tenet warned that al-Qaida is preparing to strike the US and the current threat is as 'bad as it was last summer when the agency's collection sources lit up'. Tenet said, 'You must make the analytical judgment that the possibility exists that people are planning to attack you inside the US, multiple simultaneous attacks. We are the people they want to hurt inside this country'.[117]
- *October 2002: Al-Qaida may try attack on US trains, FBI says* – The FBI issued a chilling specific warning that al-Qaida operatives 'who have Western appearance' may be planning to target US passenger trains. Terrorists may bring a bomb aboard a train, demolish a rail bridge as a passenger train approaches, or derail a train by damaging a rail bed or pulling a truck loaded with explosives across a rail line. Terrorist could also target hazardous material containers.[118]
- *November 2002: Unusual inquiries spur alerts to sea attack* – The FBI warned law enforcement agencies that terrorists may be planning and training for maritime attacks in the US The agency said local law enforcement agencies have reported 'frequent incidences of suspicious individuals asking questions about equipment and training at marine shops'.[119]
- *February 2003: Risk of terrorist attack in US up* – Senior US intelligence officials concluded the risk of a terrorist attack on US soil increased significantly in recent

weeks, but cannot agree about issuing a general warning to the public about the danger. A bulletin sent out to law enforcement agencies highlighted the heightened danger of attack on apartment buildings, hotels and other 'soft targets'.[120]

- *February 2003: Al-Qaida prompted new alert*[121] and *Data on terror attack fabricated*[122] – Evidently, the information resulting in the terror level in the US being raised to Orange in February was fabricated. Officials said the informer, a suspected al-Qaida terrorist, flunked a lie detector test after the government had issued the warning, but said information provided by the informer was not the only piece of information upon which they based their decisions.
- *May 2003: Attack fears prompt 'orange' terror alert* – Homeland Security Secretary Ridge said, 'The US intelligence community believes al-Qaida has entered an operational period worldwide, and this may include attacks in the United States'. Responses to the alert included police working 12-hour shifts in California, National Guard troops guarding subways and bridges in New York, and Capitol police SWAT teams conducting random patrols. Overseas, the US, Britain and Germany temporarily closed their embassies and consulates in Saudi Arabia.[123]
- *June 2003: Al-Qaida detainee targeted forests* – According to an FBI memo sent out to law enforcement agencies, an al-Qaida operative detained in the US, planned to set midsummer forest fires in Colorado, Montana, Utah and Wyoming. The detainee believed significant damage to the US economy would result from large, catastrophic wildfires. The Forest Service took note of the warning, but did not change any of its policies or operating patterns according to their spokesperson. A survey of law enforcement officers from the Forest Service revealed that most of them were unaware of the warning.[124]
- *July 2003: Warning: New 9/11 style attacks may come* – The Department of Homeland Security told law enforcement and airlines al-Qaida terrorists may attempt new suicide hijackings sometime in the next few months. The State Department may incorporate information about possible hijackings to an existing worldwide caution to alert American travelers. Information was gleaned from interviews of captured al-Qaida operatives and intercepted communications.[125]
- *September 2003: Al-Qaida may try using poison* – The FBI is warning that al-Qaida terrorists may try to poison food or water supplies even though the organization appears to have a relatively small US presence. The Homeland Security Department advised federal, state an local security officials to evaluate their security procedures as the second 9/11 anniversary approaches, but indicated current intelligence does not warrant an increase in the national threat level.[126]

Although the alert system was designed to communicate threats to Americans, most cities did not step up security around 11 September 2002, even though the nation was put on Threat Condition Orange – high alert – for a terrorist attack. It is though we have forgotten the lesson to be learned about the boy who cried, 'Wolf!' A survey of 309 small to medium-sized cities by the National League of Cities revealed that:

- Only 25 per cent of the cities have customized preparedness plans to conform to the five-color alert system;
- 20 per cent do not understand what the system means;
- Fewer than a third of the cities increased security at utilities, public buildings, schools, or airports;
- 27 per cent said they 'conducted business as usual';
- Less than a fifth issued local warnings are coordinated with police and emergency responders.[127]

Every year, hundreds of thousands of Americans (including flight crews) travel internationally, for business, pleasure, or both. For those traveling internationally, the US State Department has issued a travel advisory warning that attacks on 'softer' targets are likely to increase overseas as security tightens at official US buildings. These may include facilities where Americans are known to congregate or visit, such as clubs, restaurants, schools, places of worship and outdoor recreation events. Your travel plans should address the security aspect of your international travel and should include 'what if' scenarios, should you become involved in a terrorist attack on your hotel or restaurant, for example.

The deadly bombings in Bali, Indonesia in October 2002 underscores how terrorists are hitting civilians away from home – a tropical vacation paradise, a discotheque, a wedding hall, a corner cafe, all unsecured places that are no longer out-of-bounds for terrorist attacks. A thwarted terrorist attack by four Algerians on a festive market in France in December 2001 and an attack on a synagogue on the island of Djerba, Tunisia in April 2002 that killed 19 tourist (most of them German) causing a dramatic drop in tourism, are other examples of a change in tactics by terrorist organizations.[128]

We must be careful in analyzing this shift to softer targets. It could be those types of attacks may serve dual purposes. First, terrorists may be attacking softer targets because of increased security efforts surrounding hard targets. Secondly, those attacks may also be a method of diverting attention away from their planning of large attacks to be conducted in the US or other countries. This second reason should concern us most. Senator Richard Shelby, an eight-year veteran of the Senate Intelligence Committee warned of another major attack from al-Qaida terrorists. 'Oh, absolutely. It's going to happen', he said on NBC's Meet the Press. Shelby said he based his opinion on a warning of a spectacular attack contained in an audiotape broadcast in November 2002 on al-Jazeera television in the Persian Gulf emirate, Qatar. (The voice was positively identified as that of bin Laden.) 'There were several messages there. One to all of his supporters, and to us, that he is alive, and he is kicking, and he is going to be around. And I think he also sent the message he is going to attack us and attack our allies', Shelby said.[129]

The release of the tape also coincides with an increasing amount of 'chatter' or phone and e-mail messages from suspected al-Qaida operatives in Pakistan and elsewhere. Officials say the chatter, which is being intercepted by US spy satellites, may refer to unspecified terrorist attacks. 'The fear an attack is imminent and may be activated by the tape is concrete', says August Hanning, president of Germany's Federal Intelligence Service. On the tape, the voice warns the US and its allies they would be attacked if they invade Iraq. 'If you attack us, expect more attacks to come against you. Just like you killed, you will be killed. The youth of the Muslim nations will rise against you', bin Laden said on the tape.[130]

This is not an idle threat. Muslim militants use the American invasion of Iraq as a very effective recruitment tool in the US, Europe and Africa, according to counterintelligence officials. The surge in recruitment has been most visible in Germany, Britain, Spain, Italy and the Netherlands as militants within the Muslim communities are seeking to identify and groom a new generation of terrorists committed to attacks in the US, Europe and Israel.[131]

Hanning's fear 'that an attack is imminent', was echoed by Attorney General John Ashcroft in June 2002. 'We do not believe that al-Qaida maintained camps in which thousands and thousands, perhaps 10,000 to 20,000 people were trained so they might send 19 or 20 individuals to the US for one day, albeit a very tragic day, of activity. We believe there is a continuing threat. We believe it is a serious threat. We believe it is an international threat', Ashcroft said.[132] Ashcroft's message was reinforced in February 2003 when the top US intelligence officials reported to Congress. CIA Director George Tenet described al-Qaida's efforts to ready new means of attack involving surface-to-air missiles, poisons, underwater assaults aimed at ships and seaports, and the possible use of a 'dirty bomb'. FBI Director Mueller called al-Qaida 'clearly the most urgent threat to US interests' and revealed, 'The FBI had identified several hundred militant Muslims in the US suspected of having links to al-Qaida'.[133]

How much clearer can the threat messages be? To avoid becoming victims of terrorism, we must become better educated about our enemy – the terrorist – and remain ever vigilant as we go about our daily lives. You, as flight crewmembers, have the added responsibilities of PROACTIVELY preparing yourselves, both mentally and physically, to react instantly to any terrorist act aboard your aircraft. Your lives, those of your passengers, and possibly many people on the ground, are at stake. Train and train well! Train often!

Psychology of Terrorism: Part 2 – Understanding Terrorists as Weapons Systems

> I think that in the West, we do not comprehend the level of commitment of those who launch these (terrorist) attacks. If the anti-terrorism alliance hopes to prevail, the public is going to need to be better educated about the opposition they face, and what motivates them.
>
> Mike Boettcher, CNN National Correspondent

Terrorists are serious about the continued destruction of American (and our allies) lives and property, our economy and our military forces. The fight against terrorism is much more than determining the whereabouts of Osama bin Laden – it is a fight for survival of freedoms to which we have long been accustomed and taken for granted. Terrorists have attacked our homeland, and they will continue to do so until eradicated. We need to understand WHO has declared war on us. Consider these incidents with known terrorists.

- Ramzi Binalshibh was captured in mid-September 2002 in Pakistan, two days after he boasted on the Al Jazeera television network of working nearly two years to prepare the suicide hijackings of 9/11 led by Mohamed Atta, his former roommate.[134]
- Jose Padilla, a Brooklyn-born Muslim convert, was arrested in May 2002 after planning a 'dirty' radiological bomb attack and synchronized explosions in hotels and gasoline stations.[135]
- On 5 June 2002, Omar al-Faruq was arrested in Indonesia and deported to Bagram, Afghanistan where al-Qaida terrorists have been interrogated by the CIA. In September 2002, al-Faruq confessed that he was the senior representative of al-Qaida in Southeast Asia. He was ordered by two senior al-Qaida officials to plan large-scale attacks against US interests in Indonesia, Malaysia, the Philippines, Singapore, Thailand, Taiwan, Vietnam and Cambodia. The timing of the attacks was to coincide with the 9/11 anniversary. A day after this information became available; the US issued its first Code Orange terror alert.[136]
- In mid-September 2002, six US citizens of Yemeni descent arrested in Buffalo, N.Y. were charged with providing support or resources to foreign terrorists. All six men trained at an al-Qaida camp in Afghanistan last year. All marginally employed, had access to thousands of dollars in cash. One had sent an e-mail to an acquaintance in July warning of a bombing plot that 'no one would be able to bear', and that 'the next meal will be very large'.[137]
- The chief of operations for al-Qaida in the Persian Gulf region, *Abd al-Rahim al-Nashiri*, was taking flying lessons near the strategic shipping lanes in the Strait of Hormuz when he was arrested in November 2002 by United Arab Emirates authorities and turned over to the CIA. Al-Nashiri was a major planner in the attacks on the USS Cole and the US Embassy in Kenya. He was said to have been planning new terrorist attacks in the Persian Gulf region, possibly involving aerial attacks.[138]
- Reports indicated that Saif al-Adil, former security chief for bin Laden and wanted for the 1998 bombings of US embassies in Africa, and Abu Hafs, a Mauritanian who planned the failed plot to blow up US targets on New Year's Day 2000, are in hiding and planning al-Qaida operations from Iran.[139]
- Abu Zubaydah, an elusive Palestinian was promoted to chief of military operations for al-Qaida after the death of Mohammed Atef. Zubaydah was captured in a raid in Pakistan in late March 2002. Believed to be with bin Laden's immediately after the attacks on 9/11, Zubaydah was previously in charge of recruiting, training and travel for al-Qaida.[140]

Who ARE these people with such hard names to pronounce or spell for Americans – Ramzi Binalshibh, Jose Padilla, Omar al-Faruq, Abd al-Rahim al-Nashiri, Saif al-Adil, Abu Zubaydah and others?

As the US and other countries identify and attempt to locate and arrest suspected al-Qaida terrorists and members of other associated terrorist organizations (see Chapter 15 on the War on Terrorism), an alarming picture of who these people are continues to evolve. The dedication of terrorists to jihad is chilling, and the depth of their training, planning, and support is amazing. Over 3,000 suspected or known terrorists have been arrested throughout the world since September 2001. That is the good news. The bad news is that over 10,000 terrorists were trained in Afghanistan alone and we do not know the whereabouts of most of these terrorists, nor the whereabouts of thousands of other terrorists trained in other countries. Worse than that, it is estimated for every suspect arrested, nine are still at large.

According to information released in late December 2002, the US has identified 36 major players in the 9/11 attacks. The roles of these individuals included security, finance, operations, training, weapons research, religious scholarship and public relations. In addition to bin Laden, twenty major players (55 per cent) are at large.[141] Undoubtedly, these major players, and thousands of trained terrorists dispersed throughout the world at their disposal, are continuing their global plans for jihad. Additionally, they continue to recruit.

Recruitment and selection

A news article revealed basic qualifications of al-Qaida's terrorist prospects. It is important to note al-Qaida does not accept 'volunteers'. Al-Qaida finds recruits, not the other way around. In their search, recruiters focus on Islamic centers, schools and mosques around the world.[142] Among other things, al-Qaida recruiters look for a Muslim man from late teens to early thirties with a willingness to die, the ability to follow orders, and one who has patience and discipline.

Like the CIA, al-Qaida takes pains to ensure it is not recruiting an enemy agent; therefore, only Muslim men get into al-Qaida. (Women are not 'members' of al-Qaida, but the terrorist organization may use women to facilitate al-Qaida financial transactions, secure false documents, act as couriers for materials or messages, spreading propaganda, and most recently, suicide missions.[143]). Background checks conducted on recruits include interviews with family, friends and employers. One-on-one meetings test a recruit's commitment. If there is doubt regarding a recruit, al-Qaida operatives conduct surveillance on him to ensure the organization is not compromised, and that person is never privy to inter-workings of al-Qaida.

Terrorist trainees share some common traits that help make them formidable foes. They:

- Believe in a 'cause' that motivates them to succeed;
- Commit to the 'cause' voluntarily;

- Are motivated to learn and to receive instruction;
- Are anxious to apply their learned skills in real operations; and,
- Are willing to die by choice or by chance to guarantee success of their mission and their cause.[144]

As with the Mafia, there is a signed, sworn oath of allegiance and secrecy. Mobsters call it *omerta*; in al-Qaida, it is called *bayat*. Omerta is a signed promise to follow al-Qaida leadership, even to martyrdom, with penalty for breaking the oath being death.

Induction into the world of terrorism

The war in Afghanistan in late 2001 against the Taliban and al-Qaida has probably changed induction of terrorists into organizations to some degree. A process that worked well for terrorist organizations would be hard to abandon, however. When possible, it would be reasonable to expect terrorist organizations to follow the same routine as much as possible.

A typical first step after recruitment and selection is for the recruit to attend a radical Islamic school in Pakistan, or along the Pakistan-Afghanistan border region. From there, next stop is an al-Qaida guesthouse, a gateway to a terrorist training camp. Study at the guesthouse furthers the religious and political underpinnings of al-Qaida, mentally preparing recruits for their training and missions ahead.

One major objective of al-Qaida is to select recruits from all over the world to train together, to learn to trust one another and to unite with one common goal – holy war against America and her allies. Every recruit receives a copy of a 26-page booklet written by Osama bin Laden entitled, *Jihad Against America.* In the booklet, which pinpoints locations of US military bases in Saudi Arabia and Persian Gulf, bin Laden writes, 'I want to eliminate all these problems created by the Americans and the Jews'. He states that he has found a home in Afghanistan and that 'I will give you the training so you can carry on after we are gone. Our struggle will never end; it will grow stronger and more lethal by the year'. In addition, he lists various groups that are helping in jihad, including Egyptian Islamic Jihad, the Libyan Jihad Fighters, the Abu Sayyaf rebels of the Philippines, and jihad militants from Burma, Bosnia, Chechnya, Indonesia, Iraq, Jordan, Lebanon, Pakistan, Somalia, Tajikistan, Turkey, Turkmenistan, and Uzbekistan.[145]

During indoctrination at the guesthouse, the recruit is assigned to basic training lasting for six months. In basic training, the recruit receives intense mental and physical training to develop skills necessary to carry out acts of terrorism without hesitation or remorse. Based upon his performance during basic training, the trainee might be selected to continue to graduate levels of training. If the recruit advances, he gets benefits along the way – from welcome ceremonies to audiences with senior leadership.

After training, the terrorist is assigned to a cell consisting of four to five others who provide support and plan attacks, or is told to return to their countries of origin and 'await orders' to carry out attacks against the United States or others.[146] Once a plan has been developed, a mission coordinator pulls together cells that are needed to accomplish an attack once a plan has been developed, and then implements the plan.

Parallels to the al-Qaida recruitment, selection and training of terrorists have been seen in processes conducted by Jemaah Islamiyya (JI), an Islamic extremist group operating in Southeast Asia. JI first identifies potential candidates through religious study groups that include discussions of Jihad and world-plight of Muslim populations. Students expressing interest in Jihadi theology are engaged specifically over a period of 18 months and made to feel a sense of exclusivity by the recruiters. Students selected as JI members are gradually subjected to well-documented techniques of 'escalating commitment'. The JI teaches new members that anyone who leaves the group is an infidel, and that all Muslims who do not subscribe to Jihad are infidels – a dogmatism designed to convince group members that killing of other Muslims was justified. New members are required to take an oath called the 'Bai'ah', pledging allegiance to the group's leader. This is followed by 'psychological contracting' in which group members are asked to fill in forms indicating their preference of responsibilities, up to and including martyrdom. Once the contracts are signed, members cannot reverse their decisions.[147]

For better understanding of the process from recruit to trained terrorist, consider the information we have collected on terrorist training. As you do so, compare the training you have received to date, and ask yourself this question: 'Am I as prepared to defend myself and others as a terrorist is prepared to attack me?' Like most crewmembers, you will probably answer, 'absolutely not!'

Terrorist training

> We have to be terrorists ... The Great Allah said, 'Against them make ready your strength to the utmost of your power including steeds of war, to strike terror into the hearts of the enemies of Allah and your enemies'.
>
> Shiekh Omar Abdel Rahman, spiritual leader of the Egyptian members of al-Qaida to his followers in Los Angeles, December 1992.[148]

Such are the words spoken throughout the radical Islamic world to youths of all ages. Children in Afghanistan and Pakistan from as early as six years of age are brought up in militant Muslim religious schools to revere Allah, to hate America, and to prepare for martyrdom through a concept known as 'jihad', holy war. In the 1980s, these young people fought Soviet invaders, in the 1990s, they used their experience to fight for the Taliban and in the 2000s, and they continue the 'holy war' against America and its allies.

Terrorist training has been around for decades. In 1981, Ayatollah Khomeini established an international terrorist training camp at Manzareih, Iran and recruited experts in all types of modern combat and sabotage, including translators, commandos from North Korea, security experts from Syria, veteran Palestinian terrorists, advisors from Libya, and KBG officers from Russia. The first class of 150 graduated on 30 July 1981, and by 1985, there were as many as 18 functioning training facilities in Iran training thousands of terrorists, including women and suicide fighters.[149]

In June 1982, 240 organizations of 80 countries met in Tripoli, Libya for the International Conference of the World Center for Resistance to Imperialism, Zionism, Racism, Reaction and Fascism. The result was a committee consisting of Libya, Cuba, Iran, Syria and North Korea whose goal was the establishment of international terrorist training programs.[150]

Two international summits, called 'The Jerusalem Project', took place in 2001 before the September attacks in the US. Organized by two Palestinians, one from Hamas and the other from Palestinian Islamic Jihad, these events were attended by over four hundred participants who pledged to support the Palestinians and seek Arab control over Jerusalem. The attendees included representatives of Osama bin Laden's al-Qaida, the Lebanese Hezbollah, and individuals from Qatar, Pakistan, Sudan and Yemen.[151]

Military action in Afghanistan against the Taliban and al-Qaida included significant targeting of terrorist camps in that country. As members of the Taliban and al-Qaida escaped into remote areas along the border with Pakistan, they established new training camps. Attacks on known terrorist (or extreme militant) training camps in Iraq occurred during Operation Iraqi Freedom in 2003. The attacks on training camps continue in postwar Iraq. In June, American soldiers attacked a suspected terrorist training camp northeast of Baghdad, killing as many as 80 people. According to reports, most of the dead were non-Iraqis and included Saudis, Syrians, Yemenis and Africans.[152]

Two sources on terrorist training tapped during our research on terrorism are unique; the first is an al-Qaida training tape not seen on TV, and the second is a copy of an al-Qaida training manual. You may be as amazed as we were at the intensity and depth of training, considering the implications of the material to aviation and flight crews.

Al-Qaida training tape

An al-Qaida training tape (reviewed personally by an associate of ours in mid-2002) showed a number of training exercises that included small arms firing ranges, live-fire room entry and numerous mixed live-fire/role-player scenarios. He summarized his observations and lessons learned from the tape for us, and they include:

- Scenarios included assassinations, kidnappings, bombings and small unit raids on various types of targets. Detailed planning, diagramming and dry runs were followed by live-fire exercises.
- Role players made aggressive moves simulating resistance throughout scenarios. All such resistance was met with immediate and brutal countermeasures. There was no presumed compliance on part of the terrorists.

- The effort to produce detail and realism in training were impressive.
- Specific scenarios included:
  - Targeting of law enforcement officers in ambush/assassinations
  - Residential assassination
  - Assassination on golf course
  - Two and four-man live-fire room entry with target discrimination (shoot/no shoot)
  - Raid on a compound with a kidnapping
  - Drive up kidnapping of target walking down a street
  - Use of tunnels/storm drains/sewers for infiltration and escape during raids
  - Rappelling from roof of building to make entry on upper floors
  - Motorcycle drive-by target practice, and
  - Grenades thrown into second story windows by motorcycle drive-bys.
- Multiple scenarios/exercises involved raids on building with large numbers of occupants. These raids followed a standard pattern:
  - Covert entry into building and movement to initial points. (Rifles were hidden in bags/cases carried into building)
  - Initiation with extreme violent action. Any resistors are shot immediately.
  - Immediate positive control and search of prisoners. Any resistors are shot.
  - Segregation of prisoners into manageable groups (explosives were displayed to gain psychological dominance over prisoners).
  - Movement of selected prisoners in small groups to the roof where terrorists pose and make statements for the press/cameras.
  - Prisoners are executed one-by-one in front of the press/cameras.
  - All scenarios ended in execution of the prisoners and none included a plan of escape for the terrorists. They plan to kill the prisoners and die in place.
- The following points were seen repeatedly and routinely throughout training exercises:
  - Use of standard military small unit tactics with multiple elements. Coordination with sub-elements via hand-held FM radios.
  - Use of pick-up trucks by the assault element to conduct raids/assassinations with shooters concealed in the bed of the truck.
  - Use of motorcycles by the security element and as a shooting platform for drive-by shootings/assassinations.
  - Use of vehicle horn to signal withdrawal.
  - Use of explosives upon withdrawal from objective.
  - Detailed planning and rehearsal of all actions.
  - Exercise of prisoner handling procedures – from initial contact to search and control, to execution of prisoners. Terrorists practiced commands in English. Role players could be heard begging not to be killed in English.
  - Multiple man room entries.
  - Distraction devices used before room entry.
  - Multiple breach points into structures and into individual rooms.

- All scenarios were practiced live-fire, including those that involved role players. Paper targets and role players were interspersed in the same scenarios.
- Terrorists showed good muzzle awareness and control. Weapons handling was NOT haphazard. All terrorists carried and fired their weapons using the same techniques.

Lessons to be Learned from the tape

1 Although al-Qaida and other terrorist organizations are known to be seeking the ability and opportunity to use weapons of mass destruction and have used hijacked aircraft as flying bombs, they are also spending a lot of time training to carry out attacks by small groups of personnel equipped with little more than small arms and vehicles.
2 There is information to the effect that the 'perfect day' would combine attacks designed to produce maximum number of casualties and would provide a means to get 'face time' on TV news channels to deliver their rhetoric. For maximum exposure, these attacks would take place nearly simultaneously at multiple but separate geographic locations.
3 In training, we need to address differences between a typical criminal victimization and a terrorist incident in terms of early recognition and appropriate response, the difference between a typical bank robbery and a terrorist attack on a financial institution, for example.
4 If you find yourself in the middle of one of these attack scenarios, there will not be time for intervention on your behalf. If identified as a problem, you will be shot. If by feigned compliance you make it through the first cut, expect to be physically restrained and controlled with threats. Your ultimate fate, if you do not resist, is to be ritually executed in front of TV cameras.
5. The best time to act is more than likely during initiation of the attack. Once terrorists are in control, it will be very difficult, if not impossible, to take effective action.[153]

Al-Qaida training manual

An al-Qaida training manual, located by Manchester (England) Metropolitan Police during a search of an al-Qaida member's home, was introduced at the embassy bombing trial in New York in early 2002.[154] One of a ten-volume set of encyclopedias on jihad entitled, *Encyclopedia of Afghan Resistance,* it was used extensively in terrorist training camps in Afghanistan.[155] The following is a brief outline of 12 of the lessons included in the training manual:

- *Lesson One* – Principles of Military Organization
- *Lesson Two* – Necessary Qualifications and Characteristics for the Organizations' Member (Commitment, maturity, sacrifice, listening & obedience, keeping secrets

and concealing information, free of illness, patience, tranquility and unflappability, intelligence and insight, caution and prudence)

- *Lesson Three* – Counterfeit Currency and Forged Documents
- *Lesson Four* – Organization Military Bases, Apartments, Hiding Places
- *Lesson Five* – Means of Communication and Transportation
- *Lesson Six* – Training
- *Lesson Seven* – Weapons: Measures Related to Buying and Transporting Them
- *Lesson Eight* – Safety
- *Lesson Nine* – Security Plan (Definition: a set of coordinated, cohesive, and integrated measures that are related to a certain activity and designed to confuse and surprise the enemy, and if uncovered, to minimize the work loss as much as possible.)
- *Lesson Eleven* – Espionage: Information Gathering Using Overt Methods
- *Lesson Twelve* – Espionage: Information Gathering Using Covert Methods
- *Lesson Eighteen* – Prisons and Detention Centers.

> Can it happen in the US? The FBI and Navajo police launched a manhunt in February 2003 for two men believed to be Middle Eastern who assaulted a security guard at the Aneth oil field, the largest producing field in the West with all of the major oil companies having financial interest in the refinery and pipelines in the area. The field has produced more than 400 million barrels of oil since the late 1950s. One man was seen taking pictures of oil lines, the refinery and the Navajo's local government building in Aneth. The attack on the guard occurred after the two men questioned him about the operation of the facility.[156]

The information in each lesson is straightforward and chilling. Additional videos viewed worldwide on TV during the last months of 2001 showed terrorists-in-training running obstacle courses, conducting drive-by shootings, abducting passengers from vehicles, and shooting firearms and mortars.

News reports regarding terrorist training

News articles during the years after 9/11 attest to the complexity and depth of training terrorists have received and reinforce the information from the al-Qaida tape and training manual in the previous paragraphs. Selected information within each article is included.

Al-Qaida camp reveals training materials, tests – Items left behind included graded terrorist exams, a book by Osama bin Laden declaring an anti-American jihad, and instructions on how to make a bomb. What appeared to be a notebook of one al-Qaida assassin written in small English, included a systematic approach to shooting at people. Small hand-drawn images showed where to aim bullets, through the head and heart; and translations of handwritten materials in Arabic revealed chemical formulas for creating explosives of varying strengths.[157]

Al-Qaida house was built for jihad – Offices contained detonators, dynamite and chemical compounds in plastic bags. Hand grenades sat on a closet shelf beside sheets of paper bearing fake stamps for travel documents including two for Italy and one each for India, Pakistan and Malaysia. A composition book was filled with detailed recipes in English for making bombs using household products. A small notebook held Arabic instructions for using Russian mortars and artillery, advice for successful suicide attacks. Partially burned papers described how to build an atomic bomb. Notes in Arabic, German, Urdu and English explained the way explosives compress plutonium and trigger a thermonuclear reaction.[158]

Bin Laden's training camps teach curriculum of carnage – Plastic explosives, timing devices and sketches of the best places to hide a bomb on an airplane filled files of terrorist training camps near Jalalabad. Gas masks, cyanide and recipes for biological agents lined shelves of a chemical weapons laboratory. Kalashnikov rifles, silhouetted targets and lesson plans teaching children to shoot at their victims' faces were found at an elementary school. Class manuals at two main camps show recruits were trained in conventional, biological and even nuclear warfare. Recruits came from 21 countries including Burma, Bosnia, Chechnya, Egypt, France, Indonesia, Iraq, Great Britain, Jordan, Kuwait, Lebanon, Pakistan, Saudi Arabia, Turkey, Turkmenistan, Tajikistan, and Uzbekistan. A drawer in a lab contained three manuals. One, a 179-page book identifies buildings, bridges, embassies, schools, and amusement parks as targets in the West with another chapter that discussed the destruction that can be wreaked by atomic explosions. The other two manuals were entitled *Middle Eastern Terrorist-Bomb Designs* and *Advanced Techniques for Making Explosives and Time-Delay Bombs*. There were 84 pages that appear to have been downloaded from the Internet regarding bomb-making techniques involving dynamite, C3 and C4 plastic explosives. Several fake visa and immigration stamps were found in a drawer. Outside the lab were four metal poles with chains attached to their bases. At the end of one chain were the remains of what appeared to be a dead animal with white fur. Local residents said experiments with nerve gas were conducted on dogs, rabbits and other animals. Toxic chemicals – bearing labels 'Made in China', weapons and manuals, and a brochure for a Korean chemical agent alarm were found in the rubble.[159]

Terrorist notes tell ways to be Western – Thirty-five pages of handwritten notes found in a house abandoned by al-Qaida provide details on how to operate undercover in the West. The notes provide specific instruction in activities such as setting up a safe house, buying a plane ticket and establishing a 'good cover story'. No detail appears too small down to how to apply deodorant, what underwear to wear, and how to wear a wristwatch properly. Techniques for demonstrating you are not an Islamic person included advising to shave beards one week prior to travel and to play music, a forbidden Islamic practice.[160]

Seized materials expose al-Qaida – US Special Forces and CIA officers have been examining seized al-Qaida documents, computer hard drives, videotapes and telephone books. The material has already produced names and phone numbers of al-Qaida members in other countries and led to some additional arrests. [161]

Training camp is littered with terrorist exams, notes – Students were tested and graded on how to make a bomb and how to choose the best spots on a body for a kill shot. They also had to know inner workings of anti-craft artillery, how to dismantle and reassemble it, how many rounds it could fire per minute and per second, the best way to shoot down an aircraft, at what height and angle at which the weapon should be fired and how many people would be required to carry the weapon.[162]

Satellite photos believed to show airliner for training hijackers – The Salman Pak training complex was operated by Iraqi secret service and was used to teach assassinations, kidnapping, hijacking of airplanes, buses and trains and other terrorist operations according to an Iraqi defector. The defector said training involves situations where weapons are not allowed on aircraft. Terrorists are trained to use food utensils, pens and pencils to instill horror. Training involved tactics on where to sit on the aircraft, how and what to yell, and how to instill terror from the very beginning of the hijacking.[163]

Terror camps produce new graduates – The UN and intelligence officials revealed the resurgence of terrorist camps in remote regions along the Afghan-Pakistan border, including use of many small, mobile camps. The recruits, Afghans, Pakistanis, Southeast Asians and Arabs, learned to carry out bomb attacks and suicide ambushes as part of the effort to drive Americans and other troops out of Pakistan and to overthrow the pro-US government.[164]

Charges send shiver through town – Six Yemeni-Americans arrested and charged with providing material support to foreign terrorists trained at the same al-Qaida training camp in Afghanistan as John Walker Lindh, the American captured in Afghanistan while fighting with the Taliban.[165]

Information seized during the war in Afghanistan

Information seized during the war in Afghanistan reveals much greater depth in training than previously thought. Advanced subjects for some of the trainees included:

- Hand-to-hand, close quarter fighting techniques
  - Edged weapons training
  - Selecting best shot location to maximize effectiveness
- How to use:
  - heavy machine guns, rockets, artillery, and tanks

  - anti-aircraft cannons and missiles, including how much to lead a target aircraft depending on its altitude and speed
- Explosives training, including how to:
  - make explosives from chemical compounds
  - use plastic explosives and dynamite
  - blow up the infrastructure of a country, such as electric and gas plants, airports, railroads, corporation headquarters, embassies, schools, amusement parks, bridges* and hotels
  - set mines against vehicles and personnel
  - build car and truck bombs
  - use hand grenades
  - build a 'dirty bomb'.

*An example of planning attacks against bridges occurred in June 2003. Federal law enforcement officials uncovered a plot by al-Qaida operatives to destroy the Brooklyn Bridge in New York. A US naturalized citizen from Kashmir was used by al-Qaida as a scout for the planned attack. Iyman Faris, an Ohio truck driver, traveled to Afghanistan and Pakistan in 2000, met with bin Laden and worked with one of his top lieutenants. After returning to the US in late 2002, he began casing the Brooklyn Bridge and discussing via coded messages with al-Qaida leaders ways to sever suspension cables. Plotting continued through March 2003 until his arrest. In addition to the bridge plot, Faris researched information for al-Qaida about using ultra-light planes for 'escape planes', ordered 2,000 lightweight sleeping bags to be shipped to Afghanistan for use by al-Qaida, and dressed in disguise to get airline tickets allowing al-Qaida operatives to travel to Yemen. In a news conference in Washington, Attorney General Ashcroft said the case, 'highlights the very real threats that still exist here at home in the USA in the war against terrorism'.[166]

- Chemical warfare training, including how to use:
  - homemade cyanide gas as a chemical weapon in attacks on offices and apartment buildings
  - gas masks and chemical warfare equipment
  - biological agents
  - nerve gas
- Intricacies of travel, including how to:
  - buy airline tickets, travel internationally and blend into a foreign country
  - disguise oneself, even to the point of how to properly apply deodorant and to shave
  - open bank accounts, use an ATM, transfer money, obtain credit cards
  - rob banks, run credit-card fraud schemes, carry out petty theft
  - falsify, forge or obtain false documents, including passports, visas, driver's licenses, Social Security cards, green cards
  - set up a safe house
  - escape a country

- How to:
  - use the Internet, online chat rooms and e-mail
  - scout a target, surveillance techniques
  - hijack an aircraft, pilot and navigate aircraft
  - complete suicide missions.

'Complete a suicide mission'? How hard can that be! You just push a button and it is over. Actually, there is more to it than that. Suicide terrorism deserves a deeper investigation as we are seeing more and more evidence of the use of a suicide bomber as a terrorist weapon system.

Suicide terrorism

> Suicide terrorism is the readiness to sacrifice one's life in the process of destroying or attempting to destroy a target to advance a political goal.[167]

Like definitions of 'terrorism' earlier in this chapter, this definition of 'suicide terrorism' is probably out-dated, as well. The addition of 'religious goal' should at least be added to the above definition as we continue to witness jihad against the US and its allies (Christianity, Crusaders), as well as the continued suicide missions brought against the Israelis (Judaism).

Suicide missions became a tool in the military arsenal during World War II when the Japanese began training 2,200 men to become kamikaze pilots. Their effectiveness as a weapon was fully realized during the Battle of Okinawa in 1944 when 1,000 kamikaze pilots attacked 1,300 US ships, killing over 5,000 US personnel.

Suicide missions reappeared as a choice tool of terrorism in the 1980s in Lebanon, Kuwait and Sri Lanka. In the 1990s, suicide missions spread to Israel, India, Panama, Algeria, Pakistan, Argentina, Croatia, Turkey, Tanzania and Kenya. Starting in the year 2000, suicide attacks multiplied drastically and seemed to occur on a daily basis. Suicide attacks have occurred (or have been threatened) in the United States, Indonesia, Thailand, Malaysia, Singapore, the Philippines, Yemen, Colombia, France, Germany, and Italy – in addition to many of those countries from previous decades.[168]

Many organizations that have used suicide missions in the past are no longer in existence, or have been dormant for a number of years. Ten known religious and secular terrorist groups capable of using suicide terrorism as a weapon against their foes existed in year 2000. These groups included:

- Hamas – the Palestinian-based Islam Resistance Movement;
- The Palestinian Islamic Jihad;
- Hezbollah – the Iranian-backed, Palestinian-based group;
- The Egyptian Islamic Jihad (EIJ);
- Gamaya Islamiya of Egypt (IG);
- The Armed Islamic Group of Algeria (GIA);

- Barbar Khalsa International of India (BKI);
- The Liberation Tigers of Tamil Eelam of Sri Lanka (LTTE) – the only group to have killed two world leaders – the former prime minister of India, Rajiv Gandhi and the president of Sri Lanka, Ranasinghe Premadasa;
- The Kurdistan Worker's Party of Turkey (PKK); and of course,
- Al-Qaida.[169, 170]

Two years later, this list expanded and included the additional groups listed in the section on *Terrorist Organizations*, as well as others unknown to us at this time. time. Suicide terrorism provides a number of desirable characteristics that make it a choice a choice weapon for terrorist organizations:

- The success of a suicide terrorist operation is dependent upon the death of the attacker(s);
- The death of the attacker(s) protects the organization and its supporters, freeing them from worry about capture of the attacker and subsequent interrogation (and the possibility of extracting intelligence information from the prisoner through torture or psychological pressure), trial, imprisonment and humiliation; and,
- The group does not have to be concerned with developing an escape plan, often the most difficult part of an operation.[171]

Based upon successful use of suicide terrorists in the past and the advantages of their use, it is reasonable to believe suicide attacks will continue to occur and will intensify in both frequency and size. According to some reports, there are more suicide bombers ready to go than bombs available, yet suicide bombers continue to be recruited and trained, as leaders of terrorist organizations repeatedly urge their use. In February 2003, the former Afghan Prime Minister, Gulbuddin Hekmatyar who vowed jihad against US troops in Afghanistan, said, 'I ask the Muslims of the world to wage a guerilla war by using suicide attacks. Now is not the time for large-scale group assaults, but rather for individual attacks'.[172]

Small squads of suicide fighters have been raised in Jalalabad and Kabul, Afghanistan and in Kashmir, India. Suicide fighter training camps, such as those in Bajour and Mansehra, Pakistan, continue unabated to produce members of fidaiyan, or 'those who kill themselves'.[173] Pamphlets circulated in June 2003 recruiting Afghans in the southeastern part of their country are an indication that more suicide bombings are in the making.[174]

Sometimes, premature explosions take their toll on those bent on suicide. In June 2003, four Palestinian militants died when a bomb they were planting went off prematurely.[175] In July 2003, an explosion in a mosque in Fallujah, Afghanistan, where a 'bomb-manufacturing class' was in session, killed an outspoken cleric and six of his students.[176]

Suicide terrorism is not just a tool of terrorists involved in jihad. It is being used as a tool of terrorism worldwide. (Also, see Chapter 5, Explosive Devices) Russia's problems with Chechnya have been punctuated by suicide bombings. On 27 December 2002, three suicide bombers in military uniforms and with military credentials drove two military trucks into a heavily guarded Chechnya government headquarters compound and detonated bombs that had a combined force of 1000 pounds of TNT. The blast demolished several buildings, killing about 60 people and injuring over 100 others.[177] In May 2003, a woman with explosives strapped to her waist detonated them amid thousands of Muslim pilgrims, killing herself and 13 others in the apparent attempt on the life of Chechnya's Moscow-backed administrator.[178] On 5 July 2003, two female suicide bombers killed 16 other people and injured over 40 others when they blew themselves up at a crowed rock festival in Moscow. The blast, which sprayed buckshot and metal shards throughout the crowd, was the sixth suicide bombings linked to Chechnya in the past seven months.[179] Five days later, another female, arrested on Moscow's main shopping street after reports she was acting strange, was determined to be a suicide bomber after a belt of explosives was found in a gym bag she was carrying. After two hours of attempting to detonate the equivalent of two pounds of TNT, it finally exploded, killing a bomb disposal expert.[180] In September 2003, two radio-controlled bombs exploded under a suburban commuter train packed with students on their way to school, killing at least four people and injuring forty-four others. The attack, the first on a train, was thought to be a terrorist attack by Chechen militants.[181]

In an effort to destabilize Pakistan by igniting a cycle of violence between Sunnis and Shiites, Islamic militants attacked a mosque in the southern city of Quetta as hundreds of people gathered to worship, killing 47 and wounding 65. The third attack in Quetta in the past month, the use of a suicide bomber for the first time by either faction constituted a sign that religious violence was rising in the country.[182] The Shiites hold a majority of seats in a new governing council in Iraq, also made up of Sunnis, Kurds, Christians and Turkmen.[183]

The increase in suicide attacks in Israel, America, Indonesia, India, Russia and other countries underscore their continued use as effective tools of terrorism when people are more than willing to give their lives for their cause – whether religious or political, or both. In December 2002, the UN reported recruits streaming into al-Qaida training camps that were reactivated in eastern Afghanistan. In the same report, the UN warned that al-Qaida has the potential to obtain nuclear material to build a 'dirty bomb'.[184]

In February 2003, the Al-Jazeera satellite network aired a 16-minute videotape, purportedly from Osama bin Laden. In the tape, bin Laden urged Iraqis to carry out suicide attacks against Americans. Bin Laden said, 'God says, 'You should pick up arms and kill those who are infidels'. We want to be liberated from the slavery of America. We have to fight this war. We stress the importance of suicide bombings against the enemy, these attacks that have scared Americans and Israelis'.[185] Another tape followed in April 2003 in which the purported voice of bin Laden said, 'You should avenge the innocent children who have been assassinated in Iraq. Be united against Bush and Blair and defeat them with suicide attacks so that you may be successful before Allah'. The voice also urges attacks against the governments of Pakistan,

Afghanistan, Bahrain, Kuwait and Saudi Arabia in retaliation of their support of the war against Iraq. 'All of them have been imposed upon you and jihad against them is your duty', the tape said.[186]

These messages were evidently taken to heart by an Iraqi army officer in March 2003 when he killed himself and four American soldiers in a suicide attack at a roadblock north of Najaf. The officer's family was given the equivalent of US $34,000, the officer was awarded two medals and posthumously promoted to colonel. The leader of the Islamic Jihad said its volunteers have gone to Baghdad for similar missions against the American invasion. Supposedly, thousands of Arab volunteers ready for martyrdom are in Iraq, ready to 'use any means to kill our enemy in our land, and we will follow the enemy into its land'.[187]

The suicide fighter problem becomes murkier as one terrorist organization receives support by way of suicide bombers from other organizations. An example was the suicide bombing of a coastal hangout for English speakers in Tel Aviv in the late spring of 2003. The suicide bombers were Brits of Pakistani ancestry, radicalized in the Islamic extremist milieu in Britain and groomed by al-Qaida recruiters. Israeli officials found evidence Hamas was working to recruit suicide bombers through al-Qaida, a very worrisome sign. It was the first time foreigners have committed a suicide attack in Israel since the start of intifada in 2000.[188]

Collusion between terrorist organizations is evident in a videotape obtained by the Associated Press from a senior intelligence officer in Hekmatyar's Hezb-e-Islami organization in June 2003. The officer confirmed alliance of remnants of the former Taliban regime, followers of Hekmatyar, and al-Qaida. The speaker in the videotape said, 'The recent attacks in Riyadh and Morocco were planned and they were part of our martyrdom operations. You will see more such attacks in the future. Our mujahideen brothers are regrouping in Kunar, Khost, Gardez, Jalalabad, Kabul and Logar (in Afghanistan). They are engaged in preparation for the attacks'.[189]

The suicide attacks referenced in the videotape occurred in May 2003 in Casablanca, Morocco and Riyadh, Saudi Arabia. In Morocco, a Belgian consulate, a Jewish centre and cemetery, an international hotel and a Spanish restaurant were hit almost simultaneously by explosions as residents were enjoying a night out. The blasts killed at least 41 and injured dozens more.[190] Most of the dead were Moroccans, but other victims were French, Spanish and Italian. An advisor to King Mohammed VI said, 'Our feeling is this is part of the international terror and terrorism movement the world is facing'.[191]

In Riyadh, three expatriate housing compounds were attacked by at least nine suicide bombers, killing at least 91 and injuring dozens of citizens from the US, the Philippines, Spain, Germany, Australia, and several other nations.[192] Investigators in Riyadh were aware of about 50 militants belonging to three Saudi cells, including the cell responsible for the 12 May 2003 suicide attacks. One of the cells has fled Saudi Arabia and the other is still at large, according to officials.[193]

The suicide bombings involved in the dispute between Israel and Palestine are far too numerous to list. Hundreds of such attacks have been conducted with devastating effects against the population, and that conflict is beyond the scope of this book. However, the extensive use of suicide bombers by Hamas underscores their effectiveness and continued usage.

Suicide fighters

> Suicide bombers are the 'nuclear weapon' of terrorists. They are cheap (approximately $700 per bomb) and they are smart – they have eyes and a brain.[194]

Few things are more controversial in the Islamic world than use of suicide fighters. According to some Muslims' interpretations of the Koran, it expressly forbids Muslims from taking their own lives. Those holding to that belief denounce suicide as being 'not Islamic' and 'not Afghani'.[195] Other Muslims would argue the Koran supports actions of suicide bombers. These latter groups include radical and/or militant terrorist organizations with which we are familiar.

The key to the difference in beliefs lies in interpretation of certain passages of the Koran regarding the taking of one's life. According to the Koran, if one commits suicide alone, then it is a sin; however, if one commits acts of suicide against an enemy, then it is martyrdom and is to be celebrated. As the leader of Hezbollah put it, 'Acts of martyrdom are the weapons God has given to the Palestinian nation and no one can take it from us'.[196] During an interview in November 2001 by Paul Harris for the Observer, a suicide bomber said, 'When I am being killed I am going to be given the status of shaheed (martyr). I am sacrificing myself and eliminating an enemy before he causes harm. Why should that not be called Islamic?'[197] The rewards for suicide missions? The suicide bombers will:

- Be martyrs and will be revered in the population as heroes with their photographs plastered everywhere in public places and their likenesses painted on walls;
- Immediately go straight to heaven where 72 virgins await their arrival to pleasure them for eternity;
- Get to see the face of Allah;
- Have the privilege to grant life in heaven to 70 relatives; and,
- Their family will get $50,000 and elevated in status within the community.[198]

Would these rewards be sufficient for YOU to volunteer to be a suicide bomber in our war against terrorism? Are your beliefs in freedoms we enjoy strong enough to motivate you to become such a volunteer? Hopefully, we will never be forced to retaliate in this manner. What does motivate men and women to become suicide fighters? This is another difficult question to answer. Some of the suicide groups are motivated by religion, others by ethnic nationalism – or by a combination of the two. In many cases, it is difficult to tell which motivation is the strongest.

Hezbollah maintains these attackers make their decision to do this on their own, fully conscious of the consequences.[199] There are reasons to believe this is true in many cases. An al-Qaida entry application found at a destroyed training camp at Darunta,

Afghanistan makes that assertion clear. 'I am interested in suicide operations', wrote Damir Bajrami, 24, an ethnic Albanian from Kosovo. 'I have Kosovo Liberation Army combat experience against Serb and American forces. I need no further training. I recommend suicide operations against amusement parks like Disney.'[200]

One answer to the question regarding motivation comes from an underlying nationalistic feeling of oppression and suppression generated by world events, religious beliefs, and propaganda disseminated by state sponsors of terrorism. One suicide bomber said it was his religious duty to protect the oppressed and fight injustice. He believed joining the fidaiyan was the most effective way of defeating the American attacks. 'It is a way of relieving oppressed people from being oppressed. It will save them. Islam guides us to the rescue of an oppressed person. If a Muslim sees a woman or anyone being oppressed, a Muslim is obliged to go to their aid and try to rescue them. If they do not do it, then they are out of Islam', he said.[201]

The hostilities and hatred generated on a daily basis by the Israel-Palestine conflict, as well as the US support of Israel play a huge part in motivating people to retaliate against us. Capitalistic ventures in the Middle East, presence of US military forces and our conflicts with Iraq and Iran fuel the fires of hatred of the West, perpetuating terrorism as an effective offensive tool.

Conclusion

> I fear there is a lot more out there that we just do not know about, I am afraid what happened at the WTC and Pentagon was just the beginning. The worst terror may be yet to come.[202]

It is believed most of the 10,000 terrorists trained in Afghanistan were dispatched throughout the world before September 2001. In July 2002, Attorney General Ashcroft said al-Qaida maintains 'a hidden but active presence' in the USA and that its members are poised to strike again.[203] Jihad is not over by any stretch of the imagination.

Terrorist organizations are still well funded and are determined to continue jihad. They continue to recruit and train terrorists and they WILL kill again. We MUST be ever vigilant for these determined, well-funded and well-trained adversaries. As one anonymous US official said, 'I think one of the greatest dangers right now is complacency'. We already see signs of it.

If this chapter aroused some emotions from its readers that will serve as an impetus to further train and prepare – mentally and physically – for any event that may occur, then we have succeeded in reaching our objective.

Somewhere today, terrorists are training and planning to kill.
YOU may be included in those plans.
Be ever vigilant and,
Be prepared!

Notes

1 Terrorist threat in US a matter of 'when', not 'if', Senators told, *Chicago Tribune*, 28 March 1998.
2 Attack warnings issued, Associated Press, 20 August 1998.
3 Attack threat surfaced in '98 – CIA found plot to aim jet at Trade Center, *New York Times*, 19 September 2002.
4 Dangerous activities, *Arizona Republic*, 10 October 2002.
5 Dangerous activities, *Arizona Republic*, 10 October 2002.
6 Warnings not passed down, 9/11 inquiry says, *USA Today*, 19 November 2002.
7 Warning of terror translated September 12, *Washington Post*, 20 July 2002.
8 US 'dangerously unprepared' for terror attack, report warns, *Washington Post*, 25 October 2002.
9 Shackley, et al., *You're the Target*, New World Publishing, Ltd, 1989.
10 Sloan, Stephen, *Beating International Terrorism, An Action Strategy for Preemption and Punishment*, Air University Press, 1986.
11 Ibid.
12 Ibid.
13 Ibid.
14 Ibid.
15 The Road to Kabul, *TIME*, 15 October 2001.
16 Ibid.
17 Sloan, Stephen, *Beating International Terrorism, An Action Strategy for Preemption and Punishment*, Air University Press, 1986.
18 Ibid.
19 Ibid.
20 Seized materials expose al-Qaida, *Washington Post*, 15 December 2001.
21 Bio-Warfare Called 'Weapon of Choice', www.aviationnow.com, 12 April 1999.
22 US must improve image to world, 9/11 panel told, Associated Press, 10 July 2003.
23 American power, arrogance worry rest of the world, Associated Press, 13 July 2003.
24 Ibid.
25 The Culture of Islamic Hate: When Politics Shapes Religion, *Newsweek*, 15 October 2001.
26 Why the Hate?, *TIME*, 1 October 2001.
27 Al-Qaida, Hezbollah talking, officials say, Associated Press, 27 July 2002.
28 Hamas marks 15 years with menacing rally, Associated Press, 14 December 2002.
29 Radical Muslim clerics will celebrate Sept. 11, *Republic News Services*, 8 September 2002.
30 Bergen, Peter, *Holy War Inc., Inside the Secret World of Osama Bin Laden*, The Free Press of New York, 2001.
31 Osama bin Laden: Terrorist at Large – Attack on America, *Profiles*, Issue 03, Celebrity Worldwide, Inc., New York, 2001.
32 Special Report, *Jane's Intelligence Review*, Vol. 13 No. 8, 1 August 2001.
33 The Making of a Young Militant: A Terrorist's Family Ties, *Newsweek*, 15 October 2001.
34 TERROR INC. – Targeting the bin Laden network, *US News & World Report*, 1 October 2001.
35 Special Report, *Jane's Intelligence Review*, Vol. 13 No. 8, 1 August 2001.

36 'New form of al-Qaida' being reported, Associated Press, 9 May 2003.
37 Special Report: Confessions of an al-Qaeda Terrorist, *TIME*, 23 September 2001.
38 Suicide squads trained in Pakistan to hit Afghan targets, www.cnn.com, 12 December 2002.
39 McDonald's bombers planned Xmas church attacks, www.cnn.com, 16 December 2002.
40 Ibid.
41 Terror group added to US list, Associated Press, 31 January 2003.
42 Ansar al-Islam could return, Associated Press, 21 June 2003.
43 US intelligence plays down al Qaeda claim, www.cnn.com, 13 July 2003.
44 Thousands in Mideast screaming for holy war, *Wire Services*, 29 March 2003.
45 Ibid.
46 TERROR INC. – Targeting the bin Laden network, *US News & World Report*, 1 October 2001.
47 Al-Qaida continues to draw fresh funds, UN draft says, *Washington Post*, 29 August 2002.
48 Terrorism Thrives On 'Dirty Money', www.aviationnow.com, 26 November 2001.
49 'TERRORISM AND DRUG TRAFFICKING: Responsibilities for Developing Explosives and Narcotics Detection Technologies, Report to Congressional Requesters by GAO, April 1997.
50 US tracks chunks of terrorist money, *Washington Post*, 7 February 2002.
51 Tracking Terror With More Aplomb, *Wall Street Journal*, 29 April 2002.
52 Director of Islamic charities arrested, *Los Angeles Times*, 1 May 2002.
53 Charity avoids perjury counts, Associated Press, 14 September 2002.
54 Charity head charged with funding al-Qaida, Associated Press, 10 October 2002.
55 Panel rips Saudi ties to terror financing, *Washington Post*, 17 October 2002.
56 Funds likely tie 2 hijackers, Saudis, *Washington Post*, 23 November 2002.
57 FBI investigates donations by wife of Saudi diplomat, *Washington Post*, 24 November 2002.
58 Saudi donations raise fears of new attack, *Los Angeles Times*, 25 November 2002.
59 Saudis admit to lax control of terrorism-linked charities, *Bloomberg News*, 2 February 2002.
60 Special Report: Confessions of an al-Qaeda Terrorist, *TIME*, 23 September 2001.
61 Al-Qaida continues to draw fresh funds, UN draft says, *Washington Post*, 29 August 2002.
62 FBI arrests immigrant in Iranian money scheme, *Arizona Republic*, 6 October 2001.
63 UNHOLY WAR – How Islamic radicals are hijacking one of the world's great religions, *US News & World Report*, 15 October 2001.
64 Terrorism Thrives On 'Dirty Money, www.aviationnow.com, 26 November 2001.
65 Drug profits tied to Mideast terror – Fund, meth labs linked by DEA, Associated Press, 2 September 2002.
66 US foils 2 terror plots financed by drug money, *Washington Post*, 7 November 2002.
67 Phoenix man listed in Iraq-aid indictment, Associated Press, 20 December 2002.
68 Possible ties of terror, crime funds checked, *Washington Post*, 12 August 2002.
69 TERROR INC. – Targeting the bin Laden network, *US News & World Report*, 1 October 2001.
70 US Muslim arrested in terror inquiry, Associated Press, 24 July 2002.
71 Possible ties of terror, crime funds checked, *Washington Post*, 12 August 2002.
72 Most terrorists entered US legally, study says, *Hearst Newspapers*, 6 July 2002.

73 A twisted trail for terror funds, *Los Angeles Times*, 15 December 2002.
74 Terrorism 'More Lethal But Less Frequent', www.aviationnow.com, 27 May 2002.
75 Battle over Islam rages in Indonesia, *Knight Ridder Newspapers*, no date.
76 Battle over Islam rages in Indonesia, *Knight Ridder Newspapers*, no date.
77 Suicide squads trained in Pakistan to hit Afghan targets, www.cnn.com, 12 December 2002.
78 Actions hurt al-Qaida, Treasury official says, Associated Press, 2 August 2002.
79 Ibid.
80 Suicide squads trained in Pakistan to hit Afghan targets, www.cnn.com, 12 December 2002.
81 Iranian warns US of suicide attacks, Associated Press, 15 December 2001.
82 Terror camps produce new graduates, Associated Press, 24 January 2003.
83 Terrorism 'More Lethal But Less Frequent', www.aviationnow.com, 27 May 2002.
84 Special Report: Confessions of an al-Qaeda Terrorist, *TIME*, 23 September 2001.
85 Some top al-Qaida members in Iraq, US officials say, *Washington Post*, 21 August 2002.
86 Palestinian terror leader Abu Nidal reportedly dead, *Republic News Services*, 20 August 2002.
87 Possible ties of terror, crime funds checked, *Washington Post*, 12 August 2002.
88 Al-Qaida moves gold to Sudan for safekeeping, *Washington Post*, 3 September 2002.
89 US Official: Yemen has 'significant' al-Qaeda link, www.cnn.com, 3 October 2001.
90 Sloan, Stephen, *Beating International Terrorism, An Action Strategy for Preemption and Punishment*. Air University Press, 1986.
91 'Soft' targets attractive to terrorists, Associated Press, 15 October 2002.
92 Dead man walking, www.observer.co.uk, 5 August 2001.
93 Bloom, Richard W., Commentary on the Motivational Psychology of Terrorism Against Transportation Systems: Implications for Airline Safety and Transportation Law, *Transportation Law Journal*, Vol. 25 No. 2, University of Denver, Spring 1998.
94 New threats on US attributed to al-Qaida, Associated Press, 17 November 2002.
95 Iranian warns US of suicide attacks, Associated Press, 15 December 2001.
96 Sloan, Stephen, *Beating International Terrorism, An Action Strategy for Preemption and Punishment*. Air University Press, 1986.
97 Bergen, Peter, *Holy War Inc., Inside the Secret World of Osama Bin Laden*, The Free Press of New York, 2001.
98 Sloan, Stephen, *Beating International Terrorism, An Action Strategy for Preemption and Punishment*. Air University Press, 1986.
99 Bergen, Peter, *Holy War Inc., Inside the Secret World of Osama Bin Laden*, The Free Press of New York, 2001.
100 Sloan, Stephen, *Beating International Terrorism, An Action Strategy for Preemption and Punishment*. Air University Press, 1986.
101 Terrorism a worry, but business goes on, Associated Press, 6 September 2003.
102 Terrorist Mass Murder: New 'Weapon of Choice', www.aviationnow.com, 17 September 2001.
103 Colombia's kidnappers turn to aged for victims, Associated Press, 20 June 2003.
104 Report warns terrorists may pick small targets, *Wire Services*, 24 October 2002.
105 Fighters enter Iraq from Iran and Syria, *Knight Ridder Newspapers*, 14 June 2003.
106 Militants who fled Iraq may be back, *New York Times*, 10 August 2003.
107 FBI: Only 1 terror alert meant for public, *Knight Ridder Newspapers*, 14 July 2002.

108 Terrorism warning given for this week, *Knight Ridder Newspapers*, 30 November 2001.
109 Ashcroft: No end near for alerts, *USA Today*, 6 March 2002.
110 New attacks on US feared – Intercepted messages not specific, *Republic News Services*, 19 May 2002.
111 TERROR: America Is Warned, *Arizona Republic*, 20 May 2002.
112 Terror warning over model planes, www.cnn.com, 12 June 2002.
113 Color of summer: Terror alert yellow, Associated Press, 19 June 2002.
114 FBI: Terrorists may try to arrive by sea, www.cnn.com, 19 June 2002.
115 US raises alert status to 'high risk', *Washington Post*, 1 September 2002.
116 US lowers terror alert level to yellow; arrests get credit, no available data.
117 Expect more al-Qaida attacks, CIA director warns, *Cox News Service*, 18 October 2002.
118 Al-Qaida may try attack on US trains, *Wire Services*, 25 October 2002.
119 Unusual inquiries spur alerts to sea attacks, *Wire Services*, 22 November 2002.
120 Risk of terrorist attack in US up, sources say, *Washington Post*, 6 February 2003.
121 Al-Qaida prompted new alert, *New York Times*, 14 February 2003.
122 Data on terror attack fabricated, US says, *Knight Ridder Newspapers*, 15 February 2003.
123 Attack fears prompt 'orange' terror alert, Associated Press, 21 May 2003.
124 Al-Qaida detainee targeted forests, memo says, *Arizona Republic*, 11 July 2003.
125 Warning: New 9/11 Style Attacks May Come, Associated Press, 29 July 2003.
126 Al-Qaida may try using poison, Associated Press, 5 September 2003.
127 Cities colorblind to terror warnings – Many ignore nation's 5-color alert system, *USA Today*, 20 September 2002.
128 'Soft' targets attractive to terrorists, Associated Press, 15 October 2002.
129 Sen. Shelby 'absolutely expects al-Qaida attack', *Los Angeles Times*, 25 November 2002.
130 Threats often precede al-Qaeda attacks, *USA Today*, 14 November 2002.
131 War fuels terrorist recruiting, *New York Times*, 16 March 2003.
132 Terror warning over model planes, www.cnn.com, 12 June 2002.
133 Terrorism warnings sharpened, *USA Today*, 12 February 2003.
134 US officials smiling after raid hooks 'one of al-Qaida's biggest fishes', *USA Today*, 16 September 2002.
135 Bush declares US detainee 'grave danger', *Hearst Newspapers*, 29 August 2002.
136 Special Report: Confessions of an al-Qaeda Terrorist, *TIME*, 23 September 2001.
137 Charges send shiver through town, *USA Today*, 16 January 2002.
138 High-ranking al-Qaida was learning how to fly, *Wire Services*, 22 December 2002.
139 Key al-Qaida pair reported to be operating in Iran, Associated Press, 29 August 2002.
140 Officials: Captured man says he's al-Qaida brass, www.cnn.com, 1 April 2002.
141 Worldwide hunt for key 9/11 suspects continues, Associated Press, 27 December 2002.
142 Al-Qaida has a small, selective core, *USA Today*, no date.
143 FBI warns about al-Qaida using female operatives, Associated Press, 25 April 2003.
144 Terror Attacks on Americans: A survey of recent developments, www.infoplease.com, 24 November 2001.
145 Bergen, Peter, *Holy War Inc., Inside the Secret World of Osama Bin Laden*, The Free Press of New York, 2001.
146 Bin Laden's training camps teach curriculum of carnage, *USA Today*, 26 November 2001.

147 Singapore government report reveals extent of Islamic terrorist threat in Southeast Asia, www.janes.com/security/international, 20 January 2003.
148 Satellite Photos Believed To Show Airliner For Training Hijackers, www.aviationnow.com, 7 January 2002.
149 Investigators begin putting the pieces together, *USA Today*, 14 September 2001.
150 *TERRORISM AND DRUG TRAFFICKING: Responsibilities for Developing Explosives and Narcotics Detection Technologies*, Report to Congressional Requesters by GAO, April 1997.
151 Ibid.
152 Fighters enter Iraq from Iran and Syria, *Knight Ridder Newspapers*, 14 June 2003.
153 Captured Al-Qaida Training Tape, private and anonymous source, 10 July 2002.
154 Al Qaeda Training Manual, www.usdoj.gov, undated.
155 Jordan anti-terrorism and the al-Qaeda manuals, www.cnn.com, 20 November 2001.
156 Pipeline guard beaten at reservation refinery, *Arizona Republic*, 21 February 2003.
157 Al-Qaida camp reveals training materials, tests, Associated Press, 4 January 2002.
158 Al-Qaida house was built for jihad, *Washington Post*, 16 November 2001.
159 Bin Laden's training camps teach curriculum of carnage, *USA Today*, 26 November 2001.
160 Terrorist notes tell ways to be Western, *Washington Post*, 9 December 2001.
161 Seized materials expose al-Qaida, *Washington Post*, 15 December 2001.
162 Training camp is littered with exams, notes, Associated Press, 5 January 2002.
163 Satellite Photos Believed To Show Airliner For Training Hijackers, www.aviationnow.com, 7 January 2002.
164 Terror camps produce new graduates, Associated Press, 24 January 2003.
165 Charges send shiver through town, *USA Today*, 16 January 2002.
166 Al-Qaida plot to blow bridge revealed, *New York Times*, 20 June 2003.
167 Suicide terrorism: a global threat, *Jane's Intelligence Review*, 20 October 2000.
168 Nightclub terror plans revealed, www.cnn.com, 22 October 2002.
169 Inside the mind of a suicide bomber, *History Channel*, narrated by Arthur Kent, November 2002.
170 Suicide terrorism: a global threat, *Jane's Intelligence Review*, 1 August 2001.
171 Suicide terrorism: a global threat, *Jane's Intelligence Review*, 1 August 2001.
172 Afghan rebel chief urges suicide raids against US, Associated Press, 24 February 2003.
173 Suicide Mission, www.observer.co.uk, 11 November 2001.
174 Video warns of suicide attacks, Associated Press, 22 June 2003.
175 4 Palestinian militants die as own bomb explodes, Associated Press, 23 June 2003.
176 Bomb class blamed for mosque blast, *Washington Post*, 3 July 2002.
177 Suicide bombers dress as servicemen, Associated Press, 29 December 2002.
178 Woman suicide bomber kills 14 in Chechnya, Associated Press, 15 May 2003.
179 Suicide explosions kill 14 near Moscow, *Chicago Tribune*, 6 July 2003.
180 Russian officer dies trying to defuse bomb, *Los Angeles Times*, 11 July 2003.
181 4 dead in Russian rail blast; Chechens blamed, *Los Angeles Times*, 4 September 2003.
182 Militants kill 47, wound 65 in Pakistan mosque attack, *New York Times*, 5 July 2003.
183 Shiite majority in interim Iraqi governing body, *New York Times*, 11 July 2003.
184 Recruits, support strong for al-Qaida, report says, *Wire Services*, 18 December 2002.
185 Tape calls for suicide attacks, *USA Today*, 12 February 2003.
186 Suicide attacks endorsed in bin Laden-linked tape, Associated Press, 9 April 2003.
187 Family of suicide bomber rewarded by Iraq, Associated Press, 31 March 2003.

188 British bombers raise new concern, *Los Angeles Times*, 17 June 2003.
189 Video warns of suicide attacks, Associated Press, 22 June 2003.
190 Suicide blasts in Morocco kill 41 amid terror alert, www.inq7.net/wnw/2003, 18 May 2003.
191 Morocco attacks indicate a shift in terror targets, *Knight Ridder Newspapers*, 18 May 2003.
192 90 dead in Saudi suicide bombing: US officials, www.smh.com.au/articles, 14 May 2003.
193 Saudis, US bracing for terror strikes, *Wire Services*, 21 May 2003.
194 Inside the mind of a suicide bomber, *History Channel*, narrated by Arthur Kent, November 2002.
195 Suicide Mission, www.observer.co.uk, 11 November 2001.
196 Iranian warns US of suicide attacks, Associated Press, 15 December 2001.
197 Suicide Mission, www.observer.co.uk, 11 November 2001.
198 Al-Qaida training suicide bombers in Pakistan, Associated Press, 13 December 2002.
199 Inside the mind of the suicide bomber, www.cnn.com, 28 September 2001.
200 Bin Laden's training camps teach curriculum of carnage, *USA Today*, 26 November 2001.
201 Suicide Mission, www.observer.co.uk, 11 November 2001.
202 Bin Laden's training camps teach curriculum of carnage, *USA Today*, 26 November 2001.
203 Al-Qaida is active in USA, Ashcroft warns, *USA Today*, 12 July 2002.

Chapter 5

Explosive Devices

Introduction

For our purposes, 'bombs' include improvised explosive devices (IED), improvised incendiary devices (IID) and actual explosive devices (such as grenades). Improvised explosive devices (IED) contain some type of explosive material (such as C-4 plastic explosive) while improvised incendiary devices (IID) contain some type of compound that burns (such as gasoline). Unless specified differently, the use of the word 'bomb' is used interchangeably with 'explosive device'.

Unfortunately, if an unknown explosive device is on board and detonates during flight, the consequences can be catastrophic – the bombing of Pan Am 103 in 1989 is a tragic example. The good news is there have been bombs detonated on flights that caused damage and a few fatalities, but the aircraft and those aboard survived.

This chapter is not designed to replace your own airline's material regarding explosive devices, but rather to supplement your background knowledge of the subject. In doing so, we hope you will gain some appreciation for the immense magnitude of problems associated with use of explosive devices by terrorists or others acting with intent to kill innocent people, including problems associated with detection of such dangerous items. The chapter, in three parts, addresses the threat, explores preventive measures, and provides some thoughts on how to effectively deal with an explosive device aboard your aircraft.

Part 1: The Threat

Parts are parts – A brief review

Your airline security-training program undoubtedly covers standard recognition features of explosive devices; however, a quick review would probably be in order. There are three basic components of bombs, simple to remember as PIE.

P = power source, usually one of four types (or a combination) and usually some type of delay device.

- *Power sources*
  - Mechanical – spring loaded or pressure switch

- Chemical – acid eats through a barrier
- Manual – pulling a pin
- Electrical – a battery, the most common being a flashlight battery

- *Delay devices*
  - Clocks
  - Barometers
  - Electronic timers
  - E-cells
  - Cell phone

I = initiator

- Usually blasting caps, copper or aluminum in color, ¼ inch in diameter X 1–3inches long
- Matches
- Firelighters, cigarette lighters
- Ammunition primers
- Christmas tree bulbs

E = explosive charge – may be in the form of pastes, gels, resins, foam, soft or hard plastics, cords, powders, blocks, or cylindrical sticks.

- Plastic – C-4, SEMTEX, or DETA Sheet
- TNT
- PETN
- Dynamite
- Liquids or gases – gasoline, lighter fluid, butane, propane, solvents, alcohol
- Gunpowder, other powders
- Fertilizer (ammonium nitrate) and sugar

As a flight crewmember, it is important to remember PIE should you find, or be called upon to identify, a suspicious article. Even knowing PIE does not guarantee you will recognize an article as an explosive device. Terrorists, very good at disguising explosive devices, are limited only by their imaginations. Laptop computers, personal assistance devices (Palm Pilots), cell phones, pagers, CD players and electronic game players are just some of the tools for use in disguising a bomb. Bombs have also been disguised as packs or cartons of cigarettes and bottles of wine or liquor, fruit or melons, a pay phone and a car headrest.

With the advent of large numbers of terrorists who are more than willing to sacrifice their lives for their cause, the 'look' of explosive devices has changed to some extent. The suicide bomber may want to expose explosives strapped to his or her body to achieve maximum benefit of instilling terror in victims. In addition, the exposure of such a device may occur in the initial takeover phase of a hijacking attempt as a threat, again to instill fear or terror. The trend in terrorist bombs includes the use of explosives with greater power and of incorporating items used as shrapnel, such as paper clips, nuts, bolts, screws, nails, buckshot, and/or metal scraps or shards to inflict maximum damage to victims.

The threat is real

Explosives will continue to be a threat to commercial aviation regardless of how safe we are told to feel through government assurances of effective explosive screening. The FBI issued a warning in late December 2002, about terrorists' continued interest in bringing down airliners with explosives hidden in shoes and clothing.[1] The alert was tied to the 22 December 2001 anniversary attempt by Richard Reid to blow up an American Airlines flight over the Atlantic. The FBI's warning of continued threat of explosive use by terrorists reminds us law enforcement is not yet convinced of safe air travel. Subsequently, we need to continue to be ever vigilant, knowledgeable on the subject, and properly trained to react quickly to bomb threats.

Literally, dozens of pages would be necessary to list all bombing events that have taken place throughout the world since 9/11, and hundreds of pages to list those that occurred in the past decade. For instance, a suicide bombing in early November 2002 was the eighty-first suicide bombing that year in Israel alone, an average of two per week, and there have been dozens since that time. The following incidents were selected to give you an idea of the magnitude of the problem, both on and off aircraft. An incident in 1995 is included because of its relevance to US flight crews. The majority of the events occurred in year 2002. Pay particular attention to the variety of types of bombs and their components in relationship to PIE

January 1995 – A terrorist plot was uncovered to blow up a dozen US airliners over a two-day period of time when aircraft were over the Pacific Ocean. Airlines targeted were United, American and Northwest. The plot became known after a minor fire occurred in the apartment of one of the terrorists. Authorities responding to the fire found chemicals and laboratory equipment needed for bomb making in the apartment. In addition, there were documents and drawings of how to construct a bomb, including use of small electronic switches concealed inside databank watches. During the arrest and investigation of the terrorists, it was revealed terrorists had conducted two tests in preparation for the planned multiple attacks. The first test occurred on 1 December 1994 in Manila when a bomb was detonated in a theatre. Evidence gathered from that explosion included fragments of a plastic explosive, a 9v battery and a wristwatch (of the same make and model as found in the apartment). Based on the outcome of the theatre bomb, the terrorist switched brands of watches from Adec to Casio because the latter provided better stealth. The second test occurred almost two weeks later when a bomb detonated on a Philippine Airlines flight bound for Tokyo. The bomb, placed under a passenger's seat, killed the passenger and severed the aircraft's aileron control cables. The flight made an emergency landing without further incident. Evidence in the debris included a Casio watch. The plan for multiple bombings included the bomber riding on the first leg (Singapore to Hong Kong, for example), setting the timer and leaving the bomb aboard to detonate on the second leg (Hong Kong to San Francisco).

December 2000 – A Jordanian man with links to al-Qaida was arrested in Manila and 281 sticks of dynamite were seized from his home along with wiring, dry cell batteries and three cell phones used in manufacture of homemade bombs.

January 2002 – Philippine authorities arrested a key al-Qaida bomb-maker who was hiding 2,000 pounds of explosives.

January 2002 – Members of a Malaysian terrorist group in Singapore, linked to al-Qaida, were arrested after they tried to purchase 17 tons of ammonium nitrate, enough for several truck bombs as big as the one used in Oklahoma City.

January 2002 – Captured al-Qaida documents reveal their ability to manufacture explosive materials. Items included a table of explosive mixtures classified by strength, a table comparing detonators like acetone peroxide (also known as TATP – the compound found in Richard Reid's shoes), and instructions on how to make RDX and a version of C-4 (the explosive used to blow up the USS Cole). There was a list of 64 common chemicals used to make explosives. Simple products such as car batteries and hair pomade contain such ingredients. Another list detailed how to make ammonium nitrate from burned wood, metal paint and farm fertilizer. It is obvious from documents terrorists do not have to steal explosives from military bases or munitions factories, they can make their own out of easy-to-obtain, common ingredients from a grocery store, a pharmacy, a hardware store and/or a medical supply store.

June 2002 – A 500 pound fertilizer bomb in a pickup truck was detonated by remote control outside the US consulate in Karachi, Pakistan killing 12 people.

August 2002 – A 'professionally made' bomb in a Toyota station wagon was found after the vehicle was involved in a minor traffic accident in Kabul, Afghanistan and the driver arrested. The vehicle contained 880 pounds of explosives. Door cavities and a special compartment beneath the car's rear floor were packed with bricks of C-4 explosives and 20 detonators were spaced throughout the car. Tubes filled with another type of explosive were substituted for the foam of the car seats. The arrangement, attached to two car batteries (one used as a backup), was to be detonated by a suicide bomber pressing buttons by the driver's seat. Authorities estimate the bomb could have killed up to 700 people.

September 2002 – On the eve of Jewish New Year, Israeli guards manning a back-road checkpoint intercepted an Isuzu 4x4 loaded with 1,300 pounds of explosives, two barrels containing gasoline and metal shards, and a cellular phone rigged as the detonator. Authorities estimate that if the car bomb had reached its destination (which is unknown), it would have cost such loss of life that it would have changed the current political situation in just one brief moment. It was the sixth incident of such magnitude averted in the past four months.

October 2002 – The terrorist bomb detonated in a popular nightclub in the paradise resort of Bali was timed to affect the maximum number of victims, killing over 180 people and injuring almost 300 others. A large Toyota packed with C-4 explosives destroyed the nightclub and several other surrounding buildings. The target of Bali was chosen well by the al-Qaida cell as the atmosphere is relaxed along with security. The target area was filled with tourists (and rugby teams in Bali for a tournament) from 20 countries, including Australia, Germany, Great Britain, Switzerland, Canada, South Africa, Indonesia and America. A second explosion occurred minutes afterward outside the US consulate in a nearby city with no injuries reported. The terrorist group Jemaah Islamiah, linked to al-Qaida, has been blamed for the blasts.

October 2002 – A French oil tanker was set ablaze by a terrorist attack similar to that conducted against the USS Cole – a small boat packed with explosives detonated aside the ship. The attack came one week from the second anniversary of the attack on the Cole. The explosion caused the tanker to dump 50,000 barrels of crude oil into the Gulf of Aden. One crewman was lost and all others abandoned the ship that was in flames.

October 2002 – Bombings at two department stores in the Philippines killed seven and injured 144. The bombs were detonated 30 minutes apart and contained TNT. The terrorist group Abu Sayyaf, linked to al-Qaida, has been blamed for the attacks. The bombs were similar to that used earlier in the month in another bombing that killed four, including an American Green Beret.

December 2002 – Police in Karachi, Pakistan arrested three men and seized a VW bug loaded with 250 88-pound sacks of ammonium nitrate, foiling a plot to attack American diplomats as they traveled on a main road in the port city. One of the suspects was linked to a May bombing outside a hotel in Karachi that killed 14 people. All three men trained at a terrorist camp in Afghanistan run by Islamic militants fighting Indian rule in the province of Kashmir.[2]

December 2002 – Explosions ripped through a McDonald's restaurant and a car dealership in Makassar, Indonesia, killing three and wounding two. Bomb blasts have become routine in the continuing conflict between Muslims and Christians on the Sulawesi Island, 1,000 miles east of Jakarta.[3]

December 2002 – During a Christmas service in a small Christian church in the Punjab province of Pakistan, three worshipers were killed and ten wounded when two assailants in women's robes tossed grenades into the church. Police subsequently found explosives and ammunition in a shopping bag and hidden in bushes near the church.[4]

December 2002 – A gang of 20 assailants attacked a Protestant church on Christmas Eve in eastern India. After detonating several bombs, the gang robbed valuables from the congregation, raided the church safe, and fled.[5]

December 2002 – An anti-tank mine was detonated in northwestern Pakistan, destroying four video shops. Extremists there have been allowed to employ intimidation and coercive tactics in an attempt to impose strict Islamic laws that ban television and videocassettes.

December 2002 – Investigators cordoned off ten IKEA home-furnishing stores across the Netherlands after explosives were found in two of their stores in Amsterdam and Sliedrecht. The bomb from the Sliedrecht store later detonated in a police station.[6]

January 2003 – Experts defused a homemade bomb 20 minutes before it was set to explode in a Kentucky Fried Chicken restaurant in the city of Hyderabad, Pakistan.[7]

January 2003 – Three vehicles were detonated in five days in an eastern province of Colombia with a bizarre twist. The drivers of the cars were still in them when the explosives were detonated, but they were not suicide bombers, nor did they have anything to do with the Marxist guerrillas. They were civilians that had been intimidated and misled by the rebels. The driver of the third car survived and explained the setup to authorities. The man told authorities that rebels had told him they were holding two of his brothers as hostages until he drove the vehicle to a military checkpoint. At the checkpoint, he was to get out of the car, but instead, the bomb was detonated by remote control when it arrived at the checkpoint. What the man did not know until later was that his two brothers had been told the same thing as he was by the rebels. The man's brothers were the drivers of the first two vehicles that were detonated.[8]

April 2003 – A 2-inch thick manual, one volume of the *Jihad Encyclopedia* that is used by al-Qaida operatives, was found in an abandoned bomb laboratory in the Kurdish enclave in northern Iraq. The manual offers instructions in an array of lethal demolition skills, including rigging explosives, setting and concealing booby traps, and wiring an alarm clock to detonate a bomb.[9]

June 2003 – Three terror suspects were killed when a bomb they were planting under a bridge on the road from Kabul to Gardez exploded prematurely. The three men were one of 17 known teams authorities were hunting down in southeastern Afghanistan. Each team is paid $50,000 by an 'unknown source' to carry out such operations.[10]

June 2003 – Greek commandos seized and impounded a ship flying a 'flag of convenience' from Comoros after it entered Greek territorial waters and was operating in an abnormal and suspicious pattern. The ship had wandered erratically around the Mediterranean Sea for six weeks under international surveillance. The ship's load of 750 tons of industrial-grade ammonium nitrate-based explosives and 140,000 detonators was described as a floating atomic bomb. During the investigation of both the origin and destination, it was determined the cargo had been loaded in Tunisia and was destined for an address that turned out to be a post office box. Authorities speculate at this point it was a terrorist shipment and the ship's crew got cold feet delivering the dangerous cargo with US-led anti-terrorist efforts in full gear in Sudan and the Horn of Africa region.[11, 12]

July 2003 – The Bureau of Alcohol, Tobacco, Firearms and Explosives (ATFE) reported the theft of 1,100 pounds of ammonium nitrate from two construction companies, one in Colorado and the other in California. The 400 pounds of the material stolen in Colorado had been mixed with fuel oil in preparation for use. Approximately 4,800 pounds of the ammonium nitrate/fuel oil mixture were used in the Oklahoma City bombing.[13]

These events demonstrate the availability of enormous varieties and amounts of explosive materials and the escalated use of explosives by terrorists, many times directed at aviation. How many elements of PIE did you recognize?

Explosive devices involving aviation

Explosive devices on aircraft and at airports continue to be a huge threat to aviation along with bomb threats. Fortunately, the hoax threats or threats with fake explosives greatly outnumber actual cases of bombs being present; however, you may be surprised at the worldwide statistics associated with each category. As you read each synopsis, pay particular attention to the type of explosive device used and its construction relative to PIE.

Some bomb threats on aircraft: 1988–1997 (incidents involving actual explosive devices are in italics)

December 1988 – A passenger aboard an American Airlines flight handed a flight attendant a note threatening to blow the aircraft up. The flight en route from San Francisco to Dallas landed in Albuquerque and evacuated on a remote stretch of runway. No device was found. It was later determined that an eleven year-old boy had written the note.

December 1988 – Passengers and crew of an American Airlines flight exited the aircraft via the rear stairs upon landing in Richmond after a note found during flight warned

Table 5.1 Some statistics from past explosive events

1983–1987
Source: United States Department of Transportation (DOT) Criminal Acts Against Civil Aviation (1987)

- 577 fatalities due to explosions on aircraft
- 7 actual and 20 fake explosive devices were used in 35 US hijackings
- 2,589 bomb threats against US aircraft (9/week)
- 1,112 bomb threats against US airports (4/week)

1990–1994
Source: DOT Criminal Acts Against Civil Aviation (1994)

- 22 fatalities due to explosions on aircraft
- 1,407 bomb threats against US aircraft (5/week)
- 1,688 bomb threats against US airports (6/week)

1993–1997
Source: DOT Annual Report to Congress on Civil Aviation Security, (1997)

- 6,830 million passengers screened
- 5,904 arrested carrying firearms or explosives

a bomb would explode when the plane reached a certain altitude, and an additional reference to the plane's next destination, Norfolk. No device was found.

January 1989 – A Costa Rican airlines' flight was delayed at JFK after a bomb threat was made against the flight. No device was found.

January 1989 – An Atlanta-bound Delta flight returned to San Diego shortly after takeoff after the pilots were notified of a bomb threat against their flight. No device was found.

January 1989 – A notification to US airlines by the US embassy in Oslo, Norway regarding its receipt of a bomb threat against a non-specific US jet going from New York to Los Angeles on 3 January resulted in the cancellation of a United Airlines flight after seven flight attendants refused to fly. Their flight was the last flight on January 3rd and no other flights had experienced any difficulty.

November 1989 – 207 passengers and crew were killed when a bomb detonated on Avianca Flight 203 near Bogota, Colombia. Evidence in the wreckage indicated the explosive compounds RDX and PETN were used.

November 1992 – A United Airlines flight from Los Angeles to New York was evacuated upon landing at JFK International Airport after a note demanding $600,000 and a suspicious device were found in the overhead bin, exactly where a threatening letter faxed to United's headquarter in Chicago indicated they would be found. The device proved to be harmless.

July 1997 – A suicidal passenger detonated an explosive device aboard a TAM flight in Brazil. The explosion tore a hole in the fuselage, but it only injured the bomber. Another passenger was killed and several were injured by the blast.

Bomb threats on aircraft: 2000–2003 (incidents involving actual explosive devices are in italics)

May 2000 – A homemade explosive device was discovered on board a plane from Uzbekistan on the ground in Moscow. The device, consisting of 400 grams of TNT, a clock mechanism, a detonator, a battery and connecting wires, was hidden in a tea box in the rear lavatory.

August 2000 – A passenger hijacked Azerbaijan Airlines flight 254 between Nakhichevan and Baku, claiming to be armed with a grenade and a bottle of flammable liquid. Two security officials on board overpowered him. The man had two bottles, one contained kerosene, the other an unknown liquid, but no grenade.

November 2000 – A hijacker claiming to have an explosive device seized Vnukovo Airlines flight 838. The flight from Dagestan to Moscow was diverted to Tel Aviv but was refused permission to land for fear it would be blown up over the city. Israeli fighters escorted the flight to an Air Force base in the desert. The hijacker surrendered upon landing and it was discovered the 'bomb' was a blood pressure gauge.

April 2001 – A cargo hold fire warning caused a Tel Aviv-bound KLM flight to abort a takeoff from Amsterdam. Shortly after being examined by firefighters and determined to be okay, a second warning of a fire in a lavatory illuminated. A flight attendant extinguished burning paper towels and toilet paper found in the lavatory, and a third fire indication soon followed. A crewmember found and extinguished a fire in a storage area near another lavatory. At this time, the captain decided to evacuate the aircraft. Two men were charged with arson.

December 2001 – An American Airlines flight was halted just before takeoff from San Diego to Chicago after a fake training grenade used to test security screening fell out of a passenger's carry-on bag and rolled down the aircraft aisle. Supposedly, a woman picked up the wrong bag after going through security screening, had pulled an item of clothing out of it while the aircraft was taxiing out for departure, dislodging the grenade.

December 2001 – An American Airlines flight en route from La Guardia to Fort Worth made an emergency landing in Washington Dulles where passengers and crew evacuated the aircraft. The flight diverted after a passenger found a bomb threat note. Four people were injured in the evacuation. No device was found.

December 2001 – Richard Reid tried to ignite explosives hidden in his shoes during an American Airlines flight from Paris to Miami. The flight diverted to Boston Logan airport and escorted to landing by fighter aircraft. Reid bit a flight attendant who tried to subdue him. Numerous passengers and crew responded to the alarm raised by the flight attendant and Reid was subsequently subdued, tied down with approximately 25 belts and ties and given sedatives three times by two doctors onboard the flight. Reid's hollowed-out high-top sneakers contained enough PETN explosives to have downed the aircraft. Information later obtained from a laptop captured in Afghanistan links Reid to al-Qaida. Captured al-Qaida fighters identified Reid as having attended training at terrorist camps in Afghanistan.

January 2002 – A Virgin Atlantic Airways flight was diverted to Iceland while en route from London to Orlando after the crew found a bomb threat and anti-American messages written in soap on a lavatory mirror. No device was found. It was later determined that a disgruntled flight attendant had written the messages.

January 2002 – An Atlantic Coast regional jet bound for Washington Dulles airport returned to Rochester airport shortly after taking off. The precautionary landing resulted from a handwritten message 'referring to a bomb' that was scrawled on a window shade. No device was found.

February 2002 – A Hawaiian Airlines flight en route from Honolulu to Seattle was escorted into SEA-TAC airport by fighter aircraft after a bomb threat on the flight was made from a public telephone. No device was found.

February 2002 – A passenger found a written bomb threat in a lavatory of a Northwest flight en route from Cancun to Detroit. The flight returned to Cancun 24 minutes later and was evacuated. No bomb was found on the aircraft.

February 2002 – The flight crew aboard a flight from Algeria to Paris overpowered a man who had threatened to blow up the aircraft. No device was found.

March 2002 – A bomb threat telephoned by an unidentified caller resulted in a Russian jetliner dumping fuel and returning to the departure airport for landing. No device was found.

May 2002 – An SAS flight from Copenhagen to Seattle was diverted to Greenland after bomb threat messages were found in a restaurant near SEA-TAC airport and in an airport restroom. Bomb-disposal experts found no device.

May 2002 – A flight to in South Africa was delayed for over an hour after terrified passengers refused to board the flight after a bomb threat made by a passenger to airport security personnel.

May 2002 – Seven fuse-less firecrackers were discovered in the lavatory of a United Airlines flight while en route from Chicago to Hong Kong.

September 2002 – French authorities (a bomb sniffing dog) discovered 3½ ounces of explosive material wrapped in aluminum foil and concealed beneath an armrest on board a Royal Air Maroc jet during a routine check of the aircraft after it landed in the French city of Metz, coming from Marrakech, Morocco. The explosive material contained pentrite, one of the agents found in Richard Reid's shoes.

June 2003 – An explosive device was found in a life vest under a passenger seat on an Alitalia aircraft before boarding passengers for a flight from Ancona (eastern Italy) to Rome. Police searched the plane after alerted through an anonymous tip thirty minutes before departure. Authorities detonated the device, the size of a pack of cigarettes with electric cables attached.[14, 15]

Some bomb threats/attacks on airports

Thirty attacks on airports worldwide occurred from 1996 to 2000. These attacks include 14 bombings; seven attempted bombings; and 9 other incidents such as shootings, shellings (artillery or mortars), and arsons. Ten people were killed and more than 90 injured in the attacks. The most incidents in one year (13) occurred in 2000. No incidents were reported in 1999. The following descriptions of attacks on airports reveal the wide range of explosives used by attackers. Flight crews should pay particular attention to details of these attacks as airports continue to provide a relatively easy target throughout the world BEFORE security screening checkpoints.

February 2000 – Urrao Airport, Colombia: guerrillas took control of the airport and detonated an explosive charge causing damage to the runway and terminal.

March 2000 – Attempted bombing at Sheremetyevo Airport, Russia: an explosive device consisting of a grenade and a stick of dynamite placed in a jar of concentrated acid was discovered at the flight-training center. The acid served as a timing mechanism by dissolving a piece of plastic used as the safety pin for the grenade. The device was removed and remotely detonated.

March 2000 – Attempted bombing at Jakarta Airport, Indonesia: an airport worker discovered three Molotov cocktails under a bank billboard at the entrance to the terminal. The devices did not ignite.

June 2000 – Bombing at Manila Airport, Philippines: a bomb in a women's restroom exploded causing damage to windows and minor damage to the building.

July 2000 – Bombing at Cape Town Airport, South Africa: an explosive device detonated in a garbage can located outside between terminals littering a nearby parking lot with debris and severely damaging two cars. No one was injured.

July 2000 – Attempted bombing at Vientiane Airport, Laos: a small improvised device was discovered in a rest room and defused. The device was fabricated from a grenade.

November 2000 – Bombing at Vientiane Airport, Laos: a homemade device containing gunpowder and buckshot exploded outside the entrance to the terminal. The device was attached to a bicycle. Eight people were injured.

December 2000 – Bombing at Manila Airport, Philippines: five explosive devices detonated within seconds of each other killing eleven people and injuring more than 80 others. One of the devices exploded near the aviation fuel storage depot and another at the air cargo terminal.

January 2001 – Bombing at Charles de Gaulle Airport, France: a homemade device containing a few hundred grams of an unknown explosive detonated overnight in the air freight zone damaging the building.

January 2001 – Bombing at Srinagar Airport, India involved use of grenades and small arms. Eleven people were killed including the six attackers and eight were injured.

March 2001 – Bombing a Pasto Airport, Colombia: two explosions destroyed half of the airport's fire station and a vehicle and a hole (five meters deep and 40 meters long) in the landing strip.

July 2001 – Attempted bombing at Malaga Airport, Spain: two phone calls tipped off authorities of an impending explosion from a car bomb within an hour; a stolen vehicle was located in the parking garage containing a suitcase with 60 kilograms of dynamite; a three-man bomb squad took five hours to deactivate the device. It is not known why the bomb did not detonate within the hour.

July 2001 – Colombo Airport, Sri Lanka: An attack on an adjoining military base spread to the airport and involved use of mortars, rocket-propelled grenades and explosives. Three Sri Lankan Airways' aircraft were destroyed and three damaged. Six people were killed and 17 injured.

August 2001 – Attempted bombing at Belfast Airport, Ireland: telephone calls warning of an impending car bombing enabled authorities to locate the explosive-laden stolen vehicle. Explosive experts disabled the bomb made of 45 pounds of homemade explosives with use of a robot.

August 2001 – Bombing at Madrid Airport, Spain: a phone call preceded the detonation of a car bomb in a parking garage leading authorities to believe it was a 'car bomb trap' intended to be detonated when authorities found the stolen vehicle. The 60 kilograms of dynamite caused an entire floor of the parking garage to collapse damaging over 100 vehicles.

October 2001 – Attempted bombing at Islamabad Airport, Pakistan: the owner of a small bag left unattended outside the terminal could not be determined and the bag was moved to an isolated area and covered with 'bomb blankets'. Twenty-five minutes later, the explosive device detonated causing minimal damage.

November 2001 – A passenger with an expired student visa passed through a security checkpoint in Chicago O'Hare International Airport and tried to board a United Airlines flight with nine knives, a can of tear gas and a stun gun. The man had passed through security screening with a duffel bag, a fanny pack and a white plastic grocery bag. The items were caught in a random check by United personnel at the gate. The address the man gave to authorities was the same apartment as two men currently being held in conjunction with the 9/11 attacks.[16] Coincidence?

December 2001 – Security personnel snatched up a briefcase left lying at a traveler's feet in the crowded VIP lounge of the Islamabad airport and hurled it into a concrete-brick bomb bunker outside where it detonated. Several of the 150 passengers in the lounge told a security agent that a man entered the area, sat for about five minutes and then left.

January 2002 – Over 3,000 passengers were evacuated from San Francisco airport for more than two hours after security guards discovered explosive residue on the shoes of a man and the man then disappeared into the crowd and was not located. All passengers were forced to go through security screening again. Twenty-seven flights outbound flights were delayed as well as twenty inbound flights.

February 2002 – Four armed rocket launchers with timing devices for automatic firing were discovered and disarmed by a bomb squad in Karachi. The rockets were aimed at the part of the airport used by US forces.

March 2002 – Passengers and crew evacuated a Varig Airlines aircraft in Los Angeles after arriving from Rio de Janeiro. A bomb threat was made by telephone shortly before the aircraft landed.

April 2002 – Six Maoist rebels attacked the control tower at Lamidada airport in Nepal.

May 2002 – A section of the Cleveland airport was evacuated after a piece of luggage tested positive when examined by EDS.

November 2002 – Items seized at airports during the Thanksgiving holidays: 15,982 pocket knives, 98 boxcutters, 1,072 clubs or bats, 3,242 banned tools, 2,384 flammable items, 20,581 sharp objects, six guns, a toy cannon loaded with live ammunition and a brick. During the period from February to September of 2002, screeners had confiscated 813 firearms, 783,670 knives and 31,064 boxcutters.[17]

January 2003 – Three terminals at Dallas/Ft Worth International Airport were evacuated after alarms sounded to indicate a bag may have contained an explosive device.[18] Amazingly enough, neither the bag nor the man who carried it has been found.

March 2003 – A bomb concealed in a backpack exploded near an outside shelter at the international airport in Davao City on the island of Mindanao in southern Philippines, killing 19 and wounding more than 140 others. The shelter was packed with people avoiding a downpour as they waited to greet passengers from a flight that had just arrived. Shortly after, another bomb was detonated outside a clinic in a nearby town, killing one and injuring three others. Suspicion falls on Jemaah Islamiah, the Moro Islamic Liberation Front and the Abu Sayyaf terrorist groups, all operating in the area.[19]

From all of these events, flight crews should conclude that on aircraft and/or at airports, there is a clear and present danger of being involved in some manner with explosive devices. So, what is being done about the problem? We address some of the solutions next in Part 2: Preventive Measures.

Part 2: Preventive Measures

The technology is available to prevent most explosive devices from making their way aboard commercial aircraft. However, a number of obstacles to achieving that goal stand in the way, like cost, manufacturing capabilities, terminal space, passenger convenience, security worker training and knowledge to name a few. The three main areas where preventive measures have been focused are screening of passengers, carry-on baggage and checked baggage.

Screening of passengers and related problems

As far as the passengers themselves are concerned, the current generation of machines that screen the passengers cannot detect explosives.[20]

> The war on airline terrorism is being fought with 30-year-old technology. This equipment may be older than some of the individuals manning the screening stations.[21]

As evidenced by lack of technology in explosive detection, the infamous *shoe bomber*, Robert Reid, fashioned his shoes into explosives and tried to ignite them on an American flight from France.[22] Fortunately, aware flight attendants confronted him and intervened along with other passengers to subdue him. *It is worth noting the human element brought this incident to a safe conclusion and not technology.*

A General Accounting Office (GAO) report in March 2000 revealed that out of the approximately 140 million passengers that entered the US on international flights in 1997 and 1998, about 102,000 were selected by Customs inspectors for some form of additional personal search, frisk, strip search or X-ray.[23] The persons selected were based on 'Customs policies and procedures and the inspectors' professional judgment and experience'. Of the 102,000 passengers selected by this process:

- 95 per cent were frisked, resulting in a 3 per cent positive find (weapons or contraband);
- 4 per cent were strip searched, resulting in a 23 per cent positive find; and,
- 1 per cent was X-rayed, resulting in a 31 per cent positive find.

One of the repercussions of the practice of frisking passengers became widely publicized in Arizona in February 2002. Since 9/11, 32 female airline passengers have filed complaints about being fondled and groped during random body searches at Phoenix Sky Harbor International Airport and other airports around the nation. Many of the reports and allegations involve male agents targeting solitary female travelers for supposedly random pat-downs. There is no federal law requiring agents of the same sex to perform the searches. Now that the TSA has taken over responsibility for passenger screening, they appear to have adopted use of same sex frisking on female passengers.

Most airline employees are well aware of weaknesses of security checkpoints in the past as passengers – and employees – have breached security checkpoints numerous times, sometimes with great ease. Various groups, such as the FAA, DOT, GAO, and the press, have conducted a number of tests on security checkpoints with dismal results.

- During 1998 and 1999, GAO's Inspector General staff tested access controls at eight major airports and gained access to secure areas in 68 per cent of the tests and were able to board aircraft 117 times. When additional tests were conducted between December 1999 and March 2000 at the same airports, access was still gained more than 30 per cent of the time.[24]
- Throughout the remainder of 2000, DOT's Inspector General conducted a series of tests and successfully gained access to secure airport areas, including ramps and aircraft, 68 per cent of the time.
- In May 2000, GAO special agents used counterfeit law enforcement badges and credentials to gain access to secure areas at two airports, bypassing security checkpoints and walking unescorted to aircraft departure gates. The agents, who had been issued tickets and boarding passes, could have carried weapons, explosives, or other dangerous objects onto aircraft.

- The DOT Inspector General conducted 738 tests at 32 major airports from November 2001 to February 2002 and found screeners missed knives 70 per cent of the time, guns 30 per cent or the time and explosives 60 per cent of the time. Overall, screeners failed to stop prohibited items in 48 per cent of the tests. Investigators were able to gain access to the airport tarmac in 48 per cent of tests. A counterterrorism expert commenting on the results said, 'I would say it is astounding and pretty incredible, given the high state of security awareness we were under during that period. There really was not the change we thought there was after September 11th'.[25]
- In September 2002, reporters from the New York Daily News investigating airport security were able to smuggle small knives (utility knives, rubber-handled razor knives, and a pocket knife), a corkscrew, razor blades and pepper spray through security checkpoints at all 11 airports they encountered over Labor Day weekend. Airports included Newark International, Boston Logan, Washington Dulles, Portland (Maine), New York's LaGuardia and JFK, Chicago O'Hare, Los Angeles, Las Vegas, Fort Lauderdale and Santa Barbara, California. The week prior, CBS News crews tested were able to sail past security 70 per cent of the time with carry-on bags lined with lead to block X-rays.[26]
- According to government and industry officials in May 2003, undercover agents continue to regularly sneak mock bombs and weapons past federal airport security screeners, despite the $5 billion a year taxpayers are spending to safeguard aviation. The results of the tests indicated the problems are no different than when screening was accomplished by the private workforce. (Question to ponder: Just because you federalize a private employee, what makes you think that person's work ethic is going to change?) The GAO said feedback from screeners cited lack of proper training and deficiencies in screener motivation.[27]

Despite heightened security measures and raised general awareness of security issues, some people are still breaching security checkpoints or bypassing security altogether. In the month and a half after 9/11, security breaches caused the evacuation of 26 airport terminals or concourses, delayed 1,111 flights and caused cancellation of 408 flights according to the FAA.[28] Here are a few snapshots of the other incidents in the United States since 9/11.

October 2001, Phoenix – A man was arrested after he tried to board an America West flight with four ninja-style plastic knives hidden in his socks. He was stopped by security agents after passing through a security checkpoint.[29]

October 2001, New Orleans – A man carrying a loaded gun made it through a security checkpoint on onto a Southwest Airlines flight before turning the gun over to a flight attendant on the aircraft mid-flight. No charges were filed, but a security screener working at that time was fired.[30]

November 2001, New York's JFK – Part of American Airlines' terminal at JFK was evacuated, including passengers on board two aircraft preparing for departure after it was discovered security screeners were letting passengers go through the concourse after security alarms went off. Eight flights were delayed for several hours before things were sorted out.[31]

November 2001, Dallas – Passengers were cleared from three terminals and flights were halted at DFW airport after someone entered a terminal through a fire door.[32]

November 2001, Atlanta – A man ignored security guard orders and bolted through the security checkpoint, boarded an inter-airport train, and returned to his arrival gate in an apparent attempt to reclaim a camera he had inadvertently left on board the plane. The airport was shutdown for 3 hours.[33]

November 2001, Santa Ana John Wayne Airport – Flights were stopped for about three hours after a woman entered the terminal by way of an exit area. She bolted past a checkpoint and got lost in the crowd. Authorities were unable to find her. An airline spokesperson said, 'We're not sure how she got through security'.

November 2001, Seattle – Passengers at Seattle were evacuated from the terminal after a metal detector was discovered unplugged by a National Guardsman. All departing flights were stopped for more than two hours. Over 100 aircraft were affected. A domino effect created delays downstream and terminals in Oakland and Reno were closed until passengers arriving from Seattle were rescreened. At Oakland, the terminal was evacuated after a Southwest flight arrived from Seattle forcing hundreds of passengers to stand outside in high winds and drizzling rains. Hundreds of passengers were rescreened at other destinations without terminal shutdowns.[34]

December 2001, San Diego – An American Airlines jet sat on the runway for more than three hours after a dummy grenade rolled down the jet's aisle. A female passenger had inadvertently picked up the bag containing the grenade after passing through the security checkpoint.[35]

December 2001, Charlotte-Douglas International Airport – The airport was closed for an hour after it was discovered unscreened passengers had been allowed to enter a secure area through an unplugged metal detector.[36]

December 2001, Boston – American Airlines Flight 63 diverted to Boston Logan International Airport after a passenger was discovered on board attempting to light an explosive hidden in his shoe. The passenger had passed through security in Paris wearing the shoes filled with explosives.[37]

January 2002, Columbus – After calling a radio talk show and admitting he had boarded a flight with a knife hidden in his belt buckle the man was arrested after a listener notified authorities. The man could get up to five years in prison and a $10,000 fine. His bail was set at $500,000.[38]

May 2002, Cleveland – Two airport concourses were evacuated after a passenger's bag set off an explosive detector. The passenger and the bag disappeared into the crowd before security personnel noticed. The passenger and the bag were never located.[39]

August 2002, Atlanta – A security screening supervisor was fired after failing to find a .357 magnum handgun in a woman's carry-on baggage during a hand search of the bag. The woman was arrested in Philadelphia after an X-ray machine in the terminal detected the weapon as she was attempting to make a connecting flight. The Head of the TSA, James Loy, said, 'I just simply do not know how the miss occurred, but the procedures were conducted as we would hope they would be'.[40]

September 2002, Atlantic City – A Bulgarian was arrested after federal screeners found a pair of scissors embedded in a bar of soap and two box cutters in a lotion bottle in his backpack as he passed through security at the Atlantic City International Airport.[41]

January 2003, Seattle – A TSA screener started work 5:30 a.m. and was stationed at an exit lane of the screening area. His assignment was to ensure no one bypassed the security checkpoint through the exit into the concourse. At 6:00 a.m., the screener was found asleep. Concourses were cleared, flights delayed and passengers had to be rescreened before operations continued. The screener was fired.[42]

In November 2002, the USA joined 100 other countries with international airports that pin the responsibility for passenger screening on their governments. To date, only two countries – Canada and Bermuda – still leave security screening responsibilities with air carriers. America's $6 billion overhaul of airport security checkpoint personnel was completed in November 2002 when 30,000 federal screeners took over the job from airline or private companies.

The federal screeners earn US$23,600 to $35,000 annually, plus benefits. Each of the new screeners was required to undergo 60 hours of on-the-job training in addition to 40 hours of classroom instruction. Federalization of airport screeners came about because of the many problems encountered with the previous system. Low wages (often lower than the fast-food employees at the airport), monotony, stress, inadequate training and supervision, high turnover, and inadequate background checks to name a few of the problems. Extremely high turnover has seriously limited screener experience levels in the past. From May 1998 to April 1999, screener turnover averaged 126 per cent at 19 of the nation's largest airports; five of these airports reported turnover of 200 per cent or more and one reported a turnover of 416 per cent.[43] An attempt to unionize the 56,000 federal security workers by the American Federation of Government Employees was stopped by TSA chief, James Loy in January 2003.[44]

The TSA is responsible for overall security at commercial airports; however, the Immigration and Naturalization Service (INS) is responsible for oversight of international travelers. The INS report card is not pretty. In January 2003, the Justice Department Inspector General found US airports remain vulnerable to illegal entries by foreign travelers, the smuggling of aliens, drugs and other illegal contraband, and escapes by people detained for questioning. The IG also found the INS has largely failed to implement 1999 recommendations to fix problems such as badly located or inoperable surveillance cameras, inability to videotape interviews with detainees, and alarms that do not work or are not installed.[45] The INS problems are huge, as currently there are an estimated 7 million undocumented immigrants in the US and that number is increasing annually by another half-million.[46] You have to wonder about what percentage of those may be terrorists.

With federal money available, manufacturers and researchers are clamoring for their 'part'. Some of the research conducted involves total body scanners that use sophisticated X-ray technology. The machines show the person being checked essentially stripped of clothes, but reveals metallic objects wherever they are located. The machines have raised concerns over privacy and manufacturers are working on ways to blur sensitive areas or to place digital fig leaves over them. Other devices blow jets of air across the person walking through the scanning device. The air is sucked up a chimney where it is analyzed for explosive residue. Another device essentially performs a CAT scan of a suitcase in three seconds.[47] Other promising research continues in biometric ID[48] and blast-proof cargo containers.[49]

In 2003, researchers at the Reason Public Policy Institute in California recommended the current passenger-profiling system (revamped after 9/11) be scrapped and risk-based screening be adopted that focuses less on finding 'bad objects' such as nail scissors and pays more attention to identifying potentially bad people. The TSA responded they are developing such a system and a pilot program is set to begin in the Fall of 2003 with full implementation scheduled for the summer of 2004.[50]

It will be some years before we will be able to measure the effectiveness of the new federalized system and updates in technology applied to actual airport security operations. In the meantime, keep the results of the studies referred to early in this section in mind. We will continue to see weapons smuggled through security and onto our aircraft. YOU may be forced to deal with the weapons and those carrying them. As the DOT IG said, 'there remain alarming lapses and systemic vulnerabilities that must be closed'.[51]

Screening of carry-on baggage and related problems

Passengers and their carry on bags are a difficult security issue for the TSA to address without intrusive techniques that are extremely time consuming and appear impractical for mass air travel. Technologies are being developed that are less intrusive, but are not currently approved by the TSA.

One of these technologies uses identifiable mapped points on the human face as the passenger passes through the screening checkpoint to identify known terrorists and criminals from throughout the world. An alarm is sent to law enforcement stationed at the checkpoint so the individual can be stopped and investigated further. Casinos already use a variation of this equipment.

The next-generation metal detectors that passengers pass through on the way to the boarding gate will be a highly sensitive metal detector that provides an image pinpointing the exact location of metal on a person passing through the detector. This screening system is included in the ongoing Orlando International Airport trial of new checkpoint security devices.[52] However, non-metallic items such as composite weapons will continue to go un-noticed by these detectors.

Currently, if screener personnel suspect a suspicious object (explosives or weapons) within a carry-on bag they can either search the bag or test it for trace explosive residues with an Explosive Trace Detection (ETD) machine. The bag is swabbed on the handle or other areas using a piece of cloth and is put into the ETD machine where it is tested for explosive residues. First, the screeners must identify an object that appears suspicious before the bag is tested further.

If a bag is selected for additional searches, the checkpoint personnel immediately test it for explosives. However, most bags are not selected for explosive testing, and thus make it through the checkpoint without a challenge. If a bag happens to be selected for a random search then it will be tested in the same manner as a bag that is selected that contains a suspicious item. It is not unusual to be asked by checkpoint personnel for permission to check a bag. We have had our bags checked many times at the security checkpoints.

The trace explosive residue test previously mentioned will indicate positive results for explosives in many cases even though an actual explosive is not contained in the bag. For example, if you had been to the firing range shooting your weapon the day before your flight, the handle of your carry-on could test positive for explosives because trace residues from your hand have come off onto the bag handle. However, it is very possible that a bag may be packed with explosives and an ETD may not detect explosive material because no trace residue came off onto the area checked by the screener.[53]

There has been considerable effort in bringing new and more effective explosive and weapon detection technology to the front line of aviation security since 9/11. However, the human element needs to be more fully addressed in implementing these technologies. During a May 2002 test by the TSA, checkpoint screeners at 32 of the largest airports failed to detect weapons and explosives in carry-on baggage.[54]

As Table 5.2 depicts, even the best performing airport has a 6 per cent chance of letting weapons or explosives through security and onto passenger carrying aircraft. The technology to identify dangerous items in baggage must improve, or training must improve for the checkpoint personnel, or a combination of both. Because it takes humans to operate the equipment, more effort should be put into training the personnel.

Even with random and suspicious bag trace testing, the distinct possibility remains that non-metallic weapons and explosives can be smuggled through the security checkpoints and onto aircraft. The sobering fact remains the world's airline transport system is still very susceptible to attack by terrorists. The thought of weapons and bombs aboard the aircraft that we are flying often occupies our minds.

Photo 5.1 An Explosive Trace Detection (ETD) machine at a US commercial airport

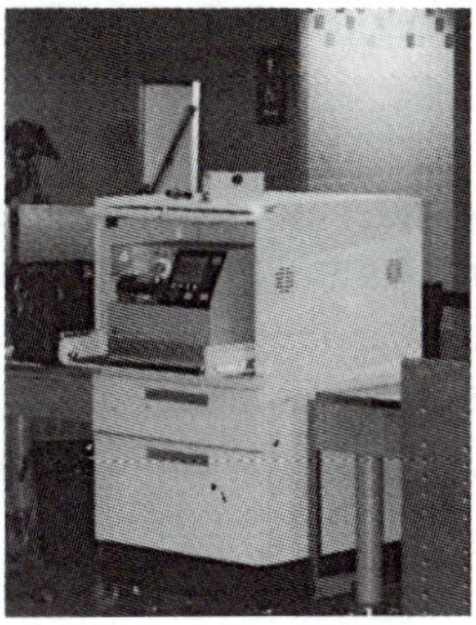

Table 5.2 Airport security checkpoint performance – failure rates of security screeners

Best	Worst
Miami – 6%	Cincinnati – 58%
Newark – 9%	Las Vegas – 50%
Ft Lauderdale – 10%	Jacksonville – 50%
Honolulu – 10%	Los Angeles – 41%
JFK – 11%	Sacramento – 40%

Source: US Transportation Security Administration (TSA), June 2002

Screening of checked baggage

> … in combination with other forms of baggage screening, bag match could be useful against some suicidal terrorists. It cannot in its own right prevent their success, but it can greatly increase the price of failure.
>
> Arnold Barnett, in testimony to the Aviation Subcommittee, H.R., January 2002

Domestic positive passenger bag match (PPBM), a requirement of Aviation Transportation Security Act of November 2001, became mandatory for all originating flights on 18 January 2002. Airlines have four options available to them to meet the requirements: hand searches, use of search dogs, X-ray machines, or ensuring all bags are positively matched to a passenger aboard the same aircraft.

In 1997, the FAA conducted a two-week experiment on PPBM that involved 11 airlines, 50 city-pairs, 8,000 flights and 750,000 passengers. The study indicated that under usual conditions, domestic departure delays could be expected in one of seven flights and the delay would average seven minutes (the average time to find and remove a bag from the cargo hold of an aircraft). The study also showed only one out of every 2,000 connecting passengers' bags was missing at departure time for the outbound flight.

About 75 per cent of all passengers, boarding aircraft in the US are originating passengers. The current PPBM regime covers this group; however, that leaves 25 per cent of all passengers – those connecting – not covered by PPBM requirements. The former FAA Head of Security believes that as long as full baggage match procedures are not implemented, the US domestic aviation system is still vulnerable.[55] Some airlines have proactively addressed this issue and are currently providing PPBM for both originating and connecting passengers.

In a testimony to the Aviation Subcommittee of the US House of Representatives on 23 January 2002, three recommendations were made regarding PPBM:

1 Even when EDS machines are fully deployed, PPBM should be continued;
2 No checked bag should be exempted from PPBM because it has passed a screening test; and,
3 PPMB should be extended as rapidly as possible to domestic *connecting* passengers.[56]

A new annex to the International Civil Aviation Organization (ICAO) standards and practices went into effect on 1 July 2002. The requirements in this annex states 'each contracting state (every member country of ICAO) shall establish measures to ensure that operators, when providing services from that state, do not transport the baggage of passengers who are not on board the aircraft, unless that baggage is subjected to appropriate security controls, which may include screening'. This annex applies to US domestic flights, as well.

Like everything else in aviation, cost is a huge factor, particularly with today's financially beleaguered airlines. However, PPBM is viewed as having the additional benefit to the airlines of reducing mishandled or lost baggage claims. Before 9/11, the average cost to an airline for a mishandled bag was US$200. There were over five million mishandled or lost bags in the US and Europe in year 2000.[57] Do the math. Since implementation of PPBM in January 2002, US airlines have reported a reduction in mishandled or lost bags from 7/1000 handled to 5/1000 handled. This equates to an overall savings of US$285 million based on year 2000 numbers.

It remains to be seen how well the current PPBM regime works. The bombings of Pan Am 103 and UTA 772 (a French DC-10) could have been avoided by the use of 100 per cent PPBM, as in each of those events a passenger checked baggage through on a multi-leg trip and then did not reboard during a connecting flight. If cost is an issue, how much money would have been saved in lives, aircraft, cargo and litigation with just these two bombing events?

In the first six months since the TSA took over the role of screening passengers' checked baggage, airline passengers have filed 6,700 complaints with the government about lost, stolen or damaged luggage. The TSA has paid US $39,000 in claims thus far to settle 485 claims. One hundred and forty-five were denied and 47 withdrawn, leaving more than 6,000 pending. Based on the established rate, claims will approach US$500,000. TSA spokesperson, Robert Johnson said the agency has handled between 250 and 300 million bags since January and the 6,700 claims are, (and we quote) 'a statistically negligible amount of complaints'.[58] Wonder if Johnson would change his mind if it was his luggage that was missing?

Of particular concern is the ease at which explosives or weapons can continue to make there way onto commercial aircraft. In November 2001, Federal officials said that less than 10 per cent of checked baggage is inspected for explosives.[59] However, in an April 2002 testimony before Congress, Transportation Secretary Norman Mineta said that 35 per cent of the checked bags are checked for explosives.[60]

Table 5.3 Screened baggage[61]

The United States government is requiring all checked bags to be screened for explosives by 31 December 2002. Estimates of explosive-detection machines needed and the amount of bags checked daily.

Airport	Machines needed	Bags checked
Dallas/Ft Worth	60	55,000
Las Vegas	60	3,000
Minneapolis/St Paul	50	50,000
San Francisco	40	200,000
Seattle/Tacoma	35	80,000
San Jose, CA	15	20–25,000
Jacksonville, FL	5	13–15,000

Even though there was, a considerable history of terrorists placing bombs on commercial aircraft, checked baggage was not scheduled to be tested for explosives by the FAA for over a decade from now.[62] That is until Congress passed the Aviation Transportation and Security Act (ATSA). ATSA mandates that all checked luggage be screened for explosives by 31 December 2002 through an approved explosive detection machine (EDS, ETD or both). However, the Homeland Security Act signed by the president in November 2002, among other things, gave a reprieve to airports on the installation of explosive technology until 31 December 2003. The TSA will work with each airport to decide what type and placement of equipment or other methods of explosive detection are best suited for that airport, giving the airports and TSA flexibility to meet the 31 December 2003 deadline.[63] TSA will not say which airports have met the 31 December 2002 deadline for security reasons.

The difference between EDS and ETD is in how the machines are operated. Trace detection equipment (ETD) requires more operators than the EDS machines. The ETD operator swabs the suspected luggage with a small piece of cloth and then processes the sample cloth for explosives. This potentially can be a time-consuming process dependent on the operator's choice of what areas of luggage to sample for explosive residue.

EDS machines scan the baggage for explosives as it passes through the machine. Current EDS equipment may process anywhere from 56 to 128 bags per hour with the next generation of EDS machines expected to check as many as 450 bags per hour.[64, 65] Current EDS machines generate false alarms on roughly three out of every ten bags. Future machines in development, but several years from production, will be capable of reducing false-positive rates to less than 10 per cent. Meanwhile, operators have to clear many bags via trace detection methods or hand searches.[66] This process is time consuming and inefficient, but it is the only method we presently have.

Starting 1 January 2003, the 23,000 newly hired government workers at US airports began verifying that no checked bag contains explosives using either EDS or ETD technology, bomb sniffing dogs or a passenger 100 per cent bag match.[67, 68] Before the 9/11 attacks, only five per cent of the roughly two million bags checked each day were screened for explosives.[69] The new procedures are an obvious improvement; however, the fact remains that essentially the same explosive testing procedures are in use now by the TSA and the airlines as were used before 1 January 2003. Nothing has significantly changed except a new deadline. The TSA and airports will not say what machines are in use at airports across the country or what combination of methods are in use at those airports for security reasons.

In early 2002, a TSA official who wished to remain anonymous, told us that at Phoenix Sky Harbor Airport there are only two Explosive Detection System (EDS) machines to test all checked baggage, when at least 60 machines are needed. These numbers have changed since then, but Phoenix Sky Harbor airport and others throughout the nation are still far short of the number of EDS machines required to do the job correctly.[70] Rather than the exception, we believe this is a widespread problem across the United States and possibly the world.

Although trace detection equipment is less expensive than EDS technology, reliability to accurately detect explosives in a bag has been called into question by some experts. The trace equipment and technology was not intended to meet the FAA's rigorous EDS certification standards. Explosive experts acknowledge it is possible for a terrorist to make a bomb that does not contaminate the outside of a bag with explosive residue, which could allow explosives to slip through security and onto an aircraft.[71]

The US government is involved in a game of catch-up while trying to figure out how to pay for explosive detections systems. Each EDS machine costs between US$700,000 and US$1 million.[72, 73] Each ETD cost approximately US$40,000.[74] The full cadre of aviation security systems has recently been estimated to cost as much as US$40 billion dollars to fully implement.[75]

The new high-intensity X-ray machines being installed can damage or ruin photosensitive materials. Kodak and other film manufacturers are warning travelers about the danger to film, including a warning on their website that states, 'Never pack unprocessed film in baggage that will be checked. These high-intensity X-ray machines will fog and ruin all unprocessed film of any speed whether exposed or not'.

Photo 5.2 Explosive Detection Machine (EDS) that is currently in use at US commercial airports

Automation and technology may eventually prevent most explosives from entering aircraft through security checkpoints and checked baggage, but until it does, what do you do if you have an explosive device on your aircraft? That is our next topic.

Part 3: Dealing with Explosive Detonation Aboard an Aircraft

Your airline security training program undoubtedly covers procedures to follow should an explosive device be involved with your flight. Your procedures should cover:

- A bomb threat made against your flight on the ground;
- A bomb threat made against your flight while airborne;
- A bomb discovered on the aircraft on the ground; and,
- A bomb discovered on the aircraft in the air.

In addition, your training should cover what factors constitute a specific or non-specific threat. Since these items are security sensitive in nature, they will not be discussed here. The intent of addressing the subject is to impress upon you the need to be intimately familiar with procedures as *time is of the essence in dealing with explosive devices*. You simply do not know how much time you have before a device detonates, even if there is a visible clock or timer running. The potential for disaster is enormous, on the ground or in the air. Your survival and the survival of all crewmembers, passengers, aircraft and cargo may depend entirely upon your immediate reactions to the threat, which means you may not have time to fumble around looking for your manual, or where the procedures are for the circumstance, or even reading them for the first time since basic training. This is not to say procedures should be memorized, but they should be easy to refer to and very familiar in location and context.

For a number of reasons beyond the scope of this book, airlines have not trained flight crews in what to expect if an explosive device detonates aboard an aircraft, either on the ground or in the air. We believe you should have some idea of the consequences. We are not explosive experts, nor do we profess to know exactly what may occur during an explosion on your aircraft. We base the following information on medical and military manuals that address these issues. We attempt to interpret the material and guidance for flight crewmembers and to make some 'best guess assumptions'. Generally, if you do suffer an explosion on an aircraft and the aircraft survives, it is going to create some major problems for you to deal with, such as the continued airworthiness of the aircraft as well as the possibility of physical and mental injuries.

What if an explosive device detonates on the aircraft on the ground? How about in flight? No one can accurately predict the outcome of any explosive event on an aircraft because of the many variables involved. The size and type of explosive charge, location in the aircraft, size of the aircraft, number of people in close proximity to the device, and whether the aircraft is pressurized or not, are some of the more important variables. We offer suggestions regarding an explosion on an aircraft that may prove to be beneficial to you should you have that unfortunate experience. Providing guidance on how to treat injuries sustained in an explosion is also beyond the scope of this book.

> *Author's note*: Keep in mind if there is an explosion on your aircraft, flight crewmembers will be affected by the explosion, just like everyone else. You may be severely injured by the blast and unable to perform tasks of assessing damage to the aircraft and/or other people. More than likely, your eardrums will be ruptured – which in itself is not fatal – but you may not be able to hear yourself speak or listen to others. (Depending upon the perforation damage to the eardrum, you may or may not recover your hearing.) You may be forced to use gestures, hand signals, or body language to communicate with others.

What happens when an explosive device detonates?

At the beginning of this chapter, we addressed the components of explosive devices, one of which was the explosive charge itself. Whatever the composition of the explosive charge, the intent of detonation is to cause a high-speed chemical decomposition of the solid or liquid explosive into a gas. A gas under high pressure and temperature now occupies the space previously occupied by the explosive. High-energy (HE) explosives such as TNT or C-4 detonate rapidly; 1 gram (g) of TNT may release 1120 calories of blast energy at the moment of detonation, generating a pressure of approximately 1,000,000 psi within the initial gas. Bombs typically carried in a parcel or suitcase may contain 1 to 14 kilograms (kg) of explosive (2–30 lbs). HE has the capability to produce a rapid release of energy and a rapid increase in pressure resulting in *brisance*, the ability to shatter nearby objects. Ordinary explosives, such as gunpowder, release energy slowly and do not possess this ability.[76]

The high pressure produced within the gaseous product is transmitted to the surrounding media as a *shock wave* traveling in all directions at speeds up to 2,500 feet per second. The shock wave has a rapidly increasing pressure front, which, upon reaching its maximum, decreases over a longer period to a pressure less than the original ambient pressure – a vacuum effect. The negative phase of the shock wave (a suction phase) lasts about 10 times as long as the positive pressure phase and rarely exceeds –1 kPa. This suction effect causes debris to be pulled into the area rather than being blown away and adds to the flying debris, causing additional damage.[77] Afterward, pressure returns to normal. The presence of reflecting or absorbing forces such as walls or people will alter wave form and peak pressure. Upon striking a solid object, a reflected pressure is magnified by two to nine times the original incident pressure. Victims who are between a blast and a building may suffer injuries two to three times greater than those that may be expected for the blast pressure.[78] We could expect similar damage on an aircraft, as all passengers and crew will be between the blast and the fuselage.

The velocity of the shock wave and duration of the positive pressure are determined by a number of factors, including the following:

1 *The size of the explosive charge* – the larger the charge, the greater the shock wave and the longer its duration
2 *The surrounding medium* – in our case air
3 *Distance from the explosion* – the further away you are, the slower the velocity of the shock wave.[79] A person 10 feet from an explosion experiences nine times more overpressure than a person 20 feet from the explosion.[80] Large wide-body aircraft can handle the effects of the blast better than small or narrow-body aircraft.

The large volumes of air that are displaced by the rapidly expanding gas of the explosion generate dynamic pressure – a blast wind. The blast wind may accelerate to a speed approaching 140 mph and may exert very high pressures in addition to those created by the shock wave. In large explosions, there may be a counter-movement of air to take up the vacuum produced by the expanding gases and displaced air. If in a pressurized aircraft and the fuselage is breached, the expanding gases will exit through the hole. A suction effect will take place, filling the aircraft almost instantly with ambient air that may be as cold as –56°C.[81]

What are the effects on human beings of the detonation of an explosive device?

There are four categories of injuries normally seen in an explosion, primary, secondary, tertiary and miscellaneous.[82]

Primary blast injuries caused by the shock wave are unique to explosions. Primary blast injuries are not commonly seen in survivors. Injuries to the chest and abdomen, when seen in those who reach a hospital, are associated with high mortality. The lungs, ears and gastrointestinal tract are most susceptible to primary blast damage. As the wave travels through the body, it causes damage by four mechanisms.

1 *Spalling* describes the occurrence of particles of fluid being thrown from a denser to a less dense medium as the shock wave passes through. In a human organ

containing both liquid and gas, such as the lungs, particles of liquid pass through the walls of the lungs into the gaseous compartments filling the lungs, at least partially, with fluid.

2 *Implosion* occurs as the shock wave passes through organs containing pockets of gas, causing each pocket to be compressed by the surrounding media. Once the shock wave has passed, the rebound expansion of each pocket occurs with even greater intensity, leading to a miniature secondary explosion. This may be seen in the ear with the rupture of the eardrum.

3 *Inertia (acceleration/deceleration)* causes a victim to be accelerated away or impacted against a stationary object. The human body tolerates being thrown by the explosion, but injuries will occur upon impact with the ground or surrounding objects. *(It is not the fall that gets you, but the sudden stop!)*

4 *Pressure differentials* result at the very moment of impact of the shock wave when a difference in pressure may develop between the outer surface of the body and internal organs. As water is essentially incompressible, the pressure within fluid-containing tissues and the vascular system remains equal. On the other hand, gas in the alveoli (*air sacs*) of the lungs is easily compressible. At impact, the pressure differential between the vascular (*fluid*) system and the alveoli drives blood from the pulmonary capillaries into the alveolar spaces, contributing to pulmonary hemorrhage (*profuse bleeding in the lungs)*) usually seen in primary blast injuries.

Secondary blast injuries result from rapid acceleration of small fragments caused by the explosion. At speeds of 50 fps, the skin is easily lacerated by flying objects and, at speeds in excess of 400 fps, penetration of body cavities may occur. Velocities of this magnitude are common in terrorist bombings and injuries resulting from flying glass, shrapnel, and debris are responsible for much of the morbidity (production of disease, such as infections). In preparing the cabin for a possible explosive event, it is extremely important that ALL loose objects be safely stowed. Pens, eyeglasses, laptop computers, CD players and other such common items, along with all galley items, have the potential to become projectiles that may cause secondary blast injuries.

Tertiary injuries occur as a victim collides with a hard surface after having been thrown by the impact of the shock wave. This is frequently a lethal event, and there is 50 per cent mortality from a vertical impact against a flat, concrete surface at velocity of 26 fps. (How many times do we see these types of injuries sustained from in flight turbulence, resulting in broken ankles or legs?) Impacts of 10 fps seem to be the limit of velocity tolerance for human beings.

Miscellaneous injuries include flash burns resulting from the intense but short-lived heat of the explosion that may reach 3,000°C. The intense heat may result in external or inhalation injuries occasionally due to release of gas from the bomb itself. External burns are usually superficial due to the short duration. Clothing offers some protection from flash burns commonly seen on the face and hands and on the lower extremities of female victims who were not wearing trousers. More extensive burns may occur if clothing ignites or if other combustible materials ignite, creating another problem – smoke inhalation.

What difference does it make if the aircraft is pressurized or not?

- *On the ground with aircraft doors open* – the aircraft is un-pressurized and the open doors would provide much relief from overpressure created by a blast. Dynamic pressure damage would more than likely be greater than damage from overpressure.
- *On the ground with aircraft doors closed* – the aircraft is usually un-pressurized or has slight pressurization applied, not to exceed .125 psi to prevent being unable to open cabin doors in an emergency. A detonation would over-pressurize the aircraft since the overpressure created by the blast would be more than the open or partially closed outflow valve could handle. Depending upon the type/size of the explosive, damage to the skin of the aircraft, windows and doors could be expected. Of course, severe damage in the immediate vicinity of the blast will occur. Depending upon location of the explosive, fuel tanks and hydraulic reservoirs may be ruptured, causing secondary explosions and fires. Oxygen generators in overhead sections of the aircraft may be activated and produce oxygen to feed the fires. Electrical cables and wires may be cut, providing an additional source of ignition for any vapors.
- *Pressurized – airborne* – the pressurization gradient for most airliners begins shortly after takeoff and builds as the aircraft climbs. Air from the air-conditioning system is used to create pressure inside the aircraft (cabin pressure) and cabin pressure is regulated by an outflow valve, usually to a maximum of approximately 8.6 psi at cruise altitude with emergency relief occurring at 8.9 psi. By regulating pressure inside the aircraft, cabin altitude is kept to well below that of the aircraft's actual (ambient) altitude. For example, at 8.6 psi cabin pressure with an aircraft cruising at 33,000 feet, cabin altitude would be approximately 5,600 feet. This process allows passengers and crew to breath normally. (Supplemental oxygen is needed above 10,000 feet for most people and is provided when the passenger oxygen system is activated – creating the 'rubber jungle' in the cabin of hanging oxygen masks.) An explosion while pressurized would normally be catastrophic from the tremendous overpressure of the aircraft, such as occurred on Pan Am 103. A large explosion will tear the aircraft apart at the seams. A small explosion may only blow a hole in the side of the aircraft, allowing the pressure to vent rapidly. If this were to occur at high altitudes, extremely low temperatures and lack of oxygen (and partial pressure of oxygen) in the cabin would occur rapidly. The time of useful consciousness would vary with the altitude, but will likely be measured in seconds, not to exceed a couple of minutes.

What will be the effects on the aircraft and what actions should I take?

- *Follow your company's procedures* – pilots and flight attendants.
- *If warned before detonation* – pilots should descend immediately to an altitude below 10,000 feet (MSA permitting), depressurize the aircraft and consider

configuring for landing. Cabin crewmembers should stow all items in the galleys and in the cabin. Anything that is loose will become a projectile.

- *If detonation occurs without warning and the aircraft survives* – pilots should accomplish an emergency descent to below 10,000 feet (MSA permitting). Take into consideration the condition of the aircraft before changing speeds in the descent. A flight control check at landing speed should be accomplished before descending for the approach to landing. Damage to aircraft systems and flight controls should be assessed and dealt with according to company procedures. Cabin crewmembers should assess aircraft and people damage in the cabin, respond accordingly, and relay information to the flight deck. Keep in mind that cabin crewmembers and pilots are going to be extremely busy, but each group may not know what damage has occurred without the other's input(s).

What are the most common injuries associated with an explosion?

- *Injuries to the eyes* are common and may range from simple abrasions to retinal detachments or global rupture. It is important to seek out these injuries and to manage them appropriately.
- *Auditory injuries* are also very common and vary in degree. Inertia from the shock wave and pressure differentials may cause linear or small perforations in the eardrum. Ruptured eardrums are more likely in the ear that is toward the explosion. Damage down in the ear cavity may induce vertigo and dizziness and is usually an indication of further head injury. If a person has hearing in both ears, there is a decreased probability of significant blast injury. Hearing impairment is very common in bomb victims. Lack of awareness of this simple fact may lead to incorrect evaluation of victims who are unable to hear commands or to respond to them.
- *Lung injury* may be caused by primary, secondary, tertiary or inhalation effects of the explosion. Blast injury to the lung is one of the most devastating threats facing victims of an explosion, particularly in a confined space such as an aircraft. Susceptibility of the lungs to blast injury depends on the peak blast pressure and its duration. In common HE explosives used in terrorist bombs, duration of positive pressure is two to ten milliseconds for a 50 to 4000 lb. charge. The shock wave will exerts pressure on the structure of the aircraft and on human tissue. Overpressures of 30 kPa (thirty times normal ambient pressure) will cause glass to shatter. Over 30 kPa there is a 10 per cent chance of tympanic membrane (eardrum) rupture, and that increases to 50 per cent chance at 100 kPa. Pressures between 500-700 kPa result in 50 per cent chance of lung damage with significant incidence of death, and at over 1,400 kPa, death is inevitable. Pressure levels high enough to cause serious injury to the lungs or other internal organs almost invariably rupture the eardrums. Survivors of a blast with pulmonary injuries may indicate cyanosis (turning blue), a cough, a chest held fully expanded, and/or difficulty breathing.
- *The cardiovascular system* is usually affected secondary to lung damage and air emboli (bubbles in the blood) represent an immediate threat to life. Symptoms

may include being unable to mentally process correctly, confusion, and/or disorientation. Monitoring is essential as air bubbles in the coronary artery may lead to death. Many of those who do not survive an explosion die to problems associated with air emboli.

- *Gastrointestinal tract* injuries are common and are caused by the shock wave as it passes through the abdominal region. Air-containing organs, such as the stomach, duodenum and colon may be ruptured by implosion, or the shearing forces of inertia may tear the organs loose. More solid organs such as the liver, spleen or diaphragm may rupture. Bright red rectal bleeding is a sign of internal damage to one or more of these organs. Secondary perforation due to projectiles is common.
- *Traumatic amputation* is a tertiary injury caused by shock wave and inertia. The limb may be mangled and grossly contaminated. A minority of traumatic amputations is due to fragment injury. Only one per cent to two per cent of those who survive will have traumatic amputation and its presence is highly suggestive of other severe injuries.
- *Secondary injuries* may include tattooing of the skin with dust and imbedded objects. Each imbedded foreign object should be treated on its own merit, but it is important to remember they may penetrate deeply. Entry wounds may be deceptive. (Three hundred pieces of wood were removed from one survivor of the Tower of London bombing in 1975 where the explosive was placed beside a cannon on a wooden carriage.)
- *Fractures* may occur in any extremity, but lower extremity fractures are more common. These injuries are often associated with extensive lacerations and soft tissue injuries.[83]
- *Psychological problems* are common and may include hysteria, crying, post-traumatic stress disorder (PTSD), and behavioral changes. One report of 1,532 patients reveals a 58 per cent incidence of psychological problems.[84] Approximately 10 per cent of uninjured or slightly injured people may experience PTSD. Many airlines have a Critical Incident Response Program (CIRP) and may be called upon to send a team to your airline to supplement your program or to perform the critical incident stress debriefing if your company does not have one. The CIRP team members are flight crewmembers that have received in-depth training in this area and provide a tremendous service to fellow crewmembers and their families.

Important points to consider

- In a major explosion, expect up to five per cent of victims to have significant blast injuries, but in some cases this may not be apparent until a number of hours after the explosion.
- Head and neck injuries are the areas most vulnerable to injury, although they constitute only 12 per cent of total body mass.
- In a study of 5,600 blast incidents, including 495 deaths, the five injuries most commonly seen in fatalities (exclusive of soft tissue injuries) were:

  - Brain injury – 66 per cent
  - Skull fracture – 51 per cent
  - Diffuse lung contusion (scattered bruising) – 47 per cent
  - Eardrum rupture – 45 per cent
  - Liver laceration – 34 per cent
- Lower limb fractures and traumatic amputations are also to be expected and leg injuries account for more than 33 per cent of injuries – definitely something to keep in mind if an emergency evacuation is performed.
- An additional 33 per cent of victims will have injuries involving the head or face, although penetrating injury to the skull is uncommon.
- Less than 10 per cent of victims will have chest or abdominal injuries. Due to the high velocity of projectiles, all penetrating wounds of the chest and abdomen should be explored.

Conclusion

As in every security system we have to work with, there are both successes and failures. Sometimes the failure of one system is caught by another system, pointing out that no system is going to work 100 per cent of the time. The threat of explosive devices being aboard aircraft is real and it is prevalent in our aviation system today. The government and industry are pursuing every effort to prevent explosive devices from being put aboard our aircraft; however, as this chapter vividly points out, there are failures in the systems in place and all types of weapons are still getting aboard the aircraft, including explosive devices.

It is evident the government must continue to make the investments in security and must continue to update security-related technologies with cooperation from private companies. The threats by terrorist groups are credible and something similar to 9/11 could occur again unless security measures are continually upgraded.

Commercial aviation must continue to look toward both technology and continued education of all aviation employees to keep the terrorist threats at bay. As we continue our fight on terrorism, it is a certainty that terrorists will attempt further cowardly attacks. Neglect and complacency toward security by all of us in the aviation world have unfortunately put us into this uncomfortable dilemma. Technology is only as good as those who build it and operate it; therefore, the human element must receive its share of attention.

It is crucial that flight crews know what to expect during an explosive device event. Armed with information in this chapter, flight crews should have a better respect for any explosive device found on an aircraft. It is imperative for the safety of everyone on board and the protection of the aircraft, that crews follow their bomb-on-board procedures thoroughly during such an event. Situational awareness, communication, and crew coordination skills are vital to decision making during any explosive device event.

Notes

1 FBI cites airline bombing threat possibility, Reuters, 24 December 2002.

2 US diplomats target of bomb plot, Associated Press, 16 December 2002.

3 3 Killed, 2 injured as blasts rip 2 Indonesia businesses, Associated Press, 6 December 2002.

4 Celebration marred, Associated Press, 26 December 2002.

5 Celebration marred, Associated Press, 26 December 2002.

6 4 video shops in Pakistan blown up, Associated Press, 29 December 2002.

7 Pakistan police defuse explosive in restaurant, *Wire Services*, 13 January 2003.

8 Colombian car bomb tactics take a new twist, www.janes.com, 17 January 2003.

9 Manual offers tips on bombs, *New York Times*, 28 April 2003.

10 Bomb error fatal to 3 in Afghanistan, Associated Press, 18 June 2003.

11 Ship seized in terror scrutiny, Associated Press, 25 June 2003.

12 Greeks begin probe of ship, Associated Press, 24 June 2003.

13 2 ammonium nitrate thefts raise homemade-bomb fears, Associated Press, 19 July 2003.

14 Explosive found on Italian plane, www.cnn.com, 12 June 2003.

15 Italian police find bomb on plane waiting to load, *Wire Services*, 13 June 2003.

16 No terrorism suspected in O'Hare weapons arrest, www.cnn.com, 6 November 2001.

17 Airports Thanksgiving seizures: 15,982 knives and a brick, Associated Press, 3 December 2002.

18 Bomb alarm empties Dallas airport terminals, Associated Press, 10 January 2003.

19 Bomb blast in Philippines kills 19; second kills 1, *Los Angeles Times*, 5 March 2003.

20 Airport security systems unable to detect plastic explosives on passengers, Associated Press, 24 December 2001.

21 Aviation experts say new equipment is needed to wage battle against terrorism, Associated Press, 2 January 2002.

22 Footwear focus of airport security after man tries to ignite explosives, Associated Press, 24 December 2001.

23 US Customs Service: *Better Targeting of Airline Passengers for Personal Searches Could Produce Better Results*, A report to the Honorable Richard J. Durbin, United States Senate. United States General Accounting Office, 25 September 2001, p. 1.

24 Dillingham, Gerald L., *Aviation Security: Vulnerabilities in, and Alternatives for, Preboard Screening Security Operations*, GAO, 25 September 2001, p. 5.

25 Weapons slip past airport security, *USA Today*, 25 March 2002.

26 Reporters smuggle knives onto flights, Associated Press, 5 September 2002.

27 'Bombs' get past airport security, *Los Angeles Times*, 11 May 2003.

28 Security breaches hinder flights, *Dallas Morning News*, 17 November 2001.

29 Man held for knives at airport, *Arizona Republic*, 4 October 2001.

30 FAA Pushes for Beefed-Up Security After Lapses at Airport Checkpoints, *Wall Street Journal*, 26 October 2001.

31 Plane terminal evacuated in Dallas, Associated Press, 3 November 2001.

32 Ibid.

33 Security breaches hinder flights, *Dallas Morning News*, 17 November 2001.

34 Few incidents reported at airports, *USA Today*, 26 November 2001.

35 Security breaches hinder flights, *Dallas Morning News*, 17 November 2001.

36 Ibid.

37 France, US Probe CDG Passenger Screening, *Aviation Week and Space Technology*, 7 January 2002.
38 Belt worn on plane held knife, Associated Press, 25 January 2002.
39 Passenger's bag sets off detector; airport closed, *Wire Services*, 4 May 2002.
40 Supervisor fired, failed to find gun in bag search, Associated Press, 28 August 2002.
41 Airport arrest over hidden weapons, Associated Press, 30 September 2002.
42 Dozing Seattle-Tacoma Airport screener fired, *Seattle Times*, 8 January 2003.
43 Dillingham, Gerald L., *Aviation Security: Vulnerabilities in, and Alternatives for, Preboard Screening Security Operations*, GAO, 25 September 2001, p. 6.
44 Transportation security chief bars union of screeners, *Wire Services*, 10 January 2003.
45 INS failing on security at airports, Associated Press, 24 January 2003.
46 Immigrants at 7 million, revised INS report says, *Los Angeles Times*, 1 February 2003.
47 Lab keeps pace with terrorists, *Arizona Republic*, 2 March 2003.
48 Airport Access Control and Biometric ID Verification: Coming to an Airport Near You, *Fenix Magazine*, July/August 2002, p. 27.
49 Another Blastproof Cargo Container Gains FAA Nod, *Aviation Week and Space Technology*, 25 February 2002.
50 Risk-based screening at airports proposed, *Chicago Tribune*, 29 May 2003.
51 FAA Pushes for Beefed-Up Security After Lapses at Airport Checkpoints, *Wall Street Journal*, 26 October 2001.
52 Transportation Security Administration Awards 1 Million Grant to InVision Technologies Subsidiary For Next Generation Explosive Detection Equipment, *Quantum Magnetics,* 16 May 2002.
53 Guns, Trace Detection in Senate Crosshairs, *Aviation Week and Space Technology*, 27 May 2002.
54 Airport Security Failures Persist, *USA Today*, 1 July 2002.
55 *Aviation Security International*, June 2002.
56 Barnett, Arnold, *Bag Match – At Last*, In testimony to the Aviation Subcommittee, US House of Representatives, 23 January 2002.
57 Bag Match – A reconciliation challenge, *Aviation Security International*, June 2002.
58 6,700 luggage claims filed in past 6 months, Associated Press, 29 June 2003.
59 Security upgrades strain airports' space, budgets, *USA Today*, 28 May 2002.
60 Ibid.
61 Ibid.
62 Guns, Trace Detection in Senate Crosshairs, *Aviation Week and Space Technology*, 27 May 2002..
63 Homeland Security Bill Includes Explosive Screening Delay, *Aviation Week and Space Technology*, 14 November 2002.
64 Third EDS Maker Expected to Get Federal Approval, *Aviation Week and Space Technology*, 30 May 2002.
65 Guns, Trace Detection in Senate Crosshairs, *Aviation Week and Space Technology*, 27 May 2002.
66 Security Deadline Angst Doesn't Deter Magaw, *Aviation Week and Space Technology*, 25 June 2002, p. 64.
67 Airports rush to meet bomb detection deadline, *The Atlanta Journal-Constitution*, 27 December 2002.
68 Few bag screening problems reported, Associated Press, 3 January 2003.

69 Fewer than 10% of checked bags inspected by airports for bombs, official says, Associated Press, 14 November 2001.
70 Ibid.
71 Guns, Trace Detection in Senate Crosshairs, *Aviation Week and Space Technology*, 27 May 2002.
72 Third EDS Maker Expected to Get Federal Approval, *Aviation Week and Space Technology*, 30 May 2002.
73 Tight Security Compels Airport design Shakeup, *Aviation Week and Space Technology*, 18 February 2002.
74 Guns, Trace Detection in Senate Crosshairs, *Aviation Week and Space Technology*, 27 May 2002.
75 Security upgrades strain airports' space, budgets, *USA Today Research*, 28 May 2002.
76 Galvagno, Captain Samuel M., *Blast Injuries*, 63rd FS, Squadron Medical Element, USAF, 7 November 2002.
77 The Emergency War Surgery NATO Handbook, Part I: *Types of Wounds and Injuries: Chapter V: Blast Injuries*, United States Department of Defense, US Government Printing Office, Washington, DC, 1988.
78 Lavonas, Dr Eric, Blast Injuries, www.emedicine.com/emerg/topic63.htm, 31 October 2001.
79 The Emergency War Surgery NATO Handbook, Part I: *Types of Wounds and Injuries: Chapter V: Blast Injuries*. United States Department of Defense, US Government Printing Office, Washington, DC, 1988.
80 Lavonas, Dr Eric, Blast Injuries, www.emedicine.com/emerg/topic63.htm, 31 October 2001.
81 Galvagno, Captain Samuel M., *Blast Injuries*, 63rd FS, Squadron Medical Element, USAF, 7 November 2002.
82 The Emergency War Surgery NATO Handbook, Part I: *Types of Wounds and Injuries: Chapter V: Blast Injuries*, United States Department of Defense, US Government Printing Office, Washington, DC, 1988.
83 Ibid.
84 Lavonas, Dr Eric, Blast Injuries, 31 October 2001.

Chapter 6

Scary Stuff: Chemical/Biological/ Radiological Weapons

Introduction

> The probability of a WMD incident is greater than ever and threatens the United States and other countries with potentially devastating consequences, including widespread death and disease, and destruction of societal infrastructure, and possibly society itself.
>
> Joseph F. Waeckerle, MD[1]

> Only a small fraction of the containers, trains, trucks and ships entering the country are ever searched, meaning the chances of ever detecting a weapon of mass destruction are almost nil.
>
> From a report by a Council on Foreign Relations congressional panel, 25 October 2002

As reality has been fed with imagination since 9/11, experts from the US and other countries have theorized a number of different attacks on America, or any of our allies. Some of the most devastating methods discussed have involved chemical, biological and/or radiological attacks. Typical headlines, such as 'Foreign flag ships a security concern'[2] and 'Firefighter planes may be inviting new terror attack',[3] and news articles expressing concerns about aviation security, such as over crop dusting aircraft that resulted in the grounding of all those aircraft types numerous times in the past year, serve to underscore widespread concern over these weapons of mass destruction. In January 2002, *New York Times* reported information, formerly classified as either secret or top secret, revealing how instructions to create biological weapons are available through the Internet.[4] To make matters even worse, we have human weaknesses in our security of top-secret information relating to the America's chemical, nuclear and biological capabilities. For instance, a former National Guard officer and his wife have been charged with illegally obtaining such documents worth millions of dollars on the black market to militias and terrorist organizations.[5]

After terrorists used aircraft as weapons of mass destruction on American soil, their use of any or all of these three types of weapons on our country can be expected. An al-Qaida spokesman, Sulaiman Abu Ghaith said, 'We have the right to fight American by chemical and biological weapons so they catch the fatal and unusual diseases that

Muslims have caught due to their chemical and biological weapons'.[6] How much more warning do we need?

All of these weapons are available to terrorists and it is only a matter of time until we experience the effects of one or more of them. Two years after 9/11, the Homeland Security Department issued an advisory the al-Qaida may try to poison our food and/or water supplies.[7] An indication of the magnitude of the problem comes from a September 2002 report that states:

- Nineteen countries suspected of having or pursuing biological and chemical weapons include Egypt, India, Iran, Iraq, Israel, Laos, Libya, North Korea, Pakistan, Russia, South Africa, Syria and Taiwan. Libya alone has produced more than 100 tons of blister and nerve agents.
- At least 17 countries either have nuclear weapons or are believed to have the means to produce them. Among those countries suspected of pursuing nuclear weapons are Iran, Iraq, Libya and North Korea.
- Sixteen nations have the missile technology capable of carrying nuclear, biological or chemical weapons to distant targets, including Egypt, India, Iran, Iraq, Libya, North Korea, Pakistan and Syria.
- Thirty-two countries produce more than 150 kinds of unmanned drone aircraft capable of flying undetected below missile-defense systems to deliver a nuclear, biological or chemical payload.[8]

According to the Center for Nonproliferation Studies at the Monterey Institute of International Studies, in the 25-year period from 1975–2000, 342 terrorist incidents occurred involving use of chemical and/or biological agents. One hundred and thirty-nine of these attacks took place on American soil. During the same period, there were 140 threats of bioterrorism that were hoaxes, 83 of which were in the US The 205 attacks on foreign soil resulted in 2,492 chemical injuries, 752 biological injuries, 150 chemical fatalities and two biological fatalities.[9]

One only has to use limited imagination to devise scenarios in which any of these weapons could be employed against us. Two national laboratories under research contract with the US government to determine the chemical/biological threat to our subway systems stated in a report the release of a chemical or biological agent in a subway could lead to exposure of more than 100,000 people through movement of trains, the ventilation shafts and street egresses above ground. Major problems exist in detection and containment of such an attack as trains continue to move throughout the system and passengers disperse throughout the city. This is particularly true if slow-acting biological agents were used, in which case it may be days or weeks before affected people begin to show up at medical facilities throughout the city, making it very difficult to determine when and where the original contamination took place.[10]

A similar situation exists in aviation. An aircraft with a biological agent on board unknowingly may spread the contamination to numerous airports and expose hundreds of flight crews, passengers and ground personnel to the agent. All of those people so exposed would continue to spread the disease as they dispersed throughout the population. Again, it would be very difficult to determine the original contamination source and to isolate the cause or the people exposed.

Biological weapons are more than antipersonnel weapons; they can also be used against crops as part of economic warfare. One fungal strain with crop-destroying potential – wheat cover smut – was tested as a weapon by Iraq in 1985. The test demonstrated wheat cover smut spores sprayed over immature wheat plants would be lethal to the crop.[11] In September 2002, the National Academy of Sciences reported that food supplies in the US are vulnerable to an agricultural terrorist attack and is 'unable to prevent it, poorly equipped to spot it, and not prepared to respond to it'. Among the diseases and pests that could be used to attack crops and livestock: Mediterranean fruit flies; the nipah virus, carried by pigs; and, karnal blunt, a fungus that attacks wheat.[12] Can you imagine the economic disaster resulting from widespread destruction of livestock and wheat and other crops in the United States?

There has been some degree of effort put forth in developing and employing devices that sniff the air for deadly agents like anthrax and smallpox. At secret locations in at least 31 cities nationwide, 'Biowatch' monitoring systems have been in place since early 2003. Some of the 31 cities include Philadelphia, New York, Washington, San Diego, Boston, Chicago, San Francisco and St Louis. Filters within the system are removed and analyzed daily. So far, the Biowatch system has not produced any false positive that would trigger an emergency response. It is estimated the cost per city for the devices is US$1 million, and if it worked only one time, it would sure be worth the price. As Bob Bostock, HSD chief for the EPA said, '(Before), the only way to tell if a biological agent had been released was to see if people started turning up sick or worse'.[13]

As we discuss the nuclear threat to our nation, consider these facts relating to the Russian Chernobyl disaster in 1986. Of the 3.5 million Ukrainians exposed to large doses of radiation, approximately 30,000 people living in the contaminated zones have since died due to radiation exposure. Of the 600,000 liquidators (clean-up workers) at Chernobyl, about 100,000 have died and another 200,000 are seriously ill and the situation for the survivors is 'dire'. The bad news? The Chernobyl cleanup was so badly bungled, another disaster could occur 'at any time'.[14] What if that scenario happened in the United States? '~~Houston~~, Washington, we have a problem!'

The three sections of this chapter review background material regarding each of the three types of terror weapons and provide flight crews with knowledge of how to deal with the consequences should they encounter any such attack while performing their jobs on an aircraft or at an airport.

Part 1: Chemical Weapons

Background

Chemical weapons have been used effectively for thousands of years, such as arrows or spears dipped in a poisonous substance before being used against an enemy. Chemical weapons may vary from rat poison to powerful nerve toxins. Israel has reported this year that some of the bombs used against them contained nails dipped in rat poison.[15] In China in September 2002, a man driven by hatred for his competitor used rat poison to contaminate food at his rival's restaurant resulting in the deaths of 38 people and sending over 200 to hospitals. (The man received a death sentence.)[16] Terrorists used sarin, a powerful nerve toxin that may be absorbed through the skin as a liquid or inhaled as a vapor, during a subway attack in Tokyo in 1995 that resulted in a dozen deaths and injured over 1,000 other people.[17] In April of 2003, the prosecutors of the man accused of masterminding the subway attacks in Tokyo labeled Shoko Asahara 'the most vicious criminal in the country's history' and demanded the death penalty, but a verdict is not expected until March 2004 or later. (Asahara's cult, formerly Aum Shinrikyo, now goes by the name Aleph.[18])

Unlike biological weapons, chemical weapons do not require being kept alive; however, they do not reproduce like their biological counterparts either. To be effective against the general population, chemical weapons require being deployed in large quantities. It is for this reason there is genuine concern regarding terrorists using drones, crop dusters or firefighting aircraft to disseminate chemicals over large populated areas. In the month following 9/11, investigators discovered that some of the hijackers involved that day had repeatedly approached a crop-dusting outfit in Florida for information on their aircraft, and had downloaded technical information on crop dusters from the Internet. The discovery prompted the grounding of agricultural aircraft three times within the month. Crop dusters can dispense from 300 to 800 gallons of chemicals per flight.[19]

Raw materials for chemical weapons are readily available with security of the substances being rated as fair to very poor. Many employees of chemical facilities are not subjected to background checks. Rail and truck facilities have limited or no security beyond staging areas. In fact, rail cars and trucks loaded with a wide array of toxic chemicals, such as chlorine, acids, liquefied petroleum gases, and cyanide compounds pass through and/or stop in residential areas daily. Barges loaded with the same or similar chemicals plow through our rivers passing through large cities on their way to their destinations.[20]

Recommendations have been made by the American Society of Engineers to install global positioning units on all trucks, especially those hauling hazardous materials. The GPS units would alert companies to any truck diverting from a planned route, allowing them to notify law enforcement authorities immediately.[21] The importance of such tracking devices was underscored in May 2002 when a truck loaded with 96 tons of sodium cyanide was hijacked in Mexico. Sodium cyanide, widely used in the mining industry, can suffocate someone if sniffed, ingested or absorbed through the skin. The amount stolen would be enough to kill over 200,000 people if deposited into a public water source. The stolen truck was later recovered, minus most of the chemicals.[22]

James Tour, a chemist, tested the ability to purchase chemicals needed to make sarin gas for a Defense Department panel. He placed an order from one of the nation's most reputable chemical suppliers and received all needed chemicals the next day. For US $130.20 plus shipping and handling, he would have been able to produce 280 grams of sarin, or a comparable amount of soman or GF – relatives of sarin. Dispensed correctly into a building ventilation system, 280 grams of sarin could kill hundreds to thousands of people depending on the size of the building and the number of occupants.[23]

An attack on any of the 15,000 chemical facilities throughout the US could have a devastating effect on thousands of lives. Hundreds of those facilities have filed mandatory worst-case scenario reports with the Environmental Protection Agency, indicating a release could spread a toxic plume for up to 14 miles downwind. Over 2,000 chemical facilities are within range of population centers of over 100,000 people. As if that were not enough, there are over 480,000 miles of pipelines that crisscross the US, mostly only three to four feet underground through populated areas. Every state in the union has chemical facilities that store over 100,000 pounds of extremely hazardous substances except Vermont. Illinois ranks the highest with 628 such facilities. Efforts have been made, and continue to be made, to limit information regarding locations of chemical sites and pipelines. Previously available on government Web sites, that information has been stripped along with locations of drinking water sources. In addition, the EPA wants mandatory 'vulnerability assessments' from each facility that cover factors such as site security, access control, storage practices and inventory control.[24]

Chemical dumps also pose security risks. In September 2002, soldiers on patrol at the Deseret Chemical Depot southwest of Salt Lake City, Utah reported spotting an intruder dressed in dark clothing who triggered an alarm. The Deseret facility is being used to destroy tons of sarin nerve gas and VX (a more toxic, but less volatile nerve agent), and tons of mustard gas (a blister agent that dissolves tissue on contact). The intruder was never found.[25] The disposal of chemical agents remains a huge problem with possible after effects lasting for many decades.

Tens of thousands of bombs and barrels filled with blister agents and nerve gas lie at the bottom of the Baltic Sea and eastern Atlantic, along with entire ships full of such weapons scuttled for disposal after World War II. The 60,000 tons of toxic chemical agents have come back to haunt the environment. There have been over 400 reports in the past two decades of fishermen snagging bombs and chemical debris in their bottom fishing tackle near the Danish island of Bornholm alone, and several fishermen have been treated for chemical burns and other poisoning symptoms. Scientists in the region have detected lethal materials, such as arsenic (100 times normal levels), lewisite and sarin mixed in with ocean bottom sediment, and highly toxic sulfur mustard gas that has been transformed into brown-yellow clumps of gel and washed ashore. Pierre Henriet, a geophysicist who has tracked dumps of mustard gas weapons in deep waters off the coast of Belgium, probably hit the proverbial nail on the head when he stated, 'It's an illusion to think we can clean up this mess'.[26]

Other large arsenals were deposited offshore of the United States, Australia, Britain, Canada, Japan and Russia. Still other sites are unaccounted for because declaring marine dumping was required only after 1985 under the Chemical Weapons Convention.

Personally, we will pass on any opportunity to eat seafood from this region or play on their beaches in that area again. We believe Mother Nature is going to slap us very hard for messing with her on this issue.

The threat is real

During Iraq's war with Iran in the 1980s, mustard gas and tabun (a nerve gas) were used in dozens of attacks against Iranian troops and Kurdish Iraqi civilians, killing as many as 5,000 people and permanently affecting thousands more who survived.[27] [28] In December 2002, UN weapons inspectors in Iraq found a dozen artillery shells filled with mustard gas at Muthanna, a chemical weapons munitions site that has produced sarin, tabun, VX and mustard gas.[29]

In November 2002, it was revealed Iraq had ordered a million doses of atropine, mainly from suppliers in Turkey.[30] Atropine is highly effective against nerve agents such as sarin and VX, both of which Iraq has acknowledged having made and stockpiled. The order by Iraq is interpreted as a move to protect their soldiers and signals the intent by Iraq to use chemical weapons in future conflicts.

From 1993 through 1998, the annual number of serious hazardous materials incidents reported to the US Department of Transportation averaged 418 per year. ('Serious incident' is defined as involving a fatality or major injury; closure of a major transportation artery or facility, or evacuation of six or more persons; or a vehicle accident or derailment resulting in the release of hazardous materials.) These incidents resulted in an average of 11 deaths per year. Terrorists could use toxic industrial chemicals that are widely produced, shipped by rail and truck tanks, and stored in both urban and rural manufacturing sites. A conventional explosive could be used to rupture a transport or storage tank creating a chemical disaster. Because of the difficulties in obtaining materials and the technical challenges of producing chemical weapons, some experts consider toxic industrial chemicals more likely weapons of terrorism.[31]

It is a known fact that many terrorists have been trained in use of chemical weapons. A video tape showing al-Qaida testing a lethal gas on a dog was aired in August 2002 on CNN.[32] The tape was one of a collection of tapes brought out of Afghanistan by a CNN reporter in early August. The President's press secretary commenting on the tapes said in a press conference, 'This is a serious reminder of the type of enemy we are up against, and the risks the world faces from people who would use weapons that bring harm to innocents. It vividly illustrates what terrorism means and the threat it imposes'. After viewing the tapes, one congressman remarked, '... after the horror of New York, we must be reminded regularly the terrorists are still around, getting ready with all the power at their command to train new cadres to perpetrate the most horrendous crimes – from suicide bombings to the use of chemical or bio weapons'.[33]

With national and international focus on determining Iraq's arsenal of biological, chemical and nuclear weapons, our government has now admitted that 101,752 Allied soldiers were exposed to varying levels of toxic chemicals during the destruction of chemical weapons depots conducted in the Gulf War in 1991. For years, the Pentagon discounted claims of mysterious illnesses by Gulf War veterans being linked to toxic exposures of sarin, cyclosarin and mustard gases; however, the Office of Veterans Affairs has ordered another study to be conducted regarding this issue.[34] To date, the findings have not been released.

In November 2002, Scotland Yard officials arrested and charged three Arabic men with possessing materials for the 'preparation, instigation or commission of a terrorist act' that included the release of cyanide gas in the London subway system.[35] In January 2003, London police raided an apartment and found traces of ricin, a poison twice as deadly as cobra venom. They arrested six men of North African origin in the apartment under the Terrorism Act and charged them with chemical weapons offenses. Seven more suspects were arrested in a later raid on a north London mosque known as a center of radical Islam.[36]

In February 2003, an Italian judge indicted 12 terror suspects including nine Moroccans, a Pakistani, an Algerian, and a Tunisian suspected of plotting a chemical attack on the US Embassy in Rome. Police raids in Rome turned up 8.8 pounds of a cyanide-based compound, firecrackers and maps that highlighted the US Embassy and Rome's water supply.[37]

In May 2003, An Arabic-language magazine, *Al-Majalla*, quoted a senior member of al-Qaida about the possibility of the group poisoning US water supplies.[38] This brings up a good question. Why did it take the HSD five months to issue an advisory regarding this issue?

The threat is real enough for the military to consider new options for dealing with chemical attacks on the battlefield. The US government has approved a special skin lotion for soldiers to apply immediately after a chemical attack to neutralize potentially fatal or incapacitating effects of the agents used. The lotion that has been used for years by the Canadian military, RSDL (reactive skin decontamination lotion), is meant to neutralize chemical agents intended to be absorbed through the skin and not inhalants.[39]

An example of the use of a chemical agent

In October 2002, a widely publicized event occurred in Russia involving use of a chemical agent. Fifty-four heavily armed Chechen rebels took over a theatre less than three miles from the Kremlin and held 750 people hostage. The rebels demanded Russia remove its forces from Chechnya; if they refused, the rebels would blow up the building killing everyone, including themselves. The elite Alpha force verified the explosive threat as their squads carried out intelligence gathering prior to the rescue attempt. They reported the building was booby-trapped with mines at the entrances and exits as well as in passageways and on theatre seats. Two large bombs were strategically placed in the balcony and in the orchestra row. Approximately 20 Chechen female rebels (war widows) with their bodies wrapped in explosives sat among the hostages. Russian officials estimated the explosives were powerful enough to not only destroy the theatre building, but also many neighboring buildings as well. (Special Forces searching the building after the operation found 30 devices.)

Negotiations between the rebels and officials repeatedly broke down during the 58-hour ordeal. In order to make their point, the rebels killed two hostages – a man and a woman – and threatened to continue killing 10 hostages every hour until their conditions were fully met. The rebel group's commander issued a statement over the Chechen news website that said, 'No one will get out of here alive and they'll die with us if there's any attempt to storm the building'. Faced with the prospect of over 700 people getting killed (plus others in and around the buildings nearby), the Russian government decided to act. Russian Special Forces pumped an unknown gas into the building in an effort to incapacitate the rebels and prevent them from detonating their explosives during the rescue attempt.

Hostages reported no visible indication of the presence of the gas, but a strange 'pungent' smell. There were no irritating symptoms like those associated with tear gas or pepper spray. The hostages reported becoming sleepy, confused, and passing out.

The chemical attack killed 116 hostages and sent 405 others to hospitals, 45 in grave condition. The Special Forces shot the rebels incapacitated by the gas. The Russian government was criticized for lack of coordination that contributed to many victims' deaths. The lead chemist who heads Russia's Union of Chemical Security organization stated that many lives would have been saved if antidotes had been provided immediately after the attack.

Russia has refused to identify the gas used in the attack, but chemical experts believe it was an opiate-based compound based on the symptoms of the victims. US officials suspect the gas was an aerosol form of Fentanyl, a fast-acting opiate painkiller that has many medical applications. Russian doctors tried atropine, an antidote for nerve agents with no success in treating survivors; however, Arcane – a drug that reverses effects of opiates – did appear to help. According to doctors, many of the victims died of heart failure, respiratory distress or blood-circulation problems, from suffocating on their own vomit or swallowing their tongues while unconscious. Acute psychological stress, lack of bodily movement, chronic conditions that became acute during the time in the theatre and lack of food and water for more than 50 hours compounded the effects of the gas and contributed to many of the deaths. Some survivors report continued side effects of weakness, being unable to walk, red skin (like a sunburn), and mental confusion.[40, 41, 42, 43, 44, 45, 46, 47, 48, 49] Five weeks after the incident, all but five of the more than 650 hostages who were hospitalized were discharged; however, an unknown number have checked back into hospitals.[50]

What does this event have to do with aviation in America? Imagine a cell of approximately 20 terrorists taking over a large airport during a busy holiday weekend to effect the release of all al-Qaida prisoners currently held in Guantanamo Bay, Cuba.

Approximately 1,000 passengers and crewmembers are in the terminal/concourse area. The terrorists block the entrances and exits to the terminal and set a deadline for their conditions to be met. The heavily armed terrorists have four large explosive devices and some of them have explosives strapped to their bodies. Negotiations continue for days and conditions in the terminal become physically unbearable as lavatories become filthy, food and water run out. An elderly man dies of an apparent heart attack. A woman has a miscarriage. Terrorists announce that anyone caught using a cell phone will be shot immediately, as a lawyer finds out shortly after the announcement was made. Severely wounded, he pleads for help. The deadline passes with no results and the terrorists kill the wounded lawyer and a TSA security checkpoint agent, and threaten to kill more hostages unless conditions are met within a new deadline. The US government reacts and within a few hours, an incapacitating chemical agent is introduced into the airport ventilation system in an effort to prevent the suicidal terrorists from killing everyone. Everyone becomes incapacitated and the Hostage Rescue Team storms the terminal and kills the terrorists; however, 232 people die and 678 people are hospitalized from the effects of the chemical agent. Oh, by the way, communication broke down and no antidotes for the 'unknown' chemical agent were on hand, either at the terminal or at local hospitals. Doctors in surrounding hospitals are overwhelmed with the number of victims and have no idea how to treat them, 102 of which are listed as in critical condition and are in intensive care. A number of airline crewmembers were reported to have been in the food court of the terminal at the time and a preliminary report from the airlines indicate that at least six crewmembers died and 13 are among those listed as being in critical condition. Names were withheld by the airlines pending notification of next of kin. Government officials decline to release information on the type of agent used, but it is believed to be a new agent that was designed to incapacitate entire cities in an upcoming conflict in the Middle East region. This ordeal provided the government and the Pennsylvania State University's Applied Research Laboratory with a chance to test the chemical agent in an actual event prior to the upcoming conflict. Got the picture?

Okay, so this is NOT a Tom Clancy novel! Do you feel the need to know more about chemicals that may be used against you? We hope you do. Will you remember the names of all the complex chemical compounds? Probably not, but *hold your breath, do not touch anything,* and keep reading anyway.

Classification of Chemical Weapons

> The day I breathed the poison gas was the day I started to die.
>
> Iranian soldier, survivor of Iraqi chemical attack, 1988.[51]

Chemical weapons are classified as nerve, blister, choking, blood and incapacitating agents.[52] As weapons of terror, they are intended for use as 'area denial' and once you leave the area, you leave the risk. In reality, they are not 'gases'. They are vapors and/or airborne particles that are heavier than air. Generally speaking, they do not work when it is freezing, they do not last when it is hot, and movement of air, such as the wind, easily disperses them.[53]

Some chemical agents with the potential for being weaponized or otherwise disseminated by terrorists include chlorine, phosgene, diphosgene, hydrogen cyanide, hydrochloride, cyanide, ammonia, sarin, soman, cyclosarin, and vesicants (blistering agents, such as mustard gas). These substances may exist as solids, liquids or gases, depending upon temperature and pressure. Chemical agents used in munitions (the most likely being chlorine, phosgene, diphosgene or sulfur mustard) are usually in liquid form for dispersal upon detonation of the explosive.[54]

Nerve agents

> You go through violent tremors, vomiting, loss of bowel control and then suffocation. You can't breathe. You can't move. You can't do anything. You're dead.
>
> Norton Zinder, Geneticist at Rockefeller University[55]

Nerve agents work by disrupting the body's chemical message system that carries signals among nerve cells. The nerve gas attacks an enzyme that regulates the nervous system causing nerves to become overactive, exhausting them and producing convulsions.[56]

Nerve agents may be recognized by their odor, varying from the smell of new mown hay or green corn to something fruity or the smell of camphor. Droplets of nerve agent look like molasses or Karo syrup.[57] Multiple symptoms usually occur during nerve agent exposure and may include a sudden headache, dimness of vision, tearing, slow heart rate, muscle pain, weakness, seizures, runny nose, excessive saliva or drooling, difficulty breathing, tightness in the chest, convulsions, contractions of bladder and bowel, nausea, stomach cramps, and/or twitching of exposed skin.[58]

The antidotes for nerve agents are atropine (a muscle relaxant) and pralidoxime chloride. The antidotes must be administered within minutes of exposure. The antidotes send the body into overdrive for five minutes, after which the toxic agent is used up. Treatment for the inflicted usually involves trying to keep the person alive long enough for the nervous system to recover and muscle control can resume, using antidotes, CPR, or both.[59] Neither antidote is a cure for nerve agents.

- Sarin (GB) [60]
  - *Description*: developed by the Germans in 1936, sarin is a highly toxic compound existing in both clear liquid and vapor states that attacks the central nervous system; enters the body by inhalation, ingestion, through the eyes and skin; evaporates after two hours at 50 degrees Fahrenheit; has no odor. Although sarin gas can seep through the skin, inhalation delivers a lethal dose 400 times faster.[61]

- *Effects*: can cause death within minutes after exposure; symptoms vary, but may include runny nose, tearing, drooling, excessive sweating, difficulty in breathing, dimness of vision, nausea, vomiting, headache and twitching; interferes with nerve impulses causing convulsions and paralysis of the lungs and blood vessels, literally suffocating its victims.
- *Treatment*: immediate decontamination by removing clothing, flushing the eyes and skin with water.
- *Antidote*: available at many hospitals.

• VX [62]

- *Description:* the most toxic of all (known) chemical compounds; comes in clear to straw colored liquid or vapor forms; considered 100 times more toxic by entry through the skin than sarin and twice as toxic by inhalation; can persist for long periods under average weather conditions and for months in very cold temperatures; can enter the body by inhalation, ingestion, through the eyes and through the skin; and, has no odor.
- *Effects*: can cause death within minutes after exposure; interferes with nerve impulses causing convulsions and paralysis of the lungs and blood vessels, literally suffocating its victims; symptoms vary, but may include runny nose, tearing, drooling, excessive sweating, difficulty in breathing, dimness of vision, nausea and twitching.
- *Treatment*: immediate decontamination by removing clothing, flushing the eyes and skin with water.
- *Antidote*: available at many hospitals.

Blister agents[63]

Blister (vesicant) agents include the mixture of compounds collectively known as 'mustard' or 'mustard gas' (H). Other blister agents are sulfur mustard (HD), nitrogen mustard (HN), phosgene oxime (CX) and Lewisite (L), an arsenic based compound.

Lewisite is differentiated from the mustards by pain beginning immediately upon skin contact. Nasal irritation, sneezing and pungent odor provide early warning of the presence of (L) vapor.

The diagnosis of blister agent-induced injury is straightforward once blisters have appeared; however, early recognition of exposure can be difficult since eye inflammation and upper respiratory tract irritation are common to a number of other chemical agents as well. In addition, although skin damage occurs within minutes of contact, it may not be recognized until blisters form several hours later. After a 1–12 hour latent period during which burning and itching may occur, redness appears on exposed skin, followed by translucent, yellowish blisters on a red base.

- Sulfur Mustard (HD)
  - *Description*: smells like onions, garlic or mustard; pale yellow or dark brown in color; in vapor or liquid forms can be absorbed through the eyes, skin and mucous membranes.
  - *Effects*: begins dissolving tissues on contact, causing skin injuries similar to burns and damage to lungs and eyes; usually not fatal, the gas can cause blindness, lung problems (bronchopneumonia), ravaged bowels, disorientation, and welts and blisters.
  - *Treatment*: do not pop the blisters, as the liquid inside will cause the affected area to spread; soap and cold water washing and fresh air immediately after contamination are the best solutions you may have to remedy an exposure (hot water and/or scrubbing both accelerate absorption and increased vapor formation).
  - *Antidote*: None.

Choking agents[64]

This group of chemical agents produces irritation of the upper and lower respiratory tracts. Agents in this category include phosgene (CG), diphosgene (DP), and chlorine (CL).

- Phosgene (CG)
  - *Description*: a vapor that smells like cut grass (if you can smell the odor, you have been exposed); approximately three times heavier than air, CG hugs the ground as a white cloud that spill into low lying places.
  - *Effects*: causes lung edema (filling with fluid) leading to suffocation; full effects of exposure may not be realized until 4–6 hours after exposure; tearing, painful cough, frothy sputum, cyanosis, chest discomfort, and difficulty breathing are symptoms of impending edema of the lungs.
  - *Treatment*: fresh air in the case of inhalation; rinsing with plenty of water in case of exposure to skin or eyes.
  - *Antidote*: None.
- Chlorine (CL)
  - *Description*: a greenish-yellow gas with a pungent odor; heavier than air; reacts violently with many organic compounds creating a fire and explosive hazard.
  - *Effects*: corrosive to the eyes, causes tearing, blurred vision and burns; inhalation may cause labored breathing and lung edema (not often manifested until hours after exposure); high exposure levels can cause death.
  - *Treatment*: fresh air in the case of inhalation; rinsing with plenty of water in case of exposure to skin or eyes.
  - *Antidote*: None.

Blood agents[65]

Blood agents cause aerobic cellular metabolism (the passing of oxygen from the blood to the cells) to come to a virtual halt. Venous blood remains as oxygen rich as arterial blood since oxygen is unable to be metabolized. Hydrogen cyanide (AC), cyanogen chloride (CK) and potassium cyanide (PC) are agents in this category. Potassium cyanide poisoning of water and food supplies has been used in the past by terrorists.

- Hydrogen Cyanide (AC)
  - *Description*: extremely flammable as a colorless gas or liquid; gives off toxic fumes in a fire and is highly explosive.
  - *Effects*: irritates the eyes, skin and respiratory tract; symptoms include burning and redness of the skin and eyes; inhalation causes confusion, drowsiness, shortness of breath leading to collapse; can affect the CNS resulting in impaired respiratory and circulatory functions; exposure can be fatal.
  - *Treatment*: Fresh air in the case of inhalation; rinsing with water in case of skin or eye exposure.
  - *Antidote*: none.

> In May 1995, an attempted hydrogen cyanide gas attack was narrowly averted by subway guards in Tokyo, only two months after the sarin gas attack on the subway. A small fire was used to create and disperse the gas from a restroom that ventilated to a station platform.[66]

Incapacitating agents[67]

Incapacitation agents have potent CNS effects that seriously impair normal function but do not endanger life or cause permanent damage in operationally effective doses. Quinuclidinyl benzilate (BZ) is a representative agent of this category. CNS symptoms run the gamut from inattention, confusion, anxiety, restlessness and hallucinations on up to delirium, and they may last for days.

Exposure to any of these chemical agents – *nerve, blister, choking, blood, incapacitating* – is a scary proposition to say the least. Flight crewmembers are ill-equipped to recognize or effectively deal with exposures to these agents, on or off the aircraft.

Common chemicals

There are some types of chemicals that are not classified as 'weapons', but non-the-less may be effectively employed against crewmembers and/or passengers – and they are relatively cheap and are easy to obtain.

Common chemicals may be effectively used to destroy or injure sight, or to impair respiration, or to destroy or injure the skin. Obviously, destroying one's ability to see greatly impairs the ability to defend oneself or others. During the takeover of aircraft on 9/11, hijackers used small plastic squirt bottles containing hair dye to dispense the chemical into the eyes of their victims. The purpose in doing this was to cause the victim to close their eyes in pain so they could not see the box cutter or knife used to cut their throats. Some of the chemicals to be considered as possible terrorist weapons fall into the categories of acids, caustic liquids and defensive sprays. There have been numerous incidents in the past several years of the inadvertent release of defensive sprays in airports and on aircraft. In addition, the transport of many chemicals on an aircraft or other mode of transportation poses a threat, both from a terrorist standpoint and from chemical accidents. An example of the latter occurred in February 2003 when a 100+ rail-car freight train derailed in the middle of the town of Tamoroa, Illinois. Over 1,000 people were evacuated in a three-mile area due to leaking chemicals and a subsequent fire. The chemical included vinyl chloride, formaldehyde, methanol, and hydrochloric acid, all hazardous to breathe and lethal in high concentrations. Each car carried 24,000 pounds of chemicals.[68]

- Acids
  - Muratic acid (used to clean ceramic tiles)
  - battery acid
  - citrus acid (lemon, lime, grapefruit juice)
- Caustic liquids
  - Bleach
  - hair dye
  - Drano
  - oven cleaner
  - others (read the labels on products in your cabinets)
- Defensive sprays
  - CN – Chloroacetophenone – a lachrymator, color-coded red (Mace)
  - CS – Orthochlorobenzalmalononitrile – an irritant, color-coded blue
  - OC – Oleoresin Capsicum – an inflammatory, color-coded orange (Pepper Spray)

Chemical defensive sprays [69, 70, 71]

- CN and CS – Tear Gas
  - Better known as Mace (a brand name), CN is a solid, not a gas or liquid, as is CS. CN and CS micro particulate solids are simply suspended a specific liquid carrier and are dispensed along with the liquid in the form of a spray. The liquid carrier evaporates quickly, leaving dust-like solids airborne or on a surface where the chemical can begin to work. CN and CS work through the tear ducts (hence 'tear gas') making it ineffective on dogs and other animals

that do not have tear ducts. CS is also an irritant to the skin. CN and CS behave in similar ways, producing copious tearing and irritation in contact areas. Both make breathing uncomfortable with the effects of CS being more intense in addition to causing a heavier mucous flow.

- Clinical effects of CN and/or CS by area of the body affected include:
  - Eyes – burning, irritation, tearing, inflammation of the eye, sensitivity to light
  - Skin – burning, redness
  - Gastrointestinal tract – gagging, retching, vomiting
  - Airways – sneezing, coughing, tightness in chest, irritation, copious secretions
  - Nose – burning pain, runny nose
  - Mouth – burning of mucous membranes, salivation
- Since CN and CS make the subject very uncomfortable and do not actually incapacitate when used in an aerosol, these chemicals do not often affect persons with mental states altered by intoxicants, disease or simple rage. It is estimated that CN or CS is only effective 60 per cent of the time and generally takes a minute or so to become fully effective. It may not affect people who are intoxicated, on drugs or mentally ill.
- CS is almost insoluble in water and only slightly soluble in ethyl alcohol and carbon tetrachloride. Because of these physical characteristics, decontamination of buildings, furniture, and other materials exposed to CS is very difficult, time consuming and expensive. Highly flammable, the use of CS was a large contributor to the conflagration that burned the Branch Davidian compound and inhabitants in Waco, Texas in 1993.

• OC (Pepper Spray)[72, 73, 74]

In August 2002, a Miami International Airport concourse was evacuated for three hours after a pepper spray can was discharged into the ventilation system causing 43 people to suffer respiratory distress. The can was disguised as a cigarette lighter. Paramedics treated the victims for breathing problems and the associated symptoms of scratchy throat, watery eyes, coughing and sneezing.[75]

- Unlike CN and CS that are manufactured chemicals irritants, OC is made from oleoresin capsicum oil extracted from cayenne or habaneras peppers and is a natural inflammatory agent. More than 200 varieties of peppers grown worldwide are rated on a Scoville scale (named for the inventor) with bell peppers being zero, jalapenos at 5,000, cayenne ranging from 2,500 to 25,000 and habaneras around 85,000.[76] Through processing by any one of over 200 manufacturers, OC oil is converted into a concentrate that has a heat rating of up to 2.5 million. The final product contains a percentage based on the 2.5 million rating and varies from 1 per cent (civilian) to 5–10 per cent (police) to 15-20 per cent (animal control – mainly bear).[77] Regardless of the difference in percentage, the effects are the same except for two important details – the larger the percentage, the stronger the effects and the longer the effects last. The direct effects of OC last for up to 45 minutes, although some symptoms have been reported as lasting as long as a week.[78]

Both authors have had extensive experience with defensive sprays. As a police officer, Waltrip was taught the proper use of sprays and being sprayed was part of his training. He has used OC pepper spray on multiple individuals with varying levels of success. Williams, a certified defensive spray instructor, has taught defensive spray classes as part of personal protection courses for men and women. To be certified as an instructor, Williams also had to be sprayed and reported the mucous lining of his nose peeled continually for over 6 months. Neither man would list being sprayed as something they would like to do on a regular basis.

- OC has the strong odor of cayenne pepper. The effects of OC are almost instantaneous and the spray is effective 95 per cent of the time, even on people who are intoxicated or on drugs. OC in the eyes causes immediate pain with difficulty in keeping the eyelids open and copious tearing (you will wonder where all that water came from!). OC dilates the capillaries of the eyes and may cause temporary blindness. OC inhaled causes an intense burning sensation in the nose, mouth, and throat, accompanied by swelling. Breathing becomes difficult and limited to shallow breaths accompanied by uncontrollable coughing and wheezing. Mucous will flow from your nose in a steady stream. OC on the skin causes a burning sensation as the OC particles enter pores. Other symptoms include vomiting, diarrhea, fatigue, headaches and disorientation.[79]
- OC spray leaves a fine oily, sticky residue, so wiping it off is difficult. In fact, by wiping you may cause the OC particles to be further imbedded in the pores of the skin. Wiping the eyes with hands or fingers that are contaminated with OC particles will only serve to make matters worse.
- If you suspect OC spray has been introduced into the aircraft, the following are suggestions that may help the crew and passengers:

Pilots –

- Isolate the flight deck;
- Don oxygen masks and use 100 per cent oxygen until on the ground and parked;
- Raise cabin altitude to open outflow valve and better ventilate the aircraft;
- Turn off recirculation fans;
- Turn air conditioning fans to high flow and lower cabin temperature;
- Turn seatbelt sign ON and make a PA;
- Consider deploying the emergency oxygen system in the cabin;

- Consider declaring an emergency if cockpit is contaminated or if any person is experiencing major difficulties.

Cabin Crews –

- Notify flight deck immediately if OC spray is detected in the cabin;
- Do not open the flight deck door;
- It will be up to you (what is new!) to take care of yourself, other crewmembers and passengers, and that may be difficult until the air conditioning flow takes airborne particles out through the outflow valve, which should take about 3–4 minutes from the time the pilots raise the cabin altitude;
- Consider use of emergency oxygen walk-around bottles or personal breathing equipment;
- If the cabin emergency oxygen system is activated, instruct passengers to don and use the masks until notified otherwise;
- If the source of the OC is near the front of the aircraft cabin, expect the vapor to travel to the rear of the aircraft to the outflow valve area;
- If the source is at the rear of the aircraft, most of the OC particles will exit through the outflow valve by normal airflow, but some may be reintroduced into the entire aircraft until the pilots turn off the recirculation fans;
- Everything that particles touch will be contaminated; do not distribute any uncovered food, ice, or opened cups or cans of beverages to anyone;
- Be aware of any person exhibiting extreme breathing problems (extreme tearing and nose-running are ugly and uncomfortable, but not deadly) and administer first aid oxygen as appropriate. *Note*: People who have asthma, bronchitis, or other respiratory illnesses, or heart problems are more susceptible to the debilitating effects of OC.80
- Do NOT apply ointments or solutions, other than water, as usually this will worsen the condition.
- Do not penetrate packaged or canned goods, but they must be rinsed off before opening to avoid contamination of the whatever is inside.
- While you are waiting for the air to clear, breath through wet napkins or paper towels and keep your eyes closed (give these to others, as well);
- Bottles of water may be used to flush eyes; fill ice buckets, coffee pots, empty soda cans or any other container with water for people to use to flush eyes/nose/mouth or wash their uncovered hands/face/arms; ice, or ice packs, will be effective in reducing pain, but not in removing the OC particles.

– If you suspect you have encountered OC spray, flush eyes, nose, mouth and throat (gargle) with copious amounts of water (emphasis on 'copious'). Wash all exposed skin with soap (if available) and water. Take a full shower when possible; however, before you do, wash your hair with your head hanging down (like over the bath tub) to prevent OC particles from traveling from your hair back into your eyes (a tip from personal experience). Clothes may be washed (or dry cleaned) normally. Do not forget to clean your shoes and wash the soles.

Part 2: Biological Weapons

> Humans are often the most sensitive, or the only, detector of a biological attack. Without knowledge of the attack, an increased number of patients presenting with signs and symptoms caused by the disseminated disease agent is the most likely first indicator that use of a biological weapon has occurred.[81]

Background

Like chemical warfare, biological agents have been used for thousands of years. Dead or diseased animals would be put into sources of water – streams, wells, and lakes. Tips of arrows and spears were dipped in feces or blood of decomposing bodies. Corpses infected with diseases such as the plague or smallpox would be thrown or catapulted over castle or city walls.[82] During the fourteenth-century siege of Kaffa (now Feodossia, Ukraine), the attacking Tartar force experienced an epidemic of plague. The Tartars attempted to convert their misfortune into an opportunity by catapulting the cadavers of their deceased into the city to initiate a plague epidemic. An outbreak of plague was followed by the retreat of defending forces and the conquest of Kaffa by the Tartars. Ships carrying plague-infected refugees sailed to Constantinople, Genoa, Venice and other Mediterranean ports and are thought to have been the source of a second widespread epidemic.[83]

During World War II, the Japanese used biological warfare against China. At least 11 Chinese cities were attacked with biological agents. The attacks included contaminating water supplies and food items with pure cultures of anthrax, cholera, salmonella and other biological agents. Cultures were also thrown into homes and sprayed from aircraft. Plague was developed by allowing laboratory-bred fleas to feed on plague-infected rats. Aircraft released as many as 15 million fleas per attack over the 11 cities. An attack on one of the four Japanese biological warfare sites led to approximately 10,000 biological casualties and 1,700 deaths among Japanese troops, mostly due to cholera.[84]

The Allies developed biological weapons for potential retaliatory use in response to a German biological attack; however, the only known German tactical use of biological warfare was the pollution of a large reservoir in northwestern Bohemia with sewage. Bomb experiments of weaponized spores of anthrax were conducted on Gruinard Island near the coast of Scotland and resulted in heavy contamination of the island. Viable anthrax spores persisted until the island was decontaminated with formaldehyde and seawater during 1986.[85]

Apparently, the US conducted its own testing of 50 chemical and biological agents from 1962 to 1973 that involved 5,842 soldiers, many of which had no knowledge of their participation in the experiments. Continuation of the investigations by the Pentagon into the experiments, called Project 112 and Project SHAD, are being supported by members of Congress.[86]

Although much of the focus today is on the military use of biological warfare, bioterrorism can come from civilian sources as well. For instance, in 1978, Jim Jones in Guyana laced Kool-Aid with cyanide, killing 900 people. In 1982, Tylenol in the US was laced with cyanide.[87] In 1984 the Rajneesh cult poisoned salad bars in Oregon with salmonella, sickening some 750 people.[88] In 1995, two members of a Minnesota militia group were convicted of possession of ricin they produced for use in retaliation against local government officials. In 1996, an Ohio man connected with an extremist group was able to obtain bubonic plague cultures through the postal service.[89] Although NOT the work of terrorists, an example in Ecuador in November 2002 illustrates how easily biological agents can be introduced into drinking water sources and the effects such an event may have on the general population. Water tainted with cow manure penetrated a broken drinking water pipeline, contaminating the water supply for Ibarra. One child died and 1,200 people were treated for diarrhea, vomiting and dehydration from E. coli bacteria in the water.[90] In April 2003, an Egyptian ship bound for Quebec, Canada was quarantined offshore after a crewman apparently died of anthrax infection. The crewman died before the ship left Brazilian waters en route to Canada. An autopsy was performed in Brazil and the body was returned to Egypt. Brazilian authorities suspect the man died of anthrax and it is unknown whether contamination on the ship was the cause.[91]

More sophisticated in some respects today, bioterrorism still has the capability to instill fear and anxiety, pain and suffering, and death among victims in an effort to annihilate an adversary, or to make them too sick to fight or function. Biological weapons are characterized by low visibility, high potency, substantial accessibility, and relatively easy delivery.[92]

The most distinguishing feature separating biological terrorism from conventional terrorism is the extraordinarily large number of casualties that could follow a major biological terrorist attack. Each act of bioterrorism could result in hundreds of thousands or millions of casualties since civilian populations are not immunized against most biological agents and do not have protective equipment readily available, such as filtered respirators and gas masks.[93] The head of the former Soviet agency that manufactured biological agents told a subcommittee of the House National Security Committee that 'causing illness or death' was the fifth most important reason for use of biological weapons. The others, in order, are: 'inciting panic and fear, paralyzing the nation, overwhelming medical services, and causing severe economic damage'.[94]

A biological weapon is more than just the use of a pathogenic microorganism or toxin. It is a system composed of four major components:

1 Payload – the biological agent
2 Munition – a container that keeps the payload intact and virulent during delivery
3 Delivery system – missile, artillery shell, aircraft, etc.
4 Dispersal mechanism – an explosive force or spray device to dispense the agent to the target population.[95]

The most likely bioterrorism attack would involve realeasing any number of biological agents into the air as a biological aerosol, a stable cloud of suspended microscopic droplets of bacterial or virus particles. This attack could be accomplished by use of low-flying aircraft, crop-dusters, or trucks equipped with spray tanks and releasing the biological agent upwind of populated areas. Aerosol canisters filled with an agent and employed through use of a timing device could be placed in subways, airports, air-conditioning/heating systems of buildings, or other crowded places. Contamination of bulk food supplies in restaurants, supermarkets, food-processing plants, or food distribution centers is another possibility.[96] The idea of infection caused by invisible agents is frightening.

Widespread panic will be a particular risk when biological agents are used to threaten or to attack a sizeable civilian population. Fear will understandably be great as people watch their fellow citizens and loved ones fall ill and possibly die in large numbers due to some biological agent. Contingency plans for dealing with public hysteria and disruption of all public services must be part of every city's emergency reaction plans. People fleeing an area of known contamination will undoubtedly spread the disease elsewhere. An important part of the response to bioterrorism will be dealing with the psychological reactions among survivors, emergency workers and the public.[97] The combination of the novelty of biological warfare and the activation of deeply rooted fears predict that strong psychological and physiological responses will occur.[98]

The threat is real

> In my view, the threat from anonymously-delivered biological weapons and from emerging infectious diseases simply dwarfs the threat that we will be attacked by a third-world ICBM with a return address.
>
> Senate Foreign Relations Committee Chairman, Joseph Biden[99]

The view of Congressman Biden is shared by many other experts and government officials. Former CIA director James Woolsey said a biological attack on the US by terrorists or an enemy state is the most serious threat the nation faces from weapons of mass destruction. Former Senator Sam Nunn, a one-time chairman of the foreign relations committee, said he would put the biological threat to the US 'near the top of the list'.[100] Dr Anthony Fauci, director of the National Institute of Health said, 'The threat of smallpox as a bioterrorist weapon is real and health officials are doing everything they can to keep the citizens of our nation safe from such an attack'.[101]

Even though biological weapons are excellent killing machines, they make poor weapons for military objectives, such as seizing territory, due mainly to the fact the agents usually have rather lengthy incubation times making the effects more long term than immediate. The delivery method and conditions (such as wind and weather) also plays a huge factor in the employment of biological agents. There has been considerable restraint by nations possessing biological weapons in not deploying these weapons for moral reasons and for the certainty of massive retaliation if the weapons were indeed used.[102] However, all of these factors are outside the thinking of terrorists today as we have witnessed during the fight against al-Qaida. Terrorist groups have no borders or defined battlefields. They seek mass destruction of civilians, as well as military personnel, and are not deterred by fear of retaliation.

The potential impact of biological weapons is well illustrated by a 1970 World Health Organization publication. It estimated that 50 kilograms of aerosolized anthrax spores dispensed by an aircraft two km upwind of a population center of 500,000 unprotected people in ideal meteorological conditions would travel more than 20 km and kill or incapacitate up to 220,000 people, nearly half of those in the path of the biological cloud.[103]

Between 1985 and 1991, Iraq developed anthrax, botulinum toxin, and aflatoxin for biological weapons. Two hundred bombs and 25 ballistic missiles laden with biological agents were deployed by the time Operation Desert Storm occurred. Of the 25 missiles, 13 were filled with botulinum toxin, ten with aflatoxin, and two with anthrax. In 1990, Iraq modified a MIG-21 fighter aircraft to be remotely piloted and equipped it with a 2200-liter belly tank fitted with a spray mechanism. In a field test carried out in January 1991, the remotely controlled jet sprayed a solution laden with a simulated biological agent over a practice target range. The results of the tests are unknown.[104]

During a bio-warfare simulation called Dark Winter conducted by the government in 2002, US Senator Sam Nunn assumed the role of 'President'. Later, in a congressional hearing Senator Nunn summarized lessons learned from the exercise. Those remarks bear repeating.

> We have effectively only 12 million doses of smallpox vaccine in America to protect a population of 275 million that is not highly vaccinated and is therefore highly vulnerable.
>
> Our simulation began with 20 confirmed 'cases' in Oklahoma City; 30 suspected cases spread out in Oklahoma, Georgia and Pennsylvania, and countless more cases of individuals who were infected, but didn't know it.
>
> The effects of a bomb are bounded in time and place. After the explosion, the nation's leadership knows if you're injured, and the extent of the damage.
>
> Smallpox, on the other hand, is a silent, ongoing, invisible attack. It is highly contagious and spreads in a flash – each smallpox victim can infect 10–20 others. Because it incubates for two weeks, it comes in waves.
>
> The most insidious effect of a biological weapons attack is that it could turn Americans against Americans. Once smallpox is released, it is not the terrorists anymore who are the threat; your neighbors and your family members can become the threat, and can even become the enemy.

> For more than 2,000 years, the first rule of war has been to know your enemy. You estimate the number of tanks and planes and troops of the enemy, their intelligence capabilities, and other resources.
>
> But in this case, the order of battle would be our own people, traveling, engaging in commerce, and spreading the disease. You don't know who initially released the virus, how much more germ agent they have, or where they are. The usual responses to attack are impossible: 'Engage the enemy, open fire, stop the advance, bring out the wounded'. You can hardly know who IS wounded.
>
> Since smallpox has not been seen in the US since 1949, very few health care professionals would recognize the virus. Initial cases could be sent back home infectious, even after appearing at doctors' offices or emergency rooms. Laboratory facilities needed to diagnose the disease are inadequate and out of date.
>
> Hospitals run at capacity all the time; a surge in patients from smallpox, combined with the inevitable infections of hospital personnel and the flight of some fearful health care professionals would create a catastrophic overload.
>
> We have 12 million doses of vaccine, enough for one in every 23 Americans. Whom do we decide to vaccinate?
>
> Do you seize hotels and convert them into hospitals? Do you close borders and stop all travel?
>
> What level of force do you use to keep someone sick in isolation? Do you keep people known, or thought to be exposed, quarantined in their homes? Do you guarantee 2.5 million doses of vaccine to the military?
>
> How do you talk to the public in a way that is candid, yet prevents panic – knowing that panic itself can be a weapon of mass destruction?
>
> Naturally, there are some skeptics anytime you describe a dire threat to the United States. *I want to tell you, I am convinced the threat of a biological weapons attack on the US is very real.* An experiment some years ago showed that a scientist whose specialty was in another field was able to weaponize anthrax on his first attempt, for less than $250,000. Hundreds of labs and repositories around the world sell biological agents for legitimate research.
>
> We need to focus more attention, concern and resources on the specific threat of bioterrorism. We are considering ways to improve infectious disease surveillance around the globe, including rapid detection through state of the art sensors, investigational and a fast and effective response.
>
> The national pharmaceutical stockpile should be built to capacity as soon as possible, and then dispersed to different sites that must be secured. We don't want to fall victim to a twin attack that releases a bio-agent and simultaneously blows up all our drugs and vaccines.
>
> Officials at the highest levels of the federal government – and at state and local levels – need to participate in exercises like Dark Winter to understand the importance of advance preparation. Theater professionals rehearse for months before the real event. This is one case where life had better imitate art for the sake of like itself.[105]

Unlike the immediate consequences of an explosive device, the consequences of a biological attack may not be realized for days or weeks, depending upon type of agent, recognition of exposure, and correct diagnosis of symptoms. Due to relative long incubation times of some biological agents, their effects may have been widely transmitted before cases are detected allowing the disease to become widespread throughout the population.[106] Information from various sources regarding incidents in the past ten years underscore the reality of the threat from chemical and/or biological warfare, whether from a rogue nation such as Iraq, or from any of the 270 known terrorist groups. Here are a few highlights.

February 1992 – Twenty-six specimens of anthrax, Ebola and other pathogens were listed as missing from the Army's biological laboratory at Fort Detrick, Maryland. The discovery was found after an inventory ordered by a new commander at the lab who found 'little or no organization and little or no accountability'. The fate of the missing specimens remains unknown.[107]

December 1998 – During Operation Desert Fox, a British missile sheared the top off a military hangar in southern Iraq, exposing a drone aircraft specially modified to disperse chemical and/or biological agents. Up to a dozen of the unmanned aircraft were spotted, each fitted with spray nozzles and wing-mounted 80-gallon tanks. It is far from certain that an aircraft-mounted chemical or biological attack would be successful, especially against troops, but at the minimum the capabilities offer new ways to terrorize civilian populations, particularly in the cities of Israel, Saudi Arabia and Kuwait. In addition, Iraq is known to have converted crop dusting gear into a germ-spraying device mounted on helicopters. It has also developed biowarfare 'drop tanks' that can be mounted on Iraqi fighter aircraft.[108]

April 1999 – Defense officials have alerted Congress to evidence of a 'dramatic increase' in interest in germ weapons on the part of terrorists, criminals and 'rogue' states. The reality is that any nation or terrorist group capable of producing beer or household pesticides has the potential to make and hide biological and chemical weapons. The biological threat is fueled by a variety of factors, from the cheap cost and easy availability of lethal agents, to poorly recognized changes in the psychology of terrorism. Some experts consider mass murder a distinct possibility, an inevitable occurrence by others.[109]

March 2000 – It was revealed that a California doctor who committed suicide had passed a bag filled with cholera, typhoid, botulism, anthrax, and bubonic plague to a South African military doctor involved in Project Coast – a project that has been trying to create deadly bacteria and other diseases that only affect Blacks. Investigators dug up the doctor's yard and found a cache of military-grade weapons and explosives. In the doctor's refrigerator, they found jars containing germs that cause typhoid and cholera.[110]

February 2002 – The CIA director said the contents of documents discovered in Afghanistan indicate Osama bin Laden was seeking a sophisticated biological weapons research program. Interrogations of al-Qaida fighters have substantiated these findings.[111]

March 2002 – US forces uncovered a laboratory near Kandahar, Afghanistan designed to manufacture anthrax that was apparently not up and running when deserted during the attacks on al-Qaida. Five other laboratories have been found that tested positive for anthrax and another biotoxin, ricin, extracted from castor beans.[112]

September 2002 – The National Academy of Sciences reported that America's food supply is vulnerable to an agricultural bioterrorist attack and the US is unable to prevent it, poorly equipped to spot it and not prepared to respond to it. An attack using biologic diseases against crops and livestock would be comparatively easy to undertake compared with the bombing of the WTC. Among the diseases and pests that could be used to attack crops and livestock are: Mediterranean fruit flies; the nipah virus, which is carried by pigs; and karnal blunt, a fungus that attacks wheat. The report states the government does not know enough about foreign pests and diseases to be able to stop them. Although such attacks would not lead to famine, it could cripple the nation's food industry, lead to quarantines on US agriculture and shake Americans' confidence in what they eat.[113]

During intense interrogation in March 2003, Khalid Shaikh Mohammed, the principal author of the attacks on 9/11 and currently a US prisoner, began to provide information regarding the biochemical abilities of the al-Qaida organization. His information, corroborated with a newly acquired cache of documentary evidence, indicates the al-Qaida biochemical weapons program was considerably more advanced than previously thought. The evidence and testimony show al-Qaida completed plans and obtained the materials required to manufacture botulinum and salmonella (biological toxins) and the chemical poison cyanide. Among the documents was a direction to purchase the bacterium that causes anthrax, and they are close to production of the toxin. Evidence also points to the enlistment of competent scientists including a Pakistani microbiologist and a Pakistani bacteriologist, who by the way had access to production facilities and materials and has since disappeared.[114]

The good news, if there is any, is that biological agents are very difficult to produce to be kept alive, to be transported and to be employed. A study in mid-2000 by the Center of International and Security Studies at the University of Maryland concluded that:

- Hoaxes and threats were more likely than actual use of biological agents;
- Small-scale sabotage attacks or attempts at personal murder were more likely than large-scale attempts at mass casualties; and,
- A crude dispersal of a biological agent in a close area was the most likely mode of attack.[115]

The first point made regarding hoaxes also proved to be very true. The US Postal Service received nearly 12,000 hoaxes, threats and suspicious mail incidents involving anthrax by November 2001, resulting in evacuation of 429 postal facilities for varying periods of time.

The next predictions came true in October 2001 when small-scale, crude dispersals of anthrax spores (less than a gram total between all the incidents) arrived by mail to selected individuals' offices in Florida, Virginia, New Jersey, Washington DC and New York, killing five people and infecting 13 others.

It was revealed in November 2002 the FBI has been working for months trying to replicate the type of anthrax used in the attacks in 2001. FBI Director Mueller stated the scientists were using reverse engineering in their process of trying to duplicate an anthrax agent as sophisticated as the anthrax samples taken from the attacks last year.[116] Their difficulty points out the fact that most terrorist organizations probably do not have the sophisticated equipment and knowledge to produce military grade anthrax leading to the conclusion that such materials would probably come from a terrorist sponsor state, such as Iraq.

The hunt for the perpetrator of the anthrax attacks continues in 2003. In June, the FBI began draining a 1.45 million gallon pond near Fredrick, Maryland in a search for evidence the person who carried out the attacks filled the envelopes with the anthrax spores under water for his or her protection. In May, some evidence was found in the pond that supported an anonymous tip regarding the procedure. The pond is near the Army Medical Research Institute of Infectious Diseases at Fort Detrick, the primary custodian of the particular strain of anthrax found in the envelopes sent to the victims.[117] A couple of months later and US$250,000 poorer, authorities had found nothing of interest in soil samples taken from bottom of the pond.[118]

Data from the Monterey Institute of International Studies indicate that 262 biological incidents occurred between 1900 and mid-2001. Of the 262 incidents, 157 (60 per cent) were terrorist cases, the remaining cases being the work of criminals. Of the 262 incidents, 173 were hoaxes, 55 were threats that did not materialize, and only 34 cases involved actual use of a biological agent with nine of those occurring in the US.[119] Even the hoaxes cause terror and widespread concern, however. In August 2002, two employees opened an envelope with a suspicious white powder in Al Gore's Tennessee base of operations. Tests on the powder were negative for anthrax. In September 2002, envelopes containing a suspicious white powder, delivered to US consulates in Munich, Hamburg, Leipzig, Duesseldorf and Frankfort, Germany and to US embassies in Denmark and Italy, prompted concern at diplomatic posts across Europe of a potential biological attack. Again, fortunately, tests results were negative.[120]

Are we prepared as a nation for a chemical or biological attack? The answer to that question depends upon whom you ask.

Yes

- Health and Human Services Secretary Tommy Thompson during an interview on CBS *60 Minutes* said, 'We've got to make sure that people understand that they're safe. And, that we're prepared to take care of any contingency, any consequence that develops from any kind of bioterrorism attack'. He stated that eight staging areas around America were stocked with 50 tons of medical supplies – including vaccines, antibiotics, gas masks and ventilators – that can be moved to the site of any bioterrorist attack. He also indicated there were approximately 7,000 personnel ready to respond to any crisis anywhere in the country.[121]

- Parkland Hospital in Dallas has a stockpile of drugs, including an antidote for sarin nerve gas, antibiotics for anthrax, and medication to relieve suffering. It also has a bioterrorism response team and has trained the staff using simulated attacks.[122] The Department of Health and Human Services reported on 1 November 2002 that Florida is the only state ready to receive the National Pharmaceutical Stockpile of medicine and vaccines in case of an emergency. Although 31 October was the deadline for states to report progress in preparing for bioterrorism, only 20 states had complied. They have until 1 December to produce detailed plans for vaccinating their entire populations within days of a smallpox attack.[123]
- After two biological scares in April 2003 (one in Florida and the other in Washington State), federal authorities said communications were quickly established between local responders and the Department of Homeland Security's coordination center. A spokesperson for the department said, 'We expect these things to happen and we're ready to respond and prepared to communicate with state and local governments'. The Centers for Disease Control in Atlanta, which also has a role to play, was not called on for its expertise in either of the two events.[124]

No

- In January 2000, the American Medical Association reported hospitals and other health care facilities were 'poorly prepared' for any bioterrorism attack. Only 25 per cent of 6,000 hospitals are at some state of readiness for a chemical or biological incident.[125]
- A study published in the Journal of the American Public Health Association in mid-2000 revealed that less than 20 per cent of all hospitals they surveyed on the East Coast had adequate disaster plans.[126]
- In November 2001, the General Accounting Office reported that Army medical department officials indicated that chemical and biological scenarios causing mass casualties would overwhelm current medical capabilities.[127]
- In November 2001, Surgeon General Koop said, 'We were not prepared for the anthrax bio-attack, regardless of source. And the fear generated by it far outweighed the health threat. Think of the distraction and the chaos involved with fewer than 50 anthrax victims, real or uncertain in the anthrax scare. How would our resources handle not 50, but 5,000? How about 50,000? How about 5 million?'[128]
- The National Association of Counties reported in January 2002 that more than half the nation's 731 counties with populations of less than 10,000 are unprepared to respond to a bioterrorism or chemical attack. About one-fourth of all counties in the US fall into this category.[129]
- A survey in January 2002 found 75 per cent of county public health departments have the authority to impose quarantines; however, 60 per cent of those departments do not have a plan to enforce or implement quarantine.[130]

- In April 2002, Senator Bill Frist (who is also a physician), said nine out of ten public health departments in the US do not have anyone trained in combating bioterrorism, and as many as one-third lack an Internet connection for fast communications.[131]
- The Council on Foreign Relations released a report in June 2003 that indicated the US is still not spending enough to prepare firefighters, police, rescue, and medical agencies to handle another catastrophic attack. Under current plans, the US will spend $27 billion over the next five years in this effort; however, the report recommends spending about $100 billion over the same period. The report stated 'the US remains dangerously ill-prepared'.[132]

More and more communities are exercising procedures for a bioterror attack, however. In November 2002, officers with assault rifles and paramedics armed with hypodermic needles invaded a local high school system in Mesa, Arizona as part of a daylong drill to see how ready health, emergency and military systems were to deal with such an attack. At 9:00 a.m., paramedics and public health nurses began giving tetanus shots to 3,000 students from six high schools and finished by 11:00 a.m. The drill included use of mock antibiotics sent in a shipment to Tucson from one of 12 secret locations that make up the National Pharmaceutical Stockpile. Department of Public Safety officers escorted the fake supplies to Mesa and guarded the cargo until it was carried into the gym where 200 adult volunteers waited for antibiotics to treat their fake anthrax.[133]

Related incidents and reactions worldwide since 9/11

- *Sweden* – police seized four suspicious letters addressed to corporations (one US) for checks by biological warfare experts.
- *Germany* – the mailroom at the federal chancellery in Berlin was sealed off after postal workers discovered a powder trickling out of an envelope. In another incident, authorities in Brazil tested a white powder found on an aircraft originating in Germany.
- *Switzerland* – an employee at a Swiss health-group in Basel underwent preventive medical treatment after receiving a suspicious letter containing an unidentified powder.
- *France* – police evacuated offices of the French Space Agency, a financial institution, a school and a tax collection agency after powder arrived in the mail.
- *United Kingdom* – 200 people were evacuated from Canterbury Cathedral after a man was seen sprinkling white powder in a chapel.
- *Australia* – dozens of government workers took decontaminating showers after their office received a letter containing a white powder. A US consulate was evacuated in a separate, but similar incident.

- *Canada* – Parliament closed after a worker developed a rash after opening mail. Two post offices in Toronto and Montreal were evacuated after workers found powdery substances.[134]

Lethal Diseases

Biological agents that exist include anthrax, plague, smallpox, salmonella, cholera, tularemia, shigella, Ebola, West Nile Virus, Venezuela equine encephalitis, botulism, ricin, monkey pox, viral hemorrhagic fever, aflatoxin, marburg, burcella, lassa fever, machupo, and iunin.[135] However, the four most feared biological agents today are anthrax, smallpox, plague and botulism. Anthrax is a bacterium that is not communicable, but can kill up to 90 per cent of its victims. Antibiotics can kill anthrax bacterium, which produces a toxin that can lead to coma and death; however, there is no antidote for the toxin secreted by the bacterium. Smallpox is a virus that is easily transmitted from one person to another and kills approximately 30 per cent of its victims.[136] Dr William Hall, president of the American College of Physicians, believes the percentage of deaths to be higher. In an interview on CNN, Dr Hall said, 'The figure of 30 per cent for smallpox comes from historical experience in other countries. We know that when smallpox has been introduced into populations who have not encountered the virus before … smallpox had a much higher fatality rate, certainly exceeding 50 per cent'.[137] Both of these agents have been produced in huge amounts by 17 nations, some of which have used genetic engineering to make the strains more lethal and resistant to antibiotics and vaccines.

Anthrax

> It was 27 days I pray to God no one on the face of the earth will have to go through.
>
> Postal worker Leroy Richmond, one of the survivors of anthrax.[138]

Anthrax outbreaks and attacks can be traced throughout centuries of time. Anthrax is thought to have been the fifth Egyptian plague in 1500 B.C., as well as the sixth plague known as the 'plague of boils'. During the 1600s, the 'Black Bane' killed 60,000 cattle in Europe. German agents in the US were believed to have injected horses and mules with anthrax prior to being shipped to Europe, causing over 300 deaths among the animals.[139] Anthrax killed 1 million sheep in Iran in 1945.[140] From 1978 to 1980, human anthrax epidemics in Zimbabwe infected more than 6,000 people and killed as many as one hundred. In 1979, anthrax spores accidentally released at a Soviet Union military facility killed 68 people.[141]

Anthrax is colorless, odorless and invisible following its release. These traits account for the 'white powder' used in the anthrax attacks in the past two years as a means for the perpetrator to have some idea of its whereabouts, although powders of any color may be used. A number of powders used in the recent attacks have not been white, but brownish in color.[142]

There are over 1,200 known varieties of anthrax, but scientists use only a dozen of those. An acute infectious disease caused by spore-forming bacterium, anthrax most commonly occurs in mammals such as sheep, cattle, goats, camels and antelopes.[143] The organism exists in the infected host as the vegetative bacillus and in the environment as a spore. The spore is the stage of the bacterial life cycle that is the usual infective form. Anthrax can occur in humans when they are exposed to the spores by one of three methods – *cutaneous* (through the skin), *inhalation*, or *gastrointestinal.*[144]

The bad news is there is no atmospheric warning system to detect an aerosol cloud of anthrax spores. The really bad news is there is no vaccine available for civilian use, as pharmaceutical companies in the past have viewed the production of anthrax vaccine as economically unfeasible. According to the Department of Defense, there were only 24,000 doses of anthrax vaccine left in the military inventory – enough to vaccinate only 4,000 military personnel. This is extremely alarming as estimates prepared by the Office of Technology Assessment for the US Congress in 1993 indicated that 130,000 to 3 million deaths could occur with the release of 100 kilograms (220 pounds) of aerosolized anthrax over Washington, DC – an attack as lethal as a hydrogen bomb. At the time of the report, Iraq had over 50 tons of anthrax.[145] In 1995, Iraq admitted it produced 8,500 liters of concentrated anthrax as part of their biological weapons program.[146]

As if the actual cases of anthrax in 2001 were not enough, the US Postal Service says it has been plagued by nearly 12,000 hoaxes, threats, and suspicious mail incidents – an average of 654 daily – that have resulted in the evacuation of 429 postal facilities for varying amounts of time.[147] There have been some other side effects, as well. In December 2001 and January 2002, more than 250 Capitol Hill employees complained of various illnesses ranging from skin irritation to headaches and nausea after opening irradiated mail.[148]

Cutaneous anthrax

About 95 per cent of anthrax infections occur when the bacterium enters a cut or abrasion on the skin (*cutaneous*). It begins as a raised itchy bump that resembles an insect bite, but soon turns into a painless ulcer. The ulcer is usually one to three centimeters in diameter and has a black center in the middle. Lymph glands in the adjacent area may also swell. About 20 per cent of untreated cases result in death. With treatment the mortality rate is less than 1 per cent.[149]

It is estimated 2,000 cases of cutaneous anthrax occur annually worldwide. In the United States, 224 cases were reported between 1944 and 1994. The largest reported epidemic occurred in Zimbabwe between 1979 and 1985 when more than 10,000 human cases of cutaneous anthrax occurred.[150] In October 2002, a man in Arizona was reported to have contracted cutaneous anthrax from a woolen Turkish rug. The previous case in Arizona was reported 20 years ago when a man contracted the disease from an animal-skin drum from Haiti.[151]

Cutaneous anthrax cases stemming from the attacks in 2001:

- New York: NBC *Nightly News*, female assistant to anchor Tom Brokaw; ABC News, infant son of producer; CBS News, female assistant to anchor Dan Rather; *New York Post* employee; *New York Post* employee; ABC employee.
- New Jersey: West Trenton postal workers (two); Hamilton Township mail processing employee and a bookkeeper; Camden County postal worker.[152]

Cutaneous anthrax historically has been treated with oral penicillin, or with doxycycline as an alternate. Amoxicillin is recommended in cases of pregnancy, lactating mother, age younger than 18 years, or antibiotic intolerance.[153]

Inhalation anthrax

Prior to 2001, only 18 cases of *inhalation anthrax* have been reported in this country since 1900, the last was in 1978 according to a medical report published in 1999.[154] Inhalation cases stemming from the attack during 2001 include:

- Florida – Photo editor at American Media, Inc. in Boca Raton (*died*); another employee at America Media
- New Jersey – two Hamilton Township postal workers
- New York – hospital supply room worker (*died*)
- Washington, DC – two postal workers at Brentwood mail processing center (*both died*); two additional Brentwood workers; State Department mailroom employee.[155]

Untreated, the mortality rate for inhalation anthrax is estimated to be over 90 per cent; however, six of 11 inhalation anthrax patients in the attacks in 2001 survived, suggesting the estimated mortality rate is high. However, early recognition and aggressive initiation of appropriate antibiotic treatment may have made the difference in those cases.[156] One of those that died thought he had food poisoning with nausea, abdominal pain and vomiting. Emergency room doctors diagnosed him as having an inflamed stomach and referred him to his primary care doctor. By the next day, it was too late and the man died five hours after being admitted. Another victim went to his doctor's office complaining of aching, weakness and a fever. He was diagnosed as having a virus and sent home. Four days later, he went to an emergency room with his original symptoms as well as chills, nausea, vomiting and a cough. He died 13 hours later. The difference in the deaths and the survivors was the length of time between the onset of the symptoms and the diagnosis of anthrax. Two other patients reported being sick for three days, one with a low-grade fever, chills, cough, a sore throat, muscle aches and shortness of breath, the other complained of a constant headache, nausea, chills, night sweats, and a sore throat. These two men received CT scans/X-rays that provided the first clue of anthrax. Doctors quickly prescribed three antibiotics and they survived.[157]

A number of the survivors of the anthrax attacks in 2001 continue to have symptoms their doctors cannot explain – fatigue, severe mood shifts, shortness of breath, chest pains and memory loss. The National Institute of Health has plans to study the survivors – particularly those who survived inhalation anthrax who are of great scientific interest because in the past nearly everyone with inhalation anthrax died and doctors have almost no information about recovery.[158]

It takes approximately 8–10,000 spores to contract anthrax via inhalation. Senator Daschle's letter reportedly had 2 grams of anthrax powder containing between 100 billion and 1 trillion spores per gram.[159]

Gastrointestinal anthrax

Exposure to *gastrointestinal anthrax* would more than likely come from eating undercooked meat contaminated with the bacterium and is very rare in the US. There were no gastrointestinal cases of anthrax diagnosed following the attacks of 2001. The incubation period for gastrointestinal anthrax is one to seven days and symptoms include nausea, loss of appetite, vomiting (to include blood), severe diarrhea and fever followed by abdominal pain.[160]

The drug ciproflaxin is used to treat victims of anthrax. 'Cipro' is a commonly used drug for respiratory and urinary tract infections, as well as skin and gastro-intestinal infections. It is generally tolerated very well with upset stomach being the most common side effect. Allergic reactions such as a rash are less common with Cipro than with penicillin.[161]

Another anthrax vaccine (anthrax vaccine adsorbed – AVA) has been licensed for use in humans and is reported to be 93 per cent effective. Manufactured and distributed by BioPort Corporation of Lansing, Michigan, the vaccine contains no dead or live bacteria. One per cent of the 10,722 inoculations of employees of the US Army Medical Research Institute of Infectious Diseases (USAMRIID) experienced side effects that included one or more of the following: headache, malaise, fever, muscle pain, nausea, vomiting, perspiring, blurred vision, generalized itching, or sore throat.[162]

The Center for Disease Control and Prevention in Atlanta, Georgia recommends vaccination against anthrax for the following:

- People who work directly with the organism in the laboratory
- People who work with imported animal hides or furs
- People who handle potentially infected animal products in high-incidence areas (outside the US)
- Military personnel deployed to areas with high risk for exposure
- Pregnant women should be vaccinated only if absolutely necessary.[163]

Inoculations against anthrax have caused some unexpected problems, however.

The General Accounting Office released a report in October 2002 that details widespread debilitating side effects experienced by 85 per cent of National Guard and Reserve pilots. The pilots had received at least one shot of the series of six inoculations to be taken over a period of eighteen months. Effects include swelling, burning, itching and pain in the arm receiving the injection, a lump in the arm, chills, fever, extreme fatigue, dizziness, headaches, blurred vision, numbness in extremities, joint pain, memory loss, blackouts, ringing in the ears, insomnia and nausea – none of which are conducive to safe flight. As a result, 18 per cent of those surveyed by the GAO said they intend to transfer to non-flying jobs, move to an inactive status, or take a general discharge to avoid the inoculations. That is in addition to the 16 per cent of pilots who have already done so. Pilots and crew, who may be the first to enter into danger areas, were the first to receive the inoculations prompting the study by the GAO.[164]

An article by CNN in October 2001 contains advice for postal workers that are also applicable if an envelope or package is found on an aircraft.

1 *Do not handle the mail piece or package suspected of contamination.* (My question is how did you come to suspect the object without handling it to begin with?)
2 *Notify your supervisor.* (In our case, the captain.)
3 *Make sure that damaged or suspicious objects are isolated and the immediate areas are cordoned off.* (Depending upon location in the aircraft, this may be accomplished with varying degrees of difficulty. For instance, what if the aircraft is full of passengers?)
4 *Ensure that all persons who have touched the object wash their hands with soap and water.* (We should be able to accomplish this in the aircraft lavatory. Personal bars of soap and bottled water are alternate sources. Remember to report the lavatory holding tank has been contaminated.)
5 *Call a postal inspector to report the incident.* (The captain should accomplish reporting the incident.)
6 *Designated officials will notify local, county and state health departments.* (Coordination for diversion or continuing to destination will determine who actually gets called.)
7 *Designated officials will notify the state emergency manager.* (At 3:00 a.m. on a weekend? Again, your final destination plays a huge part in this communication process.)
8 *List all persons who have touched the object, including contact information.* (This is a very, very important step. The reasons for this should be obvious.)
9 *Place all items worn when in contact with the suspected object in plastic bags.* (This includes all clothing, jewelry, pens, etc. Seal the bags! Clean clothing from your suitcase (or someone else's) may be donned after step 10 has been accomplished.)
10 *Shower with soap and water.* (Not possible on an aircraft, so do the next best thing. Wash all exposed skin with copious amounts of soap and water. Remember to report the lavatory holding tank has been contaminated.)

11 *If prescribed medication by medical personnel, take it until otherwise instructed or it runs out.* (This will probably occur after landing and medical personnel (and medication) are available. Remember, anthrax does not kill instantly or immediately. You will probably have time to receive the proper medication.)

12 *Call the CCDC Emergency Response at (770) 488–7100 for answers to questions.* (This may be possible through a phone patch from the cockpit. Write this number down where you know it is if you need it.)[165]

Smallpox

> The threat of smallpox as a bioterrorist weapon is real and health officials are doing everything they can to 'keep the citizens of our nation safe' from such an attack. A smallpox attack is just one of many potential bioterrorism threats, but perhaps is the most frightening.
>
> Dr Anthony Fauci, Director of the National Institutes of Health[166]

Smallpox is believed to have killed more people throughout the world than all wars and epidemics combined.[167]

- *1350 BC* – First known episode: Hittite warriors catch the disease from Egyptian prisoners. When the Hittite king and heir are fatally infected, their empire falls apart.
- *180 AD* – A smallpox epidemic dubbed the Plague of Antonine kills 3.5 to 7 million people in the Roman Empire, including Emperor Marcus Aurelius.
- *910 AD* – The Arab physician Rhazes writes the first medical account of smallpox, trying to explain why survivors didn't catch it, the earliest theory of immunity.[168]
- In 1763 during Pontiac's rebellion, British officials and fur traders at Fort Pitt deliberately gave small-pox-contaminated blankets to the Indians.[169]

The results from a national survey taken in the US during 2002 revealed the vast majority of Americans have major misconceptions about smallpox and its vaccine. Most of the 1000 polled believed (falsely) that smallpox can be treated and there have been new cases in the past five years. Only a small percentage believed there was enough vaccine for every American.[170] Hopefully, the information presented in this book will serve to enlighten others who, like the authors, were not well read on the subject. What we discovered researching the subject was sobering.

We thought we had a handle on smallpox, but the threat of its use as a biological weapon has received tremendous attention – and rightfully so. Smallpox is a very serious threat because of its potential to spread quickly and with devastating effects. A military exercise in the summer of 2001 involved a simulated smallpox attack on Oklahoma City. The epidemic quickly soared out of control spreading to 25 states and millions of people.[171]

Here is how the smallpox virus works:

- *Transmission* – People must be within six feet of a patient for a prolonged period to catch the disease; the virus can be spread through infected clothing or bed linens; the disease is not as infectious as measles, chickenpox or the flu; it tends to spread among families rather than in workplaces or schools; and, it is not usually contagious until visible symptoms appear, so patients can be identified and isolated before they unwittingly infect others.
- *Infection stage: days 1 to 5* – Victims inhale the virus through contaminated air droplets. It spreads from lungs to local lymph nodes.
- *Incubation stage: days 6 to 17* – Microbes migrate to the liver and spleen were they multiply rapidly. Patient's experience no symptoms during this stage and are not yet contagious.
- *Flu and sores stage: days 18 to 20* – Initial symptoms include fever, fatigue and vomiting. The virus shows up as sores in the mouth and throat before spreading to other parts of the skin. People are highly contagious during this stage.
- *Outbreak stage: days 21 to 37* – Small bumps appear on limbs and torso, becoming fluid-filled pustules. The disease is most deadly during this stage. The pustules scab over within two weeks, but patients remain contagious until scabs fall off.[172]

Smallpox, eradicated worldwide in 1972 through efforts by the World Health Organization, is known to exist only in laboratories or in nations known or suspected of having biological weapons.[173] These nations include the US, Russia, France, North Korea, Libya, Syria, Iran and Iraq.

In late 2002, the CIA investigated an informant's accusation that Iraq obtained a virulent strain of smallpox from a Russian scientist who worked in a smallpox lab in Moscow during the Soviet era. The scientist is known to have visited Iraq on several occasions as recently as 1990. Some experts fear the strain provided to Iraq during this period was a version that could be resistant to vaccines and could be more easily transmitted as a biological weapon. The possibility that Iraq possessed this strain is one of the several factors that has complicated the decision about how many Americans should be vaccinated against smallpox.[174] As of the publishing of this book, US and allied military personnel have not located any trace of smallpox strains in Iraq.

The head of the National Institute of Allergy and Infectious Diseases reported in September 2002 the US now has more than enough smallpox vaccine to protect everyone in an emergency. The 86,000 long-stored doses on hand would be diluted and tests indicate the diluted doses would work. A contract for an additional 209 million doses was let and the first batch was expected to be on hand in 2003.[175]

In October 2002, top bioterrorism advisors to the Bush administration revealed a bioterror response plan involving a voluntary smallpox vaccination program that would begin with 500,000 health care workers, expand to 10 million emergency responders, and extend to the rest of the population as early as 2004. The offering represented a shift in thinking from June 2002 when a government advisory panel recommended inoculating about 20,000 medical personnel. Should one case of smallpox appear in the US, officials would assume we were under attack and quickly move to nationwide vaccinations.[176]

In November 2002, it was announced the Bush administration planned to recommend that emergency room workers and first-responder teams take the smallpox vaccine. The shot would be available to other health care professionals as determined by each state. The general public eventually would be offered the vaccine, but not encouraged to get the shots.[177] Plans also got underway for vaccinating 500,000 US military troops against the disease who would be assigned to the Middle East during Operation Iraqi Freedom.[178]

The US government is stockpiling the vaccine, but has no plans for routine vaccinations for the public. Experts estimate that if every American were vaccinated against smallpox, approximately 400 people would die from the vaccine. Dr Fauci of the NIH said, 'It's extremely conceivable we will have to accept those risks and vaccinate people'.[179]

The government is requiring every state to develop plans for a smallpox attack on their state. The plans must discuss:

- How to inoculate about 7,500 doctors, nurses and rescue workers who might be exposed to the disease;
- How the state would distribute vaccines to other health care workers and to the public;
- How information would be disseminated through information technology; and,
- How it would designate 500–1,500 beds for highly contagious patients.[180]

In the event a smallpox case occurs in the US, the CCDC recommends isolating the victim, as well as a containing ring of people exposed to the victim, rather than mass vaccinations. The problem is in recognition and diagnosis of symptoms as there are only a few hundred doctors who have ever seen a case of smallpox. The disease can easily be confused for chickenpox. To aid nationally in the recognition of smallpox and anthrax victims, plans for a computerized surveillance network by the CCDC that would review thousands of diagnoses daily for unusual patterns, such as a sudden increase in reports of flu-like symptoms could signal a smallpox attack. The lead-time provided by such a system would be pivotal in saving thousands of lives by early recognition and treatment of the diseases. Since the fall of 2002, fourteen Harvard Vanguard treatment centers has reported data daily on 250,000 patients with no suspicious patterns. The national system would mirror the Harvard system and could provide early warnings of less sinister disease outbreaks such as an incident in 1993 in Milwaukee when tens of thousands of people got sick from a water-born illness.[181]

In the event of a smallpox outbreak, CDC guidelines provide for shipment within five to seven days of enough vaccine for every American from over 400 million doses are currently available and stockpiled in the US. In an attack, 20 clinics per state, each employing about 200 workers, could each inoculate approximately 6,000 people over two eight-hour shifts.[182]

The vaccine delivers 'vaccinia', a relatively harmless virus into the body and the immune system creates antibodies that attack the vaccinia. The antibodies remain in the body for years and are designed to attack smallpox if the patient is ever infected. Typical reactions to the inoculations include:

- Low grade fever;
- Soreness and redness at the vaccine site;
- Swollen and sore lymph nodes under arms;
- About one in 10 people will experience extreme discomfort with fatigue, loss of appetite, and other flu-like symptoms lasting a day or two; and,
- One out of three people will feel sick enough to miss work, school or have trouble sleeping.[183]

There are some additional dangers, however. Vaccinia is a living microbe, so it can infect and seriously harm some recipients. It was estimated that:

- One out of 100,000 people will develop a rash or sores, typically on the face, eyes or genitals from touching the vaccination site and then other body parts;
- A toxic or allergic reaction occurs in one out of 100,000 people;
- 14 to 52 people per million will develop serious eczema;
- Infection can lead to death in 14 to52 per million people;
- Swelling of the brain occurs in 14 to 52 per million people;[184]
- Deadly reactions include encephalitis, which can cause paralysis or permanent neurological damage; and/or
- Progressive vaccinia, where the vaccination site does not heal and the virus spreads, eating away at flesh, bone and intestines.[185]

One set of figures released in June 2003 regarding 450,293 military personnel who were inoculated from December 2002 to the end of May 2003, add another item to the dangers listed above – heart muscle inflammation, myopericarditis. There were 37 cases among this group, which translates to 78 per million. One civilian and one military person contracted encephalitis.[186] Another report states that 454,856 military personnel received the smallpox vaccination and at least 50 experienced myopericarditis or pericarditis symptoms. Additionally, at least 22 of the 37,608 recipients of the vaccine experienced the same symptoms.[187] Three people have died from the vaccination. (These figures translate to 146 per million, double the previous report.) Regardless of which report is the more accurate, many of the agencies involved with the smallpox vaccination effort are recommending the program be put on hold until the heart-problem issue can be further researched. This development was another setback in the smallpox vaccination effort nationwide.

The original goal of the vaccination program that began in January 2003, was to vaccinate 450,000 front-line health-care workers; however, only 16,919 had been vaccinated by March 7, 2003. The nation's largest population centers – home to more than 30 million people – have only vaccinated 296 front-line workers, including 115 in Los Angeles County, 53 in San Antonio, 41 in New York City and 35 in Phoenix. In Phoenix, the medical director for epidemiology and bioterrorism said, 'There are no cases of smallpox in the world. There is no credible threat of the disease. Right now, the risks of vaccination are greater than the risks of disease'.[188, 189] This philosophy appears to be the prevailing outlook by the medical field. As of 1 August 2003, only 38,062 volunteers nationwide had received the vaccine.[190]

Those who should avoid the vaccine entirely include: adults with small children, pregnant women, nursing mothers, people with eczema, people with weak immune systems, those with HIV or AIDS, organ-transplant recipients, chemotherapy patients, those with heart problems, and those who share living quarters or are in close, daily contact with people on this list.[191]

In a poll conducted in November 2001, 60 per cent of Americans polled indicated they would take a smallpox vaccination if offered, even knowing the risks. Tens of millions of Americans under the age of 30 are susceptible to smallpox because they were never vaccinated after the US stopped immunizations in 1972.[192]

Studies and debates continue regarding the vaccine and the pros and cons of being inoculated. The results of new research completed in August 2003 indicate people vaccinated up to 75 years ago are either immune or resistant enough to have only mild cases of smallpox. 'That's good news for the people who were vaccinated, and for people who have never been vaccinated, also', said Mark Slifka, a viral immunologist at Oregon Health and Science University. 'It means that with 145 million to 150 million Americans walking around with reistance to the smallpox virus, our "herd immunity" is high'.[193]

As of January 2003, the Centers for Disease Control and Prevention had shipped 204,000 doses of smallpox vaccine to 40 states (those meeting the deadline for submission of a state plan), but only about 700 volunteers had been inoculated by the first week in February. Employee unions are balking, big hospitals are opting out, and crucial questions about liability and compensation for vaccine side effects remain unanswered.[194]

For those opting to wait on an inoculation until a later time, the CDC guarantees that states will receive vaccines within 12 hours of any outbreak. And, even after exposure to smallpox, individuals have up to four days to get vaccinated and build up immunity to the disease.[195]

President Bush said, 'As commander-in-chief, I do not believe I can ask others to accept this risk unless I am willing to do the same, therefore I will receive the vaccine along with our military'. The President received his inoculation on 21 December 2002 with no complications.[196]

For those who are undecided about receiving an inoculation, perhaps a bit of historical data would be helpful. In Liverpool, England in 1902, a smallpox epidemic killed about half the infected adults over 50 years of age who had never been inoculated. *The epidemic bypassed every vaccinated child.* Of the adults who were inoculated as youngsters, most developed smallpox, but only 10 per cent of them died.[197]

Plague

'Plaguing us' for centuries, bubonic plague epidemics have killed 200 million people in the past 1,500 years. 'Black Death', Europe's epidemic that started in 1347, killed 25 million people in Europe and 13 million in the Middle East and China by 1352. In 1994, 500,000 people fled the city of Surat, India in fear of a bubonic plague epidemic, an event that underscores the widespread fear associated with this disease.[198] Although rare in the US today, 15 states, mainly in western United States, have experienced cases of plague in the past decade. New Mexico had nine cases in 1998, six in 1999 and one case each in 2000 and 2001.

News of the case of the plague anywhere gets widespread attention, however. After two tourists from New Mexico fell ill with the plague while in New York in November 2002, Fox News TV channel ran a headline trailer that included 'Black Death', and newspapers like the *New York Times* headlined 'A disease that ravaged medieval Europe reappears'.[199] Reuters' headline was, 'Plague Scares New York'.[200] It is so rare of a disease that even the media was surprised by its occurrence.

Bubonic plague is transmitted by bites from fleas living on host rodents, or by respiratory or blood droplets from animals to humans, or humans to humans. *Pneumonic* plague, an uncommon and highly lethal form of plague, was developed by the US and Soviets in the 1950s and 1960s and consists of small plague particles that would be disseminated through an aerosol. Pneumonic plague, an infection of the lungs, can be spread through contact with respiratory droplets generated by the victim. There is no environmental warning system to detect an aerosol cloud of plague bacilli.[201]

The incubation period of bubonic plague is from two to ten days. The first sign of bubonic plague is a swollen and very tender lymph gland, followed by fever, chills, headache, nausea, vomiting, and extreme exhaustion. Untreated, plague bacteria enter the bloodstream and causes death in 25–50 per cent of cases.[202]

Pneumonic plague would probably be the choice of terrorists due to the characteristics previously described. Following an incubation period of one to six days, symptoms of pneumonic plague appear that include high fever, chills, headache, wheezing and shortness of breath, a cough with spitting up of blood, and ultimately respiratory failure, circulatory collapse and death. Pneumonic plague is invariably fatal if antibiotics are not administered within one day after onset of symptoms. Streptomycin sulfate, tetracycline, chloramphenicol, and gentamicin sulfate are effective therapies for bubonic plague, especially if begun within 24 hours of the onset of symptoms.[203] There is a vaccine for bubonic plague, but not for pneumonic plague.[204]

Some good news regarding the plague was released in July 2003 in Phoenix, Arizona. Researchers there announced they have mapped the genetic code of Arizona plague that is not much different from other strains of the plague. The genetic fingerprinting of strains is important in identifying the bacteria's origin in the event of a bioterrorism attack, similar to the identification of the anthrax strain used in the anthrax letter attacks in 2001.[205]

Botulinum toxin

The single most poisonous substance known, botulinum is 15,000 times more toxic than the nerve agent VX and 100,000 times more toxic than sarin.[206] It is estimated that one gram of aerosolized botulism toxin (the weight of an average paper clip) has the potential to kill at least 1.5 million people. Botulinum toxin poses a major biological threat because of its extreme lethality and ease of production and transport.[207] Reports from 1995 revealed that Iraq had filled and deployed over 100 munitions containing botulinum toxin. While most cases of botulinum intoxication are caused by ingested contamination, aerosolized toxin is deadly; therefore, an aerosol attack is by far the most likely scenario for the use of this toxin, however it could be used to sabotage food supplies, as well.[208] In 1995, Iraq told the UN it had more than 5,000 gallons of botulinum toxin and had loaded much of it in bombs and warheads. That amount is enough to kill the entire population of the earth three times over.[209]

Botulism is easily acquired and is therefore the highest priority by the National Institute of Health. It is found in the soil and can contaminate poorly prepared food. In fact, about 120 Americans get botulism each year. 'If it were added to the food supply, it could result in a significant number of very serious illnesses', said one official.[210]

There are seven distinct but related neurotoxins produced by different strains of the bacillus (designated A through G), and all seven types act by a similar mechanism and induce similar effects when inhaled or ingested. Botulism does not penetrate skin, but results from being absorbed through an opening in the skin or through a mucosal surface such as a lung. Botulinum toxins have caused numerous cases of botulism when improperly prepared or canned foods are ingested and many deaths have occurred from such incidents.[211]

The toxin attacks the peripheral nervous system resulting in muscle paralysis and victims may experience difficulty in speaking, vision, and/or swallowing. Skeletal muscle paralysis follows, manifested as a symmetrical, descending and progressive weakness that may culminate abruptly in respiratory failure.[212] Respiratory failure secondary to paralysis of respiratory muscles is the most serious complication and generally the cause of death.[213]

An antitoxin is available, but must be administered early after diagnosis. Recovery can take from weeks to months, depending upon the severity of the illness, and may require use of life support systems.[214] The government only has about 1,000 doses of the antitoxin.[215]

Dealing with Chemical/Biological Weapons Aboard Aircraft

Suggested steps (not tested or approved by civil or federal authorities) to isolate the agent and prevent further exposure:

- Do not open the cockpit door to avoid exposure to the flight deck crew;
- Communicate with flight deck by interphone;
- Flight deck crewmembers should don their oxygen masks with 100 per cent selected;
- Distribute moistened paper towels to cabin crew and passengers to breath through;
- Maximize skin coverage with shirtsleeves down and uniform jackets worn;
- Provide blankets to passengers so they can cover themselves;
- Lower cabin temperature to the lowest practical setting;
- Decrease cabin pressure to evacuate and dilute the agent;
- Cabin crew should check for the device; once located, nobody should move it or touch it;
- Cabin crew should create a barrier between the biohazard and the cabin atmosphere (see your dangerous goods procedures) with layers of plastics bags, wet blankets etc.;
- Passengers from the immediate contaminated area should be moved and isolated elsewhere in the cabin;
- Rubber gloves and personnel breathing equipment could be worn by cabin crew to perform duties;
- Discontinue any food or beverage service;
- Secure the cabin as usual for landing;
- After the aircraft is on the ground, passengers and cabin crews must remain together and quarantined until checked by trained medical personnel;
- To avoid becoming contaminated, the flight crew must not be in direct contact with passengers and cabin crews; and,
- The aircraft must be checked by properly trained personnel for contaminated air ventilation, any unusual trace of hazards in the cabin, galleys (for infected food/beverage), or lavatories, etc., before being allowed to continue in service.

Decontamination and quarantine

These two areas have received little attention from the perspective of the aviation industry. When experts in these areas were approached on the subjects during the Homeland Defense Security Training Conference in October 2001, typical reactions were 'deer in the headlights' looks. To date, no one has addressed what to do with a planeload of people that is contaminated with a biological agent or how to decontaminate the aircraft effectively so it can be returned to service.

Williams has personal experience as a military pilot with chemical warfare gear, and procedures used to decontaminate aircrews, ground crews and aircraft. Understandably, there is extreme difficulty involved with the decontamination processes. Decontamination of buildings in Washington after the anthrax attacks was very expensive and took weeks. It is reasonable to expect that decontaminating an aircraft would likewise be an extremely difficult and expensive proposition and the aircraft would likely be out of service for quite a long time.

The following suggestions are offered as food for thought in dealing with the situation after landing if your aircraft is contaminated with a suspected or known biological agent:

- Brief the cabin crew and passengers on: what is expected to occur, including the facts they will not be able to leave the aircraft, air conditioning will be discontinued, food and beverage service will not be available, use of lavatories must be kept to an absolute minimum, and aircraft supplies will be limited to what is currently on board the aircraft; cell phone use will be permitted once informed that external ground power is connected to the aircraft; everyone's patience and understanding would be greatly appreciated; and, that you will keep everyone informed as the situation progresses.
- Do not pull up to the terminal gate and allow the jetbridge to be attached and the aircraft door to be opened. Unfortunately, you must keep the 'bugs' captured on your aircraft.
- Park the aircraft away from the terminal and, if possible, downwind of populated areas.
- Coordinate for ground power to be connected and once established, shut down the aircraft completely. Ground power is preferred over the APU since fuel for the APU may become a factor in a prolonged situation.
- WARNING: The APU may be utilized for electrical power ONLY. Running the air conditioning will pump the 'bugs' out through the outflow valve.
- Do not open any aircraft door or cockpit window – again, keep the 'bugs' to yourself – until advised to do so by a properly equipped HAZMAT team or a civil response team.
- Do not allow ground servicing crews to approach the aircraft. No panels or doors must be opened, particularly cargo doors. Lav service should not be attempted as the 'bugs' may have contaminated the holding tank fluid.
- It may be necessary to delay treatment of any medical emergency on board until properly equipped and trained personnel are available.
- Expect extended delays in responses from HAZMAT, emergency responders, and civil response teams as they attempt to coordinate their approach to the situation.

Part 3: Radiological Weapons

Background

Radiation is a general term that is applied to the transmission of energy including nuclear energy, ultraviolet light, visible light, heat, sound, and X-rays.[216] Radiation, as it applies to this chapter, refers to *ionizing radiation* from nuclear sources. Ionizing radiation cannot be seen felt or heard. The three major types of ionizing radiation are alpha particles, beta particles and gamma rays.

Alpha particles can be stopped by a layer of clothing, paper or the outer layer of skin, whereas *beta particles* cannot. Irradiated alpha and beta particles can be inhaled through contaminated dust or smoke particles, or they can be ingested through irradiated foodstuffs, or introduced into open wounds. Both alpha and beta particles cause cell damage until they are removed, or until they decay. *Gamma radiation* is extremely dangerous as these rays pass through clothing and the entire body, inflicting extensive cell damage. The body itself does not become radioactive.[217]

Ionizing radiation causes changes in cell division, cell structure and cell chemical activities. If the body absorbs enough radiation, leukemia and other cancers may result, and at a certain dosage level, death is a certainty.

The threat is real

> The threat of terrorists setting off a crude nuclear bomb in a major city is real and should be urgently addressed.[218]
>
> A report from the Nuclear Threat Initiative, 2003

> Over the next three decades, the spread of nuclear weapons technology and its possible use by terrorist groups represent the nation's greatest security challenge.[219]
>
> CIA Director George Tenet

> The worst threat on the probability/consequences matrix is nuclear.[220]

The National Nuclear Security Administration (NNSA), a relatively new organization under the Energy Department, maps threats to the US from attacks involving vehicles, cyber, biological, chemical and nuclear means. The threats are mapped using a two-axis matrix that lists 'probability of occurrence' on one axis and 'consequences' on the other. The last quote above is from a report by the NNSA.

World events beginning in September 2001 and continuing into 2003 continue to underscore this opening remark. Efforts by North Korea, Iran and Iraq to develop nuclear capabilities bring the subject to the news on a daily basis. It is difficult to imagine a nuclear holocaust precipitated by any of these countries or by US reactions to these threats. Although Iraq may not possess a nuclear weapons capability at this time, they reportedly had 500 scientists working in the areas of chemical/biological/nuclear weapons prior to Operation Iraqi Freedom in the Spring of 2003.[221] In June

2003, an Iraqi scientist turned over to US officials, a two-foot high stack of documents and about a dozen highly engineered metal components necessary to build a gas centrifuge plant capable of enriching uranium to weapons grade. The items had been buried in his rose garden for the past 12 years. Iraq's nuclear program was dormant and awaiting until US and UN pressure was lifted before restarting the program. One of the documents showed how to hide materials and deceive UN weapons inspectors. According to the scientist, the documents and parts were broken up into four different sets. He assumed the other three sets were hidden by other scientists.[222, 223]

The US was poised to retaliate against Iraq with a nuclear device should Iraq have used chemical or biological weapons against forces from the US and/or our allies. In September 2002, President Bush signed a classified document that would allow the use of nuclear weapons in response to biological or chemical attack.[224] In fact, a poll conducted by the *Washington Post* and ABC News found that 60 per cent of Americans favored the use of such a device against Iraq under those circumstances.[225] It is feasible that friendly forces could be caught up in a nuclear strike and/or its aftermath in confrontations with any of the three countries noted.

The nuclear programs in Iran and North Korea have received a lot of attention in 2003. The collusion of the two countries in the nuclear arms arena was highlighted in June 2003 by the detection of an Iranian cargo plane picking up containers in North Korea during what was suspected to be a shopping trip for ballistic missiles or their components.[226] Additionally, Iran reported in early 2003 it had discovered uranium reserves and was setting up production facilities for peaceful use of nuclear energy. Just a few months prior, the US said satellite imagery indicated structures at one of Iran's nuclear plants were being covered with earth, indicating Iran is building 'a secret underground site where it could produce fissile material'.[227]

The US has its own nuclear program and conducts studies regarding nuclear topics on a regular basis, some of which involve effects of nuclear disasters, whether accidental or terrorist-related. Sandia Laboratories in Albuquerque maintains a computer simulation system that allows NRC to predict spread of radiation from any of 103 nuclear plants in the US based on their location, geography and area population densities, and prevailing or seasonal weather patterns within hundreds of miles of sites. Damage assessments, including number of prompt casualties, long-term cancers, affected population centers and duration of evacuations for specific areas can be estimated for any region of the country.[228] An official Nuclear Regulatory Commission study performed in October 2000 at Sandia was based on various accident scenarios ranging from worker mishaps to plane crashes into a spent fuel pool building. The study concluded effects of a spent fuel meltdown would be enormous.[229]

The extent of possible radiation damage described in the NRC report, released in February 2001, is far more severe than anything previously disclosed. The study revealed a catastrophic meltdown in the spent fuel pool of a nuclear power plant could cause fatal, radiation-induced cancer in thousands of people as far as 500 miles from the site. Prompt fatalities would occur in immediate vicinity of such a site where radioactive particles would be expected to fall. Millions of people within the 500-mile zone would have to be evacuated for periods ranging from 30 days to one year. People living within 10 miles of a nuclear plant may never be allowed to return. Within 500 miles of Indian Point nuclear plant in Buchanan, NY, there are nearly 82 million people living in the US and another 11 million in Canada.[230]

Since 9/11, other groups have also conducted studies involving nuclear disasters. In early December 2002, about 70 people from the federal government, several port authorities and private companies participated in an exercise on port security. Participants responded to three scenarios, all occurring on the same day:

1 A radioactive bomb smuggled into the Port of Los Angeles;
2 A dirty bomb found in a freight container in Minneapolis that had been shipped through Canada; and,
3 The arrest by the Georgia Ports Authority of three men, one of which is on the FBI's terrorist watch list, for trying to steal cargo.

The consequences of the port closings were dramatic. Participants found that it would take 92 days to work through the backlog of cargo, costing the US economy US$58 billion. Ships were stranded, importers and exporters sustained lost sales and spoiled goods, and manufacturers began to close plants. One participant from the American International Marine Agency insurance company said, 'A lot of light bulbs went off. The bottom line is that we're not totally prepared'.[231] The need for preparation was underscored in March 2003 when federal intelligence and energy officials expressed their concern that al-Qaida terrorists would build an improvised nuclear device and smuggle it into the US aboard a cargo-container ship. The concerns of officials center on responses made by captured al-Qaida planner Abu Zubaydah to the question, 'What type of "new" attack would surprise America?' His immediate response was 'nuclear'. Al-Qaida is suspected of having a secret nuclear-bomb lab in Sudan, Pakistan or Yemen.[232]

It is really good to know that people at high levels and representing a wide spectrum of interests are taking terrorist threats seriously and are attempting to proactively find areas of vulnerability and to work on viable solutions. It is highly recommended to be a participant in any security drill or exercise, especially if it involves aviation. Lessons learned in simulated events involving any or all of the forms of threat are invaluable. According to the experts, the nuclear threat exists in three main forms and four probable scenarios. The main forms include:

- Detonation of a thermonuclear device (two scenarios);
- Detonation of a 'dirty bomb'; or,
- An attack on a nuclear power plant or storage facility.[233]

Four probable scenarios for a nuclear attack include:

1 A Russian suitcase bomb obtained on the black market and smuggled into the US and detonated;
2 A terrorist group might build its own nuclear bomb out of smuggled nuclear material;
3 A 'dirty bomb' – a conventional explosive wrapped with radioactive materials – smuggled into the US or used against an overseas target of interest; and,
4 An attack on a nuclear power plant or nuclear waste storage facility.[234]

In a presentation to the Senate Intelligence Committee, CIA Director George Tenet said, 'The overwhelming disparity between the US forces and those of any potential rival drives terrorist adversaries to the extremes of warfare – toward the suicide bomber or the nuclear device as the best way to confront the United States'.[235] Based on that statement alone, each of the four scenarios deserve a closer look and more background information.

Scenario #1: A Small Atomic Demolition Munition, SADM

US and Soviet authorities are believed to have built several hundred portable atomic bombs. The Small Atomic Demolition Munition, or SADM, weighs approximately 100 pounds and may be carried in two parts. The warhead consists of a tube (18–24 inches in diameter) with two pieces of uranium, which, when rammed together would cause the atomic blast. The firing unit would more than likely require decoding prior to activation. Originally intended to slow an invasion of Europe, one of the numerous missing SADMs from former Soviet Union could be sold to terrorists who would seek to smuggle it into the US or within range of an overseas military base or other target of interest. Two Russians were arrested in Miami in 1997 after offering to sell a SADM to undercover US Customs agents.[236]

Scenario #2: A thermonuclear device

Nuclear weapons are true weapons of mass destruction with effects being a combination of heat, blast, electro-magnetic, pulse, and radiation. Retired Armor Master Gunner SFC Red Thomas gave us some good advice in a nutshell regarding survival of a nuclear device. We reprint his comments in part with his permission.

> If you see a bright flash of light like the sun, where the sun isn't, fall to the ground! The heat will be over a second. Then there will be two blast waves, one out going, and one on it's way back. Don't stand up to see what happened after the first wave; anything that's going to happen will have happened in two full minutes. These will be low yield devices and will not level whole cities. If you live through the heat, blast, and initial burst of radiation, you'll probably live for a very, very long time. Radiation will not create fifty-foot tall women, or giant ants and grass hoppers the size of tanks. These will be at the most one-kiloton bombs; that's the equivalent of 1,000 tons of TNT. Here's the real deal, flying debris and radiation will kill a lot of exposed (not all!)

> people within a half mile of the blast. Under perfect conditions, this is about a half-mile circle of death and destruction, but when it's done, it's done.
>
> EMP stands for Electro Magnetic Pulse and it will fry every electronic device for a good distance, it's impossible to say what and how far but probably not over a couple of miles from ground zero is a good guess. Cars, cell phones, computers, ATMs, you name it, all will be out of order.
>
> There are lots of kinds of radiation, you only need to worry about three, the others you have lived with for years. You need to worry about 'Ionizing radiation', these are little sub atomic particles that go whizzing along at the speed of light. They hit individual cells in your body, kill the nucleus and keep on going. That's how you get radiation poisoning; you have so many dead cells in your body the decaying cells poison you. It's the same as people getting radiation treatments for cancer; only a bigger area gets radiated.
>
> The good news is you don't have to just sit there and take it, and there's lots you can do rather than panic. First; your skin will stop alpha particles, a page of a newspaper or your clothing will stop beta particles, you just gotta try and avoid inhaling dust that's contaminated with atoms that are emitting these things and you'll be generally safe from them.
>
> Gamma rays are particles that travel like rays (quantum physics makes my brain hurt) and they create the same damage as alpha and beta particles only they keep going and kill lots of cells as they go all the way through your body. It takes a lot to stop these things, lots of dense material. On the other hand, it takes a lot of this to kill you.[237]

Experts worry that terrorists or hostile nations may get their hands on enough uranium or plutonium to build a nuclear bomb from one of hundreds of research reactors around the world. The US is focusing on elimination of 24 reactors in 16 countries built and fueled with help from the former Soviet Union. The reactors are designed to use highly enriched uranium used to make nuclear bombs, as well as to create nuclear isotopes used for medical treatments and other peaceful purposes. Research reactors are a big concern because they offer a ready source of precisely the material needed to create a nuclear bomb, and security at some of them is frighteningly lax. A number of countries and terrorist organizations have gone 'shopping' for enriched uranium and plutonium, including Iraq (before Operation Iraqi Freedom) and al-Qaida terrorists.[238, 239, 240] Prior to Operation Iraqi Freedom, Iraq had stepped up attempts to import industrial equipment used to enrich uranium for use in nuclear weapons. Several shipments of materials destined for Iraq were intercepted in 2002, at least one coming through Sudan from China.[241] In the months after Operation Iraqi Freedom, the UN and the International Atomic Energy Agency found and secured tons of uranium thought missing from Tuwaitha Yellowcake Storage Facility (about a mile from Tuwaitha nuclear research center) located 12 miles south of Baghdad. The facility was believed to have contained 500 tons of natural uranium and uranium dioxide, and 1.8 tons of low-enriched uranium that could be further processed for arms use, and 150 transportable radioactive devices from Iraqi hospitals and research facilities. The radioactive isotopes were the most immediate concern as they could easily be slipped out of the country and sold on the black market to terrorists bent on development of a 'dirty bomb'.[242] The uranium could also be sold to any nation in support of their nuclear weapons program.

These problems were compounded with the discovery that other nuclear sites in Iraq also been heavily looted. A US Department of Defense (DOD) team composed of eight nuclear experts, accompanied by a US Special Forces detachment, visited all seven nuclear facilities in Iraq in April 2003 and reported none of the facilities intact. There was fresh evidence Iraq's most dangerous technologies and assets have been dispersed beyond anyone's knowledge or control.[243] It is not clear what has been lost in looting and destruction of any of these facilities, but it is well known looters roamed unrestrained among various types of nuclear material and scientific files that would speed development of a nuclear or 'dirty bomb'. What is also known is many files and containers of nuclear material are missing.[244]

There appears to be quite a lot of 'missing' nuclear material already on the black market. Since 1993, the International Atomic Energy Agency has documented 18 cases of weapons-grade nuclear smuggling and hundreds of cases of trafficking in radioactive materials. In 1999, US Customs agents seized ten grams of weapons-grade uranium hidden inside a car traveling into Bulgaria. In June 2002, international nuclear inspectors found two kilograms (4.4 pounds) of highly enriched uranium was missing from a defunct nuclear facility in post-Soviet republic of Georgia. The uranium dioxide pellets are of the highest grade, enriched to over 90 per cent of fissionable isotope U-235. Additional questions remain to be answered regarding missing equipment from the facility that might be used by another country to make additional amounts of bomb material.[245]

A Harvard study funded by the Nuclear Threat Initiative, a private group co-chaired by former Senator Sam Nunn, reported (at least four times in 2001 and 2002), that terrorists carried out reconnaissance at Russian nuclear warhead storage sites or transport trains. Much of the study focused on US efforts to safeguard nuclear materials in Russia.[246] The following event highlights the concern in this area.

In December 2001, Russian police arrested seven people accused of trying to sell highly enriched weapons-grade uranium. A criminal gang was offering the two-pound capsule containing uranium-235 for US$30,000. (Here is the scary part.) In the economic turmoil following the Soviet collapse, police have *regularly* seized low-grade nuclear materials stolen by people who tried to sell them for profit.[247, 248] One must ask the obvious questions, 'How much did the police miss?' and, 'Who bought it?' and, 'Where is it now?'

As another example of the problem, two Turks were arrested and 35 pounds of weapons grade uranium seized in September 2002 in Ankara, Turkey. It was believed the uranium was smuggled from an eastern European country.[249]

The US has pictures taken from spy satellites over the past seven years showing Iranian and Russian construction crews building a nuclear power plant in Bushehr on the Persian Gulf. The plant poses huge problems for the Bush administration in its doctrine of pre-empting threats to US national security.[250] In an effort for the US to 'buy its way out' of dealing with this issue with Iran, the Bush administration is offering a US$10 billion dollar incentive to Russia if it would halt construction of the reactor at Bushehr and stop helping Iran develop potent missiles and weapons of mass destruction. The potentially lucrative deal involves storage of radioactive material from around the world.[251]

Representatives of the Taliban and al-Qaida between 1999 and 2001 contacted at least 10 of Pakistan's top nuclear scientists, and several accepted the representatives' offers. Pakistan has at least 24 nuclear warheads.[252]

There is also the possibility of terrorists gaining access to one or more of our own nuclear missiles. Based upon access security, perimeter defense, area security monitoring and the rapid response of security forces assigned to guard these sites, the possibility of terrorists gaining access to a nuclear weapon is very remote. Approximately a fourth of all United States Air Force (USAF) security forces are assigned to the 20th Air Force, the unit responsible for guarding all missile sites – a 45,820 square mile area in the north-central section of the US about the size of Pennsylvania. The security forces operate under a rigid set of rules of engagement. 'You will be prompt. You will be brutal. You will be overwhelming. You will devastate the situation. There will be no hostage negotiations. Our security forces are very, very ugly and obvious. The message is: Do NOT come here to do your evil, violent thing'.[253] Personally, I believe them. There are simply other less complicated ways to plan an attack with a radioactive device. Take the next scenario, for example.

Scenario #3: A 'dirty bomb'

A 'dirty bomb' is a radioactive device fashioned from conventional explosives (such as dynamite, TNT or C-4) wrapped with radioactive materials obtained from such sources as medical devices or nuclear waste. Although a dirty bomb (measured in hundreds of pounds) does not have the explosive impact of a nuclear weapon (measured in thousands of tons), it is far easier to develop. Radiation dispersed by a dirty bomb could render a large city uninhabitable for weeks, months, or even years.

Experts believe a dirty bomb concocted by a terrorist group would be one of two types, one deadly but more difficult, the other powerful in terms of terror. The former would entail 100 pounds of conventional explosives bundled with plutonium or spent fuel rods from a nuclear reactor. Intense alpha rays would make this weapon extremely lethal. Without protection, handlers would soon die of overexposure. Alpha rays would permeate an area the size of a football field, exposing victims to six times the lethal dosage. Outside the blast area, winds could carry a lethal plume up to two-thirds of a mile.[254]

The latter bomb would consist of 100 pounds of conventional explosives bundled with cobalt-60 or cesium-137. Cobalt-60 is an isotope used to irradiate food and kill bacteria and in cancer radiation therapy. Cesium-137, also used to treat cancer, is widely used in industry for measuring devices, food irradiators and other applications. Cesium chloride powder is probably the material best suited for dirty bombs. 'It is radioactive, and the powder disperses well', said a US Energy Department official in March 2003.[255]

During the first six months of 2003, US Department of Defense and Russian scientists have experimented with simulated 'dirty bombs' in New Mexico's desert and in Russia's Ural Mountains to determine how such a bomb would behave and the reach of the radiation effect as a result of blast and wind.[256] Formal results have not been published and it is unlikely they will be made public for obvious reasons.

The immediate deaths from a dirty bomb would depend upon the size of the explosive used. Stress and fear-induced heart attacks are more likely to cause deaths after the explosion than the radioactive material according to the American Institute of Physics. If you were smoking a cigarette half a mile away, it would be far more dangerous to your health than the radiological part of a dirty bomb explosion. The effects created by a dirty bomb go beyond the actual casualties it may cause. Scientists believe a dirty bomb detonation would set off widespread panic and severely disrupt the economy. It is indeed a weapon of 'terror'. Much of the area surrounding the blast would be contaminated, perhaps thousands of people would need to be evacuated to avoid becoming contaminated, and the massive clean-up costs would be horrendous and take months, if not years. Place the bomb in the center of a political or financial capital and the economic consequences could be enormously devastating.[257, 258]

If ingested, the radioactive dust and particles dispersed by the blast could cause cancer. The maximum dosage of gamma rays would not cause any immediate radiation-related deaths in the blast zone. Winds could carry particles small enough to be inhaled. Adverse health effects would be long-term, with risks of sickness rising with the amount of particles ingested. As one nuclear weapons specialist put it, 'it is not how many people will die right away, but how many might die of cancer many years later'.[259]

It is the radioactive particles that pose the greatest danger from a dirty bomb. If you can avoid getting the particles on you or inhaling them, you will probably not receive enough radiation to cause long-term effects, such as cancer. If you are a victim of a dirty bomb attack, there are three things you should do to best protect yourself from radiation:

1 Remove all outer clothing; by doing so, you will remove most of the sources of radiation (the radioactive particles from fallout);
2 Wash hands, face and other exposed skin areas with soap and water; if possible, take a shower; and,
3 Use anything available to serve as a filter to breath through – a mask, clothing, towel, napkin, etc. – anything that would limit or prevent your inhaling radioactive particles.[260]

The threat of a dirty bomb is real. Consider the ramifications of information from these articles since 9/11:

- Jose Padilla, a.k.a. Abdullah al Muhajir, a former Chicago gang member, was arrested in May 2002 at O'Hare International Airport. Padilla had flown to Chicago from Pakistan to gather information for a suspected 'dirty bomb' attack on US soil by al-Qaida, possibly targeting Washington, DC. He was sent on the mission by al-Qaida because they knew as a US citizen he would be able to travel freely in the US without drawing attention to himself. Padilla came to the attention of US officials as a result of information supplied by Abu Zubaydah, a senior aide to bin Laden picked up by US authorities in Pakistan earlier this year.[261, 262] Later in June, a federal counter-terrorism task force arrested a South Florida Muslim leader and founder of a large Muslim charity who had direct ties with Padilla.[263]
- Sealed bottles and drums of radioactive liquids, uranium-238 (low-grade uranium), cyanide, and other poisonous chemicals were found in a large underground tunnel complex near the edge of an airbase controlled by US forces in Kandahar, Afghanistan in December 2001.[264] US officials have concluded al-Qaida intended to use the uranium-238 found in the complex to make 'dirty bombs'.[265] At the time of the arrest of Padilla, it was suspected, but not confirmed, al-Qaida possessed a 'dirty bomb'. These suspicions were confirmed in January 2003 after British intelligence agents infiltrated the al-Qaida network and found documents that showed al-Qaida members had built a device near Herat in western Afghanistan. The Taliban regime helped al-Qaida construct the device by providing medical isotopes and the device has not been recovered.[266]
- In May 2002, the Nuclear Regulatory Commission reported that US businesses and medical facilities lost track of 1,495 pieces of equipment with radioactive parts since 1996. Six hundred and sixty parts have been located, but 935 remain missing. The vast majority of missing items contains tiny amounts of radioactive material and poses little threat. However, some of missing equipment contains potentially lethal amounts of radioactive cobalt or cesium that could be used in the manufacture of a dirty bomb. Lost or missing radioactive material has been a chronic problem for more than a decade. An Energy department inventory begun in 1995 determined that tens of thousands of the agency's radioactive sources could not be fully accounted for.[267]
- There are about two million licensed radioactive sources in the US and an average of 300 reports of lost, stolen or abandoned radioactive material each year, according to the Nuclear Regulatory Commission. The International Atomic Energy Agency, a division of the UN, has documented almost 400 cases of trafficking in nuclear or radiological materials since 1993.[268]
- A small pellet of radioactive iridium-192 disappeared just south of California border between Tijuana and Tecate, about 70 east of San Diego. It is unclear whether the 8-inch by 6-inch cylinder was stolen or fell of a truck. Mexico's state-owned oil company uses the radioactive material to x-ray its pipeline.[269]

After a massive search by soldiers and firefighters, a trash picker at a municipal trash dump in Tecate found the undamaged cylinder three days later.[270]

- In June 2003, authorities in the former Soviet republic of Georgia reported the discovery in a taxicab of a container of nerve gas and two boxes of highly radioactive material – Cesium-137 and Strontium-90 – that could have been used to make a dirty bomb. The announcement underscores the vulnerability of the former Soviet Union's vast crumbling nuclear infrastructure and chemical weapons arsenal to thieves and terrorists.[271]
- Also in June 2003, authorities in Thailand, acting on information from American investigators, seized 66 pounds of cesium-137 from a Thai man peddling it for use by terrorists in manufacturing dirty bombs. The radioactive material was believed to be from Russian stockpiles and smuggled into Thailand through Laos. What is really troubling, of course, is the fact that al-Qaida, and other terrorist groups affiliated with al-Qaida, have long used Thailand as a hub of operations in Southeast Asia.[272] It is not beyond the scope of reality that other such sales have gone undetected.

The prospect of a 'dirty bomb' being used by terrorists in the US has prompted additional screening requirements at all US land borders, airports and seaports. As of March 2003, all of the estimated 500,000 people a day will be screened for radioactive materials. The screening process requires that all travelers, their vehicles and their luggage and possessions pass within monitoring distance (several feet) of one of the 7,000 portable radiation detection devises purchased for the program. Cargo sent by sea and air will continue to be screened only on a selective basis; however, plans are underway to provide screening of all such cargo within a year.[273]

Scenario #4: An attack against a nuclear power plant or storage facility

The Energy Department is advising US companies of a growing threat of terrorist attack on vital domestic energy facilities. An internal Energy Department report 'Energy-related terrorism in the United States would be a particularly significant threat in a military crisis with the Soviet Union. However, in the absence of a superpower confrontation, there is the possibility that potential Third World adversaries could sponsor attacks on the energy infrastructure in the United States'.[274] The report was prepared for Congress in 1987 – 15 years ago – yet, it is just as true today.

An attack on a nuclear power plant with conventional explosives is far likelier than a nuclear device being employed against the United States. The Nuclear Regulatory Commission has recognized this fact and has staged mock raids on US nuclear facilities for years. Unfortunately, some of these mock assaults were successful, sometimes releasing more radiation in simulation than Chernobyl.

Chernobyl was an actual nuclear accident in 1986 that caused some 30,000 deaths and the evacuation of 135,000 people from the surrounding 'exclusion zone'.[275] A six-mile radius belt around the reactor at Chernobyl is still uninhabitable. A huge shell-like structure, designed to keep water out and dust in for 100 years, is being planned to completely enclose the reactor. Robots and live personnel, where possible, will tackle the removal and storage of 200 tons of uranium and a ton of lethally radioactive plutonium that remains inside the ruins.[276] Moscow is only 415 miles from Chernobyl. Produce from the surrounding areas, particularly closer to Chernobyl, still has very high concentrations of radioactive isotopes. Moscow has a corps of atomic food inspectors that continually monitor fruits and vegetables being sold in the city's 69 open-air produce markets. Edibles such as mushrooms, blueberries, cranberries and lingonberries constitute the bulk of the 3,000 pounds of produce that is confiscated annually and destroyed.[277] A successful attack by terrorists on any of our nuclear facilities could have a similar effect on our nation's food products that could last for decades.

The fear of an attack on a nuclear facility was perhaps closer to happening than we had imagined. In June 2002, in an Associated Press interview with two high-ranking al-Qaida leaders, Ramzi Binalshibh (who was arrested in later months), and Khalid Shaikh Mohammed (the head of the al-Qaida military committee), disclosed the first targets considered by al-Qaida were nuclear facilities. The decision was made to go to other targets for fear the attack on a nuclear facility would go out of control. However, the leaders indicated attacks on nuclear facilities were still being considered.[278] Diagrams of American nuclear power plants found by US forces in Kabul, Afghanistan in January 2002 indicate al-Qaida's interest in striking them.[279]

The NRC released documents in March 2002 indicating terrorists may now be employed at nuclear reactors in the US, just as terrorists enrolled in flight schools prior to hijacking commercial jetliners and crashing them into the WTC and Pentagon. The documents also show the nation's 86 most sensitive nuclear power plants fail to screen workers for terrorist ties and do not know how many foreign nationals they employ.[280]

Nuclear power plants throughout the nation were put on a heightened state of alert in mid-May 2002 after the Nuclear Regulatory Commission received information from the intelligence community. Details of the information were not made public, but obviously, there was a general threat that targeted these facilities.[281]

The Nuclear Regulatory Commission has conducted a study to determine the ability of containment vessels to withstand direct hits by a B767. A containment vessel is approximately 160 feet high and 130 feet wide and houses the nuclear reactor and fuel. Tests conducted by two consulting firms for the Electric Power Research Institute in 2002 concluded that a Boeing 767-400, fully loaded with over 28,000 gallons of fuel and flown into the center of a nuclear reactor at 350 mph would not penetrate the four-foot thick concrete structure. Federal regulators are waiting for completion of their own tests before drawing final conclusions.[282]

There are other means of attacking a nuclear facility, however. The chairman of a Senate subcommittee assessing the vulnerability of nuclear power plants to terrorist attacks described a list of problems at power plants that include poor preparation for dealing with commando-style attacks, unrealistic assumptions of what constitutes enemy threats, and personnel troubles that undermine security.[283]

Federal regulations call for plants to be prepared to deal with 'a determined violent external assault, attack by stealth or deceptive actions of several persons'. The attackers are assumed to have light weapons, a four-wheel drive vehicle and help from an accomplice in the plant. Regulations do not call for protections against attackers with aircraft or boats, even though many plants are on lakes, rivers and seashores or in zones where flying is not tightly restricted. Results were 'poor' at nearly half the plants during security drills conducted by the NRC since September 2001. Prior to 2001, drills were held at each facility every eight years.[284]

Transportation and Storage Problems

Highly radioactive nuclear waste remains dangerous for hundreds of thousands of years. Half of the plutonium planned to be stored in Yucca Mountain, Nevada will still be radioactive 380 million years from now. The proposed site is designed to be leak-free for 10,000 years. Storage and transportation to storage sites have become monumental problems as nuclear wastes pile up from nuclear plants, bomb factories, university labs, and nuclear submarines and aircraft carriers. Adding to these problems are security and accountability of the materials.[285]

More than 161 million Americans live within 75 miles of the 131 nuclear waste sites in the US Most of these sites were intended for temporary storage and are overflowing with nuclear waste waiting to be transported to permanent storage facilities. (The Callaway nuclear plant located 100 miles from St Louis has 613 tons of nuclear waste in temporary storage.) No state wants to have a permanent nuclear waste site; however, a nuclear waste repository at Yucca Mountain (90 miles from Las Vegas) is being proposed by the Bush administration. If it opens, it will receive 77,000 tons of radioactive waste from 72 commercial nuclear power plants and five federal facilities.[286] The Washington-based Environmental Working Group has launched a website the public can use to see how close their homes, schools and jobs could be from the proposed transportation routes to Yucca Mountain from all across the nation. The Group estimates that one out of every three Americans live within five miles of one of the proposed routes. Concern for possible attacks on shipments or transportation accidents prompted the Group to act.[287]

Questioned about the possibility of an attack on a shipment of nuclear waste, a spokesperson for the Nuclear Energy Institute was quoted as saying, 'You can talk about what-if scenarios until you're blue in the face, but we have a transportation record that stands for itself. It has been 45 years, 3000 shipments and no release of radiation'. There are a couple of rebuttals to this statement. First, 45 years ago terrorism as we know it was non-existent. Second, today's drivers could possibly be conspirators themselves as the Justice Department disclosed in August 2002.[288]

Twenty people were charged with fraudulently obtaining licenses to haul hazardous materials, including some who may have links to the terrorists staging the attacks on the WTC and Pentagon. The new charges focus attention on the prospect of a new terrorist threat, not from the skies but from the roads. The DOT and FBI are warning the trucking industry to watch for any suspicious activity in connection with hazardous materials including chemicals, radioactive waste and other substances that could be used to create weapons of mass destruction. The investigators began to focus on hazardous waste permits after the arrest of a former cabdriver in Boston with ties to al-Qaida who had obtained a Michigan permit to haul hazardous wastes.[289]

The US Department of Energy began shipping weapons-grade plutonium from a heavily polluted Rocky Flats nuclear plant near Denver, Colorado to a Savannah River storage site in South Carolina in mid-2002. Plans are to move 34 metric tons of plutonium to the Savannah River site, 160 miles southwest of Charlotte, NC by the end of 2003, as part of the process to shut down Rocky Flats by 2006. The government has been shipping plutonium to and from the Savannah River site by truck and rail for the past 50 years. At the Savannah River site, plutonium is converted into mixed oxide fuel (MOX) for use in Duke Power's nuclear reactors in the Charlotte area.[290, 291]

In July 2002, a ship loaded with 550 pounds of nearly weapons grade plutonium left Japan on an 18,000-mile voyage to Great Britain. The plutonium was being returned because it was defective. International environmental groups, Pacific Island nations and member of the US Congress opposed the shipment charging that security was minimal and the ship leaked. There was also fear of a terrorist attack on the ship similar to that made on the USS Cole.[292]

Radioactive waste continues to be the proverbial 'albatross' around America's neck. Plans to clean out and solidify radioactive waste in rusting tanks located in Hanford, Wash, near Aiken, SC and in Idaho face major technical problems and cost over-runs. After the Energy Department tried in 1999 to cut billions of dollars and several years off the clean-up schedule by redefining some of the material as 'incidental' (which would allow tens of millions of gallons of radioactive waste to be left shallowly buried), a US District judge ruled the attempt as illegal. The waste is supposed to be buried only in a deep geologic repository.[293]

Dealing with Radiation

How do you recognize symptoms of radiation sickness and how can they be treated? You will more than likely be aware of a nuclear detonation; however, if you are not near the blast of a dirty bomb, you may not realize what has occurred until hearing about it, or seeing reports of it on television. You may hear the explosion, but not associate it with a nuclear threat. Therefore, it is important for you to know the symptoms of radiation sickness and what to expect as far as treatement.

Symptoms of radiation sickness[294]

Nausea and vomiting – Nausea and vomiting occur with increasing frequency as radiation exposure increases with their onset occurring as late as 6–12 hours after exposure. They usually subside within the first 24 hours. The occurrence of vomiting within the first two hours is associated with a severe radiation dose, while vomiting within the first hour of exposure is associated with doses that are fatal.

Hyperthermia (abnormally high fever) – The occurrence of chills and fever within the first day after exposure is associated with a severe and life-threatening dose. A significant rise in body temperature within the first few hours of exposure indicates a potentially lethal dose.

Erythema (abnormal redness of the skin) – A person who receives a high dose of whole-body radiation will experience redness of the skin within 24 hours of exposure. If only a portion of the body is exposed, the redness will be confined to the affected area.

Hypotension (lowered blood pressure) – A significant drop in blood pressure is indicative of a lethal dose of radiation.

Neurologic dysfunction – Symptoms include mental confusion, convulsions and coma. All persons who demonstrate obvious signs of central nervous system injury within the first hour of exposure have received a lethal dose of radiation.

Anti-radiation pills

Anti-radiation tablets protect the thyroid gland against cancer in the event of a nuclear accident. Evacuation is the Number One protection, but potassium iodide is an additional layer of protection being provided.

More than 650,000 people who live and work within ten miles of Three Mile Island nuclear plant are eligible for anti-radiation pills that are being distributed free by that state's Health Department. About 42,000 pills were distributed by mid-August 2002. Fifteen other states have ordered the pills through the Nuclear Regulatory Agency.[295]

The Postal Service confirmed in December 2002 it had shipped more than a million doses of potassium iodide pills to post offices. 'We're not distributing them to employees', spokeswoman Sue Brennan said. 'We've deployed them to locations and will only use them if, God forbid, there's a radiation event.'[296]

In May 2003, US military officials expressed enthusiasm about an experimental drug that could protect first responders to any nuclear event. The drug, HE-2100, offers protection when administered before radiation exposure as well as a few hours after exposure, making it highly desirable for military personnel or other first responders either entering a radiated zone or leaving one. HE-2100 buttresses the immune system, in particular the infection-fighting powers of bone marrow, which is most vulnerable to radiation. The drug protects the bone marrow's ability to continue creating infection-fighting cells, called neutrophils, even after radiation exposure. HE-2100 stimulates neutrophil production by causing cells that become neutrophils to mature and to be released into the bloodstream. Supporting the body's immune system is vital since most fatalities from exposure to radiation are a result of infections such as influenza and pneumonia.[297]

Conclusion

In reality, the US is wide open for any chemical/biological or radiological attack by terrorists, both foreign and domestic. It is virtually impossible to guard every mile of our borders and oceanfront property. We do not know the enemy within, who they are or where they are. We do not know the timetables of terrorists. Although we have tightened – and in some cases, initiated – security at nuclear facilities, chemical plants, power plants, laboratories, hospitals, etc., they all remain vulnerable to varying degrees. Our nation's water and food supplies could be easily contaminated at any time. Any of our nation's transportation systems could be used to spread various types of CBR agents.

Although there has been a lot of attention focused on CBR issues, the fact remains America is largely unprepared for any such event. People are being trained, supplies are being produced and distributed, security is being tightened, scenarios are being exercised and emergency response plans are being updated, but the general public is not being educated on the dangers of CBR events. It is the general public that will bear the brunt of any CBR attack. Each section of this chapter includes paragraphs emphasizing 'The Threat Is Real'. Education on the subject of CBR warfare will not create paranoia, but rather provide the impetus to become mentally and physically prepared for any such event.

Be cognizant of 'strange' events occurring worldwide, particularly in areas of known CBR agents, such as the Middle East. The US Army assigned two teams of medical investigators to determine a puzzling flare up of cases of pneumonia among troops deployed in Iraq, Kuwait, Qatar and Uzbekistan. From 1 March through 30 July 2003, about 100 cases were reported, with 15 of the cases severe enough to require attaching the patients to mechanical respirators. Two people died, both served in Iraq.[298] Although CBR agents have not been found to blame, there has not been any other logical explanation either. One has to wonder …

Airports and aircraft are still viable targets for terrorists. As a flight crewmember, being knowledgeable on the subject of CBR warfare can mean the difference between life or death for yourself, your crew and your passengers should any of these type events occur on your aircraft, at your destination while en route or on the ground, during your layover, or while at home. As a flight crew, you may be the only people on board the aircraft who have any knowledge at all about these events and what they may mean to both immediate and long-term survival.

For now, and in the foreseeable future, all you may be equipped with to handle any CBR event is your knowledge of the subject. As Dr William Hall said, 'The key here is for every American to have a plan'.[299] What is YOUR plan?

Notes

1 Domestic Preparedness for Events Involving Weapons of Mass Destruction, Vol. 283, No. 2, www.jama.ama-assn.org, 12 January 2000.
2 Foreign flag ships a security concern, Associated Press, 16 June 2002.
3 Firefighter planes may be inviting new terror attack, Associated Press, 18 October 2002.
4 Expert: Bioweapon plans can be ordered on Net, www.cnn.com, 14 January 2002.
5 Pair had top-secret chemical, nuclear information, FBI says, Associated Press, 6 February 2003.
6 Feds believe suspect was targeting Washington, Associated Press, 11 June 2002.
7 Al-Qaida may try using poison, Associated Press, 5 September 2003.
8 Mass-destruction weapons abound all over the globe, Associated Press, 11 September 2002.
9 Garrett, Joan Sullivan, Countering Bioterrorism: Developing an Emergency Response Plan, MedAire, Flight Safety Foundation and National Business Aircraft Association 47th Corporate Aviation Safety Seminar, Phoenix, AZ, May 2002.
10 Policastro, Dr Anthony and Dr Susanna Gordon, The Use of Technology In Preparing Subway Systems For Chemical/Biological Terrorism, Homeland Defense Training Conference, Track 5 – Safety & Security: Response to Critical Incidents and Other Emergencies, Washington, DC, October 2001.
11 Iraq's Biological Weapons – The Past as Future, Vol. 278, No. 5, www.jama.ama-assn.org, 6 August 1997.
12 US is unprepared for bioterror attack on food, report says, *Knight Ridder Newspapers*, 20 September 2002.
13 Security tool's worth doubted, Associated Press, 20 July 2003.
14 Russia, Ukraine are bickering about Chernobyl culpability, *Christian Science Monitor*, 25 April 2003.
15 Bombs had rat poison, Hamas says, Associated Press, 13 December 2001.
16 Death sentence over Chinese poisonings, www.cnn.com, 30 September 2002.
17 Japan steps up security after subway gassing, *Washington Post*, 21 March 1995.
18 Death penalty sought in nerve-gas assault, Associated Press, 25 April 2003.
19 Ag Aviators: Terrorists Would Face Big Hurdles, www.aviationnow.com, 8 October 2001.
20 Trains, trucks become potential terrorist targets, *Northwest Valley News*, 24 May 2002.
21 Ibid.
22 Search widens for sodium cyanide, *Chicago Tribune*, 23 May 2002.
23 Musser, George, Better Killing Through Chemistry, *Scientific American*, December 2001.
24 EPA to Require Terrorism Checks at Chemical, Water Plants, Associated Press, 7 June 2002.
25 Chemical dump alarm sounds, but no intruder is discovered, Associated Press, 6 September 2002.
26 Discarded War Munitions Leach Poisons Into the Baltic, *New York Times*, 20 June 2003.
27 Iranians show gas attack horror, Associated Press, 16 October 2002.
28 Nerve gas a miserable death, *Newsday*, 21 March 1995.
29 UN inspectors find missiles full of deadly mustard gas, Associated Press, 7 December 2002.

30 Iraq seeks antidote for nerve gas, *New York Times*, 12 November 2002.
31 Featured CSA Report: Medical Preparedness for Terrorism and Other Disasters, www.jama.ama-assn.org, 29 October 2001.
32 Video shows al-Qaida testing lethal gas on dog, *New York Times*, 19 August 2002.
33 Tapes show bioweapons experiments by al-Qaida, *New York Times*, 19 August 2002.
34 829 more Gulf vets exposed to gas, Associated Press, 27 April 2002.
35 3 charged in London terror plot, Associated Press, 17 November 2002.
36 Investigation of deadly poison leads to arrest of North African, Associated Press, 24 January 2003.
37 Italy indicts 12 terror suspects; 9 suspected in chemical plot, Associated Press, 7 February 2003.
38 Poisoning US waters may be al-Qaida plan, *Wire Reports*, 30 May 2003.
39 Lotion to fight chemical attacks, Associated Press, 29 March 2003.
40 American is among 116 hostage fatalities, *Knight Ridder Newspapers*, 27 October 2002.
41 American recalls the hostage takeover, *Washington Post*, 29 October 2002.
42 As rescuers arrive, fear: 'We will all be blown up', *New York Times*, 26 October 2002.
43 Experts suggest Valium gas used in Russian theater raid, Associated Press, 27 October 2002.
44 Moscow raid 'novel', but deadly, Associated Press, 26 October 2002.
45 Putin vows no surrender to terrorism blackmail, Associated Press, 27 October 2002.
46 Rescue lethal to hostages, Associated Press, 28 October 2002.
47 Russian troops raid theater, Associated Press, 26 October 2002.
48 Theatre hostages: 'A lot of blood', Associated Press, 24 October 2002.
49 Siege gas 'was morphine spray', www.cnn.com, 29 October 2002.
50 Ills plague Moscow hostages, Associated Press, 17 December 2002.
51 Iranians show gas attack horror, Associated Press, 16 October 2002.
52 Emergency War Surgery NATO Handbook: Part I – *Types of Wounds and Injuries*, Chapter VI – *Chemical Injury*; US Department of Defense, 6 November 2002.
53 Thomas, SFC Red (retired), Putting Chemical, Biological & Radiological Agents in Perspective, http://urbanlegends.about.com/library/bl-red-thomas.htm, October 2001.
54 Emergency War Surgery NATO Handbook: Part I – Types of Wounds and Injuries, Chapter VI – Chemical Injury; US Department of Defense, 6 November 2002.
55 Nerve gas a miserable death, *Newsday*, 21 March 1995.
56 Ibid.
57 Thomas, SFC Red (retired), Putting Chemical, Biological & Radiological Agents in Perspective, http://urbanlegends.about.com/library/bl-red-thomas.htm, October 2001.
58 Emergency War Surgery NATO Handbook: Part I – Types of Wounds and Injuries, Chapter VI – Chemical Injury; US Department of Defense, 6 November 2002.
59 Nerve gas a miserable death, *Newsday*, 21 March 1995.
60 Textbook of Military Medicine: Medical Aspects of Chemical and Biological Warfare, Chapter 7 – Vesicants, Department of Defense, 6 November 2002.
61 Musser, George, Better Killing Through Chemistry, *Scientific American*, December 2001.
62 Textbook of Military Medicine: Medical Aspects of Chemical and Biological Warfare, Chapter 7 – Vesicants, Department of Defense, 6 November 2002.
63 Ibid.
64 Ibid.

65 Ibid.
66 Policastro, Dr Anthony and Dr Susanna Gordon, The Use of Technology In Preparing Subway Systems For Chemical/Biological Terrorism, Homeland Defense Training Conference, Track 5 – Safety & Security: Response to Critical Incidents and Other Emergencies, Washington, DC, October 2001.
67 Textbook of Military Medicine: Medical Aspects of Chemical and Biological Warfare, Chapter 7 – Vesicants, Department of Defense, 6 November 2002.
68 Train spills hazardous chemicals, Associated Press, 10 February 2003.
69 DuVernay, Bert, Chemical Aerosol Training, *The Firearms Instructor*, Spring 1993, Vol. 9.
70 Clede, Bill, Oleoresin Capsicum, *Law and Order*, March 1993, Vol. 41, No. 3.
71 Textbook of Military Medical Aspects of Chemical and Biological Warfare, Chapter 12 – Riot Control Agents; Department of Defense, 6 November 2002.
72 DuVernay, Bert, Chemical Aerosol Training, *The Firearms Instructor*, Spring 1993, Volume 9.
73 Wilson, Lynne, Pepper Spray Madness, *Covert Action Quarterly*, 2 November 2002.
74 Pepper Power, www.udap.com, 2 November 2002.
75 Miami airport closure: Mace or pepper spray suspected, www.cnn.com, 21 August 2002.
76 Clede, Bill, Oleoresin Capsicum, *Law and Order*, March 1993, Vol. 41, No. 3.
77 Pepper Spray, www.eliminator-pepper-spray.com, 2 November 2002.
78 Chemical Cops: Tear Gas and Pepper Spray Can Be Deadly, www.commondreams.org, 2 November 2002.
79 Ibid.
80 Pepper Spray's Effects on a Suspect's Ability to Breathe, National Institute of Justice, December 2001.
81 Clinical Recognition and Management of Patients Exposed to Biological Warfare Agents, Vol. 278, No. 5, www.jama.ama-assn.org, 6 August 1997.
82 Why we should be concerned about Biological Warfare?, Vol. 278, No. 5, www.jama.ama-assn.org, 6 August 1997.
83 Biological Warfare – A Historical Perspective, Vol. 278, No. 5, www.jama.ama-assn.org, 6 August 1997.
84 Ibid.
85 Ibid.
86 Rumsfeld urged to continue probe of biotests on troops, Associated Press, 2 July 2003.
87 Garrett, Joan Sullivan, Countering Bioterrorism: Developing an Emergency Response Plan, MedAire, Flight Safety Foundation and National Business Aircraft Association 47th Corporate Aviation Safety Seminar, Phoenix, AZ, May 2002.
88 Most US hospitals found unprepared to handle chemical, biological attack, www.cnn.com, 11 January 2000.
89 Why we should be concerned about Biological Warfare?, Vol. 278, No. 5, www.jama.ama-assn.org, 6 August 1997.
90 Manure in water pipes kills tot, sickens 1,000, *Arizona Republic*, 7 November 2002.
91 Canadians to search ship for anthrax links, *Canadian Press*, 25 April 2003.
92 Why we should be concerned about Biological Warfare?, Vol. 278, No. 5, www.jama.ama-assn.org, 6 August 1997.
93 Biological Terrorism, Vol. 278, No. 5, www.jama.ama-assn.org, 6 August 1997.

94 Anthrax's Real Power is as Agent of Fear, Not Death, Says a Former Soviet Aide, *Wall Street Journal*, 18 October 2001.
95 The Threat of Biological Weapons, Vol. 278, No. 5, www.jama.ama-assn.org, 6 August 1997.
96 Clinical Recognition and Management of Patients Exposed to Biological Warfare Agents, Vol. 278, No. 5, www.jama.ama-assn.org, 6 August 1997.
97 Biological Terrorism, Vol. 278, No. 5, www.jama.ama-assn.org, 6 August 1997.
98 The Threat of Biological Weapons, Vol. 278, No. 5, www.jama.ama-assn.org, 6 August 1997.
99 Biden: Bioterrorism more of a threat than missiles, www.cnn.com, 5 September 2001.
100 Ibid.
101 Official: Threat of smallpox bioterrorism real, www.cnn.com, 3 November 2001.
102 Musser, George, Better Killing Through Chemistry, *Scientific American*, December 2001.
103 Clinical Recognition and Management of Patients Exposed to Biological Warfare Agents, Vol. 278, No. 5, www.jama.ama-assn.org, 6 August 1997.
104 Iraq's Biological Weapons – The Past as Future, Vol. 278, No. 5, www.jama.ama-assn.org, 6 August 1997.
105 Biological Threat to US Homeland is 'Very Real', www.aviationnow.com, October 29, 2002.
106 Garrett, Joan Sullivan, Countering Bioterrorism: Developing an Emergency Response Plan, MedAire, Flight Safety Foundation and National Business Aircraft Association 47th Corporate Aviation Safety Seminar, Phoenix, AZ, May 2002.
107 Pathogens lost by lab, report says, Associated Press, 21 January 2002.
108 Iraqi planes toting bioweapons a concern for US *Washington Post*, 5 September 2002.
109 National Labs Man Front Lines of War Against Terrorism, www.aviationnow.com, 26 November 2001.
110 Doctor tied to S. African germ-war program, Associated Press, 3 November 2002.
111 Bin Laden seeking bio weapons, CIA says, *Washington Post*, 7 February 2002.
112 CIA says bin Laden seeks biological tools, Associated Press, 27 November 2001.
113 US is unprepared for bioterror attack on food, report says, *Knight Ridder Newspapers*, 20 September 2002.
114 Al-Qaida gaining on biochemicals, *Washington Post*, 24 March 2003.
115 Musser, George, Better Killing Through Chemistry, *Scientific American*, December 2001.
116 FBI tries to replicate anthrax from 2001, *Washington Post*, 3 November 2002.
117 FBI drains pond in search of evidence in anthrax mail, Associated Press, 10 June 2003.
118 Soil from drained lake has no anthrax bacteria, *Wire Services*, 1 August 2003.
119 Musser, George, Better Killing Through Chemistry, *Scientific American*, December 2001.
120 Consulate mail yields a suspicious powder, Associated Press, 12 September 2002.
121 Thompson: US prepared for bioterrorism, www.cnn.com, 30 September 2001.
122 Most US hospitals found unprepared to handle chemical, biological attack, www.cnn.com, 11 January 2000.
123 Only Florida ready for bioterror attack, Associated Press, 3 November 2002.
124 Official coordination, caution are shown in bioterror scares, *Gannett News Service*, 23 April 2003.

125 Most US hospitals found unprepared to handle chemical, biological attack, www.cnn.com, 11 January 2000.
126 News mags: Biological, chemical terror threaten US, www.cnn.com, 1 October 2001.
127 US unprepared for bioterrorists, *Knight Ridder Newspapers*, 8 November 2001.
128 Experts: Gov't must sharpen message of bioterrorism, www.cnn.com, 29 November 2001.
129 Small town fears in face of bioterrorism, www.cnn.com, 28 January 2002.
130 Ibid.
131 Anthrax scare in St. Louis, www.cnn.com, 6 May 2002.
132 Report says nation not ready for attack, *New York Times*, 29 June 2003.
133 Bottlenecks arise in mock attack, *Arizona Republic*, 22 November 2002.
134 WHO tries to calm anthrax fears, www.cnn.com, 16 October 2001.
135 Infectious Disease and Biological Weapons, Vol. 278, No. 5, www.jama.ama-assn.org, 6 August1997.
136 Official: Threat of smallpox bioterrorism real, www.cnn.com, 3 November 2001.
137 Dr William Hall, Medical impact of bioterrorism, www.cnn.com, 19 October 2001.
138 One year later: Anthrax lessons learned, www.cnn.com, 29 October 2002.
139 Timeline: Anthrax through the ages, www.cnn.com, 16 October 2001.
140 Anthrax as a Biological Weapon, 2002, Vol. 287, No. 17, www.jama.ama-assn.org, 1 May 2002.
141 Soviet anthrax accident killed 60, www.cnn.com, 16 October 2001.
142 Ron Atlas: Outsourcing bioterrorism, www.cnn.com, 22 October 2001.
143 10 things you need to know about anthrax, www.cnn.com, 14 October 2001.
144 Clinical Recognition and Management of Patients Exposed to Biological Warfare Agents, Vol. 278, No. 5, www.jama.ama-assn.org, 6 August 1997.
145 Anthrax as a Biological Weapon, 2002, Vol. 287, No. 17, www.jama.ama-assn.org, 1 May 2002.
146 Soviet anthrax accident killed 60, www.cnn.com, 16 October 2001.
147 N.J. postal facility closed after cleanup bungled, www.cnn.com, 7 November 2001.
148 Anthrax scare in St. Louis, www.cnn.com, 6 May 2002.
149 10 things you need to know about anthrax, www.cnn.com, 14 October 2001.
150 Anthrax as a Biological Weapon, 2002, Vol. 287, No. 17, www.jama.ama-assn.org, 1 May 2002.
151 Pinal County resident tested for skin anthrax, *Arizona Republic*, 24 October 2002.
152 FBI turns to public in anthrax investigation, www.cnn.com, 2 November 2001.
153 Anthrax as a Biological Weapon, 2002, Vol. 287, No. 17, www.jama.ama-assn.org, 1 May 2002.
154 Anthrax death spurs wide probe, *Washington Post*, 6 October 2001.
155 FBI turns to public in anthrax investigation, www.cnn.com, 2 November 2001.
156 Anthrax as a Biological Weapon, 2002, Vol. 287, No. 17, www.jama.ama-assn.org, 1 May 2002.
157 Anthrax appears treatable if caught early on, *USA Today*, 13 November 2001.
158 Anthrax survivors still puzzle, *New York Times*, 5 October 2002.
159 Anthrax as a Biological Weapon, 2002, Vol. 287, No. 17, www.jama.ama-assn.org, 1 May 2002.
160 Ibid.
161 Dr Craig Smith: Anthrax treatments and bioterrorism preparedness, www.cnn.com, 26 October 2001.

162 Anthrax as a Biological Weapon, 2002, Vol. 287, No. 17, www.jama.ama-assn.org, 1 May 2002.
163 10 things you need to know about anthrax, www.cnn.com, 14 October 2001.
164 Anthrax shots hurt military recruiting, *Chicago Tribune*, 24 October 2002.
165 A dozen tips for handling mail packages suspected of anthrax contamination, www.cnn.com, 15 October 2001.
166 Official: Threat of smallpox bioterrorism real, www.cnn.com, 3 November 2001.
167 US fears smallpox stockpiles worldwide, Associated Press, 6 November 2002.
168 The Plan to Fight Smallpox, *NEWSWEEK*, 14 October 2002.
169 Elizabeth Finn: The history of the smallpox virus, www.cnn.com, 5 November 2001.
170 Many in US poll believe smallpox can be treated, *Washington Post*, 20 December 2002.
171 Smallpox feared as next terror tool, *New York Times*, 14 November 2001.
172 The Plan to Fight Smallpox, *NEWSWEEK*, 14 October 2002.
173 Smallpox feared as next terror tool, *New York Times*, 14 November 2001.
174 Iraq may have Russian smallpox virus, *New York Times*, 3 December 2002.
175 Ample smallpox vaccine affirmed, Associated Press, 30 September 2002.
176 Bioterrorism experts back smallpox vaccines, Associated Press, 5 October 2002.
177 ER workers likely to be 1st for smallpox shots, Associated Press, 27 November 2002.
178 Smallpox plan awaits Bush OK, Associated Press, 7 November 2002.
179 Official: Threat of smallpox bioterrorism real, www.cnn.com, 3 November 2001.
180 Feds want state plan on fighting smallpox, *Arizona Republic*, 4 December 2002.
181 Bioterror attack warning system will get a tryout, *Boston Globe*, 4 October 2002.
182 The Plan to Fight Smallpox, *NEWSWEEK*, 14 October 2002.
183 Smallpox shot being debated, *Arizona Republic*, 27 January 2003.
184 Ibid.
185 Bush given smallpox vaccine, *Los Angeles Times*, 22 December 2002.
186 Heart warning issued on smallpox shot, Associated Press, 25 June 2003.
187 Experts urge hold on smallpox shots, *Atlanta Journal-Constitution*, 20 June 2003.
188 Few getting smallpox vaccination, *Los Angeles Times*, 15 March 2003.
189 Bioterror strategy readied, *Arizona Republic*, 26 March 2003.
190 Bush smallpox plan too narrow, panel says, *Los Angeles Times*, 13 August 2003.
191 State cautions on vaccination if there's a smallpox outbreak, *Arizona Republic*, 12 December 2002.
192 Poll suggests US fears of bioterrorism continue, Associated Press, 19 November 2001.
193 US is likely still immune to smallpox, *Cox News Service*, 18 August 2003.
194 Most unwilling to get smallpox vaccinations, Associated Press, 6 February 2003.
195 Panel urges feds to go slow with smallpox inoculations, Associated Press, 18 January 2003.
196 Bush given smallpox vaccine, *Los Angeles Times*, 22 December 2002.
197 Elizabeth Finn, The history of the smallpox virus, www.cnn.com, 5 November 2001.
198 Garrett, Joan Sullivan, Countering Bioterrorism: Developing an Emergency Response Plan, MedAire, Flight Safety Foundation and National Business Aircraft Association 47th Corporate Aviation Safety Seminar, Phoenix, AZ, May 2002.
199 2 cases of plague create stir in East, Associated Press, 10 November 2002.
200 Plague Scares New York, *Reuters*, 12 November 2002.
201 Garrett, Joan Sullivan, Countering Bioterrorism: Developing an Emergency Response Plan, MedAire, Flight Safety Foundation and National Business Aircraft Association 47th Corporate Aviation Safety Seminar, Phoenix, AZ, May 2002.

202 Ibid.
203 Clinical Recognition and Management of Patients Exposed to Biological Warfare Agents, Vol. 278, No. 5, www.jama.ama-assn.org, 6 August 1997.
204 Dr David Bryman, Airplanes and Biological Terrorism, Fenix Flight Magazine, July/August 2002.
205 Arizona plague's DNA is mapped, *Arizona Republic*, 2 July 2003.
206 Clinical Recognition and Management of Patients Exposed to Biological Warfare Agents, Vol. 278, No. 5, www.jama.ama-assn.org, 6 August 1997.
207 Garrett, Joan Sullivan, Countering Bioterrorism: Developing an Emergency Response Plan, MedAire, Flight Safety Foundation and National Business Aircraft Association 47th Corporate Aviation Safety Seminar, Phoenix, AZ, May 2002.
208 Iraq's Biological Weapons – The Past as Future, Vol. 278, No. 5, www.jama.ama-assn.org, 6 August 1997.
209 Botulinum toxin considered threat, Associated Press, 26 March 2003.
210 Ibid.
211 Clinical Recognition and Management of Patients Exposed to Biological Warfare Agents, Vol. 278, No. 5, www.jama.ama-assn.org, 6 August 1997.
212 Botulism Surveillance and Emergency Response, Vol. 278, No.5, www.jama.ama-assn.org, 6 August 1997.
213 Clinical Recognition and Management of Patients Exposed to Biological Warfare Agents, Vol. 278, No. 5, www.jama.ama-assn.org, 6 August 1997.
214 Garrett, Joan Sullivan, Countering Bioterrorism: Developing an Emergency Response Plan, MedAire, Flight Safety Foundation and National Business Aircraft Association 47th Corporate Aviation Safety Seminar, Phoenix, AZ, May 2002.
215 Botulinum toxin considered threat, Associated Press, 26 March 2003.
216 Grant, Harvey, and Robert Murray, David Bergeron, *Brady Emergency Care*, Prentice Hall Division, Englewood Cliffs, NJ, 1990.
217 Ibid.
218 Nuclear risk high, report concludes, Associated Press, 13 March 2003.
219 CIA director says global nuclear arms race looms, *USA Today*, 12 February 2003.
220 National Labs Man Front Lines of War Against Terrorism, www.aviationnow.com, 26 November 2001.
221 Iraqis hand over list of scientists, Associated Press, 29 December 2002.
222 Scientist reportedly turns over nuke records, *USA Today*, 26 June 2003.
223 Ex-Iraqi scientist give US weapons parts, Associated Press, 26 June 2003.
224 Bush gets wide options in war, Associated Press, 1 February 2003.
225 6 in 10 Americans favor nuclear use, poll finds, *Washington Post*, 19 December 2002.
226 Iranian cargo plane detected in N. Korea, *Wire Services*, 17 June 2003.
227 Iran discovers uranium reserves, Associated Press, 10 February 2003.
228 Nuclear plants called easy marks, *Arizona Republic*, 6 October 2002.
229 US nuclear plants could survive aircraft attacks, official says, *Hearst Newspapers*, 18 July 2002.
230 Spent fuel meltdown a hazard at 500 miles, Westchester, *N.Y. Journal News*, 12 November 2002.
231 Drill exposes impact on terrorism on ports, Associated Press, 5 December 2002.
232 Officials fear al-Qaida nuke attack, *New York Daily News*, 14 March 2003.
233 Nuclear attack: Now anything seems possible, www.cnn.com, 9 November 2001.
234 N-terror: 'Clear and present danger', www.cnn.com, 2 November 2001.

235 CIA director says global nuclear arms race looms, *USA Today*, 12 February 2003.
236 A-bomb matter missing from ex-Soviet lab, Associated Press, 29 June 2002.
237 Thomas, SFC Red (retired), Putting Chemical, Biological & Radiological Agents in Perspective, http://urbanlegends.about.com/library/bl-red-thomas.htm, October 2001.
238 Dirty bomb material found at al-Qaida facility, Associated Press, 7 December 2001.
239 Hunt is on for bomb-grade uranium, Associated Press, 24 August 2002.
240 Uranium reportedly found in tunnel complex, *USA Today*, 24 December 2001.
241 US says Iraq was foiled trying to get nuclear gear, Associated Press, 2002.
242 Missing Iraqi uranium found, Associated Press, 21 June 2003.
243 Nuclear site is surveyed; was looted, *Washington Post*, 4 May 2003.
244 7 nuclear facilities in Iraq damaged by looters, *Washington Post*, 11 May 2003.
245 A-bomb matter missing from ex-Soviet lab, Associated Press, 29 June 2002.
246 Nuclear risk high, report concludes, Associated Press, 13 March 2003.
247 Russia arrests 7 in sale of arms-grade uranium, Associated Press, 7 December 2001.
248 N-waste smuggling suspect arrested, www.cnn.com, 20 September 2002.
249 Turkish police nab 2, 35 pounds of uranium, Associated Press, 29 September 2002.
250 Emerging nuclear plant in Iran poses test for US, *Washington Post*, 29 July 2002.
251 US offers Russia $10 bil to end Iraq cooperation, Associated Press, 24 October 2002.
252 Terrorists courted nuclear scientists, *USA Today*, 12 November 2001.
253 No Questions: Protecting US nuclear missile sites requires tougher, clear-cut responses, *Aviation Week and Space Technology*, 12 May 2003.
254 Explosion, not radiation, 'dirty bomb' worst fallout, www.cnn.com, 10 June 2002.
255 US, Russia test 'dirty bombs' to analyze terror threat, Associated Press, 15 March 2003.
256 US, Russia test 'dirty bombs' to analyze terror threat, Associated Press, 15 March 2003.
257 Scenario of a 'dirty bomb', *Boston Globe*, 11 June 2002.
258 Dirty tricks with dirty bombs, www.cnn.com, 11 June 2002.
259 Crude but deadly device most feared nuclear weapon, Associated Press, 11 June 2002.
260 How a 'dirty bomb' may harm you, Associated Press, 11 December 2001.
261 Arrest of 'Dirty Bomb Suspect Stirs New Fears About al-Qaeda, *Wall Street Journal*, 11 June 2002.
262 Ashcroft: Captured Man Planned 'Dirty Bomb' Attack, Associated Press, 10 June 2002.
263 2nd 'bomb' suspect held, *Republic News services*, 12 June 2002.
264 Official: Men discovered substance in jar, bottles, *USA Today*, 24 December 2001.
265 Al-Qaeda interested in 'dirty bomb', US says, www.cnn.com, 4 December 2001.
266 Al-Qaida built a 'dirty bomb' in Afghanistan, BBC reports, Associated Press, January 2003.
267 Radioactive parts pose a terror risk, *Washington Post*, 4 May 2002.
268 Nuclear plant security under intense review, Associated Press, 26 September 2002.
269 Radioactive pellet vanishes near border, Associated Press, 28 July 2002.
270 Missing iridium pellet if found in city dump, Associated Press, 31 July 2002.
271 Radioactive material found in cab in Georgia, *Wire Services*, 17 June 2003.
272 Thai police seize radioactive matter, *New York Times*, 14 June 2003.
273 US to screen all entrants to catch radioactive material, *New York Times*, 1 March 2003.
274 Energy firms at risk of attack, Associated Press, 6 February 1989.
275 Terror Weapons: The Next Threat?, *TIME*, 1 October 2001.
276 Chernobyl reactor to be enclosed by movable shell, *Washington Post*, 3 January 2003.
277 Glow-in-dark fruit a problem for Muscovites, *New York Times*, 15 September 2002.
278 Al-Qaida first thought to hit nuke targets, Associated Press, 9 September 2002.

279 Al-Qaida computer could be a bonanza of intelligence data, Associated Press, 1 January 2002.
280 Lawmaker: Nuke plants vulnerable, *USA Today*, 26 March 2002.
281 Bush pushes OK of atomic dumpsite, *Los Angeles Times*, 25 May 2002.
282 Nuclear plants can take jet hit, data says, Associated Press, 23 December 2002.
283 US nuclear plants could survive aircraft attacks, official says, *Hearst Newspapers*, 18 July 2002.
284 Security criticized at nuclear plants, *New York Times*, December 17, 2001.
285 Bush pushes OK of atomic dumpsite, *Los Angeles Times*, 25 May 2002.
286 Moving nuclear waste is a target, *St. Louis Post-Dispatch*, 6 July 2002.
287 Nuclear routes' proximity detailed, *Gannett News Service*, 11 June 2002.
288 Nuclear threat downplayed, Associated Press, 31 January 2002.
289 Trains, trucks become potential terrorist targets, *Northwest Valley News*, 24 May 2002.
290 Plutonium transfers to S. Carolina start, *Knight Ridder Newspapers*, 3 August 2002.
291 Security extremely tight in nuclear fuel transfer, Associated Press, 23 August 2002.
292 Nuclear fuel shipment leaves Japan fearful, *Arizona Republic*, 5 July 2002.
293 Feds' radioactive-waste plan ruled a 'whim' that breaks law, *New York Times*, 4 July 2003.
294 Emergency War Surgery NATO Handbook: Part I – Types of Wounds and Injuries; Chapter VII: Mass Casualties in Thermonuclear Warfare. US Department of Defense, 6 November 2002.
295 Pa. Distributes anti-radiation pills, Associated Press, 16 August 2002.
296 Feds want state plan on fighting smallpox, *Arizona Republic*, 4 December 2002.
297 New pill could protect from radiation exposure, *Washington Post*, 19 May 2003.
298 Pneumonia in troops puzzling, *New York Times*, 6 August 2003.
299 Dr William Hall: Medical impact of bioterrorism, www.cnn.com, 19 October 2001.

PART II
PREPARING FOR THE THREATS

Chapter 7

Awareness for Survival

Introduction

There are five unique and readily identifiable phases of awareness that each of us encounter throughout our lives. We are always in one level or another as we go about our daily activities. For instance, you are in a particular phase right at this moment – hopefully the right one (YELLOW) – as you read this book. It is important that your awareness phase match the criticality of the moment. The lack of recognition of warning signs has caught many people unaware of a dangerous situation. For some, even thought they recognized the danger, they were unable to react due to the lack of knowledge or training on how to respond.

Marine Colonel Jeff Cooper observed various phases of awareness as he observed the deaths of his troops in Viet Nam. The soldiers died because they were not in the proper phase of awareness for the situation they faced, or as he phrased it, 'levels of consciousness'. The concept behind Cooper's 'levels of consciousness' was expanded and applied to aviation, particularly in application to human factor issues involved with both incidents and accidents. The concept, also successfully applied to law enforcement, security and personal protection programs, was renamed 'phases of awareness', and expanded upon by one of the authors.

We have identified the phases as colors for simplicity. The causal factors, characteristics, and importance of each phase is explored to emphasize how vital awareness is to your survival. The phases of awareness are WHITE, GREEN, YELLOW, RED and BLACK.

You will pass through most of these levels on a daily basis, depending on your activities. You may go from one level to another almost instantaneously. The phases are not progressive, necessarily, although it is possible for one phase to lead to another phase. The majority of normal movement is between WHITE, GREEN and YELLOW, with RED and BLACK reserved for more extreme conditions, as we will explain. If you are interested in learning more about this subject, you are in YELLOW, and we are ready to begin our exploration into phases of awareness. If you are sleepy, you are in WHITE. Please close the book, take a nap, and resume reading when you are refreshed and in YELLOW.

A quick overview and comparison of all five phases provided in Table 7.1 highlights the states of activity and awareness found in each phase. You may want to refer to this chart during the discussion of each phase. It should be obvious that we are most vulnerable to security threats (as well as threats to safety) during WHITE and BLACK when we are unaware of our environment or unable to cope successfully with significant, life-threatening events that may occur in the environment.

Table 7.1 Phases of awareness

Phase	State of activity	State of awareness
WHITE	Inactive	Unaware of environment
GREEN	Active	Aware
YELLOW	Proactive	Heightened awareness
RED	Reactive	Focused awareness
BLACK	Unable to react effectively	Overwhelmed, limited awareness

Phase of Awareness: WHITE

WHITE is an extremely important phase of awareness to us as it is where we mentally and physically rest. As an adult, if you get your normal eight hours of sleep each night, you will spend at least a third of your entire life in WHITE. This does not take into consideration naps, dozing, micro-sleeps, daydreaming, 'staring into space', being a 'couch potato', 'taking a break' and other such activities that when tallied, add many days of your life to the time you spend in WHITE.

Rest, both mentally and physically, is so important to your health and well because your brain and body generally let you know when you need it. For most of us, the problem lies in our not paying attention to our brain and body as we go about our lives. We tend not to get the proper rest we need, either mentally or physically. 'There will be plenty of time to rest when I'm dead', is a common response in attempting to rationalize our busy agendas. However, the brain and the body will only take so much abuse; then they revolt, and either or both of them will take you to WHITE.

Watch the ending of a marathon as runners literally stagger (and sometimes crawl) across the finish line. Their bodies are telling them that they need rest. Look at the faces of an airline crew getting off the aircraft in the morning after flying all night. Their faces will tell you they need rest, also.

The average attention span of the normal adult is about 20–25 minutes; then, the brain takes a break and goes to WHITE. You may be in WHITE for only a few seconds, or it could be much longer, but the brain needs the mental relief and it is going to take it. (While you are reading this book, you will involuntarily go to WHITE numerous times. It is up to us to motivate you to return to the book.)

WHITE involves a lot more than mental and physical rest. WHITE sometimes involves being actively engaged in activities outside your occupation, or your current primary task. Some of these activities are mentally relaxing, others physically relaxing.

For instance playing golf as a hobby (although there are many golfers who would refute this statement) may be physically tiring, but mentally relaxing. Reading a book may be physically relaxing, but mentally tiring. Regardless of the activity we choose, that activity is usually a method of finding the mental or physical rest we need.

While we are engaged in these activities, however, we are usually unaware of what is going on around us. For instance, while playing golf, have you ever had someone's golf ball land near you, and you had no clue where it came from? While reading a book, has someone ever slipped up on you? The real danger lies in being so preoccupied with the 'relaxing' activity that we let our guard down and leave us vulnerable to any type of attack. Preoccupation is only one of many factors that can lead us into WHITE.

Sleep and rest cannot be mentioned without also addressing one of the most common factors affecting flight crews – fatigue. There have been numerous studied conducted on the topics of sleep and fatigue in aviation and we would encourage you to read them, if you have not already done so. Fatigue can occur mentally and physically, or both. Either way, fatigue requires proper rest in order to recuperate and restore the body and mind, putting you in WHITE. When you are mentally and/or physically fatigued, your brain and body effectively tune out the surrounding environment. In doing so, you become vulnerable to attack. Rest and recuperation must be conducted in a safe place, free from vulnerabilities. Flight crews have fallen asleep in subway cars and in restaurants from fatigue after flying all night. What are their vulnerabilities in those locations?

Unfortunately, there are too many examples of people in WHITE placing themselves and others in jeopardy. In January 2003, a security screener assigned to exit lane duty at an international airport in northwestern US, clocked in at 5:30 a.m. The exit lane station was intended to prevent people from bypassing security and entering the concourse through the exit. At 6:00 a.m., a co-worker noticed the guard was asleep, resulting in concourses cleared, planes delayed and travelers required to be rescreened.[1] The guard was in WHITE and it cost him his job. It could have cost us much more!

Distractions can easily take us into WHITE, or as we will determine in a later phase, YELLOW. Let us say you are paying attention to your duties on the aircraft, either on the flight deck or in the cabin. Everything is 'normal'. Suddenly, a passenger appears to faint and slumps over in his seat. Does that event detract from the inflight service by the flight attendants? Does the call to the flight deck distract the pilots? Yes, it certainly does. The distracted flight attendants may not notice the man who immediately got out of his seat, rows ahead of the 'distraction', and is approaching the flight deck door. Does the call to the flight deck create a distraction that causes an altitude or heading deviation? (It has.) In these examples, distractions have caused members of the flight crew to lose awareness of their environment, leaving them vulnerable to dangers. These distractions took the crewmembers to WHITE.

In December 2001, authorities at an international airport in the southeastern US closed the airport for an hour after finding a metal detector at the security checkpoint unplugged. Security agents at that checkpoint had been distracted and failed to check their equipment.[2] They were in WHITE. Any type of weapon could have gotten through security and onto an aircraft.

In all of the above cases, aviation personnel jeopardized the safety and security of passengers, flight crews, and aircraft by being unaware of their environment in WHITE. We do not know all the details behind those incidents and other factors may have influenced the behavior of those in WHITE. Lack of motivation, boredom, monotony, stress, habit-patterns, complacency, and effects of alcohol or illness and/or medications are just a few of the many other factors that cause human beings to go to WHITE. Acting alone, or in combination with each other, these factors can result in one's lack of awareness of the surrounding environment and the vulnerability to danger.

WHITE is our default mode. It is where the brain and body like to be, and if left alone without any stimulation, that is where they will go. This is a good thing as far as mentally and physically resting is concerned; however, it is a bad thing when it comes to being aware of your environment and any associated threats.

It is important to recognize when you, or anyone else that affects your life, is in WHITE. If we recognize WHITE, we can manage it most of the time. WHITE seems rather obvious when someone is asleep or napping. Although, micro-sleeps, the relatively short periods of time when you might think you are awake, but are actually asleep, are not uncommon. Pilots have reported micro-sleeps on final approach, for instance, particularly after flying coast to coast all night. During the micro-sleeps, they were in WHITE. You may have experienced something similar while driving. You are on a long stretch of interstate highway late at night, and you think you are awake; suddenly, your head jerks and you realize that you have been asleep for a moment. The rush of adrenaline after that discovery (and the sound of the tires leaving the pavement) probably kept you wide-awake for a while. The lack of visual or auditory stimulation, monotony, time of night, and a long day may have all contributed to your being in WHITE while driving.

If you are asleep on an aircraft, you are in jeopardy unless someone you trust is watching over you. In July 2003, two passengers videotaped and photographed a sleeping charter pilot during a 55-minute flight from Walker's Cay to Fort Lauderdale-Hollywood International Airport. The co-pilot saw the passengers taping and photographing the captain, but did not wake him. Neither did the passengers. According to the company's general manager, the captain denied being asleep, but added, 'When I saw the video, it looks very bad'. An FAA spokesperson said, 'When two pilots are necessary for a flight, they are both required to remain awake, alert and performing their flight-related duties'.[3] The captain resigned because of being in WHITE at the wrong time.

Another characteristic of WHITE is daydreaming, sometimes described as 'lost in thought', 'just thinking', or 'spaced out'. During daydreaming, you may be unresponsive. A good indication that someone has been daydreaming is when they ask, 'What did you say', or 'what is going on?' when it should be obvious. During daydreaming, you are probably inattentive to what you are doing and completely unaware of what is going on around you.

Complacency can easily lead you into WHITE. Complacency is sometimes the result of habit and/or repetition. As a flight attendant, you may routinely pull a serving cart from the back of the aircraft forward with your back to the front of the aircraft. You have done this hundreds of times with no problem; however, today as you begin your normal routine, you do not notice the passenger with the knife approaching you from behind. Why? Because nothing ever happened to you all the times, you have done the same thing before. You fell from the trap of complacency into WHITE, and became a victim.

Pilots are susceptible to complacency, as well. A flight attendant calls the flight deck and says a passenger would like to know where we are. The response is 'I don't know ... just tell them we are somewhere over Kansas'. The autopilot and computer-controlled aircraft does such a good job navigating and flying the aircraft, we have the tendency to become complacent. What if the flight attendant had said instead, 'Captain, there is a man with a knife against my throat, and he wants to know where we are right now'. Would you make the same reply, 'Tell him we are somewhere over Kansas'?

Stress can be a big player in taking you to WHITE, and its effects can be distracting, as well. Just before departure of a commercial flight, the gate agent passed a note to the captain that read, 'Call the chief pilot as soon as you land'. The agent then closed the cabin door and the ramp agent said over the interphone that the aircraft was ready for pushback and engine start. What do you think was on the captain's mind during engine start, taxi, takeoff, climb, cruise, descent and landing? What did the chief pilot want? What have I done wrong? Is there a family emergency? The list of questions could go on forever. The captain was completely distracted the entire flight and was the first person off the aircraft at the destination airport. He immediately called the chief pilot who said, 'Next time you are through here, stop by my office and pick up your 15-year pin'. The stress generated by this simple message took the captain to WHITE for the entire flight.

One of the best ways to determine if you and/or others, are in WHITE, are to observe communications. We know snoring and head bobbing are good indications of someone sleeping. A person that is unresponsive to questions or conversation, whistling or humming, joking or making light conversation at an inappropriate time, silent when they should not be, or singing aloud while wearing earphones, is indicating they may be in WHITE.

Phase of Awareness: GREEN

Whereas WHITE is considered, an *inactive* phase (at least in terms of security awareness) GREEN is the *active* phase. In GREEN, you are actively accomplishing the task, or tasks, at hand, depending upon your type of work. For example, pre-flighting the aircraft, loading the computer on the flight deck, accomplishing checklists, obtaining ATC clearances, answering the radio, boarding passengers, securing the galley, serving beverages, and every other task involved in preparing a commercial aircraft for departure.

In GREEN, you are paying attention to what you are doing and mentally processing the world around you. We enter into GREEN because we are motivated and/or stimulated to do so. For instance, most readers of this book were probably was told as a child, 'You can go out to play after you finish your homework'. We were motivated to pay attention to our homework, stimulated by the sounds of other kids playing outside.

What motivates us to pay attention to our work? For pilots, motivators may include safety of flight, pay and benefits, expectations of others in getting from point A to point B on time, and lessons learned from mistakes of others that led to disasters. For flight attendants, it may be the joy of working with people, travel, and other company benefits (pay is probably not a motivator). We know that if we do NOT pay attention to performing our jobs, safety of flight may be jeopardized for everyone and customers may not choose to fly the airline because of poor safety record of the airline, and/or poor service.

Other, subtler, motivators may include how we feel, both mentally and physically. In GREEN, we are more than likely mentally and physically rested. We are wide-awake and alert. We feel good and are able to handle stress easily. We are confident in performing our duties because we are adequately trained and equipped to do the job. We catch and correct errors before they become problems.

People in GREEN are performing their jobs according to their training and expectations. Communications are business-like, correct, timely, and pertinent. Crew briefings and checklists are performed as designed and at the correct times. All calls from ATC are heard and acknowledged by the pilots. Passengers receive proper attention by the flight attendants. Customer service problems are recognized and resolved effectively. GREEN may be a very busy phase, but everything is taken care of according to normal procedures.

GREEN is good. Security threats are recognized and resolved in GREEN. In July 2003, security screeners spotted a handgun as it passed through the X-ray machine at a security checkpoint in Florida. The handgun was inside a teddy bear carried by a 10-year old boy, which underscores the importance of searching anyone that passes through the checkpoint, regardless of age. Before reaching the checkpoint, a girl, described as being between 10 and 14 years old, asked the boy if wanted the bear. His mother indicated it was okay for him to have it. The boy and his parents were unaware of the gun inside the bear.[4] (Ever wonder why airlines caution against carrying anything offered to you by a stranger?)

The security screeners were in GREEN, alert, attentive, and performing their job as trained and expected. What if they had been in WHITE and/or the metal detector had been unplugged as in the incident mentioned previously? The firearm could have easily been carried onto an aircraft very innocently by an unsuspecting child. The person that put the firearm in the teddy bear, or an accomplice, could have retrieved it later during flight. Your imagination can complete this scenario.

Phase of Awareness: YELLOW

YELLOW is the *proactive* phase. It is the phase of awareness in which all learning takes place, making it an extremely important phase and one in which we all spend a great deal of time throughout out lives.

We pack our brain with information in YELLOW. When we read, we are gathering information, as well as when we listen to others, or when we watch and listen to the television. In YELLOW, we actively search for information and our senses provide inputs for mental processing. (You are in YELLOW right now, as you read, analyze and study what is said in this book.) We are motivated to learn.

Training is accomplished in YELLOW. Pilots experience all types of emergencies during flight simulator training to store the recognition and resolution of those events in their brains for future use. Flight attendants train in cabin mockups, fighting on-board fires, dealing with medical emergencies and performing emergency evacuations, for the same reasons.

In YELLOW, we ask questions, analyze, give opinions and/or answers, and make plans. What, why, where, when, how and 'what if', are frequently used words in YELLOW, We hear a sound, for example, and ask, 'What was that?' We accomplish a pattern match with what has been stored in our brain, and an answer is provided. If there is no pattern match (we have never heard the sound before), we begin analyzing it, asking more questions and looking for answers. Once we identify the sound, we store it in our brain for future use in pattern matching. If we hear it again, we will recognize it.

Many times, YELLOW results from a heightened awareness. A light illuminates on the instrument panel, catching our attention. A passenger rings her call button in the cabin, getting the attention of the flight attendant. The light and the call button are designed to attract attention. We proactively respond to their signals and resolve the issue at hand.

In YELLOW, we notice and analyze inconsistencies, discrepancies and things that do not 'look right'. The oil pressure on the #2 engine is low, but the quantity and temperature are normal. What is wrong with the oil pressure? During flight, a passenger is unresponsive and foaming at the mouth. What is the matter with him? No one is around the briefcase under a seat in the boarding area and it has been unattended for at least 15 minutes. Should I tell anyone?

There is a cardboard box about one foot-square sitting on the flight deck jump seat when you enter the aircraft to pre-flight. As the first officer, you take a close look at it, discovering that it is labeled 'Human Eyeballs'. You have previously transported human organs for transport, so you look for the required paperwork. There is none. You ask the agent working the flight where the box came from and about the missing paperwork. No one seems to know anything about it. You are in YELLOW. What are you going to do? Are you going to open the package to verify its contents? Are you going to remove it from the aircraft? Are you going to call security? Were you trained to deal with this problem?

YELLOW stimulates our curiosity. YELLOW can be stimulated by strong sensory cues, such as a warning light. YELLOW is also where the sixth sense is activated. The sixth sense, intuition, is the conduit of communication connecting the unconscious portion of the brain with its counterpart, the conscious portion of the brain. The feelings that 'things just are not right and 'I should not do that' are powerful indicators that intuition is at work. The unconscious portion of the brain is 'seeing something' that the conscious portion is overlooking, generating an uneasy feeling. Studies have shown that the sixth sense to be correct about 90–95 per cent of the time.[5]

A danger associated with YELLOW is focused attention. The light that comes on, the bell that rings, the person yelling causes us to focus our attention on that event to identify and rectify the situation, and that is not only a normal but a required response. The danger lies in focusing entirely on the distraction to the point that we forget about everything else that is happening.

The 1972 Eastern Airlines L1011 accident is an example of how focused attention on a minor item led to the entire flight deck crew becoming distracted and crashing the aircraft into the Everglades in Florida. As the aircraft was configured for landing in Miami, the green light indicating the nose gear was extended and locked down did not illuminate. Both pilots and the flight engineer focused their attention on trying to fix the light. None of the crew noticed the aircraft begin a slow descent and no one correctly interpreted approach control's query as to their intentions. The plane continued its descent into the swamp, killing 101 people, and injuring 176 others. The entire crew was in YELLOW.

This crash highlights another danger in YELLOW. We tend to draw others into YELLOW with us. In the Eastern crash, all three flight deck crewmembers got involved and no one flew the aircraft. Caution must be exercised when getting others involved in resolving problems. Managing this problem becomes even more crucial in a two-person cockpit. The pilot not working the problem MUST fly the aircraft and not allow any distractions to take away from this vital task.

One logical progression from YELLOW is to phase RED. As an example, an engine fire light comes on, getting our attention. We go to YELLOW as we analyze the problem, and then to RED as we react to the situation as we have been trained. A flight attendant in YELLOW analyzes a sick passenger and responds to the situation in RED, as trained.

Phase of Awareness: RED

RED, the *reactive* phase of awareness is very involved and complicated, as you will see shortly. During RED, you respond with what you know. It is too late to start the learning process when you are in RED. A situation has occurred requiring a definite response, not a question. An emergency evacuation is a good example where both flight deck and cabin crews have very specific responses that they have been trained to utilize during such an event. It is common in post-event interviews for crews not to remember how they responded, but they performed flawlessly anyway. They reacted in RED.

RED occurs when the brain recognizes a high threat situation. An engine fire light coming on during takeoff or a masked man with a knife approaching you in the galley are quickly recognized as high threats by the brain through mental processing of certain learned cues. You normally shift from GREEN (or WHITE) to YELLOW as you identify the threat, followed quickly by a shift to RED as you react to the situation. Your reaction to the recognized threat depends upon your experience with similar situations and your trained responses to them – such as practicing engine fire on takeoff in the simulator or instantly using defensive techniques against the man with the knife.

In RED, we react with one of two types of responses, learned or instinctive responses. If an instantaneous response is not required (instinctive), the brain searches its files for a solution to the perceived problem. Once it finds a match from what you know, it selects the course of action to take – the learned response. You call for the proper checklist and perform any memory items. You simply react to the situation as trained, or from what you know from your experience. (If the search does not find a match, you may go to either YELLOW – to analyze the situation further – or to BLACK, as discussed later.)

The brain tries to protect itself and the body automatically through use of instinctive movements that are used when danger is sensed; for instance, quickly closing or shielding your eyes with your hand when blinded by a strong light, or dropping a wine glass and catching it before it hits the floor. We do not practice those reactions, but the brain realizes that something bad will happen if it does not instantly signal the body to do something, and it reacts instinctively.

In RED, the activation of your instinctive survival mode depends upon the perceived severity of the moment or event. Better known as the 'Fight or Flight' syndrome, many protective impulses are generated without any conscious inputs almost instantaneously.

Characteristics of RED vary according to whether it was a learned or an instinctive response that is triggered. Usually, if a learned response is triggered, the brain continues to function normally; however, blood pressure may rise above normal and muscles become tense. Communication is usually confined to commands and responses as procedures and checklists are followed. Passenger announcements become clipped, matter-of-fact, hurried and directive. (To the first officer) 'Tell departure control we have an engine problem and are declaring an emergency. We are following the engine out procedure and want vectors for an immediate landing. We have 150 souls on board and 3 hours of fuel.' (To the passengers) 'Ladies and gentlemen, this is the captain. We have experienced a problem with an engine on the right side of the aircraft. The situation is under control. We will be returning to AAA airport and will be landing in approximately 10 minutes. Flight attendants, prepare the cabin for emergency landing.'

If the brain senses grave danger, the Fight or Flight syndrome may be triggered. When this happens, dramatic neurological and physical changes take place almost immediately. Normally, the right and left sides of our brain work in conjunction with one another, providing us with the abilities to reason and to create. When fight or flight is triggered, the brain goes into a survival mode, shifting control of the brain to the hypothalamus – a walnut-sized area of the brain located at the bottom center of the brain. The main frame of the brain virtually shuts down and the blood supply to it is restricted. You will not be able to balance your checkbook or decorate a room when you are in RED, as both sides of the brain are shut down.

The hypothalamus, in simple terms, is hard-wired to the files stored in your brain; however, it has a very limited ability to collect and process new data. If you have learned a procedure or made a plan to deal with a particular situation, the hypothalamus can find it in the files and retrieve it for your use. If you have never seen or heard of the event and/or have never mentally processed any procedure or plan to deal with it, the hypothalamus comes up blank, sending you to BLACK, which we will discuss next.

As soon as control is shifted to the hypothalamus, it begins to prepare your body to either fight for your life, or to run away (flight). Although the following is a list of items that will happen in this situation, keep in mind that they happen at the speed of electrical impulses generated by the central nervous system (CNS) and they are simplified, reducing the medical jargon.

Blood – A signal is sent to the heart to increase output. The result is a faster heartbeat and an increase in blood pressure and pulse rate. (This sudden increase in blood pressure and rate has been known to cause death to people with weak vascular systems – hence the saying 'scared to death'.) Blood flow increases dramatically to the large muscle groups. The small muscle groups and capillaries in the skin are constricted and the blood normally going to them is diverted to the large muscle groups (neck, shoulders, arms, thighs, calves). After incurring major injuries, such as cuts or gunshot wounds, people have been known not to bleed until after the adrenaline wore off and circulation was restored to the extremities and to the skin. Digestion shuts down and the blood used in that process is diverted to the large muscle groups, as well.

Oxygen – The large muscles demand oxygenated blood, so a signal is sent to the lungs to increase output. The result is an increase in breathing frequency and depth. The tendency is to breath through the mouth rather than the nose since more air can be ingested. Breathing through the mouth can cause 'dry-mouth', or 'cotton-mouth', making it difficult to talk.

Blood sugar – The muscles need sugar to burn for energy, so a signal is sent via the pituitary gland to the liver to increase sugar output into the blood stream.

Adrenaline – The CNS can only sustain all this activity for a short time; therefore, it sends a signal through the pituitary gland to the adrenal gland to increase output. Adrenaline flows through the body approximately 200 mph, very fast in a short distance. The adrenaline sustains the functions initiated by the CNS. When the adrenaline rush is over, the brain and body want to relax. Where do we recuperate mentally and physically? In WHITE, of course, putting us back into the danger zone of letting our guard down.

People have been known to go immediately asleep after the adrenaline wore off. Additional side effects of adrenaline wearing off will be discussed in BLACK.

Muscles – Most everyone has read or heard about feats of strength of people under the influence of adrenaline. The large muscle groups, energized from blood saturated in sugar and oxygen, become extremely powerful. This is a good thing, if you are in hand-to-hand combat. It is not so good if you are attempting to make small corrections while maneuvering an aircraft, as muscle movements are large and jerky. Braking on the ground may be excessively heavy. The enlarged muscles in your neck may press on your vocal cords, making your voice squeaky and high-pitched. The lack of blood flow to your small muscles groups, such as your fingers, may cause a loss of dexterity. Selecting settings by knobs or making inputs into a computer may become very difficult.

Perspiration – With all the bodies' pumps running full bore, body temperature rises. A signal is sent to the perspiration glands to increase perspiration in an attempt to cool the body down. (Look at the soggy armpits of pilots coming out of simulator after a check ride, or of a flight attendant after a series of emergency events in a cabin trainer.)

Sensory perception – All of the senses are heightened and sharpened. You may hear things you have never heard before (which may be confusing). Hair follicles are stimulated and you may experience 'goose bumps', with the hair standing up giving you a better sense of touch. Your sense of pain may be greatly diminished, temporarily. You may experience a metallic taste as your taste buds are stimulated.

Depending upon the condition of your eyes, you may experience better than normal vision (even without glasses); however, the size of the images may be exaggerated.

> During an interview with the captain of a flight involved in a hijacking, a question was asked relating to the type of firearm used by the hijacker. The captain indicated that the firearms had to be a .50 caliber or larger. If fact, the caliber was a 7.65mm, much smaller than the captain thought.

Another significant feature of the fight or flight syndrome is 'Tachi Psychi'. During Tachi Psychi (temporal distortion), heightened visual ability combines with the speeding up of the visual processing centers and the accelerated triggering of the motor control functions, causing a perceived slowing down of time.[6] 'Everything seemed to be in slow motion', is a common statement indicating a person has experienced this time warp. For about 80 per cent of people experiencing temporal distortion, time slows down; for the remaining 20 per cent, time seems to speed up.

While reacting to a fight or flight situation, the tendency is to focus on that situation very intently and narrow down to very specific items, such as looking directly at a person's eyes that is yelling at you and forgetting to look at his hands. (Looks do not kill, hands do.) This 'tunnel vision' is necessary to some extent as the brain is verifying its inputs, but can be detrimental to recognizing what else may be occurring elsewhere.

Communication during the fight or flight syndrome is difficult both for those trying to talk and for listeners trying to understand. Guttural grunts, groans, and incoherent and/or incomplete sentences are common, in addition to the use of expletives. Commands and responses tend to be shouted or shrieked in a high-pitched, staccato-like manner, interspersed between breaths of air.

The brain's limited capacity to mentally process new information during the fight or flight syndrome may create confusion and add to the stress levels already experienced. *Please pay attention to this very important point. If you are involved with someone who has shifted into the fight or flight mode and you have not shifted, the job of mental processing belongs to YOU.* It has been our observation that if the person in the flight or fight mode is given directions or orders, that person will comply or carry them out without hesitation. Out of ideas, they will latch on to any directive given to them. In reviewing a head's-up-display (HUD) videotape of a pilot experiencing an engine failure in a single-engine fighter, and subsequently going to RED, members of his flight gave him numerous directions. 'Start down, now'. 'Come left'. 'Come twenty degrees left'. 'Get rid of your drop tanks, now'. The pilot immediately complied with each command and successfully landed the aircraft, engine out. One could easily conclude from viewing the entire tape, that if the pilot had been by himself, or if no one had given him directives, the aircraft would have been lost. This was not an isolated case, either.

If you are involved with a high-stress security-related event, such as a terrorist attack or a hijacking, and if you are not in the fight or flight mode yourself, you must remember that YOU may have to direct other crewmembers that have shifted to the fight or flight mode.

The key to coming out of the fight or flight mode lies in control of your breathing. If you force yourself to breath 'normally', you can break out of the mode. This sounds a lot simpler than it is; however, restoring normal breathing slows the lungs and heart, relaxes the large muscle groups, begins circulation to the areas deprived of blood, and returns control of the brain to the main frame allowing mental processing to restart. You recover both mentally and physically. Encouraging others to 'breath normally' can help them break out of the mode, as well.

Phase of Awareness: BLACK

In terms of action, BLACK is a phase of *ineffective action(s).* While discussing the 'levels of consciousness' with Colonel Cooper, phase BLACK was introduced to him. (His levels were white, yellow, orange and red.) Colonel Cooper regarded BLACK as just 'deep red'; however, after years of applying the phases of awareness to aviation accidents, BLACK was determined to be a definite phase by itself. Numerous incidents occurring during personal protection courses taught by Bud Williams, also verified BLACK as a definite phase.

BLACK contains many negative features, such as desperation, panic, being out of control, confusion and/or ineffective actions, and should be avoided at all costs.

Unfortunately, cockpit voice recordings have captured these traits in too many accidents. It is reasonable to assume that a number of these factors were present in the aircraft involved in the 9/11 attacks. We want to help you avoid being in BLACK.

It is possible to enter BLACK in several ways. The most common way is through lack of knowledge and/or training. In YELLOW, we pack our brains with information and data. When the hypothalamus searches for information during RED and does not find anything stored in your brain pertaining to the situation, the hypothalamus does not know what to tell your body to do. Instead of letting you hurt yourself by making a wrong move, the hypothalamus causes you to freeze in position. You cannot move, and may not be able to speak (the brain does not know what you should say, either). Communication may be total silence, or unintelligible sounds. 'Freezing' differs from panic, which may involve sporadic and exaggerated movement. Musical performers know that stage fright produces a trembling in their hands and that if the stage fright is severe enough, they can do nothing at all.[7] The expression 'paralyzed with fear' has a very sound basis. Obviously, if you freeze in position and are unable to move, you will easily become a victim of the high-stress situation.

In describing the details of a traffic accident involving an emergency vehicle and a passenger car, an EMT said:

> I remember seeing her car pulling forward. Then I saw her face and the panic on it as she looked through her windshield at me. She froze right in the middle of the intersection. And I knew I was going to hit her ...

If you experience 'freezing' during training, it is crucial that you repeat the scenario until you are able to work through it without freezing. The best way to avoid BLACK is through education and training. If your personal knowledge and accompanying security training is inadequate in preparing you for aviation-related events, you are a candidate for going to BLACK and freezing.

The brain's search for information in RED does not require a perfect pattern match. If it can find anything close that it can adapt for use, it will tend to grab on to it. For instance, you see a passenger approaching with a box cutter in his hand. Your training did not include defense against a box cutter, but did cover attacks with a knife. Your brain can use your defense against the knife in commanding your body to respond to the box cutter.

One of the problems associated with not finding a perfect pattern match is that after the brain grabs onto something similar, chooses and adapts it for use, and commands the body to react, the brain may perceive the actions it commanded are not effectively dealing with the situation. It then restarts its search for the perfect match. In doing so, it finds something else that is similar and may choose it, adapt it for use and issue new commands to the body. This repetitive process may happen extremely fast, resulting in the body becoming confused as to what it is trying to accomplish. In a similar manner, the wrong diagnosis of a problem or incorrectly prioritizing a list of problems can result in taking you from RED into BLACK by causing confusion, leading to panic. Panic results when nothing seems to be taking care of the problem, another symptom of being in BLACK. Although an infrequent event, the inability of a pilot to handle multiple emergencies in flight simulators has caused the pilot to panic. Panic can also be determined from cockpit voice recordings of some accidents. In both of these cases, words describing communication during panic were 'incomplete', 'erratic', 'unintelligible', 'screaming', and/or repeated questions with no apparent answer, such as 'why is not it working?' As a person realizes that nothing is working to correct the situation and even may be making the situation worse, a high level of frustration may be induced, feeding panic. 'Just do SOMETHING!' may be a characteristic response. Other communication during this time may include a generous sprinkling of expletives.

Another way of entering BLACK is through a side effect of the adrenaline rush experienced during the fight or flight syndrome. When adrenaline wears off, the body wants to rest, both mentally and physically as previously stated. However, adrenaline wearing off may also have another negative side effect. During the fight or flight syndrome, the blood flow to the capillaries in the skin, the small muscle groups, the digestive system and to the main frame of the brain is very constricted. In order to return normal circulation to these areas, the hypothalamus may cause the body to shake and/or jerk uncontrollably. The shaking and/or jerking may be much more violent than shaking or shivering when the body is cold. The uncontrollable shaking is included as a feature of being in BLACK because it is 'uncontrollable'. During this period of shaking, you may not be able to react physically to a situation or be able to communicate effectively.

A couple of examples vividly demonstrate the debilitating effects of adrenaline wearing off. The first example comes from an incident on a Boeing 757. The second involves a woman who successfully negated a physical/sexual assault.

> A cargo fire light in the forward cargo hold illuminated on descent into the destination airport. Blowing both bottles of fire extinguishing agent into the forward hold did not extinguish the fire light until on final approach. All checklists were completed, flight attendants and passengers briefed, and the cabin was prepared for a possible emergency evacuation. The captain flew an instrument approach to Category II weather minimums, breaking out right at minimums. He landed, cleared the runway at a high-speed turn-off and brought the aircraft to a stop as quickly as possible. The airport fire and rescue personnel responded immediately. A firefighter opened the forward cargo hold, did not detect any smoke or fire, and gave the okay to continue taxiing to the gate. After making an announcement to the flight attendants and passengers that everything was okay, the captain said, 'Tell ground control that we are going to sit here for about another five minutes.' After relaying this message to tower, the first office asked the captain about the delay. The captain replied, 'Because my legs are shaking so bad that I cannot keep my feet on the rudder pedals for the brakes!' The captain had experienced the fight or flight syndrome and the accompanying adrenaline rush.

> A radio talk show host was making a short daytime road trip in her car. As she pulled off the interstate highway at a rest stop to use the restroom, she noticed only one vehicle present, an eighteen-wheeler with its engine running. The woman took her handgun

with her into the restroom (YELLOW). Upon leaving the facility, a very large man confronted her with a rope in his hands. She quickly drew her handgun and pointed it at him while backing him out of the facility towards his truck (RED). She quickly got into her car and drove off rapidly down the interstate. About five minutes later, she pulled off to the side of the road. She said her legs were shaking and twitching so badly she could not keep her feet on the accelerator or the brake. Her neck muscles were jerking her head in all directions, making it difficult to monitor her rear view mirror. The effects of adrenaline wearing off completely rendered her unable to function normally, putting her in BLACK. (She recovered after about 15 minutes, continued on her trip, stopping at the next exit to call the police and report the incident.)

The startle response is a momentary spike into BLACK. More than likely, all of us have experienced a situation where someone scares you by jumping out from behind a blind corner, or jabs you in the ribs from behind, slams a book down on your desk when you are not watching, or something very similar, activating the reflexive startle response. The sudden jerk of your body, or part of it, or your gasp are ineffective in dealing with the perceived threat, but are activated by the brain in BLACK. You may recall getting goose bumps, followed by a sudden flush of warmth afterwards as the blood flow throughout the body as it accelerated.

A characteristic that is unique to BLACK is that of a person giving up during the attempt to find a remedy to the situation. When a situation is perceived to be beyond the capabilities to handle by an individual in BLACK, the person simply gives up trying. This phenomenon can be recognized, particularly in cockpit voice recordings or ATC tapes after an aircraft accident, by a call to a supreme being, such as 'Oh, God!' 'Lord, help us!', or other similar calls. Some communications indicate the finality of the situation, such as 'It's over', or 'We're going to crash!' Unfortunately, in a few known cases involving aircraft disasters, the aircraft could have been recovered had the crew not gone to BLACK in this unique manner, and given up.

Putting the Phases into Perspective

From the descriptions provided for each phase, it can easily be deduced that GREEN and YELLOW are the two phases that provide the best likelihood of early detection of any security-related event. YELLOW and RED are necessary phases to effectively deal with a life-threatening event. Each of us will spend a significant amount of our lives in WHITE, but we must manage and control our time spent there. We must do everything possible to avoid being in BLACK.

It would be preferable to live constantly in GREEN; however, more brain bytes are consumed in GREEN than in WHITE – it simply takes more energy to stay alert 100 per cent of the time and the brain/body are not going to let you do that. Living constantly in YELLOW is not an option either because it takes more energy and brain activity than GREEN, so the brain/body are not going to let you do that. RED requires an extremely high level of brain energy, especially with the fight or flight syndrome operating at a peak in both of those areas. As much as some people would like to live in a constant adrenaline rush, it is certain the brain and body are not going to let you do that, as well. BLACK represents complete overload of the brain and body and quickly drains energy from both the brain and the body. You would not live very long if you stayed in BLACK indefinitely.

What this means is that we must recognize, control and manage the phases of awareness we experience as we accomplish our routine jobs and encounter life-threatening, high-stress situations. Here are some things that are under your control and upon which you should rate yourself as to how well you accomplish them:

- Being in good health; proper diet and nutrition, controlling intakes of alcohol and tobacco, getting routine physical examinations;
- Being in good physical condition; exercising on a routine basis, controlling sleep and rest cycles to maximize alertness on the job;
- Controlling your stress levels through stress reduction techniques;
- Insisting on thorough, pertinent, practical training on security issues from your airline, both in the classroom and in flight or cabin simulators;
- Reading and studying security-related books, articles, course materials;
- Providing additional individual preparation through attending advanced training, seminars, conferences, and course offerings pertinent to security events;
- Paying attention to and analyzing daily news articles (occurring daily) relating to any of the subjects in this book;
- Conversing and sharing information and experiences with other crewmembers about security-related events;
- Reviewing security procedures and sharing contingency plans during flight crew briefings;
- Controlling distractions, both in the cabin and on the flight deck; and,
- Practicing the recognition of the phases of awareness as they occur in your life and in others and knowing how to apply the advantages of each phase to the situation at hand; knowing the limitations of each phase; and, knowing how to avoid any negative aspects of each phase.

In summary, the phases of awareness are real. You will experience most or all of them in your lifetime. Some of the phases are helpful to you in accomplishing your daily, routine tasks as well as responding appropriately during a crisis situation, while other phases are detrimental to those efforts. You must know the difference and place yourself in the most advantageous phase for what is occurring in your life at the moment. That could be WHITE, sleep. It could be GREEN as you perform routine tasks, or YELLOW as you note discrepancies. It could be RED, fight or flight. One thing is certain; you never want it to be BLACK. Your practice in recognition of these phases during your day-to-day life will help you quickly recognize them should you encounter a high stress situation where your life, or the lives of others, depend upon your actions. You will be surprised at how many times you will find yourself in WHITE!

Notes

1 Dozing Seattle-Tacoma Airport screener fired, *Seattle Times*, 8 January 2003.
2 Security breaches hinder flights, *Dallas Morning News*, 19 December 2001.
3 Pilot resigns; was taped sleeping, *Associated Press*, 19 July 2003.
4 Airport scan reveals gun inside 'gift' bear, *Arizona Republic*, 17 July 2003.
5 Williams, Clois, and Steve Waltrip, *Behavioral Assessment of Threat*, Diversified Training Company, April 2003.
6 Adrenal Stress Effects, www.rmcat.com/page17.html, 23 July 2003.
7 Adrenaline, www.peterharris.org/roadsafety/adrenaline/html, 23 July 2003.

Chapter 8

Mental Preparation: Developing a Survival Mindset

Introduction

Mental preparation, extremely important in developing a mindset of survival, is not any different from preparing for any other emergency aboard an aircraft. Pilots prepare in the flight simulator and flight attendants prepare in the cabin trainer for the worse case scenarios. It does not matter if you are a 60-year-old flight attendant/pilot or a 21-year-old flight attendant/pilot you can still mentally prepare for a possible violent physical confrontation. How? By development of a mindset of survival through a personal commitment to never giving up when faced with danger. Unfortunately, crewmembers are living in a new reality. The times we live in have changed and we must change with them, or risk being led like lambs to the slaughter.

During the development of a flight crew security program, we interviewed a major airline captain who, while serving as a military pilot in Vietnam, was downed behind enemy lines. The purpose for our interviewing Captain Gordon Paige was to learn from him how he and others survived in extremely difficult circumstances. Captured by the North Vietnamese, Captain Paige was held at the infamous Hanoi Hilton. Captain Paige spoke of the various stages of his captivity. The difficulties he experienced during his eight months in captivity took tremendous individual inner strength. Very discouraged after his capture, he grew mentally stronger daily as he accepted his dilemma. He and the other POWs developed a mental strength that took time to build. Paige received encouragement from his fellow POWs, who encouraged one another to survive and make the best of their miserable conditions. It was not easy, but they did what they needed to do to survive and to come home safely.

Although, crewmembers may not ever end up as a captive in a hijacking event as long as Captain Paige was a POW, they would experience much of what he did in a different way. Crewmembers are in fact captives to the continued terrorist threats and actions. Commercial aviation and all who are a part of it are captive to threats and actions of terrorists. We are captive because current threats are deadly serious and out of our control.

Even though Captain Paige's experience with the mindset for survival occurred over an extended period, we should take advantage of the time we now have to develop and prepare our minds for survival. Otherwise, we may find ourselves in a hijacking situation with no mental preparation of how to react. Like Captain Paige and his fellow POWs, crewmembers should encourage one another to be strong so they can be mentally prepared to face very difficult circumstances such as the flight crews experienced on 9/11. Crewmember lives depend on one another more than ever for mutual support and survival. By learning what those crews experienced on the fateful 9/11 flights, crewmembers can better understand terrorists' minds and tactics. The crews on 9/11 did not have this advantage. Today, armed with knowledge of the survival issues crewmembers faced during those attacks, crewmembers can prepare mentally and physically to defend themselves for any life or death situation on board an aircraft. In this chapter, we will attempt to prepare you mentally against terrorist threats. Whether you heed our warnings and accept our advice is strictly up to you. We know it is a hard topic to accept. Developing a survival mindset is an individual approach. We will give you some basic principles to follow in developing a survival mindset that we believe are foundational to survival in the dangerous world of air transportation and aviation insecurity.

Setting the Stage

Terrorists have the advantage by virtue of surprise. They know when, where, how, and what kind of an attack they are going to make. However, they do not know how prepared crewmembers actually are to defend against their attack. Your lack of mental and/or physical preparation is what terrorists are counting on for their success. Crewmembers can use this to their advantage by preparing and responding mentally in ways the terrorists cannot predict. Terrorists may commit violent acts intended to shock and horrify those who witness these acts. Nevertheless, if crewmembers are mentally prepared to withstand a horrible act, no matter how bad it may be, then the terrorists have lost more than half of the surprise of a hijacking. It is imperative that you respond to extreme violence with extreme violence. Do it quickly and with all your strength. Otherwise, it may be too late. To react in this manner, takes mental preparation for most of us.

The radical terrorists from 9/11 are the worst possible type of enemy you face as a crewmember. They are cold-blooded murderers who think they are going to heaven for killing you or anyone else they designate as their enemy for their own twisted and sick beliefs. If you can fully understand this, then you can prepare for it by developing a mental toughness and a determined will to live.

Should you face the situation of a radical terrorists taking over your aircraft and committing a horrifying murder to set the tone of the hijacking, it is imperative you maintain control of your emotions. This sounds difficult, if not impossible, but you can do it. You should understand they are counting on you to be shocked and stunned into inaction, horrified that such a cold-blooded act could take place in front of you. Your subsequent inability to react is exactly what they want. You will play into their hands if you are so shocked that you stand there with your mouth open, unable to act (Phase of Awareness BLACK).

There will be plenty of time later (and there will be a later!) to worry about the horror of the incident. You must be able to respond to terrorists at the same level or greater than the cruelty they are committing aboard your aircraft. Faced with the most violent situation you have ever experienced, your mind must be free to act without inhibition when fighting for your life with trained terrorists who will certainly try to kill you.

Lets face it, going up against terrorists who have trained for years on how to kill you is a tremendous task for anyone. Yet, being prepared to deal with horrifying events as they occur will greatly increase your odds of survival and all of those aboard. Do not be fooled by government reassurances and others who think that terrorists cannot make it through the security checkpoints without detection. We all have read news reports of how weapons and bombs can successfully be smuggled onto commercial airliners. Do NOT count on security checkpoints to stop a terrorist and weapons from getting onboard an aircraft.

We are not one bit confident that any of the high tech solutions will stop cunning, planning, and preparation of intelligent terrorist hijackers. Why should we be? We are crewmembers who trusted the FAA, FBI, CIA, or any one of the other government agencies that did not stop the terrorists from carrying out the attacks on 9/11. Authorities know terrorists were planning some extreme terrorist acts, but 9/11 happened anyway, and all our brother and sister pilots and flight attendants were murdered. Assurances by politicians that we are safe now from terrorists do little to comfort us. As flight crewmembers, we must become an integral part of the solution to airline security and not place our confidence in security measures put into place by the government and aviation industry. If we do not recognize that times have changed and become a proactive part of the seamless security, we will no doubt become victims of our own inaction.

According to the FAA/TSA, the old 'Common Strategy' hijacking techniques worked very effectively up to the day of 9/11. This is not true at all. The techniques worked in a different era when hijackers wanted to go to Cuba. As the motives changed and violence of hijacking increased throughout the 1980s and 1990s, the Common Strategy remained the same – a serious mistake. Flight crews must now be more than bystanders when confronted with violent situations aboard aircraft. They must be trained to deal with violent encounters with overwhelming force. Flight crews must accept this reality and not react by putting their heads into the sand and pretending another 9/11 disaster is not possible.

Mindset

Just days after the terrorists' attacks on 9/11, Steve Waltrip, asked by a concerned and worried flight attendant how she could 'possibly defend herself' from trained terrorists, told her the first step would be to develop a mindset of survival so that it would be much more difficult for an attacker to win. It is true that terrorists may have had years of training leading up to an attack, but you have your brain, your will to survive, and hidden strengths that you may not know exists within you. Your mind, your wits, and the hidden physical strengths are possessions terrorists will never be able to take from you. The sudden shock of an attack or infliction of a serious wound would surprise anyone. Once you realize that you are in the midst of an extreme life or death situation, you can and must use the gift that God gave to each and everyone of us, your brain.

State of mind and proper mindset are keys to success in overcoming any dire situation. At this very moment, you must believe in yourself and that you can overcome any threat that comes before you. You must never give up!

September 11 is a date that no crewmember at that time will ever forget. The haunting memories of what occurred will forever be burned into our memories. Among many other things, crewmembers will remember this day as the day their rules regarding hijackings changed forever. It has now become known these men trained for years on the weaknesses and traits of our aviation security systems. The terrorist hijackers took martial arts courses, trained in the use of knives, took flying lessons and prepared themselves mentally and physically for their mission. They were determined men who approached their homicidal task with religious zealotry and military discipline.

The mindset set of a radical terrorist is a strange and determined mix of religion and politics. They will stop at nothing to accomplish their overall goals and will sacrifice their lives to achieve that goal. To read more on the thinking processes of a terrorist read Chapter 4, Investigating Terrorism, for a better look at their training and preparation.

How can we as everyday working people ever expect to overcome the murderous/suicidal attacks that occurred on that horrible day? How could we ever prepare for such individuals as those? We can and we will overcome such wicked determination that was conceived in secret and carried out with great success. You are capable of developing a mindset using fundamental methods to overcome their advantages.

Camaraderie

One of the most important aspects of a survival mindset is *camaraderie.* Crewmembers must believe they are in an aircraft with other crewmembers that are willing to come to their assistance when needed. Whether you personally like them or not, you must be able to count on them when the 'chips are down', and 'all hell is breaking loose.' Camaraderie is an underlying aspect of all groups of people who must rely upon each other for survival. You see this in members of the military, police, fire fighters and any other group of individuals tied together by survival situations. Each crewmember must be able to rely on every other crewmember for collective survival.

It is extremely important that crewmembers *develop a bond with other crewmembers.* We must rely on each other for our survival so we need to build a strong bond that goes beyond the details of everyday, routine tasks. We must care for each other to the extent that we would fight to the death for each other. We may not talk about it much, but that bond must be present, and we must believe others feel as we do about that bond.

Crewmembers must *agree on a common goal of mutual survival.* Mutual survival begins with believing that all members of the crew are needed and can be relied upon in successfully defending one another. Nobody expects you to be a 'Rambo' and take on a whole plane of hijackers by yourself, but together crewmembers can survive a serious assault. There have been many media reports of terrorist training camps throughout the world where they train for years to overpower, kill, and defeat by unconventional methods. Regardless of this fact, crewmembers must believe they can defeat a terrorist attack within the aircrew team. Your survival is predicated upon the survival of other crewmembers on your plane. You need other crewmembers as much as they need you.

Commitment to the crewmember team that we are working on is essential in building trust. Thorough crew briefings with every crew you fly with during the day, open the lines of communication and set the stage for building trust with other crewmembers. The commitment demonstrated in the briefing will give you the satisfaction and peace of mind to feel comfortable in today's new reality of air transportation. The aviation world will continue to be a very dangerous place, and the trust we develop with each other is essential to survival. Letting each other know when anything suspicious or identified as dangerous is occurring is a positive way in which to build and reinforce trust.

Crewmembers must protect each other from vulnerability and assault. When Steve Waltrip was a police officer, it was essential that officers protect each other from vulnerability. For example, an officer would not let someone walk up behind another officer without letting him or her know about it. In an airplane, the same thing could happen. As crewmembers protecting each other, we should attempt to notify other crewmembers of potential threats whenever possible. Crewmembers must realize how serious the threat is to them by trained terrorists. Terrorists are very capable of developing tactics to counter the best defensive approaches we can develop. Do not trust any passengers who may approach you or come up behind you. As innocent as it may seem, if a terrorist knows some of your tactics, they will counter them and try to catch you off guard. It is a common belief the recent terrorist attacks across the world have been carried out by men. However, many women are trained and are capable of being involved in terrorist attacks.[1] Do not assume because it is a woman approaching you that she is not capable of extreme violence against you, as well.

There must be no question to our commitment to one another. As we have been saying repeatedly, it is imperative that you understand the commitment you must have for one another. Your mutual survival may someday be based upon this very fact. The need to protect each other must be instilled upon each crewmember. We believe the defensive approaches taught to crewmembers should be based upon the trust and camaraderie we have with each other. Camaraderie, trust and commitment should not be ignored in the development of airline security procedures.

Six Important Principles for a Survival Mindset

The six principles embodied in this section will assist you in developing a mental picture of the steps required in building a survival mindset.

Survival principle one: Knowledge

Knowledge is the first step in developing a survival mindset. Talking with others who have had experiences in defending themselves is helpful in understanding the mental processes involved. However, a determined mindset can also be learned in a multitude of ways. The alcoholic can learn it by quitting alcohol. The parent can learn it through the terminal illness of a child. These are difficult circumstances for anyone to deal with, but are common to the human condition. We start developing a determined mindset through the experience of life's difficulties.

You should apply the difficult experiences in your life in establishing a baseline for a determined survival mindset. We have all had difficult experiences in life. Nothing quite works in life like our difficult experiences in establishing tenacity. The knowledge you have gained by life's travails need to be applied in a continual review of how you would react in a given situation. For example, did you give up on your search when you did not get that job you wanted? If you did give up, take that experience and analyze it to learn how you could have done better, then give it another try. Be honest with yourself and use this experience as another brick in your mindset foundation. Determination and tenacity are requirements of life and an effort should be made to strengthen these traits in your life.

When Steve Waltrip was a rookie cop going through the field training program at the San Jose Police Department, he was faced with a difficult training officer who believed in making a new officer's experience on patrol as stressful as possible. The training officer would volunteer Steve for the most difficult assignments during the shift and when that assignment was complete, he would quickly volunteer him for another assignment without letting him write the report from the previous assignment. Steve would often have three to five reports to write at the end of the ten-hour shift. Reports, such as rape, assault with a deadly weapon, domestic violence or any other important incident, would require a significant amount of detail. The reports would often take four to five hours to complete. Steve also had to study so he could pass the oral and written quizzes the training officer would demand of him during the week. This schedule gave precious little time for sleep or relaxation during the workweek. The training officer explained that this sort of treatment was essential and was a 'trial by fire' so he could 'temper the steel' within Steve. As difficult as this period was emotionally, the training officer was preparing Steve for the rigors of being a 'street cop.' As Steve began working solo on patrol, he ultimately realized the training officer was correct in his rigorous training approach. Many times, he had to rely upon an inner strength that was partially developed by the training officer during those difficult days. Nothing takes the place of knowledge gained through experience and intense training.

Without knowledge of what to expect when confronted with trying circumstances, a person can only guess, or ignore the prospect altogether. When actually confronted with a problem never before encountered, the response and the ability to think through the situation will vary between individuals. However, you can learn from others who have experienced difficult circumstances and apply them to your life. If you have nothing to gage your reaction to violence upon, then accepting the advice of experienced individuals is the best recourse.

We know that terrorists hijacked four airliners on 9/11 with relative ease. Crewmember security training was geared for passive resistance. For example, cooperate with the hijackers, but look for opportunities to delay or cause mechanical problems. Terrorists learned what crewmembers were going to do and took advantage of it. At this point, our only recourse is to change our tactics and how we view being taken hostages on a one-way flight to death.

With the knowledge we now have about our enemy, the terrorist hijacker, we can become better educated and mentally strengthen our minds to take into account their ruthless tactics. With this valuable knowledge, we now know what fate awaits us if we cooperate with terrorists in the hijacking of an airliner. If you are ever hijacked by a group of terrorist hijackers who by all observations are anything near what the 9/11 hijackers look and act like, then you will certainly die if you or others do not take coordinated action. Facing this challenge will take mental toughness on your part.

Unlike the crewmembers on 9/11, you have a unique opportunity to develop beforehand knowledge of our enemy and what mental steps need to be taken. Take advantage of this situation, learn from the experiences of others and apply that knowledge to your job. We all have a powerful weapon in the form of our brains. The time it takes to develop the knowledge will be worth it. You are worth it. Knowledge is power, and power provides the opportunity to survive. Knowledge is the development of being able to discern when the best time it is to act for your own protection. Knowledge is not carelessness or recklessness, unless there is no other recourse. Knowledge is not caution beyond being able to make a decision. Knowledge is knowing the best time to make a decision of action that could mean your survival.

Survival principle two: Training

Training establishes skills that increase your knowledge and competence at staying alive. Training gives you the experience to react correctly in a confrontation. If you do not possess any training in self-defense, your ability to defend yourself and others is greatly diminished. The fact you are reading this book demonstrates your willingness to learn. We learn through training. We encourage actual hands-on training to gain the defensive skills that are necessary in today's environment. Although, the information in this book is important, it will not replace individual instruction of self-defensive techniques.

Training is the crucial application of knowledge. Training is also crucial to the development of a survival mindset as it establishes personal experiences in developing the strong mindset of survival. You can still learn by examination of your life's experiences, but nothing truly replaces a test of those experiences. The best test we have in expanding our survival mindset is through realistic, challenging training. Challenging training pays dividends that can be applied to real life experiences. Although there is no training that replaces the experience gained from real life incidents, training needs to come as close to real life as possible. How realistic is your training?

Survival principle three: Awareness

If a person has all the knowledge in the world about survival mindset and self-defense training, but is not aware of what is going on around them they can easily become a victim. Awareness of your environment, those around you and the threats that exist are crucial to avoiding becoming a victim. Certainly, an attacker can surprise anyone, but allowing oneself to become a potential victim by being unaware is an invitation to disaster. Awareness is so important that we have dedicated a complete chapter to that issue.

Doing your job well is important, but you should have your priorities straight. Your individual survival should be your number one priority in life. You did not make the rules the hijackers established for us on 9/11, but you should make accommodations for them by remaining aware of your work environment. No, you are not being 'paranoid' by staying aware of your environment you are just accepting the reality of this dangerous world and dictating your actions to counteract this threat.

Survival principle four: Willingness and ability to act

The willingness to act when confronted with a violent situation is essential to survive it. Violent confrontation is not an easy thing to contemplate, but it is essential that you accept it when it occurs and act as necessary to defend yourself. Willingness is a frame of mind that should be thought through and developed before a confrontation occurs. You must be willing to do what you must to survive and take any necessary steps to accomplish that goal. Accepting that you might have to take difficult and disturbing action to survive is a key element to a survival mindset. If you are not willing to take whatever action you must to survive, you have already given up.

Willingness to act when confronted with violence is an acceptance of responsibility for your own survival. Willingness we speak of is anticipating action when action is needed. This action may need to be taken immediately, or at some other point in time. However, willingness to act should not be squandered through overlooked opportunities. When faced with violence, opportunities to overcome it may not occur again if you are not willing to act at the first chance. Usually, but not always, the best opportunity to act is immediately upon recognition of the threat.

That is why it is so important to remain aware of your environment to prevent being caught off guard.

Ability to act is simply the willingness to act put into motion. When faced with an inevitable physical confrontation, you have the choice to act or not act. If you do not act when the opportunity is available, you have squandered the ability to take advantage of the situation. You must be able to recognize when an opportunity exists to gain the upper hand against an attacker. With all your strength, you need to respond to the threat with overwhelming willingness and ability.

We cannot change what occurred on 9/11, but we owe it to the deceased crewmember's memories to approach our jobs in a completely different way. They would have wanted us all to become stronger through better crew security training. An integral part of that training is developing a mindset of survival, something the crews of 9/11 did not have the benefit of during their moments of extreme danger.

Competency is acquired through knowledge and training. Since you are reading these words, you are in fact training to become empowered with knowledge and ability. We applaud your attitude and encourage you to continue your training to become stronger and stronger against terrorist threats that will continue to face crewmembers for a long time to come.

Survival principle five: Avoiding pitfalls of complacency, dependency, and denial

We are asking you to make a survival mindset a part of your everyday thinking. The worst thing you can do is be satisfied with those survival beliefs. Continually review you beliefs and thoughts to strengthen your personal resolve. Complacency of any skill will cause deterioration of that skill. You must always remain aware of your human condition. Humans will always be in a constant state of change. Be resilient to this change and make the changes to adapt to your environment. Continually work to improve your mindset attitude through the experiences of life. Use your experiences in life to improve your skills. Look forward what you can learn from the challenges of life.

You can look at life's challenges in two ways. One, you do not accept the challenge and miserably fail at it; or two, you accept the challenge in an effort to improve yourself as a human. A survival mindset is about life and not giving up on it. You are a valuable asset to the airline you work for and must continually strive to not only improve as an employee and crewmember, but also improve as a human being. Take it upon yourself to learn about protecting yourself and remain vigilant of those skills as well as the environment that is around you.

Some crewmembers have come to be wholly dependent upon others for their security. The fact is that no matter where we live, we are all ultimately responsible for our own personal safety. If you are attacked in your home by a stranger, chances are a police officer will not be standing on your doorstep waiting to help you. We need to do what we have to do to protect ourselves under any circumstance. This is why we are so passionate about providing crewmembers with the tools to make knowledgeable and educated decisions about their personal protection. However, this approach takes work and personal commitment. If you believe you are not as trained as you should be in security, then you need to make an effort to change that. You are ultimately responsible for your own education. The authors agree that airlines need to make a quantum shift in their attitudes toward crewmember security training, but meanwhile the threats continue and crewmembers are left with what they have. We encourage each of you to gain as much knowledge and information about the threats and what you can personally do about them. If you are like us, you will discover that you will feel much more secure by gaining knowledge in how to protect yourself.

Denial is another enemy to crewmember security. Denial is believing that another event like 9/11 could occur, or that it would not happen to you. Do not be fooled by the complacency that has crept into the lives of crewmembers. We can become victims again by not believing terrorists are capable of carrying out other devious attacks on commercial aviation. Threats by terrorists that include explosives, chemical/biological agents, and hijackings among other things, are a clear and present danger to our lives and jobs. Imagine what would happen to the airline industry around the world if another terrorist event occurred on a commercial airliner. The effects of 9/11 have ravaged our industry and another incident could cause many airlines to become extinct. What do you think would be the consequences to the airline you work for now? The outlook for commercial aviation would be dismay indeed.

Survival principle six: Never give up

This is the most important principle. No matter what the circumstances you are facing you should not ever give up. It should be more than a goal, but a way of looking at life and surviving life's dangers. This does not mean you will not be frightened by danger, but rather that you will not give up on the situation you are faced with. There is always hope. No matter how dismal it may seem.

In 1986, an incredible display of a will to live was demonstrated by an FBI agent in a Miami gunfight has become a remarkable testimony to the survival mindset. The incident began when two men suspected of being bank robbers were under surveillance by eight FBI agents in three cars. The incident turned very ugly when the FBI agents attempted to make the suspects stop their car. After the men crashed their car into a tree, a gun battle ensued that left two FBI agents dead and four others seriously wounded. The suspected bank robbers were also killed in the shootout. The deadly confrontation took approximately 4 minutes with 132 rounds of ammunition fired by both the FBI and the suspects. Amazingly, after the suspects received fatal gunshot wounds they continued to fight and killed two FBI agents. An FBI agent, severely wounded in the arm and bleeding profusely from his wound, was determined not to let the murderers escape. With only one useable arm, he fired his 12-gauge shotgun five times at the suspects. Both suspects, their vehicle being disabled by the crash into the tree, attempted to drive away in one of the dead agents' cars. Approaching the suspects, the wounded agent fired his pistol at them at close range, hitting them with five of the six rounds he fired from the gun.

The FBI agent, Edmundo Mireles, demonstrated not only a strong will to survive, but also the ability to stop the suspects from escaping while suffering from a severe wound. He could have given up after receiving his serious wound, but made a conscious decision to continue to fight. It should also be noted here that even though one of the suspects had received two fatal gunshot wounds, he continued to fight and killed two agents, one of which had fired one of the fatal rounds into that suspect's body. This incident provides us with an interesting view into a survival mindset possessed by both good and bad individuals.

This is just one example of the many individuals throughout history who have demonstrated extreme bravery under exceptionally trying circumstances. You have this courage and determination somewhere deep inside of you, also, that needs to be both acknowledged and relied upon when confronted with trying circumstances. Who knows, you may find yourself along any of life's journeys and be called upon to physically and mentally excel beyond your wildest dreams. Trust and believe that you are capable of feats beyond what is humanly possible to do what needs to be done. The phrase, 'Never give up' is not just mere words to encourage you, but a way of life that needs to begin now as you read these words.

Never giving up means you will do what needs to be done no matter what the circumstances. You will either win or lose, but either way you will not give up and will give 100 per cent effort of yourself. Never give up is an attitude. An attitude of *no matter what you do to hurt me, until my last breath I will not give in to you.* Your goal is to win a violent confrontation, but regardless of the outcome, you commit to not giving in when faced with dire circumstances. Dying of lung cancer, Steve Waltrip's father was face to face with death, but refused to die and go peacefully into the afterlife. He literally wanted to get out of his deathbed and run away; however, his father was physically unable to run away and could not get away from the realization of death. Yet, still would not give in. Physically unable to hang on any longer, Steve's father would only go after he and his wife encouraged him to go peacefully. Steve learned an important lesson he will remember for the rest of his life about his father and the human spirit day his father died. Never give in, not now, or ever.

Contemplating a life or death struggle with another person is not a pleasant thing to think about, but you may have no other options available. Responding with a committed resolve may make the difference in surviving the incident. Through Steve Waltrip's police career, he was confronted with many violent individuals who had no intention of going peacefully to jail or to the mental ward. Although, Steve always preferred to have a situation end peacefully, that just was not always possible. If the incident looked to Steve as trending toward resistance and violence he would find the first available opportunity to act to get the individual handcuffed. Without any warning, he would quickly and overwhelming act to get the person restrained with handcuffs so the incident could be deescalated without serious injuries. This technique works well because often the aggressor is not expecting you to react quickly and is surprised by your decisiveness. If forced into reacting to a violent encounter you should always act without warning, decisively and overwhelmingly in defense of yourself or someone else.

All the principles of mindset can be summed up in by this important mental concept: NEVER GIVE UP!

Surviving a Violent Attack

> Now remember, if things look bad and it looks like you're not going to make it, then you got to get mean. I mean plumb mad dog mean. Because if you lose your head and you give up, then you neither live nor win. That's just the way it is.
>
> Clint Eastwood in the movie *The Outlaw Josey Wales*

Fair fight ... NOT!

First, you need to recognize there is no such thing as a fair fight. Those hijackers on 9/11 did not believe it and neither should you. One of the hardest things for nice people to do is to not fight fair. Throughout our lives, many people have been told to *be nice, get along, play fair,* and *do not get into a fight* – all of which the vast majority of people throughout the world have tried to accomplish. Unfortunately, those exact concepts will get you killed in a violent confrontation such as a terrorist attack. This point must be emphasized repeatedly and strongly. If you are defending your life and the lives of others, you CANNOT FIGHT FAIR! THERE IS NO SUCH THING AS A FAIR FIGHT! In the event of a life and death struggle, you must be willing to do the unimaginable to other human beings who are bent upon your destruction. Hair pulling, eye gouging, biting repeatedly, hitting below the belt, spitting in the face, stabbing with writing pens, pouring hot coffee on someone, screaming obscenities and other such not nice behavior may not only be necessary, but may be your only way of defending yourself.

Your violent reactions to an attack must be quick, overwhelming, and immediate.

> The object of war is not to die for your country, it is to make the other dumb bastard die for his. (General George C. Patton, United States Army)

The quote from General George Patton during WWII sums up the mental attitude that we must develop to successfully deal with violent confrontations. When faced with a violent confrontation on an aircraft, we must do everything within our power to make the aggressor(s) pay dearly for his attempt to end our lives with destruction. There is no mistaking it, we are at war; war against radical terrorists who believe that killing us and/or dying for their cause will give them a special place in heaven.

> I heard people throwing up, yelling 'I'm going to die!' Others yelled, 'We're NOT going to die!' (Karen Seong, World Trade Center 9/11 Survivor)

One of the survivors of the 2001 terrorist attacks in New York was interviewed by a reporter after 9/11 and made the statements above. The differences in mindset are readily apparent between the people she observed that day. The people yelling, 'I'm going to die' epitomize people who are NOT mentally prepared and DO NOT have a MINDSET OF SURVIVAL. Those who were yelling, 'I'm going to die', were already giving up and were ready to die. The ones yelling, 'We're NOT going to die' exemplify the mindset of the survivor. These individuals were not willing to give up and were in a much better emotional position to survive the events of 9/11.

Never give up!

Being empowered with knowledge, and to some degree experience, provides a tremendous boost in the confidence a person has in building the mindset to survive. Proper training provides competence and confidence in one's abilities. We want to assure you that with confidence that you can protect yourself and that you can survive a violent attack. Our goal is to never hear you say, 'I'm going to die', or even worse 'We're going to die'. The change from singular to plural is extremely important to all of us as flight crewmembers and the *all for one and one for all* theme is the essence of the Airline Security Creed at the front of this book.

The will to live

The bodies of over 2,800 human beings were buried when the World Trade Center crashed down into 3 billion pounds of debris. Incredibly, 20 people survived the collapse and lived to tell about it. One of those incredible survival stories occurred to Port Authority police officers Will Jimeno and Sgt John McLoughlin who survived both tower collapses while attempting to rescue workers from the north tower of the World Trade Center. This is a story of two men who survived beyond what a normal person would be able to endure. Through experiences such as theirs, we begin to understand the will to live. As brief as this story may appear here, it was definitely not a brief experience for these men who will endure the scars, both physically and mentally for the rest of their lives. This is their incredible story.

> After the terrorist attacks on 9/11, Sgt. John McLoughlin, 48, a veteran police officer trained in rescues, was outside the World Trade Center and wanted three volunteers that knew how to operate the 30-pound self-contained breathing device used by firefighters. Jimeno, 33, a rookie police officer, had learned how to use the breathing device at the police academy and stepped forward. So did Officer Antonio Rodrigues, 35, Officer Dominick Pezzulo, 36 and Officer Chris Amoroso, 29, who had already carried people to safety from the WTC.

The men were pushing carts of air packs in the shopping mall that connected the north and south towers when they heard a boom and then a rumble. They did not know it at the time, but the south tower of the WTC was collapsing. Sgt. McLoughlin told the officers to run toward a freight elevator nearby. Officer Pezzulo was the closest to the elevator with Jimeno right behind him, followed by Sgt. McLoughlin. An incredible thunderous roar engulfed them as a rain of concrete and steel buried the men. After the collapse, Sgt. McLoughlin asked the men in his charge to 'Sound off!' Unfortunately, only Officers Pezzulo and Jimeno answered. Officer Jimeno called out for Officers Rodrigues and Amoroso for several minutes until Officer Pezzulo told him to stop because, 'They're in a better place'.

Jimeno was pinned by a concrete wall that had fallen on his lap and the air pack on his back propped him upright at a 45-degree angle. Pezzulo was buried near Jimeno. Through the rubble, they could see a hole that let in light 20 feet above them. McLoughlin was 20 feet away and a little below them in a crevice that was the size of a coffin.

Pezzulo was able to get himself free and repeatedly tried to lift the cement off Jimeno, but was unable. Pezzulo took out his gun and fired out through the opening 20 feet away hoping that someone would hear the gunshots, but nobody heard the shots.

As they continued to struggle to get free, a second rumble began as the north tower began collapsing on them. Jimeno and Pezzulo looked each other in the eye. Jimeno fearing the worst signaled with his hand to Pezzulo that he loved him in sign language. 'If it is going to hit me, I will die seeing my friend', Jimeno thought to himself. The rumble became as loud as a thousand freight trains. Falling concrete slammed Pezzulo to the ground and he let out a loud and excruciating cry. Pezzulo said he was 'hurt bad' and both of them knew he was dying. They spoke quietly, about life, about their families, about being cops. They told each other they loved one another. Pezzulo asked that they would not forget his efforts at trying to save them. Pezzulo died facing the light from the hole now 30 feet above them.

Sgt. McLoughlin's legs had been crushed in the second collapse and he could not see Officer Jimeno. The sergeant spoke into his radio, but the only response he heard was static. Flames began to shoot into the hole from above. Jimeno thought burning to death was not a good way to go. The fire enveloped Pezzulo's gun and it started firing. The gun fired 15 bullets that ricocheted off concrete and all Jimeno could do was cover his face. The bullets and the fires then faded, but they were still alone and pinned 30 feet below the top of the ruins.

They talked to keep each other awake and alive. Occasionally, they yelled for help, but mostly they talked about personal and intimate things. They talked about their kids, families and feelings they had never shared with anyone.

Then, they heard a voice coming from above them. A man yelled into the hole and gave the last name of a man he was searching for and wanted to know whether he was down there. 'No', Jimeno yelled, but the man walked away leaving them. 'Don't leave us!' Jimeno yelled, but the man was gone. Jimeno began yelling in frustration. Sgt. McLoughlin told Jimeno not to get mad because they did not know whether the man was hurt and they did not have any other information to go on.

As night fell Jimeno and McLoughlin were passing in and out of consciousness. Jimeno, had a vision of Jesus walking toward him, dressed in a white robe. Tall grass waving in the wind could be seen over one shoulder and a large lake over the other. He was bringing Jimeno a bottle of water.

> When Jimeno awoke he suddenly felt at peace with dying. However, with that peace came a renewed spirit to fight and he told Sgt McLoughlin, 'We're going to get out of this hellhole'. Jimeno began banging a pipe in front of him to make noise. He got out his firearm, but could not shoot it because his hands were too swollen to pull the trigger, so he banged it like a hammer.
>
> McLoughlin encouraged him to keep yelling. They found themselves breaking into laughter because Jimeno recalled a line from the movie G.I. Jane: 'Pain is good. Pain is your friend. If you are feeling pain, you are still alive.' To a pair of men whose legs were pinned under the rubble of the WTC this was funny.
>
> At about 10:30 p.m., 12 hours after the second building collapsed Jimeno heard a distant voice. 'United States Marine Corps!' a man yelled from far away. McLoughlin and Jimeno began to scream in unison. 'Keep yelling', the voice said. 'We'll find you'. As the Marine poked his head in the hole, Jimeno looked at his face above and said, 'Please don't leave'. The Marine said, 'I'm not going anywhere'.
>
> It took New York Police Department rescue specialists three hours to free Jimeno and another eight hours to rescue McLoughlin. Rescue workers wrapped Pezzulo's body in an American flag before they removed it. He was buried 19 September 2001. Both men required extensive medical treatment. Sgt. McLoughlin's injuries required 27 operations on his legs. Officer Jimeno spent 3 months in the hospital and rehabilitation. Both men received the Port Authority's Medal of Honor.[2]

There are many lessons to learn from the experiences of Sgt McLoughlin and Officer Jimeno. They endured the death of their friends during the first tower collapse, but did not give up. They were trapped under the rubble and did not give up. After the second tower collapsed, Officer Jimeno talked with Officer Pezzulo until he died, and he still did not give up. After the second collapse, a fire threatened to burn the officers to death and caused Officer Pezzulo's gun to shoot wildly, and they still did not give up. They thought they may be rescued, but the potential rescuer deserted them, they still did not give up. After the rescue they continue to suffer physically and mentally, but you know what? They are not going to give up.

What type of a person does it take to endure what these police officers experienced? People exactly like you who are placed into a difficult position of survival. Could you have kept your heads as these officers did? Only you can answer that question, but preparing your mental frame of mind now by developing a mindset of survival will make your chances of surviving in a life or death situation much better. Many good, strong and wonderful people died in the terrorist's attacks on 9/11, but those who were in a position to survive did so by their shear will power. There will be time to release emotionally later when you are in a safe place and where your survival is not threatened. Be strong; keep your chin up and never, ever, under any circumstance, give up!

Courage in the face of danger

At sometime in our lives we may be called upon to be courageous in the face of danger. We may not want to be courageous, but we may have to if we wish to survive an extremely difficult situation. The passengers and crew aboard United 93 realized the terrorist attacks were occurring in New York and Washington DC using commercial jet aircraft. They were faced with a harrowing and difficult decision. Do they let the terrorists crash the airplane into their selected target, the White House, capitol building or some other important location? Or, do they attempt to stop the terrorist by sacrificing their lives? No one should ever give up fighting for life when faced with a grave situation like that which occurred to the passengers and crew of UAL 93.

Cee Cee Lyles, the second flight attendant on UAL 93 knew that terrorists were crashing airplanes. She left a heart-rending message on the answering machine at home for her husband and children. Among other thing, she told her husband that she '… heard planes were going into the World Trade Center'.[3] She later contacted her husband on her cellular phone and told him that her plane was being hijacked. At the end of their conversation, she said that it looked like passengers were forcing their way into the cockpit. Her husband then heard screams and the whooshing of air.[4] It is obvious by this call that, faced with certain death, the passengers and crew were taking their destiny into their own hands by attempting to stop these murderous men from accomplishing their wicked plan.

Sandy Bradshaw, also a flight attendant on UAL 93, reached her husband by cell phone. She told her husband that most of the passengers were herded to the rear of the plane. She said she was boiling water to throw on the hijackers. What sort of bravery and courage do you think it took to confront '3 guys with knives'?[5] Especially, when you know the terrorists have already killed two others by slitting their throats.[6] Sandy and the others were going to attempt to '… take the airplane back …'. How can you describe this kind of courage? It is beyond words.

A passenger, Jeremy Glick, with full knowledge of what occurred at the WTC, told his wife from a cell phone on UAL 93 that he and three other guys were thinking of attacking the hijackers. His wife encouraged him and said, 'You need to do it.'[7] He said, 'Okay … I'll be right back.' Apparently, at the same time Todd Beamer was having a discussion with a telephone operator and mentioned they were going to 'jump' the hijackers and attempt to regain control of the plane. When questioned by the operator Beamer said, 'At this point, I do not have much choice'. Beamer then said the words that have inspired the world with its courage in the face of certain death, 'Okay. Let's roll'.[8]

Throughout the course of human history individuals have been faced with what seems are insurmountable odds. They have shown their humanity and accepted their situation with courage and bravery that few of us have ever been called upon to demonstrate. The passengers and crew of UAL 93 had a courage that certainly will be counted as one of the greatest personal sacrifices of history. Do you think you could have shown such courage under similar circumstances? It is our hope that none of us will ever have to find out what it is like. Yet, if you do find yourself in such a predicament, try to remember the courage of the passengers and crew of United Flight 93, and 'Okay, let's roll!'

> Greater love has no one than this, than to lay down one's life for his friends. (John 15:13)

Survival Mindset in Action: FedEx 705

A life or death struggle occurred between three pilots and a deadheading flight engineer on 7 April 1994 in a DC-10, soon after departure from Memphis, Tennessee. This event was a frightening example of how quickly a violent attack can occur. Often an attacker has planned his actions and goes to great pains to conceal his true intentions. This was such an incident.

> In the violent attack, the hijacker was a fellow employee who wanted to kill the pilots and take over the aircraft. However, there has been speculation that he wanted to commit suicide by crashing the DC-10 into the Federal Express headquarters in Memphis.
>
> The attacker was Auburn Calloway, a flight engineer at FedEx who was facing a disciplinary hearing that could have resulted in his termination. Angry at the way his case was being handled by management, he wanted to even the score in some twisted way. Calloway got his financial affairs in order by early afternoon of April 7th. In hindsight, it was evident he was dedicated to his plan. He was in fact a very dangerous man who had developed a warrior mindset during the years it took for him to earn a black belt in karate.
>
> Calloway arrived at the airport and passed through a security checkpoint without passing through a metal detector, which was common for cargo airlines at the time. Calloway was planning to ride as a passenger on FedEx 705 from Memphis to San Jose, California. He had in his possession a guitar case containing four hammers, a spear gun, and a scuba diver's knife. The cargo DC-10 had a few seats in the galley area for use by company employees and Calloway was listed as the sole passenger on the flight. Calloway took his guitar case onto the DC-10 and placed it into the galley area where he could easily access it later during the flight.
>
> The flight crew consisted of Captain David Sanders, First Officer Jim Tucker, and Flight Engineer Andy Peterson. They had arrived on time and had conducted their preflight duties. The crew did not know about the pending disciplinary charges against Calloway. Engine start, taxi and takeoff were completed normally and the aircraft proceeded on the flight-planned course toward San Jose. Passing through 19,000 feet in the climb, the crew was involved in light conversation. Meanwhile, in the galley area, Calloway opened his guitar case, removed a 21-ounce framing hammer and began to implement his plan.
>
> Entering the flight deck, Calloway immediately attacked Peterson, the flight engineer, with two quick and brutal blows to his head. Calloway then quickly struck Tucker with a vicious and crushing blow to his head. Both Peterson and Tucker were stunned bleeding profusely from the massive head injuries. Sanders, the captain, seeing the attack on Tucker could not believe what he was seeing. Quickly turning his attention to Sanders, Calloway swung, but Sanders' raised hands deflected the blow. His second swing did not fully connect because Sanders was moving his head back and forth to avoid the attack. The third swing caught the engine fire handle on the cockpit ceiling and was deflected away from Sanders. Making one last attempt, Calloway caught Sanders on the right side of his head, nearly ripping off Sander's right ear; then, he turned suddenly and departed the flight deck.
>
> Even though they were dazed and disoriented by the attack, Peterson and Tucker were aware of the attack on Sanders, but both could hardly move; yet both men realized

they would have to muster an inner strength they had never been called upon to rely on before. Stunned by the attack, Sanders was attempting to release his seat belt when Calloway re-entered the flight deck with a spear gun and a hammer.

Peterson was weak from the loss of blood from a gushing wound on the side of his head and his vision was extremely narrowed by the injury. However, he saw Calloway with the spear gun. With Calloway's attention on Sanders, who he was threatening to kill with the spear gun, Peterson somehow reached out, grabbed the spear gun and fell to his knees. Sanders released his seat belt and moved quickly toward Calloway, who was in a struggle over the spear gun with Peterson.

Even though Tucker's head injury was extremely serious and the right side of his body was numb, he was aware of the violent confrontation going on around him. He knew he had to do something to help in the life and death struggle that was taking place between Calloway, Peterson and Sanders over possession of the spear gun. Tucker grabbed the flight controls with his left hand and pulled back as hard as he could. He then made a hard banking left turn. The g-forces from the maneuver caused Calloway, Peterson and Sanders to fall back through the flight deck door into the galley area.

Tucker, continued to roll the DC-10 through 140 degrees of bank, inverted the aircraft and began descending at a rapid rate. He continued to maneuver the aircraft skillfully and realized that any negative-g-forces could rip the cargo from their tie-downs in the cabin, which could then smash through the top of the aircraft. During this time of incredible aircraft maneuvering, Tucker somehow alerted Air Traffic Control as to the struggle aboard the flight. ATC assisted as best as they could under the circumstances and began notifying the proper law enforcement authorities.

Meanwhile, the life and death struggle continued in the galley area. Calloway was pinned to the floor by Peterson while Sanders was attempting to remove the hammer from Calloway's hand. During the struggle, Calloway got his hand loose and struck Sanders with the hammer. Sanders fought to keep from losing consciousness and the thought crossed his mind they might lose the fight. Fortunately, just at that moment another of Tucker's maneuvers imposed g-forces that caused Calloway's hand to fall to the floor. Sanders saw his opportunity and successfully got the hammer away from Calloway.

Peterson still had his hands on the spear gun and was lying across Calloway's mid section pinning Calloway to the floor. With the hammer raised above his head, Sanders ordered Calloway to stop struggling and give up the spear gun. When he continued to fight, Sanders hit Calloway across the top of his head two times. Calloway began to plead for mercy and asked Sanders not to hurt him any longer. Yet, Calloway would not let go of the spear gun.

When Peterson began screaming in pain as Calloway began biting him in the shoulder, Sanders struck Calloway two more times across his head, fracturing his skull with the hammer. Even though Calloway was injured, he continued to struggle with Peterson and Sanders.

At Sander's request, Tucker put the DC-10 on autopilot and even though he was gravely injured and paralyzed on his right side, released his seat belt, got out of his seat and entered the galley to help subdue Calloway. The men and the galley were covered with blood. Tucker successfully took the spear gun away from Calloway. Tucker, placing the spear gun against Calloway's chin, warned him not to move or he would kill him. However, Tucker knew that he was bluffing because of his growing weakness and paralysis.

Sanders returned to the flight deck and took control of the DC-10. Realizing he needed to get the aircraft down as soon as possible, he attempted to call ATC, but found that he could not speak. His jaw had somehow become dislocated during the fight. Pressing his hand against the right side of his jaw, he pushed hard and heard bone, muscle and tendons snapping back into place. He made contact with ATC and they re-directed Sanders, who was now in control of the aircraft, back to the Memphis airport.

While maneuvering the aircraft back to the airport, Sanders had to again engage the autopilot and leave his seat to help subdue Calloway, who appeared to be gaining the advantage in his struggle with the two injured crewmembers. Tucker reassured Sanders they once again had Calloway under control and Sanders returned to the captain's seat. Sanders had lined up for Runway 36 Left, but realized that leaving his seat for a few moments to assist his crew had put them too high for landing. He banked around sharply for another attempt at the runway, lowered the gear and flaps, and landed on Runway 36 Left.

Beginning at approximately 3:28pm and with touchdown at 4:04pm, the thirty-six minutes of life and death struggle must have seemed like an eternity to the flight crew. Even though the landing was successful, Calloway was continuing to struggle and seemed to gain strength by the minute. Tucker was losing the ability to talk or fight and Peterson, although refusing to give up, was extremely weakened by his head injury and loss of blood.

Sanders opened the right front exit door and the emergency slide deployed; however, airport police officers were unable to climb the slippery vinyl slide. A paramedic successfully climbed the slide and was thrown a pair of handcuffs by a police officer so Calloway could be restrained.

All four men were transported to the hospital for treatment. Peterson and Tucker were in critical condition. Peterson had two open wounds on his head, deep bruises on his arms, a large gash across his arm from the spear gun, and assorted bites on his shoulders. Tucker, the most seriously injured of the three, was paralyzed on his right side and his speech was slurred. Tucker had a large, open head wound from the crushing blow of the hammer that had driven bone fragments into his brain and would need immediate brain surgery upon arrival at the hospital. Sanders had puncture wounds on his arms, his right ear dangled by a piece of skin, and he had six open gashes on his head. Calloway had a fractured skull and deep cuts from the blows of the hammer by Sanders.

All three crewmembers survived the attack and received the Air Line Pilots Association's highest award for heroism, which only eighteen pilots have received since the award's inception in 1966. Auburn Calloway, sentenced to life in prison in a Federal penitentiary with no possibility for parole, is currently serving his sentence in Atlanta Federal Penitentiary. [9]

Captain Sanders, First Officer Tucker and Flight Engineer Peterson demonstrated an incredible will to survive during this unexpected violent attack. The horror and fear all three of these men felt by this attack were immense. However, they were placed into a life or death situation where they needed to act decisively or die. These men, through some inner strength that we all possess, found the strength to act when action was needed. This was truly an amazing story of survival that we can use to inspire us in preparing us for the worst. We encourage you to be strengthened by the performance of these individuals because we all are capable of the survival mindset they demonstrated on that fateful day.

Conclusion

Being mentally prepared for what may await us in the skies is essential in the reality that exists in the world today. Not understanding this concept could cost you and others their lives. Do not be dependant upon the government for your security in the skies. We expressed our concern about the lack of training and true airline security in the introduction to this book. We are not politicians and do not have any hidden agendas. We speak from our honest belief that crewmembers are not adequately prepared for another round with trained terrorists. What is certain is the government is prepared to shoot us down with fighter jets, if needed. That approach protects the halls of government, not passengers or crewmembers.

Crewmembers are not receiving essential training requirements and guidance from the government to confront cold-blooded terrorists. Pretending the government is providing comprehensive protection for airline security would be a major mistake on our part as crewmembers. Consider this for a moment. If you are an active crewmember, think about when and where sky marshals are riding on the aircraft. The sky marshals' strategy is clearly aimed at protecting the centers of government activity as much as possible. By these actions, it is evident to us the government has little confidence in flight attendants or pilots to defend themselves. More importantly, they have not shown a real interest in providing crewmembers with essential survival training. Crewmembers are left to there own devices in self-defense. This chapter is an important aspect to the development of crewmembers becoming an active part to the airline security equation and not the problem. Taking responsibility for your own safety is an important part of a survival mindset. We encourage you to accept this concept and always look for ways of improving and strengthening your personal security.

> The bottom line is that when the aircraft door closes, the jet bridge has pulled back, and the airplane is pushed back into the alley, we ultimately have nobody to depend upon but ourselves. (Steve Waltrip)

NEVER GIVE UP!

Notes

1 Zoroya, Gregg, Woman describes the mentality of a suicide bomber, *USA Today*, 22 April 2002.
2 Cauchon, Dennis, and Martha Moore, Miracles Emerge From The Debris, *USA Today*, 6 September 2002.
3 Longman, Jere, *Among the Heroes: United Flight 93 and the passengers and crew who fought back*, 2002, p. 177.
4 Ibid., p. 180.
5 Ibid., pp. 173–6.
6 Ibid., p. 162.
7 Ibid., p. 153.
8 Ibid., pp. 203–4.
9 Hirschman, Dave, *Hijacked: The True Story of the Heroes of Flight 705*, 1997.

Chapter 9

Conflict Management

Introduction

The intent of this chapter is to provide crewmembers with useful conflict management information that can be useful in dealing with others in the course of doing their job, whether they are on the flight deck or in the cabin. We are not so presumptuous to believe we have all the answers for dealing with conflicts and confrontations. We do have experience in law enforcement, CRM, and human factors that provide an insight into human relationships and a sound basis for our tried and proven conflict resolution techniques. Dealing with passengers on a daily basis is not easy. Just like police officers, flight crewmembers can grow weary of dealing with individuals and their associated problems. We will not bog down the reader with complicated solutions, exhaustive studies, and drawn out explanations to conflict. We provide simple and effective techniques that will make crewmembers' jobs much easier as they interact with the traveling public and each other.

Conflict

What is conflict? For the purposes of this chapter, we define conflict as *when what you expect to happen is different from what is actually happening*. It is important to keep this definition in mind as you proceed. Conflict happens to all of us and is inevitable as we go through life. Crewmembers see conflicts occurring daily in their workplace – flights that are running late or cancelled, passengers stressing over standing in line and being treated like a terrorist at the security checkpoints, and over-sold and crowded aircraft. Company bankruptcies, tense labor negotiations, furloughs or downsizing, and management bonuses after labor groups have taken pay cuts are just a few of the many sources of conflict within the aviation industry. Seat duplications, irate and/or intoxicated passengers, personality conflicts between crewmembers, inoperative passenger entertainment systems, no air-conditioning on the ground in the summer and lack of information to the passengers during delays are only a few of the added sources of conflict while confined on an airliner. As if the point needed to be made, crewmembers have conflicts.

Some crewmembers are able to handle uncomfortable situations professionally and in their stride while others continually escalate the situation into a full-blown confrontation with passengers or other crewmembers. What makes the difference? The difference lies in the training and experience of the person willing to adjust their personal approach to conflict management. An unwilling person will reject the ideas presented in this chapter, making it necessary for us to learn to deal with them, as well. It is very important to the authors to underscore the fact from our airline experience (totaling almost 50 years), flight crews – both cockpit and cabin crew – do a remarkable job in handling unpleasant and sometimes dangerous encounters with passengers and other crewmembers. For many of them, this chapter may be regarded as 'preaching to the choir'; however, you may still find some of the techniques different and useful. Please continue doing the fine job that you are, particularly in today's crazy environment.

Striving for on-board tranquility is extremely important to the flight crew. Crewmembers should recognize that passenger rudeness and deliberate disobedience is often not a personal challenge to the crew's authority. Fear of flying, loss of control, confinement in a small space, prohibition against smoking, too hot or too cold, lack of food, other inconsiderate passengers, and other stresses are all associated with stress leading to hostilities by passengers. That does not make them right, but they are factors that crews must react to and manage.

Many of these fears can be exhibited by passengers in several ways such as, 'Why can't I have another drink?', 'Why can't I sit in this seat?'. Actions such as getting out of their seat when the seat belt sign is illuminated, or not putting on their seat belt, may or may not be a deliberate attempt to challenge a crewmember's authority. A passenger's reactions often mirror the crewmember's responses.

A basic understanding of human nature may be useful to the crewmember in dealing with difficult passengers. For example, a crewmember confronting a passenger with the 'rules' may illicit negative responses. A passenger may become defensive by feeling helpless to their conditions, i.e. cramped by being confined in the aircraft cabin, and react with resentment. By being knowledgeable of the basis for reactions, the crewmember can learn responses that will not escalate the situation beyond what is desired, a peaceful resolution.

The primary role for cabin crewmembers is safety, but often the passengers do not recognize this fact until an emergency occurs. Although unfair and inaccurate, the perception of the traveling public is the cabin crew's job is to serve them and to anticipate and meet their personal needs. Before 9/11 if an incident could not be resolved by the cabin crew, one of the options was to have a pilot exit the flight deck and talk with the passengers. The 'authority figure' exhibited by the pilots in both their demeanor and uniform often resolved the problem. After 9/11, pilots are not going to leave the flight deck to handle disturbances in the cabin for obvious security reasons, leaving it entirely to the cabin crew to manage the situation in the cabin. It is very important to continue educating the traveling public about the primary role of the cabin crew – safety. Given the time and our patience, the traveling public may begin to understand the importance of the cabin crew to the role of safety and security.

Preserving 'SELF'

Preservation of 'SELF' should be a major goal of crewmembers as they go about their jobs. Our attitudes and responses to conflicts are critical to our personal happiness and well-being. Approach this aspect of your job positively and the outcomes of your actions will prove more fruitful and beneficial for you as a person. When confronted with conflict the following techniques may be helpful in preserving 'self':[1]

Do not take it personally. The person is probably not directing their anger at you personally, but is directing it at the environment, conditions, and/or airline. Be professional, avoid getting angry and stick to the facts. There are two ways of determining if you are taking conflicts too personally; if you think about them as you are going to sleep, or if you have dreams about them. If you are experiencing either of these symptoms, you ARE taking it personally and you must work on overcoming this tendency. This is easy to say, but hard to do when someone has been screaming profanities into your face.

Take a deep breath. Then, take a few more. Controlling your breathing controls the voice and blood pressure. Anger, a natural response in many encounters, puts you in phase of awareness RED. Remember, the way out of RED is control of breathing. It works!

Acknowledge the person's hostility. Ignoring the issue only serves to escalate the other person's anger and determination to continue the conflict. Show concern and empathize with the other person's problem or situation.

Allow the anger. Avoid being judgmental. Allow the person to vent their anger without your over-reacting. Actively LISTEN. (While you are listening, breath deeply.)

Find and share something in common. Connect with their anger. Regardless of whether you completely agree with them or not, tell them you also do not care for the situation. Ensure them you are working to solve the problem to everyone's satisfaction. Avoid putting the person into a position where they have no way out without humiliating themselves.

Ask for clarification. Focus on their attention on the issue, not yours. Try to see the issue from their perspective. Talking about the issues directs attention, leads to defusing and may provide solutions to the problem.

Settle for disagreement. If the person will not compromise on his or her position, and then accept the fact that you may not agree with them. That does not mean the conflict is over, it simply means you may need to resort to another technique.

Mediate conflict. Restate the issue and tell why it must be resolved. Although you may not have taken the other person or the situation personally, the other person may have taken YOU personally. Ask others to step in and help you resolve the differences. Your withdrawal from the situation may be required in this case.

Working to preserve your dignity as a human being during conflicts may not guarantee the situation will be resolved to your satisfaction; however, remember that you are probably not taking the disgruntled passenger home with you and that you must preserve your concept of 'self'.

Interpersonal Relationship Skills

> Do unto others, as you would have them do to you.
>
> The Golden Rule

> In early spring 2002, a scheduled flight out of Phoenix was in the final stages of departure from the gate when a late arriving passenger rushed on-board the aircraft. As he attempted to stow his bag in the overhead compartment above his seat, a flight attendant several rows away said she had a place for his bag in the overhead compartment at that location. He continued to attempt to put his bag into the crowded overhead compartment over his seat without acknowledging the flight attendant. She raised her voice to the point it could be heard throughout the Boeing 737, and repeated her desire to put his bag at her location.
>
> It appeared with some re-arranging of some of the other bags within the compartment over his seat, his bag would fit without a problem. The man struggled in his attempt to get his bag into the overhead compartment. The flight attendant was obviously irritated as the man ignored her for the second time.
>
> The flight attendant went to the passenger, pulled the bag away from him, and said loudly, 'I'm putting your bag back here!' He did not resist her but quietly said it was his bag and he preferred it to be in the overhead compartment that was over his seat. She ignored him. After the flight attendant had put his bag into the compartment several rows aft, she returned to where he was seated and confronted him. With a raised voice that could be heard throughout the aircraft, she indignantly said, 'Don't take that attitude with me!' The man's response could not be heard, but afterwards she pointed her finger at him and began to lecture him about how she was responsible for his safety. He was obviously embarrassed and did not respond to her haranguing. The flight attendant eventually walked away after completely humiliating the man.

This is an (actual) example witnessed by the authors of escalating a situation when it was unnecessary. It is easy to 'Monday morning quarterback' and to say the flight attendant should have done this or done that, but you will have to agree, this is an example of poor interpersonal relationship skills by the flight attendant. Fortunately, the man did not become violent or disruptive during the flight. What the flight attendant accomplished was the humiliation of a paying customer in front of many other passengers. What kind of referral do you think he, or anyone who witnessed the event, will be giving this airline to others? How could the flight attendant have handled this situation differently?

One of the keys to successful conflict management is taking the right approach to the presence of conflict. The real key to conflict management is to understand that it is not about WHO is right, but WHAT is right. Managing conflict is *DIFFICULT* and most of us have never had adequate training to deal with managing conflict. Most of us try to avoid conflict altogether. It is relatively easy to practice dealing with conflict in a classroom setting; however, it is much more difficult when confronted with the real thing. Emotions and egos on both sides, as well as fatigue, stress and frustrations can complicate the issues.

Like it or not, as a flight crewmember, effective conflict management is your *RESPONSIBILITY*. Why? Because your personal SAFETY is at risk. It may well be that the safety of the entire crew, passengers and aircraft are at risk, particularly if you succeed in infuriating the wrong person on the wrong day. This is in NO way a justification of any misdeed by a passenger; however, human beings can be very unpredictable creatures. You simply do not know exactly what may cause a person to commit an act of violence and you want to stay completely away from that threshold.

The following is a simple, but effective way to approach conflict with others:

1 *Do not place blame*. Find and focus on the issue, not the person. Empathize, if you can do it truthfully.
2 *Stay unemotional.* Emotion consumes logic. Think about the arguments you have had in the past. Did any of them get resolved after they got emotional? Probably not.
3 *Show respect for the other person.* This may be very difficult when the other person is disrespectful of you. Again, do not take it personal. Hear the other person out and concentrate on their perception of the problem.
4 *Listen.* Actively listen. Stop talking and focus on what is being said. Avoid the temptation to start formulating your response before the other person is finished.

Sure-fire Ways to Escalate a Conflict

Wait a minute! Are you teaching us HOW to escalate a conflict? We thought this was all about conflict resolution! Well, it IS about conflict resolution, but how many times have you escalated a situation unintentionally? In order to understand how to defuse a confrontation, we need to understand what will escalate it, either intentionally or unintentionally.

Thousands of incidents have occurred in the history of aviation where confrontations that turned violent have injured or killed people at airports and on aircraft, many of them airline employees. An incident that occurred in 1999 demonstrates the seriousness of escalating a situation.

> On July 22, 1999, a Continental flight from Newark to Orlando began boarding after a two-hour delay. A couple's 18-month old daughter somehow managed to wander alone down the jetway. The mother ran after her, but was stopped by the gate agent who allegedly pushed the woman. The enraged husband confronted the gate agent; however, witnesses testified the gate agent grabbed the husband by the neck and a struggle ensued. During the scuffle, the husband put the gate agent in a bear hug and both of them fell to the floor. The gate agent's neck was broken and he was comatose for five days. The passenger claimed he acted in self-defense and was acquitted of all charges by a jury on April 3, 2001. The gate agent lost 80 per cent of the mobility of his neck.[2]

In this unfortunate incident, if the gate agent would have known and used the four steps of approaching conflict management discussed previously, the matter could have been resolved peacefully. Now, he has a permanent disability and a passenger had to endure an arrest and prosecution. How can you avoid making the same mistake? Know and avoid saying certain things or making aggressive actions that have a high probability of escalating the situation. Here are some things passengers just do not want to hear.

'Those are the rules!'

The seatbelt sign is illuminated and a passenger gets up to use the restroom. You tell him to return to his seat and fasten his seatbelt, pointing to the seatbelt sign. He looks at you, says he needs to use the restroom and points out that you are up moving about, as well. You then say, 'Sir, go back to your seat because *those are the rules*'.

Simple 'cop-outs' like this just do not go over well with a passenger, or with anybody for that matter. You are not giving them a reason, but rather a pat answer that will do nothing but make them ask, 'Why?' Forget for a moment that as a crewmember you understand the reasons why the seatbelt sign is illuminated. How would you respond to someone telling you, 'those are the rules'? Would you want to know whose rules or why flight attendants are up and moving around when passengers cannot be? Crewmembers confronting a passenger using this statement are exerting their control over the person and may be forcing a verbal confrontation. You may be right, that is the 'rule', but what has that accomplished if it ends up in a difficult confrontation with a passenger?

A reasonable explanation can go a long way with most people. A better response to a passenger refusing to sit down may be something like, 'Sir, the Captain has turned on the seatbelt sign for your safety. My job requires me to take the risks of being up and moving about. The airline is concerned for your safety and the safety of others, and none of us wants to see you hurt by turbulence. I hope you will understand. Please return to your seat and fasten your seatbelt'. Will this work 100 per cent of the time? Probably not, but it will work in the vast majority of cases. Most people appreciate a considerate explanation of the circumstances. A reasonable explanation given in an unemotional tone of voice, demonstrates to the other person that you care about them personally, their safety and the safety of others. Authoritative approaches to handling people are usually not effective in the long run. You may gain compliance by a passenger, but you may have to explain to your supervisor why they wrote a complaint letter against you. The Golden Rule works wonders with people and should serve as a guide in everything we do.

'What do you want me to do about it?'

Usually transmitted in a sarcastic tone of voice, this response shows indifference to the other person and their problem. If you want to really escalate a situation, then go ahead and use this insensitive phrase. Most people would interpret this statement to mean, 'I do not care about you or your problem'. Instead of becoming a problem solver, you have just become a large part of the problem.

You can use your own imagination to figure out what was said just before this response. It would be reasonable to assume that a person has asked you for your assistance in dealing with a problem. It may not seem to you to be a difficult problem, it may even be a trivial question, but it is their problem and they are asking you for help. They feel you have the knowledge and experience to find a solution to their problem. You represent your airline. You are the keeper of the solutions. When people come to you asking for a solution, you should feel honored they look to you as the person who can solve their problem. Rise to the occasion and demonstrate your skill by helping to solve their problem. Show concern and be empathetic.

Go back to the man who was trying to put his carry-on in the overhead bin above his seat. Pretend he had indicated to the flight attendant that he was having a problem with his bag, and she replied, '*What do you want me to do about it?*' What would have been his natural response? What if she had used an alternative approach? For example, 'Let me see if I can rearrange some of these bags and make room for yours. If I cannot make room, there is an open space a little further back. There, now it should fit'. She made the passenger happy by showing she cared, and she did it in front of other passengers – free public relations. She successfully avoided embarrassing the man, and avoided any type of confrontation. Remember, the Golden Rule works wonders with people and should serve as a guide in everything we do.

'What is your PROBLEM?'

Not really a question, but an imperial statement, if you really want to start a verbal face off with a passenger try saying, 'What is your problem?' (with emphasis on the word 'problem'). It is a sure-fire way of escalating the situation! Do not be surprised if you are punched in the nose, or, as a minimum, embroiled in a nasty verbal confrontation using a statement like this. What you are really saying is the person is a nuisance, and you do not want to be bothered with his or her trivial problems. Many times, this response is directed at a person's behavior. A situation where a passenger is telling loud and crude jokes is brought to the attention of a flight attendant, eliciting the response from the flight attendant, '*What is your problem?*' More than likely, the passenger's reply will be something like, 'You and this crummy airline ...'. Well, you DID ask!

This is the kind of statement Waltrip has made to his kids when they are fighting and carrying on with inappropriate behavior. For example, Sam strikes Josh, for something that is perceived by Sam as a major infraction (looking out his side of the car, etc.). Dad (Waltrip) confronts Sam and says, 'What is your problem?' Not meant as a question, but what he is really saying is, 'You have a problem!' It would be more appropriate for Dad to say, 'We need to work on your interpersonal communication skills relative to conflict resolution within our family unit'. Just joking, of course. Yet, when there is a problem at work or home, we need to look carefully at what is causing the problem and seek ways to resolve it rather than aggravating it.

An alterative approach might be, 'Sir (or ma'am), may I speak with you in private? Several passengers have complained about your language and we would appreciate if you would refrain from telling any more crude jokes or using foul language. Okay?' Remember, the Golden Rule works wonders with people and should serve as a guide in everything we do.

'It is for your own good'

This is an example of a person 'talking down to another' person. What the speaker of these words is really saying is, 'You are so stupid that you do not know what is good for you. Let me decide for you'. This is an insulting phrase and will probably result in the response, 'What do you mean it is for my own good? I know better than you what is good for me'.

You are passing through the cabin before departure and see a young man wearing earphones. The passenger has the music turned up so loud, you can hear the music from his CD player as you pass by. You tap the person on the shoulder and motion for him to remove his earphones. He does, and you tell him he has to turn off his CD and leave his earphones off until you get airborne. He asks, 'Why?' You respond, '*It is for your own good*'. Would you be pleased at being talked to in such a demeaning way? How would you respond? Chances are you would not respond favorably. A brief explanation is better than no explanation. How does this sound as an alternative approach? 'Excuse me sir, the FAA requires you to remove your earphones and turn your CD player off until we are airborne. There may be important announcements affecting your safety that could be made by the pilot or any of the flight attendants in the event of an emergency. We would not want you to miss them. Thanks'.

Remember, the Golden Rule works wonders with people and should serve as a guide in everything we do. (Are you beginning to get this message?)

'Why can you not be reasonable?'

This question usually results from the frustration you may feel when, after some amount of negotiations, the other person still does not agree with you. When these words are uttered, it is almost assured the other person will become more unreasonable. 'What do you mean I am unreasonable. You are the one that is unreasonable. I have told you ten times that I am starving! All I want to do is run to get something to eat and I will be right back'. People do not want to admit they are being unreasonable, even if they know it. It is human nature. Gracefully accepting humiliation in the form of a chastisement in front of others is not our best trait as human beings. Why fight human nature when you could easily deflect a verbal confrontation by demonstrating some understanding of human nature.

If you really believe the other person is being unreasonable, as an alternative approach may be to try summarizing your interpretation of THEIR position in an unemotional, very polite tone of voice. For example, 'Okay, sir, let me see if I understand you correctly, you want to get off the airplane, find a fast-food place, get something to go, and get back before we depart in five minutes. I am hungry too, so I would like to go with you, but we would both miss the flight. I will see if I have any extra snacks, and if so, you are welcome to them. Okay?'

The tone in which you address the person in this case is very important to arriving at any kind of resolution. A sarcastic tone invariably will undermine your position and cause the other person to be even more resolute in their position. Remember, the Golden Rule works wonders … (Okay, you ARE beginning to get this message!)

'Why? Because I said so!'

An obviously condescending statement, the speaker is attempting to show his or her superiority. The speaker thinks he or she is coming from a position of authority and wants you to know it. Unless the person spoken to feels they are going to be physically assaulted and lose, they will probably rebel against this statement. You may even get a laugh out of them, and then something like, 'Yeah, right! Who made you king for the day?'

A businessman that came on-board in the first wave of passengers and is sitting in first class with his laptop computer out during the boarding process, he is obviously working very intensely on something. He seems oblivious to other passengers and to your attempts to serve him a pre-departure beverage. It is now time for departure and he is still working feverishly. You approach him and ask him to turn off his computer and stow it until airborne. He asks why, and in your haste, you snap, '*Why? Because I said so!*' What kind of response do you expect from this person?

An alternative statement might go something like this. 'Sir, I know you are extremely busy and I hate to interrupt you, but for everyone's safety, I must ask you to turn off your laptop and stow it until we get safely airborne and a flight attendant makes the announcement that it is okay for everyone to use certain electronic devices. You were so busy during boarding that you missed your pre-departure beverage, but I will be glad to bring you something as soon as we begin our service after airborne. Thanks for understanding'.

No one, not even a child, likes to be treated like a child. Treat others with genuine respect and with a genuine attitude of caring for their safety. You may not like them as a person, but caring for their safety is still your responsibility. Remember, the Golden Rule works wonders.

'Calm down!'

Whenever we resort to telling someone to '*calm down*', the situation is already out of control to some degree. Obviously, emotions are high among those involved in the situation. Most often, this phrase is spoken in a loud voice. Yelling '*calm down!*' in someone's face is not conducive to making him or her want to comply with you. When a person is upset, the last thing they need is someone telling them their concern is unwarranted. Effectively, that is what is happening when told to '*calm down*'. No matter how trivial the situation is to you, a person's troubles are important to them. Show concern and be empathetic. Speak slower, softly and lower your voice. The gentle concern you show in your voice and actions will encourage them to actually calm down.

An alternate approach would be to say, 'Folks, this is going nowhere. Can I have everyone's attention, please? Let us try to sort things out one at a time. Everyone will get a chance to talk, so please wait your turn. While you are waiting for your turn, please take a deep breath and listen to what the other person is saying. I am going to start with this lady on my right and work around to my left. Okay, ma'am, what is going on here?'

Yes, the Golden Rule works wonders.

People First, Objectives Next

In all of these examples, an underlying notion comes through loud and clear – people just want to be able to express themselves and to be understood in a respectful manner. A wise Pastor offering some very good advice about dealing with people, said, 'Put people before objectives'. This is great practical advice. If we care more about getting someone to put their seat back up, than we do about the person, our priorities are wrong. People should always be more important than objectives. However, we can get people to accomplish our objectives as long as we put them first. If our motives and priorities are correct, a passenger will more readily comply with crew requests. When we lack knowledge of human understanding, or do not apply what we know about natural human reactions, we face the risk of escalated conflict.

The average passenger just wants to be treated fairly and honestly. Putting passengers first makes a simple statement about how you and the airline feel about them. If all we care about is getting them to comply with our orders, the resultant passenger dissatisfaction will be reflected in their attitudes toward us personally, as well as the company for whom we work.

Unfortunately, needless confrontations will arise which may result in injury to flight crews. There is certainly no excuse for the passenger who lashes out physically in an unprovoked face-to-face encounter with a flight attendant or pilot. These individuals need to be punished to the full extent of the law. However, the stark realities of sky rage incidents are that many could have been avoided by some simple principles of human understanding by the crew. We need to put people first over objectives and to make everyone's flight a good experience to remember.

Passengers come aboard aircraft with every conceivable problem under the sun. Someone once described an aircraft as a city filled with a wide range of emotions, with some people going to a funeral and some to a wedding. Everyone has problems and part of our job as flight crewmembers is to get the passengers to their destinations without adding any other problems to their lists. We should consider ourselves problem solvers, not problem makers. Flight attendants are generally some of the best problem solvers we have ever seen, and they are not given the credit they deserve. What do flight attendants do that makes them so good with people?

The first thing that is readily evident about these quality flight attendants is they genuinely like people. During the interview before they were hired, they probably said, 'I like to work with people' … and, they do. It shows. Observe how they treat others. They treat others, as they would want to be treated. They show respect and treat others as if they are the most important person at that time. They are sincere, personal and genuine to others. If you watch them closely, you will see them get a passenger cooperate with them with whatever they want to accomplish, and make them feel good about it too. It is a win-win situation for everyone involved.

After stopping someone for a traffic violation, there are police officers that make it a goal to get the driver to say 'thank you' after getting a traffic ticket. Under the circumstances, how could that be possible you wonder? Simply, by treating them kindly and accepting the fact that nobody is perfect. Police officers who practice this approach realize they do not need to belabor the issues with a driver that had just violated a traffic law. When an officer is respectful and discusses the violation with the driver in a completely non-threatening manner, a 'thank you' from a motorist is not an uncommon reply.

Traffic accidents are a different example. When Waltrip was a police officer, he would be called to investigate an accident between two or three vehicles. On occasion, a driver would berate himself or herself for not being more careful. Waltrip did not have to say anything about their carelessness, because they already recognized it. Of course, there are always exceptions. For example, the reckless driver who always thinks he is right no matter what. In this case, Waltrip may get an ear full of how it was the other guy's fault and how he is such a good driver and would never do anything to cause an accident. Waltrip would conduct his own investigation regardless of what the driver said and come to a conclusion based upon his investigation. Even if it were the reckless driver's fault, Waltrip would gracefully and respectfully discuss the findings. Waltrip would not back down from the truth, but humiliating the reckless driver by berating him for his inconsiderate driving skills was not appropriate. Unfortunately, not all police officers take this approach in dealing with people. Neither do all flight crews.

The fact of the matter is that regardless of how much proof and evidence there is against some people, they refuse to accept fault. We must accept the fact there are people just like this that board our airplanes, either as passengers or as crewmembers. In spite of everything to the contrary, they believe they are right. We can find some degree of this stubbornness in all of us. When we deal with people, we need to understand there are going to be some who believe they are right no matter what.

Just how do we get some people to do what we want aboard an airplane without getting into a battle over who are right? Applying the golden rule is a great place to start. Getting a difficult person to cooperate with you when they want to do something entirely different is an art. Some very talented flight attendants successfully deal with difficult people everyday. They are experts at it and never seem to elicit a complaint. They put themselves into the other guy's shoes and they treat others, as they would want to be treated. They simply live the Golden Rule.

Conclusion

There are a huge number of books and courses on conflict resolution on the market. We would encourage anyone to read and study techniques on the mechanics of resolving confrontations. We all need to be able to effectively defuse and solve conflicts before they escalate into physical attacks, on or off the aircraft. What we say and how we say it plays a major role in this endeavor. Focus on the issue, not the person. Keep emotions out of it. Show respect for the other person, and truly listen to what they are saying. Treat others, as you would like to be treated.

'Okay, I have done all of that, and the situation still escalates. What now?' You must be able to protect yourself, other crewmembers and passengers, and the aircraft from acts of violence. Prepare yourself accordingly.

Notes

1 Dahlberg, Angela, *Air Rage*, Ashgate Publishing, 2001.
2 Passenger Acquitted In Breaking Gate Agent's Neck, *USA Today*, 4 April 2001.

Chapter 10

Flight Crew Use of Force

Author's Note

In this chapter, the authors address flight crews' use of force against an aggressor on an aircraft operated in the United States. The authors apologize to international readers who will notice that this section takes on a distinctive American perspective to the legal ramifications of self-defense on an aircraft. This is because both the authors are American, live in the United States and have had experience in this country's use of force laws. They have chosen to address this subject from their personal backgrounds. Although, this chapter addresses the laws of the United States, the application of many of the use of force principles expressed in this chapter could also apply to other countries throughout the world. The authors encourage crewmembers from around the world to learn the use of force laws of their own countries, and how those laws affect their ability to defend themselves on the aircraft.

Introduction

Among other requirements of the Aviation and Transportation Security Act (ATSA) of 2001 (United States), it is required that crewmembers be trained on the 'appropriate responses to defend oneself'. ATSA also authorizes flight crews to use 'any means possible' to prevent the armed takeover on an aircraft. In addition, the Homeland Security Act that became law in November 2002 gives airline pilots the authority to carry and use a firearm against a hijacker that forces their way into the flight deck. The Act also has mandated self-defensive training for cabin crewmembers. The bottom line is that flight crews are authorized to use force up to and including lethal force in protecting themselves and the aircraft. In light of these legislative directives and policies, the airlines need to focus and direct flight crewmembers in properly controlling the use of force before flight crews become involved in unnecessary use of force litigation. Prohibiting or discouraging crewmembers from acting in self-defense is fraught with legal potholes and labor discord. This is not an issue that will be resolved by issuing broad, ambiguous company directives or making the issue extremely complicated for crewmembers. Crewmembers need clear, concise, and easy to understand use of force policy that makes sense. A policy, rule, or other directive that appears self-serving, irrelevant, restrictive, and /or lacks direction or purpose will more than likely be disregarded by the average crewmember.

Mandated crewmember security training emerged from the Aviation and Transportation Security Act (ATSA). This legislation dictated that all crewmember training be completed by mid-October 2002. For the airlines in the United States, this training was completed on time. Both the law and the mandatory training address crewmember use of force that, like it or not, requires action on how to deal with this issue. Clearly, government attitudes and beliefs about self-defense have changed significantly since before 9/11. The simple fact that we live in a different world fraught with terrorist threats has changed the thinking processes of government regulators. Unfortunately, government or airline guidance on crewmember use of force is severely lacking on this very important issue.

Our experience with various airlines revealed a huge deficit in addressing this issue. A use of force policy is a sensitive area for the airlines to address. The liability issues affecting the airlines are tremendous, but a lack of direction for crewmembers is also fraught with legal pitfalls. Many crewmembers have sought out their own self-defense training and the overall lack of standardized training in understanding the ramifications of using force may prove to be troublesome. In fact, the liability issues for airlines may be worse than having the airline provide defensive training in the first place. For the airlines' own self-protection, it makes fiscal and practical sense to control as many of the aspects of crew defensive training as possible and to provide guidance through a use of force policy.

Use of force is a major issue and careful guidance is needed for both crewmembers and airlines alike. Based upon our experience we believe the information in this chapter will provide essential guidance as it has for one established air carrier in the United States.

Importance in the Development of a Policy of Guidance

An increase in the consumption of alcohol by the traveling public is combining with the stresses of air travel to create a dangerous mix aboard an airliner. As aircrews have noticed since 9/11, overall stresses have increased dramatically with the results being an increase in unpleasant encounters with passengers. The airlines need to recognize that crewmembers and passengers may interpret a sky rage incident for an act of terrorism and may respond with violence against an aggressive passenger. Without any specific crewmember training or guidance on this issue, what will that response actually be and where does the liability for injury or death lie?

It is extremely important that airlines become aware of the heavy monetary price they can pay for not developing and properly directing flight crews in the use of force. One only has to look at police departments across the nation to realize they have paid large monetary settlements for the improper use of force by police officers. In this chapter, we provide guidance from our personal experiences with Use of Force Polices and Procedures and how they relate to the law in the United States. The authors have consulted with legal counsel on crewmember use of force issues. The applications discussed in this chapter will assist airline legal departments in developing a crewmember use of force policy that is legally sound.

Airlines need to give policy guidance to their flight crewmembers on the defensive uses of force by ensuring their training leads to a full understanding of the scope and limitations on any use of force. The authors are unaware of any airline that has developed comprehensive guidelines and policies regarding use of force by flight crewmembers except for one established airline in the United States. This lack of direction may ultimately prove to be a major mistake for the unlucky airline whose crewmembers use force against a passenger and end up in civil litigation over the matter. One successful lawsuit could potentially cost the airlines millions of dollars. Should airlines and crewmembers take this chance?

Flight crewmembers need guidance through an airline policy that articulates and justifies their use of force in a legitimate manner. Both the airlines and their flight crewmembers need this guidance to protect them from any liability issue that could arise from a lack of a clear policy on a use of force incident. When developed, the use of force policy should give guidance, but not constrain or restrict a crewmember in what they defensively need to do to end a physical attack aboard an aircraft in a reasonable manner.

Professional law enforcement agencies within the United States have developed policies governing use of force by its officers. Law enforcement officers are constrained and directed to operate within the use of force policies of their department. Any variation outside of these policies could cost an officer his career and freedom as evidenced by the Rodney King incident in Los Angeles in the early 1990s.

Photo 10.1 Crewmembers are involved in many instances of violence aboard aircraft

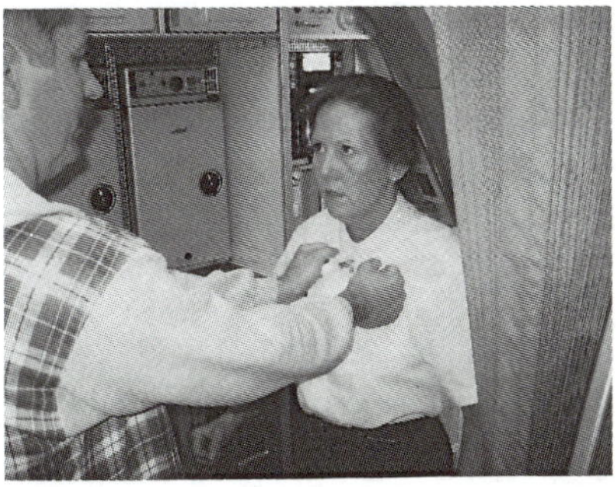

In this well-known case, the Los Angeles Police Department (LAPD) asserted the officers acted slightly outside the scope of the department's use of force policy. Of the four officers directly involved, two went to prison, one was severely disciplined and the other's employment was terminated. Additionally, all the officers who were present, including those from other police agencies that did not actively participate in the arrest of King, were disciplined by their respective departments. Even the police helicopter pilot and observer in the helicopter circling overhead were disciplined. Furthermore, the LAPD paid US$3.8 million to settle the subsequent civil lawsuit brought by King's attorney.[1] Unnecessary use of force incidents continue to plague the LAPD as evidenced by the US$28 million to settle unnecessary use of force complaints in 2000 alone.[2]

As we all know, law enforcement officers place themselves in the middle of many violent situations. As such, police need clear and concise direction in the implementation of the use of force. Airlines obviously do not have the same responsibilities as law enforcement agencies and never will. However, at the very least, airlines should develop policies involving flight crew use of force to protect themselves from civil liability issues that could result in large monetary losses because of a lack of a well-reasoned and defined policy on use of force.

It should go without saying that flight crewmembers should never be expected to perform a police function. Entering this area is undesirable, unrealistic, and could possibly escalate an avoidable incident into a physical confrontation the crew is not trained to handle. Law enforcement matters should always be left to trained officers of the law unless of course, there is no other option. Flight crews should avoid, if reasonably possible, any type of physical confrontation with a passenger. Under normal circumstances, flight crews should be limited to a purely defensive use of force to repel an aggressor, defend another from physical attack, and/or restrain a passenger with restraint devices if deemed reasonably necessary under the circumstances. As we all witnessed on 9/11, extreme measures may be required by flight crewmembers to overcome those who are determined to cause mass destruction of life and property. The use of force policy needs to cover the wide spectrum of uses of force that may occur on an aircraft.

Police are legally justified to make an arrest and defend themselves or others in the commission of their duties. However, many police officers have been arrested for violating US civil rights laws in using excessive force when making an arrest of a citizen. It has become clear by the implementation of the Airline Transportation Security Act (ATSA), and the Homeland Security Act (HSA) that flight crews are expected to use force onboard an aircraft if necessary, and therefore need to be covered by a use of force policy.

Violence Aboard Airliners is a Reality

In January 2002, Southwest flight 1702 (B-737) from Los Angeles to Las Vegas was pulling away from the gate when a 6′ 2″, 210-pound man approached the rear of the aircraft with a shoe in his hand. When a flight attendant tried to prevent him from opening the rear door the man hit her in the head with his fist. The man did open the door, but two male passengers moved to subdue him.

In February 2002, United Airlines flight 855 (B-777) from Miami to Buenos Aires had an incident that involved a flight crew's use of force. A drunken, unarmed man partially forced his way into the flight deck with 'Kung Fu' style kicks to the lower half of the cockpit door. The captain made a desperate plea for help over the public address system and a number of crewmembers and passengers responded immediately. As the man tried to enter the flight deck through the lower half of the cockpit door, the first officer hit him in the head with the crash axe, leaving a 2-inch gash on the aggressor's head. With the assistance of passengers, the crew managed to handcuff the man and drag him back into the passenger compartment. One flight attendant received minor injuries during the altercation.[3]

These are just two of the many examples of violence aboard aircraft. The chapter on disruptive passengers and sky rage gives numerous examples where flight crews needed to use force against aggressors. Many of the altercations aboard aircraft involved the excessive use of alcoholic beverages.

Table 10.1 Number of passenger incidents reported in the United States

Year	Sky rage	Disruptive passenger
1995	90	174
1996	182	292
1997	297	450
1998	301	142
1999	302	302
2000*	41 (January only)	500

Sources: FAA, ATA, ALPA, ITWF, Associated Press documents.

Even in light of the terrorists' attacks on 9/11, violence aboard commercial airliners still occurs. A possible explanation may be that alcohol consumption levels among the traveling public has increased significantly since 9/11. Some airports have recorded increases of the sale of alcohol to passengers by as much as 16 per cent.[4] It is common knowledge that alcohol consumption is associated with a reduction in an individual's inhibitions and is a significant factor in physical confrontations. As indicated by the statistics in Table 10.2, alcohol is the number one factor in sky rage/disruptive passenger incidents.

Table 10.2 Major issues leading to disruptive passenger disturbances

Too much alcohol consumed by passenger	88%
Passenger's demanding/intolerant personality	81%
Flight delays	78%
Stress of air travel	75%
Smoking ban	70%

Source: UK CAA 1999.

Variations in Use of Force Policies

Law enforcement agencies vary in the application and implementation of their use of force policies. Although, policies vary, they have been largely impacted by Federal and State court case law. The use of force guidelines that are now in place at law enforcement departments have largely been developed with court opinions as a guide. The ultimate test of a use of force policy has evolved over the years through court challenges. A tremendous liability could be suffered by a law enforcement department that does not adhere to the levels of force that are reasonable and prudent as interpreted through statute and the courts. Therefore, a use of force policy is a naturally evolving process. Over time, it becomes evident that, on occasion, a police department's use of force policy is obsolete or is viewed by the courts and local citizens as too abusive. The result is a change of policy that reflects levels of force that is acceptable to these entities.

Escalation of Force

Most law enforcement agencies incorporate within their policies an ascending level of force during an incident. This is often referred to as the 'escalation of force'. Practically speaking, working one's way up on the scale of force does not always occur. However, the scale is a general guide and is the preferred departmental method to approach a potential incident. A generalized police 'escalation of force' is as follows:

- Presence;
- Voice;
- Hands;
- Chemical spray (OC pepper /mace);
- Stun gun/Taser;
- Impact weapon (baton, asp, or other impact weapon); then,
- Lethal force

The first five items are normally considered non-lethal methods of force. That is not to say hitting someone over the head with a police baton would not cause death. Deaths have occurred using weapons, normally intended for non-lethal purposes, in an unauthorized manner.

We propose the airlines develop an escalation of force similar to that of law enforcement. An example of this escalation of force could be as follows:

- Presence;
- Voice;
- Hands and/or enlisting the aid of others;

- Makeshift weapons (Only during a serious bodily threat to the crewmember or a passenger); then,
- Force, by whatever means, that is equal to lethal force

With a codified escalation of force, crews will begin to understand the importance of beginning at the lowest possible levels of force when confronted with a potential violent incident. However, because of the actions of an attacker, airlines need to understand that a crewmember may not be able to work their way up on a use of force scale. In a perfect world, starting at the lowest levels of force is always desirable. The escalation of the incident should rest solely upon an attacker and not on the crewmember. If possible, the crewmember's goal should always be to de-escalate an incident. Taking this approach does not mean the crewmember must become a victim while an attacker assaults them. The airlines should not directly, or indirectly, encourage crewmembers to take the 'first punch' before they act defensively to reasonably protect themselves from injury.

Considerations and Factors

Police as well as flight crewmembers must understand the limitations on the proper use of force before a potential violent confrontation. It is impossible to predict with any certainty how a situation will develop during every incident involving the use of force. This concept needs to be fully understood by airline management. Flight crewmembers must also realize there are acceptable levels of force to repel an attack, and they must be careful not to over react. Adhering to some basic principles will protect both crewmember and the airlines from any undue liability.

A number of factors should be considered before any use of force. These factors should include, but are not limited to:

- The conduct of individual(s) reasonably perceived by the flight crew at the time;
- Individuals who may be reasonably thought to be under the influence of drugs/alcohol at the time of the incident (mental capacity);
- Proximity or availability of weapons;
- Availability of other options (backing away from the situation, verbally defusing a potentially dangerous escalation, etc.);
- Potential for injury;
- Size/weight, age, gender and any other significant physical disparities; and,
- Any other exigent circumstances (hijacking, flight deck breach, violent attack upon a crewmember/passenger or any other extreme threat to human life).[5]

After an incident involving a crewmember's use of force, supervisors should closely examine a reasonableness of the application. The incident should be judged from the perspective of a reasonable flight crewmember on the scene at the time. *Second-guessing* a crewmember from any other perspective is unrealistic. Flight crewmembers should be entrusted, but expected to exercise restraint and discretion in any application of the use of force. Well-reasoned and common sense defensive approaches should be applied by crewmembers when confronted with an attack. The defensive approaches will vary depending on the abilities of the individual crewmember. Some crewmembers may have had previous self-defense training and may be able to respond effectively, while others may have had no training and respond with instinctive defensive methods that are inadequate. *Additionally, crewmembers should not have to sustain physical injury before applying a reasonable amount of force to defend themselves, or others, from injury or death.*[6]

Photo 10.2 Flight attendant being physically grabbed on the arm by a passenger

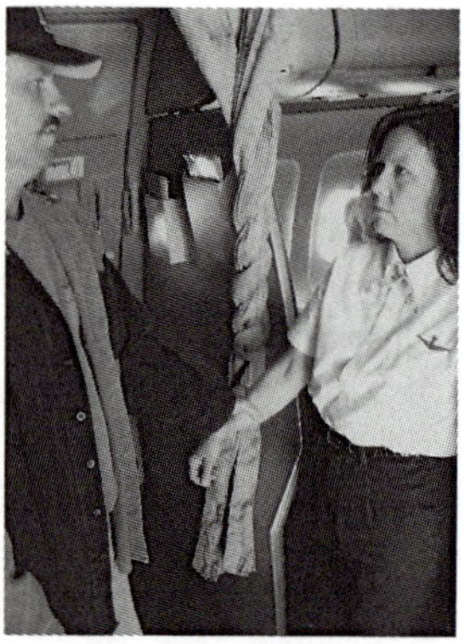

Question: What amount of force should this flight attendant take against this angry passenger?

Answer: Only that amount of force that is *reasonable* based upon the *totality of the circumstances.*

Reasonable Application of Force

What amount of force can a crewmember use to defend themselves aboard an airliner? Quite simply, a reasonable application of force is that amount of force that is moderate and rational based upon the *totality of the circumstances.*[7] Nevertheless, in any given situation a use of force for self-defense should only be applied to that extent needed to overcome an attack and stop the aggression. Unlawful or unreasonable force is that amount of force that goes over and above the amount of force needed to subdue an individual for an illegal violent act on an aircraft. For example, if a flight attendant were faced with a verbally obnoxious passenger, it would be an unlawful use of force to strike the passenger with a full can of soda. Based upon the *totality of the circumstances,* a verbal defusing of the incident would be the appropriate level of force in this situation.

It is doubtful crewmembers will ever be required to possess the same level of understanding of use of force applications as law enforcement officers. Law enforcement officers in their line of duty, place themselves directly into the middle of many violent or potentially violent situations; therefore, their understanding of use of force principles is paramount to their mission. Airline crews should not become involved in trying to resolve a violent incident unless there is absolutely no other choice available to them.

At the time of this writing, the Homeland Security Act has been signed into law allowing American pilots to carry firearms on the flight deck.[8] All applicable laws pertaining to governmental law enforcement and to applications of use of force apply to those pilots who are selected as FFDO candidates, complete the training, and are deputized as Federal Flight Deck Officers (FFDO). In-depth training in use of force is extremely important for the FFDOs, as the threshold of understanding for law enforcement is much higher than for the general population.

Flight crews will need to recognize they will have to exercise good judgment and reasonable discretion in any application of force. If the airline and/or crewmember find themselves in front of a court, the judge will closely view a reasonableness of the application of force. It will be measured from a *reasonable person perspective*, which measures force against an *average prudent individual*.[9] However, as time passes and airlines and flight crews become more familiar with use of force concepts, legal standards will eventually be raised to a higher threshold of understanding for airline and crewmembers alike.

Unlawful Use of Force

Flight crews must remain cognizant of the ramifications upon their livelihoods and freedom by an unlawful use of force incident. Even in light of Section 144 of the Aviation and Transportation Security Act, which reads:

> An individual shall not be liable for damages in any action brought in a Federal or State court arising out of the acts of the individual in attempting to thwart an act of criminal violence or piracy on an aircraft if that individual reasonably believed that such an act of criminal violence or piracy was occurring or was about to occur.[10]

Notice the word reasonably. Reasonable is an important aspect to any use of force policy because it is directly related to the law and the right to defend oneself or others. We are convinced that if a crewmember were to exceed the *reasonable* limitations of this section, Federal law would be violated by depriving the individual in question of their civil rights, and the crewmember could be held responsible either civilly, criminally, or both.[11]

In the current aviation environment, we have expectation, direction and validation of crew defensive use of force aboard aircraft. Yet, no real guidance from airline or government on to what extent the force should be. Would the government let federal law enforcement officers make up their own minds on what type of force should be used in a given situation? Definitely not.

There are two federal civil rights laws that law enforcement officers and crewmembers particularly need to be concerned about:

1 Title 18, USC., Section 241, Conspiracy of Rights:

> This statute makes it unlawful for two or more persons to conspire to injure, oppress, threaten, or intimidate any person of any state, territory or district in the free exercise or enjoyment of any right or privilege secured to him/her by the Constitution or the laws of the United States, (or because of his/her having exercised the same).
>
> Punishment varies from a fine or imprisonment of up to ten years, or both...[12]

2 Title 18, USC., Section 242, Deprivation of Rights Under the Color of Law:

> This statute makes it a crime for any person acting under color of law, statute, ordinance, regulation, or custom to willfully deprive or cause to be deprived from any person those rights, privileges, or immunities secured or protected by the Constitution and laws of the US This definition includes, in addition to law enforcement officials, individuals such as Mayors, Council persons, Judges, Nursing Home Proprietors, Security Guards, etc., persons who are bound by laws, statutes, ordinances, or customs.
>
> Punishment varies from a fine or imprisonment of up to one year, or both ...[13]

Although, crewmembers need to be concerned with both these federal civil rights sections, we want to emphasis the last section, Title 18, USC, Section 242. Notice the definition to whom this section applies – ... *individuals such as ... persons who are bound by laws, statutes, ordinances, or customs.* With the Aviation and Transportation Security Act of 2001, Mission Statement of the Common Strategy 2, and the Homeland Security Act, we believe these civil rights laws specifically apply to flight crews in the United States.

The main point is that crewmembers are now operating in a new environment in which they are not familiar. Law enforcement officers spend a great deal of time attempting to understand their legal position in regards to use of force. A subject that is often discussed in the press, police officers think about it continually. Police officers have to because if they do not, it could mean the loss of their job and freedom by not gauging their actions correctly. We are now in a new reality of air transportation and crewmembers, not closely examining use of force issues, could see their jobs and freedom affected. It is imperative that crewmembers begin to address these issues before they are over-run by events that will continue to occur.

If crewmembers could face prison and loss of employment in an unnecessary use of force incident, what could be the legal repercussions to the airlines? Some cities have paid dearly for police unnecessary use of force, and so could an airline:

- Between 1994 and 1996, New York City paid out US$70 million.
- Between 1991 and 1996, Los Angeles paid over US$79 million.

- Between 1986 to 1997, Detroit paid more than US$100 million.
- July 1993 and November 1996, Philadelphia paid over US$32 million.[14]

Managing Use of Force

In August 2000, a 19-year-old passenger became irate for no apparent reason and attempted to force his way into the flight deck of Southwest flight 1783. After he attacked several passengers and acted irrationally, at least six male passengers restrained him. After landing at Salt Lake City airport, airport police boarded the flight and found the 19-year-old man unconscious. Doctors later pronounced him dead at a local Salt Lake City hospital. A County Coroner later determined the cause of death to be from the amount of force applied while passengers were restraining him.[15]

According to some witnesses in news reports, the young man was being assaulted by passengers while he was completely restrained. Although, the US Attorney filed no criminal charges, there are some important issues to examine on the use of force in this particular case. As we previously discussed, a use of force can only be used at a level just enough to overcome an attacker. Prosecutors could view any further force beyond this point as an unlawful use of force.

The question becomes, can passengers and flight crews have a person completely restrained, and continue to use force against them? Ultimately, we believe the answer to the question is 'no' and believe Southwest 1763 incident is an anomaly of law. Even in the light of 9/11, if passengers and crews repeatedly used excessive force against violent passengers it is almost certain prosecutors would press criminal charges against those they felt responsible. An excessive use of force is still an excessive use of force, even if it is against a drug-crazed or psychotic individual. Society does not tolerate excessive use of force from police and we should not from passengers and/or flight crews.

When force is used against another for any reason, the need to demonstrate reasonableness will be examined by law enforcement and prosecutors. Prosecutors will take a close look at the incident and determine if any abuses of the law occurred. Some prosecutors are more zealous than others are, and if there is any hint of abuse, they will file criminal charges against those they believe are responsible.

Managing an incident involving a person, restrained by scared and angry passengers, is a challenge. In a dynamic incident involving violence, emotions among crew and passengers will be running high. Some people may become so blinded by their fears and anger they may be driven to behave in ways they normally would not. However, it is imperative that cooler heads prevail. A crewmember must step in and stop any unintentional death or unnecessary injury. As unwelcome as it may be for crewmembers, they must attempt to stop well meaning, but excited passengers from killing an obviously restrained person. This may be where the feminine, softer and gentler approach may be useful in keeping matters under control. This is NOT a chauvinistic statement. Some use of force studies have been conducted suggesting gender may play a significant role in avoiding a physical confrontation while attempting to restrain an individual.[16]

If a flight crewmember does not attempt to stop passengers from over-restraining an individual, but could have, they and their airline may be held civilly responsible for their lack of action. It is also conceivable a crewmember could face criminal charges in some situations when they could have acted to stop overly zealous passengers and did not.[17] If this were the case, both the crewmember and the airline in question could suffer greatly.

Managing passenger use of force is a difficult task to master for any crewmember, but an unavoidable one in light of the current mood among the traveling public. Flight crews must do everything in their power to stop a death from occurring aboard an aircraft. Proper training and company guidance will greatly reduce this risk to all.

Once it is obvious to a crewmember that a violent person is successfully restrained by passengers, they should step in, and if physically necessary, push or pull others off the individual. We recommend all flight crews keep a small roll of either duct tape or a fibrous box tape with them on their person for restraining purposes.

As alcohol consumption continues to rise at airport terminals, sky rage incidents will no doubt begin to rise at some point. With the fear and anxiety pervasive among the traveling public, flight crews may need to become managers of potential conflicts aboard their aircraft. Both airlines and flight crews need to be prepared and ready to deal with any future incidents like the one that occurred aboard Southwest Airlines flight 1763.

Lethal Force

A discussion of a use of force would not be complete without discussing a use of deadly force. A use of deadly force is also referred to as lethal force. Either way, it is the ultimate application of the use of force. Airlines and flight crews should carefully consider this aspect of the use of force.

The airlines should not discourage through policy or procedure any measure that inhibits flight crews from considering using deadly force under the following exigent circumstances:

> In necessary self-defense or defense of another person, and there is a reasonable cause to believe there is an imminent danger of death or serious bodily injury.[18]

An attacker is overwhelming crewmember A. Crewmember B believes death or serious injury could occur to crewmember A. Striking the attacker over the head with a full soft drink container could result in the attacker's death, probably not, but it is a possibility.

After the use of lethal force against a violent attacker, the justification must be limited to the facts known or perceived by the crewmember at the time. Facts unknown to the crewmember, no matter how compelling, should not be a factor, nor be considered in later determining if lethal force was justified. This same approach is used in determining the justification of lethal force by law enforcement in analyzing circumstances surrounding a police officer's use of lethal force.

Deadly force should not be looked upon as a deliberate killing of another person. It should be viewed in the respect that when a use of lethal force is applied, it *could* result in death. We should never set out to *kill* another person when discussing lethal force. A flight crewmember's only motivation should be to stop an attacker from seriously injuring or killing us or another person.

Flight crews have to prepare themselves to face the fact the force they may need to use in an extreme situation, like 9/11, may result in death to an attacker. Nobody is saying we have to like considering using deadly force to protect human life. To some people the taking of a human life to save a human life may seem to be a contradiction in terms. Nevertheless, let us consider the greater good: to save an innocent person (including ourselves) from serious injury or death, we may be forced to use lethal force to stop the attacker.

The airlines need to understand some situations may be serious enough for flight crews to resort to lethal force and that right should be acknowledged through a policy statement such as:

> When a threat to human life exists, circumstances dictate no other available or reasonable alternative, and after all reasonable methods have been exhausted or are impractical, deadly force should be a major consideration.[19]

An aggressive intruder breaching the flight deck is an example of a very grave situation. Obviously, the breaching or attempted breaching of the flight deck door is a life or death situation for everyone aboard. If time permits after verbal warnings, a flight crewmember is justified in using lethal force of any kind to stop the breaching of the flight door.

Personal Decision

Most crewmembers may never have contemplated the deliberate taking of another person's life in self-defense. As the events of 9/11 prove, a personal decision needs to be made by each crewmember whether, if they were ever faced with such a dire situation, they would be willing to use deadly force to defend themselves and/or others. If they are unwilling to resort to such an extreme measure in the defense of their life, or the life of another, then unfortunately they should consider taking up another occupation. If a crewmember were to decide against continuing their career because they are unable or unwilling to use lethal force, this would be completely understandable. There would be nothing to be ashamed of, and should be viewed as a courageous personal choice.

The airlines should expect that some crewmembers might be repulsed by the thought of using any type of force against others, let alone lethal force. Unfortunately, like it or not, flight crewmember job descriptions have changed dramatically since that horrible day in September. Regrettably, all crewmembers need to accept the fact they must fulfill a new aspect of their occupations. Nobody ever would have believed anyone would be seriously discussing flight crew self-defense or a use of force before the attack on 9/11. It is a sad reality, but one the airlines and their flight crews must accept if they are to successfully continue in their jobs.

Seeking Medical Aid

After any incident involving use of force, injuries may have occurred. Sometimes they may not be readily evident at the time, but after the adrenaline wears off, pain will become noticeable. Only after the incident has stabilized and any threat by an attacker is eliminated, should crewmembers seek medical attention for those injured. As angry as a crewmember may be with any individual(s) for attacking them or the aircraft, anyone that is injured and needs medical attention should be accommodated – this includes the aggressor(s).

When an injury occurs during an arrest, police are required to seek out medical aid and administer first aid if required. Likewise, flight crews will need to request medical aid and administer first aid to the extent possible.[20]

Federal Flight Deck Officers

There are both pros and cons to airline pilots carrying firearms, but the evidence and common sense clearly indicate armed pilots will increase the security aboard an aircraft. However, numerous details need to be worked out by the US government before the program is fully implemented. Training is one of those important details and is crucial to a successful implementation of the federal flight deck officer (FFDO) program. What we want to discuss here are some of the issues potential flight deck officers should begin to understand about the job they are facing. Most pilots do not have law enforcement experience. Many have not been exposed to some of the complicated legal issues that occur to police officers on a regular basis. It is our hope that in the FFDO program there will be a consistency of training, knowledge, performance, and standards that are common to all forms of law enforcement in the United States.

Pilots have often asked why they are required to have a law enforcement function when armed on the aircraft, as the law requires. The answer quite simply is for liability reasons. The government will accept the liability for an event, but only if the armed pilot is considered a quasi-law enforcement employee of the United States. The government quite naturally wants some standards applied to the individuals who will carry these weapons.

Training

Although it is important, there is much more to carrying a firearm than proper gun handling techniques or going through the motions of shooting at a target three feet away. The training requirements for flight deck officers should be commensurate with the overall responsibility of the position. Naturally, the training requirements should involve less training than what federal law enforcement officers go through, but it should definitely not be by a significant amount so that it jeopardizes the quality of training and the traditions of American law enforcement.

Training should reflect the responsibility that is being proposed in the law. As an armed pilot, you may be enforcing laws (on a limited basis) of the United States, and nothing less than a complete understanding of what those laws are and the limitations of the commission take time to learn. As a law enforcement officer and under the right circumstances, you may legitimately take the life of another person. This awesome responsibility should not be taken lightly, or without thinking through and understanding the consequences of such a commission. For example, look how the press and public react when a local police officer uses his firearm in the line of duty. Imagine what will happen if a pilot uses a firearm in the line of duty. The incident would be covered in worldwide news and would be thoroughly examined by several law enforcement entities. A flight deck officer should have a complete understanding of the modern application of the use of force concepts and under what type of conditions force can be used. This is not as easy as it may sound.

Armed Pilot Use of Force

Use of force by pilots with a firearm is an extremely important issue. If a pilot were to shoot a suspect forcing their way into the flight deck, the press, FBI, FAA, TSA, DOJ, ACLU and the airline will want answers to how and why it occurred. The incident may be a completely justifiable event, but this will not stop the 'armchair quarterbacks' from second guessing your decision. This could cause a lot of anguish for you and your family. Many fine officers have gone through some very difficult mental issues before they could come to grips with the fact they killed another human being. We are talking about some big tough police officers that carry a weapon everyday of their lives. What makes any pilot think they are different?

Just for a moment, think about what your children will go through with their friends and classmates at school when word gets out that you killed someone on a plane. It is going to be very difficult for them because they may be on the receiving end of insults by their classmates. 'Wait', you say, 'I'll be the hero and everyone will appreciate the fine job I did'. Think again, because even if the incident was a clean and justified shooting there will always be detractors. Just because it is clear to you does not mean it will be perceived that way in the press and with civil rights groups. You will not be able to argue your point because you will be the subject of an intensive investigation and will not, and more importantly, should not engage in public commentary of an investigation until after it is completed. Even after the investigation is completed, TSA policy will probably prohibit you from making public comment on the incident. Additionally, do not forget the inevitable civil trial for unnecessary use of force that will require you to testify on the witness stand and be cross-examined by hostile attorneys.

Pilots should have a working knowledge of what they are facing in the world of civil rights, laws and other challenges in this era of 'rights' before they step into the position. The fallout of any incident will not be easy, but the risks can be greatly reduced by understanding what you can and cannot do while acting as a federal flight deck officer.

Pilots should remain cognizant of the ramifications upon their livelihoods and freedom by an unlawful use of force incident. The following excerpt of section of the Aviation and Transportation Security Act that needs to be repeated here:

> Section 144
>
> *An individual shall not be liable for damages in any action brought in a Federal or State court arising out of the acts of the individual in attempting to thwart an act of criminal violence or piracy on an aircraft if that individual reasonably* believed that such an act of criminal violence or piracy was occurring or was about to occur. (Authors' emphasis)

Notice the word reasonably. If a flight deck officer were to exceed the *reasonable* limitations of this section, Federal law could possibly be violated by depriving the individual in question of their civil rights. The pilot could be held responsible either civilly, criminally, or both. A flight deck officer must have an understanding of escalation and use of force that is at least equal to any federal law enforcement officer. After all, a flight deck officer is in fact a law enforcement officer when acting within the scope of their authority.

Why is an understanding of use of force principles so important? Because, it is imperative flight deck officers be able to demonstrate discretion and judgment in any situation involving their authority. After an incident, law enforcement investigators may ask a FFDO if there was any other way they could have handled the situation. A FFDO will be thoroughly questioned by investigators and the facts very closely examined. The truth will become known, one way or another. A law enforcement official will read you what is referred to the 'Reverse Miranda', where you cannot refuse to give a statement to investigators about the incident. You will not automatically be believed until you can convince the FBI and the US Attorney that what you did was justified. This may be a shock to you, but this is exactly what occurs in the real world to cops who are involved in a shooting or other serious use of force issues. Perception is what counts, and if you followed the rules you can greatly reduce your risks of a negative decision regarding your actions. That, however, is not always a guarantee.

The Homeland Security Act (H.R. 5005) is now the law and spells out the language regarding the Flight Deck Officer program. The verbiage is interesting and you need to read carefully between the lines to understand fully what is actually being said. Here are selected portions of that flight deck officer program legislation as they relate to use of force:

> Sec. 44921. Federal flight deck officer program
>
> (g) AUTHORITY TO USE FORCE- Notwithstanding section 44903(d), a Federal flight deck officer may use force (including lethal force) against an individual in the defense of a commercial aircraft in air transportation or intrastate air transportation if the officer *reasonably* believes the security of the aircraft is at risk (Authors' emphasis).
>
> (h) LIMITATION ON LIABILITY-
>
> (2) LIABILITY OF FEDERAL FLIGHT DECK OFFICERS- A Federal flight deck officer shall not be liable for damages in any action brought in a Federal or State court arising out of the acts or omissions of the officer in defending an aircraft against acts of criminal violence or air piracy unless the officer is guilty of gross negligence or willful misconduct.

There we go with that word *reasonably* again. The perception of being *reasonable* can be a slippery slope that is waiting for the flight deck officer who does not take seriously the current political environment in which we live. Do not say you cannot become a victim of circumstances because you can. Law enforcement officers must always be careful in everything they do, 24 hours a day, seven days a week.

It is very important to remember State and Federal laws legitimize law enforcement officers in the use of force, including deadly force. Nevertheless, some officers have later been held responsible because their actions were interpreted by others as 'gross negligence'. These officers have been convicted in a court of law and sent to prison. We assure you prison is not a nice place for former law enforcement officers, which includes a federal flight deck officer. Preparing yourself now for the potential pitfalls of becoming an FFDO would be a wise course of action.

In an early section of this chapter, we were discussing federal civil rights laws and how they are applied to flight crews. As an armed pilot with law enforcement authority, you will be held to a higher standard than unarmed flight crewmembers. You will be expected to know the limitations of your legal authority to use force and especially deadly force. Do not forget about the two federal civil rights statutes that have sent law enforcement officers to prison: Conspiracy of Rights and Deprivation of Rights Under the Color of Law.

The main point we want to make is that pilots are now operating in a new environment that most are not familiar. Law enforcement officers spend a great deal of time attempting to understand what their legal position is in regards to use of force and the law. They have to because if they do not it could mean the loss of their job and their freedom by not gauging their actions correctly. We are now in a new reality of air transportation and not thinking on these things could effect your job and freedom. It is imperative that pilots begin to address the use of force issues before they become over-run by events that will no doubt occur in the future.

Armed pilots need to recognize they will have to exercise extremely good judgment and reasonable discretion in any application of force. A pilot could find himself or herself in front of a court or a grand jury where a reasonableness of the application of force will be closely examined. Speaking of a courtroom, how would you testify? What should your demeanor be like? What do you do when confronted with a hostile attorney? What kind of report did you write? Are there any discrepancies in it for an attorney to exploit? If there were discrepancies, just how are you going to explain them away? The point is the potential fallout of your actions could be worse than the incident itself. A wise police officer always tries to think quickly through what the eventual outcome could be before they act. Asking 'what if' questions are a common practice of police officers. Sometimes there is no other choice but to act and then accept what happens next. Nevertheless, if you act within the scope and boundaries of your authority, you will reduce your risks as much as feasible. Having a thorough knowledge of those limitations is a requirement of the job.

Service: A Personal Sacrifice

Serving as a law enforcement officer you will sacrifice your personal rights and privileges you now enjoy as a civilian. Your family and friends will be affected by your choice. Imagine what would happen if you had to use deadly force against a terrorist to successfully repel a hijacking while serving as a FFDO. You would be considered a hero to most of the world, and that would be great. However, let us now consider how the terrorists' friends (other terrorists) and relatives (terrorist supporters) will react. Forevermore, you would be a marked man or woman by terrorists who will no doubt put a bounty out on your head. How do you think it will feel to have a death warrant hanging over you and your family's heads for the rest of your lives? These are serious issues you need to consider before becoming a FFDO. Service as a flight deck officer will be a personal sacrifice. Is it a sacrifice that you are willing to make?

For anyone who has carried a weapon on a daily basis, it has ultimately become a burden. Your behavior on and off duty will need to remain stellar at all times and that includes not consuming alcohol while in possession of your weapon. The TSA supervisors of the armed officer program could view a traffic confrontation, a dispute with your neighbor or an argument with a co-worker very negatively, which would reflect poorly on the flight deck officer program and the TSA. Your behavior will always be scrutinized on or off duty. Any incident that brings negative attention to you could be detrimental to your continued participation in the federal flight deck officer program. The flight deck officer program will depend heavily upon the knowledge and common sense of its pilot corp. Anything less could cause a lot of trouble for the armed pilot and the future of the program. Most pilots want this program to be a success and your knowledge and understanding will be what achieves that goal.

Report Writing

A very important aspect to any use of force incident is report writing. The lack of proper documentation or a poorly written report could be an embarrassment and cause severe legal problems to both the airline and crewmember. The report should contain facts, observations, perceptions, witness statements, and any other pertinent information. The answers to the *Who*, *What*, *When*, *Where*, and *How* of the incident need to be included in the report. If all of these five foundational items are covered in a report, a fairly good image of what occurred should emerge.

Report writing is a crucial aspect to the conclusion of a use of force incident. The crewmembers should collect witness statements before deplaning unless there is some extenuating circumstance, such as an injury that requires medical attention to either the crewmember or the witness passenger. The witness statements that are collected directly after an incident are usually much more credible than if taken several days later. Impressions and discussions with others can change a witness's perception of what really occurred. If needed, the witness can at some later date refresh their memory with the written statement that you took from them.

After a witness statement is taken, be sure to read it back to them to get their approval. Direct quotes should be noted on the report with quotation marks. It is okay to paraphrase their words, but be sure to read back your impressions so they can agree. Be sure to note in the report that you read back their statement and they agreed to what you wrote.

The effort to write a complete and concise report may take some time, especially after any major incident where there will be demands on your time by those who want to debrief you. However, it is extremely important to get your facts straight in your mind before making any statements that you may regret or are misinterpreted by others. Taking time to sit down with other crewmembers that were aboard the aircraft during the incident and that can relate to you their impressions of what they are going to include in their report, can make your writing report much easier. We are not talking conspiracy to make up untruths about an incident, but as important as any use of force incident is, taking the time to sit down and analyze the situation closely will make an important report understandable. Writing untruths of what occurred can cause some major legal problems for you that can involve criminal violations such as conspiracy, interfering with a criminal investigation, and perjury, to name just a few.

Be truthful, because the truth will emerge anyhow, and if you appear honest in your report then it will reflect positively on you.

Writing an important report should not be rushed and taking the necessary time to document the incident will be worth it for everyone involved. Be honest, forthright, and sincere in your documentation of the incident.

Conclusion

It is impossible to give a clear direction in every possible aspect of the use of force. General guidelines through company policy should give crewmembers the needed latitude to act when faced with a use of force incident. The airlines are being placed into a very difficult position in the new air transportation reality that has occurred since 9/11. Heretofore unheard of procedures and policies have to be developed to cope with the inevitable fallout of the ad-lib defensive procedures that have been implemented by crews, as well as the legitimate teaching of self-defensive tactics to flight crews. Codification of reasonable and logical policies of crew defense will protect crewmembers and the airlines from unlawful uses of force and any liability fallout that may occur as much as possible. These policies should be well thought out, consistent, fair, easy to understand for the crewmember and easy to implement for the airline.

Any use of force policy developed should not be so restrictive that flight crews feel intimidated by the airline's use of force policy when they need to act decisively to save a human life. As a former police officer (Waltrip) who has worked under extremely restrictive policies, I can assure airline management that this can be a consideration that could preoccupy the mind of a crewmember if the policy is designed to purely protect the company. Human life may be predicated upon a policy that does not stop a crewmember from acting when action is needed because they are apprehensive of a restrictive use of force policy whose only goal is to protect the airline from civil liability. Waltrip has had many discussions with police officers that have felt the pressure of having to act in a given situation and knowing in the back of their mind the department they worked for was more interested in protecting their own interests than protecting the officer from injury. A restrictive and legalistic use of force policy will be counterproductive to the safety of flight crews. The priority should be placed on human life in the development of a use of force policy and we think it can be done while protecting an airline from liability issues as much as possible under the current legal culture.

The traveling public should support and understand the development of use of force polices, and will be comforted by the fact that crewmembers will act quickly and decisively when faced with a potentially deadly incident. The traveling public will interpret such action as a serious aspect of security and we believe will support this concept. What airline would not gain favor by advertising their flight crews are trained and prepared to deal with potentially deadly incidents? However, we discourage revealing any specific company security procedures regarding crewmember self-defense, especially in light of the amount of intelligence the hijackers gathered and assimilated to carry out the 9/11 attacks.

The events of 9/11 will not be forgotten by anyone, especially by the traveling public. Time will not totally erase the horror of that day. The airlines were vulnerable, and the terrorists took advantage of it. Even with all the governmental assistance, it is ultimately the responsibility of the airlines and flight crews to prevent such a horrible event from ever occurring again. It is our duty to the men, women, and children who board all of our airlines everyday to do everything in our power from preventing such devastating events from ever occurring again.

Notes

1 Meyer, Greg, *After Rodney King: What Have We Learned*, 1994.
2 Data mining for policing the police, *Computerworld*, 2 April 2001.
3 Co-Pilot uses axe to keep man out of cockpit, www.cnn.com, 8 February 2002.
4 Mattern, Hal, Sky Harbor retail increases, *Arizona Republic*, 27 May 2002.
5 Stanislaus County Sheriff's Department, *Manual of Policy and Ethics – Use of Force*, 1998.
6 Ibid.
7 *Webster Dictionary*, 1997 Edition.
8 H.R.5005 Homeland Security Act.
9 *Ballentine's Law Dictionary*, 1969 edition.
10 *S. 1447, Aviation and Transportation Security Act of 2001*, 19 November 2001.
11 *Title 18, USC., Section 242, Deprivation of Rights Under the Color of Law.*
12 FBI web page.
13 FBI web page.
14 Leadership, and Professionalism in Policing, Institute for Integrity, policefoundation.org.
15 Autopsy finds passengers killed man in 'air rage' case, *Associated Press*, 16 September 2000.
16 Garner, Joel, and others, *Understanding Use of Force By and Against the Police*, US Department of Justice, National Institute of Justice, November 1996; and Adams, Kenneth, *What we Know about Police Use of Force*, US Department of Justice, October 1999.
17 *Title 18, USC., Section 241, Conspiracy Against Rights.*
18 San Jose Police Department, *Police Duty Manual – Use of Force*, 1995.
19 Stanislaus County Sheriff's Department, *Manual of Policy and Ethics*, 1998.
20 San Jose Police Department, *Police Duty Manual – Use of Force*, 1995.

PART III
DEALING WITH THE THREATS

Chapter 11

Profiling

> We all wish for complete or utopian security but we must accept that this is only fantasy. We live in a world of uncertainty where the most difficult puzzle is man himself. This shall always be, because man studying man can never be completely objective.
>
> Laurence J. Peter, *The Peter Prescription*, 1972

Introduction

> Five passengers who were removed from or prevented from boarding flights last year after the September 11 terror attacks filed suits against four major US airlines, accusing them of racial profiling and discrimination. All five passengers, who are of Middle Eastern or Asian descent, had passed through airport security checkpoints.[1]

One staff attorney involved in the litigation told CNN the airlines 'speak in the abstract about the need for safety and security related to September 11, but nothing they've done in any of these cases advance the need or interest in safety and security'. He hopes the litigation will lead to 'better training of pilots and flight attendants about when there is legitimately a security risk'.[2]

The intent of this chapter is to help fill the need for training of flight crews in effective and proactive profiling. Your particular airline may already address this issue and this information is not intended to rebut their approach to profiling. If profiling is not addressed, you will find this information useful in your daily flying routine. A simple, yet very effective approach is taken with the issue that will be repeated constantly. It is '*absence of the normal*' and '*presence of the abnormal*'.[3] As you will discover, these two premises are applicable to the vast majority of situations, regardless of sex, race, color, religion, or origin. The contentious matters of why we should or should not racially or ethnically profile are not for discussion. We must focus on cues that will aid us in detection of terrorists before committing their deadly acts. For airline personnel, this is the essence of true profiling.

As you study this chapter, you will gain a better idea of how to subtly interview every passenger by observing cues generated by both conscious and subconscious brain functions. Verbal and non-verbal communication, mannerisms, and uncontrollable body responses to high stress, such as sweating profusely in normal temperatures, are a few of the cues discussed. Used in conjunction with your intuition about the situation, skill in profiling can prove to be a powerful defensive tool in identifying those who are planning to do you harm. The examples are straightforward and provide tools you can use to make informed decisions about those aboard your aircraft. You will probably be surprised at the effectiveness of these techniques as you begin to observe people more closely at the airport and on the aircraft.

Defining Profiling

For the purposes of this chapter, 'profiling' addresses subjective methodologies. Objective profiling is accomplished through machinery and technology; subjective profiling is accomplished through direct human interface. There are advantages and disadvantages of each method; therefore, we need to employ both types of profiling. Failures of objective profiling permit undesirable passengers, sometimes armed, to arrive at the departure gate or aboard aircraft, emphasizing the importance of training flight crews (and gate agents) in the effective use of subjective profiling. Subjective profiling is often used in criminal profiling.

The difficult practice of *criminal* profiling involves the use of sociology and psychology to provide investigators with a general description of criminal behavior and personality based on clues left at the crime scene. Identification of terrorists who have not committed a crime is made even more difficult since there is no crime scene from which to gather clues. As experts agree, identification of terrorists is a very difficult and inexact science. Take for example the profiling of the sniper(s) involved in the shootings in the Washington, DC area in 2002. Analysts and criminal profilers bombarded the media with their theories. The general consensus was a lone white male with white supremacist ties. As we know now, it was two men – one black and the other Jamaican, and both converted Muslims. 'A lot of analysts were dead wrong, including me', said Brian Lewis, a crime analyst and terrorism expert (Cox News Service).

If trained and experienced profilers can make such huge mistakes, what guarantee is there that flight crews will not make similar mistakes? There simply is no guarantee. Please re-read the quote at the beginning of this chapter. Humans are looking at other humans. There will be mistakes, but that does not mean that subjective profiling should be abandoned. Sometimes there are many available cues that may be used to good advantage in recognizing a potential threat. Knowledge of these cues, how to recognize and interpret them, can be an extremely effective method of identifying potential threats. Take this case for example.

> Captain Williams was able to closely observe US Customs agents for about a month at one major international airport as they manned security checkpoints. The particular unit observed was the top unit in the US for detecting contraband coming into the country. Agents accomplished this record solely through use of non-verbal cues exhibited by passengers, resulting in further personal search – frisking, strip search, or x-raying. As one woman was being questioned at the security checkpoint, she became extremely nervous and began to vomit 'slugs' of cocaine. (A slug is produced by filling fingers of a rubber glove with a drug, tying it off with dental floss, and then cutting off the filled

finger. Slugs are swallowed by the 'mule', a person carrying the drug. Typically, the mule would be given a laxative upon completion of their delivery and the slugs would be excreted.) X-rays of the woman revealed 96 slugs of cocaine extending from her throat down through her intestines.

It seems one cannot peruse a newspaper without seeing some article on 'racial profiling'. Use of the term outside its definition has led to a negative connotation to this term. Misuse, combined with the ugliness of racial politics and the all-too-frequent incompetent and corrupt use of racial profiling has led to a continual furor over the subject. Used within its correct definition, racial profiling can be a very effective tool in narrowing the search for terrorists worldwide. Racial profiling is the identification of racial factors, such as skin color, hair texture, facial structure, physical attire, spoken language, accent, surname, and travel history, all of which profiling experts and statistical analysts have associated with a specific behavior, such as an act of terrorism.[4] The term 'stereotyping' is commonly misused in conjunction with the term racial profiling. 'Stereotyping' denotes the use of membership in a group to make inaccurate judgments about an individual. If racial profiling continues to lead accurate predictions about incipient aviation terrorism, stereotyping, by definition, is not occurring.[5]

Views on racial profiling are very polarized. The chairman and CEO of a Washington-based security firm, GlobalOptions, said, 'We are concerned about people from a particular region of the world. They tend to be young and they tend to be male. We ought to spend most of our time looking for them'.[6] The legislative counsel for the ACLU said, 'Profiles are notoriously under inclusive. Who knows how the next terrorist will appear? It could be a grandmother, a student, we just do not know'.[7] From 11 September 2001, to November 2002, there were 688 charges filed by Middle Easterners and Asians alleging backlash discrimination stemming from the attacks of 9/11, up 20 per cent from past years.[8] In June 2003, President Bush issued two distinctive sets of guidelines governing the conduct of all seventy federal law enforcement agencies. The guidelines include a broad prohibition on profiling in traditional and routine law enforcement investigations and a looser set of standards for national security cases.[9] In response, advocacy groups for minorities criticized the guidelines maintaining the position the profiling ban is too lax, doesn't require agencies to monitor their own compliance, doesn't require collection of data on who is being stopped or why, fails to ban religious and national-origin profiling, and applies only to federal authorities.[10]

Transportation Secretary Mineta told an Arab-American group in Detroit in mid-2002, 'It is very tempting to take false comfort in the belief that we can spot the bad guy based on appearance alone. Some are yielding to that temptation in their arguments for racial profiling, but false comfort is a luxury we cannot afford'.[11] In today's environment, it will be extremely difficult for security personnel, Federal Air Marshals, and airline personnel to NOT racially profile to some extent; therefore, it is crucial that any such endeavor is accomplished within the bounds of the definition.

Keep the true definitions of racial profiling and stereotyping in mind as you continue to see news articles and reports concerning these issues. Our approach to profiling avoids the pitfalls associated with both racial profiling and stereotyping approaches.

Difficulties in Profiling

One of the major difficulties in finding terrorists anywhere in the world is they do not wear signs around their necks or on their backs that say 'Terrorist'. What is a terrorist supposed to look like? The al-Qaida terrorist group alone is known to have cells in over forty countries worldwide, including the US, and it is only one of over 370 known terrorist organizations. Terrorists are not limited to any one race or religious sect, or to national boundaries. The chapter on terrorism in this book provides an in-depth look at terrorists. If you have not read that chapter, please do as some of the important cues in recognition of terrorists are generated by their selection and training.

Although a very small number indeed, the few lawsuits and dozens of complaints regarding incorrect profiling of passengers of Arabic, other Middle Eastern, and Asian ethnicity compared to the millions of passengers who have traveled since 9/11 have gained a lot of attention from the news media. The unfortunate individuals who were incorrectly targeted by flight crews and passengers highlight the need for education and training in subjective profiling. A good example of the lack of training in this area involves an incident aboard an aircraft flying from Chicago to La Guardia Airport in New York.

> A young movie star from India and her family, as well as some other actors, were traveling on the flight. As they approached New York, she and members of her group started talking excitedly, pointing and gesturing at landmarks, and moving from one window seat to another. A passenger, not understanding the language (or their actions) alerted a flight attendant who then notified the flight deck crew. Within minutes, two F-16s joined on the B-757 and escorted it through landing. The actress and her entourage were detained and questioned for four hours. One of the actress's remarks is right on the button: 'Do I look like a terrorist?'[12]

Would a *well-trained cabin crew* have made the same decisions? It is important to point out the flight deck crew is NOT going to come out of the cockpit to make their own assessment of the situation. More than likely, they are going to take the word (decision) of the cabin crew, and if an error is to be made, it will be on the side of safety. The responsibility for analyzing events in the cabin falls almost completely in the lap of the cabin crewmembers, and like it or not, many of the captain's decisions in the cabin are going to be heavily influenced by the cabin crew in today's flight environment. Not only must the entire flight crew analyze the event, but they must be able to educate passengers regarding security issues and reduce their fears and anxieties, as well. It is essential to aviation safety and security that skills training in situational awareness, communication, crew coordination, and decision-making are taught effectively to all flight crews.

The Subjective Approach to Profiling

> On our aircraft, the captain is in charge and has to weigh a lot of factors in the overall safety of everybody on the airplane. We would not remove someone based on race, religion, or national origin. It's based on behavior.
>
> Joe Hopkins, Airline Spokesman for United Airlines[13]

Subjective profiling adds another dimension to the layers of detection we must use to identify terrorists or others bent on destruction or disruption of flights. It CAN be an extremely useful tool, but it requires training to use. Without training, subjective profiling can be very ineffective and can create tremendously time-consuming and expensive repercussions for the airlines. In October 2001, the US Commission on Civil Rights set up a hotline to handle claims of airline discrimination, as well as harassment and hate crimes. During one 12-hour period, the volume of calls peaked at approximately 70 calls per hour.[14] Many of the reports involved specific instances of being removed from aircraft (or prevented from boarding) because of 'uneasy feelings' expressed by flight crewmembers or other passengers. *PAY ATTENTION!* This is not to say that you should not remove a passenger that is exhibiting abnormal behavior for fear of litigation. Any passenger that creates an 'uneasy feeling' to anyone, whether they are a gate agent, crewmember or other passenger, should be *scrutinized more closely* to determine the source of those feelings.

Profiling by airline personnel – ticket counter and gate agents, ramp workers, baggage handlers, and flight crews – must be based on something other than racial or criminal profiling for a number of reasons. Lack of training in these two types of profiling, their inherent inaccuracies, and possibility of litigation if incorrectly used are just of few of the reasons. One thing we can do is to observe passengers, their baggage, and other airline workers whether that opportunity is for only a few minutes or for hours. What we need to look for are 1) '*absence of the normal*' and/or 2) '*presence of the abnormal*'.[15] Searching for and finding either of these two clues should signal the observer to further investigate the situation. This technique works in spotting routine problems, medical emergencies, aircraft emergencies and in identifying terrorists or others with the intent of doing harm. Is it 100 per cent accurate? No, it is not, but it is a tool for you to use. To better find and deal with situations that may occur on your flight or anywhere else in the aviation environment. First, we need to define what is meant by 'normal' and 'abnormal', and then look at how to use this important tool.

What is 'Normal'?

Each of us has our own mental models, preconceived notions, of things on earth that have been formed throughout our life by our experiences and influenced by others. For instance, if I said the word 'picnic', what immediately comes to your mind? For me, it is a red and white-checkered tablecloth spread out under the shade of a huge oak tree, and on the cloth is a wicker basket full of fried chicken, potato salad, iced tea and my mother's famous chocolate cake. (Obviously, I had a good experience with picnics when I was growing up.) Your mental model of a picnic may be completely different. So, which mental model is 'normal'?

'Normal' for the purposes of this chapter is defined as expectations of behavior based on our own life experiences, including the display of characteristics, dress, ethnicity or behavior with which we can personally identify. Try these examples. How would you describe the following people on a flight? Do not peek at our answers until you make your list.

1 A normal business traveler going to work
2 A normal business traveler returning home from work
3 A normal tourist going to Disneyworld
4 A normal tourist returning from Disneyworld

Our answers

1 Business dress (suit), briefcase, laptop computer, cell phone, *Wall Street Journal*, business papers, garment bag, preoccupied, alone or with a partner (male or female), not prone to drink alcoholic beverages, traveling in first, business or coach class.
2 May be dressed down from business attire, tie loosened, briefcase, notes, calculator, cell phone, prone to having an alcoholic beverage, joking, conversational, traveling in coach, business or first class.
3 Part of a family, casually dressed, brochures of Disneyworld, electronic games, colorful back pack, CD or tape player, excited, traveling in coach.
4 Part of a family, casually dressed in Mickey Mouse ears and/or clothes with other Disney characters' logos, colorful back pack bulging with souvenirs, tired and sleepy, traveling in coach.

More than likely, your mental models of these typical passengers were described in the same or very similar terms. As this brief exercise shows, we all have preconceived notions as to what each type of passenger on an aircraft will look like and how they will behave. How would you describe a person going off to college? A person going to a wedding? A terrorist?

Yes, a terrorist. You probably have a mental model of a terrorist based upon the attack on America in 2001 and all the focus by our government and other nations on finding terrorists worldwide, as well as the extensive media coverage of the many events that have occurred since that time. Your mental model is more than likely not based upon direct contact and personal observations of a terrorist. Your model is probably flawed by your bias as to what a 'normal terrorist' is like, but for you that model defines 'normal'. We should look for in every passenger in every situation the 'absence of the normal'. Even then, absence of the normal does not necessarily mean that a person is a terrorist! It simply means that a closer look at the situation is warranted.

Normally, people are truthful – at least that will be the assumption we will build upon in support of defining 'normal'. Most of us have had experience dealing with people who lied to us when we thought they were telling the truth. Based upon our experience then, most of us would probably agree that it was difficult to determine the person was lying to us at the time. How do you know if someone is telling you the truth? The two following quotes make the point.

> The man who speaks the truth is always at ease. (Persian proverb)

> If you tell the truth, you don't have to remember anything. (Mark Twain)

A person telling the truth is generally alert, composed, and attentive with no significant mood swings. They will sit upright, lean forward and establish an open relaxed position. Their head will be straight or tilted to the side and not tilted downward. They may make smooth posture changes that are random with no patterns to them in a non-rigid position and hold their palms up with their elbows pointed away from their bodies. They may smile, and appear to be sincere. Their body motions will correspond to their statements and they do not appear to have anything to hide. For example, they do not shake their head horizontally when answering 'yes' to a question. They are congruent. Their behavior is consistent with their demeanor. They will not shy away from direct questions. When spoken to, they do not become more nervous during the conversation but become relaxed as rapport is established. Your intuition will not signal any significant changes in how you feel about them. Their manner, gestures and words seem to match and their words ring true.

What if something is not right about the behavior exhibited by another person, or if their words and actions are not congruent, or if you believe they are not telling the truth? What then? Two distinct possibilities exist: 1) our assessment was entirely wrong; or, 2) something is abnormal. Let us assume our assessment was accurate and there is something abnormal present or going on.

What is 'Abnormal'?

> 'Abnormal': markedly irregular, deviating from the normal or average.
>
> Webster's Ninth New Collegiate Dictionary

> I could see that he wasn't acting normally. From the minute he got onto the plane, he was fidgety, moving around, getting up to go to the toilet, getting up to check his bag in the overhead compartment.
>
> Passenger describing a would-be hijacker aboard an El Al flight

It must be emphasized that 'abnormal' does NOT mean unacceptable or wrong, nor is it connected in any way to gender, race, color, or ethnic origin. It simply means *untypical for the situation.* It must also be kept in mind that your mental model of 'untypical for the situation' may be entirely different from the mental model of the person you are observing. Watching someone walk down the street and totally avoid all cracks in the sidewalk may be 'untypical' or 'abnormal' for you, but may be entirely normal for that individual. 'People watching' is a great pastime and a vital part of our method of profiling, but correctly interpreting what you see is a skill that must be developed through detailed study of human behavior and through experience.

Regardless of the mental image of the 'coolness' of James Bond created by Hollywood, people under high stress exhibit certain characteristics, many of which they are unable to mask or hide. It is important in recognition of 'abnormal' for you to be familiar with some of these characteristics. The following table provides a breakdown of some of the most common stress cues and where they can be observed, both on and off the aircraft.

It is very unwise to develop a mental model from only one or two of the cues listed in the table below. A person who is shaking may not be indicating high stress from being involved in an impending security-related event, but rather may just be cold. A person with their arms folded across his chest may not be signaling reluctance to being approached, but simply their normal habit pattern. What DOES matter is collecting all the cues available, processing them as a whole within the context in which they were collected, and formulating conclusions based upon absence of the normal and presence of the abnormal. See Table 11.1.

Looking for 'Absence of the Normal' and 'Presence of Abnormal'

Looking for absence of the normal goes well beyond profiling based upon gender, race, color, language, dress, etc. Absence of the normal focuses on 'what is missing from this picture?' Presence of the abnormal focuses on 'what is in the picture that should not be. Many times, absence of the normal is accompanied by presence of the abnormal. Take these events for example:

Table 11.1 Stress cues and their sources

Where to watch	What to watch for
Head (eyes, mouth/lips, brows, cheeks, hair, neck)	• avoiding eye contact • furtive glancing around • dilated pupils and/or rapid eye blinking • dry lips • flushed cheeks and/or neck • rapid pulsating of arteries in neck and/or temple • furrowed brow • stroking or pulling at hair • nervous, crackling laughter and/or speech • biting lips or inside of cheeks • constantly licking lips • grinding teeth • excessive and/or deep yawning or sighing • frequently rubbing eyes • frequently touching nose, ears, lips • gulping, swallowing hard, clearing throat continually, pulsating adam's apple • grabbing throat or back of neck with palm
Hands and arms	• hands trembling or shaking • clenched fists, white knuckles • jingling of coins or other pocket contents • tapping fingers • sweaty palms • nail biting, cracking fingers • lint picking (no apparent lint) • arms folded over chest • sweaty armpits • uncommon use of hand signals or gestures • scratching (without an itch) • grasping hands in front, letting go, repeating (women) • grasping hands behind back, letting go, repeating (men) • grabbing arm above elbow, letting go, repeating (men)

Table 11.1 cont'd

Where to watch	**What to watch for**
Legs and feet	• foot, toe or heel tapping • crossing and uncrossing legs • constantly swinging leg • trembling of knees • rapid clinching and unclenching of inner thighs • continual pacing • locking ankles (women more than men) • sweat spotting at waist and behind knees of pants • constantly shifting weight from one foot to the other
Other body movements or indications to look for	• overall tenseness • trembling or shaking • goose bumps • frequent tugging at or adjusting clothes or jewelry • frequently looking at a watch • profuse perspiration (when it's not hot) • diarrhea (constantly going to the restroom) • rocking motions • curling up in fetal position • using objects as barriers (may be a weapon) • thumbs hooked in top of pants
Nervous attitudinal behaviors	• aggressive • in a hurry, rushing • frustrated (beyond normal) • over-friendly, flirtatious • chain smoking • abnormal alcohol consumption • over-protective of baggage or objects
Other potentially abnormal/ hazardous behaviors to watch for	• requests to check-in excessive baggage • passengers making 'secret contact' • someone 'casing the joint' • late arrivals to the gate or aircraft • excessive time spent in lavatories

> As a flight engineer on the A-300 Airbus with Eastern Airlines in the late 1970's, F/E Williams answered a call from the cabin crew while at cruise altitude over the Atlantic en route from San Juan to New York. There was a female passenger holding a baby in coach that had been completely wrapped in a blanket from the time the lady boarded the flight. During the several hours that had elapsed after takeoff, the lady refused any beverage or food for herself. In addition, none of the cabin crew had seen her feed the baby or to give the baby any milk or water. The baby had not made one sound the entire time, nor had it moved. The lady had not left her seat the entire time, either. Something was not right as normal activities and behavior of a woman traveling with a baby were missing. US Customs was alerted in New York and a search by their agents found something both unimaginable and unbelievable. The baby, which was dead, had been completely gutted, filled with packets of cocaine, and crudely sown back up. Absence of the normal was the key in recognizing and acting upon this horrible event.

> On 14 September 2001, Captain Williams flew for the first time since the events of the 11th. Not unlike any other flight crewmember flying during that time, Captain Williams was very concerned about the possibility of another terrorist event occurring involving a commercial jet. As a result, Williams completed his cockpit pre-flight and set-up and then stood in the cockpit door, watching passengers as they boarded the flight and looking for anything or anyone unusual. About the tenth person to board was a man carrying a large, expensive-looking baby carriage. The man handed it to the flight attendant at the door of the aircraft and asked her to check it for him – a 'normal' occurrence. However, the man did not have a wife or baby traveling with him – something 'abnormal'. The man was asked to step off the aircraft and to unfold the baby carriage. A search of the many pockets was conducted, during which time Captain Williams had the gate agent find out as much information regarding the passenger as was possible. As it turned out, the man and his wife and infant daughter were among the thousands of passengers that had gotten caught up in the situation resulting from the grounding of all flights a couple of days earlier. His wife and daughter had taken a previous flight that was full and he was joining them at their destination on this later flight. His wife had the infant and he had the baby carriage. Although the incident was benign, it demonstrates the concepts of absence of the normal – no wife or infant- and presence of the abnormal – a man traveling alone with a baby carriage.

The Richard Reid *shoe bomber* incident is worth studying as it provided clues that alerted flight attendants of a significant threat to their flight. The following Time Magazine article excerpt provides some insight into behaviors we need to profile, 'absence of the normal, presence of the abnormal'. Although the following is a small part of a larger article written by Cathy Booth Thomas, it will give you a good indication of Reid's unusual behavior.

> One minute Christina Jones and Hermis Moutardier were flight attendants who adored flying to glamorous destinations and in the next minute, they were on the front line of a war. American flight 63 was jammed with 185 passengers that morning as baggage problems delayed the takeoff from Charles de Gaulle Airport for an hour, but after takeoff, the flight seemed routine.

> Then a passenger aroused the flight attendants' curiosity. A 'huge' man, 6 ft. 4 in. and weighing more than 200 pounds, refused to eat or drink anything, even water – odd behavior on a transatlantic flight that could last up to ten hours. Jones had been cautioned by another flight attendant to be wary of passengers who didn't accept food on a long flight, so she asked the man three times if he wanted anything. 'Usually I think, 'Yeah! Less work for me'. But something about him…seemed strange', she recalls.
>
> Moutardier joked that maybe he was on a diet, but she too asked him if he wanted to eat. 'I talked to him in French, assuming he was French. He said he did not speak French. I wanted to be nice, so I asked where he was from, and he told me Sri Lanka'. She did not believe him and she was right. He turned out be Richard Reid, a British citizen who investigators believe was an operative in the al-Qaeda network.
>
> About two hours out of Paris, passengers began to report smelling smoke. Moutardier cruised the aisle looking for the source of the burning smell. She found Reid sitting alone by a window seat trying to light a match. She warned him that smoking was not allowed on the flight. He promised to stop, then began picking his teeth with the matchstick.
>
> A few minutes later, Moutardier saw him bend over in his seat. 'I thought he was smoking and it made me mad. I was talking to him saying, 'Excuse me,' but he ignored me. I leaned in and said, 'What are you doing?" As she pulled at him, he turned, giving her a glimpse of what he was hiding. What she saw terrified her. 'He's got the shoe off, between his legs. All I could see is the wiring and the match. The match was lit'.[16]

The rest of the story is history as Jones, Moutardier, other crewmembers and passengers subdued Reid after a significant fight and restrained him until landing where he was placed under arrest. They were all very lucky that Reid was not successful in lighting off the fuse that could have brought the airplane down into the Atlantic Ocean. The FBI later reported there were enough explosives in one of the shoes to blow a hole in the plane's fuselage. Much gratitude and thanks are due to both Jones and Moutardier for their awareness and actions that helped save the lives of 185 passengers and crew.

What were the significant items present or absent from this event? The cabin crew involved with this event had been told to look for anything unusual, not specifically the 'absence of normal and presence of abnormal' that we are speaking of, but none-the-less a head's up, general alert. It was the absence of the normal – the refusal of anything to eat or drink on a flight of extended duration – that prompted further investigation by the cabin crew. It was the presence of the abnormal – having a shoe off and trying to light it with a match – that prompted action by the cabin crew, assisted by passengers.

If we are to learn from any event, we must probe a bit deeper and think through some 'what if' scenarios. We are NOT finger pointing as we read and study in a comfortable setting; however, we need to look at how a similar situation could be handled differently.

'But something about him ... seemed strange'

This comment deserves our attention. What was it about Reid that elicited this comment from Jones? Could it have been his unkempt appearance? His mannerisms? His verbal or non-verbal communication? Intuition? The refusal of a normal food service? From the article above, we do not know; however, it was probably a combination of a number of these cues that Jones processed both consciously and subconsciously. Jones was uneasy enough to tell Moutardier of her concerns, but neither were alarmed enough to alert other crewmembers or the captain. Jones could have asked him if he was feeling ill, or asked if he may want something to calm his nervous stomach, or engaged in other small talk to gather information in making a further determination of what his behavior meant.

She did not believe him and she was right.

Moutardier questioned Reid – a very good move on her part – to better determine her mental model of him. In doing so, she stated that she did not believe him (being from Sri Lanka). Why did she not believe him? Was it what he said or the way he said it that elicited the belief that he was lying? Again, we do not know; however, we do know the signals she was receiving were strong enough to elicit this feeling. How do YOU know if someone is lying? Did it matter if Reid was lying about being from Sri Lanka? On the other hand, were his untruthful statements an indicator that nothing he said or did could be trusted? If Moutardier still wasn't sure about Reid she could have had another crewmember discreetly talk with him; however, having another crewmember enter the conversation may tip the person off that he or she is being scrutinized leading to further complications in gaining the truth and/or further information.

When she correctly perceived Reid was lying about being from Sri Lanka, Moutardier did not follow up with further questions. Because it could have provided useful information and probably demonstrated without a reasonable doubt that he was lying and should be considered a threat. For example, a possible dialogue between a flight attendant (F/A) and Reid could have possibly gone along these lines:

F/A: 'Where are you from?'
Reid: 'Sri Lanka'.

F/A: 'Oh really, where in Sri Lanka?' *(observing for deceptive clues)*
Reid: 'Oh ... um, Colombo'. *(showing reluctance in his answer)*

F/A: 'Oh interesting, I've never known anyone from Sri Lanka.
Were you born there?'
Reid: *(shifting in his seat, becoming uneasy and looking away)* 'Yes'.

F/A: 'How's the weather there?'
Reid: *(looking away trying to think about how he should answer)* 'How's the weather there? Oh, nice'.

F/A: 'Is it hot or cold or both?'
Reid: *(crossing his arms, shifting in his seat and looking over his shoulder)* 'Is it hot or cold? It's ah … warm'. *(Reid knows he is lying and is becoming concerned that Moutardier will discover he is lying.)*

The flight attendant, recognizing he is definitely lying but not wanting to tip him off, continues in a non-threatening concerned approach. She will not let on through her own voice and body language that she knows he is lying to her. She perhaps notices Reid is starting to look away from her and seems to be delaying his answers to her simple questions.

F/A: 'How many people live in Sri Lanka?'
Reid: *(he doesn't know the answer, but needs to think of one quick)* 'Hmm … about two million'. *(he is getting very aggravated with this lady's questions)*

F/A: 'What do you do for a living there?'
Reid: *(obviously agitated)* 'I'm a shoe salesman'. *(oh, that slipped!)*

F/A: 'I'm in the market for some shoes, what kind of shoes do you sell?' *(observing his agitation, she knows he has something significant to hide)*
Reid: *(knowing he can't answer he goes on the offensive)* 'Hey, excuse me, *(his voice rising with controlled agitation)* but I'm tired and I want to get some sleep now'.

F/A: 'Oh, okay, let me know if you need anything by ringing your call button *(pointing to it)* on the overhead panel'.
Reid: *(not looking at her pointing to the button and refusing to make any eye contact)* 'OK'.

This conversation could have gone any one of a million ways, but the point is that when you suspect deception you need to follow up with questions designed to find the truth. Even if you are cut off by the passenger, it is a clear indicator that something is wrong. Who does not like to talk about themselves and where they are from? Our lives are central to the world we live in. The world literally revolves around us. Becoming agitated because someone is interested in us is not normal for anyone.

What could the flight crew have done if they strongly suspected Reid of pending violence or attack when two hours out of Paris over the North Atlantic? What would YOU have done? There is no simple answer, but if you strongly suspect someone of trying to do you and other people harm at 35,000 feet then you have to do 'something'. That something may be to have an able bodied person (ABP) sit near the suspect until the captain is notified and a course of action decided upon. If there is law enforcement or deadheading crewmembers aboard then they can be called upon to assist you by observing the suspect. There is an old saying, 'The best defense is a good offense'. In this particular case, a strong showing of self-protective measures could have deterred Reid from attempting to blow up the airplane. If in the end the passenger did not have any mal-intent aboard the airplane then, 'oh well, we are sorry'. Demonstrating a united front of strength, awareness and interest is important if there is good reason to believe something is not right about a person.

... passengers began to report smelling smoke. Moutardier cruised the aisle looking for the source of the burning smell

How did the passengers make their reports? Did they ring the call buttons or did they stop a flight attendant passing through the aisle? If you were a flight attendant that a passenger had stopped and passed this information to, what would you do? We hope you would do exactly what Moutardier did – she cruised the aisle looking for the source. What if Moutardier had delayed her investigation until after the meal service was complete, or for other reasons? When Moutardier found the source, she acted appropriately, on what she saw. In addition, she continued monitoring Reid. Would you have blown the incident off after seeing the person just lighting a match and issuing a verbal warning about not smoking on the flight?

A few minutes later, Moutardier saw him bend over in his seat

What was Moutardier doing? Without realizing it, she was looking for absence of the normal and presence of the abnormal. All of Reid's actions to that point contributed to the interpretation of his bending over as the presence of the abnormal, one of many typical behaviors exhibited by deceptive people. Deceptive behavior is often the most difficult aspect of people to recognize. Because of this challenge, it is crucial to learn the subtleties and the nuances of what deceptive people practice.

How to Recognize Deception

> Deceivers are the most dangerous members of society. They trifle with the best affections of our nature, and violate the most sacred obligations.
>
> George Crabbe

A deceptive person may look to relieve stress through a multitude of behaviors, such as continual yawning, stretching, changing the position of their body, scratching, pulling, picking, stroking, inspecting, lip-biting, finger-tapping, playing with objects, looking repeatedly at their watch, rapidly chewing gum and other similar nervous behavior. When spoken to, the deceptive person may not pay attention, or cross their arms, continually look away, have their hands tightly folded across their lap, clench their fist, or forcefully laugh at an inappropriate time in the discussion.

A deceptive person may seem evasive in their responses by being non-committal, not remembering details about simple questions or providing a lot of information to a simple question, which could be a rehearsed story. If upon questioning other individuals with whom they may be traveling, the same exact story is given, then it may well be a rehearsed story to cover up their true intentions. The person may appear overly polite and volunteer unsolicited items about themselves.

A deceptive person may also be anxious about the flight departure even though the flight may be running on time. They may complain to you stating some excuse about why you should get the flight out early. Their excuse may be vague and stammered – 'My sick mother is picking me up at the airport and we need to get going'. Simple follow up questions that indicate your concern may cause some problems for them such as:

- 'I'm sorry, what's wrong with your mother?'
- 'How old is she?'
- 'Should she be driving if she is sick?'
- 'What kind of car does she drive?'
- 'Does she live with anyone?'
- 'How does she get along at home being sick?'
- 'Does anyone help her?'
- 'Does she live in a house with stairs?'

If the person is being deceptive, their responses may become choppy and they may seem like they are searching for a right answer. Since they have not thought through the web of lies they are beginning to weave for themselves, they may become defensive and will become increasingly concerned about their lies being discovered. They may begin to repeat your questions in an attempt to mentally buy time so they can think of a suitable answer, for example:

> You: 'How old is she?'
> Person: 'How old is she? *(pauses, searching for an answer)* she's 82'.
>
> You: 'Can she drive?'
> Person: 'Can she drive? Yes'.
>
> You: 'What kind of car does she drive?'
> Person: *(Nervous laughter. Squirming in his seat. Avoiding eye contact.)* 'What kind of car does she drive? … Ah … a small car'.

You: 'Really? My mom likes a bigger car. She drives a Lincoln. What model car does your mother drive?'
Person: *(Becoming obviously agitated, facial frown, shifting in seat again and deeply sighing)* 'She drives a small car. *(Changing the direction of discussion and attempting to dismiss you)* Now can we get going?'

This is an example of an exchange with a deceptive person. Details beyond the initial statement may be difficult for them to answer. Nothing rings factually like the truth. Simple questions beyond an initial one will not be difficult for a truthful person to answer. Remember, you are asking questions in a non-accusatory manner. Do not give the person the third degree and tip off what you are seeking – THE TRUTH.

You must think on your feet, show empathy, and ask concerned questions to discover the truth. How can anyone argue with someone who is showing concern for them or their family? Do not miss an opportunity to ask simple questions of individuals that bring attention to themselves' such as in the example provided. A person using delay tactics, as in the above example, must keep track of their lies. A quick response to a simple question can also be an indicator of guilt.[17] Remember, it is the extremes in vocal and/or body language behavior that will indicate deception.

Politicians are usually very good at deception in both verbal and body language. Verbally, in that when asked a question they do not want to answer, they shift the answer into something they really want to talk about. Reading body language is a different story and a more difficult skill to master. Deception may be indicated when words do not match the associated non-verbal actions.[18]

In all the examples provided the absence of the normal prompted further investigation. The presence of the abnormal prompted action. Although this sequence is not cast in concrete, events will frequently unfold in this manner. Your ability to receive and correctly interpret normal and abnormal cues from an individual has a high correlation with the rapport you establish with that person. Customer service training addresses the importance of rapport in establishing and meeting customer needs. The same concept of rapport applies to identification of threats aboard an aircraft.

Profiling Tools

Building rapport

Building rapport is an extremely important step to establishing trust and communicating with another person. Your uniform gives you instant credibility for asking questions. Your personal appearance and your approach to individuals serve to either open or close the door to establishing rapport with passengers. As odd as it may sound, our intention should be to try to get them to trust us and not the other way around. This becomes a bit tricky when we are both suspicious and trying to be pleasant at the same time. Always on your mental guard when talking to passengers, your suspicions and intuitions should be concealed from those around you. You can still be suspicious and pleasant at the same time without appearing phony, but it takes practice.

Mirroring the actions of the person you are talking to may be helpful in getting that person to open up to you. People are usually more comfortable when talking to others that are acting the same way they are acting. Mirroring speech patterns, posture, and gestures encourages rapport. If a person crosses their arms or puts their hands in their pockets, or displays other similar mannerisms, you should attempt to mimic them without appearing too obvious and thus phony.

Once rapport is established, it can be easily ruined through inappropriate verbal communication. Giving unsolicited advice, trying to tell a bigger or better story, using complicated vocabulary, and interrupting and/or changing the subject will undermine development of rapport, as will not paying attention or not listening to the other person. Asking good questions is the key to gaining the information you are seeking in the short time you have available as you interface with passengers. Granted, the more time you have for gathering information the better mental picture you may be able to draw about a person; however, due to time constraints in the normal boarding process for instance, you may be forced to make quick assessments based upon your training and experience and assisted with your intuition.

Observing and interviewing – critical skills in profiling

Observing passenger behavior and employing subtle interview techniques are effective profiling techniques. The body language of passengers you observe can speak louder than words they speak. The word interview conjures up thoughts of formal job interviews, or sitting in a police station where you are asked a line of questions. Interviewing should be so subtle the passenger does not know they are being screened through simple and pleasant questioning. As you make subtle inquiries and gather information, you should appear to the passenger as a concerned crewmember who has their best interest in mind. The answers to subtle questions and the observations of non-verbal signals through body language provide us with much needed information as we judge whether a passenger poses a threat to the flight, or not. Making the effort to observe and speak with as many passengers as possible will greatly assist flight crews in the determination of threats aboard the aircraft.

The actual words spoken in answer to your question(s) are not as important as the manner and tone used by the respondent. Communication experts say that only 7 per cent of verbal communication involves the words chosen for use. The other 93 per cent involves body language (55 per cent), tone and inflection (38 per cent). If you ask a passenger how he is doing and he sarcastically answers, 'Oh, just great'. It was not the words, but the manner and tone/inflection of the voice coupled with body language that alerted you to the fact that this person is not happy about something. The information you will obtain through discussions (interviews) and observations can be used to determine not only potential hijackers that may be on your aircraft, but with other potential problems that may arise from passengers who may pose a safety threat to your flight, or who may create a medical emergency while airborne.

Interviews or conversation should occur in a non-threatening discussion style format that has specific goals to discover information about the person spoken too. This an informal process to acquire information that can be used on follow-up questions to discover if a passenger's behavior is consistent with your observations. Just like the example we used with the 'Oh, just great' passenger whose words obviously did not match the other signs he exhibited.

In the short time you have to speak with passengers as they are boarding the aircraft you will need to measure conversations carefully. As the passengers are entering or passing through the cabin of the aircraft, engage them in conversation. Move through the cabin and speak with the passengers, especially those you have a 'gut feeling' about. Rapport building in this short time frame is difficult; yet, it is extremely important to gaining the information you need to assess passenger threat potential.

The objective of the subtle interview is to get the passenger talking. You want them to talk 70–80 per cent of the time.[19] As they are speaking, actively listen. Pay close attention and respond appropriately. Head nods and saying things like, 'uh-huh' 'I see' and 'Oh' create rapport with the other person. Avoid asking questions that can be answered with a 'yes' or a 'no'. Ask open ended questions that force conversation. Open-ended questions typically begin with how, when, where, why and what. You want them to speak so that you can carefully study their body movements, speech patterns, demeanor, mood, and whether you notice their level of comfort is decreasing or increasing. If their comfort level is increasing, that is a good sign you are building a good rapport with them and they are relaxed. On the other hand, if they are getting more tense and nervous as they talk with you, a cause for concern exists. Most people would begin to relax as they spoke with a caring crewmember, but if they are planning some highly stressful evil deed their increased stress level may begin to show as you speak with them and manifest itself in an increasing level of nervousness.

Lt Scott Cornfield from the San Jose, California Police Department is an expert at conducting interviews and interrogations. He has gotten confessions from hardened criminals that you would not think was possible. Regarding interviewing people he said, 'the demeanor I get … the demeanor you get'.[20] What he means is that being non-confrontational with those you are talking with is the most productive to getting the information you want in an interview. First impressions are lasting and if it is obvious that you are trying to accomplish this goal by confrontational questions then you will be either perceived as rude or obviously seeking information. Smile and be pleasant. People who scowl and who appear aloof will not get the truthful open responses they are seeking from other people. An unintended consequence of this approach is that you may be too blunt and to the point, which may tip off a trained terrorist as to your intentions. Remember, trained terrorists may have received years of training, including how to counter these techniques. We are not dealing with blundering idiots. Under estimating the ability of trained terrorists to determine your intentions could be a major mistake.

Intuition

Terrorists explored the weaknesses in our airline security system and carefully exploited them to their great advantage on 9/11. One of our biggest mistakes prior to the attacks was that we did not take time to recognize the cues that were present ever so clearly in hindsight, and to act upon our intuition as we watched terrorism explode worldwide. Before 9/11, most Americans did not quite understand the enemy we faced. We now understand them to be crafty, persistent, dedicated, patient, tenacious, and willing and able to sacrifice their life for their beliefs. We must learn from our mistakes and make an oath to each other never to let this happen again by devising and learning methods to counteract their evil intents. Developing and paying attention to your intuition is an important part of countering terrorism.

Intuitive profiling tactics must be developed that are not seen or heard. You must open your mind and believe that you can detect through intuitive processes dangerous individuals that get on your airplane. Your brain can be consciously trained and used effectively to scan the environment and intuitively analyze the clues present. Your brain also perceives and processes cues subconsciously, creating what is known as 'the sixth sense'. When you do not know why you are feeling a certain way about a person or situation, your intuition or sixth sense is processing cues that are present and trying to give you a warning – an uneasy feeling – about the situation. Studies have shown the sixth sense is correct approximately 95 per cent of the time; therefore, pay close attention to those uneasy feelings – they are probably correct. Dr. Arthur Deikman has written, 'Intuition is a process that is fundamentally different from and superior to reason in discovering truth'.[21] Some psychologists have suggested that intuition is not a supernatural or unconscious process, but is a subliminal perception of data or insight already available to unconscious cueing.[22] By whatever means it is accessed by your brain, it is a tool that you can use to greatly assist you in your duties as crewmembers.

Intuition has been linked to military leaders who used it to prevail over their enemies or to save the lives of their men. Other leaders have gone into battle ignoring the 'still small voice' and suffered for it. An example of a military leader who understood and followed that inner voice was Col. John Alexander, commander of a Special Forces team in Vietnam.

> While leading a small patrol deep into the jungle in enemy territory, Col. Alexander felt a sudden urge to stop in his tracks. Something did not feel right to him and he did not know why. He looked down and saw that a booby trap wire was strung taut against the back of his boot. The wire was connected to the pin of a hand grenade just a couple of feet away from him. If he had not stopped when he did, he would have either been crippled or killed by the explosion. The grenade was disarmed and he was spared. His intuition, his sixth sense, stopped him in his tracks and probably saved his life.[23]

Another example of reacting to an intuitive feeling comes from the personal experience of Waltrip.

> Police Officer Waltrip made a traffic-stop on a car that had a front headlight out in San Jose, California. After the car pulled over to the side of the road, Officer Waltrip observed three male occupants patiently sitting in the car and they did not appear to be doing anything suspicious; however, something did not feel right about the situation. Acting on his intuition, Officer Waltrip called on his police radio for assistance. Waltrip did not approach the car until the other officer arrived a few minutes later. After Officer Waltrip and the other officer cautiously approached the vehicle, Waltrip asked the driver to step out of the car with his hands completely in sight. The driver complied and he and both officers backed up to the rear of the patrol car. During the pat down of the driver, Waltrip discovered a pocket full of .357 caliber ammunition, but no weapon. Waltrip questioned the driver as to the whereabouts of the gun and the driver said it was on the floor of the car. After handcuffing the driver and placing him in the back of the patrol car, Waltrip and the other officer removed both remaining passengers from the car at gunpoint. In a search of the vehicle, Waltrip found the fully loaded gun under some papers on the floor on the passenger's side, along with a large amount of cash. The cash was from a large drug sale that had just transpired.

Officer Waltrip probably saved his own life, and that of his partner, by paying attention to his intuitive feelings.

Developing an intuitive ability is an inexact science. A common belief is that women are more intuitive than men are, but this is not necessarily true. Women do tend to ask more questions than men do. As a result, their brains are storing more data that is helpful in the subconscious processing of cues from all five senses, thereby creating a better intuitive capability. However, we all have the capability to be intuitive.

Learning to trust your intuition is another part of the equation. Try to put all negativity aside and listen to your inner voice as you go about your life. Experiment with your intuition as you encounter people throughout the day and in different settings, such as at work or at home, in restaurants and shopping malls, etc. What does your intuition tell you about each person with whom you come into contact? In conversations with people, are their words congruent with their actions? Without letting on about your experiment, ask questions. Does their story ring true? You are not trying to catch someone in a lie, but are trying to hone your skill as a student of human behavior – a skill of being able to accurately interpret human behavior that could one day save your life.

Conclusion

Everyone who steps aboard your airliner needs profiling in one way or another. It is essential that you keep your mind open as you speak with passengers and other crewmembers. The possibility of terrorist groups changing their strategies is very real. Air rage incidents rarely begin 'out of the blue'. Looking back at these incidents it is often clear the events were brewing and the behaviors of the individuals concerned were becoming increasingly aggressive.

Learning how to *read people like a book* will greatly increase your ability to recognize events before they occur. Accurately interpreting hostile signs can be used to defuse a situation before it gets out of hand or to give you time to prepare for the worst. Looking for the 'absence of the normal and presence of the abnormal' as discussed in this chapter will provide you with an advantage over air rage incidents that will continue to occur. As much as terrorists around the world hate Americans and their friends, eventually another incident will occur. Profiling is another tool in your toolbox of self-defensive measures; your ability to use profiling as an effective tool is dependent upon your knowledge of what it can do for you. Repetition is the key to developing any type of skill. Therefore, profiling must be practiced on a daily basis to become an effective weapon against terrorism. The proper use of profiling could save your life.

Notes

1 Airlines sued over bias vs. Mideast-looking people, Associated Press, 5 June 2002.
2 ACLU Sues Four US Airlines, Alleging Middle-Eastern Bias, *Dow Jones Newswires*, 5 June 2002.
3 Violence in the Skies Seminar; *Green Light Limited*, London, United Kingdom; New Orleans, Louisiana, July 2002.
4 Higgins, Michael, Looking the part, *ABA Journal*, November 1997.
5 Bloom, Richard, Racial Profiling: Should It Be Used for Aviation Security, *The Leader*, Fall 1999.
6 Offices try to prevent harassment of Muslim staff, *USA Today*, 14 September 2001.
7 Airlines sued over bias vs. Mideast-looking people, Associated Press, 5 June 2002.
8 9/11 generating more ethnic backlash, discrimination, Associated Press, 4 December 2002.
9 Policy that bars race profiling is unveiled by White House, *New York Times*, 18 June 2003.
10 Race-profile ban decried as too lax, Associated Press, 25 June 2003.
11 Ethnic profiling of air passengers debated, Associated Press, 5 July 2002.
12 Do I look like a terrorist? Star spurs jets to scramble, Associated Press, 19 July 2002.
13 Airlines face post 9/11 racial profiling, discrimination suits, http://www.CNN.com, 4 June 2002.
14 Airlines, passengers confront racial profiling, http://www.CNN.com, 3 October 2001.
15 Violence in the Skies Seminar; *Green Light Limited*, London, United Kingdom; New Orleans, Louisiana, July 2002.
16 Thomas, Cathy Booth, Courage in the Air, *TIME*, 9 September 2002.
17 Cornfield, Lt. Scott, Interviews and Interrogations '97, San Jose Police Department.
18 Dimitrius, Jo-Ellan Dimitrius and Mark Mazzarella, *Reading People*, Ballentine Books, 1999.
19 Cornfield, Lt. Scott, Interviews and Interrogations '97, San Jose Police Department.
20 Ibid.
21 Deikman, Arthur J., Mystical Intuition. *New Realities Magazine*, May/June 1987.
22 Jo-Ellan Dimitrius and Mark Mazzarella, *Reading People*, Ballentine Books, 1999.
23 Alexander, Col. John, Maj. Richard Groller, and Janet Morris, *The Warrior's Edge*, William Morrow and Co. Inc., 1990.

Chapter 12

Flight Crew Survival Tactics and Techniques

Introduction

The authors have learned a respect for proper defensive tactics because of their experience as a personal protection specialist (Williams) and as a police officer (Waltrip). Just as a lack of proper tactics on the street can cost a police officer his life, a lack of proper defensive tactics can get a crewmember injured on an aircraft, or much worse. The proper use and implementation of tactics can save an officer's life, as it did for Waltrip when he was a street cop. It is hard to quantify such a claim, but since he is alive and co-authoring these words, he did something right. Because of our life's experiences, we have concluded that effective defensive tactics used by crewmembers will save lives.

Although, there are obvious differences between the roles of police and flight crews, there are shared dangers in today's world. Primarily, because there are individuals in the world (terrorists or combative passengers) who would like to cause a great deal of harm to crewmembers. A properly trained police officer will use trained tactics in everything he or she does in public. Likewise, properly trained pilots and flight attendants should use trained tactics to protect them in everything they do around the traveling public. The basic principles we have developed in this chapter are practical. If used properly, they can make the difference in preventing injuries to crewmembers.

There is a definite psychological advantage to employing tactics. The least of which, they help crewmembers feel more confident in the job they are doing. It is impossible to have a single defensive tactic for every situation you could possibly experience, but a fundamental understanding of how they work and how they can be implemented in situations, will help avoid becoming a victim. For the purposes of our discussion of tactics in this chapter, keeping crewmembers alive is our focus and motivation. Tactics involve thinking and using your brain to avoid dangerous situations. The protection of other crewmembers, passengers and the aircraft are the bottom line in the development of this chapter.

Definitions and Understandings

With the implementation of reinforced cockpit doors and the assurance of greater flight deck protection, there may be a tendency for some flight attendants to believe that the pilots do not care about what happens in the cabin as long as the pilots are safe. Both the authors are airline pilots and believe these feelings of ill will are misguided, and for the vast part untrue. All crewmembers need to move beyond the thinking that pits one set of crewmembers against the other, because it simply undermines the team concept. We all must recognize that we have a common goal of survival. The ultimate responsibility of the aircraft rests upon the shoulders of the captain; however, other pilot(s) and flight attendants assigned to a particular flight are an extremely important aspect to the entire flight crew's survival. The captain needs to recognize each crewmember's strengths and weaknesses and be able to delegate actions as necessary to the crew. Flight crew security is just another aspect of crew resource management (CRM). Proper treatment and respect to all crewmembers is crucial in resolution of any potential security incident.

Flight crews should understand they can use strategies to gain the advantage against those that want to do them harm. The terrorist actions of 9/11 are an example of why we must develop and implement tactical strategies to deter, or if needed, stop an attack by a hijacker or disruptive passenger. Crewmembers do not have to become victims. This is one reason why crewmembers need to be empowered with well-reasoned and logical tactics.

An important aspect of any kind of training, and especially emergency training, is the development of a mental state of mind for a successful outcome. This means crewmembers must develop the confidence to know what to do in a security emergency and respond appropriately when an incident unfolds. In the case of security training, it means developing a warrior state of mind. If a violent passenger attacks you, you must respond with some sort of self-defense that will assure your survival. A crewmember that has never had a problem with a passenger in 20 years and believes they do not need any of this 'tactics stuff', is ignoring the reality of the current state of the world. It is plausible some of the crewmembers on one of those four airliners on 9/11 never had any problems with passengers, either, and we all saw what happened on that horrible day. We strongly recommend that crewmembers learn and prepare before a security emergency occurs. Prepare yourself for winning 100 per cent of the time and do not settle for anything less. As you read this chapter, envisage how you can respond to a security event. Try developing your own tactics as they relate to your crew duties. You may be surprised to find how good you may be at inventing your own tactics.

Saddam Hussein had provided training bases for terrorists from around the world. Before his removal as president by a military coalition of countries during Operation Iraqi Freedom, Saddam used the hatred of the terrorists as a tool to accomplish his own devious plans. An aspect of that terrorist training is hijacking airplanes, and spreading terror across the world.[1] It is important to emphasize that there are countries globally that support terrorism. Those countries will continue to be a serious threat to flight crews around the world. The threats crewmembers face are as real today as they were on 9/11, and maybe even more so. Hijacking attempts will continue regardless of how safe governments or airlines say it is. Stay focused to the possibility of further attempted hijackings. We have entered a new chapter of airline history and 9/11 may just be the opening chapter of what air travel may be in this new millennium. It is imperative flight crews do what they can to make it safer. Stay alert!

Crewmembers must face the new reality that lies before them in airline travel. Inconveniences are going to be an integral part of commercial aviation from now on. Just accept it as a requirement of doing business and deal with it. Crewmembers must acknowledge and accept a new level of security that will require their active participation. You must realize that for the continued safety of air travel around the world, crewmembers must become part of the security equation. Like it or not, it has become an unpleasant fact, and to resist change will make it more difficult for you, raise your stress levels and shorten your life.

Developing methods to protect yourself and others should be the major goal of flight crew tactics. This is a pioneering concept to the world's commercial airlines. The airline of Israel, El Al, has developed very effective techniques to protect themselves from hijackings. Israel has been a major target of wrath from people from their part of the world for decades. They have understood by the actions of terrorists that they are a target and have planned accordingly. Likewise, crewmembers and airline executives need to understand fully that the world's commercial airlines have become a target to terrorists from across the globe. This is a very serious threat to crewmembers, and unfortunately, will continue to be the case for a very long time to come.

A crewmember's role is no longer limited to the technical aspects of completing a scheduled flight. There are now other important security roles for airline crewmembers to perform. The primary focus of course, should be on safely completing the flight. Yet, how can crewmembers safely complete a scheduled flight if they are ignorant of dangerous security concerns? Safety and security go 'hand in hand'. A scheduled flight cannot be completely safe unless it is reasonably secure from any threats. Furthermore, if a security threat becomes evident to the flight crew, they should reasonably be able to deal with it knowledgably.

Just because an organized terrorist hijacking attempt has not occurred to an airline since 9/11, does not mean airline travel is safe from hijackings. Let's face it, 9/11 changed forever the manner in which crewmembers need to do their jobs. The typical crewmember's perspective of past airline security being satisfactory was misguided, and in fact, nothing but an illusion. In actuality, effective airline security in the area of flight crew training had not existed for about 30 years. We need to develop new methods to deter hijacking and/or other violence aboard airliners.

Who do you think is better at understanding the intricacies and nuances of a crewmember's job: a crewmember with experience in security or a security administrator with no experience in a crewmember's job? During one symposium the authors attended in the spring of 2003, a regional director for the TSA began his presentation with a personal introduction that began, 'I have no experience in aviation'.

Immediately we thought, then why is he in an important decision-making position that affects aircrews, airlines and the traveling public? After finishing his presentation that underscored the fact that he really did not know anything about aviation, he left the building before anyone could ask him a question. We need administrators, but we need people who are knowledgeable about aviation.

Administrators have their role, but discounting crewmember input in the development of strategies is a mistake. We encourage crewmembers and airline management personnel from around the world to be open minded to the aspect of self-defense and tactics. Airlines and the government must value and treat crewmembers as more than dispensable tools to help the airline make money. Crewmembers are human beings who want to make a living to support their families, and have the right to go home safely at the end of their trip pairing.

Simply stated, a tactical approach in the way crewmembers go about their jobs will save lives. Just as Waltrip believed his tactical behaviors as a police officer helped prevent an attack against him, flight crews applying defensive tactics will deter hijackings. Make no mistake about it, demonstrating confidence, determination, and an ability to act will show others that you are prepared. You might not be a Bruce Lee, but you can demonstrate by your body language that you can take care of yourself if needed. Later in this chapter, we will go into detail about how the way you stand and talk will demonstrate to others that you are trained to defend yourself.

Environment

Stay aware of your surroundings. That is easy to say, but hard to do sometimes. As discussed in Chapter 7 – Awareness for Survival, a crewmember's awareness is the key to survival in critical situations. Police officers are often astonished to interview witnesses to a crime who could provide little information, even though they were present during the incident. Not only did they fail to recognize that a crime was about to occur, but many witnesses did not even realize a crime was occurring until the victim alerted them to it.

Crewmembers can ill afford to be in the 'WHITE' zone (oblivious, unaware) while on duty during a flight. If, as a crewmember, you find yourself in a position where you are naturally drifting off into an unaware or 'WHITE' state of mind, find another crewmember that can 'watch your back' and protect you until you come out of this phase. In this way, you are not jeopardizing yourself, or other crewmembers, by your lack of awareness. Likewise, other crewmembers may need some time to regroup at some point, and then you can return the favor.

Since it is conceivable that passengers could turn out to be hijackers on your flight, it is imperative that you watch passengers carefully as they are being boarded. Gut feelings or a hunch may not be enough to have a passenger removed from the flight; however, you must watch those individuals carefully and discreetly before the aircraft door closes, so a more informed decision may be made on how you may need to proceed (remember Chapter 11 – Passenger Profiling?). If you have any suspicions at all, be sure to tell the other crewmembers of your intuitive feelings so they can be aware of the passengers in question, as well. Additionally, be sure to keep the captain informed as much as possible because he or she is the Inflight Security Coordinator, and needs to know of your suspicions. The captain may want to explore the alternatives, which may include a face-to-face conversation with the persons in question.

Do not be intimidated by looking at others and observing unusual behavior. When a person has something to hide, they put up emotional barriers to hide this behavior. A person in authority simply looking at them, may at times, break down these emotional defenses. This may sound unusual, but often when a police officer is looking at someone who has something to hide (drugs, warrants, etc), it will cause an incredible amount of stress for the individual. Sometimes these individuals panic and begin running away from the officer for no other reason than their emotional barriers were broken down by the officer looking at them. There are times when a person with something to hide from the law, will start to fidget uncontrollably because they become extremely uncomfortable by the presence of a police officer. Their stress was caused by a simple presence of a person of authority. Crewmembers need to be aware of these types of behaviors. We would like to see potential hijackers become visibly uncomfortable by the sight of any uniformed crewmember because they know they are skilled at observations of passengers.

Be observant to your environment and note behavior of passengers that you can articulate as unusual. However, be careful not to act on these suspicions until you have concrete proof of suspicious activity. Nevertheless, the suspicious activity you do notice can be a useful marker and may provide the early warning you need to survive a violent attack.

Crewmembers need to accept some important concepts about the current airline world. Primarily, their level of awareness needs to be at a continually high state of readiness (YELLOW), especially to activity that does not appear normal. As discussed in Chapter 11 – Passenger Profiling, do not forget about the *absence of the normal* and the *presence of the abnormal.* Be vigilant and do not disregard suspicious activity. If you are not sure of what you saw or heard, discuss it with another crewmember. If there is still a question, bring it to the attention of the captain. In light of the current world affairs, crewmembers can no longer disregard the suspicions they have of passengers that before 9/11 would have gone unchallenged.

Additionally, watch for unusual activity among the passengers (unusual hand signals, gestures, code words, passengers that follow a crewmember's every move, or any other unusual activity). Hijackers may strategically place themselves around the cabin so when they decide to act they will have an excellent overview of the aircraft. There is a chance that they might want to communicate with each other by using signals of one sort or another. Be alert and do not overlook this type of activity.

A chilling true story, told to us in person, accentuates the need to remain aware of your surroundings and to act on your suspicions. The flight attendant's true name and airline will remain anonymous to protect him from any reprisals.

> Joe is a flight attendant for a major airline and was at a layover hotel near JFK on the morning of 9/11. As he began to get dressed for work, he turned on the television where a breaking news story caught his attention about a plane that had crashed into the WTC. A short time later as he was watching the news story unfold, the second hijacked airliner crashed into the WTC. Joe and his fellow crewmembers spent the next two days watching news reports, experiencing the emotions that accompanied those horrific events, and consoling one another.
>
> Two days later, a crew scheduler called Joe at the hotel and told him to report for duty for a scheduled flight out of JFK that afternoon. Joe did not feel comfortable about it, but reported to work as requested. In fact, Joe was very uncomfortable with having to work a revenue flight just two days after the tragic events of 9/11. As an ex-military man, he recognized the fact that further hijacking threats existed. He felt the flight should proceed only with the crewmembers that had been stranded with him for the two days after the terrorist hijackings.
>
> He began talking about his feelings on this issue with the captain who minimized Joe's gut feelings. Joe explained to the captain that he was a veteran who knew when something did not look or feel right. The captain did not want to hear it, and began discussing how he was now considering removing Joe from the flight as being unstable and unable to complete his duties. Joe felt insulted and ended his discussion with the captain because he felt the captain was not taking his concerns seriously with an important security issue.
>
> Shortly thereafter, passengers began boarding the aircraft and Joe began greeting them as they entered through the main cabin door. Among the passengers were over a dozen crewmembers that had also been stranded by the events of 9/11. None of the crewmembers noticed anything unusual as the boarding process continued.
>
> Among the passengers boarding, Joe noticed a Middle Eastern man entering the aircraft. He sensed something unusual about the man and felt uncomfortable as he made eye contact with the man as he boarded. Several other Middle Eastern men boarded the flight and Joe did not sense anything unusual about them. Something about the first man made him suspicious but, he could not identify what it was that caused his concern.
>
> As the passengers continued to board, another flight attendant stationed in the back of the aircraft called to the forward flight attendant station where Joe was standing. She said there were three Middle Eastern men in the rearward part of the aircraft seated in various locations that were communicating using hand signals and what seemed like code words. Joe told her he would come to the back aircraft and observe the individuals for himself. When he arrived in the back of the aircraft, the other flight attendant identified the men. One of the men happened to be the man he felt uneasy about as the man was boarding.
>
> Joe was convinced a security threat existed and set about to investigate these men further, without raising any of their suspicions. One of the individuals was sitting under the entertainment control monitor in the rear portion of the aircraft. Joe feigned adjusting the monitor in an effort to make small talk with the individual. Joe asked the man where he was going and he replied that he was connecting to a flight to 'Mexico'. Joe knew from news reports that the US borders were still closed and that there were

currently no flights in or out of the country. Joe looked down and saw the individual's ticket cover and ticket. The ticket did not have 'Mexico' as its final destination, but rather 'El Paso'.

Joe was now thoroughly convinced a serious security issue existed aboard his aircraft. He began moving forward to the front of the aircraft to alert the captain to the developing security situation in the back of the aircraft. As he passed the men in question, Joe noticed that all three of them were now watching him very closely as he passed through the cabin.

Joe approached the captain and told him of the developing security concerns in the back of the aircraft. The captain told him that the flight was now delayed by air traffic control (ATC). Acknowledging the captain, Joe began to move to the back of the aircraft to check how things were developing. Most of the passengers were now more or less boarded and seated in their assigned seats. Again, as Joe passed into the back of the aircraft the suspicious men watched him very closely as he passed them. When he passed the last man, Joe turned to look back and saw one man lift his hand and signal to the two other men. The man extended all five fingers on his hand in what Joe immediately thought was a signal to the others that there were five crewmembers on the flight. He quickly turned around and headed for the front of the aircraft to alert the captain of the very suspicious activity of these men.

After Joe relayed the information about the men to the captain, the captain finally became concerned and directed the first officer to call airport security. The captain also told Joe the airport was now closed because two men had tried to get through a security checkpoint with fake pilot identifications. Joe turned, exited the flight deck and entered the galley area of the A320. He then heard a door in the jet-bridge slam open and the sound of several individuals running down the jet-bridge. He stepped to the front door of the aircraft and was startled to see approximately eight FBI, Marshals, Customs, and INS agents who were armed with shotguns, machineguns, and handguns.

Joe gave the agents the seat locations and a general description of the individuals in question. The agents entered the aircraft, had all the passengers aboard raise their hands above their heads, and threatened to shoot anyone who made a suspicious move. Fortunately, everyone complied except a passenger who thought he would get a photo of the exciting developments. A US Marshal slapped the camera out of the passenger's hands, pointed a shotgun into the passengers face and asked him if he wanted 'to get shot'.

After the officers took the three suspicious men off the aircraft in handcuffs, another Middle Eastern man walked off the aircraft stating he was with the other three men. Naturally, all the passengers were horribly shaken by the experience, and most of them wanted to get off the aircraft immediately. Since the airport had been closed due to the earlier security incident, all passengers were deplaned and the flight was eventually cancelled a couple of hours later.

As Joe and the rest of the crew were walking toward the hotel pickup area in front of the terminal, he noticed one of the Customs Agents who had responded to the incident on the aircraft. Joe approached the Agent to thank him for responding so quickly to the incident aboard the aircraft. The Agent told Joe that he did not blame the crew for being careful about who boarded their aircraft because one of the men taken off the plane was on the Immigration and Naturalization Service terrorist list and was a wanted criminal.

Joe was startled by the Special Agent's response, but was glad that he had followed through on his suspicions and had possibly prevented a hijacking of his aircraft.

Again, be vigilant and do not overlook suspicious activity aboard the aircraft! Be vigilant for deliberate distractions somewhere on the aircraft before a hijacking. For example, hijackers may create a loud commotion in the back of the aircraft to focus the attention of passengers and flight attendants to that location. All of the flight attendants may rush to the back of the aircraft to investigate and react to the incident. Unfortunately, the front of the aircraft would be unattended, giving other hijackers at the front of the aircraft the opportunity to force entry into the flight deck. Therefore, when your attention is diverted it may provide an opportunity for hijackers to act. It is imperative to aircraft security that a flight attendant remains in the front area of the aircraft at all times.

Remain aware that hijackers may be very discreet and difficult to detect. Terrorists have been training and plotting the world over to devise methods to kill and have openly stated their desire to cause destruction.[2] The terrorists who hijacked the airliners on 9/11 were discreet and obviously did not make anyone suspicious of their intentions until they violently took over the flights. Be prepared and on your guard because terrorists are continuing to train to kill you and anyone else, who gets in the way of their deadly ambitions.[3]

Crewmembers need the ability to alert other crewmembers that hijackers are attacking them, or of other serious trouble. Every crewmember should have in their possession a whistle. The whistle will be discussed in further detail in Chapter 13 – Unconventional Self-Defense. This whistle should be kept with crewmembers at all times so they can alert others to the immediate need for assistance. The crewmember should only use the whistle as a major warning to other flight attendants and pilots. Upon hearing the whistle, the pilots should begin an immediate descent until they can determine a threat no longer exists aboard the aircraft. Therefore, blow the whistle at the first sign of a physical attack, or other serious assault upon anyone in the aircraft. If there are two inebriated passengers fighting, then law enforcement personnel can address the issue while the flight is on the ground.

During a disturbance in the cabin, the flight deck should enter into a phase of 'lockdown'. During the lockdown, there should not be any foot traffic between the flight deck and the cabin. In the past, the flight deck has often been a place of sanctuary for a flight attendant who wanted to escape a disturbance in the aircraft or to take a break. Unfortunately, this is no longer a viable alternative for flight attendants, and if used for this purpose may in fact, lead to a breach of the flight deck by hijackers or others. If a threat of any level exists in the cabin, flight attendants need to alert the pilots, so together they can develop a plan on what actions need to be taken.

Team Issues

In the United States, the airlines have taken security measures to protect the flight deck, such as re-enforcing the flight deck door and making them resistant to gunshots or explosives. The Aviation and Transportation Security Act of 2001(ATSA) in the

United States, made provisions for airline pilots to have firearms on the aircraft, and the Homeland Security Act of 2002 (United States) codified this in follow-up legislation. Starting in June 2003, volunteer pilots in the United States began firearms training under the guidance of the Transportation Security Administration (TSA). Upon completion of this training, the pilots were sworn in by the United States government as Federal Flight Deck Officers (FFDO). This program will continue to be controversial to both pilots and flight attendants worldwide as there continues to be a significant divide in opinions between these two crewmember groups on this issue.

Unfortunately, the attention focused on the protection of the flight deck has driven a wedge between pilots and flight attendants. Human nature being what it is, the flight attendants definitely have a right to feel hurt by the lack of attention to their protection. Many flight attendants feel as if they have been pushed aside as being expendable, while pilot protection is being emphasized. Regardless of the perceived disparity in security emphasis, flight attendants are crucial to the success of the safety and security of any given flight. A flight attendant may be the only thing between life and death for passengers during an in-flight emergency or security incident.

We need to dispel the belief that the pilots are trying to hide behind their reinforced door and do not care what happens to the flight attendants. Generally, pilots are usually very defensive of the safety and security of the flight attendants and passengers. Once informed of a physically aggressive passenger or hijacker, most pilots would be more than willing to get out of their seat, go into the cabin of the aircraft, and in the most kind and gentle way, subdue a violent passenger who has caused harm to a crewmember or passenger. Unfortunately, the new reality of heightened security has all but closed that option. In today's world, it would be unwise for a pilot to exit the flight deck in an effort to settle a problem or other security issue in the cabin of the aircraft. Tactically, it would be a major mistake to subject one of the pilots to severe injury by attempting to intercede into an incident in the cabin. The pilots are required to fly the airplane, and if one of them is injured and unable to perform their duties, the passengers and flight attendants just better hope the health of the other pilot is excellent. The passengers and flight attendants need the pilots, but at the same time, the pilots need the flight attendants. The pilots need the flight attendants to prevent an unauthorized person entry into the flight deck, to protect the passengers and to deal with in-flight emergencies in the cabin. Pilots need flight attendants and flight attendants need pilots.

All crewmembers should recognize they are a team and are drawn together by mutual survival. Crewmembers need to bond and recognize who the real enemies are to their survival. Building emotional walls between crewmembers is not the solution to defeat those who think they can hijack aircraft and do with it as they please. Crewmembers must work together to prevent any further hijacking of commercial aircraft. Crewmembers must put forth a united front, and demonstrate to anyone who thinks they can attack or injure a passenger and/or crewmember that they cannot get away with it, and will most certainly pay a heavy price for trying.

Pilot Awareness and Actions

As mentioned earlier in this chapter, terrorists may attempt to cause a distraction or other commotion in the cabin to divert attention away from their true intentions. If, an incident occurs on the aircraft, it may in fact, be an incident between traveling passengers. All the same, crewmembers need to protect the flight deck at all costs and leaving the flight deck during a passenger incident may jeopardize the safety of the flight. Do not ever leave the flight deck during a disturbance in the cabin. Pilots, be aware of the diversionary tactics terrorists may employ by luring you out from behind the reinforced flight deck doors. A reinforced door will not do pilots any good if terrorists lure them out of the flight deck allowing them to rush into the cockpit and take over the aircraft. How are you going to get terrorists out of the flight deck with a locked, impregnable door? Pilots must practice sound tactical approaches to flight deck security as anything less could be lethal for all.

Pilots should act quickly and decisively if yelling, screaming, or a whistle is heard from the cabin. Yelling and screaming is a very good indication a disturbance of an unknown level is occurring in the cabin. You may not have the time to investigate before you take immediate action. The pilots should consider the whistle to be a sure sign that a serious incident is occurring in the cabin. Do not question the whistle signal, because to delay could be detrimental to the flight attendants and passengers. Additionally, the flight attendants will expect you to take immediate action by starting a descent. You must trust the flight attendant's judgment and take action that everyone is expecting you to take. Teamwork is required to get the aircraft on the ground safely.

What occurs if a kid or a practical joker blows a whistle on the plane? How do you know that this is not a deliberate plan of hijackers? For example, a hijacker could have a child blow the whistle, which would ultimately get the flight attendants to notify the pilots of the prank. Then, the hijackers could take advantage of the complacency of the flight crew generated by this situation and take action. Hijacker tactics such as this must not fool you. It is not a joking matter for an individual to discuss 'bombs' or other weapons at an airport and law enforcement authorities deal harshly with people who do this. Thus, blowing a whistle on an airplane should not be a joking matter and the pilots must consider it as a serious incident until it can be resolved on the ground. If it was just a joke, then it was not very funny and the government should deal harshly with passengers who would do this.

In reality, if a flight attendant calls the pilots on the interphone and claims the whistle was a hoax or a joke, the pilots will not have any way of knowing whether a hijacker is forcing the flight attendants to make the call. Unless, the aircraft has remotely mounted cameras, the pilots will not be able to verify the aircraft is secure visually. This brings up a good question. Why is it that probably the best tool available for pilots to discern what is actually happening in the cabin has not been a mandatory modification to all commercial aircraft?

Until a remote alerting device is developed for use by cabin crews, we must use something that can alert all the crewmembers. The whistle seems to be a good intermediate step as it is cheap, legal to carry and easily recognized when blown.

Crewmembers are part of a team, and as a team, pilots must fulfill their responsibilities within the team. If pilots use the procedural actions that the flight attendants expect, it will assure the flight attendants that help is on the way. You must help reduce the risk of injury to the flight attendants, passengers and the aircraft by responding as anticipated. At the first significant sign of a disturbance in the cabin, declare an emergency, state the unknown nature and begin an immediate descent toward a suitable airport. Declaring an emergency, stating the unknown nature of the disturbance, and beginning a descent is the prudent and safe approach to everyone's security.

If after an unknown disturbance is heard in the cabin and the pilots begin an emergency descent, it is likely, the flight deck will become a place of multiple communications between ATC, pilots, flight attendants, and the airline. The myriad of communication issues may become a distraction for the pilots as they attempt to coordinate the resources to make a safe landing. What may be a viable alternative for the pilots of a two pilot aircraft is to split up the aircraft duties. The captain usually makes important decisions pertaining to a given flight. Two pilots can be busy with normal flying duties, but then throw in a security emergency, communications with the flight attendants, ATC/company notifications, and we have a recipe for disaster. The solution may be to have the first officer handle all the communications with ATC and fly the aircraft to a suitable airport. The captain, as the in-flight security coordinator, can deal with the incident by coordinating with company personnel and any other related duties until the situation is under control. It is our recommendation that during any type of a security issue on the aircraft, the captain should manage the incident and the first officer should fly the aircraft.

Flight crews need to establish a foundational trust with one another in this new era of airline security. However, nothing will undermine this trust more than disregarding the concerns crewmembers have about issues that are important to them. You may be an excellent captain or first officer, but you need help in successfully completing any given flight. No one can do it alone, except maybe Rambo, but he is not an airline pilot. With this in mind, always remain sensitive to the entire crew's security concerns.

The incident described earlier about the flight attendant in JFK who felt the captain disregarded his security concerns accentuates the seriousness of overlooking those concerns. The result of treating crewmembers unprofessionally may result in undesired and lasting negative effects. Even after the incident proved Joe was correct in his suspicions, the captain did not apologize for the humiliating way he treated him. As captain, do not undermine the trust your crew has in you by being unresponsive to their legitimate security concerns. If, you do not agree with the flight attendant's security concerns then you should handle the difference professionally. A condescending and rude dismissal of a flight attendant's concern will cause ill will between the flight crew and may ultimately become the real security issue. If you were wrong, admit it, apologize and move on.

The pilots must always keep in mind the flight attendants are the first line of defense and they are the last line of defense. Pilots are somewhat secure from an immediate assault from a hijacker since they are behind a reinforced flight deck door. Pilots expect flight attendants to protect the flight deck from any unauthorized entry by hijackers, even to the point of injury or worse. Certainly, the protection of the flight deck is crucial to the security of the flight, but flight deck crews should not overlook the courage flight attendants are demonstrating everyday. Pilots need to acknowledge the extreme sacrifices flight attendants make on their behalf.

Aircraft Security

In this new era of aviation security, many new security procedures by airlines and governments have been in a steady state of flux. One of the problem areas has been how pilot and flight attendants go to and from the flight deck. Procedures will vary somewhat from airline to airline, but the fact is the flight deck door is opened while in flight to bring food items into the flight deck or for the pilots to go to use the lavatory. The periods in which the door is opened the pilots should be especially vigilant against forced entry by hijackers. Recognize the vulnerability of the flight deck when flight attendants or pilots are going in and out of the flight deck. Be alert; look around you as you pass in and out of the flight deck. Be observant to who may be watching you and studying how you go in and out of the flight deck.

Stay alert to the fact hijackers may study periods of vulnerability of the flight deck and when it would be the best time to commit to their cause. The terrorists that hijacked the airplanes on 9/11 had obviously studied the established procedures of airline security and found the weaknesses, which they murderously exploited. As airlines establish security procedures, they will have an element of predictability. As time passes, flight crews will become increasingly comfortable with the procedures, which terrorists will undoubtedly study for their planning purposes. Keep in mind terrorists may be using your flight to gather intelligence so they can plan a future hijacking of your company aircraft. Be alert and watch passengers who may be interested in watching how you do your job. Take the following incident for example.

This particular incident involved suspected terrorists who were testing the procedures of the cabin crewmembers with various types of actions aboard the aircraft while the flight was enroute to Mexico City.

> Diane (her name changed in this account to protect her identity) is a flight attendant for a major domestic US airline and has been a flight attendant for 25 years. An incident occurred in April 2003 that she wants all crewmembers to know about. This experienced crewmember recognized something did not feel right about several passengers on a flight to Mexico City.
>
> The flight began normally as boarding agents checked passengers onto the aircraft. During the boarding process, Diane noticed four men who boarded together and who all appeared approximately 26 years old. They all sat in the middle rows of the aircraft. At

first unconcerned about the men, she began to feel uneasy about them as she began her in-flight emergency briefing. The way the men were looking at her startled her. They were all looking at her as if they wanted to kill her. Remember, she is an experienced flight attendant who has had a lot men look at her during her career. She felt strange about them, trusted her 'intuition' and told the other two flight attendants on the flight about her concerns.

The flight proceeded normally until just after the flight leveled off at cruise altitude. All four of the men choose to move to different locations on the aircraft. Two sat in row 4, just behind first class and the other two attempted to sit in the last row of the aircraft. She wanted to maintain control of these men and had to think of something to get them to move back to their original seats. She told the men they had to return to their original seats because the rows were being 'protected' for flight attendants who needed to sit down quickly in case the flight experienced 'turbulence'. They reluctantly complied with her request.

Every time she walked through the aircraft cabin, she noticed the men 'glaring' at her with a stern look. When she was with the other flight attendants in the back of the aircraft, the men would continually look back to verify where all the flight attendants were located. When Diane spoke with the men, she noted they spoke perfect English. Yet, when they spoke to each other, they were speaking a language she thought might be 'Arabic'. Speaking Arabic alone would not normally get her attention, but the fact that they were behaving the way they were concerned her. Moreover, this behavior did not stop. The men were also passing a white envelope back and forth between them across the aisle. Diane never did discover what was in the envelope, but all the same felt concerned by their behavior.

While still en route, one of the men went into one of the rear lavatories where he remained for an 'unusually long amount of time'. After he came out of the lavatory, Diane went in and searched the trashcan, under the sink, behind the toilet and anywhere else that something could potentially be hidden. As she opened the paper dispenser and removed the paper, she saw that a piece of the backing of this area had been tampered with. The sheet metal was pulled back and wiring and other inner components of the aircraft were visible through the opening. She was not sure the man caused the damage, but the unusual behaviors of these men, the length of time he occupied the lavatory, added to her suspicion. Was he looking for a future place to stash a weapon, explosives or other dangerous items?

Diane advised the captain of all of the strange behavior of these men and both he and the first officer became very concerned. The pilots 'locked down' the flight deck and got the crash axe out of its holder. As the flight approached Mexico City, the pilots called air traffic control and asked to have the police waiting for them.

Meanwhile, as the flight descended through 10,000 feet, the men all stood up and began to make phone calls on their cellular phones. She approached them and told them to sit down and turn off the phones. They all complied, but a short time later, she heard a cell phone ringing. One of the four men still had his phone turned on. Again, she told the men that using the cellular phones was not allowed until arrival at the gate. Even upon landing, two of the men immediately stood up, turned on their cell phones and began talking in Arabic.

She felt that these men were either 'testing' or 'gathering' information about the airline. There was not a moment during the three-hour flight that these men were not involved in some sort of 'testing activity'.

> When the flight pulled into the gate, they were met by Mexican police who detained the four men and took them to Customs for processing. The police later turned the men over to US Drug Enforcement Officers, who later released them. Curious to the outcome of this incident, Diane contacted the airline's corporate security the next day. The airline security officer told her that one of the men was on a US 'terrorist watch list' and all of the men were traveling on 'Iraqi passports'. She inquired whether this incident would be released to crewmembers so that they could be aware of suspicious individuals on scheduled flights. The security officer said it was not the company's policy to release this information to crewmembers and did not want her to discuss the incident with any one else. She later discovered through a follow-up discussion with a company security official that the FBI later apprehended one of the individuals upon his return to the United States on the same airline. The man was a known Al Qaeda terrorist.

This incident proves that terrorists are still out there, probing and plotting their next action against aviation. Stay alert to passengers who behave in a suspicious manner and do not be reluctant to take action. Diane's reaction and responses to these men was exemplary. However, the response to the incident by her airline was completely unsatisfactory. Why is it so difficult for the airlines and the government to keep crewmembers appraised of occurrences that have ramifications to them? It is past time for the airlines and governments of the world to keep aircrews in the security informational loop.

The public has begun to learn some of the security procedures established at the airlines through the press, crewmember discussions with non-airline people, and/or by the terrorists who are probing the barriers of aviation security. Terrorists may be either legal immigrants or actual citizens of your country and working for an airline. Do not expect security procedures to remain exclusively confidential to flight crews. Airlines are trying to reduce security procedure exposure, but we need to be realistic and recognize this is not completely possible. In the United States, airline crewmembers are operating under the security procedures of 'Common Strategy 2'. Yet, if airlines were to use this information in its current form year after year, crewmembers tomorrow could certainly find themselves in the same predictable position as on 9/11.

Do not use the aircraft defensively unless you have direct knowledge of the situation in the cabin of the aircraft, the incident is desperate and needs your direct involvement. Many flight attendants have heard captains say during the pre-flight briefing, 'If I hear any yelling or screaming from the back of the aircraft you'll have about 2 seconds to grab onto something and hang on'. This means the captain plans to fly the aircraft into wild gyrations in an attempt to throw hijackers off balance.

Although well intended, this is the wrong method of defending the flight attendants, passengers and the aircraft. Imagine an unknown violent confrontational incident occurring in the cabin that you can hear through the reinforced flight deck doors. You do not know what is occurring in the cabin, but want to take action anyhow. You begin violent positive and negative maneuvers and anyone who is not seat-belted into a seat is violently thrown against the ceiling and floor. However, in this particular situation the flight attendants, with the assistance of passengers, were gaining advantage over the hijackers. That is of course, until you, Captain Al Knowing got involved. Now the heroes in the cabin have become severely injured by your actions and the hijackers are taking advantage of the situation you provided for them. Do not act in an irrational manner that will needlessly get innocent people injured or killed.

There is a time when the defensive use of the aircraft is acceptable. If you were certain that unless you used the aircraft as a defensive weapon, hijackers would be free to force their way into the flight deck. Additionally, as a last resort, when the flight attendants have been overcome in the cabin by attackers, and if you did not use the aircraft defensively, hijackers would gain control of the aircraft. Only under those circumstances should the pilots use the aircraft as a weapon. Pilots must be 100 per cent sure of their actions because death could occur by the abrupt maneuvering of the aircraft. At a minimum, the defensive use of the aircraft should meet the requirements of the following statement:

> In necessary, self-defense, defense of another person, and there is a reasonable cause to believe that there is imminent danger of death or serious bodily injury.

An unauthorized person forcibly entering the flight deck will fulfill the above definition. The word 'forcibly' needs to be properly defined to clarify any misunderstandings. 'Forcibly', (for all intentional purposes, is 'force') is defined as using, 'physical coercion against a person or thing' or 'the power to control or persuade'.[4] To put it in terms we can all understand, if an unauthorized individual enters the flight deck during flight without permission under ANY MEANS, and you reasonably believe that person is danger to everyone aboard, then defensive use of the aircraft would be justified. The pilots should automatically assume if an unauthorized person forcibly enters the flight deck, they intend to do harm to everyone on the aircraft.

We must also conclude that if an unauthorized individual forcibly enters the flight deck, other crewmembers, law enforcement, or passengers have failed to stop them. Since the survival of all aboard depends on the control of the aircraft by the pilots, they will have to take appropriate and decisive action to prevent the aircraft from falling into the wrong hands. It needs to be understood by all crewmembers that the pilots will use the aircraft defensibly, as a last resort, when an unauthorized individual is forcibly accessing the flight deck.

Flight Attendant Tactics

Many flight attendants have bitterly complained to the authors about how vulnerable they felt in the cabin in the days following 9/11. Furthermore, several flight attendants have told us that at one particular US major airline, 200–300 flight attendants had resigned out of fear. Unfortunately, many flight attendants across the globe have resigned because of the fear of terrorism. No one can blame these flight attendants from quitting a job that could get them murdered.

The following techniques have been taken directly from our experiences as a police officer and personal protection specialist. These tactics can make a significant difference in potentially reducing the chance of becoming a victim of violent passengers, as well as from hijackers. These tactics will provide crewmembers with a good foundation in building self-protective behavior.

By virtue of their position, flight attendants have become responsible for the security and safety of commercial airline travel. Without any specialized survival training, they are expected to protect the pilots, passengers, aircraft and themselves. Many flight attendants continue to feel vulnerable to attack because many of the airlines have yet to train them effectively on how to defend themselves against a violent attack. Even in light of the security training requirements of the Aviation and Transportation Security Act of 2001 (USA), airlines have been reluctant to act decisively to provide comprehensive defensive training for flight attendants. In the United States, crewmembers can only hope that the self-defense provisions of the Homeland Security Act of 2002 will fulfill their expectations of true aircrew security training. Only time will tell.

Pilots, passengers, airlines and the government are asking flight attendants to accomplish a new and dangerous aspect of their job without the training to fulfill that responsibility. After 9/11, some flight attendants sought out self-defense training on their own accord. This is commendable considering there was not any guidance from the airlines or the government. Many crewmembers continue to feel vulnerable by the lack of direction of the airlines. We would like to see any fear these crewmembers are experiencing completely eliminated through realistic and thorough training. By incorporating concepts discussed in this book into their curriculum, airline training departments can provide an excellent base line for crewmember security training.

As flight crewmembers, we have also been discouraged by a lack of action by the airlines and the government on aircrew security training. Yet, all of us must recognize the enormity of the task airlines are faced with after 9/11. It is not an easy problem to solve in determining what levels of defensive training will be acceptable, especially if there is nothing for a comparison. If airlines were to follow the advice of all martial arts experts (who have somehow become self-anointed experts on aviation security), anything short of achieving a black belt is unacceptable. This is especially true if training was conducted at the 'expert's' training centers where they would reap all the financial benefits. No, it is much more complicated than that, and we need to recognize the issues that face the airlines. For example, what levels of defensive training will be sufficient for aircrews? How are the crews to be trained? Where will crews be trained? What type of self-defense training do they receive? Who will give the training? What happens if a crewmember does not want self-defense training? How will the airline regulate the training the crews receive? Will there be a policy regulating crewmember use of force? What are the liability issues of crewmembers using force against a combative passenger? These questions are important for consideration by both airlines and the government. Whatever crewmember security policies the airline institutes, they will probably be guided by government mandates. The policies will need to be reasonable in application and defensible in court. The bottom line is that the airlines need to determine what self-defensive plan will work the best for their flight attendants and pilots. One thing is certain; flight crews should not have to rely upon the outer rings (Chapter 1, Airline Security Model) of security for all of their protection. If the Richard Reid 'shoe bomber' incident proved anything to crewmembers, it is that security needs to be emphasized at all levels of aviation.[5]

Talking with Passengers and Basic Crewmember Safety

Two important aspects of tactical self-protection are the communication exhibited by crewmembers and their state of awareness. People notice if a person is alert or unaware to their presence and movements. This especially seems to be the case when someone wants to attack or harm you. Perpetrators will pay particular attention to your demeanor and your communication with them. Your stance as you face others is extremely important to self-protection because it conveys your preparedness. An uncaring or unconcerned demeanor and stance will indicate your vulnerability to attack. If you are conveying a self-assured stance and demeanor, you are indirectly telling others you are alert and capable. Being self-assured does not mean that you should be aggressive or rude.

A crewmember should always stand in a bladed stance while talking with passengers for several reasons, primarily to maintain your balance at all times. If you are standing in a bladed stance and someone pushes you, it is much easier to maintain your balance. To stand in a bladed stance, you face forward lining up both feet next to each other. Imagine a straight line drawn on the floor in front of you from right to your left that runs perpendicular to the direction you are looking. Spread your feet approximately shoulder width. With your dominant foot (your dominant foot is the right if you are right handed or left if you are left handed) step back so that your foot is approximately at a 45 degree angle from the imaginary straight line. Additionally, bend your knees slightly so you can maneuver quickly if needed.

Compare the way you normally stand to a bladed stance by conducting a short experiment. Stand as you normally would (feet apart, but directly under you) and have someone push you (not hard) at your chest. You may notice you will lose your balance easily. Now, try repeating the experiment in the bladed stance. If you do it correctly, you will find you are able to maintain your balance.

In addition to the balancing benefits of the bladed stance, you will convey through your body language that you are confident, capable, and willing to act decisively if forced into a confrontation. The way you stand is just a small part of how you need to broadcast to others your preparedness, or lack of it.

Not only is the way you stand important, but also the position of your hands. The hands should be kept between your waistline and lower chest area while talking to

Photo 12.1 Bladed stance

passengers. While keeping your hands up, clasp them gently or make small gestures with them, so passengers will think that you 'talk with your hands'. Placing your hands in a position to defend yourself allows you to save precious time if attacked by a passenger. The positioning of your hands will appear non-threatening to passengers if you do it correctly. At first, this may feel unnatural, but with practice it will become second nature and you will be ready and prepared to defend yourself.

Watch every passenger's hands while they are in your presence. If assaulted by a passenger, the attack would probably be accomplished with the use of their hands. If you watch the position of a passenger's hands as they talk to you, it will give you a definite advantage in knowing if an attack is coming. It is conceivable an attacker could kick you in the head, but the attack is more than likely coming from the attacker's hands. This assumption is not a certainty of course, as an attacker could give you a low kick. However, they will more than likely use their hands or use a weapon held in their hands while on an airliner.

Do not turn your back on a passenger. We also need to be realistic and accept the fact that there will be times we turn our back on a passenger. Do not make a habit of it and avoid doing it on a regular basis. Especially avoid turning your back when an upset or combative person is close to you. Turning your back is an invitation to be assaulted by them. What you are really saying by your body language is, 'go ahead hit me'. Reducing the opportunities for someone to assault a crewmember is something that takes practice and should become a part of everyday life for crews. Using proper crewmember safety tactics will deter an attack by an aggressor.

If someone is going to attack you with a weapon, other than a firearm, they will need to be in close enough to carry out the assault. Although difficult to accomplish in an aircraft, try to keep your distance from people. Try to stay at least an arm length away from passengers. This is not your arm length, but the passenger's arm length because if their arm is longer than yours is they can still assault you. Remember this equation, 'Distance = Time and Space to React'. Keeping your distance from a passenger will help to reduce the possibility of someone striking you. Again, we need to be realistic about crewmember life aboard a commercial airliner where passengers and flight attendants move back and forth down the 22-inch aisles. Herein lies the argument for crew camaraderie, looking after each other.

There are times when passengers will approach and come close to a crewmember with a question. Try to avoid allowing this to occur. It is okay to step back or move away from a person as they move closer to you. Often, when you step back from a passenger, it is normal for them to move toward you to maintain the closeness. If this occurs, remain aware of your surroundings and what is behind you. If you are moving back to keep your distance from a passenger and you back up against the aircraft door, your options for escape are limited. Avoid putting yourself into this predicament because if a passenger did attack you, your rearward movement options are non-existent. Before it gets to that point, raise your hand and politely, but firmly, say something to the effect of, 'Sir, I apologize, I hope you understand, but please do not get too close to me'. Most people will respond positively and stay back as you request, but if they do not, this is a signal of impending aggression on their part. Then, it is time to get firm and order them, 'Stay back!' in a loud voice that can be clearly heard by others on the aircraft. Be ready with your whistle and be prepared to defend yourself. This may appear somewhat aggressive, but we live in extraordinary times and you have a right to protect yourself. Let your common sense and good judgment guide you in this area, but realize your level of vulnerability.

We have all experienced people who are the 'touchy-feely' types. They like to touch you on the arm or shoulder while they are talking to you. You should not let anyone be close enough to touch you. If a person comes up behind you and you do not see them, as you become aware of their existence move away from them. Do not let anyone touch you as a touch could be a precursor to an assault. Do not allow an unknown person to touch you under any circumstance.

Be on guard and prepared under all circumstances to protect yourself from attack. Just because you are speaking with a woman or an elderly person does not mean they will not attempt to assault you. There is something in the human condition that people will sense about another when they are vulnerable to attack. It may be some sort of primal trait humans inherited through the ages. When someone is contemplating and waiting for an opportunity to attack, the attacker will act when he or she senses their victim is vulnerable. Conversely, the opposite is often true. People can sense when another person is prepared to defend himself or herself. Not appearing vulnerable to others may make the difference in not being attacked by an aggressor. Even hijackers would have to think twice about their mission if there is a planeload of flight attendants who are not leaving themselves open for attack. The tactics written in this section will work if you practice them and make them part of your routine. The old Boy Scout motto is not just a hollow phrase, but words of sage advice, 'Be Prepared'.

Do not make yourself deliberately vulnerable to attack by not adhering to sound principles of flight crew safety and tactics. Always standing in a bladed stance, properly positioning hands, watching the hands of others, keeping your distance from passengers, not letting anyone touch you, adhering to sound principles of crewmember safety, looking people in the eyes, and being observant send signals to others that your are prepared and can handle yourself. These fundamentals of flight crew tactics will go along way in protecting a crewmember and preparing them from those who think they can do with them what they want.

Cart in the aisle: Serving drinks/meals

A flight crewmember must be ready and willing to protect other crewmembers. The concept of 'I will watch your back if you watch mine', is the attitude crewmembers need to incorporate into their everyday thinking. This approach is beneficial to the crewmember team during periods of unavoidable vulnerability such as when the flight attendants are serving drinks or meals. On airlines that operate with more than one or two flight attendants, two will often serve meals and drinks from a cart pushed down the middle of the aisle of the aircraft. There are some obvious tactical disadvantages when the flight attendants serve seated passengers from a cart. First, their attention is diverted away from any possible danger behind them. Second, the situational awareness to the other parts of the aircraft is significantly reduced by the focused attention to their service duties. However, we can considerably reduce flight attendant risks by following a few simple tactical guidelines. The primary thing to remember is both flight attendants must watch behind the other for possible threats.

As just previously mentioned, when serving from a cart a flight attendant's attention is focused on their duties. Therefore, if a passenger approaches from behind them, they may not see them until they are tapping the flight attendant on the shoulder asking for another drink. At such a moment, teamwork needs to play a major part in the crewmember concept of security. If a passenger approaches a flight attendant from the rear, the other flight attendant who is in a better position to see them approaching says, 'behind you'. The flight attendant turns and faces the passenger. The flight attendant talking with the passenger should position themselves in a balanced bladed stance with their hands positioned correctly. They attempt to keep the passenger at more than the passenger's arm length while monitoring the passenger's hands. The flight attendant who pointed out the approaching passenger watches the exchange closely while remaining situationally aware of the aircraft, being ever vigilant to diversionary tactics. If needed, the supporting flight attendant should move the cart to allow the engaged flight attendant a path to retreat.

> If the passenger becomes physically aggressive, the monitoring flight attendant 'blows the whistle, enlists the aid of others, and buys time so the pilots can successfully land the aircraft'.

Disturbance in the back of the aircraft (not necessarily a physical fight)

Recognize hijackers may use deceptive actions to begin an aircraft takeover. Causing a disturbance to divert attention away from their actual intent is nothing new in offensive actions by organized militant groups. The crew should always remain vigilant to the possibility to any diversionary tactics of hijackers. When an incident begins (whatever it may be) in the cabin, it is essential that you stay aware of the environment around you. Do not let your guard down and completely focus on the incident unless there are other crewmembers that can stay vigilant and 'watch your back'.

The diversion could be a physical disturbance, a plan by terrorists to draw out law enforcement or others in the aircraft that want to assist the flight crew. Quickly, the hijackers would be able to identify the responders and may single them out for 'elimination' allowing them freedom to carry out their malevolent intentions. Be aware of such tactics if you ever come to the help of another crewmember. Be cautious and 'watch your back' carefully.

A hijacking could begin with a passenger feigning a heart attack or some other serious medical problem. The passenger could get everyone's attention and could divert the attention of the crewmembers away from other areas of the aircraft. The feigned medical problem may prompt at least one flight attendant into asking the pilots for entry into the flight deck to contact a medical guidance organization on the radio. The request by a flight attendant for entry into the flight deck would more than likely be granted by the pilots, reducing the number of flight attendants in the cabin by one. The hijackers could then spring into action neutralizing the two flight attendants in the rear galley one at a time. Dressed in flight attendant garb, one or two of the hijackers could proceed to the front of the aircraft without suspicion where they could intercept the flight attendant coming out of the reinforced flight deck door. As the flight deck door opens, the hijackers could forcibly enter the flight deck, kill the pilots with knives made from composite material they smuggled aboard in their carry-on baggage undetected through the security checkpoint at the airport. Meanwhile, other hijackers, seated in the first class section could block access to the front of the aircraft giving their hijacker friends time to takeover the flight deck unrestricted. The terrorist hijackers would now be in the flight deck, protected by the government mandated super reinforced doors that are now on all United States commercial airliners. How would you solve this dilemma?

It is imperative to stay aware of your environment and to direct other crewmembers to remain extra vigilant during high workload activity in the cabin. Your ability to remain aware of the environment around you is extremely important to your survival. Do not let an incident that demands a lot of attention lull you into becoming a victim. Just be aware that an incident in the cabin may be a diversion and could be staged by hijackers.

The flight attendant assigned to the first class section of the aircraft should not ever leave the front of the aircraft, unless it is transitory in nature, and in the case of extreme emergency. The only protection between the flight deck door and passengers is a flight attendant. Hijackers should never have any opportunity to gain unobstructed access to the flight deck. If the 'first' is in the back of the aircraft talking with their flight attendant friends, the flight deck door is dangerously unguarded. Nobody should have even the slightest chance to force entry into the flight deck. The 'first' should usually remain in the front of the aircraft to run interference on anyone who would attempt to gain unauthorized entry into the flight deck. If hijackers were to gain entry into the flight deck, it has been horribly proven that disastrous results will occur. If the 'first' attempted to stop an unauthorized entry, an ensuing scuffle, yelling, or whistle could alert the pilots and/or the other crewmembers to an incident in the front of the aircraft. If this were to occur, the pilots should immediately begin a descent to the nearest suitable airport where law enforcement can intervene. The protection of the aircraft and all aboard is dependent upon a team effort by all the crewmembers.

During a disturbance of any kind in the cabin, the first class flight attendant should stay in front of the aircraft and loiter near the flight deck door. To successfully accomplish this goal, the flight attendant assigned to the first class section of the flight should remain alert to the possibility of offensive actions that could occur during a disturbance in the cabin and prepare accordingly. This problem is worsened by a single flight attendant operation where the only flight attendant on board must respond to a medical (or other type of disturbance) emergency anywhere in the cabin. It would be wise and prudent for the single flight attendant to inform the pilots of the need to respond prior to actually responding, giving the pilots ample warning of the need for additional awareness to the situation.

Uncooperative or disruptive passenger seated

If a passenger refuses to stow his tray table or raise his seat, or causes any other minor disturbance, his or her actions can ultimately become a major incident. By adhering to the following tactics, a flight attendant can significantly avoid injury. As mentioned previously, during any incident involving a disturbance in the cabin, one should always remain vigilant to potential diversionary tactics of hijackers.

At some airlines, if a passenger refuses to cooperate with one flight attendant, then another will attempt to resolve the problem. [Author's note: The following tactics assume a minimum of three cabin crewmembers available in addressing the issue described.] For safety purposes, if a passenger fails to respond to a flight attendant's direction, the remaining two flight attendants should become involved. If the situation were to escalate into violence with the uncooperative passenger, the flight attendant initially involved would be able to 'blow the whistle, enlist the aid of others, and buy time so the pilots could safely land the airplane'.

For example, after being unable to get a passenger to follow directions to raise his seat, flight attendant #1 tells the other two flight attendants of the passenger's refusal to follow directions, the seat number, and any other pertinent information about the passenger. Flight attendant #1 calls the pilots on the interphone and lets them know a potential passenger disruptive incident may be developing in the cabin of the aircraft. The flight deck now goes into a 'lockdown mode' and the door will not be opened until the incident is resolved. Flight attendant #1 would guard the cockpit door in an attempt to protect the aircraft if the incident is a diversionary ploy by hijackers.

Number 2 and #3 flight attendants should approach the uncooperative passenger in an attempt to peacefully resolve the problem. Flight attendant #3 should be positioned two or three rows behind the passenger and should monitor the discussion between flight attendant #2 and the passenger in question.

Flight attendants #1 and #3 should remain vigilant to the environment in the front and back of the aircraft and be suspicious of diversionary disruptive tactics.

Flight attendant #2 should stay more than an arm length away from the uncooperative passenger and should begin a discussion with them. Before 9/11, many airline cabin trainers instructed flight attendants to move close to the passenger and get down on a knee to be at the passenger's eye level. This action was meant to demonstrate concern and interest in the passenger and was obviously public relations driven. This approach places the crewmembers in a vulnerable position to injury. The authors strongly recommend crewmembers disregard this procedure.

If the uncooperative passenger physically attacks flight attendant #2, flight attendant #3 'blows the whistle, enlists the aid of others, and buys time for the pilots to safely land the airplane'.

Flight attendant #1, stationed at the front of the aircraft, should also blow the whistle, thereby assuring the pilots have become aware of an attack or other serious incident in the cabin.

Flight attendant #3 assists flight attendant #2 with the attacking passenger. Flight attendant #1, after blowing the whistle, will call the pilots on the interphone, and if necessary, will use the public address system (PA) to enlist the aid of others to assist flight attendants #2 and #3.

Because of the possibility of hijacker diversionary tactics, flight attendant #1 stays aware of the surroundings, keeps the PA microphone in hand in case it may be needed to enlist the aid of others.

If the situation did not become physical and the passenger cooperated with the request of flight attendant #2, then the incident is closed. However, if the uncooperative passenger continued to refuse the request, the flight attendants should not force the issue and escalate the incident into a physical confrontation. The flight attendant may be 100 per cent correct in trying to get the uncooperative passenger to adhere to the aviation regulations, but will not be able to perform normal duties if injured by an irate passenger. Do not enforce a regulation to the point of escalating the incident into violence. Be polite, firm and explain the need for the passenger to adhere to the regulation, but do not subject yourself to violence.

Important actions during a physical confrontation or serious threat

Unless you have been continually training for the last several years in defensive tactics, you will lose a hand-to-hand confrontation with trained terrorists. However, the authors have attempted to assist you, the crewmember, by developing a survival mindset. You must have a warrior spirit to survive a violent confrontation. We need such a spirit when faced with a physical threat. We may become discouraged when faced with a violent encounter, but not to the point of giving up our lives. When a person gives up, they will lose whatever they are trying to accomplish, and if it is a fight for their life, then they are as good as dead. The authors encourage you to take self-defense lessons to greatly improve your ability to survive a violent encounter. You do not need to be a martial arts expert, but a basic understanding of self-defense will always be a big advantage.

When physically confronted by a combative passenger, or a terrorist hijacker, you should follow some basic survival rules. Attempt to repel a physical attack as much as possible through whatever means to survive. If that means biting, scratching, gouging, kicking or any other unfair method of fighting to win and survive, then that is exactly what you ought to do. Many people have been taught that 'there are rules' when engaging in a physical confrontation. The first thing we need to understand about repelling a violent attack on-board an aircraft is that there are no rules. There is no such thing as a fair fight.

Flight crewmembers should all have a whistle at all times while assigned to a flight. Crewmembers will blow their whistles when there is an assault on a crewmember, or during a hijacking attempt. A whistle is naturally loud, ear piercing, and is an effective tool to alert the pilots of a disturbance in the cabin.

If hijackers were to gain access to the flight deck as they did on 9/11, then all aboard will certainly perish. Flight crewmembers must defend the aircraft by preventing the flight deck from being breached. You must consider that this is a life or death defense of your life and the life of the passengers. Do not allow an unauthorized person access the flight deck.

Whenever you are confronted by a physical confrontation or a serious threat, you should make a loud disturbance using your voice, or if possible, blow the whistle. Doing so can alert other crewmembers (deadheading, commuting, or working the flight), law enforcement officers, and passengers who can assist you. Follow these general steps when a passenger forces you into a physical confrontation:

1. Defend yourself while yelling, 'STOP!'
2. Blow the whistle or yell.
3. Enlist the aid of others.
4. Buy time so that the pilots can safely land the aircraft.

Flight Attendant or Pilot Taken Hostage

As we have been emphasizing repeatedly in this chapter, defense of the flight deck is the defense of the aircraft and all aboard. Becoming a hostage of an armed violent individual is a difficult thing to consider. Yet, we should recognize a possible tactic on the part of hijackers would be to take a pilot or flight attendant hostage in an effort to gain access to the flight deck. Defending the flight deck against a hijacker is a desperate situation that has no easy solutions or answers. Nevertheless, what is certain and absolute, is that crewmembers must defend the aircraft by defending the flight deck. To allow an organized terrorist hijacker to gain access to the flight deck is a ticket to your death.

If you recognize the situation materializing on the aircraft is a hijacking, you should take action immediately. For example, if you saw a flight attendant being taken hostage at the other end of the aircraft, blow the whistle as loud as you possibly can. Giving an early alert to the pilots by blowing your whistle is one method in preventing a successful hijacking. The pilots should begin an emergency descent as soon as possible. The quick response to the whistle at the first sign of danger should give you and everyone else on the aircraft the possibility of making it to the ground safely. Making it to the ground safely is extremely important because it means your aircraft will not be used as a guided missile to kill innocent people. Keeping the aircraft from falling into the wrong hands also means the aircraft will not be shot down by a military fighter jet. Any way you look at, if the aircraft comes into the possession of hijackers, your death, and all those aboard, will shortly follow.

Photo 12.2 Flight attendant taken hostage

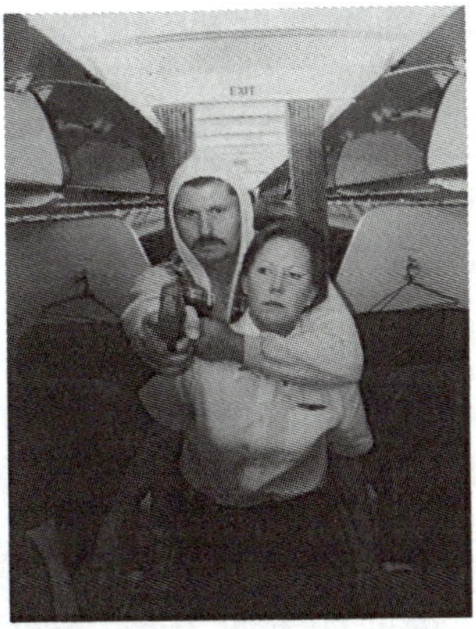

There are no hard and fast rules when dealing with a terrorist hijacker. If taken hostage, indicate cooperation but begin brainstorming for ways to stop them. The slimmest of opportunity may be your only chance to take advantage of the situation and stay alive. You are in a dangerous dilemma where there may not be any clear indication of escape. If a coordinated effort can be accomplished with another crewmember, then do it. If you do not have anyone but yourself to stop access to the flight deck, then you need to do what you have to do to stop it.

Develop an understanding with all crewmembers that the flight deck will not be assessed by a hijacker(s). Crewmembers must all be in the same determined frame of mind in preventing unauthorized access to the flight deck. We hope this is why you are reading this book, so you can prepare and devise methods of action before hand, giving you a mental plan to prevent a flight deck intrusion. Waiting until a hijacking occurs to think about how you are going to defend the flight deck is too late. Regardless of seniority or time on the job, all crewmembers must understand and agree a hijacker will not gain access to the flight deck under any conditions.

Before 9/11, the threat of a suicide hijacking never entered crewmembers' minds. Common strategy methods called for complete cooperation with hijackers. What every crewmember in the world needs to remember is that those heroic crewmembers on those doomed hijacked flights gave their lives on 9/11 in the line of duty. As horrible as it is, all crewmembers need to learn the lessons of the new world they work and live in. We owe it to the memories of those who perished to never let such a horrible event to occur again. To accomplish this goal, airline crewmembers must drastically change the way they go about their business.

Your survival depends upon being mentally prepared to overcome hijackers. If you can recognize, and most importantly, accept the rules of the new world of air transportation we live in, your chance of surviving a suicide hijacking will increase dramatically. Recognition of the fact that you may be taken hostage by a hijacker to gain access to the flight deck should begin to mentally prepare you for the possibility of such an event. The development of defensive tactics with other crewmembers to prevent hijacker access to the flight deck will greatly assist you in defense of the remainder of the aircraft. Keep calm and look within yourself to formulate methods to prevent flight deck access by hijackers. All crewmembers need to realize that the pilots or flight attendants will not open the flight deck door under any circumstances for a hijacker.

Cabin Security Coordinator

From training and regulations, most crewmembers are aware of the positions and duties of the Ground Security Coordinator (GSC) (ground personnel) and the In-flight Security Coordinator (ISC) (the Captain). In thinking outside the box, we propose the creation of a Cabin Security Coordinator (CSC) (lead flight attendant). The justification for this position comes because of new security measures in effect stemming from the hijacking events of 9/11. Under any abnormal circumstance, the flight deck crew will not, more than likely, leave the flight deck or allow the flight deck door to be opened;

therefore, flight attendants must physically manage whatever situation is occurring in the cabin. Communication with the flight deck may be limited, or non-existent, particularly when a serious threat exists aboard and aircraft. Therefore, a single point of contact and leadership is needed in the cabin and we feel this person should be the lead flight attendant.

The position of CSC does not contradict in any way, the duties and responsibilities of the ISC (or GSC), but rather serves to enhance and support those responsibilities. If communications on a given flight were normal, the ISC would coordinate with the CSC during flight in the same manner as with the GSC on the ground. The CSC would provide leadership and direction to the flight attendants in the cabin should communication with the flight deck be restricted or impossible.

In addition to normal duties of the lead flight attendant, the CSC would:

- Brief all flight attendants in the crew on security-related items and updates during the pre-flight briefing;
- Be the point of contact with the flight deck crew whenever communications with the flight deck are needed and possible;
- Be the coordinator between the GSC and ISC regarding removal of undesirable passengers during the boarding process;
- Supervise and direct flight attendants in the crew during any incident involving disruptive passengers or sky rage, or any other incident with a potential for violence;
- Enlist the aid of, and direct law enforcement officers (LEO) and/or willing passengers as appropriate, to assist in a physical confrontation with an aggressor;
- Supervise and direct flight attendants and/or others in use of force and restraints;
- Assure medical attention is provided for those injured in a confrontation, including an aggressor, if applicable;
- Assess threat level in the cabin during and after an event has occurred;
- If necessary, direct a medical triage;
- Assess damage to the cabin and/or aircraft after an incident and relay information to the flight deck crew, if possible;
- Ensure witness statements are obtained following an incident in the cabin; and,
- Write a comprehensive report chronicling the incident.

We firmly believe the duties specified above, and the change in the security environment in which crewmembers operate, justify the creation of the position of Cabin Security Coordinator. Additional training would be required for this position and should be incorporated into existing flight attendant training curriculum.

Deadheading or Commuting Crewmembers

Deadheading or commuting to work on a flight is commonplace for many crewmembers. At some point or another, most crewmembers will have to deadhead somewhere. You are an available resource to aid the assigned crew and should remain aware of the cabin environment. Unless, you are sitting next to another crewmember that can remain aware of the surroundings, do not slip off into a nap, especially while traveling in uniform. Since anyone in uniform could be threat to hijackers, you may be unprepared for the danger you may have to face if you are found unaware. If a violent hijacking takeover were to occur during the flight, you may be one of their first victims to be killed. This may serve two purposes for the hijackers; eliminate you as a potential threat and instilling a state of horror that petrifies everyone on-board into inaction, thereby allowing the hijackers a free reign. Do not allow this to happen to you.

As a potential resource to the crew, you must remain alert to assist them if needed. Your assistance could be the difference between life and death if a hijacking attempt were to occur. An extra set of hands, feet, eyes, and a brain could be enough to push the odds into the favor of survival during a violent hijacking attempt.

General Tactics

Preferably, travel out of uniform. This may not always be practical because on arrival at the airport you may need to report immediately to work, or turn the flight around and fly it back from where it came. You can reduce your risk for identification as a crewmember if you are not wearing your uniform. In a small way, you are undercover and could be an important resource to the crew.

If traveling out of uniform you should be discreet, with whom you discuss your employment. Do not discuss your employment with the passenger seated next to you because the person (like a hijacker) may not be the person you think they are. The nice man next to you, who just appears interested in you, may in fact be a hijacker who is gathering useful information for his cause. Do not discuss your employment with anyone at the airport except people you know, and then quietly and discreetly.

Remain aware that hijackers may plan methodically and attempt to collect information so they can eliminate any potential threats. It is has been widely reported in the press that the hijackers from 9/11 were all dressed in average western wear and acted normally. Nothing in their behavior caused suspicion, which made them just like anyone else on the flight. There will no doubt be solo hijacking attempts like the shoe bomber Richard Reid, who may have acted on his own initiative.[6] Do not volunteer information about yourself to anyone you do not know, and who may in fact be plotting to kill you.

Be aware of those who are seated around you for any suspicious and/or unusual behavior. We keep getting back to the awareness issue, which is extremely important in all of the security issues we have discussed thus far. Staying aware of your surroundings cannot be emphasized enough in this book. Without remaining aware, the flight attendants on American Airlines flight 63 would not have noticed Reid before he attempted to ignite the explosives in his shoes. Another person who deserves recognition is the flight instructor who noticed something unusual about the man the press has termed the 20th hijacker. The instructor wondered why Zacharias Moussaoui was interested in learning how to fly a commercial jet, but showed no interest in taking off or landing. The instructor reported his suspicions to the FBI in August 2001.[7] Moussaoui was quickly arrested by the FBI and later charged as a conspirator in the 9/11 hijacking case.

If you are deadheading or commuting, you should position yourself tactically to be of assistance to the crew. However, your personal safety comes first. Therefore, if you are in uniform, the safest place for you to sit is at the window seat. If a hijacker wanted to eliminate you, he may not be able to do it quickly since you are slightly more inaccessible than if you were in the aisle seat. Sitting at a window seat gives you a little bit of an advantage, it may be just enough. Remember the equation from earlier in the chapter, Distance = time and space to react? There are times when a person needs to use every advantage they can to succeed, and this could be one of those times, where sitting in a window seat may make the difference.

If traveling out of uniform, the best tactical position for you to assist the crew would be in the aisle seat. Ask the ticket agent to seat you in an aisle seat for better access to the aisle. They cannot always give you what you request, but it is definitely worth asking. Sitting in an aisle seat allows you to easily get up and assist the crew if the situation dictates it.

If you are in civilian clothes, be sure to identify yourself discreetly to the cabin crew, and make sure they know where you are seated. If the flight crew has no idea who you are and a security incident begins to occur, and you get up to assist them, they might misidentify you as a hostile. Not only should you be a team player while working a flight, every effort should be made to help if the situation dictates it. However, since everyone needs to be tactically on the same level, discreetly identifying yourself to the working crew gives him or her more options if they need your help.

Awareness does not begin when you get on the airplane, but should become a way of life. Developing an awareness mindset takes practice. You must make an effort to focus continually on the things around you so that eventually you become aware of the things around you automatically. With this approach in mind, before gate agents board the passengers, watch the passengers in the boarding area to detect unusual or suspicious behavior. Do not stare at people. Be discreet, and do not make your observant behavior too obvious to those around you. If you become too obvious, it could cause others to become suspicious of you, resulting in your becoming a target of suspicion to law enforcement. In addition, you may unknowingly identify yourself to the hijackers as a potential threat to them.

Conclusion: Why Tactics?

Many fine police officers have died in the line of duty for a lack of proper tactics. Their unfortunate deaths have resulted in the development of many police tactics to prevent further deaths to other officers. On 9/11, flight crews died violent deaths at the hands of terrorist hijackers. Just as police have learned from the unfortunate deaths of fellow officers, crewmembers worldwide should learn valuable lessons from the deaths of crewmembers on 9/11. As the development of police tactics stemming from the experience of others has helped save additional lives of officers, we contend that the *development of flight crew tactics has the same potential to save lives*.

Will the aviation industry learn the difficult lessons of terrorism? Regardless of the actions or inactions of the aviation industry, crewmembers need to honor those crewmembers that lost their lives on 9/11 by applying tactics and techniques to prevent another such catastrophe. The deaths of crewmembers at the hands of terrorists must not be repeated. Their deaths must mean more than just financial reorganization of the airline industry. Crewmembers must not wait for the airline industry or the government to develop methods of self-defense because it may never occur.

If flight crews use tactics, they will better understand their respective roles in this new era of terrorism. The times have changed, and like it or not, crewmembers must change with them. The security training codified in the United States' Aviation and Transportation Security Act and the Homeland Security Act signaled a significant change in aviation philosophy. This legislation has legitimized a crewmember's right to defend against a brutal attack. Crewmembers do not have to become victims again! We are confident that if you follow the guidelines we have laid out in this chapter, they will serve as a baseline of basic tactical knowledge that will further your understanding of pro-active self-defensive behavior.

Tactics will help flight crews feel more confident in their own abilities to detect and deter a terrorist hijacking. After 9/11, we spoke with many flight attendants and pilots who were very frightened of what could happen to them without self-defensive training. Many flight attendants at airlines across the world sought out their own individual self-defense training. These crewmembers felt good about their new skills and were more at ease while at work. Defensive training is a definite advantage when the time comes to defend yourself against an attack. Nevertheless, it is not enough to learn how to give somebody a karate chop to the neck. You can be a tenth degree black belt in any specialty of the martial arts, compete in tournaments and win trophies, but could get seriously assaulted by turning your back on the wrong person. We are talking life or death here, and if you lose control of an aircraft to a hijacker, it means you will die. Although we encourage everyone to learn self-defense, that alone will not guarantee your survival. Incorporating self-defense into an overall tactical approach in the way you work is most desirable.

Well-trained flight crews will positively affect public confidence in airline security. The public expects and deserves to be protected by the airline they choose to fly. When the airlines advertise they are training the flight crews in defensive tactics, it raises the confidence level of the traveling public. The result is what all crewmembers want: the traveling public to return to the airlines and to enjoy the freedom of unimpeded and uneventful travel throughout the world.

Throughout this chapter, we have attempted to touch upon some of the things to consider while preparing to defend yourself and the airplane. In fact, many other tactics are being used by crewmembers worldwide. We encourage you to continue to look for the security weaknesses of airline travel and find new and creative ways to close any gaps in safety and security.

Notes

1. Interview with Sabah Khodada, PBS, *Frontline*, 14 October 2001.
2. Elliott, Michael, Special Report: Hate Club, *Time Magazine*, 12 November 2001.
3. Interview with Sabah Khodada, PBS, *Frontline*, 14 October 2001.
4. *Webster's New World Dictionary*, 1980.
5. Footwear focus of airport security after man tries to ignite explosives, Associated Press, 24 December 2001.
6. Ibid.
7. Moussaoui's flight instructor feared jet could be used as a weapon, Associated Press, 21 December 2001.

Chapter 13

Unconventional Self-Defense

***WARNING:* THE SELF-DEFENSE TECHNIQUES DISCUSSED IN THIS CHAPTER ARE FOR DEMONSTRATION PURPOSES ONLY AND NOT MEANT TO REPLACE COMPETENT PERSONAL INSTRUCTION.**

Introduction

Crewmembers must not only be mentally prepared for violent confrontations, but must also be physically prepared. In this chapter, we will identify items on the aircraft that can be used as unconventional weapons, review areas of the body that are susceptible to pain, identify various empty-handed defensive methods, and demonstrate methods to come to the aid of others. It is not feasible to expect all crewmembers to train to the point of being experts in self-defense. However, we strongly believe crewmembers should receive training in basic self-defense, and attend recurrent training sessions to assist in maintaining a minimum level of skill. This approach should be a condition of a crewmember's employment at an airline. Learning basic self-defense is not rocket science, but does require effort and the desire to learn on the part of the crewmember.

Our belief is that all crewmembers deserve to be trained in self-defense and not dismissed by the 'experts' as being incapable of learning at least a minimum of self-protective techniques. The resultant training to come out of ATSA (USA) in 2001 and implemented throughout the majority of airlines discouraged comprehensive self-defense training for crewmembers. This point has become a very contentious issue with crewmembers in the United States since their views were based upon the events of 9/11. Crewmembers worldwide deserve better security training than most of them received by their respective airlines. Crewmembers are *the last line of defense* for the survival of passengers. If they fail at this task, the alternative is for the aircraft to be intercepted by an air force fighter jet and shot down, or experience a reenactment of the events of 9/11. Neither of these two alternatives are acceptable.

Crewmembers should not accept the limited *in the box* thinking that makes them vulnerable to attack and injury. The best method to protect against attack is by being prepared against a worst-case scenario. To accomplish this goal, a crewmember should have training in self-defense, as well as a workable, up-to-date knowledge of airline security issues.

Some techniques and tactics we will discuss in this chapter are extremely violent and intended for discussion and illustration purposes only. *Nothing will take the place of actual instruction, and this chapter will not replace hands-on training. Therefore, we will not attempt to train you on unconventional makeshift weapons, or on how to deploy them. If faced with a situation where you need to employ an unconventional makeshift weapon for your defense, you are truly in a desperate condition and will have to rely upon the instinctive use of any makeshift weapon.* The use of an unconventional makeshift weapon should be evident to you, or anyone else, when faced with a violent incident like the hijackings on 9/11. *READ THE CHAPTER ON FLIGHT CREW USE OF FORCE AND THE LEGAL RAMIFICATIONS OF USING FORCE INAPPROPRIATELY CLOSELY.*

In a life or death situation, all types of force should be a consideration for survival. The subject matter we will be discussing is unpleasant and may make you ill contemplating the use of unconventional makeshift weapons against another human being. Yet, a proper mental frame of mind is necessary to use a makeshift weapon for defensive purposes. Your survival or that of another crewmember may depend using a makeshift weapon against a violent attacker. The bottom line is, either you want to survive, will do anything to accomplish this goal, or you are willing to die at the hands of cowardly murders. We hope you will never be in a situation where your options for survival are taking extreme acts as described in this chapter. Crewmembers should be mentally and physically capable beforehand to deal with a deadly situation if it occurred on the aircraft. A deadly confrontation is not a place you want to figure out how to defend yourself. It is important for you to realize that your only option for survival may be to recognize the potential in deploying makeshift weapons for survival.

We hope this chapter, along with the others in book, will help you to understand your personal value and give you the knowledge to help you survive extremely difficult and violent circumstances. Knowing and understanding your defensive options will increase your odds at surviving an extremely violent confrontation. We do not guarantee that the information in this chapter will protect you from injury, but in a desperate confrontation, even some knowledge about protecting yourself is better than none.

Personal Safety Considerations

Many defensive methods exist for crewmembers to use for their protection. For emphasis, we will briefly summarize basic tactics covered in Chapter 12 because we believe they are important concepts for you to grasp. This approach may be somewhat redundant, but fits into the self-protective approach we are attempting to develop in this chapter. Tactics we want to emphasize include:

- *The way you stand:* An important part in tactical self-protection is how you face others and communicate with them. People notice if another person is alert to their presence or unaware of their movements, especially in the event someone wants to attack or harm you.

- Your stance is extremely important in self-protection. The primary reason for establishing and maintaining a bladed stance is for balance. Additionally, through the balancing benefit of the bladed stance, your body language sends the message you are aware, confident, capable and willing to act decisively if need be. You should *always stand in a bladed stance while talking with passengers.*

Photo 13.1 Bladed stance

- *Hand positioning:* Keeping your hands above your waistline in a non-threatening manner will correctly position them to defend against an attack. Doing this every time you talk with a passenger, gives you the extra time needed to respond in case of a violent attack. A simple tactical method, it can easily be accomplished in a non-threatening manner while talking with passengers.
- *Observe hands of others:* An attacker will use his or her hands to hurt or kill you. As simple as watching the hands of others may appear, failure to follow this advice may be detrimental to your health. Either empty handed, or with a weapon, the hands are used to attack. Staying aware of the location of a passenger's hands can give you the added time to respond to an attack.
- *Do not turn your back on others:* We need to be realistic here. You are a crewmember on an airliner within confined spaces. However, do not make yourself an easy target for attack. Turning your back on an angry or intoxicated passenger is like saying to them, 'go ahead, hit me, its okay'. Avoid making yourself an easy target for a potential hijacker (or sky rage bent passenger) by turning your back on them.

- *Do not let anyone touch you:* If a person can touch you, he or she can easily attack and overcome you. If you can be touched, you are in the zone for an attack.

Weapons Available to YOU

Your body parts

We all have readily available weapons built into our bodies that we can use for self-defense. When faced with dire circumstances we must be willing and able to do what we must to survive.

Again, we are not advising you on how to employ your 'built in' weapons, but are pointing out the benefits of knowing that they are available to you. We have trained airline crews in the use of these and other self-defensive methods. The following are some examples of how your body parts can be used as weapons against an attacker.

- *Head:* Head butting frontward and/or backward against the face of an attacker can be very effective when in close proximity to their face, such as a bear hug from behind. Be prepared for an injury to your head caused from using your head as a defensive weapon. When you use your head against an attacker's face, you may sustain a cut to your head, probably from one or more of their teeth. Even a small cut to the head may bleed a lot, and although unsettling, it will not prevent you from defending yourself. A forward head butt should be attempted using your forehead area to strike the opponent and you should avoid impact on your nose and/or eye areas. (See Photo 13.2)
- *Teeth:* Biting is another effective method to cause pain to an attacker who may have your subdued. A human bite can cause excruciating pain and will eventually lead to an infection of the area that was bitten.
- *Forearm:* The forearm is an effective weapon in an up-close situation with an attacker. With the proper technique, a forearm strike can deliver a powerful blow to an attacker who is in close proximity to you. A blow delivered by the forearm to the nose, eyes, cheek, or neck of an opponent can be devastating. (Photo 13.3)
- *Hands:* Your hands are great for grabbing, twisting, pushing, pulling, slugging to the stomach/diaphragm area, and to deliver palm strikes. Avoid using your fist to the boney part of the face of an attacker because of the potential of injury to your hand. Palm strikes are the safest method for you to use to avoid an injury your hand and wrist, and can be powerful if delivered properly. Notice in Photos 13.4 and 13.5 that the palm strike began with the open palm at waist height and is delivered in conjunction with a twist of the hips towards the opponent for additional power. In these photos, the flight attendant has secured the attacker's arms by reaching over them with her left arm, preventing the attacker from being able to dodge her right-handed palm strike.

Photo 13.2 Rearward head butt

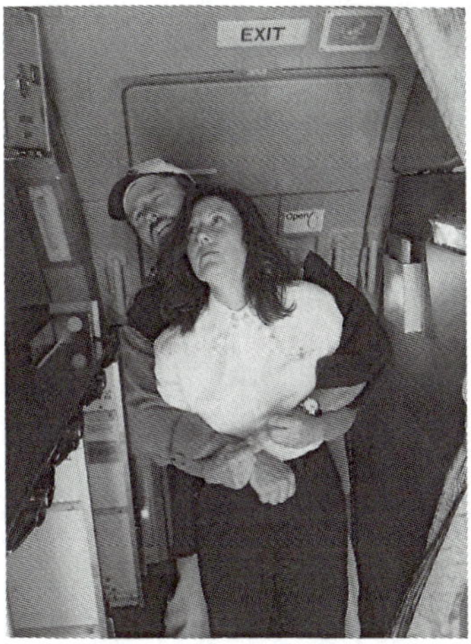

Photo 13.3 Forearm strike

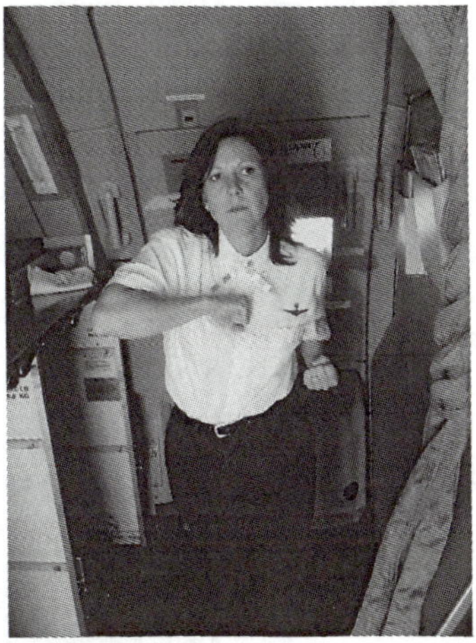

Photos 13.4 and 13.5 Palm strike in action

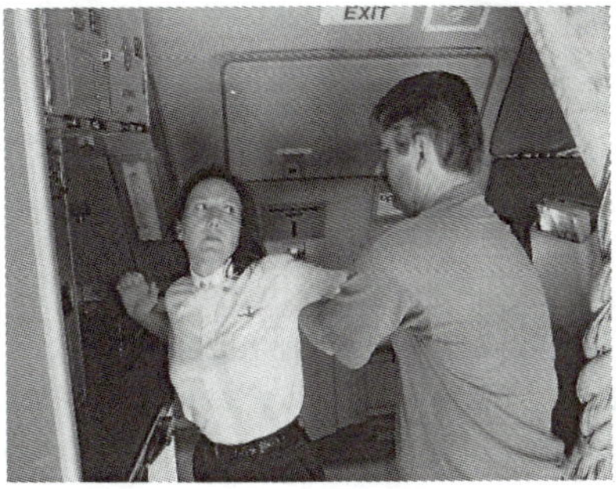

- *Fingers and Thumbs:* A finger or a thumb forced into the eyes and throat of an attacker can be disabling to them. Caution should be used if you try poking your fingers hard into the eyes of an attacker because you may break a finger, limiting your ability to defend yourself. Instead of using your fingers to poke, gouging at the eyes will reduce the risk of breaking a finger. Be aware that anytime you place your hands (or other body parts) in close proximity to your opponent's facial area, you are in danger of their use of teeth to protect themselves. In Photo 13.6, the flight attendant, in a chokehold by the attacker, has reached with her left hand behind his back and used her fingers in his eye sockets to pull his head backwards. If she placed her left thigh behind his knees, pulling his head backward in this manner and lifting his right leg with her right arm would cause him to fall away from her.

Photo 13.6 Finger gouging to the eyes

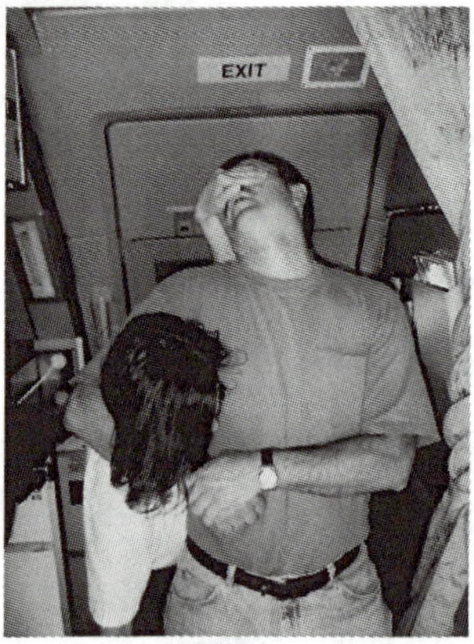

- *Knees:* Knees can be used effectively to an attacker's face when the attacker's face is at knee level, or to his groin area when up close. As with the kick, be careful when kneeing to the groin of a man, because of the natural protective tendencies of males to their groin. It may be a good diversionary tactic to get the attacker's attention in protecting his groin, then strike with your knuckles to his or her throat or deliver a palm strike to his face.
- *Feet:* Kicks should be delivered with the ball of the feet to the knees of the attacker when they are standing, or to the rib cage area and face when he or she is on their knees. Kicks must be delivered swiftly while maintaining balance. Although powerful, kicking is a vulnerable method to use because if the attacker gains control of your leg, he or she can take you down to the floor quickly and very hard. We also discourage a kick to the groin of a male, unless there is no other choice. Again, most men are very protective of this area, and once your foot is at this level, the attacker can grab your foot, putting you into a vulnerable position to be injured. A knee to the groin is a much better option in the confines of an aircraft. If you do choose to kick the attacker, it is much safer for you to

kick no higher than the attacker's knees. Kicks to the shin, calf and ankles can cause pain and some immobility.

Unconventional Makeshift Weapons

Unconventional makeshift weapons should only used as a last resort against an attacker who is attempting to takeover the aircraft, cause a death, or other serious injury to a crewmember, or another person.

Makeshift weapons are weapons we will not attempt to teach you how to use on an attacker. However, they are readily available to you in case you need them in a desperate situation. This is where a fair fight will not be an option!

As a sober reminder, some of the very same weapons we are discussing were reportedly used by terrorists in the training camps of Iraq before the toppling of Saddam Hussein's regime, as well as other terrorist training camps throughout the world.[1] *Many of these very same makeshift weapons can be easily taken through security checkpoints without suspicion and brought aboard an aircraft where they can be used against you!*

On your person

- *Pens, pencils* – Very effective as stabbing weapons to the eyes and throat, stomach, heart, or lungs (soft tissues) of a violent attacker.
- *Keys* – Not always readily available, but they can be used to slice or poke into the eyes, throat, stomach, and groin. Keys are not a very practical weapon because of their size and difficulty in grasping, but an option if nothing else is available.
- *Sprays* – Nose sprays, perfume, breath sprays, deodorants, foot sprays, when given time to access can be used to temporarily blind the attacker so he can be subdued. The effectiveness of blinding an opponent was highlighted during the attacks on 9/11 when some of the hijackers used hair dye in small plastic spray bottles to blind crewmembers during the aircraft takeover phase.
- *Small flashlights* – Held in the fist, with the bottom of the flashlight pointing downward, can be used as a blunt striking instrument much like a kubaton to the eyes, face, throat, neck, stomach or other bodily areas.(*A kubaton is a small weapon used in martial arts. It is usually metal and approximately six to eight inches long and about a ½-inch in diameter.*) For more information on how this weapon is used, refer to any of the martial arts training manuals available on the open market, or seek out professional instruction.

On the flight deck

In a situation where someone forces their way into the flight deck, pilots should be prepared to do what must be done to defend it. This is an obvious lethal force situation where the pilots must do anything necessary to defend against hijacker(s) who want to take over the aircraft. *The number one priority is not to let the aircraft be taken over by hijackers. The pilots must survive to get the aircraft safely onto the ground.*

- *Pens, pencils* – A very effective weapon for stabbing into the eyes or throat of an attacker.
- *Large flashlights* – Grab the flashlight by the lens and use it as a club.
- *Crash axe* – A very sharp tool, but the pilots must have the time to access the weapon. Caution must be used not to injure the other pilot or to damage needed flight deck components. Accessing the crash axe may be difficult when a hijacker is forcing his or her way into the flight deck. Additionally, a trained attacker can easily defend against the crash axe in the confines of a flight deck. The fact that the crash axe is mandatory equipment aboard commercial aircraft is not a secret. Terrorists are no doubt aware of the existence of the crash axe and will be prepared to defend against it. This weapon is the most lethal available to unarmed pilots, but its use is mostly impractical due to the confines of most aircraft flight decks. Instead of swinging the axe, grab it with one hand close to the head of the axe and the other on mid-handle, and employ it using very short, jabbing motions.
- *Landing gear pins* – Heavy, bulky and awkward, but an option as an impact weapon.
- *Extinguishers* – Halon sprayed into the face of an attacker would take his or her breath away and temporarily blind them, giving you time to subdue him or her. However, lets review the basics of how a halon extinguisher works. Halon removes the available oxygen surrounding the area of the fire in an effort to starve it of oxygen, and thus extinguishing it. Anyone around the spray dispersion would also have difficulty breathing, which of course would include you. The loss of oxygen in the flight deck would force the pilots to don their oxygen masks, making them unable to subdue the aggressor effectively. With oxygen masks donned, pilots can use the public address (PA) system on the aircraft to enlist the aid of others on the aircraft to come to their assistance on the flight deck.
  The extinguisher could also be used as an impact weapon, but full bottles of halon are heavy and difficult to handle. Additional danger could exist if the head of the extinguisher were to break off. Not only would all the contents of the halon extinguisher immediately enter the flight deck, the metal bottle would become a projectile, inflicting severe injury to anyone unlucky enough to be in the way. Although, using halon extinguishers have their advantages, the negative outweighs the positive and should only be used as a last resort.

In the cabin

- *Galley items* – A full can of soda could be used as an impact weapon against an attacker. Wine bottles, ice tools, coffee pots, hot coffee and peanuts are all available in the galley. (Do not laugh! Peanuts pushed all the way into an eyeball with the thumb are very effective.)
- *Seat cushions and blankets* – Both can be used as makeshift defensive shields to be used against knives or clubs. Blankets can be used as an offensive weapon to assist another crewmember by throwing it over the head of an attacker and pulling backward quickly. See *Enlisting the Aid of Others* at the end of this chapter.
- *Emergency equipment* – Seatbelt extenders can be used for choking and striking, fire extinguishers as impact weapons and blinding agents.
- *Baggage* – Light passenger carry-on baggage can be used as a striking weapon. Small carry-on baggage is mostly ineffective as a weapon, but is an option. Laptops and briefcases can be used as shield against edged weapons.
- *Passenger items* – Belts, ties, panty hose, T-shirts, etc., can be used to restrain an attacker. They can also be used to choke an opponent.

Hitting Where it Hurts

The facial and neck areas – eyes, nose and throat, – are vulnerable areas that are sensitive and can cause a great deal of pain if struck. When defending against a vicious opponent, these and other sensitive areas are vital targets that could mean the difference between life and death.

- *Eyes* – Gouging your fingers or thumbs into the eyes will damage and possibly blind an attacker; therefore, the eyes must be considered primary targets when faced with a serious bodily threat against you, other crewmembers and/or the aircraft. Again, avoid jamming hard with your fingers because you could possibly break one or more fingers against the face or head of the attacker.
- *Nose area* – A hard palm or forearm strike to the nose area will cause severe pain and watering of the eyes. A broken or bleeding nose could be the result of a hard palm strike, and is naturally very painful. The pain you inflicted upon the attacker may give you the time needed to subdue, or to escape where you can enlist the aid of others.
- *Throat* – A knuckle jab to the throat can cause breathing difficulty, and thus deflate the aggression of an attacker. A hard strike to this area may cause severe physical damage to the throat, which possibly could result in his death.
- *Groin* – The groin area of a male is particularly vulnerable to injury and can either be kicked, struck with a fist or an object, or grabbed and squeezed hard. Remember, most men are naturally protective of this area, but it should be a consideration if the opportunity presents itself.

The Whistle!

The simple police whistle has been around for many, many years and has served as a universal alert for police and others. It is loud and catches the attention of everyone in the surrounding area. Have you ever been in a stadium with 30,000 screaming fans and still heard the referee's whistle from the field? It is a simple, but effective method to get the attention of those all around.

If a whistle were blown in the back galley of a single deck jet, pilots, flight attendants and passengers would all hear it. If any flight attendant blows the whistle, all other flight attendants on the aircraft should also blow their whistles to relay. This process not only provides signals throughout the aircraft, but also acknowledges that the original signal was heard. Upon hearing the whistle, the pilots should respond by initiating a descent to the nearest suitable airport.

The whistle is simple, cheap and easy to use. Most everyone has blown a whistle at some time in their life and knows how it works. All cabin crewmembers should have a whistle and have it available for use on every flight.

The use of the whistle is the fastest, surest manner in which to alert all cabin crewmembers as well as the flight deck crew. Therefore, *at the first serious sign of violence aboard the aircraft, a crewmember should blow their whistle immediately, either as the first signal or as a relay signal.*

Photo 13.7 The whistle

Early Warning/Detection: The Key to Surviving an Attack

One of the keys to surviving a violent attack, whether perpetrated by a disruptive passenger, a hijacker, or a terrorist, is *early warning* that an attack is imminent.

Early warning for flight crews is attained through the techniques and tactics we have been examining throughout this book, including:

- Awareness of security issues
- Being in the correct level of awareness while working, and
- Timely notification of all other flight crewmembers at the first indication or recognition of an event occurring, or the first perception that an attack is imminent.

Know and Use Space-Distance Factors

The confined spaces of flight decks, galleys, and aisles of aircraft, limit the offensive tactics of aggressors as well as crewmember defensive actions. This should be a very important factor designed into any crewmember defensive response. Many martial arts defensive and offensive maneuvers are very effective if *space* is available or not an issue. However, many of those maneuvers cannot be deployed successfully in the close confines of an aircraft. An example would be what is commonly known as a *'round house'* kick, which requires a wide area to perform. The 'round house' kick is a sweeping 360-degree turn and is impractical in airliners.

In reacting to a violent confrontation where you cannot maintain an adequate distance from the attacker, crewmembers should employ self-protective techniques designed to escape quickly from the immediate scene. For the most part, this may only be a temporary condition in an aircraft; therefore, we must look at employing defensive maneuvers, perhaps one after another, until aid from others arrive and is effective in subduing the aggressor.

Keeping a distance between you and another person will give you added time and space to react to an attack. If possible, stay more than an arm length away from another person. This is not your arm length, but the arm length of the other person. Remember this equation in keeping your distance from an attacker:

Distance = Time and Space to React

If a person wants to move closer to you, move back away from them, stay aware of what is behind you and how much room you have. Do not back yourself into a corner if you can help it. If possible, give yourself an avenue of escape. If you do not have much room behind you, ask the passenger to keep their distance. If it appears to be a typical passenger who is moving closer to you, respond with something like, 'Sir (or Madam), I apologize, I hope you understand, but could you please keep from getting too close to me?' Most people will comply with your reasonable request. If a passenger does not comply with your request, you may need to repeat your request quickly, with added emphasis. If the passenger has mal-intent, this may be the point in which they begin to act. Be prepared and ready to defend yourself.

Enlisting the Aid of Others

A significant part of any flight crew security-training program should be enlisting the aid of others (crewmembers or passengers) when confronted with an attacker, or other potentially dangerous situation. If a crewmember is being attacked, we need to have a plan of action on how we are going to assist them. When coming to a crewmember's call for assistance you may be coming to their aid from the rear of the attacker. The following sequence of pictures (photos 13.8 through 13.11) is a good defensive method to employ against an attacker. For simplicity sake, all the techniques we are depicting for use in this chapter (blankets, belts, & hair or head/pulls) are similar concepts and thus, are easier to remember. The following photos depict examples of coming to the aid of another with the available weapons aboard the aircraft and utilizing head and/or hair pulls. When accomplished correctly, each of these defensive techniques will result in the attacker's head snapping backwards. *Where the head goes, the rest of the body will soon follow.* If able, the person you assisted is free to help you continue to fight, subdue and restrain the attacker.

- *Blankets* – Approaching the attacker from behind, quickly loop the blanket over the attacker's head/face. Take a step backwards with one foot, while quickly pulling hard back and downward at about a 45-degree angle. Use your hips to assist you in applying a significant amount of twisting force to either side as you step back. Continue pulling downward so the attacker's head and body will come down onto the floor. Photos 13.8 through 13.11 demonstrate this technique.
- *Belts* – Approaching the attacker from behind, with the belt looped through the belt buckle, flip the belt over the attacker's head/face at approximately his or her nose/eye level and quickly tighten the loop. Immediately, take a step backwards with one foot, while quickly pulling back and downward hard at about a 45-degree angle. Use your hips to assist you in applying a significant amount of twisting force to either side as you step back. Continue pulling downward so the attacker's head and body will come down onto the floor. Once the attacker is on the floor, keep the belt tighten by placing one foot on the attacker's neck and continue pulling the belt taut.
- *Hair (or head) pull* – Approaching the attacker from behind, grab the hair on top of the attacker's head and step back with one foot while quickly pulling back and downward hard in line with their spine and in a straight down movement. If the attacker does not have hair, reach over the top of their head, grab the top ridge area of their eye sockets, and pull back and downward. If you used your right

hand, step back with your right foot. Use your hips to assist you in applying a significant amount of force as you step back. Continue pulling downward so the attacker's head and body will come down onto the floor. Keep your grip on the attacker's hair and apply tension through use of a dragging motion by stepping away from the attacker's head.

Photos 13.8 to 13.11 A passenger coming to the assistance of a crewmember

Photo 13.8

Photo 13.9

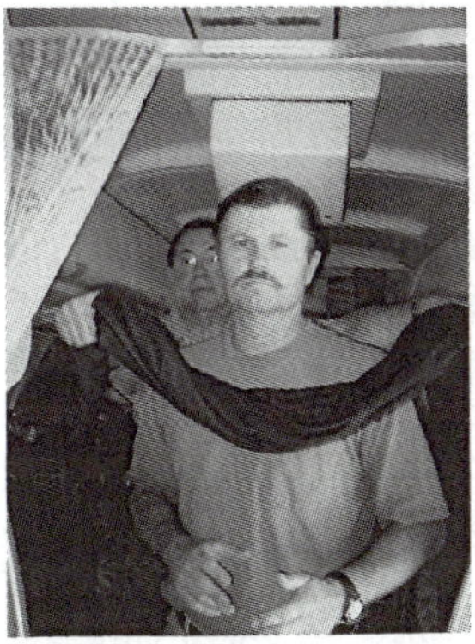

Photo 13.10

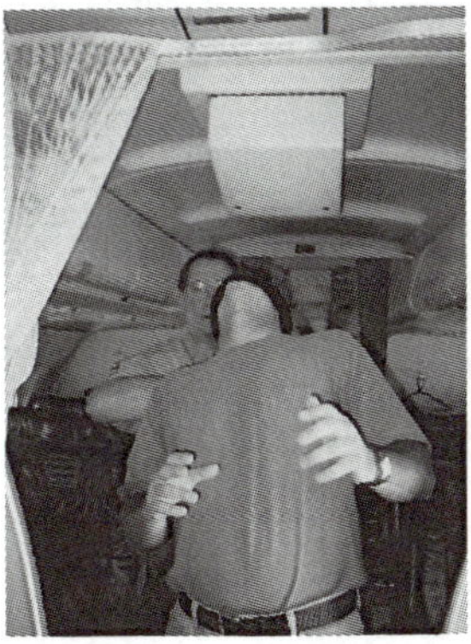

Photo 13.11

Restraining a Violent Passenger

> *Restraint training requires specific training and it is not our purpose to provide that training here. Our desire is to give crewmembers some concept on how to restrain a passenger in as safe and effective manner as possible under the circumstances.*

When a passenger displays aggressively violent behavior, or a reasonable belief exists that they will become violent, the passenger should be restrained with a restraint device to prevent injury to himself or herself, or others. We recommend fibrous boxing tape to restrain a passenger. Fibrous tape is a simple restraining device and is easy to apply once a person is subdued. The restraining of a passenger is obviously a serious situation. The crew must consider the passenger in question to be a serious enough of a threat that if they were not restrained, a potentially dangerous situation jeopardizing the safety of flight could occur.

Before any attempt at restraining a violent passenger, flight attendants should attempt to contact the captain and the situation discussed. However, there may be instances that occur in the cabin requiring an instantaneous decision and quick response by flight attendants. In these cases, the flight attendants should use their common sense and act quickly to reduce any injuries or aircraft damage. In these situations, it would be impractical to contact the captain before attempting to restrain a violent passenger.

The cabin crew should enlist able-bodied persons/passengers (ABP) to assist them in restraining a passenger. How many ABPs are needed will depend on several factors, such as where in the aircraft the incident is occurring, how many ABPs volunteer, space limitations, how many violent passengers are involved, and other real or potential threats aboard the aircraft.

With ABPs available, flight attendants should manage the confrontation with the aggressive passenger. If possible, a crewmember should attempt to resolve it peacefully by asking the passenger to cooperate in allowing himself or herself to be restrained. A crewmember should always ask the passenger to cooperate. If they begin to resist, a crewmember must say aloud, 'stop resisting' as many times as necessary during the restraining process. The flight attendant should direct the ABPs in the method and manner of restraint. Crewmembers should observe closely that the passenger is not intentionally injured by the ABPs who may become involved in a physical confrontation with the passenger during the restraining process. Always check the passenger for injuries after they are restrained, and arrange for medical attention if needed.

You should know that any time a person's freedom is threatened by restraint, a distinct possibility exists that they may become violent. Sometimes, no matter how well you handle the situation, a person may become violent when their liberty taken away from them. Naturally, you should have already assessed the situation and made the determination the individual is a serious threat to the safety of flight. An alternative approach may be to arrange ABPs around the passenger in question with instructions to restrain the person if they continue to be a threat.

Do not overlook serious and aggressive behavior as you may come to regret it at some point during the flight. When in doubt, discuss it with the captain unless time does not permit.

Restraining a passenger will fall into three basic categories: Restraining the passenger while they are violently resisting, are passively uncooperative, or are cooperative.

Photo 13.12 Crewmembers practicing restraining a violent passenger on a life size/weight mannequin

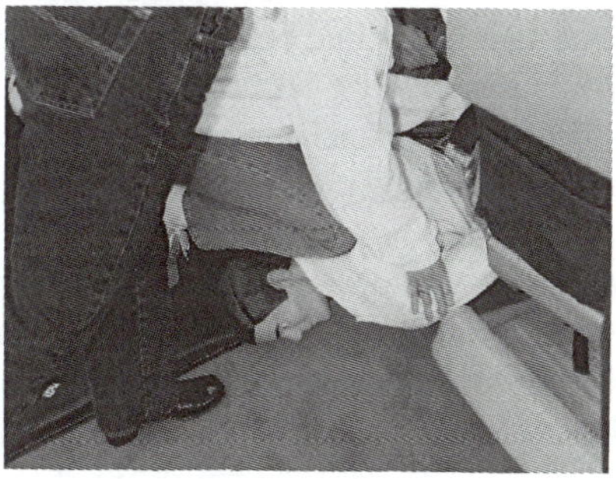

A passenger who violently resists

If the passenger is resisting violently, a crewmember should direct the ABPs in restraining techniques. A flight attendant should enlist a minimum of three to four ABPs to assist in restraining a single violent passenger. Possibly more ABPs to control other passengers from becoming involved would be a consideration. If there is time, the crewmember should brief the ABPs on the desired restraining technique. The crewmember should direct the ABPs to guide the passenger face down onto the floor of the aircraft. This will be difficult, considering the narrow width of most single aisle airliners. If the ABPs are unable to guide the passenger onto the floor, direct them to place the passenger over the armrest of the nearest aisle seat. Once the passenger is restrained by the ABPs, a crewmember should direct the ABPs to tape the restrained person's wrists behind their back using an over and under figure eight method. Ensure the tape is not wrapped too tightly around the person's wrist. Restricting blood circulation could lead to undo physical injury to their hands. Do not under-restrain either, especially, a violent person who could continue to be a threat (i.e. Richard Reid – the *shoe bomber*). If the passenger is kicking and flailing about, then direct the ABPs to restrain the legs using the same figure eight pattern as with the wrists. After secured, monitor the restrained person's blood circulation, when able. If symptoms indicate circulation has been impaired, re-tape more loosely and then cut away or loosen the previous taping.

If the passenger continues to flail with their legs, then *hobbling* the passenger is a viable option. A violent flailing passenger is hobbled to prevent an injury to others as well as to themselves. Hobbling involves attaching tape or a line between the secured wrist and the ankles. If the passenger is in a seat, then hobbling can occur by taping their legs to the frame of the seat. If in a seat, the restrained passenger attempts to head butt or bite others, their body and/or head can be taped to the seat itself. If they are spitting, a crewmember or ABP can loosely tie cotton material such as a cotton napkin or a shirt around their face. Use caution and verify the person can breath normally, otherwise, they could suffocate.

A restrained passenger, face down on the floor of the aircraft with their hands and feet restrained, as well as hobbled, must be turned onto their side. If not turned onto their side, the stress of their hands tied behind their back and ankles and drawn up toward their wrists, could negatively affect their breathing ability. Additionally, laying the restrained person on their stomach may put a significant amount of pressure on the stomach area, leading to asphyxiation and death to the passenger. Therefore, after they are restrained, ensure they are turned onto their side. A crewmember must be careful not to injure a passenger after they are restrained.

If an aggressive passenger decides to cooperate and allow you to restrain them, then that is wonderful; but do not be fooled by pleas of mercy because once you have made the decision you must stick with it. Let law enforcement sort it out upon arrival.

Passively uncooperative passenger

A passively uncooperative passenger a crewmember is attempting to restrain is one who will not cooperate with being restrained. They may not fight, but may not be willing to get out of a seat, turn around and let strangers put a restraining device on them. Try to avoid such an encounter by luring the passenger to a galley area where they can be restrained more easily. If the person continues to be uncooperative, station two ABPs on either side of the person and one ABP behind the person.

Be careful of your ABPs who may get confrontational with the passenger and escalate the incident into a violent one. A passively uncooperative passenger may easily become violent during the attempt at restraining them. Be careful and maintain control of the passenger by directing the ABPs to maintain control of the person's arms.

Always try to have two ABPs controlling each of the passenger's arms. Have an ABP or a crewmember secure the passenger's hands behind their back with whatever restraining device approved for your airline. As previously mentioned, the authors prefer the simplicity of fibrous tape. Move the passenger to the last row of the aircraft and seat them in a middle seat between two ABPs. Have the ABPs maintain a vigilant watch on the passenger.

Cooperative passenger

A cooperative passenger is handled in much the same manner as the passively uncooperative passenger. If possible, ask the passenger in question to accompany you and the ABPs to the rear of the aircraft where the restraining can take place in the same manner as described in a moment. If this is not feasible and they are seated, ask them to get up and step into the aisle. With two ABPs on either side, ask the person being restrained to turn toward a window. Have the ABPs control each arm of the person and ask the passenger to put his/her hands behind their back. Have an ABP or a crewmember secure their hands behind their back. Move the passenger toward the back of the aircraft and seat them in a middle seat between two ABPs.

Always be cautious of a cooperative passenger becoming violent Additionally, anyone traveling with him or her could become confrontational with you and/or the ABPs.

Conclusion

The intention of this chapter has been to familiarize crewmembers with the unpleasant prospect of defending against extremely violent attacks. However, one-on-one training is essential in conveying the practical aspects of employing unconventional weapons and tactics. Regardless of whether governments or airlines mandate training for crewmembers, we encourage you to seek your own self-defense training. Do not count on others to provide you with the training you need. Your life is more valuable than waiting for the training you deserve. You may be correct in believing the airlines should train crewmembers in self-defense, but that will mean little if you are attacked by an aggressive passenger and injured because you do not know how to defend yourself. Being correct will not make you any less injured. Take responsibility for your own life and become involved in protecting it from attackers. Crewmembers need to become part of the solution and take responsible steps to assure this goal. Crewmembers can become a valuable tool in the fight against terrorism, but will need to take the initiative in making it happen. Ask yourself how much your life is worth and spend accordingly to protect it.

Note

1 Interview with Sabah Khodada, *PBS Frontline*, 14 October 2001.

Chapter 14

Post Incident Considerations

It ain't over, 'til it's over!
Yogi Bera

Introduction

An area directly affecting both flight deck and cabin crewmembers that has been sorely neglected in security training programs throughout the industry is that of post incident considerations. For those who have not been involved with a high stress situation, such as a hijacking, bomb threat, or violent disruptive passenger, pay close attention to the information in this chapter. Dealing with the situation on the aircraft in the air, although important and necessary, is only one part of your problem. We do not want the other parts to be a surprise to you.

Today, as in the past, the airlines, unions and the government have kept flight crews in the dark as to what to expect AFTER an incident on an aircraft. Flight crews have somehow muddled through the aftermaths of incidents not knowing what to expect, forced into being reactive rather than proactive after an incident. We believe it is essential to provide at least an elementary background of information that may be helpful to crewmembers if ever faced with the aftermath of a violent situation. That is the purpose of this chapter. Before we begin, think about the following scenarios and related questions:

- You have had a bomb threat on your aircraft while airborne and have located a suspicious-looking package. Procedures are followed, and two of the three cabin crewmembers are in the process of securing and packing the device at the least risk location when the device detonates. Both cabin crewmembers are sucked out of the gaping hole in the side of the aircraft. As the remaining cabin crewmember, how do you handle this situation? As the captain, what are your concerns?
- Your flight has experienced a violent, intoxicated passenger who has succeeded in breaking the nose of one cabin crewmember and the arm of a passenger. In the process of subduing and restraining the passenger, another cabin crewmember was bitten severely on the arm. It appears one of the irate passenger's shoulders is out of joint and he is bleeding from his left ear. As one of the uninjured cabin crewmembers, how do you handle this situation? As the captain, what are your concerns?

- During flight, four male passengers simultaneously attack all cabin crewmembers throughout the cabin. Passengers, hearing the screaming of the crewmembers, rush to their aid. During the melee, all four terrorists are killed and the flight deck is not breached; however, all cabin crewmembers have sustained injuries, some life-threatening. During the fights on board, one terrorist detonated a grenade, killing himself and three passengers and injuring another four people, including a cabin crewmember. The grenade also blew a hole in the cabin floor near the over-wing area. There are numerous cuts and stab wounds on at least a dozen people and several people appear to have broken bones. One of the terrorists in the rear of the aircraft smashed a small bottle of some type of liquid before being choked to death by a large man. Toxic fumes are permeating the cabin causing some of the other passengers to wretch and pass out. As one of the less-severely injured cabin crewmembers, how do you handle this situation? As the captain, what are your concerns?

We realize these are UGLY scenarios; however, any one of them could occur on your flight. Are you prepared to handle any of them? This chapter addresses five major areas for crewmembers to assess after a violent situation has been brought under control on the aircraft, along with a review of related topics. Additionally, we explore post incident stress it may pertain to flight crewmembers' mental health and to their careers. We will intentionally ask more questions than we will provide answers. We want YOU to think!

Five Areas to Assess

The five major areas to assess immediately after stabilizing a violent event on an aircraft are:

1 *WHO* is able to respond verbally and physically in the cabin
2 The extent of *INJURIES* you may have on board
3 Any *DAMAGE TO THE AIRCRAFT* that may affect your descent, approach and/or landing, and
4 *FURTHER THREATS* aboard your aircraft that you need to consider prior to or after landing.
5 What *RESOURCES* do you have at your disposal?

Who is able to respond?

This seems like a simple question, but the answer can get quite complicated. In most training scenarios we have seen, cabin crewmembers are still able to respond somewhat normally during the scenario. This simply may not be the case. Furthermore, the answer is complicated by the size of the aircraft and number of cabin crewmembers on board. Since we do not know who you (the reader) are, and the type of aircraft you fly, you must think through this question based upon your situation.

You may be one of 16 cabin crewmembers on a large wide-body aircraft, a single cabin crewmember on a regional jet or corporate aircraft, or anywhere in between. The important thing is that you think through the answer to this question based upon your experience and situation. If the lead (#1, senior, etc.) flight attendant is incapacitated, who is going to assume leadership in the cabin, and how is that accomplished? What do you tell the captain when establishing contact with the flight deck? What if you can respond verbally, but are unable to respond physically to accomplish what remains to be done in the cabin?

This is NOT just a cabin crew question! As the flight deck crew, how do you assess who is able to respond in the cabin? How do you know if it is a cabin crewmember, a passenger, Air Marshal, or a terrorist? How do you establish communication with the cabin if all cabin crewmembers are incapacitated?

As flight deck and cabin crewmembers, answering this first question is extremely important because it sets the stage for how we address the remaining three areas to assess. Knowing who is communicating in the cabin is vital to the decision making of the captain.

What is the extent of injuries on the aircraft?

It is important to assess injuries of everyone aboard the aircraft. Again, this sounds simple, but can get complicated very easily as there may be injuries inflicted that you have never been trained to diagnose or to treat. Your ability to move about throughout the cabin may be limited due to your own injuries, or to the condition of the cabin. Where do you start?

As callous as it may seem to readers not familiar with crewmember duties and responsibilities, the first people to assess are all crewmembers. You need to know the status of every crewmember, their injuries (if any), their ability to communicate effectively and accurately, and their ability to perform duties as required. (Do we dare ask if you even know all crewmembers on the aircraft, both on the flight deck and in the cabin?)

If perpetrators breach the flight deck but are neutralized successfully, what is the condition of the flight deck crew? The advent of two-place aircraft has increased the responsibilities per person on the flight deck and the results of numerous scenarios could turn flying the aircraft into a one-pilot operation, or worse – both pilots wholly or partially incapacitated. Who are other resources on the aircraft that could fly the aircraft, or aid the pilots in flying the aircraft? Are there additional flight deck officers on board, such as required on many international and/or long flights, or deadheading company pilots qualified on the aircraft? Would you rather have help from a pilot from another airline that is qualified on your type aircraft, or one of your own company pilots qualified on a different type of aircraft? Are there military or corporate pilots aboard? If you have a choice, whom do you want on the flight deck and how do you address the subject of the flight deck door? How do you get medical aid to flight deck crewmembers that have sustained injuries?

The cabin crew must take stock of each other's injuries and capabilities before continuing with any type of duties or administering aid to others. If the flight deck crew were to land the aircraft within ten minutes and call for an emergency evacuation, what would you do to prepare the cabin under any of the three scenarios we described in the introduction, and how would you direct the evacuation, particularly if you were the only fully or partially functioning cabin crewmember?

These types of scenarios are where Crew RESOURCE Management skills are extremely important, emphasis on RESOURCE. The entire crew must assess their available resources on the aircraft, crewmember-wise.

Next in importance, assess the condition of passengers, particularly those that can assist you such as non-revenue airline personnel, medical personnel, law enforcement personnel and military personnel. Every person is important on the aircraft; however, by extending treatment and/or medical care to those who can further assist you, you may increase your ability to treat many more people much more quickly.

Having enlisted the aid of passengers in resolving a violent attack in the cabin, there will most probably be passengers who have sustained serious injuries, along with flight attendants. It COULD easily be a real mess back there! How do you accomplish triage? Who gathers the information to pass along to MedLink or other agencies regarding the type and extent of injuries sustained in the cabin? What supplies do you have available to you to tend to 'fighting wounds', such as gun shot, knife or puncture wounds, crushing wounds and broken noses, jaws, fingers, arms, or severe damage to eyes. Do you know how to stabilize a large number of people who are in shock? Are you waiting on your airline to train you for such situations, or are you proactively pursuing that knowledge elsewhere?

Consider use of resources outside the aircraft, as well. Medical assistance can be coordinated through medical service providers like MedLink and company medical departments. Cabin crews must realize that in dire emergencies such as the scenarios we described, the flight deck crew will be extremely busy coordinating and implementing the emergency descent, approach and landing. There may be little time for coordinating medical assistance in some cases. However, if the flight is over the middle of the Pacific or Atlantic Oceans, there may be plenty of time to seek assistance. Good judgment and common sense should rule in making this determination.

How are the aggressors? Are they subdued and properly restrained so as not to pose an additional threat as the flight continues? Tending to their injuries is the very LAST priority we should have. In the case of a disruptive passenger, after the passenger has been subdued and properly restrained and injuries to crew and passengers has been accomplished, it would be appropriate to tend to injuries to the disruptive passenger. Like it or not, you may be the victim of a violent attack by a passenger, but you are not the judge and jury in this situation. You have a high probability of being in court to defend your actions, as well as any that you directed against this individual.

You want the judge and jury to know that YOU:

- verbally tried to defuse the situation
- warned the attacker of the consequences of any violent behavior
- successfully defended yourself (and others) against the violent attack, and
- sought medical assistance for the attacker after the attack was terminated – showing compassion as a human being for someone who may be severely injured. It does not take much of an imagination to consider the alternative of NOT providing medical assistance to the aggressor.

What damage has occurred to the aircraft?

With chaos erupting in the cabin generating all kinds of sounds, it may be very difficult to ascertain the condition of the aircraft. Obviously, monitoring aircraft systems and 'feel' is important. Communication with the cabin crew may be limited or delayed, depending upon what is happening in the cabin. Before putting your aircraft into a high performance envelope, it may be to your advantage to take time to assess the condition of the aircraft PRIOR to initiating your emergency descent. Here are some things to consider.

Safety of flight items – Has there been any damage to the aircraft that affects flight integrity? Has the aircraft sustained any damage to doors and/or windows, or holes in the fuselage from bullets or from detonation of explosive devices, that would limit the speed of the aircraft in an emergency descent? If pieces of the aircraft have come off, did any of them strike flight control surfaces or enter the intake of an engine? Do you need to make a controllability check prior to slowing the aircraft down at low altitude?

Systems related items – Have any of the aircraft's systems been damaged, and if so to what extent? If there has been aircraft damage that makes an approach and landing marginal, what are you going to do?

Pressurization – *A*re there any large or small holes in the fuselage that are not supposed to be there? Is pressurization holding? Do you hear any strange whistling noises or sounds of air escaping? Do you need to consider descending and depressurizing the aircraft in case of the presence of an un-detonated explosive device onboard?

Fuel – Are any fuel leaks visible from the flight deck or cabin? Are fuel gauges indicating a loss of fuel? Are you drastically overweight for landing? Can you dump fuel if necessary? Do you have enough fuel to get to the airport selected for landing, whether that is your planned destination or an alternate airport?

Electrical – Are all buses powered? Is the APU available as a backup? Do you have any electrical shorts anywhere? Do you smell electrical smoke in the cockpit or cabin? Is it necessary to cut power to the galley buses based on damage in the cabin? What lighting is available inside and outside the aircraft?

Avionics and instruments – Do you have a full set of instruments? Are you able to aviate, navigate, automate, and communicate effectively? Do you have normal communication with the cabin crew? Is your transponder working normally? Can you communicate either directly or indirectly with the fighter aircraft that may intercept your flight? Is TCAS working? Is your weather radar working?

Hydraulic power – Are all hydraulic systems powered? If not, what do you have? Will you be required to modify your approach and landing based on flap and gear configurations? Do you need to configure early to test controllability due to any aircraft damage that may have occurred?

Based upon your assessment of the condition of your aircraft, do any normal procedures change? What resources are available to you to give you expert technical advice? Does your company have a maintenance department person in your dispatch area that can give you technical assistance? Do you know how to contact them? How do you contact representatives from the manufacturer of your aircraft? Do you have this information readily available?

What further threats exist on the aircraft?

Aggressors – Are all the known aggressors subdued? Are they properly restrained so as not to be a further threat? If it is a terrorist event, what measures have you taken to identify any additional 'sleeper' terrorists onboard? Have you considered checking passenger identifications or passports against the flight manifest? Do you need to lock down the cabin and control access to lavatories? Do you have passengers watching each other for abnormal behavior? If you had a 'disruptive passenger incident', have you considered the possibility it might be a diversionary tactic to a more violent act?

What if terrorist succeeded in taking over the cabin, but have not been able to breach the flight deck? What do you expect to happen once you have landed the aircraft under this condition? Once the aircraft comes to a stop after landing, will you abandon the flight deck or stay with the aircraft?

Firearms, edged weapons – Have confiscated weapons been secured? How many are there? Where are they? Who has control of them? Do you know how to make 'safe' a loaded firearm? Unload it? Use it, if necessary? Are knives, box cutters, or other edged weapons secured? Could an undesirable person get to them?

Explosive devices – Are there any additional explosive devices on board? How many? Where are they? Have any of them been moved to the LRBL? Have the LRBL procedures been carried out? Have you notified the flight deck of the explosive devices onboard? Has the flight deck alerted the appropriate agencies of a bomb on board? Where will you park the aircraft? Will you perform an emergency evacuation (you are at Chicago O'Hare International Airport in January and it is –20°F outside)?

Chemical/biological devices – If there are suspected chemical or biological agents on board, what will you do after landing? Will you perform an emergency evacuation under these conditions? Will you allow anyone to open any door from inside or outside the aircraft? Do the responders know the condition of your aircraft, and are they equipped to handle a aircraft with chemical or biological agents on board? How can you obtain medical assistance from ground personnel who are not equipped for a chemical/biological event?

Are there any identifiable chemical or biological weapons onboard? How many and where are they? What procedures have you used to mitigate their effects? Where will you park the aircraft? Do you expect to be quarantined, and if so, for how long? Do you run the APU under these circumstances? Are ground electrical units and/or air conditioning units available? How will someone get them to you if you are parked in a remote area of the airport? What is the status of your aircraft lavatories, potable water, food, beverages, blankets, pillows, etc.? What do you tell your passengers?

As you can probably tell by all the questions we raise, these four major areas to assess immediately after stabilizing a violent event on an aircraft are extremely important to consider BEFORE an event occurs. Whatever the event that may occur aboard your aircraft, odds are that procedures you currently have in place do not address many of the questions we have posed. As usual, it will fall on the shoulders of flight crews to find the answers. As we cannot dictate your company policies and procedures, we reserve our opinions on these questions. It is up to you to bring these issues to the attention of your company and resolve them in the best interest of all concerned.

What resources do you have at your disposal?

As you know from 'normal' operations with 'normal' aircraft and or people problems, a multitude of people are ready to help you meet your specific needs. This is especially true during any security-related event.

Our purpose is not to tell you specifically who to call, but to remind you of some of the agencies that can support your needs, IF THEY KNOW ABOUT THEM! As with everything we do, accurate and timely COMMUNICATION is extremely important to the successful conclusion of any abnormal event.

MedAire (or other medical advice provider) – If your airline contracts with MedAire, you have a wealth of information at your fingertips for dealing with the medical mess in the cabin, or even the cockpit for that matter. MedLink can provide a wide range of services that may be essential in coping with the situation on board your aircraft. In addition to the normal medical advice, they can provide you with immediate information on how to handle non-normal injuries, as well. The injuries you may have on board will more than likely not be the types you would expect during normal operations. MedLink can help you with advice on:

- Triage;

- Injuries sustained from fighting and/or abrupt aircraft maneuvering; and/or,
- Chemical burns or exposure to biological agents.

For MedLink to be a resource for you, you must contact them and relay sufficient information for them to be able to assess conditions and formulate a plan for you, including advice on diversions for medical reasons. *(Your situation may dictate landing at a different location than suggested by MedLink – remember the Captain has final authority in making that decision.)* Accurately completing the MedLink form will greatly aid in coordinating their help. (By the way, how do you get the form to the flight deck?) *[WALTRIP'S NOTE: SLIP IT UNDER THE DOOR]* MedLink can notify and coordinate with the appropriate agencies for medical assistance as well as patient transport to area hospitals if they know your destination.

Agency coordination – Based upon your communication with ATC, and possibly your company, numerous agencies may get involved without your directly contacting them. It is extremely important to make your exact conditions known in aiding the people on the ground that are trying to help you. Carefully choose your words to avoid any misunderstandings, misinterpretations, or unwarranted concerns. During a night flight over the Atlantic in 2002 involving an aircraft that was mistakenly squawking the hijacking code, a crewmember made the comment (something like), 'It's awfully dark and scary up here'. That statement, along with the hijacking transponder code, prompted an international response to a non-hijacking event. It is easy to understand how that transmission was interpreted under this condition.

You may be aware of many of the resources available to you from your training; however, we would be remiss if we did not include them in our review of the topic. Some of the agencies at your disposal are included in these groups:

- Communications
  - Air Traffic Control (ATC, Tower, Ground Control, Clearance Delivery)
  - AIRINC
  - Atlanta Radio
  - 121.5 Emergency frequency
  - Company radio (Dispatch, System Operations Control)
  - Flight Service Stations
- Aircraft problems or concerns
  - Maintenance Control
  - Company radio
  - Dispatch, SOC
  - Aircraft manufacturers (Boeing, Airbus, etc.)
- Medical advice
  - MedAire, or other medical advice provider
  - Dispatch, SOC
  - Emergency Medical Technicians, paramedics

    - Airport Rescue and Fire Fighting units (ARFF)
    - Local area hospitals (phone patch)
- Specialty agencies
    - HAZMAT teams
    - ATF (explosives, bomb squads and dogs)
    - DEA (drugs, drug sniffing dogs)
    - Civil Support Teams (chemical/biological threats)
    - FBI Hostage Rescue Team
    - Delta Force
- Law Enforcement Agencies
    - FBI
    - Federal Air Marshals
    - Customs and Immigration
    - Airport police
    - Local agencies (city, county, state police)
    - National Guard.

Keep in mind the more information passed by one transmission to another, the greater the chance for errors and misinterpretation of the information transmitted. The more concise and direct you are in formulating your transmission, the better your chances of being understood correctly. Of course, feedback is essential in closing the communication loop to confirm that your transmission was received and interpreted correctly. It may seem elementary, but if you are able, insistent upon feedback.

The 'Friendlies'

Everyone is a 'bad guy' until proven differently.

One of my (Williams) biggest revelations during Exercise Polar Star, a joint FAA-FBI mock hijacking exercise, came during the conclusion of the 18-hour ordeal. During the exercise, I was 'injured'. After the aircraft landed at our destination, I was removed from the aircraft and placed in an Emergency Response vehicle. Since all my identification had been taken during the hijacking process, I was unable to prove my identity. To my surprise, I was treated as if I was a hijacker for about two hours, until the episode was concluded and all the players sorted out by the FBI Hostage Rescue Team. YOU know you are a 'good guy', but proving it under certain conditions may be next to impossible; therefore, go with the flow and exercise patience. The responders, whether they are the FBI, DEA, ATF, or law enforcement officers from various jurisdictions, have a tough job to do in sorting everyone out and stabilizing the situation, which takes time.

You may have had a long, stressful day already, but plan for the event not to be over quickly. Relax and start writing down in detail everything you can remember that happened. Try to correlate your thoughts with timeframes, if possible. Get your entire crew to do the same (separately). You will need this information during debriefings that will follow. You just thought your day was already long! Armed with the knowledge that you will be treated as a bad guy will help you get through this phase with less anguish and misunderstanding of what is happening.

The military fighters on our wing are here to protect us.

Actually, no. If your security training does not address the issue adequately, we urge you to review (and know) the ICAO fighter interception procedures. Although they are not classified, we will not discuss the procedures in this book. What we want to point out about that issue is the fighters WILL SHOOT YOU DOWN under certain circumstances. Having been a fighter pilot for 19 years (Williams), I can truthfully say to shoot down an unarmed airliner would be the ultimate nightmare for any fighter pilot; however, an aircraft that has obviously been taken over by terrorists cannot be allowed to continue their destructive mission and possibly kill thousands of people on the ground.

You must know the correct intercept procedures and follow any directions given to you by the fighters, or passed through ATC if unable to communicate directly with the fighters. Following their directions may conflict with where you want to land (for fuel, weather or other considerations), or where your company wants you to land. If you cannot communicate your intentions with the fighters, directly or indirectly, our recommendation for your safety is to follow the directions of the fighters.

Debriefings

One of the processes that airline crews are not very familiar with is that of debriefings. Military pilots brief and debrief every mission; not so within the airline industry. Pilots and flight attendants vanish mysteriously as soon as their trips end. Military pilots know the importance of debriefings, but unfortunately lessons to be learned from commercial flights are ignored for various reasons, such as duty times, pay for the extra time debriefing, facilities to conduct debriefings, etc. You will have debriefings after a major event, such as a hijacking attempt, so do not let it come as a shock. Your day (or night) is not over by any means.

We wish we could provide you a schedule of events concerning your debriefing, but that is impossible. From personal experience and from interviewing crews that have been hijacked, we can truthfully say that no two events are debriefed the same, but they are debriefed. Some of the players in your debriefing may be (not necessarily in order of appearance):

- *Your company* – For reasons that should be obvious, such as litigation, possible violations of rules, public relations and the press, expect some company management personnel to want to talk to you as soon as possible.

- *Your union* – For those who belong to a union, your union representatives will want to hear your story as soon as possible to put any union resources to work on your behalf, whether that is legal representation or a Critical Incident Response Team.
- *Law enforcement* – The law enforcement agency that has jurisdiction for your flight will want to debrief you. This could be airport police, city or county police, or state police.
- *FBI* – FBI representatives will want to debrief you as soon as possible. They will expect full details from each crewmember, even those who may not have been involved in the incident. More than likely, this will be your longest debriefing.
- *FAA, ATF, DEA, TSA* – Depending on what occurred during your event, you may be debriefed by any or all of these agencies.
- *The Press* – Your event will make national and/or international news. Reporters from newspapers and television will want to interview you. Please follow your company policy on this issue. Most companies will want their public relations or public information personnel to speak to the press concerning your event. Remember, what you say could be used in litigation arising from the event. Exercise extreme caution in this area. Terrorists, to identify both weak and strong points for future attacks, could use any information you give regarding the event.

The debriefings may take approximately two to six hours total, depending on how many separate debriefings occur. You will probably be very fatigued by the end of debriefing, if not beforehand. Keep this in mind as fatigue contributes to memory loss, confusion, and lack of clear thinking. This is why we recommend making detailed notes as soon as the event is over when event is much fresher on your memory and you have not been confused by the many questions sure to come your way. It is much easier to refer to your written notes as time passes and debriefings continue to occur one after another. A very important point to remember is that your interpretation of the event, including your observations and involvement, may be totally different from other crewmembers. Avoid the temptation for 'everyone to tell the same story'. Just tell it like you saw it and let the experts put the facts together. That is what they are paid to do.

You may be the only person in your crew that has read this book or has any other knowledge of the debriefing process. It is crucial that you share this information with other crewmembers to help calm their fears and to alleviate some of the stress from the entire episode.

Your relatives, friends and co-workers will want you to recount the event. Possibly, security personnel and training department personnel from your company will want you to repeat the story for what they can reap from it to improve security and crew training. Again, exercise caution in releasing information that may be detrimental to flight crews in future events.

Violence and its Aftermath

The purpose of this section is to prepare you for the consequences of a violent attack. As much as we attempt to avoid becoming a victim, this may be unavoidable. You can train and prepare yourself physically and through playing out scenarios in your mind, but that will not prepare you for the psychological repercussions of a violent attack. By preparing yourself now for the feelings you may experience after a violent event, it will help you mentally survive the fallout of a violent confrontation. As humans, we are susceptible to psychological reactions to violence or threats of violence. This is why we will take some time to discuss this important aspect of violence. We are not psychologists, but rather have experience in living and working in violent situations and would like to share with you helpful suggestions to assist you in coping with violent encounters.

There are four factors that you should be aware of when confronted with violence. The *physical, emotional, psychological and social factors* of a violent encounter should be considered by crewmembers. Any or all of these factors will influence you is some manner, having minor to major effects on you.

Physical factors

The body responds physically to physiological responses resulting from a crisis such as a violent struggle for your life. The body's symptoms to violence may include nausea, sweating, sensations of hot or cold, uncontrollable shakes and fatigue. When confronted with violence you may immediately begin to feel sick to your stomach and begin what feels like a cold sweat. It may later feel like you are extremely hot as blood flows to areas of the body that were restricted during the 'fight or flight' syndrome. As adrenaline begins to wear off you may get uncontrollable shakes that are outwardly obvious, and since your body has been 'running a marathon', you may feel extremely tired and sleepy. As the blood flow returns to the skin, the small muscle groups and the digestive system after the 'fight or flight syndrome' is over, you may find that you have been cut or injured and didn't even know it at the time. Pain also may increase as the body immediately regulates how much you can endure and gradually gives you more as your tolerance increases. There is the distinct possibility that you may go into shock, depending upon circumstances. Can you recognize the symptoms of YOUR going into shock, or when others may be in shock? How do you respond to shock?

Emotional factors

The emotional factors to violence may include fear, disbelief, shock, anger or rage and rationalization. When it is clear you are being confronted with a violent threat, the natural reaction is fear. Fear is dangerous as it causes one to withdraw. You must overcome fear with rage in order to survive. Often, disbelief that someone is attacking you will stop you in your tracks as you try to assimilate what is occurring. Shock goes hand and hand with disbelief as you may become immobilized, not knowing exactly how you should respond. You may experience anger or rage you have never felt before. You CAN fight with anger or rage. After the incident, you may begin to rationalize your actions and your feelings.[1]

To counteract these physical and emotional symptoms you must project the desired outcome of the event – your survival. Train yourself in how you need to respond to a crisis. Play out scenarios in your head and play out how you would react to them. How you respond to a crisis varies with each individual, but training can help curtail any natural reflexes to a violent confrontation.

Most reactions to violence are normal and you may have already experienced some of them at some point in your life. Feeling fear to a threat of violence is a normal reaction and a person who says they do not experience fear when confronted with violence is either lying or crazy (the NO FEAR crowd).

The disbelief that someone is actually trying to hurt you may cause you to freeze and not react. This is something you can learn to control. As we discussed in Chapter 7, you need to put some thought to potential threats so that your mind has something to draw upon during a serious threat. With no forethought, or with no preparation or training, your brain will have nothing to reference during a confrontation, causing you to freeze in position and/or to react incorrectly against the threat you are facing.

Anger against a violent encounter is a correct response to the threat. Directed anger will cause you to act whereas fear and emotional withdrawal will indicate to the aggressor that you have given up and he can do with you as he wishes. A 'kinder and gentler' approach to a violent encounter will almost guarantee your becoming a victim. *Becoming a victim is not in our game plan and should not be in yours either.* Being angry over the attack and responding aggressively and overwhelmingly IS part of the plan. Being nice about defending yourself against a ruthless attacker is the wrong approach to a survival mindset. If attacked, the situation has moved beyond defusing the situation verbally. It is now time to act in self-defense and you must become angry to accomplish your goal – SURVIVAL.

Rage is a potential response to a violent confrontation. However, the difference between rage and anger in this context is that rage is uncontrolled whereas anger can be directed. When an individual goes into rage, they have lost control and are responding with pure emotion. Rage is anger that is in total panic. You must control your anger and not let it slip into a rage. Rage will cloud your thought processes to the point of misdirecting your self-defense. While in rage, you will almost certainly over-react to the situation. Rage is the extreme opposite response to disbelief and shock. Both ends of that emotional spectrum can be avoided completely with good mental preparation.

Psychological factors

The psychological responses to a violent confrontation may cause a continual mental replaying of the event, nightmares, self-doubt and religious conflicts. It is completely normal to replay a violent encounter. It is extremely important for you to understand what actually occurred to you and this may take time as your brain attempts to process this information. As long as you do not become obsessed over the incident for months on-end, replaying the event occasionally can lead to closure on the event.

Nightmares are another reaction to what happened to you. Your mind is actively replaying the incident out in your mind as you sleep. This may be disturbing, but should diminish as time passes. Self-doubt is also a symptom of violence. This may occur if you believe you could have done something more useful to defend yourself. You suddenly feel vulnerable that you are incapable of taking care of yourself. When Waltrip was a police officer, he experienced many violent confrontations. He would always replay the events in his mind to learn and gain knowledge for future incidents, but there was always an element of doubt and thoughts of 'what could I have done differently?' After a suicidal woman was shot and killed by police after she attacked them with a fighting knife, a city council member said, 'I don't think people realize the guilt police deal with the rest of their lives (after a shooting), and they always question if they could have done something different. You carry this guilt on your chest for your entire career, and it tears them up inside'.[2] The point is even a police officer that encounters violence as a part of his job will feel doubt. Do not be disturbed by any self-doubt you may experience after a violent confrontation.

Your religious convictions may clash with your contemplating violence or your response to a violent incident. This is also something Steve Waltrip faced as a police officer. Steve is a Christian and had many inner conflicts with the actions he sometimes had to take as a police officer. He responded by trying to view the incident in the context of the greater good. For example, should he let a woman be assaulted violently by her boyfriend, or should he step in with his police issued baton and strike the man to make him stop? Likewise, would you do everything in your power to stop a terrorist hijacker, or do you let him hijack the plane, crash it and kill potentially thousands of people? For the greater good to prevail in this world, we must sometimes make difficult decisions that may cause a conflict with our beliefs. How do you reconcile those beliefs? We recommend that you view a violent confrontation in the greater good. For good to survive in this world, attempts, potentially violent attempts, must be made to stop evil from prevailing. As Edmund Burke once said, 'All that is necessary for the triumph of evil is that good men do nothing'. Evil will not triumph if we approach self-defense with this attitude. We can use our religious beliefs not only to comfort us with these thoughts, but also to reconcile any potential conflicts with our self-imposed restrictions of self-defense.

Social factors

A little known and therefore little considered consequences of being a survivor are the social issues you may experience. You may feel that what you experienced is personal and others are incapable of understanding what you are feeling. This may be true to a point, but do not shut out your friends and family. You may get very tired of repeating the incident, but if this happens, respond by simply saying that you do not want to repeat the story over again and that you hope they will understand. There may come a day when you are more willing to share the encounter and the feelings you experienced with them. Do not isolate yourself from the people who love and care about you. It is okay if you need some time to yourself, but you are not alone in your experiences and you will get through this potentially difficult time. As always, experiences and feelings will vary by individual.

Your family will be your greatest strength, but their response may vary. Children may be frightened of what occurred to you and may not want to be around you. Understand they are responding to their own feelings. They will ultimately understand and will come around on their own. Not wanting to intrude upon your privacy, your friends may not contact you. Avoid feeling abandoned because they are trying to give you some space. Seek them out so they understand the door is open to communicate with you.

Your spouse or significant other, startled by your protective response to the incident, may not know how to comfort you. They may feel some fear that you took the steps you did to defend yourself or others. This sometimes happens to a police officer's spouse when the realization occurs after they discover their husband, the father of their children, took the life of another person in the line of duty. It is important to know that you and your family may experience a multitude of emotions and responses that cannot be fully appreciated or anticipated beforehand.

After a violent confrontation on an aircraft, you will be facing an intense law enforcement investigation. You will be interviewed intensely, and probably be asked to wait for hours while witnesses and other participants are also interviewed. Sitting around waiting to be interviewed by police and FBI is not a pleasant experience. You will need comforting and advice and this is where a union representative, another crewmember from a Critical Incident Response Team, or supervisor may be very helpful. Union and/or company legal guidance may be needed later because of potential civil litigation arising after the incident.

What do all of these factors have in common? Stress. Every person handles stress differently than the next person. We each handle stress differently ourselves, depending upon our mental and physical well-being and the stressors working on us at any one time. There are many books and articles on stress and we do not intend to open that topic in this book; however, in keeping with the theme of post incident considerations, we must breach the topic of posttraumatic stress.

Posttraumatic Stress Disorder

Posttraumatic stress disorder (PTSD) is an anxiety disorder that can develop after exposure to a terrifying event or ordeal in which grave physical or psychological harm occurred, or was threatened. Traumatic events that can trigger PTSD include violent personal assaults such as rape or mugging, natural or human-caused disasters, accidents, or military combat. PTSD can be extremely disabling.[3] Only trained medical personnel familiar with the symptoms can diagnose PTSD.

PTSD is defined in terms of the trauma itself and the person's response to the trauma. The person's response to the trigger event involves intense fear, helplessness, and/or horror.[4] The effects of a violent confrontation may cause you many uncomfortable feelings in the days following the event. However, these feelings of confusion and terror will usually pass as time goes by. You may return to a normal routine as the traumatic event begins to fade, but not always. This may be a sign you are suffering from PTSD and need the help of a trained professional. If left untreated, the negative symptoms to violence may last a lifetime.[5] It is important to note that having strong reactions to trauma is normal and there is a range of expected reactions depending on a person's prior exposure to trauma and genetic factors. Most important, you should understand there are effective treatments for PTSD.[6]

Those at risk of PTSD include military troops who served during wars or armed conflicts, rescue workers involved in the aftermath of disasters such as the terrorist attacks on New York City and Washington, DC, and survivors of the Oklahoma City bombing, the 1994 California earthquake, the 1997 North and South Dakota floods, and hurricanes Hugo and Andrew. Survivors of accidents, rape, physical and sexual abuse, and other crimes; immigrants fleeing violence in their countries; and people who witness traumatic events are among those at risk for developing PTSD. Families of victims can also develop the disorder.[7] A recent study found PTSD in 15 per cent of 500,000 Vietnam veterans and 18 per cent of 10 million women who were victims of physical assault. It is estimated that eight to ten per cent of the population will suffer from PTSD sometime in their lives.[8]

Common symptoms of PTSD

In general, PTSD is the overwhelming of the body's normal psychological defenses against stress. After a traumatic event, abnormal function of normal defense systems result in certain symptoms exhibited in one or more of three ways.

Physical symptoms may include an exaggerated startle response; difficulty with concentrations and memory; mood instability, especially anger and depression; sleep disturbance; and hyper-vigilance. People with PTSD also experience emotional numbness and sleep disturbances, depression, anxiety, and irritability or outbursts of anger. Feelings of intense guilt are also common. Most people with PTSD try to avoid any reminders or thoughts of the ordeal. It is possible for the body to react so strongly the fight or flight syndrome may be triggered, along with all of its symptoms.

Intrusive symptoms may include recurring, distressing recollections, such as thoughts, memories, dreams, nightmares and/or flashbacks; physical or psychological distress at an event that symbolizes the trauma; and grief, or survivor guilt. Many people with PTSD repeatedly re-experience the ordeal in the form of flashback episodes, memories, nightmares, or frightening thoughts, especially when exposed to events or objects reminiscent of the trauma. Anniversaries of the event can also trigger symptoms.

Avoidant symptoms include avoiding specific thoughts, feelings, activities or situations related to the traumatic event; diminished interest in significant activities or situations that may trigger memories of the trauma; and diminished range of emotions/psychological numbness.[9] There may be psychogenic (emotionally caused) amnesia for the event that can lead to a variety of reactions. For example, the person may develop a diminished interest in activities that used to give pleasure, detachment from other people, and sadness the future will be shortened.[10]

Diagnosis and initial approach to PTSD

Anyone may experience any combination of the above-described symptoms during the first month following a significant traumatic event. This is normal. PTSD, diagnosed when symptoms last more than one month, can develop at any age, including childhood.[11] If the duration of symptoms is more than a month and causes significant distress or impairs the person's ability to function, then the diagnosis of PTSD can be made.[12] Symptoms typically begin within three months of a traumatic event, although occasionally they do not begin until years later. If the duration of symptoms is more than three months, a diagnosis of chronic PTSD can be made. If the onset of symptoms occurs six months after the event, or later, the situation is referred to as a delayed onset of PTSD and the prognosis is often worse.[13] Once PTSD occurs, the severity and duration of the illness varies. Some people recover within six months, while others suffer much longer.[14]

Dealing with PTSD

Allowing an early peaking of the symptoms associated with PTSD is appropriate and preferable in treating the illness. *This is an important fact for flight crews to remember. Seeking immediate treatment from professionals is highly recommended even though you may feel like you can handle the situation, or that you are unaffected by the event.* The specific goal of a debriefing by a professional psychiatrist is not to push the trauma away, but to get the person to talk about all aspects of the trauma and how it is affecting them. Studies have shown that early intervention techniques reduce both acute (short-term) and chronic (long-term) PTSD.[15] For example, a study of 12,000 schoolchildren who lived through a hurricane in Hawaii found that those who got counseling early on were doing much better two years later than those who did not.[16]

Understand that we are not attempting to introduce you to some sort of 'psycho-babble' as we approach this subject. We believe it is important for you to understand some of the complexity involved in dealing with PTSD since we know fellow crewmembers that have experienced PTSD first-hand.

Research has demonstrated the effectiveness of psychodynamic psychotherapy, cognitive-behavioral therapy, and exposure therapy in which the patient gradually and repeatedly relives the frightening experience under controlled conditions to help him or her work through the trauma. Other types of therapy that are useful include visualization techniques and peer group support. We offer a short blurb about each of these types of treatment.

Psychodynamic psychotherapy focuses on past traumas and how they may be rekindled by the present experience. This type of long-term therapy is usually required in treating people with a history of previous severe trauma in childhood, such as sexual or physical abuse.

Cognitive-behavioral therapy involves separating intrusive thoughts from the associated anxiety they produce. Cognitive therapy seriously diminishes the power of reminders to cause severe reactions; therefore, it is used to treat people who exhibit avoidance symptoms. The goal is for the person to no longer need to avoid situations or places that may be reminders of the trauma. Treatment may also involve use of audio or videotapes and by keeping a journal.

Exposure therapy consists of education about common reactions to trauma, breathing exercises, and repeated exposure to the past trauma in graduated doses. As a result of exposure therapy, the traumatic event can be remembered without resulting in feelings of anxiety or panic. *Stress inoculation training*, a variant of exposure therapy, can be used for management of anxiety. Stress inoculation training involves carefully monitoring the person's thoughts that follow from thinking about the traumatic event, and then using a script that was created in therapy to attempt to change the thoughts that follow the thinking about the event.

Visualization techniques and *confidence builders*, such as positive self-talk and social skills, may also be used in reducing anxiety. In visualization techniques, the person trains him or herself to recall and visualize a particularly peaceful or pleasant place or situation whenever thoughts of the trauma occur.[17]

Numbing, including emotional unresponsiveness, detachment from others, and loss of interest in life's pleasures, is the most difficult symptom to treat. Peer group support is extremely important in dealing with these issues. Many airlines and unions have Critical Incident Response Programs (CIRP) and/or Employee Assistance Programs (EAP). If your company or union does not have one, personnel from other airlines and/or unions will readily volunteer to help you. The CIRP and/or EAP will furnish professional counselors and specially trained co-workers who provide confidential assessment and short-term counseling to employees and their families in order to assist in dealing with being a victim of violence and other related matters.

Even if your airline furnishes a CIRP and/or EAP personnel, it is strongly recommended that you seek the advice and guidance of a professional counselor. You are not showing weakness by seeking out this guidance, but rather are showing an understanding and maturity of this fragile existence we call life.

Scientists are attempting to determine which treatments work best for which type of trauma.[18] A survey of PTSD experts concluded that for milder acute PTSD, stress debriefing and early individual psychotherapy are especially important. For more severe acute PTSD, medication, critical incident stress debriefing, and group and individual psychotherapy should be started in combination. Chronic PTSD is treated with group and individual psychotherapy in combination with stress debriefing, and medications.[19]

Studies have also shown that medications help ease associated symptoms of depression and anxiety and help promote sleep. All types of PTSD, except sleep disturbance, will respond to the selective serotonin reuptake inhibitors (SSRIs). The only drug approved by the FDA at this time for PTSD is the SSRI, sertraline (Zoloft). If the person is manic depressive, a mood stabilizer may be added, such as lithium or divalproex sodium (Depakote). For sleep distrubance, trazodone (Desyrel) solpidem (Ambien), or nefazodone (Serzone) are oftern recommended.[20]

Co-occurring depression, alcohol or other substance abuse, or another anxiety disorder are not uncommon for individuals who suffer from PTSD. The likelihood of treatment success increases when these other conditions are appropriately identified and treated as well. Headaches, gastrointestinal complaints, immune system problems, dizziness, chest pain, or discomfort in other parts of the body are common and doctors often treat the symptoms without being aware they stem from PTSD. For this reason, when diagnosed with PTSD referral to a mental health professional experienced in treating people with the disorder is recommended.[21]

Conclusion

There are events that occur to us as children or adults that are so overwhelming and inherently frightening they cause temporary, and in some case permanent, changes in our physical and/or psychological responses to stress. When there is a significant traumatic event, everyone can expect to be temporarily overwhelmed and develop at least some of the symptoms of posttraumatic stress disorder.

> After 19 years of flying fighters and 30 years of flying commercial aircraft (Williams), I know I can handle stressful situations; however, I will be the first to admit the traumatic events on 9/11 had a huge effect on me, at least temporarily. After watching the unbelievable events unfold over and over on television for about 36 hours non-stop, I had trouble sleeping. When I slept, I would replay those horrific scenes repeatedly in my dreams. As commercial flights began to operate once again, I flew a three-day trip. The briefing with my first crew was full of emotion and some of the responses of the cabin crew almost overwhelmed me. One flight attendant, with tears streaming down her cheeks, said if anything were to happen in the cabin, they (the flight attendants) would all be dead. Another flight attendant said her five-year old son asked her if she was coming home that night. Later, as I told others about their responses, I would choke up and tears would come into my eyes. It was almost 18 months before I could relate the responses of the cabin crew without triggering overwhelming emotions. The anger directed at those responsible will probably never cease.

We have not covered all symptoms of PTSD in this section. You may experience other feelings that we have not touched upon because not everyone reacts the same when confronted with violence. If you experience any symptoms resulting from a traumatic event, seek qualified professional help immediately. Focus on being a survivor and DO NOT GIVE UP!

Notes

1 National Institute of Mental Heath, *Facts About Post Traumatic Stress Disorder*.
2 Woman shot by police suicidal, *Arizona Republic*, 8 September 2003.
3 National Institute of Mental Heath, *Facts About Post Traumatic Stress Disorder*.
4 Posttraumatic Stress Disorder and 9/11, MedicineNet.com, 12 November 2002.
5 The Assaulted Staff Program, *Coping With the Psychological Aftermath of Violence*, Raymond B Flannery, Jr, PH.D, Chevron Publishing Corp. 1998.
6 Posttraumatic Stress Disorder and 9/11, MedicineNet.com, 12 November 2002.
7 National Institute of Mental Heath, *Facts About Post Traumatic Stress Disorder*.
8 Posttraumatic Stress Disorder and 9/11, MedicineNet.com, 12 November 2002.
9 National Institute of Mental Heath, *Facts About Post Traumatic Stress Disorder*.
10 Posttraumatic Stress Disorder and 9/11, MedicineNet.com, 12 November 2002.
11 National Institute of Mental Heath, *Facts About Post Traumatic Stress Disorder*.
12 Posttraumatic Stress Disorder and 9/11, MedicineNet.com, 12 November 2002.
13 National Institute of Mental Heath, *Facts About Post Traumatic Stress Disorder*.
14 Ibid.
15 Posttraumatic Stress Disorder and 9/11, MedicineNet.com, 12 November 2002.
16 National Institute of Mental Heath, *Facts About Post Traumatic Stress Disorder*.
17 Posttraumatic Stress Disorder and 9/11, MedicineNet.com, 12 November 2002.
18 National Institute of Mental Heath, *Facts About Post Traumatic Stress Disorder*.
19 Posttraumatic Stress Disorder and 9/11, MedicineNet.com, 12 November 2002.
20 Ibid.
21 National Institute of Mental Heath, *Facts About Post Traumatic Stress Disorder*.

Chapter 15

The War on Terrorism

Introduction

One concept that occasionally gets lost in the shuffle of daily activities is that terrorists have declared war on America and its allies, particularly Israel. It is a war we did not ask for, but one we will continue to fight for a very long time. It is not appropriate for the purpose of this book to discuss how we got to this point in history, but suffice it to say, our foreign policies have precipitated much of the hatred of the US and its allies. We cannot change that situation, but must instead focus on how to win this war.

There have been some admirable attempts by the US and its allies to fight battles in the war on terrorism. The war has already cost billions upon billions of dollars, and it will continue to be an expensive campaign for years to come. The alternative is not palatable. We are winning a few battles, but we must win the war.

This chapter is in two parts. The first addresses the US fight against terrorism and the second explores international efforts to combat terrorism. We cannot begin to cover the fight in its entirety in one chapter, or even one book. It has been an enormous effort on the parts of many dedicated men and women, and we salute each of their efforts on our behalf. It is up to every American to determine how they best can wage war on those determined to destroy us. We must also support all those who put themselves in harm's way so that others may continue to enjoy the freedoms we sometimes take for granted. Here are some of their efforts.

Part 1: America's War on Terrorism

In America, the war on terrorism has seen some successes. It will be years, perhaps, before we know to what degree those successes are in the grand scheme of things. It is difficult to tell if the prevention or intervention in one event has had any effect on other events. Perhaps the arrest of an airport employee with fake credentials prevented a weapon (of your choice) from being slipped aboard an aircraft that was intended for use during flight to commit a terrorist activity. We simply do not know. We can only speculate and use our imaginations, as painful as that might be, to step through scenario after scenario similar to the events on 9/11. We should place a very high value on every success, regardless of how important or how insignificant they may appear on the surface.

In December 2002, FBI Director Robert Mueller revealed that nearly 100 terrorist attacks, some intended to take place in America, have been thwarted since 9/11. A number of the intended attacks involved ships. Mueller credited better intelligence gathering and coordination, and information from al-Qaida detainees in custody, including architects of would-be attacks.[1]

Attorney General John Ashcroft declared in June 2003 the investigations and convictions since 9/11 have severely disrupted global terrorist organizations. The results of some of the efforts include:

- Discovering and dismantling terrorist cells in Buffalo, New York, Detroit, Seattle, and Portland, Oregon;
- Deporting 515 undocumented immigrants linked to 9/11;
- Freezing more than US$125 million is assets linked to terrorist groups;
- Convicting 23 people on charges related to financing terrorist operations;
- Arresting 1,200 people for document fraud involved with employment at the nation's airports;
- Breaking up 9 major immigrant smuggling rings; and,
- Stopping 11 terror suspects as they tried to enter the United States, including one known member of al-Qaida.[2]

As you read about the efforts that have been made in this country, keep four things in mind.

1 A number of agencies, including the FBI and CIA, have taken many hits regarding security in the homeland; however, many of their fine agents have performed admirably on the behalf of all Americans, both before and since 9/11. Those agents seem to have been overlooked in all the commotion and mayhem that has occurred since 9/11, and they deserve our deepest appreciation.

2 According to reports, 8 million illegal immigrants are living in the United States, with that number growing daily.[3] The Inspector General's office of the Justice Department reported in January 2003 the nation's 159 international airports remain vulnerable to illegal entry by foreign terrorists and smugglers because the INS has not followed security recommendations made in 1999.[4] Who are these 8 million people, how are we ever going to identify them? What threats do they pose to the rest of us? What if only one per cent of these unknowns are terrorists? What if one per cent of the 43 million foreign visitors to the US each year are terrorists? Do the math!

3 It will take years to fully integrate the 22 federal agencies compromising the Homeland Security Department that became a single terrorism-fighting entity on 1 March 2003.[5] Homeland Security's US$33 billion budget and 170,000 employees represent the largest reorganization in the US government since 1947, and this huge wheel will move ever so slowly. With the jockeying for positions within this new organization, the internal politics, the focus on finding a 'home'

for Homeland Security, and all the other things associated with creating and managing such a huge organization, who is paying attention to national security? If you were a terrorist, would you attack the US again, before this department gets organized?

4 Although successes, all the efforts to date are but a drop in the proverbial bucket of what will continue in the future.

Security initiatives

The FBI acknowledged that it is using unmarked aircraft to monitor people who might have terrorist connections. The acknowledgement came after frequent, unexplained flights over some cities in early 2003, raised fears among residents. The FBI official indicated they are watching 'many foreign nationals'.[6] Some of the aircraft are equipped with night surveillance and eavesdropping equipment. With the electronic surveillance equipment, agents can pursue listening devices placed in cars, in buildings, along streets, and can monitor or listen to cellphone calls. Several of the fleet of more than 80 aircraft, equipped with infrared devices, allows agents to track people and vehicles in the dark. Other aircraft are rigged for photography missions. All 56 FBI field offices have access to the aircraft.[7] The American Civil Liberties Union (ACLU)is all over this activity, as you can well imagine.

The American Bar Association (ABA) has entered the fray over Americans and US residents held by the government as 'enemy combatants', a type of wartime prisoner held without charge or trial and not allowed legal advice. The ABA's said it is un-American to deny legal rights to anyone in this country when apprehended. The 400,000-member ABA is asking lawmakers to amend the surveillance power given to the government by Congress after 9/11, and to order more oversight of wiretapping and searches. Lawyers from the Bush administration said crimes have been foiled with information obtained from combatants and that giving the enemy combatants lawyers would ruin interrogations and threaten the public good.[8]

The restricted airspace over Washington, DC, expanded in February 2003 from a 15-mile radius to a 30-mile radius around Washington, extends to an altitude of 18,000 feet. James Loy, undersecretary of the Transportation Department and head of TSA said, 'The Washington capital region is home to a number of particularly symbolic targets which must be protected. Terrorists are known to favor targets in the transportation sector and to consider our civil aviation system as an arsenal of improvised weapons'.[9]

In February 2003, the Homeland Security Agency released new threat-preparedness material that can be read on the Web at: www.ready.gov, or received in the form of a brochure by calling 1-800-BE-READY. The preparedness initiative, promoted by a major national public awareness campaign, will utilize as much as US$100 million in donated radio and TV airtime, newspaper and Yellow Pages space, and billboards.[10]

A medical facilities program entitled the National Disaster Medical System is being prepared throughout the US at approximately 2,000 hospitals in mid- to large-size cities. The system, designed to ensure military personnel will have immediate access to treatment in the event of large numbers of casualties, is also available in case of natural disaster or other catastrophic events, such as 9/11 or worse, stretch medical facilities to their limits.[11]

The US Attorney's Office has finally gotten serious about prosecuting anyone who brings weapons to security checkpoints. In March 2003, an assistant US attorney said, 'If they (passengers) get to the scanner and we find a weapon in their carry-on, we will assume they meant to sneak it on the plane, and we will prosecute'. Violators will be charged with carrying a weapon or explosive on an aircraft and will face up to 10 years in prison, a US$250,000 fine, or both. Several prosecutions have occurred since 9/11, including a retired police officer who attempted to pass through security with four knives hidden in his socks, a woman carrying a 3-inch knife, and a man who had a firearm hidden in a videocassette recorder. The police officer was acquitted by a jury and the other cases are pending.[12]

One security initiative in 2003 was very short-lived. The Defense Advanced Research Project Agency (DARPA) from the Pentagon announced on 29 July that it was setting up a commodity-style market to help its generals predict terrorist attack, coups and other turmoil around the globe. Investors in the program would use their expertise to buy and sell futures contracts on world events. The program, Future Markets Applied to Prediction, was cancelled on 30 July after withering criticism from lawmakers.[13]

Another initiative that began in February 2003 met with protests from privacy advocates and some lawmakers. The first version of Computer Assisted Passenger Prescreening System (CAPPS) contained numerous serious flaws and was revised with inputs from privacy advocate groups. CAPPS II began a six-month test program in August 2003. Under CAPPS II, the TSA will not use bank records, credit records or medical histories and commercial data providers will not be allowed to acquire or retain passenger information. All passenger data is supposed to be deleted from the government system as soon as travel is completed. Here is how the system is supposed to work:

- Travelers provide the airline with basic information when making a reservation, such as name, date of birth, home address and home phone number.
- The airlines send the information to the government's computer system three days before the flight. Within five seconds, the system cross-checks the data against commercial databases, such as phone books and magazine subscription lists to determine the authenticity of the passenger's identity.
- The program also checks personal information against government databases and watch lists to assess the likelihood that a passenger is a terrorist threat. Those deemed an 'elevated' or 'uncertain' risk will be required to undergo secondary screening with a hand-held wand.

- Anyone deemed a high risk is supposed to be brought to the attention of law enforcement, including those with outstanding criminal warrants.

The government will continue taking public comments and will issue a notice detailing elements of the final plan before it is implemented nationwide in early 2004.[14]

In early August 2003, the government suspended two programs that allowed foreigners to stay in the US without visas while awaiting flights to other countries. The State Department said al-Qaida and other terrorist organizations had planned to use the two programs to get access to flight to and from the United States. The lack of screening for visas could have allowed potential terrorists to enter the country without being checked against federal lists of terrorist suspects. The suspension does not affect passengers from 27 visa-free countries, mostly in Europe, the Far East and Southeast Asia.[15] Our question is, why not ALL countries? Terrorist have been captured with credentials from all of the excluded areas and Southeast Asia is currently the new hotbed for terrorism. Without the benefit of inside intelligence information, the excluded nations would appear to be a giant loophole framing the faces of smiling terrorists.

Technological advances and initiatives

Lockheed-Martin, awarded a five-year, US$12.8 million contract in early 2003 is developing a system to check background information and assign a threat level to all commercial passengers. The system will check credit reports and bank accounts and compare those with passenger names on the government watch list. A TSA official indicated that no data from the background checks would be stored. This seems to be a far-fetched statement, and one on which you might not want to place any bets. Of course, the ACLU is all over this idea, screaming about unconstitutional invasions of privacy and profiling issues. Delta will try the system at three undisclosed airports beginning in April 2003 and the system could be in place nationwide by the end of 2003.[16] Do not bet on that, either.

The National Security Council, Homeland Defense Department, FBI and transportation safety agencies, as a group, are coordinating efforts to protect commercial flights against surface-to-air missile attacks. An official stated, 'The government has long been concerned about the possibility of a shoulder-fired missile taking down a plane. (Please define the phrase, 'long been concerned'.) US airports are being surveyed as to assess their vulnerabilities and airport security personnel have been put on alert. Various technologies are being looked at to protect planes, including the use of decoy flares'.[17] The interest in this item stems from two events. The first was an attack on an Israeli jet in Kenya in November 2002 that involved the use of two SA-7 missiles fired from a four-wheel-drive vehicle located a mile from the airport. The other was an attempt to shoot down an American plane taking off from Prince Sultan air base near Riyadh, Saudi Arabia. That attempt was determined after security forces found the discarded missile at the perimeter of the base, indicating that either the missile or the operator failed and the weapon abandoned. US security official concluded the threat to commercial aviation could be serious because the missiles are portable and plentiful. Where do you think most SA-7 missiles are located, around US airports or near foreign airports? Where are more terrorists that would use these weapons, around US airports or foreign airports? That is not to imply that we should not be more aware around America's airports, but to raise the question about airports all around the world that are more apt to provide targets of opportunity for this type of attack. You can still drive a vehicle within a mile of almost any US airport today. How much effort is going to be required to fix that problem?

In January 2003, the FAA announced a notice of proposed rulemaking (NPR) that calls for a modification to transponders on passenger and cargo aircraft that would allow pilots to activate the hijacking code in a single, simple action. The transponder would keep broadcasting the signal and be designed to thwart any attempts to deactivate it, or cut offs its power. Activation of the hijacking code would also send a visual signal to the crew that it has been activated. The proposed deadline for modifying the estimated 7, 394 aircraft is 29 March 2005.[18]

Beginning in January 2004, foreign visitors arriving at US airports and seaports will have their travel documents scanned, their fingerprints and photos taken and their identification checked against terrorist watch lists. The new security system is entitled 'US Visitor and Immigration Status Indication Technology', or US VISIT.[19]

The TSA security laboratory is experimenting with X-ray back-scatter technology as a possibility to replace magnetometers now being used at airport security checkpoints. The new machines, priced between US$100,000–200,000 each show the person passing through the machine as naked. Scientists are trying to modify the machines with an electronic fig leaf that fuzzes out sensitive body parts and/or distorts the face of the person to make them unrecognizable.[20] This machine should certainly solve the monotony and boredom problem associated with security screeners. Let us hope the fig leafs do not fall from the human trees in the fall and winter seasons.

In May 2003, the Pentagon announced it is developing a radar-based device that can identify people by the way they walk for use in a new anti-terrorist surveillance system. The system, Total Information Awareness, has raised privacy alarms on both ends of the political spectrum.[21] The US is also considering an eye-scan ID system currently used successfully in the Netherlands.[22]

DARPA, the Defense Advanced Research Projects Agency, is helping the Pentagon develop new technologies for combating terrorism and other uses. Some of DARPA's projects include an urban surveillance system that would use computers and thousands of cameras to record and analyze the movement of every vehicle in a foreign city. Dubbed the 'Combat Zones That See', the project is designed to assist US military troops to fight in cities overseas. The system automatically identifies vehicles by size, color, shape and license tag, or drivers and passengers by face. A similar system, used in Great Britain, involves the use of an estimated 2.5 million cameras. It is estimated the average Londoner is photographed over 300 times a day. As a comparison, there are 16 closed-circuit television cameras watching major roads and gathering places in the District of Columbia. DARPA reported the use of 40 million cameras in use worldwide, with 300 million expected by 2005.[23]

If you think 'Big Brother' is watching you, you are probably correct. Another project of DARPA includes developing software that scans databases of everyday transactions and personal records worldwide to predict terrorist attacks and creating a computerized diary that would record and analyze everything a person says, see, hears, reads or touches.[24]

An even bigger 'eye' looms on the horizon. The Office of Naval Research is working with Honolulu-based Science and Technology International to develop 200-foot long surveillance blimps. Packed with leading-edge sensors and high resolution cameras, the blimps could scour the landscape or oceans, spotting and tracking targets on the ground or deep under water. The blimps could police US harbors to pinpoint terrorist divers, suspicious boats or other unusual activity. They could also be employed to provide increased surveillance at military bases and along the country's borders.[25]

The US is considering a biometric security access system currently in use at the London City Airport for its 1,600 employees. To enter any of the secure areas, an employee must pass a smart ID over an electronic reader and then have their 'biometric finger template' – a fingerprint recognition process- checked to confirm their identity. The system can be expanded to encompass other forms of recognition, such as iris or voice recognition, and could be expanded in use to include passengers.[26]

Results of background, immigration, or other checks

Background investigations conducted on airport employees, resulted in the arrest of 30 employees at Portland International Airport by Federal agents, on charges of using fake documents to get jobs. The workers were responsible for baggage handling, construction, and food and custodial services.[27]

The TSA interviewed 340,000 applicants in ten months out of the 1.7 million applications it received in the mail and on-line, as well as from the 89 job fairs it held in 56 cities. TSA chief James Loy said, 'As you might imagine in an effort of this scope, there have been problems'. As of June 2003, 1,208 screeners out of the workforce of 55,000 screeners hired to work in 440 airports nationwide, were terminated because of 'suitability issues'. Of those terminated, 503 had failed to reveal an arrest or conviction of a crime, including 85 convicted of felonies. The attempt to meet the hiring deadline resulted in as many as 30,000 of the 55,000 workers not being cleared at one point, even though they were actively working.[28]

'In my mind, I was doing a noble thing'. This statement was made by a Jordanian graduate student at the University of Texas in February 2003 who considered becoming a suicide bomber if the US invaded Iraq. Tahir Ibrihim Aletwei also said at his deportation hearing, 'If someone had approached me to do something against the country (USA), I was willing to do it'.[29] Aletwei was deported, posing the questions,

'How does he feel about the US now, and will we see his name attached to another act of terror in the future?'

You will probably find this incident strange and a candidate for the Darwin Award. An Afghan man was arrested in February 2003 after he flagged down a Tucson police officer and said the two Hispanic men he was with were kidnapping him. The police took all three men into custody. As it turned out, the Afghan had been in a dispute with the Hispanics over money after paying them to get him across the border. After being turned over to the Border Patrol, the men were interviewed by the FBI. The Border Patrol refused to disclose how the men got across the border.[30]

Of the approximately 82,000 Arab and Muslim men living in America that registered with immigration authorities in 2003, more than 13,000 were living in America illegally. In June 2003, the INS announced that most of the 13,000 men would be deported, although only a handful was linked to terrorism.[31]

Zakaria Mustapha Soubra, an aeronautical safety student at Embry-Riddle Aeronautical University in Prescott, Arizona, was deported in May 2003 after being held for over a year without bond. Soubra, admitted he had served as an organizer for the radical Islamic group Al Mohujiroun and had demonstrated against US foreign policy. One 765 Muslim-nation foreigners detained for immigration violations, Soubra was arrested based on a technical violation of his student visa. He is the only one out of eight Arab or Muslim aviation students in Arizona identified publicly.[32]

In August 2003, authorities arrested two Pakistani men at the Seattle-Tacoma International Airport after their names were flagged on an anti-terrorist 'no-fly' list. One suspect paid cash for a one-way ticket to New York, but when the ticket agent called authorities, walked away leaving his ticket on the counter. The other man also paid cash for his ticket in a separate transaction. Authorities, trying to determine what the men were doing in the US, are holding the men on immigration charges.[33]

Investigations/arrests of known terrorists, or those connected to terrorists

As of June 2003, FBI agents investigating al-Qaida-related matters in 40 states, claim to have disrupted 35 terrorism-related incidents since 9/11. The on-going investigations include inquiries into possible terrorist-cell operatives and sources of funding for terrorist organizations. Many of the 35 incidents involved the arrests of al-Qaida sympathizers and suspected operatives in more than a half-dozen states.[34]

In January 2003, the FBI questioned as many as 50,000 of the 300,000 Iraqis living in the US in search for potential terrorist cells, spies or people who might provide valuable information during Operation Iraqi Freedom. The largest Iraqi communities in the US are found in Michigan, California, Texas, Illinois, Pennsylvania and Tennessee. Some of the Iraqis were upset.[35] Too bad.

A federal grand jury has arrested Semi Osman, born in Sierra Leone, on citizenship charges after allegations that he entered into a sham marriage to gain citizenship in the United States. Osman holds a British passport. He, along with other members of the Dar-us-Salaam mosque in Seattle, are under investigation for ties to al-Qaida recruiter, Abu Hamza al-Masri.[36]

A Pakistani college student pleaded guilty in August 2002 to conspiring to make jihad by plotting to destroy electrical power stations, the Israeli Consulate and other targets in Miami-Dade and Broward counties through arson and/or explosion. Imran Mandhai faces 5 years in prison and deportation to Pakistan. His father, hoping his son can continue to study computer science behind bars said, 'The government has programs, don't they?'[37] (The student will probably be too busy staying alive to study!)

Abdul Malike, a New York cabdriver from Afghanistan, arrested in May 2003 after attempting to buy explosives, bulletproof vests, and night-vision goggles, had gone to a Miami harbor to seek information on bridges and cruise ships. The prosecutor said Malike, who may not have acted alone, had 'sinister intentions' and was expecting financing for his explosives and other items from Pakistan.[38]

Iyman Faris, a Kashmiri-born naturalized US citizen, pleaded guilty in May 2003 to providing material to support a terrorist organization. Under the directions of Khalid Shaikh Mohammed of al-Qaida, Faris (a.k.a. Mohammed Rauf) plotted to destroy the Brooklyn Bridge in New York and to carry out an unspecified simultaneous attack in Washington, DC as recently as April 2003. Faris, a truck driver in Ohio, had carried cash and cell phones to al-Qaida during a visit to Afghanistan in early 2002. While in Afghanistan, Khalid Mohammed personally advised Faris of his interest in deliveries to cargo planes, as 'he was interested in cargo planes because they would hold more weight and more fuel'. In the US, Faris provided bin Laden with intelligence information about ultra-light aircraft being considered for use as escape vehicles for terrorists. He also scouted for equipment used to sabotage rail lines and to cut suspension cables of bridges.[39]

As a result of interrogations of Khalid Shaikh Mohammed (suspected mastermind of 9/11) and Ramzi Binalshibh (head of al-Qaida in Indonesia), and Malaysian chemist Yazid Sufaat (who provided fake papers for Moussaoui to enter the US), it appears that Zacarias Moussaoui was being groomed as part of a broad plot that included additional suicide hijackers in a second wave after 9/11. Moussaoui, a French citizen, the lone man charged as a conspirator in the 9/11 attacks, was originally thought to have been the '20th hijacker' on 9/11.[40]

A Saudi man who accused America West Airlines of racial profiling after he and another Arizona State University student, Hamdan Al-Shalawi, were handcuffed and removed from a flight last year, was arrested by the FBI in June of 2003 and held at an unspecified location and on unspecified charges.[41] Both men were acquaintances of Zakaria Soubra, the ERAU student deported in May 2003.[42]

The Justice Department charged 11 men with training to join an overseas terrorist group, Lash-kar-e-Tayyaba, responsible for the deaths of 14,000 Indian soldiers and 300 civilians in its fight to evict India from Kashmir. As of July 2003, eight of the 11 are being held until their trial, three remain at large. During a search of one of the captured men's residence, authorities found a cache of assault weapons, ammunition and a document called the *Terrorist Handbook*, containing instructions on how to make explosives.

The men trained in military tactics using paintball games in Virginia and practiced with firearms at shooting ranges in numerous locations. The indictment says the men traveled to a terrorist training camp in Pakistan shortly after 9/11.[43]

Maher Hawash, a software engineer who tried unsuccessfully to enter Afghanistan to fight against US troops, pleaded guilty in August 2003 to aiding the Taliban and agreed to testify against another six persons, all part of the 'Portland Seven'. Hawash will serve at least seven years in federal prison under a deal approved by US Attorney General Ashcroft.[44]

In August 2003, the FBI arrested Hemant Lakhani in New Jersey and two money transfer agents in New York. The three men were part of a conspiracy to smuggle 50 shoulder-fired SA-18 Igla missiles from Russia into the United States for US$5 million. Lakhani, a British national born in India, began talking about selling the missiles shortly after 9/11 to a man who represented himself as a member of a Somali terrorist group. The terrorist group's representative was actually an unidentified FBI informer who recorded 150 conversations with Lakhani. The two New Yorkers were charged with operating unlicensed money transmitting businesses after arranging illegal money transfers for the deal. Lakhani faces up to 25 years in prison and US$1.25 million in fines, while the other two men face up to five years in prison and a US$250,000 fine.[45]

Interruption of terrorist funding

(This topic is covered in some detail in Chapter 4, Investigating Terrorism; however, the enormity of the problem deserves the additional space.) As of December 2002, the Treasury Department froze US$112 million in terrorist-related funds and convictions of 23 terrorists secured in 22 states.[46] The US Treasury and State departments offer up to US$5 million for information that allows the government to stop the flow of money to terrorists. The 'Rewards for Justice' program paid more than US$9.5 million to 23 people since its inception.[47]

The Treasury Department and the Department of Justice have seized US$6.8 million domestically and more than US$16 million in outbound currency being smuggled to Middle Eastern countries. The Justice Department seized at least 15 foreign-based bank accounts in the US in recent months and confiscated money belonging to overseas banks in Israel, Oman, Taiwan, India and Belize.[48]

DEA chief Asa Hutchinson announced in August 2002 that his department had uncovered evidence that points for the first time to a US drug operation that financed terrorism. Evidence collected in raids and arrests in 2002 involved 136 Middle Eastern men in Chicago and Detroit. They are accused of importing the chemical pseudo-ephedrine from Canada and reselling it to illegal manufacturers of methamphetamine, a popular street drug. Profits were funneled to the Iranian-backed terrorist organization, Hezbollah, and to specific terrorists' accounts in Lebanon and Yemen.[49]

In Texas, a Dallas grand jury indicted five brothers with money laundering and shipment of computers and computer parts to Syria and Libya. The arrests and indictments in December 2002 were in addition to raids in Michigan that resulted in the arrest and indictment of seven people involved in illegal money transfers of up to US$50 million to Yemen.[50]

US officials left Malawi in southern Africa with five al-Qaida suspects in their custody despite a court order forbidding deportation. The five men, two Turks, a Saudi, a Sudanese and a Kenyan, arrested in a joint operation with the CIA and Malawi intelligence officials, are accused of funneling money to al-Qaida. The whereabouts of the men are unknown.[51]

Sheik Mohammed Ali Hassan al Moayad of Yemen and a Yemeni assistant, Mohammed Mohsen Yahya Zayed were arrested in January 2003 in a sting operation in Germany. The men were accused of funneling money, weapons and recruits to al-Qaida and other terrorist groups. Moayad bragged to an FBI informant that he handed bin Laden US$20 million just before the 9/11 attacks. The complaint alleged Moayad and Zayed raised much of their money from US contributors, New York businesses, and the Al Farooq mosque in Brooklyn.[52]

A University of South Florida professor, long accused of ties to terrorism was charged in February 2003 with running US financial operations of the Palestinian Islamic Jihad, an organization linked to more than 100 suicide bombings and other attacks. Sami Amin Al-Arian, a Kuwaiti, allegedly ran worldwide finance operations and laundered money to be funneled to the families of those carrying out the suicide attacks. A grand jury indicted Al-Arian, three other men arrested with him, and four men who are believed to be somewhere overseas. The indictments contain 50 separate criminal counts, including conspiracy to kill people overseas, provide support to terrorist organizations, perjury, and immigration fraud.[53]

In another event involving a university, Ali Saleh Kahlah Al-Marri, in the US on a student visa and studying computer science at Bradley University, was arrested and charged on numerous counts in May 2003. Al-Marri was charged with possession of at least 15 unauthorized and counterfeit credit card numbers, and lying in account applications at three banks to help finance the al-Qaida network.[54]

The US House Committee on International Relations was told in July 2003 that al-Qaida and other terrorist groups are using counterfeit goods to fund their operations with the global trade estimated between US$400 to US$450 billion a year. The secretary general of Interpol (the agency that coordinates information among law enforcement agencies in 181 countries) said supporters of al-Qaida have been found with huge amounts of counterfeit items, including CDs, DVDs, cigarettes and knock-offs of designer handbags.[55]

In August 2003, Enaam Arnaout, a Syrian-born US citizen, was sentenced to 11 years in prison and fined over US$300,000 for defrauding donors by diverting money intended for refugees to Islamic military groups in Bosnia and Chechnya. Arnaout's Benevolence International Foundation funneled about US$20 million to Muslim countries, supposedly to help widows, orphans and refugees.[56]

America's efforts abroad

Under President Bush's rules for the war on terrorism, American citizens working for al-Qaida overseas can legally be targeted and killed by the CIA. Although CIA officials claim that he was not the target of the attack, one American has been killed under this authority. In November 2002, a CIA-operated Predator drone fired a missile that killed a carload of al-Qaida operatives in Yemen. The real target was a Yemeni named Qaed Salim Sinan al-Harethi, the top al-Qaida operative in Yemen. The CIA did not know that a US citizen, Yemeni-American Kamal Derwish, was in the car. Derwish was allegedly the leader of an al-Qaida cell operating in suburban Buffalo, NY, where a half-dozen other members were arrested previously.[57]

The US announced plans in December 2002 to finance the construction of 177 checkpoints along Afghanistan's borders. The checkpoints, staffed by 12,000 border police, would serve to stem the flow of illicit drugs, terrorists and contraband into and out of the country. Each checkpoint would cost approximately US$300,000.[58]

Speaking of borders, the US and Canada agreed in 2001 to a 30-point plan to enhance border security while maintaining the flow of people and goods. The plan included creating 'fast-lanes' for pre-cleared trucks and people, increased sharing of intelligence, more coordinated immigration policies and joint border enforcement teams. A new US system for keeping track of foreign visitors entering from Canada by targeting people born in Iran, Iraq, Libya, Sudan and Syria, has angered the Canadians. Canada warned its citizens born in those countries to avoid travel to the US. Canada protested to Washington after a Syrian-born Canadian was detained during a transit stop in New York and deported to Syria.[59]

The US is trying to align itself with three countries located on the Horn of Africa that it has previously criticized for their records on human rights. Eritrea, Ethiopia and Djibouti are strategically important to the protection of sea lanes in the Persian Gulf. The long coasts and porous borders, coupled with political unrest and corruption, have made the area a hub for drug and arms running and a haven for al-Qaida operatives.[60]

Omar Abdel-Rahman, an al-Qaida operative ranked just below Khalid Shaikh Mohammed in the organization's hierarchy, was captured in Pakistan in February 2003. Known as the 'Lion of God', Abdel-Rahman once ran a terrorist training camp in Afghanistan. Abdel-Rahman and his brother, who was captured in Afghanistan in 2001, are sons of a radical Egyptian cleric now serving a life sentence in a federal prison for plotting to destroy bridges and tunnels in New York City.[61]

In April 2003, US authorities reported a worldwide manhunt for Adnan El Shukrijumah, known within al-Qaida as 'Ja'far the Pilot', who was an overseas acquaintance of Jose Padilla. Padilla was arrested in Chicago in 2002 on charges of plotting to use a 'dirty bomb' in an attack on the United States. El Shukrijumah is a well-connected operative with a range of skills that match al-Qaida's continuing interest in staging attacks with planes and attacks against soft targets in the United

States. El Shukrijumah has six aliases, passports from Saudi Arabia, Canada, Trinidad and Guyana, and is a licensed pilot.[62]

Also in April 2003, a US special forces unit in Baghdad captured Abul Abbas, the Palestinian terrorist who was convicted in the 1985 hijacking of the Achille Lauro cruise ship and murder of an invalid American, Leon Klinghoffer. The capture was made by the same team of US commandos that rescued American Army POW, Jessica Lynch from an Iraqi hospital. Abbas, the first major terrorist found in Iraq since Operation Iraqi Freedom began, had tried in vain to cross the border in Syria.[63]

In May 2003, President Bush and President Gloria Arroyo of the Philippines pledged expanded collaboration in campaigns against terrorism. The US promised more than US$95 million in military aid and a new deployment of US forces to help defeat Muslim rebel groups in the Philippines. Bush also designated the Philippines as a major non-NATO ally, a status that will enable the country to conduct joint research and development with the Pentagon and to bid on certain US military contracts.[64]

US troops in Iraq arrested a group of suspected Islamic militants in June 2003, included several connected with Abu Musab al Zarqawi (an associate of bin Laden). Also included in the group are members of Ansar al Islam and Partisans of Islam, a Kurdish Islamic extremist organization. Officials believe the group oversaw a plot in London to produce ricin, plotted the murder in October 2002 of US diplomat Lawrence Foley in Jordan, and was planning other attacks in Western Europe.[65]

The US decided in June 2003 to place teams of US inspectors at major seaports in Muslim nations and other strategically located ports to prevent terrorists from using cargo containers to smuggle chemical, biological or nuclear weapons into America. The inspectors will be provided with radiation monitors, chemical detectors and other equipment to inspect high-risk metal cargo containers before they are put on US-bound ships.[66] The inspectors have their work cut out for them as more than 6 million containers enter the US from overseas each year.

In July 2003, American forces captured the Iraqi intelligence agent reported to have met with the 9/11 hijacker, Mohammed Atta in Prague five months before the attacks. Ahmad Khalil Ibrahim Samir Ani, who was taken into custody in Iraq, is believed to have worked as an Iraqi spy under diplomatic cover, serving as vice consul at Iraq's embassy in Prague.[67]

Part 1: Summary

The efforts highlighted in this section are by no means the majority of all the fine efforts by thousands of people in America that are dedicated to preserving our way of life and freedoms we enjoy. From the efforts provided, we hope you will have a better understanding of the magnitude and depth of problems we face in America's war on terrorism within our borders and overseas. These efforts continue 24 hours a day, seven days a week. There will be mistakes. There will be failures and successes.

Appreciate the efforts for what they are … a fight for all of us, our security, and our peace of mind.

Part 2: The International War on Terrorism

Gaining multi-national support

The tragic events of 9/11 in America, quickly disseminated worldwide through television and other modes of communication, triggered huge emotional responses from many nations. The firmness of the American President in expressing the determination of the US to eliminate terrorism throughout the world was unmistakable. During a trip to Europe in May 2002, Bush's reminder to our allies they, too, are potential targets of terrorists sparked mixed responses in Europe. Bush faced large crowds of protestors throughout his visit, a stark contrast to the sympathy expressed for Americans just after September 11th. American foreign policies regarding nuclear proliferation, trade sanctions and global warming, as well as the imminent attack on Iraq, seemed to be more important to Europeans than tracking down bin Laden, the al-Qaida and other terrorist organizations. The first battle, to gain the attention and support of our allies, was an uphill engagement.

Evidence of some of the attempts in gaining global support for the fight against international terrorism comes from headlines dating back to the first of the year 2002:

- 'Global manhunt on for terror figures' – *Chicago Tribune*, 18 January 2002
- 'Bush takes terror fight to Europe' – *Los Angeles Times*, 23 May 2002
- 'Terrorism Alerts Trigger Call for Global Action' – *Aviation Week and Space Technology*, 27 May 2002
- 'NATO told it must act on terror threat' – Associated Press, 7 June 2002
- 'Bond is forged to fight terrorism' – *Chicago Tribune*, 2 August 2002
- 'Global terrorist hunt intensifies with capture, arrests' – *Los Angeles Times*, 13 June 2002
- 'Bush wants world help in Mideast terror fight' – Associated Press, 15 August 2002.

'It's not our fight' seemed to be the banner flying over a number of countries, an attitude underscored by NATO Secretary-General Robertson's remarks in June 2002. When Defense Secretary Rumsfield asked whether NATO was ready to become an offensive force against terrorist threats, Robertson replied, 'We are a defense alliance, we remain a defense alliance. We don't go out looking for problems to solve'.[68] NATO *was* willing to accept additional and upgraded military equipment from the US, however. Surprise, surprise!

After another rash of suicide bombings in Israel, President Bush again called for international support in trying to stop terrorist killings. Peace efforts between the

Israelis and the Palestinians change on an hourly basis with no end to their struggles in sight. Bush's 'Road to Peace' has seen numerous detours as attacks by both sides continue, sometimes abated, but always continued. The US has had better success in Southeast Asia.

In July 2002, the Association of Southeast Asian Nations (ASEAN) consisting of the US, China and 11 other countries, reached an agreement intended to interrupt the flow of financing for terrorist groups. On 1 August 2002, the US and ten nations in Southeast Asia signed an agreement pledging to plug holes in security, share intelligence information and enhance police cooperation. The accord covers Brunei, Cambodia, Indonesia, Laos, Malaysia, Myanmar, the Philippines, Singapore, Thailand, and Vietnam.[69]

There have been numerous successes between international intelligence and international police agencies in identifying and tracking terrorists and terrorist cell activities. The depth and magnitude of their efforts are also to be applauded. There is no way to predict what might have occurred had these efforts been neglected.

A cross-section of international responses

Many of our allies, some of which may only be friends for convenience or for the moment, have made efforts to combat terrorism in their own countries as well as to pursue those in support of or responsible for the attacks on America in 2001. The list of countries fighting terrorism is not at all inclusive, nor are all the efforts presented; however, the intent is to give the reader a broad glimpse of activities taking place outside America in the war on terrorism. The list is in alphabetical order by country.

Australia

Australia boosted security in December 2002 at its embassies overseas, and warned terrorists may attack within Australia. Australia also closed its mission in the Philippines. The Prime Minister said he was prepared to act against terrorists in neighboring Asian countries and the UN charter should be changed to allow nations to strike pre-emptively against terrorists planning to attack them. To no one's surprise, the PM's statements riled neighboring Asian countries.[70]

Canada

Law enforcement officials in Canada in January 2003 confirmed that as many as 19 people of Middle Eastern and Pakistani origin might have entered the US illegally from Canada. Officials are trying to determine whether all 19 are operatives for al-Qaida or affiliated terror groups.[71] Information was gathered during a breakup of a sophisticated document forgery ring in Ontario where the 19 men were provided false passports, false names and photographs. A raid on the homes of Michael John Hamdani and a friend turned up an array of big screen TVs and other luxury goods, US$600,000 in forged American Express and Thomas Cook checks, a state-of-the-art counterfeiting operation complete with silk-screen equipment, ink stamps like those used by consular officials, and stacks of high-grade fake passports and other identity documents.[72]

Canadian Security Intelligence Service agents arrested a Moroccan, Adil Charkaoui, in May 2003. Charkaoui faces deportation from Canada as a 'national security threat' after intelligence officials identified him as a dormant agent of al-Qaida. Charkaoui has been a resident of Canada since 1995.[73]

Egypt

Egyptian police arrested 13 members of the banned Muslim Brotherhood and confiscated literature and leaflets in raids at homes and at an organizational meeting in January 2003.[74]

France

In November 2002, French authorities arrested six suspected associates of Richard Reid, the shoe-bomber. The arrests were part of an investigation of a Pakistani-dominated network that allegedly built Reid's shoe bombs and sheltered, funded and supervised him before the attempt on the American Airlines jet in December 2001. One of those captured was wanted in a failed attempt to bomb a synagogue in Strasburg during Christmas 2000 and the mastermind behind the plot to attack Los Angeles Airport with a car bomb on New Year's Eve 1999. The six were part of 17 extremists belonging to three Islamic networks arrested in raids during November.[75] Also in November, French authorities detained 3 people in their continuing investigation of the bombing of the Ghriba synagogue on the resort island of Djerba in April that killed 19 tourists.[76] French intelligence agents arrested eight suspects in connection with the same attack earlier in the month, and found documents in the home of one of the men that relate directly to the attack.[77]

In December 2002, French authorities broke up a terrorist cell with ties to al-Qaida and Chechen rebels planning bomb or toxic gas attacks in France and Russia.[78] During the month, they also arrested Abderazak Besseghir, an airport worker of Algerian origin at Charles de Gaulle Airport, after finding a pistol, plastic explosives, detonators and a fuse in the trunk of the man's car.[79] French police detained three suspected Islamic militants in the outskirts of Paris in in connection with an alleged plot to attack the US Embassy in Paris.[80]

French authorities arrested a Moroccan in June 2003 in connection with an investigation into the 9/11 attacks in the US. Karim Mehdi had arrived from Germany at Charles de Gaulle Airport en route to the French island of La Reunion off the southeastern coast of Africa.[81] Also in June, French counterterrorism investigators arrested a German, Christian Ganczarski, suspected of taking part in an al-Qaida bombing of a Tunisian synagogue in 2002, and of having ties to a Hamburg cell that plotted the 9/11 attacks.[82]

French authorities arrested more than 150 members of a long-established armed Iranian opposition group in July 2003, accused them of organizing terrorist acts, and seized US$1.3 million in US$100 bills. The crackdown on the Mumahideen Khalq was deemed necessary to prevent their use of France as an international base of operations to supplement their activities in Iraq.[83] The leader of the group and eight others were released after posting bail two weeks later.[84]

Germany

German officials, taken aback by how some of the 9/11 hijackers took advantage of Germany's privacy laws to formulate their plan, began an extensive security crackdown in November 2001. Distressed at being caught so unaware, they are scrutinizing almost every Muslim man age 16-40 for ties to terrorism plots or radical movements. Investigators are combing government, bank and university computer databases for clues.[85]

Investigators in June 2002 identified the man who first recruited Mohamed Atta and other Hamburg-based hijackers into al-Qaida. They do not know the whereabouts of the man, Mohamed Zammar, but suspect he is custody of another nation.[86] Germany and the US will soon reach an agreement on how Berlin can supply evidence against Zacarias Moussaoui, accused on six counts of conspiracy in the 9/11 attacks. Germany has some evidence of his connection with al-Qaida that could help convict him; however, as of June Germany is refusing to provide the evidence so long as Moussaoui faces the death penalty.[87] Also in June, German authorities were on the alert for a possible surface-to-air missile attack against German passenger planes. The alleged plot also included the use of model aircraft laden with explosives to attack commercial jets as they took off or landed.[88]

German police questioned and released seven suspected Islamic extremists in July 2002 who were believed to be plotting new terrorist attacks. Five months of surveillance did not turn up enough evidence to hold the men.[89]

German investigators said in August 2002 they have evidence that Atta and two accomplices trained at al-Qaida camps in Afghanistan from late 1999 to early 2000. Less than six months later, Atta and the two men enrolled in flight schools in the US. Four other Arabs from Hamburg attended training camps about the same time, including two of the other hijackers who flew planes into the WTC and the Pentagon on September 11th. The German investigators have also established a clear link between al-Qaida and a recent attack on a Tunisian synagogue. In the attack, a truck filled with liquid propane ignited and the resulting explosion killed 14 German tourists, 6 Tunisians, a Frenchman, and the suicide bomber.[90] Also in August, terrorism indictments brought against six men accused them of conspiring to help al-Qaida members who were plotting to attack the US. One of the men is accused of being an al-Qaida banker who funneled thousands of dollars to the suicide hijackers.[91]

A Turkish man and his American fiancée were arrested and explosive chemicals and five pipe bombs in their apartment were confiscated in September 2002. They are being held on charges of planning a terrorist attack on a major American military base in

Heidelberg on or near 11 September 2002. The woman worked at a supermarket for US personnel at the base. There was no immediate indication of links to al-Qaida.[92]

German authorities working with the FBI arrested two Yemeni men in Frankfurt in January 2003. One of the men captured, Ali Hassan al Mouyad, was an aide and close friend to recently captured Abd al-Rahim al-Nashiri (al-Qaida chief of operations in the Persian Gulf and key planner of the attack on the USS Cole). The other man, Mohammed Moshen Yahya Zayed, was a one-time imam at a mosque in Yemen and an al-Qaida financier.[93] Also in January, German police arrested the head of the Al-Aqsa Foundation on charges of supporting terrorists after a year-long FBI sting operation. Sheikh Mohammed Ali Hassan Moayad allegedly sent US$3 million to Hamas and other militant Palestinian groups.[94]

German police raided six houses in western towns in February 2003, and arrested 3 people in connection with the Hamburg cell involved in the 9/11 attacks. Two of the three men were working to build a cell that was planning attacks on a Rhein Main Air Base near Frankfurt, the other was accused of supporting the cell.[95] Also in February, a German court returned the first verdict in the attacks of 9/11, convicting Mounir el Motassedeq – a Moroccan – on 3,000 counts of accessory to murder for helping the Hamburg-based al-Qaida cell that led the attacks. A close friend of Mohammed Atta, the former electrical engineering student was sentenced to 15 years in prison, the maximum under German law.[96]

In March 2003, four Algerians were convicted of a plot to blow up a French Christmas market and a synagogue in Strasbourg in December 2000. The four belonged to an al-Qaida terrorist cell, and had trained at terrorist camps in Afghanistan.[97]

In May 2003, German prosecutors charged a Moroccan, Abdelghani Mzoudi, with accessory to mass murder in the 9/11 attacks in the United States. Mzoudi is the second veteran of an al-Qaida training camp to be charged with providing logistical support in the 9/11 plot.[98] Also in May, a Turkish man was convicted of illegal possession of explosives and lesser charges of drug violations. Osman Petmezci was convicted of stealing gunpowder and chemicals to make liquid potassium nitrate, a potential bomb material. Petmezci had originally faced charges of planning a bomb attack on a US military base in Germany on the anniversary of 9/11.[99]

In July 2003, a German court approved the extradition of Mohammed Al Hassan Al-Moyad and his assistant, Mohammed Mohsen Yahya Zayed, to face charges in the United States of supplying weapons, militants and millions of dollars to al-Qaida. The extradition was approved with a number of stipulations protecting the two men.[100]

Abdelrazak M., an Algerian emigrant who lived in Germany for several years with his family, was arrested in August 2003 in Hamburg on suspicion of preparing explosive attacks on crowded tourist resorts on Costa del Sol in Spain. Addelrazak M. and four or five other fanatical Muslims left Hamburg in March for Syria to join Iraqi forces in attacks on invading US troops. The men were arrested in Syria and held for several weeks before being allowed to return to Germany.[101]

Great Britain

The Blair government formulated more security steps for aviation in an attempt to tighten the noose on international terrorists in October 2001. Other measures address terrorist group financing and bioterrorism.[102]

About 250 people, mostly Muslims, attended a meeting in July 2002 with several militant Muslim leaders to condemn the US and what they said is the oppression of Muslims in the West. Leaders from Britain's mainstream Muslim community said the militants did not represent the opinions of the 1.5 million Muslims in Great Britain. The militant group aspires to turn Britain into an Islamic state.[103]

A raid on an Islamic mosque in London in January 2003 resulted in the arrest of six North African men and one Eastern European man. The raid was part of an ongoing investigation of a terrorist network involved in the production of ricin and the slaying of a police detective. A search of the mosque turned up canisters of tear gas, stun gun, an imitation firearm and potentially significant documents. The mosque has functioned openly as a center of recruitment, ideological incitement and support of terrorist acts.[104]

John Reid, of Britain's Labor Party, said Britain faces the kind of threat that destroyed the World Trade Center and damaged the Pentagon on 9/11. In February 2003, Britain was on heightened alert with about 17,000 police and 450 soldiers engaged in counterterrorist operations.[105] 'The al-Qaida network has a substantial presence in Britain', said John Stevens, the head of London's Metropolitan Police. 'We are taking action', he added.[106] Security was boosted around London's Heathrow International Airport by hundreds of troops and tanks as police anticipated terrorist attacks timed to a Muslim holiday.[107] Anti-terrorism police detained seven people in four cities in England and Scotland during raids in February 2003. The men were linked to a cell of North African extremists charged with plotting attacks with ricin in London.[108]

British officials announced in July 2003 that two Britons and an Australian were among six who face possible terrorism charges before US military tribunals. Human rights activists and attorneys for the British detainees objected to the prospect of secret trials, with military lawyers appointed to defend the suspects, and the possibility of the death penalty. David Hicks, a former rodeo rider and kangaroo skinner, converted to Islam and traveled the world to join Muslim guerrilla movements in Kosovo and Kashmir. Hicks received training at al-Qaida training camps in Afghanistan and was captured fighting with the Taliban in Kandahar in December 2001.[109]

Greece

Greek police captured a leader of the November 17 terrorist organization in June 2002. Xiros, a religious icon painter and one of a priest's sons, was severely injured 29 June when a bomb he was carrying exploded.[110] Police penetrated the group as Greece came under increasing international pressure to improve security ahead of the 2004 Olympics. In all, seven members have been arrested, three of which served the group as executioners.[111] Greeks have been stunned by the suspects' seemingly ordinary lives and jobs. Occupations included an electrician, a retired printer, a bee keeper, a mechanic, a musical instrument maker and real estate agents. Three brothers are sons of a Greek Orthodox priest.[112]

In July 2002, Greek authorities charged two alleged members of November 17 with the assassination of American and British servicemen. The wave of arrests has apparently foiled a plot by the terrorist organization to attack a convoy of NATO peacekeepers driving from Greece to Kosovo along the Macedonian border.[113] Also in July, a 46-year old telephone operator suspected of ambushing a CIA chief in 1975 was charged with general terrorist and weapons accusations that could bring a life sentence. The 20-year statute of limitations prevented Greek prosecutors from bringing murder charges against the man. Serifis is believed to be the group's second-in-command. The suspected leader, Giotopoulos is already in custody.[114]

The November 17 group mocked reports of its demise in August 2002, warning that it could grab hostages to exchange for capture suspects. The statement, carrying the group's star, was delivered by the method previously used to distribute the group's manifestos.[115]

The main hit man for November 17, nicknamed 'Poison Hand', surrendered in September 2002 at police headquarters. November 17 has been blamed for 23 killings, including four American officials, scores of bombings and rocket attacks, and bank robberies since 1975. Other members are still believed to be at large, including some of the founders of the terrorist group.[116] Also in September, Greek Premier Simitis said that authorities have wiped out the November 17 terrorist organization. Sixteen suspected members have been arrested, including the alleged chief assassin.[117] However, a week later anti-terrorist police arrested a woman who had been living with the reported main executioner of the November 17th terrorist organization on suspicion of participating with the group. She is the first woman arrested in connection with the group.[118]

Christos Tsigridas, an admitted member of the Revolutionary Popular Struggle (ELA), was imprisoned in Athens in February 2003. The ELA is believed to have worked with the Venezuelan-born terrorist, Carlos the Jackal and responsible for more than 100 bombings.[119]

In June 2003, the Greek coast guard impounded a cargo ship that had wandered the Mediterranean Sea for six weeks under international surveillance. Investigation of the ship revealed 750 tons of industrial-grade explosives and 8,000 detonators. According to shipping documents, the cargo was bound for a company with only a post office box for an address.[120]

Indonesia

Indonesia authorities have their hands full with terrorist activities. Even if the US was successful in dismantling al-Qaida, radical Islamic groups in Southeast Asia will still be capable of terrorist acts. 'With their radical agenda and their enhanced skills acquired from al-Qaida, these groups, if left unchecked will pose a grave threat to the security of Southeast Asia for a long time to come', said one Indonesian official.[121]

Eighteen Muslim extremists were arrested in September 2002 in a plot to bomb Singapore's airport, Defense Ministry, and water pipelines in the hope of igniting a holy war in Southeast Asia and creating an Islamic state. Thirteen members were previously arrested. Seven 'secret' cells were discovered that are part of Jemaah Islamiah, a group linked to al-Qaida, some of whose members trained in Afghanistan. One of those arrested, Omar Faruq (an Iraqi) confessed to being the top al-Qaida operative in Southeast Asia.[122]

Authorities in Malaysia arrested four Islamic militants in November 2002, who had been planning a suicide attack against western targets in Singapore. Suicide bombers represent a drastic change in Islamic philosophy in Indonesia where Muslim leaders have long prided themselves on practicing a moderate form of Islam that would not sanction suicide attacks.[123] Also in November, Imam Samudra, the Afghan-trained ringleader of the Jemaah Islamiah group behind the bombings of two nightclubs in Bali in October, was arrested while waiting for a ferry bound for the island of Sumatra.[124]

In December 2002, Indonesian police in Jakarta arrested Ali Gufron, a senior commander of a regional terrorist network (JI) and a key player in the Bali nightclub attacks in October that killed nearly 200 people. Gufron is also wanted in Singapore in connection with a plot to blow up the US Embassy there.[125]

Indonesian police interrogated 18 new terror suspects in April 2003, including a man they claim was handpicked to take over Jemaah Islamiyah. Abu Bakar Bashir, the founder of JI who was arrested in 2002, went on trial in April on charges stemming from the Bali bombings. Police said some of the men admitted involvement in last year's deadly Bali bombings as well as other bombings. The men were plotting a new wave of attacks ahead of national elections in 2004.[126]

Amrozi bin Nurhasyim, known as the 'smiling bomber', expressed a readiness to die as a martyr in July 2003, and appeared overjoyed when sentenced to death for the October 2002 attacks on Bali nightclubs that killed 202 people.[127]

In August 2003, investigators arrested nine people in the August bombing of the Marriott Hotel in Jakarta that killed 12 and wounded 150 people. Supposedly, there were 10 suspects in the attack, including the suicide bomber.[128]

Iran

In August 2002, Iranian officials detained and expelled to Saudi Arabia 16 al-Qaida fighters who sought refuge in Iran after fleeing Afghanistan.[129]

Iran reported in February 2003 that it had arrested and deported more than 500 infiltrators suspected of links to the al-Qaida network. The infiltrators were sent back to their country of origin.[130]

Iranian officials told a UN representative in May 2003 that Iran has several unnamed al-Qaida operatives in custody. Iran has previously denied al-Qaida members in the country.[131]

In August 2003, Iran said it would not hand over senior al-Qaida captives to the US, and confirmed it is holding a large number of small and big elements of al-Qaida.[132]

Israel

A nighttime raid by Israeli commandos in January 2002 against a cargo ship in the Red Sea thwarted a Palestinian arms-smuggling operation linked to top Palestinian officials. The sophisticated attempt included the transport of 50 tons of Iranian-made guns and mortars, packed in pressurized, watertight pipes attached to buoys, apparently intended to float in the sea and be hauled to shore by boaters.[133]

In July 2002, Israel killed Shehadeh, a senior leader of the Islamic group Hamas responsible for dozens of deadly attacks on Israelis, and a Hamas colleague. Taking out Shehadeh, the founder of Hamas' military wing, foiled his plans to mount a major attack within the next few days against Jewish settlers in the Gaza Strip. The operation was to involve multiple suicide bombers. Seventy-two suicide bombings during the current conflict killed 256 Israelis.[134] Nearly all of Israel's most-wanted terror suspects in the West Bank have been arrested or killed. The Islamic extremist group Hamas denied that Israel has made a dent in its higher echelon and said that Israel had not penetrated the group's highest rank.[135]

In June 2003, five Israeli Arabs were charged with funneling an estimated US$10 million to the Islamic militant group Hamas. Israeli Arabs are mostly sympathetic to the Palestinian cause, but this case marks the first time that prominent Israeli Arab leaders have been charged with crimes that have political overtones. Prosecutors said the defendants raised millions of dollars from the US, Europe and Muslim countries.[136]

Italy

Eight men were arrested in July 2002 for aiding al-Qaida network as authorities combed canals in Venice for bombs after receiving a tip the Jewish quarter might be targeted by terrorists.[137] An anti-terrorist police report said Islamic militants linked to al-Qaida made plans for terrorist attacks last year in Italy. US authorities have called Milan an important logistical base for al-Qaida. Also in July, hundreds of hours of recorded conversations of Europe's most important al-Qaida outpost revealed there was a cell in Milan that supplied false passports and other documents to al-Qaida operatives who may have succeeded in entering the US. The Milan operation was headed by Egyptian terrorist Abu Saleh, the head of al-Qaida's documentation committee. In a conversation in February 2001 (not translated until March 2002) Saleh was heard to say to a passenger,

> Three brothers will soon need dual-citizenship passports, including one with both Syrian and US nationalities. Make sure the passports bear stamps. The higher-ups want the job to be done properly, to make sure they won't get caught as they reach their final destination. That document job must be flawless. They should raise no suspicion at

> airport or border checks. You have got to get across quickly and easily without being noticed. These passports won't be used for their final destination straight away. First of all, they will have to be put to the test, and then they will be used to reach their final destination. Because you can't blow the whole thing right at the beginning.[138]

Five men in Bologna, including four Moroccans, were arrested in August 2002 inside a basilica after their behavior aroused suspicions they were plotting a terrorist attack. The men were arrested after they were spotted using a video camera to shoot tape of both the fresco that depicts Mohammed in hell and a medieval-era crucifix on the main altar. 'It was clear they were checking the lay of the land and filming it while making hostile and aggressive comments in a place of worship', said the prosecutor investigating the case. The Italian secret service had sent a report to the Parliament two weeks previously warning of elevated risks by Islamic fundamentalists on 'ecclesiastic institutions and bodies' as targets.[139]

Authorities arrested five North African suspects in October 2002 in the Italian cities of Milan, Naples, San Remo and the island of Malta. The al-Qaida cell, based in Milan, was part of a European network with contacts in Iran, Malaysia and Afghanistan that is suspected of plotting attacks on US targets.[140]

Five Moroccans were arrested in northern Italy in January 2003 after a routine search for illegal immigrants turned up 2.2 pounds of explosives and maps detailing central London, and addresses and plans of NATO bases in Italy.[141]

An Italian judge indicted 12 terror suspects in February 2003, including nine Moroccans suspected of plotting a chemical attack on the US Embassy in Rome. The Moroccans were arrested after a raid turned up 8.8 pounds of a cyanide-based compound, firecrackers and maps highlighting the Embassy and Rome's water supply. The other three, a Pakistani, an Algerian, and a Tunisian, were part of a separate group trying to set up a logistical base for terror attacks.[142]

Police killed a wanted Red Brigades terrorist and arrested his female companion (another Red Brigades member) in March 2003 after a gun battle on a train. The man, whose false identity papers were being checked by police, started shooting, killing one officer and wounding another before he was gunned down.[143]

Jordan

In December 2002, Jordanian police arrested a Libyan and a Jordanian as suspects in the murder of a US diplomat in October. Officials also reported that a top al-Qaida operative supplied the two men with guns and money for a terrorist campaign in Jordan. The two men confessed to the killing of Laurence Foley and said they had planned to carry out further attacks in Amman.[144]

In July 2003, two of Saddam Hussein's daughters and their nine children received sanctuary in Jordan on humanitarian grounds, granted by King Abdullah II.[145]

Kenya

Kenyan authorities arrested six Pakistanis, four Somalis, an American and a Spaniard in November 2002 on an Indian Ocean beach before they could escape the country by boat. All but two of the men were traveling on 'suspicious passports' from Somalia where it is possible to obtain a travel document in less than an hour. The arrests were part of the investigation into the simultaneous bombing of an Israeli hotel that killed 16 people and the firing of two surface-to-air missiles at an Israeli airliner a few days earlier.[146]

Morocco

In June 2002, Moroccan officials arrested a senior lieutenant of Osama bin Laden believed to have helped terrorists escape from Afghanistan and start planning new attacks in Europe, Asia, and Africa. Abu Zubair, a Saudi nicknamed the Bear because he weighs more than 300 pounds, helped bring al-Qaida recruits to Afghanistan for training.[147]

Three Saudi suspects caught in May were arraigned in Morocco in July 2002 on suspicion of plotting to sail a dinghy loaded with explosives from Morocco into the Strait of Gibraltar to attack US and British warships. The suspects also plotted to blow up a cafe in Marrakech and plotted a suicide attack against the national bus company.[148]

In August 2003, a Moroccan court sentenced four men to death for their involvement in the Casablanca suicide bombings in May that killed 32 bystanders. The four were among dozens of defendants belonging to a clandestine Moroccan group, the Salafia Jihadia, linked to al-Qaida.[149]

Netherlands

Eight men were arrested in September 2002 on suspicion of helping finance al-Qaida and recruiting fighters for bin Laden's network. Their nationalities have not been determined. The men were arrested in different parts of the Netherlands.[150]

Pakistan

In July 2002, a Pakistani judge convicted four Islamic militants in the kidnap-slaying of the *Wall Street Journal* correspondent, Daniel Pearl. Seven more suspects remain at large.[151]

Police and intelligence officials announced in September 2002, they had arrested an Islamic militant who organized the June 14 car bomb attack on the US Consulate in Karachi, and was plotting to assassinate Pakistan's president. Sharib Ahmad, the most wanted militant in Pakistan, was arrested with five other men in a raid that also netted firearms, ammunition, 2,000 pounds of explosives, 70 hand grenades,

40 rocket-propelled grenades and an anti-tank recoilless rifle.[152] Later in the month, Pakistani police arrested five Pakistani men who were planning to set off a car bomb in Karachi on 11 September and attack McDonald's and Kentucky Fried Chicken restaurants. The group is accused of carrying out a car bombing in June outside the American Consulate, killing 12 Pakistanis.[153] Also in September, five Islamic militants who survived a fierce gun battle, were questioned by Pakistani intelligence officials. Assault rifles, grenades and other weapons, CDs featuring bin Laden and a satellite phone were found in the raided apartment.

Also during a very busy month of September, Ramzi Binalshibh, a senior operative of al-Qaida involved in the planning of September 11th attacks, was captured after a brief gunfight in a middle-class apartment building in Karachi. His capture reinforces the belief that al-Qaida is re-establishing its operations in Karachi and other cities with the help of Pakistani militants. Karachi is believed to be a transit point for moving al-Qaida personnel, money and material.[154] Another al-Qaida suspect, a Yemeni, arrested with Binalshibh has been identified as one of the killers of *Wall Street Journal* reporter, Daniel Pearl. In addition, the most-wanted militant, Sharib Ahmad, in Pakistan was arrested in September, along with five other Harkat ul-Mujahideen al-Almi militants (a radical Islamic splinter group). The raid netted a huge cache of weapons, ammunition, and a ton of explosive chemicals. Ahmad organized the 14 June car bomb attack on the US Consulate in Karachi and an unsuccessful attempt to assassinate Musharraf in April with a car bomb that failed to detonate because of a faulty detonator.

In January 2003, Pakistani authorities arrested and accused an American doctor and his family of links to top al-Qaida operatives and sheltering terrorists in their compound in eastern Pakistan. The family of five consists of three naturalized Americans and two Canadian citizens, all of Pakistani origin. Some of the al-Qaida members sheltered by the family included Abu Yasir al-Jaziri (responsible for al-Qaida's business interests), Sheik Said al-Misri (al-Qaida's financial chief), and Abu Faraj (head of al-Qaida's North African network and a deputy to Khalid Shaikh Mohammed, the 9/11 mastermind).[155] Also in January, Pakistani police and FBI agents stormed a house in Karachi and arrested three al-Qaida suspects after a hail of gunfire and grenades. It was the third major arrest of terrorism suspects in less than a month. Karachi is a haven for al-Qaida members who fled Afghanistan.[156]

A combined Pakistani-CIA raid in March 2003 netted the mastermind of 9/11 and other major terrorist activities. Khalid Sheikh Mohammed (a Kuwaiti), described as important to al-Qaida operations as bin Laden, was handed over to US authorities and taken to an undisclosed location outside Pakistan. Mohammed, a graduate of North Carolina A&T University and a master of languages and disguises, is fanatical in his hatred of the United States.[157] The raid also netted Mustafa Ahmed al-Hawsawi, a Saudi citizen believed to be the 'paymaster' of the 9/11 plot. In the months prior to 9/11, Hawsawi established bank accounts and credit cards used by the 9/11 hijackers.[158] An Egyptian captured in a previous raid sold the two kingpins out for US$27 million and relocation to Great Britain.[159] Also during the month, Yassir al-

Jaziri, responsible for communications between al-Qaida leaders, was captured in Lahore. Intelligence documents, a computer and CDs were confiscated at the home where Jaziri was arrested.[160]

In June 2003, Pakistani authorities arrested an Egyptian al-Qaida operative and seized a videocassette purportedly for bin Laden warning of attacks against the US interests in Saudi Arabia. Police also recovered US, Afghan, Saudi and Pakistani currency of an undisclosed amount.[161]

Philippines

In December 2001, officers of the country's Internal Security Department (ISD) arrested 13 members of the banned Islamic terrorist group Jemaah Islamiyya (JI) that has links to al-Qaida.[162]

September 2002 – 21 members of a militant Islamic network with ties to al-Qaida were arrested from a follow-up investigation of the 15 arrested previously for planning to bomb locations throughout Singapore. Nineteen of those arrested are members of Jemaah Islamiyah, the group responsible for the bomb plot as well as numerous bombings in Indonesia and the Philippines.[163]

In February 2003, government troops found boxes of documents including manuals on assassination, ambush and bombing techniques, and pictures of rifle-clad children trained as guerrillas in the house of a Muslim separatist leader in southern Philippines. The house, captured after a weeklong battle, served as the command post for the Moro Islamic Liberation Front (MILF).[164] Also in February, the US sent 1,700 troops to the Philippines to fight Muslim extremists in the southern part of the country. The American troops and Philippine troops were to fight side by side under the controversial plan. (The Supreme Court of the Philippines had previously ruled that US troops could only shoot in self-defense.[165]) The operation was to last as long as necessary to disrupt and destroy the estimated 250 members of Abu Sayyaf. Then, in March, the plan changed to be in line with the Supreme Court ruling and the US troops could only train Philippine soldiers for operations on Jolo Island.[166] A US training mission in 2002 failed to quell the Muslim guerrillas and the group regrouped on Jolo Island.[167]

Authorities announced in March 2003 they had detained five members of the Moro Islamic Liberation Front in connection with an airport bombing in southern Philippines that killed 21 people.[168]

In April 2003, Philippine intelligence reported terrorist plans to attack US corporations and warships in Singapore and crash a hijacked airplane at the country's international airport. Singapore was deemed a perfect target for attacks as some 17,000 Americans reside in the city-state and approximately 6,000 multi-national companies are located there. The attacks were prevented after The arrest of 15 individuals from Jemaah Islamiah prevented the attacks.[169]

In June 2003, authorities arrested a suspected Abu Sayyaf rebel who helped kidnap 20 people, including three Americans in 2000. Samir Hakim, among the original members of Abu Sayyaf, purchased weapons for the organization.[170]

Saudi Arabia

Saudi Arabia announced in June 2002 that it arrested 13 al-Qaida suspects accused of plotting attacks against 'vital sites' in the country, including an unsuccessful attempt to fire a ground-to-air missile at an US warplane taking off from a Saudi air base. The group had explosives in different parts of the country. The men are from two cells that regrouped in Saudi Arabia, one under the direction of a Sudanese national and the other under the command of an Iraqi.[171]

Saudi police detained three al-Qaida suspects in May 2003 who were plotting to hijack a plane to use in a suicide attack similar to those on 9/11. The three were allegedly part of a larger cell that was in the process of carrying out suicide attacks against landmarks in Saudi Arabia.[172] Also in May, Saudi authorities claimed to have foiled plans by suspected terrorists to carry out attacks on US interests in Saudi Arabia. Officials searched for 17 Saudis, an Iraqi and a Yemeni who hijacked a vehicle and fled after a gunfight with police disabled their vehicle. Authorities confiscated hand grenades, five suitcases containing 800 pounds of advanced high explosives, AK-47 assault rifles, ammunition, computers, communication equipment, travel documents, tens of thousand of US dollars in cash, and Saudi disguises.[173] Saudi authorities investigated suspected illegal arms sales by members of the country's national guard to al-Qaida operatives after weapons seized in the raids were traced to national guard stockpiles.[174]

Saudi officials expressed confidence in June 2003 they would capture more key suspects in the deadly attacks in Riyadh in May after the suspected mastermind turned himself in to authorities. Authorities are interrogating Ali Abd al-Rahman al-Faqasi al-Ghamdi about other cell members, terrorist financing, and additional plots. Ghamdi is believed to have close links with al-Qaida and is among the 19 militants that escaped during the incident described in the previous paragraph.[175] A series of raids in Mecca led to the capture of 50 of Ghambi's followers earlier in the month.[176] Also in June, police in Mecca killed five al-Qaida militants and arrested others during a raid on a booby-trapped apartment near the main Mecca mosque. More than 70 bombs of different sizes were found, along with numerous other weapons that included semiautomatic rifles, knives, communication devices, bomb-making material and masks. Two Chadian, an Egyptian and a Saudi were among those arrested. Officials said the suspects were planning to carry out attack in Mecca.[177]

At farms outside Riyadh in July 2003, Saudi Arabian police arrested 16 terror suspects and unearthed a cache of 20 tons of bomb-making chemicals, detonators, rocket-propelled grenades and rifles. Saudi forces also found night-vision goggles, surveillance cameras, bulletproof vests, passports and forged ID cards. It was not disclosed whether any of the detainees were linked to the Riyadh bombings or a plot foiled on 15 June to attack landmarks in the holy city of Mecca.[178]

Singapore

Authorities in Singapore in January 2002 arrested 15 purported militants linked to al-Qaida training extremist groups in Malaysia and Indonesia on suspicion of plotting bombings in Singapore, 13 of which have possible connections with three of the terrorists involved in the September 11th attacks. Detailed information on bomb construction and photographs and video footage of targeted buildings were found in their homes and offices, along with forged passports and immigration stamps and material linked to al-Qaida. The US Embassy and several office buildings that house American companies were among the targets, along with US Navy vessels in the waters of Singapore. Seven truck bombs to be used were each bigger than the bomb that was used to blow up the federal office building in Oklahoma City. Eight of the fifteen had been to al-Qaida training camps in Afghanistan.[179] Also in January, a videotape found in Afghanistan helped lead Singapore authorities to capture reported members of a terrorist cell called Jamaah Islamiyah who were planning to blow up Western embassies, US naval vessels, and a bus that transports American military service members. The terrorist cell is part of a regional network with additional cells in Malaysia and Indonesia.

In August 2002, the ISD arrested 19 members of JI and 2 members of a Philippine separatist group, Moro Islamic Liberation Front (MILF), after the security serviced learned of plots to bomb government and western targets in Singapore.[180]

Spain

Galeb Zouaydi, the Syrian-born businessman arrested in April 2002 in Madrid, was charged with crimes of terrorism linked to the 9/11 attacks. Zouaydi financed al-Qaida operatives with donations from individuals and organizations in Saudi Arabia and the profits he earned on real estate projects in Madrid. Zouaydi was a close financial associate of top al-Qaida members in Europe and sent money to terrorist groups in the US, Germany, Turkey, Jordan, Syria, Saudi Arabia, Belgium, China, and the Palestinian territories.[181]

Three al-Qaida suspects, all from Syria, were taken into custody in July 2002, including one who had videotaped several American landmarks – the Golden Gate Bridge, the Sears Tower, the Statue of Liberty, Disneyland, Universal Studios, and the World Trade Center. It was a further indication that Spain may have been used as a setting for crucial logistical support in the September 11th attacks.[182]

Spanish police arrested 16 people in January 2003 suspected of being al-Qaida terrorists in a raid aimed at an Algerian network plotting attacks in Britain and France. The police also confiscated electronic equipment and remote-control devices used for making bombs, and flasks containing suspicious chemicals. The suspects, mostly young Algerians, were accused of giving logistical support to terrorist plotting attacks using bombs and chemicals in Paris, the production of ricin in London, and the killing of a British detective during a raid in London. Spain has not been hit by Islamic terrorism, but is a hub for recruiting, financing and networks dealing in fake documents. Spain has arrested 35 people believed to be linked to al-Qaida since 9/11.[183]

In March 2003, Spanish investigators arrested five men in the bombing of a synagogue in Tunisia in April 2002. At least four of the men were Tunisian. Evidence gathered by Pakistani and US agents pointed out al-Qaida operatives in Spain and Switzerland.[184]

Sweden

In September 2002, Swedish authorities charged Kerim Sadok Chatty, a Muslim convert whose mother is Swedish and father is Tunisian, with planning to hijack a plane and illegal possession of a weapon. Chatty's pistol was found in his toiletries bag during a check prior to boarding a Ryanair flight to London. Intelligence sources said Chatty was intending to hijack the plane and crash it into a US Embassy in Europe.[185]

Syria

Syria revealed in July 2002 that a key figure in the 9/11 plot who fled Hamburg last October, has been held in secret detention in Syria. Mohammed Haydar Zammar recruited Mohamed Atta.[186] Although listed as a state sponsor of terrorism, Syria has increased intelligence sharing with the US in hopes of avoiding a full breach between Damascus and the US Syria has shown an openness in working against al-Qaida that has surprised many in the Middle East. When Saudi and other fighters began drifting through Syria after the collapse of the Taliban rule in Afghanistan, Syria detained more than 20 fighters. Information provided by the Syrian government saved American lives by heading off a militant attack planned earlier this year on US troops stationed in the Persian Gulf area.[187]

Thailand

In June 2003, Thai police arrested three men that were members of a terrorist cell planning to attack embassies and entertainment spots.[188]

A top al-Qaida operative, Riduan Isamuddin (also known as Hambali), was captured in Thailand in August 2003 by Thai authorities working in conjunction with US FBI and CIA intelligence officials. Isamuddin, the operational head of Jemaah Islamiyah, has been tied to nearly every major terrorist plot since the 1993 attack on the World Trade Center. Isamuddin, assigned by al-Qaida to recruit new pilots to conduct additional 9/11-style suicide hijackings in the US, was purportedly the mastermind behind the Bali bombings in October 2002 that killed 202 people, as well as a series of bombings in the Philippines that killed 22 people in December 2000. Isamuddin is believed to have organized and financed the bombing of the Marriott Hotel in Jakarta, Indonesia in August 2003 in which 10 people died. According to

Philippine intelligence officials, Isamuddin was plotting to blow up embassies of the US, Britain, Israel and Australia in Singapore with powerful fertilizer bombs in trucks driven by suicide terrorists. In addition, Isamuddin was preparing an attack on the Asia Pacific Economic Cooperation forum to be held in Bangkok in October 2003, and to be attended by leaders of 20 nations, including President Bush. Isamuddin, being held at an unspecified location outside Thailand, has been labeled 'one of the world's most lethal terrorists'.[189]

Yemen

In December 2002, Yemeni security forces battling al-Qaida members holed up in a building suffered one casualty, but wounded two suspects who escaped. The two terrorists that escaped are on the most wanted list as suspects in the October 2002 attack on the French tanker Limburg.[190]

Acting on FBI information in January 2003, Yemen authorities arrested at least 30 Muslim militants suspected of the murder of three American missionaries and the deputy leader of Yemen's socialist party, and believed to be part of a terrorist cell in Yemen plotting attacks on foreigners and secular political leaders.[191] As of January 2003, Yemen is holding 104 people suspected of belonging to al-Qaida.[192]

Ten key suspects in the USS Cole bombing escaped from a Yemeni prison in April 2003, through a hole in a bathroom wall inside the tightly guarded central intelligence building in Aden. The prison break will likely have major repercussions for Yemen's security apparatus. The ten fugitives were part of a 17-man group arrested following the Cole bombing.[193]

Yemeni security forces arrested five militants linked to al-Qaida in August 2003, suspected of involvement in an attack on a military convoy in June 2003.[194]

Part 2: Summary

The international fight on terrorism continues. The events listed in this section are only a few of the magnificent efforts by peoples of many nations to combat international terrorism. As you can ascertain from the articles presented, international laws vary greatly between nations in dealing with terrorists and further complicate the war on terrorism. As months and years pass, other battles large and small will be fought against those who have declared war on America and her allies. We will lose some battles and will win many. Terrorist attacks occurring on the soils of other nations, will prompt them to join the fight on terrorism.

Two of the many factors involved in the war on terrorism involve foreign policies of the United States relating to the Middle East and our dependence upon oil from that region. In a survey of 275 political, media, cultural business and government leaders from 24 nations, 160 of those surveyed said US policies were responsible for the 9/11 attacks.[195] Until we see major reform in those policies and we greatly diminish our dependence upon their oil supplies, we are doomed to continue fighting the main blaze of terrorism. Wildfires of terrorism that will inevitably flare up somewhere in the world, need to be doused through international cooperation, supported by a global lack of tolerance for terrorist activities.

The war will be won, but not soon and not easily. There will be victory and defeat on both sides.

Notes

1 100 attacks foiled, FBI says, Associated Press, 15 December 2002.
2 Anti-terror successes win Ashcroft's praise, *Hearst Newspapers*, 5 June 2003.
3 Chief of border, transportation security faces big task, *Gannett News Service*, 1 March 2003.
4 Lax INS security at airports a terror risk, report says, *USA Today*, 24 January 2003.
5 Homeland Security takes duties of 22 US agencies, Associated Press, 1 March 2003.
6 Plane flying over city is FBI on surveillance, Wire Services, 1 March 2003.
7 FBI has 'air force' watching America, Associated Press, 15 March 2003.
8 ABA mulls rights of terror suspects, Associated Press, 10 February 2003.
9 Restricted airspace over D.C. expanded, Associated Press, 9 February 2003.
10 Ridge unveils new Web site, manual for terror readiness, *Knight Ridder Newspapers*, 20 February 2003.
11 Civilian hospitals set to help with wounded in event of war, Associated Press, 8 March 2003.
12 Zero tolerance for firearms in effect at airport, *Arizona Republic*, 1 March 2003.
13 US cancels terrorism program, *Boston Globe*, 30 July 2003.
14 US reworks privacy guards for checking airline travelers, Associated Press, 1 August 2003.
15 Visa-less waits at airports suspended, Associated Press, 3 August 2003.
16 Airline flier backgrounds to be checked, Associated Press, 1 March 2003.
17 US out to deter missile assaults on passenger jets, Associated Press, 16 January 2003.
18 FAA Launches Rulemaking On Transponder Hijack Mode, *Aviation Week and Space Technology*, 27 January 2003.
19 New security program to fingerprint foreigners, Wire Services, 20 May 2003.
20 X-ray vision for airport screeners? Associated Press, 2003.
21 Pentagon may track gaits as ID system, Associated Press, 20 May 2003.
22 Security concerns boost eye-scan ID, *New York Times*, 18 May 2003.
23 Pentagon project tracks vehicles, faces, Associated Press, 2 July 2003.
24 Pentagon project tracks vehicles, faces, Associated Press, 2 July 2003.
25 Blimps to fight terrorism, Associated Press, 8 August 2003.
26 Airport rolls out biometric security, www.cnn.com/2003/WORLD/europe, 27 May 2003.
27 Agents arrest 30 Portland airport employees, Associated Press, 20 December 2001.
28 TSA Hiring Jumble, *Aviation Week and Space Technology*, 9 June 2003.
29 Jordanian who told FBI of terror mind-set ordered deported, Associated Press, 9 February 2003.
30 Afghan man arrested in Tucson, *Arizona Republic*, 20 February 2003.
31 Deportation awaits 13,000 Muslim men, *New York Times*, 7 June 2003.
32 Deportee assails 9/11 'paranoia', *Arizona Republic*, 15 June 2003.
33 2 on no-fly list arrested in Seattle, *Washington Post*, 14 August 2003.
34 Al-Qaida probes underway in 40 states, Wire Services, 27 June 2003.
35 FBI hunting Iraqi spies, terror cells across US, Associated Press, 25 January 2003.
36 www.cnn.com, 31 July 2002.
37 *South Florida Sun-Sentinel*, 9 August 2002.
38 NYC cabdriver held on terror charges, Associated Press, 28 May 2003.

39 Ohio man plotted terrorist assaults, *Washington Post*, 20 June 2003.
40 Evidence ties Moussaoui to 2nd plot, officials say, Associated Press, 29 March 2003.
41 Terrorism defendant back in jail, Associated Press, 4 July 2003.
42 Silent FBI holds Saudi from Tucson, *Arizona Republic*, 21 June 2003.
43 Feds charge 11 with plotting to join terror jihad in Kashmir, Associated Press, 28 June 2003.
44 Ore. Software engineer pleads to terror charge, Associated Press, 7 August 2003.
45 Suspect wanted to smuggle in 50 missiles, FBI says, *Newsday*, 14 August 2003.
46 US indicts 7 in crackdown on terrorist funding, *Deccan Herald*, 20 December 2002.
47 US offers US$5M for tips on terrorist funding, Wire Services, 14 November 2002.
48 Justice's seizures of money rile allies, State Department, Associated Press, 30 May 2003.
49 DEA finds drug-money ties to terrorists, Wire Services, 3 August 2002.
50 Feds nab suspected terror backers, Associated Press, 20 December 2002.
51 US takes five al-Qaida suspects out of Malawi, Wire Services, 2003.
52 US announces arrests of 3 it links to al-Qaida terrorism, *Knight Ridder Newspapers*, March 2003.
53 Prof held as terror financier, *Orlando Sentinel*, 21 February 2003.
54 Defendant denies role in financing al-Qaida, Wire Services, 30 May 2003.
55 Terrorists use fake goods to fund operations, Interpol official says, Associated Press, 17 July 2003.
56 Muslim leader sentenced, Associated Press, 19 August 2003.
57 CIA can kill citizens who aid al-Qaida, Associated Press, 4 December 2002.
58 US planning Afghan checkpoints, *Los Angeles Times*, 9 December 2002.
59 US says security rules apply to Canada, too, Associated Press, 21 December 2002.
60 US opening new front in war on terror in Horn of Africa, *Knight Ridder Newspapers*, 11 December 2002.
61 US announces arrests of 3 it links to al-Qaida terrorism, *Knight Ridder Newspapers*, March 2003.
62 Fugitive said to be al-Qaida pilot, *USA Today*, 4 April 2003.
63 US nabs Achille Lauro terrorist, Wire Services, 16 April 2003.
64 US, Philippines united on terror, *Washington Post*, 20 May 2003.
65 Troops arrest group in Iraq with suspected al-Qaida ties, *Knight Ridder Newspapers*, 11 June 2003.
66 US to place inspectors at Muslim nations' ports, *New York Times*, 12 June 2003.
67 Iraqi agent linked to 9/11 plot in custody, *Los Angeles Times*, 9 July 2003.
68 NATO told is must act on terror threat, Asso*ciated Press*, 7 June 2002.
69 Bond is forged to fight terrorism, *Chicago Tribune*, 2 August 2002.
70 Australia gets tough on terror, Associated Press, 2 December 2002.
71 19 may be in US illegally, officials say, *Boston Globe*, 3 January 2003.
72 Shadows in Our Midst, *TIME*, 13 January 2003.
73 Canada links man facing deportation to al-Qaida, Wire Services, 28 May 2003.
74 13 arrested as members of banned Egypt group, Wire Services, 3 January 2003.
75 6 suspected Reid associates arrested in anti-terror raids, *Los Angeles Times*, 27 November 2002.
76 French detain 3 more in synagogue bombing, Wire Services, 19 November 2002.
77 French arrest 8 suspects in Tunisia synagogue blast, Associated Press, 6 November 2002.

78 Terror cell with links to rebels dismantled, Associated Press, 28 December 2002.
79 Paris airport worker detained after explosives found, *Washington Post*, 31 December 2002.
80 Three suspected Islamic militants detained near Paris, www.smh.com, 10 December 2002.
81 French hold Moroccan in Sept. 11 investigation, Wire Services, 6 June 2003.
82 French query German about Tunisia bombing, Wire Services, 7 June 2003.
83 France raids Iran opposition group, *New York Times*, 18 June 2003.
84 French court releases 9 held in terror sweep, Wire Services, 3 July 2003.
85 Germany tightens security in 'sleeper' search, *USA Today*, 26 November 2001.
86 German fugitive built terrorist core, *Washington Post*, 12 June 2002.
87 Germany, US near terror evidence deal, *New York Times*, 12 June 2002.
88 Plane threats put Germany on al-Qaida alert, *Knight Ridder Newspapers*, 13 June 2002.
89 8 terror suspects are questioned, Associated Press, 5 July 2002.
90 Germans trace path of al-Qaida, *New York Times*, 24 August 2002.
91 Germans trace path of al-Qaida, *New York Times*, 24 August 2002.
92 Germans charge pair over plans against US, *New York Times*, September 2002.
93 Germans arrest 2 Yemeni men with possible links to al-Qaida, *Washington Post*, 11 January 2003.
94 US tags charity as terrorist fund-raiser, *Washington Post*, 30 May 2003.
95 7 detained in British anti-terror raids; 3 held in Germany, *New York Times*, 7 February 2003.
96 Moroccan convicted of aiding 9/11, Wire Services, 20 February 2003.
97 4 Algerians convicted of plot to blow up Christmas market, *Los Angeles Times*, 11 March 2003.
98 Moroccan is charged by Germany in 9/11 plot, *Washington Post*, 10 May 2003.
99 Turk gets term for explosives conviction, *Washington Post*, 7 May 2003.
100 Germany to extradite alleged al-Qaida supporters to USA, *USA Today*, 22 July 2003.
101 Islamist cell leader arrested, *Chicago Tribune*, 5 August 2003.
102 Britain Readies New Measures To Buttress Aviation Security, www.AviationNow.com, 22 October 2001.
103 Militant Muslim leaders in London condemn US, Associated Press, 13 July 2002.
104 British police raid extremist mosque, *Los Angeles Times*, 21 January 2003.
105 Briton says nation facing threat line one on 9/11, Wire Services, 13 February 2003.
106 Al-Qaida presence big in London, police say, Wire Services, 17 February 2003.
107 London boosts security against possible terror, Wire Services, 12 February 2003.
108 7 detained in British anti-terror raids; 3 held in Germany, *New York Times*, 7 February 2003.
109 Westerners among detainees, *Washington Post*, 5 July 2003.
110 Greek police close terror net, *Arizona Republic*, 20 July 2002.
111 Greek police crack terror group, Associated Press, 19 July 2002.
112 Greeks are stunned by terror suspects, Associated Press, 24 July 2002.
113 Greek terror suspects are charged; reportedly planned NATO attack, Associated Press, 22 July 2002.
114 Suspect in CIA slaying charged with Greek terrorism, Associated Press, 26 July 2002.
115 Greek terrorist group 'still alive', Associated Press, 1 August 2002.
116 Key terror suspect in Greece surrenders, Associated Press, 6 September 2002.
117 Greek premier claims terror group dismantled, Associated Press, 9 September 2002.

118 Woman tied to terrorist is arrested in Greece, Wire Services, 13 September 2002.
119 Suspected Greek leader of terror group jailed, Wire Services, 6 February 2003.
120 Greeks begin probe of ship, Associated Press, 24 June 2003.
121 Southeast Asia radicals pose terror risk, Singapore warns, *New York Times*, 1 January 2003.
122 Singapore uncovering network of terror cells, *Los Angeles Times*, 20 September 2002.
123 Malaysia arrests 4 terror-plan suspects, *Washington Post*, 27 November 2002.
124 Bali officials arrest alleged ringleader in nightclub bombing, *Salt Lake Tribune*, 22 November 2002.
125 Key suspect in terrorist network nabbed in Indonesia, *New York Times*, 5 December 2002.
126 Indonesian police question 18 new terror suspects, Associated Press, 25 April 2003.
127 Death for bomber faces appeal in Bali, Wire Services, 11 July 2003.
128 Indonesia arrests 9 in blast, Associated Press, 18 August 2003.
129 Iranian officials expel al-Qaida members, *Arizona Republic*, 11 August 2002.
130 Iran deports over 500 suspected terrorists, Wire Services, 17 February 2003.
131 Iran admits holding al Qaeda operatives, www.cnn.com, 23 May 2003.
132 Iran won't hand over terror captives to US, Wire Services, 5 August 2003.
133 Israel seizes ship loaded with weapons, *Baltimore Sun*, 3 January 2002.
134 Israel defends raid on Hamas, *Los Angeles Times*, 24 July 2002.
135 Israel says security sweep is a success, Associated Press, 5 July 2002.
136 5 Arabs accused of aiding Hamas, *New York Times*, 25 June 2003.
137 8 tied to al-Qaida held in Milan, Associated Press, 13 July 2002.
138 Italy surveillance hints al-Qaida 'sleepers' in US, *Chicago Tribune*, 30 June 2002.
139 Italians arrest 5 plot suspects, *New York Times*, 20 August 2002.
140 Italian authorities crack reported terrorist cell, Wire Services, 12 October 2002.
141 London map discovered in Italy raid on 5, Associated Press, 25 January 2003.
142 Italy indicts 12 terror suspects; 9 suspected in chemical plot, Associated Press, 7 February 2003.
143 Red Brigades terrorist killed in train shooting, Wire Services, 3 March 2003.
144 2 arrested in Jordan in killing of diplomat, Associated Press, 15 December 2002.
145 Saddam Hussein's daughters in Jordan, Associated Press, 31 July 2003.
146 12 held in Kenya attacks, Associated Press, 30 November 2002.
147 Morocco arrests al-Qaida bigwig, *Knight Ridder Newspapers*, 19 June 2002.
148 Al-Qaida plots are described after arrest of 3 in Morocco, Associated Press, 20 July 2002.
149 4 given death sentences for Morocco bombings, Wire Services, 19 August 2003.
150 Dutch probe possible al-Qaida fundraising, Wire Services, 3 September 2003.
151 Pakistan convicts 4 militants in slaying of reporter Pearl, Associated Press, 15 July 2002.
152 Suspect arrested in consulate attack, *Washington Post*, 19 September 2002.
153 5 suspected Islamic militants questioned after gunbattle, *New York Times*, 13 September 2002.
154 Raid in Pakistan is detailed, *New York Times*, 15 September 2002.
155 5 in family linked to terrorists, Associated Press, 16 January 2003.
156 9 arrested in Pakistan terror sweep, Associated Press, 10 January 2003.
157 9/11 MASTERMIND NABBED, *Washington Post*, 2 March 2003.
158 Sept.11 'paymaster' was captured, too, *Washington Post*, 5 March 2003.

159 Hunting in the Barren Hills, *Newsweek*, 17 March 2003.
160 Suspected al-Qaida official questioned, Associated Press, 17 March 2003.
161 Al-Qaida suspect is arrested with warning from bin Laden, Associated Press, 28 June 2003.
162 Singapore government report reveals extent of Islamic terrorist threat in Southeast Asia, www.janes.com/security/international, 20 January 2003.
163 21 terrorism suspects arrested in Singapore, Wire Services, 17 September 2002.
164 Documents taken in southern Philippines, Wire Services, 17 February 2003.
165 US troop use in Philippines controversial, Associated Press, 22 February 2003.
166 Philippines insist: No US battle vs. rebels, Associated Press, 2 March 2003.
167 1,700 US troops to open front in Philippines for terror fight, *New York Times*, 21 February 2003.
168 5 held in fatal bombing of airport in Philippines, Wire Services, 6 March 2003.
169 Reports detail plot for Singapore terror, Associated Press, 7 April 2003.
170 Rebel kidnap suspect arrested in Philippines, Wire Services, 25 June 2003.
171 Al-Qaida in Saudi Arabia, *Washington Post*, 19 June 2002.
172 Saudis detain al-Qaida suspect in hijack plot similar to 9/11, Associated Press, 22 May 2003.
173 Saudis claim to have foiled terror plot, Wire Services, 8 May 2003.
174 Guard is linked to al-Qaida arms sale, *Washington Post*, 19 May 2003.
175 Saudis hope to net additional terrorists, Associated Press, 28 June 2003.
176 Suspect in Riyadh blasts surrenders, *USA Today*, 27 June 2003.
177 Raid nets al-Qaida suspects, Associated Press, 16 June 2003.
178 Saudi police arrest 16 after finding cache of weapons, *USA Today*, 22 July 2003.
179 Tape shows Singapore attack plans, www.cnn.com, 12 January 2002.
180 Singapore government report reveals extent of Islamic terrorist threat in Southeast Asia, www.janes.com/security/international, 20 January 2003.
181 US Calls Spanish Terror Arrest a Big Break, *Wall Street Journal*, 29 April 2002.
182 3 held in Spain in inquiry into al-Qaida; videos on 1 suspicious, Associated Press, 17 July 2002.
183 Spain nets 16 terror suspects, *Los Angeles Times*, 25 January 2003.
184 Spanish officials nab 5 in synagogue blast, *Los Angeles Times*, 8 March 2003.
185 Authorities look for terror ties to Swede, Wire Services, 3 September 2002.
186 Key terrorist suspect held in Syria, *Washington Post*, 19 June 2002.
187 Syria is evolving as newest ant-terror ally for US, *Washington Post*, 26 July 2002.
188 A Famed Resort Where Tourists Fear to Tread, *Pattaya Journal*, 14 June 2003.
189 Top al-Qaida operative captured, Associated Press, 15 August 2003.
190 Officer killed as Yemenis battle al-Qaida suspects, Wire Services, 21 December 2002.
191 Yemen arrests 30 militants in death of US missionaries, *USA Today*, 2 January 2003.
192 Ibid.
193 10 main suspects in USS Cole attack escape from prison, Associated Press, 12 April 2003.
194 5 tied to al-Qaida held in Yemen convoy attack, Wire Services, 1 August 2003.
195 World's leaders fault US policies, *Chicago Tribune*, 21 December 2001.

Epilogue

Aviation Security in an Era of Uncertainty

The intent of this book was not to provide all the answers to questions and events facing crewmembers, but rather, to raise their awareness of what the future may hold for them. We do not have a 'crystal ball' in which we can see the future. We have, as much information as you or the next person, but what is evident is that an entirely new set of issues is coming to the forefront of the airline world. Those issues are a direct result of the changes that are occurring at the airlines because of the many security initiatives that have been instituted since 9/11. Furthermore, as airline security evolves important safety issues arise such as, what effect will the security initiatives have upon the delicate balance of safety? There is no doubt that safety *will* be affected, but *how* is the question.

Other questions are also important to aviation safety such as what effect, if any; will crewmember security training have upon deterring airline hijackings by terrorists? If an attempted terrorist hijacking does occur, will crewmembers be able to stop it through the training they received at their respective airline? Will security initiatives cause an aircraft accident? What has become of the working relationships between crewmembers because of the security changes? What happened to leadership on the crewmember security front? These questions need to be adequately addressed before we blunder into a serious safety incident unaware. When these and other such questions are answered, airline travel will continue to be the safest mode of transportation for the public and crew.

The financial condition of the airlines since 9/11 has generated a major struggle between crewmembers and airline management personnel. Furloughs and airline restructuring has disrupted relationships and caused friction, which may cause an erosion of airline safety and the security net. We will not get into the labor vs. management issues, but should briefly mention them here because it is an important aspect of the total safety/security equation. When crewmembers are concerned for their livelihoods, it creates distractions that are difficult for them to ignore as they go about their jobs. The unfortunate consequence of these distractions is the safety and security of the traveling public. Will their safety and security be jeopardized while crewmembers and management spar over financial issues? These important issues should be resolved before the distractions lead to unwanted safety incidents.

In writing this book, we did not investigate these complex issues because the landscape is not yet clear. The aviation environment is changing rapidly and it is difficult to ascertain the facts on many of these issues. Further investigation of these issues can occur when the aviation environment becomes stable enough to analyze the information. So instead, we have attempted to provide immediate ideas for airlines and crewmembers on how to become empowered with knowledge through training. We have attempted to demonstrate to you, the reader, a passion we have for the security and safety of crewmembers, airlines and passengers. This is a continuing effort and we will continue on this path until crews get the training they deserve.

We would like to close this book with some sobering thoughts that are important for airlines and crewmembers to consider in this new era of airline transportation. As you read these closing sections, try to mentally process your knowledge and what we have written about in this book to find solutions to these important issues. Aviation safety/security is a collective effort and we need you to help accomplish this extremely important goal.

Could the Events of 9/11 have been Prevented?

> Exploitable vulnerabilities had to exist in order to turn the idea into a reality.[1]

Yes, they could have, but not under the system that was in place at the time. It was a very flawed system. Sadly, it remains so. Parts of the report, *The Final Report of the Congressional Joint Inquiry Into 9/11*, were released to the public in July 2003. Studies on the topics of foresight and hindsight have been conducted that appear to ring true in the Congressional report. These studies have found that people will:

- Greatly overestimate what they knew in foresight of the event;
- Over estimate what others knew in foresight of the event; and/or,
- Misremember what they themselves knew in foresight of the event.[2]

Before this book goes to print, you will probably have read the report and listened to the many 'authorities' provided by the media to add their interpretations of the document. When it all comes down to it, what is actually left is hindsight. Yet, this hindsight is NOT 20/20. This hindsight is obscured by those afraid for their high-paying jobs and the stigma of having fingers pointed directly at them. It is hindsight that reeks of cover-up, and most assuredly, of trying to point the finger of blame elsewhere. Hindsight that is certainly not perfect. Some psychologists call perfect hindsight of an event 'outcome knowledge'.

Hindsight is an interesting trait of the human existence. After a tragedy, it often becomes clear the signs leading up to the event were both troublesome and crystal-clear. Individuals can clearly view an event after it occurred in contrast to those that had only a piece of the puzzle before the event. After the event, the knowledge of what occurred changes the perspective from a partial view of facts into a full view of facts. This 'big picture' understanding after the fact influences what our knowledge actually was before the event. People will often believe they had a better understanding of the event before it occurred. For example, after a traffic accident, it is often acknowledged that if some rule or driving principle had been adhered to, the accident could have been avoided. True, but how many times did the drivers overlook similar rules or principles before all the victims became aligned in a series of events that led to the accident? Have you ever seen a reasonable and sane person drive their car onto the roadway with the deliberate intent of getting into a traffic accident? Probably not. The cause of the accident frequently does not become clear until after the event has occurred when it can be analyzed objectively.

It is inevitable that each of the points about 'perfect hindsight' will come into play during any investigation into the events surrounding the attacks on 9/11 as we look for someone to blame. Where does the blame lie? It lies with every American who went about their lives oblivious to the rest of the world, and thought, 'it could not happen here, not in America'. It lies in every American who had knowledge of the weak, sick and vulnerable system and allowed it to exist for decades. It lies with every voter who elected officials who did not have the interest of Americans at the center of their attention. It lies with government bureaucracies that vied for attention, importance and funding rather than doing their job for the American people. It lies with our intelligence community who, for many reasons, did not share information and 'connect the dots' that a disaster was inevitable. It lies with government and security contractors who were more interested in lining their corporate pockets than shielding Americans from harm. It lies with every airline that permitted inadequate, non-effective and out-dated training to be given to their flight crews in the interest of 'cost'. It lies with the FAA who was supposed to oversee those programs, but whose Principal Security Inspectors turned a blind eye instead as they pursued the course of 'promoting commercial aviation'. It lies in pilot and flight attendant unions as they permitted their members to endure inadequate training while they built corporate kingdoms. It lies in each pilot and flight attendant who attended security training, viewed it only as a 'square-filler', accepted the pitiful course, and went on about their business. You see, 9/11 could have been prevented, but not under the system in place at the time. We all share in the blame.

Most assuredly, there will be people who will lose their jobs over the events of 9/11. The recommendations from the Final Report almost demand it.

> The Inspectors General at the Central Intelligence Agency, the Department of Defense, the Department of Justice, and the Department of State should review the factual findings and the record of this Inquiry and conduct investigations and reviews as necessary to determine whether and to what extent personnel at all levels should be held accountable for any omission, commission, or failure to meet professional standards in regard to the identification, prevention, or disruption of terrorist attacks, including the events of September 11, 2001.[3]

Some government organizations will cease to exist, while others will be absorbed into others.

> Based on their oversight responsibilities, the Intelligence and Judiciary Committees of the Congress, as appropriate, should consider promptly, in consultation with the Administration, whether the FBI should continue to perform the domestic intelligence functions of the United States Government or whether legislation is necessary to remedy this problem, including the possibility of creating a new agency to perform those functions [4]

New organizations will spring up, oddly enough manned by many of those who lost their jobs elsewhere. The Congressional Joint Inquiry recommends the creation of a Director of National Intelligence (and all the accompanying staff) and a National Intelligence Officer for Terrorism (and all accompanying staff).[5] Billions upon billions of dollars will be spent in addition to the billions already spent on 'homeland security'. Corporations will do anything possible to tap into the honey-pot of taxpayers' money in vying for government contracts. Universities and non-profit organizations will vie for grants to conduct studies upon studies, year after year. This is the American way and, unfortunately, we are not going to change it. What we have to do is to be knowledgeable about the system, understand its shortcomings and deficiencies, and design our lives around it. Ask not what your country is going to do for you, but what you are going to do for yourself. That is the bottom line.

'An Object in Motion ...'

The overall task of supplying security protection by individuals being more complex is one of the unfortunate aspects of the increasing security protections since 9/11. It is difficult for people who are directly or indirectly involved in the security system to understand how security initiatives affect the satisfactory level of safety. Since the approach to aviation security has grown more complex, will it cause those involved in it to be so focused on their jobs that a major safety problem could be overlooked? To be successful, as more security directives, procedures and policies from the government and airlines are published, the responsibilities for security and safety must overlap as well to prevent one area from causing holes in the other.

Safety and security must not only co-exist, they must also complement and support one another. A good example of a security initiative that directly affects safety is the 'reinforced cockpit door'. Not only is it a barrier to someone shooting at it in an armed takeover attempt, but also it is a barrier to communication and coordination between the flight deck and cabin crews during normal flight, as well as during any abnormality, such as a sick passenger. During routine operations, the cockpit door has to be opened during certain times; anytime it is opened, it is possible to breach the door and gain access to the flight deck. There is also a safety issue regarding the door during an accident. Can the pilots get out safely through the door, and/or can crewmembers or emergency response crews get into the flight deck if the pilots are trapped or incapacitated? The door was a relatively simple 'security fix' that had a negative impact in several ways on safety.

Isaac Newton was a mathematician in the seventeenth and eighteenth centuries and established certain laws of physics that continue in use today (remember the apple falling on his head?). Although Newton's law applies to physical objects, it has certain applications to aviation security and other human actions that seem to be applicable to current events in the world today. A brief look at two of Sir Isaac Newton's laws of physics can be used as examples to formulate some thoughts on whether terrorism will continue to be a threat to airline travel. One of Newton's laws of physics briefly states, 'For every action, there is an equal and opposite reaction'. The other states, 'an object at rest tends to stay at rest and an object in motion tends to stay in motion with the same speed and in the same direction unless acted upon by another unbalanced force'. Rolling a cue ball across a pool table could be an example of both laws. The push of the cue stick on the ball is the force; the weight of the ball, the spin of the ball (English), the friction of the felt surface, and any impact with other balls or the side rails (outside forces), are in opposition to the force and direction provided by the cue stick. Unless the ball goes into the pocket, it will eventually stop and the forces will become equal. If the cue ball is never struck, it (and all the other balls) will remain at rest on the table.

What do Newton's laws of physics have to do with aviation security? We suggest that for every action that is taken by terrorists, there is a reaction taken by the government. The question remains, will either side eliminate the other so that actions/reactions will cease (eight ball in the side pocket)? With Newton's laws in mind, it can be said the 9/11 terrorist actions caused the United States to react with military force in Afghanistan in an attempt to stop terrorism. After the 'action' of 9/11, many aviation security deficiencies were highlighted and attempts were made by the government to beef up airline security in 'reaction'. The reaction to 9/11 was deeply felt across the societies of the world and flying passengers took alternate modes of transportation for fear of further terrorist attacks. The reaction to 9/11 continues today as aviation security continues to be a focal point by the government and the press. This book is in fact a reaction to the events of 9/11.

The similarity to Newton's law of physics can be witnessed in our attempts to combat terrorism. The behavior of all physical objects can be described by saying that objects tend to keep on doing what they are doing. If this principle also applies to our human condition and unless some other unbalancing action occurs in this fight on terrorism, then terrorism will certainly continue. The force of the road on the braking wheels provides an unbalanced force to change a car's motion when coming to a stop. Since there is no unbalanced force to change an occupant's state of motion, an occupant of the car will continue in motion toward the initial direction of movement of the car. The person in motion tends to stay in motion with the same speed and in the same direction unless it is acted upon by an unbalanced force such as a seat belt.

What is the unbalancing force that will stop the motion of terrorism? Where are our proverbial 'seat belts' that will prevent us from impacting the windshield when the government 'puts on the brakes'? Will your airline provide them? Your union? You can answer this question for yourself, but it seems plausible that terrorism will not be completely eliminated nor will terrorist eliminate the free countries of the world. As bombs continue to drop on the Middle Eastern countries and western troops are involved in the affairs of these countries, it seems rather obvious that action and reactions will not stop any time soon by either side. We support all attempts to stop the terrorism that affects the free peoples and governments of the world; however, is enough being done? Have we used 'overwhelming force'?

What Can be Done to Make Aviation a 'Hardened Target'?

The chapter on terrorism indicated terrorists might have moved their emphasis away from 'hardened targets', such as government buildings and military bases, to 'softer targets', such as restaurants, apartment complexes, etc. There have certainly been attacks throughout the world that underscore this belief. The fallacy of this line of thinking is that by hardening targets, terrorism will cease or 'go somewhere else'. There will always be soft targets, and some hardened targets are softer than other hardened targets. We are NOT defeating terrorism by hardening targets, we are just shifting their attack and focus to other areas; regardless, it would be logical to assume the aviation industry would prefer to be a 'hardened target'. How can this be accomplished?

First, it must be understood there is no 'perfect solution' to aviation security. There are numerous things that can be done to strengthen the system, but as long as human beings are involved in any way, there will be human error. Aviation safety has progressed over decades to becoming the safest mode of transportation today. Aviation security may need to take the same road, only this time instead of dirt ruts to go down, there are super-highways. We should be able to get there quicker if we utilize what we know about designing a safety system that works. It is not perfect, we still have accidents and incidents; however, it works at an acceptable level. As such, aviation security must be designed to provide overlapping protocols, much along the same lines as James Reason's 'Swiss cheese' model for aviation safety.[6] In Reason's model, each 'slice' of Swiss cheese represents a layer of protection. The vertical slices are arranged one behind the other. Any error passing through one slice should not be allowed to pass through a hole of the slice behind it; however, sometimes two or more holes line up and allow errors to pass through several layers of protection before being stopped. If the event holes line up in all the layers of protection, an accident will occur.

Aviation security should be designed to serve one or more of the following functions (layer of protection, or slices of Swiss cheese):

- Develop an understanding and awareness of serious security threats;
- Provide adequate alarms and warnings about imminent serious security threats;

- Establish safety barriers between the security threat and other potential losses;
- Contain and neutralize the security threat should they evade the barriers;
- Provide a means of escape and rescue of innocent passengers and crew if the barriers cannot contain the security threat;
- Establish safety barriers between the security threat and other potential losses;
- Establish clear guidance on how to deal with a terrorist incident or other serious security threat;
- Conduct realistic and in-depth training for all aviation personnel in proactive security awareness and responsibility, and effective reactive response procedures; and/or,
- Provide a continual assessment of the security system that immediately addresses weakness and failures within the system.[7]

As one begins at the top of this list and works their way down, it becomes apparent that such a layered system provides the 'hardening' of the aviation target. We know HOW to harden the target, but WHO is going to do it? Your government or your company? You?

Could Another Terrorist Attack Occur in the US?

Possibly the only people who hope so are the terrorists who are living among us in small cells. It is very reasonable to believe that another horrific event will occur. It will take years before we can get the immense homeland security effort and the combined intelligence community in place and up to speed. Even then, we are leaving large gaps in our security that may never be adequately addressed. Peter Guerrero of the GAO testified that it could cost hundreds of billions of dollars to secure the country's entire transportation network, which includes 3.9 million miles of roads, 600,000 bridges, 361 ports, and more than 5,000 public-use airports.[8] 'The magnitude of the problem here is almost beyond comprehension', said Senator Frank Lautenberg, D-N.J.[9]

Aviation security efforts to date have been slow, ineffective, and insufficient. A perfect example of this came almost two years to the day from 9/11, when a man had himself crated and shipped by a cargo airplane from New York to Dallas on 6 September 2003. Michael Boyd, an aviation consultant, said, 'This is just one more proof that we don't have a clue what's in our airplanes ... it shows the back door of the airport is wide open. We're no more safe than we were two years ago'.[10] Two incidents at New York's Kennedy International Airport in August 2003 reflect the same back door being open. In one incident, three teenage boys were found wandering along a side road near one the airport's runways after their raft had been washed ashore for more than an hour. In the other incident, two reporters and a boat captain aboard a boat near the runways were detained after attempting to flee the scene.[11]

Unfortunately, there is nothing to indicate there will be a change in the efforts to thwart aviation-related attacks to date. At least, not until another disaster occurs. If you think this is a harsh statement, look at your current security training as well as what is planned for your next training cycle. Are the courses in-depth, so they address the real issues and are they geared towards saving your lives, or are they simply white wash? Last year, a major US airline sent training vendors a Request for Proposal (RFP) to supply their flight crews with 30 minutes of hands-on defensive tactics. Yes, you read it correctly, *three-zero* minutes. What could anyone possibly teach you in thirty minutes that would save your life against a terrorist that has been training for years on how to kill you? TSA 'guidance' allows a wide range of interpretations as to what airline security training should entail. Any airline that attempts to 'just fill a training square', the Principal Security Inspector (PSI) that approves the training program, the crewmembers' unions that allow it to happen, and the employees that herd like sheep into the classroom will all share in the blame for the next event. You see, the inadequate system that was in place on 10 September 2001 is still in place today; therefore, another 9/11 (or something even bigger) can easily happen. Big wheels move ever so slowly. If you read carefully the other chapters of this book regarding terrorist and their tools, chemical/biological/ radiological weapons and explosives, you will see numerous references from high-ranking officials in our country who predict another horrific event will occur. Terrorists continue to tell us it will happen. Is anyone listening?

It would be nice to believe the efforts of the governments around the world addressing the problem of terrorism will stop it, but do you really believe that is possible? As private individuals who have limited capabilities to control certain things, we suggest that crewmembers need to be continually vigilant to the threats around them and stay aware of how those threats may affect them, wherever they may live and work throughout the world. It is certain that some sort of terrorism in one degree or another will continue be a problem to the free peoples of the world for a very long time. Guarding as much as possible of what we value in life, and defending that right, will always be a challenge for each of us.

It is your individual responsibility as a free person to be aware of these challenges. It is our collective responsibilities to BE the overwhelming force against terrorism. We must not *meet* the challenges of terrorism, we must *eliminate* them. '*Let's roll!*'

Notes

1 Thomas, Andrew, FAA most responsible for 9-11?, WorldNetDaily interview by Jon Dougherty, www.worldnetdaily.com/news/article, 24 July 2003.
2 Fischoff, Baruch, Hindsight does not equal foresight: the effect of outcome knowledge on judgment uncertainty, *Journal of Experimental Psychology: Human Performance and Perception*, 1975.
3 Recommendations, Final Report of the Congressional Joint Inquiry Into 9/11, p. 9, www.fas.org/irp/congress/2002-rpt/recommendations.html, 10 December 2002.
4 Ibid., p. 4.
5 Ibid., pp. 1–3.
6 Reason, James, *Human Error*, New York: Cambridge University Press, 1990.
7 Ibid.
8 Transportation security tighter, but gaps remain, lawmakers say, Associated Press, 10 September 2003.
9 Ibid.
10 Stowaway shows air security flaws, *USA Today*, 10 September 2003.
11 2 journalists are accused of breaching JFK security, *Newsday*, 14 August 2003.

Index